AI in Language Teaching, Learning, and Assessment

Fang Pan
London School of Economics and Political Science, UK

A volume in the Advances in Educational Technologies and Instructional Design (AETID) Book Series

IGI Global
PUBLISHER of TIMELY KNOWLEDGE

Published in the United States of America by
IGI Global
Information Science Reference (an imprint of IGI Global)
701 E. Chocolate Avenue
Hershey PA, USA 17033
Tel: 717-533-8845
Fax: 717-533-8661
E-mail: cust@igi-global.com
Web site: http://www.igi-global.com

Library of Congress Cataloging-in-Publication Data

Names: Pan, Fang, editor.
Title: AI in language teaching, learning, and assessment / edited by Fang Pan.
Other titles: Artificial intelligence in language teaching, learning, and assessment
Description: Hershey, PA : Information Science Reference, 2024. | Includes bibliographical references and index. | Summary: "The book focuses on drawbacks of the application of AI in language education, resources available to ensure the ethical and safe academic deployment of AI, and benefits of applying AI through language teaching, learning, and assessment"-- Provided by publisher.
Identifiers: LCCN 2023054112 (print) | LCCN 2023054113 (ebook) | ISBN 9798369308721 (hardcover) | ISBN 9798369308738 (ebook)
Subjects: LCSH: Language and languages--Study and teaching--Computer-assisted instruction. | Second language learning--Computer-assisted instruction. | English language--Study and teaching--Computer-assisted instruction. | English language--Study and teaching--Computer-assisted instruction for foreign speakers. | Artificial intelligence--Educational applications.
Classification: LCC P53.28 .C37 2024 (print) | LCC P53.28 (ebook) | DDC 418.00785--dc23/eng/20231226
LC record available at https://lccn.loc.gov/2023054112
LC ebook record available at https://lccn.loc.gov/2023054113

This book is published in the IGI Global book series Advances in Educational Technologies and Instructional Design (AE-TID) (ISSN: 2326-8905; eISSN: 2326-8913)

British Cataloguing in Publication Data
A Cataloguing in Publication record for this book is available from the British Library.

Advances in Educational Technologies and Instructional Design (AETID) Book Series

Lawrence A. Tomei
Robert Morris University, USA

ISSN:2326-8905
EISSN:2326-8913

Mission

Education has undergone, and continues to undergo, immense changes in the way it is enacted and distributed to both child and adult learners. In modern education, the traditional classroom learning experience has evolved to include technological resources and to provide online classroom opportunities to students of all ages regardless of their geographical locations. From distance education, Massive-Open-Online-Courses (MOOCs), and electronic tablets in the classroom, technology is now an integral part of learning and is also affecting the way educators communicate information to students.

The **Advances in Educational Technologies & Instructional Design (AETID) Book Series** explores new research and theories for facilitating learning and improving educational performance utilizing technological processes and resources. The series examines technologies that can be integrated into K-12 classrooms to improve skills and learning abilities in all subjects including STEM education and language learning. Additionally, it studies the emergence of fully online classrooms for young and adult learners alike, and the communication and accountability challenges that can arise. Trending topics that are covered include adaptive learning, game-based learning, virtual school environments, and social media effects. School administrators, educators, academicians, researchers, and students will find this series to be an excellent resource for the effective design and implementation of learning technologies in their classes.

Coverage

- Educational Telecommunications
- Instructional Design
- Web 2.0 and Education
- Curriculum Development
- Higher Education Technologies
- Online Media in Classrooms
- Collaboration Tools
- Bring-Your-Own-Device
- Game-Based Learning
- Hybrid Learning

IGI Global is currently accepting manuscripts for publication within this series. To submit a proposal for a volume in this series, please contact our Acquisition Editors at Acquisitions@igi-global.com or visit: http://www.igi-global.com/publish/.

The Advances in Educational Technologies and Instructional Design (AETID) Book Series (ISSN 2326-8905) is published by IGI Global, 701 E. Chocolate Avenue, Hershey, PA 17033-1240, USA, www.igi-global.com. This series is composed of titles available for purchase individually; each title is edited to be contextually exclusive from any other title within the series. For pricing and ordering information please visit http://www.igi-global.com/book-series/advances-educational-technologies-instructional-design/73678. Postmaster: Send all address changes to above address.

Titles in this Series

For a list of additional titles in this series, please visit: www.igi-global.com/book-series

Practices and Implementation of Gamification in Higher Education
Veronica Membrive (University of Almeria, pain)
Information Science Reference • © 2024 • 320pp • H/C (ISBN: 9798369307168) • US $230.00

Optimizing Education Through Micro-Lessons Engaging and Adaptive Learning Strategies
Peter Ilic (University of Aizu, apan)
Information Science Reference • © 2024 • 398pp • H/C (ISBN: 9798369301951) • US $230.00

Fostering Pedagogical Innovation Through Effective Instructional Design
Mohamed Khaldi (Ecole Normale Supérieur, Abdelmalek Essaadi University, Tetouan, Morocco)
Information Science Reference • © 2024 • 467pp • H/C (ISBN: 9798369312063) • US $245.00

Protocols and Tools for Equitable Dual Language Teaching
Esther Gross (The Center for Educational Technology, Israel) and Jenifer Crawford (University of Southern California, USA)
Information Science Reference • © 2024 • 300pp • H/C (ISBN: 9781799883548) • US $225.00

Utilizing Visuals and Information Technology in Mathematics Classrooms
Hiroto Namihira (Former Otsuma Women's University, Japan)
Information Science Reference • © 2024 • 300pp • H/C (ISBN: 9781668499870) • US $220.00

Implications of Chatbots on Teaching and Learning
Mohammad Daradkeh (University of Dubai, UAE)
Information Science Reference • © 2024 • 330pp • H/C (ISBN: 9798369302453) • US $230.00

Fostering Foreign Language Teaching and Learning Environments With Contemporary Technologies
Zeynep Çetin Köroğlu (Aksaray University, Turkey) and Abdulvahit Çakır (Ufuk University, Turkey)
Information Science Reference • © 2024 • 338pp • H/C (ISBN: 9798369303535) • US $230.00

Embracing Cutting-Edge Technology in Modern Educational Settings
Ken Nee Chee (Universiti Pendidikan Sultan Idris, Malaysia) and Mageswaran Sanmugam (Universiti Sains Malaysia, Malaysia)
Information Science Reference • © 2024 • 334pp • H/C (ISBN: 9798369310229) • US $240.00

IGI Global
PUBLISHER of TIMELY KNOWLEDGE

701 East Chocolate Avenue, Hershey, PA 17033, USA
Tel: 717-533-8845 x100 • Fax: 717-533-8661
E-Mail: cust@igi-global.com • www.igi-global.com

Table of Contents

Section 3
Practice: Use of AI in Language Education

Detailed Table of Contents

The integration of artificial intelligence (AI) in language education, exemplified by tools like ChatGPT, has sparked significant discourse. Since its introduction, ChatGPT has established itself as an indispensable educational tool and its relentless advancement remains undeniable. Therefore, comprehending the impact and educational potential of AI becomes paramount. This chapter explores the research contexts that provide insights into the background relevant to the integration of ChatGPT in language education. It also delves into the benefits and the current research issues in AI-enhanced language education. In essence, this chapter aims to shed light on the current landscape of AI in language education and its potential implications for teaching and learning. As the realm of language education experiences evolving innovation, this chapter emerges as a guiding beacon and illuminates pathways to harness the potential of AI in language education while upholding ethical standards and ensuring meaningful pedagogical transformations.

Incorporating artificial intelligence (AI) into language education signifies a paradigm shift that promotes originality and inclusiveness. The partnership between AI developers and educators effectively tackles obstacles and establishes a foundation for continuous progress. Anticipating the future, the progression of AI holds the potential to deliver intricate customization, customizing educational encounters to suit the unique requirements of each individual. Responsible incorporation of AI into teaching methodologies transforms them into a collaborative model that empowers educators to engage in individualized interactions.

Ethics remain of the utmost importance, encompassing bias mitigation and privacy. In essence, the integration of AI into language education signifies an impending era in which the combined powers of technology and human proficiency foster the development of capable individuals who are prepared to navigate an interconnected, digitally globalized society.

As artificial intelligence (AI) continues to increase its presence and accessibility within education, the need to address AI's impact on assignment design and the production of original coursework is heightened. Within the context of an undergraduate language and culture course, this chapter thus offers reflections on the integration of AI tools and their effect on shaping assessment methods. The authors also highlight that there indeed remains a great need for continued research in the realm of AI and education going forward, especially where enhanced AI-detection technologies, institutional policies, academic rigour, and learner expressiveness are concerned.

Artificial intelligence (AI) has emerged as a transformative force in second language (L2) education, reshaping teaching and learning methodologies. This chapter explores AI's impact on L2 educators and learners through insights from questionnaires and a follow-up conversation. Initial apprehension towards AI is counterbalanced by curiosity about its potential to enhance educational practices. The chapter provides practical guidance, showcasing how AI tools can be aligned with key language learning skills and offering structured examples of activities to enhance these skills. It highlights AI's role in providing immediate feedback, simplifying complex concepts, and creating inclusive classrooms tailored to individual learning styles and needs. The discussion also addresses educators' recognition of AI's potential and underscores the need for clear guidelines and training in ethical AI implementation. As AI technology evolves, it promises a more personalized, dynamic educational journey, enriching the L2 learning process.

Artificial intelligence influences education, particularly language instruction. Despite its expanding attention, few studies have examined teachers' views on AI in education. This qualitative study explores EFL teachers' AI-related views and insights. The study uses semi-structured interviews with 21 instructors from diverse universities to uncover complex attitudes toward AI, pedagogical ideologies, perceived

Section 3
Practice: Use of AI in Language Education

Preface

Welcome to *AI in Language Teaching, Learning, and Assessment*. This book marks a pivotal exploration into the dynamic realm of artificial intelligence (AI) within the context of language education. In recent times, the advent of technologies like ChatGPT has ignited fervent discussions about the role and impact of AI in educational settings (Kasneci et al., 2023; Perkins, 2023).

WHY AI AND LANGUAGE EDUCATION?

I still vividly remember my first conversation on ChatGPT. I was talking with a Spanish teacher back in early December 2022. She was deeply impressed by its myriad possibilities extending from simulating human conversation to generating intricate responses that encompass diverse tasks such as answering queries, crafting essays, and composing music. But at the same time, she was worried about academic misconduct and its impact on assessment methods, and even expressed concern over the possible replacement of language teachers in the future, which I greatly empathized with. We did not know how much it would impact our teaching and how educational systems would respond to it, but we were certain it would change the current pedagogical environment profoundly and that we must be ready for such changes.

We were right. The introduction of ChatGPT has spurred divergent opinions, both commendations and apprehensions, within academia (Meyer et al., 2023; Shen et al., 2023). While some educators envision its potential as an asset for teaching, learning, and assessment (Hong.,2023; Kohnke, 2023; Kohnke et al., 2023; Rudolph et al., 2023), others voice concerns regarding its effect on academic integrity and ethical considerations (Cotton et al., 2023; Rane et al., 2023; Teng, 2023), incorrect or misleading information (Borji, 2023), and other issues such as biased or inappropriate content (Baidoo-Anu et al., 2023; Sallam, 2023).

Undeniably, the drawbacks associated with AI in education merit attention (Qadir., 2023). However, the inexorable march of technological advancement necessitates an adaptable educational landscape - one that embraces emerging technologies while upholding ethical standards (Kamalov., 2023; Perera et al., 2023). Thus, there arises an imperative need to delve deeper into AI, navigating its complexities to harness its positive potential in education. Motivated by precisely these points, I set about creating AI in Language Teaching, Learning, and Assessment.

EXPLORATION, ASPIRATION, AND COLLABORATION

This book zooms in on the intersection of AI and language education, aiming to explore how AI can be effectively supervised, ensuring academic integrity while bolstering its role in teaching, learning, and assessment.

Throughout its chapters, this book endeavors to address pivotal inquiries such as unpacking the challenges inherent in AI application within language education and strategies to mitigate them, identifying resources to ensure the ethical and secure deployment of AI in academic settings, scrutinizing the merits of integrating AI in language teaching, learning, and assessment, presenting and analyzing successful cases illustrating the effective utilization of AI in educational contexts, and pioneering discussions on potential advancements and future trajectories for AI in language education.

Chapters from the below countries or regions are included in the book: Canada (Lobalsamo, Segreti, Jamali & Gaspari), Hong Kong (Lee & Chen), Ireland (Liu, Sanmartín), India (S. Singha, R. Singha & Jasmine), Malaysia (Ng & Ravana), Turkey (Dincer & Bal, Uysal & Yüksel), United Kingdom (Bengsch), United States (Barrios-Beltran, Czerkawski, Khazaal, Lee, Lys, Wang). Their objectives are to offer insights, contemporary research perspectives, and educational cases that stimulate academic dialogues while advocating for the judicious use of AI in language education. All the chapters aspire to disseminate best practices within the language teaching community and foster collaboration to navigate potential biases or discriminatory outcomes arising from AI deployment.

I invite readers on an enlightening journey through the nuances of AI in language education, urging collaborative efforts toward harnessing its potential for the betterment of educational landscapes worldwide.

STRUCTURE OF THE BOOK

This book caters not only to those passionate about language education but also to language learners, educators, researchers, scholars, and AI developers seeking to explore and apply AI in educational domains. It is a comprehensive resource offering a roadmap to bridge the realms of AI technology and language education.

The chapters encompass a wide spectrum of topics, including but not limited to the synergy between artificial intelligence and pedagogy, explorations into AI's influence on teaching materials, assessing the impact of AI in educational evaluation, the convergence of AI and applied linguistics, and pioneering advancements in AI-driven language education development.

This book is divided into three sections:

Section 1: Preview - AI and Language Education
Section 2: Perspectives - What People Say About AI
Section 3: Practice - Use of AI in Language Education

There are three chapters in Section 1.

1. The Integration of ChatGPT in Language Education: Exploring Contexts, Assessing Impacts, and Unpacking Implications

Liu delves into ChatGPT's integration in language education, discussing research contexts, benefits, and current issues. Through comprehensive exploration of AI in language education, Liu offers insights into its implications for teaching and learning.

2. Enhancing Language Teaching Materials Through Artificial Intelligence: Opportunities and Challenges

Addressing the paradigm shift in language education, S. Singha, R. Singha, and Jasmine provide a comprehensive overview of AI and language education by exploring AI's potential for personalized learning and ethical considerations. They emphasize collaboration between AI developers and educators to navigate biases, privacy, and customization, ultimately fostering capable individuals in a digitally connected world.

3. The Reality of Artificiality: The Impact of Artificial Intelligence on Language and Culture Course Assessments and Rubrics

Reflecting on AI's impact on assessment design in a language and culture course, Lobalsamo, Segreti, Jamali, and Gaspari address AI tools' influence on assignment creation and original coursework production. Their chapter emphasizes the need for continued research in AI and education, especially regarding AI-detection technologies and academic rigor.

There are five chapters in Section 2.

4. Enriching the Teaching-Learning Experience by Using AI Tools in the L2 Classroom

Through insights from questionnaires and follow-up conversations, Barrios-Beltrán assesses AI's impact on L2 education, presenting insights from questionnaires and activities aligned with language learning skills. The chapter emphasizes AI's role in immediate feedback, simplifying complex concepts, and creating inclusive classrooms, advocating for ethical AI implementation and educator training.

5. A Qualitative Journey on Instructors' Perceptions of Artificial Intelligence in EFL Education

Dincer and Bal delve into EFL instructors' perspectives on AI in education, uncovering intricate attitudes and concerns through a qualitative study by interviewing 21 diverse university instructors. They reveal insights into AI's adaptability, pedagogical impact, technical proficiency requirements, and ethical/security concerns. Their chapter emphasizes the need for ongoing research to effectively integrate AI in language instruction while acknowledging the challenges and benefits educators encounter.

6. AI-Powered Lesson Planning: Insights From Future EFL Teachers

Focused on pre-service EFL teachers, Uysal and Yüksel examine AI-driven lesson plans designed for 5th-grade writing classes. Using a mixed-methods approach, they assess the efficacy of AI-generated plans, identifying strengths in engagement and structure while noting areas for improvement in differentiation and assessment. Their chapter underscores the necessity of AI literacy in teacher training for effective AI utilization in diverse language teaching contexts.

7. Discussions of Using AI in Language Education in Hong Kong

Investigating Hong Kong's discourse on AI in language education, Lee and Chen analyze newspaper articles from 2018-2023. They delve into debates and viewpoints from various stakeholders, shedding light on perceptions of AI's effectiveness and challenges in language education.

8. What Are Students Saying About AI as an Academic Tool?

Ng and Ravana delve into the impact of AI, including ChatGPT, on the academic experiences of learners. Their chapter aims to uncover students' intentions and perceptions regarding the use of AI in language learning. Grounded in the Theory of Planned Behavior, they present insights from Malaysian tertiary education institutions, shedding light on how students view AI-powered tools for academic writing and its influence on their language learning behavior.

There are seven chapters in section 3.

9. Integrating ChatGPT Into a Culture-focused Flipped Curriculum for Chinese as a Foreign Language: Experiments and Implications

Focusing on ChatGPT's role in a culture-focused flipped curriculum for Chinese as a foreign language, Wang discusses its performance in generating scenarios and scripts for intercultural communication practice. While noting ChatGPT's linguistic accuracy, Wang explores challenges in generating context-specific scripts, suggesting its use as a reference tool rather than a primary learning resource.

10. Redefining Traditional Pedagogy: The Integration of Machine Learning in the Contemporary Language Education Classroom

Examining the shift in language instruction due to digital transformation, Bengsch explores Machine Learning's potential in personalized language learning experiences, presents a speaking practice prototype app "TalkToMe," and addresses ethical concerns, aiming to bridge traditional methodologies and AI-driven education.

11. Creating Stories: Generative Artificial Intelligence Tools as Writing Tutors

Lys explores the use of prompt-driven ChatGPT in developing children's stories by a group of advanced German learners. The chapter highlights ChatGPT's role as a thinking partner, aiding students in brainstorming, vocabulary expansion, and language pattern learning. The discussion focuses on project setup, prompts used for content elicitation, and the integration of AI-generated illustrations.

12. Redesigning a Foreign Language Course With the Help of AI: Benefits and Challenges

Focusing on the redesign of a foreign language (Arabic) course, Khazaal evaluates the use of AI to align with Sustainable Development Goals (SDGs). It explores how AI facilitates experiential learning, encouraging students to reflect on sustainability issues. Khazaal highlights positive contributions and challenges of AI in achieving the redesign goals, particularly in elements related to High-Impact Practices (HIPs) and significant learning.

13. Utilizing a ChatGPT Workshop to Foster Ethical Awareness and Enhance L2 English Writing Revision Processes in University Academic Settings: ChatGPT Workshop for Effective and Ethical L2 English Writing

Exploring a ChatGPT workshop's design for multilingual university students, Lee focuses on enhancing L2 English writing skills. The chapter emphasizes ethical use, providing personalized feedback, and improving revision processes while offering recommendations for educators and future AI-related research.

14. Leveraging AI and Pluralistic Approaches for Language Teaching: A Focus on Inter-Comprehension Between Related Languages

Sanmartín introduces pluralistic teaching approach utilizing ChatGPT, aiming to enhance inter-comprehensive awareness among English speakers studying Spanish. Sanmartín provides parallel contrastive analyses of translations, focusing on structurally asymmetrical grammatical phenomena between Romance languages and English.

15. Designing Language Learning Experiences With Generative AI Tools

Czerkawski emphasizes the opportunities AI presents for language learners, highlighting its potential for personalized learning experiences and timely feedback. The chapter underscores the broader applications for instructors, suggesting ways to leverage generative AI in curriculum design and addressing diverse learner needs. Despite the advantages, Czerkawski acknowledges the challenges of effective design for language learning environments using AI and advocates for the adoption of learning experience design (LXD) principles to ensure meaningful outcomes.

IN SUMMARY

In navigating the nuanced terrain of AI in language education, this book has ventured into diverse realms and unveiled multifaceted insights and perspectives. Each chapter has contributed a crucial piece to the mosaic of understanding AI's impact on language instruction.

Through qualitative studies, experimental implementations, and analyses of AI tools like ChatGPT, our contributors have delineated both the promises and the challenges associated with integrating AI into language teaching and learning. The discourse on AI's capacity to adapt to individual learning needs, its ethical implications, and its potential to revolutionize pedagogical dynamics have been both enriching and thought-provoking.

We have explored the potential of AI as a creative writing partner, a facilitator for intercultural communication, and a tool for enhancing the quality of language learning materials. As we journeyed through the evolving landscape of AI in language education, ethical considerations such as privacy, academic integrity, and bias mitigation, have stood as guiding beacons illuminating the way forward.

However, this exploration is not merely an endpoint but a catalyst for continued discourse and growth. It underscores the imperative need for ongoing research, pedagogical adaptation, and educator preparedness to harness the potential of AI while safeguarding the integrity of language education.

As the educational horizon continues to evolve, the integration of AI within language education signifies not just a technological shift but a paradigmatic transformation. It signifies a collaborative alliance between human proficiency and technological prowess, fostering an environment where AI serves as a catalyst for personalized, dynamic, and inclusive language learning experiences.

I hope this compilation serves as a comprehensive guide, a catalyst for discussions, and an impetus for further exploration of AI's role in language education. May it inspire educators, researchers, developers, and policymakers to collaboratively pave the way for an educational landscape that embraces innovation, ethics, and inclusive pedagogical practices. Together, let us embark on this transformative journey in language education, where the synergy of AI and human expertise propels us toward an ever evolving, empowered educational future.

Fang Pan
London School of Economics and Political Science, UK

REFERENCES

Baidoo-Anu, D., & Ansah, L. O. (2023). Education in the era of generative artificial intelligence (AI): Understanding the potential benefits of ChatGPT in promoting teaching and learning. *Journal of AI*, *7*(1), 52–62. doi:10.61969/jai.1337500

Borji, A. (2023). A categorical archive of ChatGPT failures. *arXiv preprint arXiv:2302.03494*. doi:10.21203/rs.3.rs-2895792/v1

Cotton, D. R., Cotton, P. A., & Shipway, J. R. (2023). Chatting and cheating: Ensuring academic integrity in the era of ChatGPT. *Innovations in Education and Teaching International*, 1–12. doi:10.1080/14703297.2023.2190148

Hong, W. C. H. (2023). The impact of ChatGPT on foreign language teaching and learning: Opportunities in education and research. *Journal of Educational Technology and Innovation*, *5*(1), 37–45.

Kamalov, F., Santandreu Calonge, D., & Gurrib, I. (2023). New era of artificial intelligence in education: Towards a sustainable multifaceted revolution. *Sustainability (Basel)*, *15*(16), 12451. doi:10.3390/su151612451

Kasneci, E., Seßler, K., Küchemann, S., Bannert, M., Dementieva, D., Fischer, F., Gasser, U., Groh, G., Günnemann, S., Hüllermeier, E., Krusche, S., Kutyniok, G., Michaeli, T., Nerdel, C., Pfeffer, J., Poquet, O., Sailer, M., Schmidt, A., Seidel, T., ... Kasneci, G. (2023). ChatGPT for good? On opportunities and challenges of large language models for education. *Learning and Individual Differences*, *103*, 102274. doi:10.1016/j.lindif.2023.102274

Kohnke, L. (2023). L2 learners' perceptions of a chatbot as a potential independent language learning tool. *International Journal of Mobile Learning and Organisation*, *17*(1–2), 214–226. doi:10.1504/IJMLO.2023.128339

Kohnke, L., Moorhouse, B. L., & Zou, D. (2023). ChatGPT for language learning and teaching. *RELC Journal*, 1–14.

Meyer, J. G., Urbanowicz, R. J., Martin, P. C., O'Connor, K., Li, R., Peng, P. C., Bright, T. J., Tatonetti, N., Won, K. J., Gonzalez-Hernandez, G., & Moore, J. H. (2023). ChatGPT and large language models in academia: Opportunities and challenges. *BioData Mining*, *16*(1), 20. doi:10.1186/s13040-023-00339-9 PMID:37443040

Perera, P., & Lankathilaka, M. (2023). AI in higher education: A literature review of chatgpt and guidelines for responsible implementation. *International Journal of Research and Innovation in Social Science*, *VII*(VI), 306–314. doi:10.47772/IJRISS.2023.7623

Perkins, M. (2023). Academic Integrity Considerations of AI Large Language Models in the Post-Pandemic Era: ChatGPT and Beyond. *Journal of University Teaching & Learning Practice*, *20*(2), 7.

Qadir, J. (2023, May). Engineering education in the era of ChatGPT: Promise and pitfalls of generative AI for education. In *2023 IEEE Global Engineering Education Conference (EDUCON)* (pp. 1-9). IEEE. 10.1109/EDUCON54358.2023.10125121

Rane, N. L., Choudhary, S. P., Tawde, A., & Rane, J. (2023). ChatGPT is not capable of serving as an author: Ethical concerns and challenges of large language models in education. *International Research Journal of Modernization in Engineering Technology and Science*, *5*(10), 851–874.

Rudolph, J., Tan, S., & Tan, S. (2023). ChatGPT: Bullshit spewer or the end of traditional assessments in higher education? *Journal of Applied Teaching & Learning*, *6*(1), 342–362.

Shen, Y., Heacock, L., Elias, J., Hentel, K. D., Reig, B., Shih, G., & Moy, L. (2023). ChatGPT and other large language models are double-edged swords. *Radiology*, *307*(2), e230163. doi:10.1148/radiol.230163 PMID:36700838

Teng, F. (2023). Scientific writing, reviewing, and editing for open-access TESOL journals: The role of ChatGPT. *International Journal of TESOL Studies*, *5*, 87–91.

Acknowledgment

Firstly, I would like to acknowledge the contribution of all authors involved in this project. My sincere gratitude goes to all who contributed their time and expertise. The ideas and contributions that everyone has put into this book have been truly inspiring.

Secondly, I would like to acknowledge the valuable contributions from the reviewers to improve the quality, coherence, and content presentation of the chapters. Most of the authors also served as referees and their valuable input is highly appreciated. I would like to extend special thanks to Prof. Miao-Fen Tseng, Dr. Alison Standring, and Dr. Peter Skrandies who assisted with the review process. Without their significant support, this book would not be possible.

Last but not least, I would like to give my sincere thanks and love to my family and friends who supported me during the process of editing this book.

Section 1

Preview: AI and Language Education

Chapter 1
The Integration of ChatGPT in Language Education:
Exploring Contexts, Assessing Impacts, and Unpacking Implications

Weiming Liu
https://orcid.org/0000-0002-2468-6911
Dublin City University, Ireland

ABSTRACT

The integration of artificial intelligence (AI) in language education, exemplified by tools like ChatGPT, has sparked significant discourse. Since its introduction, ChatGPT has established itself as an indispensable educational tool and its relentless advancement remains undeniable. Therefore, comprehending the impact and educational potential of AI becomes paramount. This chapter explores the research contexts that provide insights into the background relevant to the integration of ChatGPT in language education. It also delves into the benefits and the current research issues in AI-enhanced language education. In essence, this chapter aims to shed light on the current landscape of AI in language education and its potential implications for teaching and learning. As the realm of language education experiences evolving innovation, this chapter emerges as a guiding beacon and illuminates pathways to harness the potential of AI in language education while upholding ethical standards and ensuring meaningful pedagogical transformations.

Language education fosters meaningful communication and interaction. At its core, it equips learners with indispensable skills to bridge linguistic divides and facilitates connections and collaborations across geographical borders. As teaching and learning innovations continue to be tested and researched, new insights are gained that influence teaching practices globally (Moeller & Catalano, 2015). Online platforms, interactive apps and immersive language experiences have opened doors to enhance education. In this digital age, technology is reshaping global communication, and digital literacy has become increasingly significant in foreign language use. This shift necessitates acquiring additional skills and

DOI: 10.4018/979-8-3693-0872-1.ch001

a nuanced ability to navigate multimodal practices. Such practices include utilising diverse multimedia channels and creatively exploring newly enhanced technological options to align with the evolving landscape of language education (Auer et al., 2022; Golonka et al., 2014; Shadiev & Yang, 2020; Ziegler & González-Lloret, 2022).

The rapid advancement of technology brings about a transformative era in language education, with a profound impact stemming from the integration of artificial intelligence (AI). A new wave of AI tools is emerging. They can be used to create new content, including text, images and computer programmes (Kukulska-Hulme et al., 2023). One such platform is ChatGPT, a cutting-edge AI language model, developed by OpenAI. The remarkable ability of ChatGPT to handle complex tasks has garnered significant attention in research articles within the domain of language education. While existing research has examined various aspects of ChatGPT in the context of language education, a noticeable gap persists in comprehensively understanding its empirical integration. This chapter aims to bridge this gap by analysing a collection of journal articles. It explores the specific research contexts in which ChatGPT has been integrated. It also discusses the benefits and challenges of an AI-enhanced learning environment. Furthermore, the chapter delves into the potential implications of such technologies on teaching and learning practices. As the field of language education evolves, the chapter emphasises the importance of adhering to ethical standards and highlights the significant improvements that AI can bring to pedagogical practices.

LITERATURE REVIEW

The role of AI in language education continually evolves and reshapes teaching and learning methods with the goal to enrich the language learning experience. The integration of AI has ignited substantial interest and debate among educators and researchers (Crompton & Burke, 2023; Huang et al., 2023; Rebolledo Font De La Vall & González Araya, 2023). The introduction of ChatGPT into language education has been hailed as a significant breakthrough in the field of AI (Roumeliotis & Tselikas, 2023). It is designed to engage in conversations with its users, respond to commands and produce text that appears to have been created by a human (Kukulska-Hulme et al., 2023). As a prominent AI language model, ChatGPT has attracted considerable attention in the field of language education and has become an increasingly prevalent and powerful tool for language learning and teaching.

Numerous researchers (Baïdoo-Anu & Ansah, 2023; Baskara & Mukarto, 2023; Cai, 2023; Hong, 2023; Kasneci et al., 2023; Kohnke et al., 2023) have collectively underscored ChatGPT's significant pedagogical impact, highlighting its wide range of educational affordances. ChatGPT enriches language learning by providing a dynamic and interactive experience that cultivates authentic conversations with the chatbot. It serves as both a tutor and teacher for language learners, with a primary focus on enhancing personalised learning experiences. ChatGPT is capable of offering language instruction, creating materials and developing activities tailored to individual learners' needs, interests, pace and language proficiency level. Another notable affordance of ChatGPT lies in its ability to provide immediate feedback. Its conversational capabilities enable learners to receive real-time feedback, helping them to refine their language proficiency and conversational fluency. This feature is invaluable for promptly identifying and rectifying language errors. Furthermore, ChatGPT supports self-evaluation, allowing learners to generate quizzes for self-assessment. This self-monitoring feature helps learners to track their progress and make informed decisions about their language learning journey. In addition, since the interactions occur with a machine, the secure and comfortable nature of the practice alleviates learners' concerns about making mistakes in front of others. This sense of security plays a crucial role in building confidence and encouraging active participation. Moreover, researchers argue that ChatGPT fosters a motivating learning environment. It gives learners control and keeps them engaged, further enhancing the effectiveness of language learning.

ChatGPT is a versatile and competent assistant that plays a notable role in supporting language educators. It offers a rich repository of content and examples to enhance teaching materials and curriculum development. Researchers have explored its potential as a teaching tool and its capacity to alleviate teachers' workload and provide substantial opportunities for teachers and educational institutions to enhance foreign language teaching and assessments. They have also shed light on how educators harness this platform to enhance language education (Hong, 2023). Simultaneously, it frees educators to focus on delivering personalised instruction and addressing the unique learning needs of individual students. As a result, ChatGPT serves as a facilitator in the educational process by delivering essential facts and fundamental knowledge when empowering educators to concentrate on the more nuanced aspects of teaching (Cai, 2023).

While the potential of ChatGPT in language education is evident, it is essential to acknowledge the challenges that come with its integration. Kohnke et al. (2023) distil these challenges into three core debates. The first debate delves into the ethical aspects of the use of ChatGPT in education in relation to concerns about potential cheating and its impact on assessment methodologies. Their second debate scrutinises the accuracy of chatbot responses, while their third discussion brings to light the cultural bias inherent in the source database and algorithms. The limitations of ChatGPT, such as its social bias and tendency to produce factually incorrect or irrelevant outputs, have been acknowledged by researchers (Cai, 2023; Kukulska-Hulme et al., 2023). Furthermore, Cai (2023) argues that ChatGPT lacks the adaptability of an experienced human teacher who can tailor their approach to specific situations and consider multifaceted factors and instincts, including dealing with handwritten tests that necessitate conversion into a digital format. Employing ChatGPT in language learning may also raise concerns about the potential replacement of human language teachers and the ethical implications surrounding the use of a machine learning system for generating texts (Baskara & Mukarto, 2023).

Some researchers have explored the practical application of ChatGPT in language education. They have studied its role as a tool for English language instruction (Kostka & Toncelli, 2023), its usability in formal English language learning (Shaikh et al., 2023) and its potential to generate chatbot dialogues for enhancing the process of learning English as a foreign language (EFL) (Young & Shishido, 2023). Another central theme revolves around comparing EFL learners' satisfaction when presented with teacher-mediated writing opportunities versus ChatGPT-assisted ones (Ahmed, 2023). Additional studies have aimed to uncover students' experiences with ChatGPT and their perspectives on its role in language learning (Xiao & Zhi, 2023) and EFL learners' perception and utilisation of ChatGPT beyond the classroom (Liu & Ma, 2023). Researchers have also examined the impact of ChatGPT on students participating in a second language writing practicum (Yan, 2023) and within the context of language learning videos on YouTube (Li et al., 2023). Furthermore, research has delved into the perceptions of faculty members (Mohamed, 2023), EFL lecturers (Alexander et al., 2023; Guo & Wang, 2023) and researchers on ResearchGate (Bin-Hady et al., 2023). However, there has been a noticeable absence of a comprehensive examination of these studies. This review examines these articles, addressing the following research questions (RQs):

RQ1: What are the research contexts in which the identified studies were conducted?
RQ2: What are the benefits of using ChatGPT to enhance language learning?
RQ3: What are the challenges with using ChatGPT in language education?
RQ4: What are the implications of integrating ChatGPT in language education in diverse educational settings?

METHODOLOGY

Building upon the research questions raised in the introduction section, this section details the methodology, including the search terms and databases used, the selection criteria for literature and the process of identifying relevant studies. Furthermore, this section elaborates on the data coding and analysis process employed to derive meaningful conclusions from the selected studies.

Keywords and Inclusion Criteria

To identify relevant English-language empirical journal articles for this project, a keyword search was conducted. Specific keywords, such as "ChatGPT language education", "ChatGPT language learning" and "ChatGPT language teaching" were chosen because of their direct relevance to language education. Given its widespread usage, the English language was chosen to ensure broader accessibility of findings within the global academic community. Additionally, this strategy was designed to circumvent potential challenges linked to translating and comprehending non-English publications.

The selection process involved the use of the Scopus and Web of Science databases. Complementing each other, these databases were utilised to identify a comprehensive range of articles on ChatGPT in language education. In addition, a forward citation search was conducted to further enrich the article selection process, given the relatively recent emergence of the use of ChatGPT in the field. In summary, the following inclusion criteria were applied to screen the articles identified through the search:

- Journal articles
- Investigations of the integration of ChatGPT in language education
- Reports of empirical data
- Publications in English

Identification of Journal Articles

The specified search timeframe extended from the initial integration of ChatGPT as a tool for language education to September 2023. The process of selecting relevant journal articles consisted of three stages. In Stage 1 (S1), Scopus was used to identify high-quality peer-reviewed journal articles. In the first phase of Stage 1, the keywords "ChatGPT language education", "ChatGPT language learning" and "ChatGPT language teaching" yielded 107, 132 and 37 journal articles, respectively. In the second phase, unrelated articles were removed from the three lists. The elimination process entailed a comprehensive examination of the topics and abstracts of each article to ascertain their alignment with ChatGPT's specific focus on language education, learning and teaching. The articles under consideration were empirical studies. Any articles that did not directly pertain to these themes were subsequently excluded. As a result, this phase retained 6, 8 and 3 articles on the three lists, respectively. The third phase involved cross-checking for any duplicates between the articles on the three lists. In the end, nine articles remained. Table 1 indicates the three search phases and results during the process of identifying and selecting relevant articles.

Table 1. Journal article selection process in Stage 1 (S1) via Scopus

Phases	Activities	Keywords Used	Number of Journal Articles Found
Phase 1 (S1)	Search	ChatGPT language education	107
		ChatGPT language learning	132
		ChatGPT language teaching	37
Phase 2 (S1)	Topic and abstract evaluation	ChatGPT language education	6
		ChatGPT language learning	8
		ChatGPT language teaching	3
Phase 3 (S1)	Cross-checking	N/A	9
Total			9

Note. N/A = not applicable

In Stage 2 (S2) of the process of identifying journal articles, the Web of Science database was used. "Article" was set as the document type. The same set of keywords were employed as in Stage 1. This selection process consisted again of three phases. In the first phase, the keywords produced 117, 113 and 26 journal articles, respectively. The second phase removed unrelated articles, resulting in the identification of 4, 5 and 2 journal articles, respectively. The third phase of this stage involved cross-checking for any duplicates between the three lists. In the end, five articles were retained. Table 2 outlines the journal article selection process in Stage 2.

Table 2. Journal article selection process in Stage 2 (S2) via Web of Science

Phases	Activities	Keywords Used	Number of Journal Articles Found
Phase 1 (S2)	Search	ChatGPT language education	117
		ChatGPT language learning	113
		ChatGPT language teaching	26
Phase 2 (S2)	Identification	ChatGPT language education	4
		ChatGPT language learning	5
		ChatGPT language teaching	2
Phase 3 (S2)	Cross-checking	N/A	5
Total			5

Note. N/A = not applicable

As illustrated in Table 3, the first phase in Stage 3 of the process of identifying journal articles involved a cross-check for duplicates between the journal articles generated during Stage 1 and Stage 2. It was discovered that the 9 journal articles identified during Stage 1 included the 5 journal articles that were identified during Stage 2. A forward citation search was carried out using both Scopus and Web of Science to explore how the 9 journal articles were referenced in subsequent works. Three additional journal articles that cited some of the initial 9 journal articles met the inclusion criteria. As a result, a total of 12 journal articles progressed into the final investigatory phase. The details of these 12 selected articles are summarised in Table 4 in the Appendix.

Table 3. Journal article selection process in Stage 3 (S3)

Phases	Activities	Database	Number of Journal Articles Found
Phase 1 (S3)	Cross-checking for duplicates	Scopus and Web of Science	9
Phase 2 (S3)	Forward citation search	Scopus and Web of Science	3
Total			12

Data Coding and Analysis

The research data management and analysis for this study were primarily conducted using Microsoft Excel 2016 as the data storage and generation tool. To organise and structure the information in the articles, the process commenced by coding the selected articles and then categorised the findings under relevant themes. The themes served as a framework for interpreting the data and understanding the broader patterns and insights present in the research. The categorisation process yielded four main themes: research contexts, benefits, challenges and implications. Each of these main categories was further divided into several sub-categories. These sub-categories provided a detailed insight into the collected data and the iterative nature of this process allowed for a deeper and more nuanced understanding of the subject matter. Through coding, categorisation and analysis, the aim was to identify patterns, relationships and variations within the data.

RESULTS AND DISCUSSION

This section explores the research contexts of the identified studies, examines the benefits and challenges of integrating ChatGPT into language education and discusses its implications.

Research Contexts

The research contexts encompassed various aspects, including research sites, participants, research methods and data collection tools. Each of these elements played a crucial role in building a comprehensive understanding of the research environments and the processes involved in academic investigation.

Research Sites

The selected studies, comprising a diverse range of research sites, reflected a global interest in this field. In Europe, studies were carried out in Norway (Shaikh et al., 2023) and Cyprus (Alexander et al., 2023). The project in the United States (Kostka & Toncelli, 2023) contributed to North American insights. In the Middle East, studies in Saudi Arabia (Ahmed, 2023; Mohamed, 2023) explored the impact of the tool. Studies in China (Guo & Wang, 2023; Xiao & Zhi, 2023; Yan, 2023) and Japan (Young & Shishido, 2023) represented East Asian perspectives. Research on ResearchGate (Bin-Hady et al., 2023) represented an international academic community and research context. Research on YouTube (Li et al., 2023) underscored the utility of the platform in various language learning contexts. The study spanning multiple countries (Liu & Ma, 2023), including China, the United States and other Anglophone countries reflected the global applicability of ChatGPT in language learning.

Participants

The studies under investigation examined the use of ChatGPT in language education from various angles and engaged with diverse groups of participants. Some studies focused on educators and researchers, such as Alexander et al. (2023) who worked with a smaller group of six university English as a second language (ESL) lecturers teaching C1 level English academic writing courses. Guo and Wang (2023) engaged with five Chinese EFL teachers, with a focus on the importance of evaluating and implementing ChatGPT. Mohamed (2023) involved 10 EFL faculty members researching educators' perceptions. Bin-Hady et al. (2023) interacted with 20 researchers on ResearchGate from various universities around the world who had different linguistic backgrounds. They all were interested in technology-based language learning and teaching.

Other studies examined the perspectives of language learners. Liu and Ma (2023) investigated the use of ChatGPT in informal digital learning settings among 405 EFL learners. Meanwhile, Ahmed (2023) included 64 first-Year university EFL students to investigate the interest in ChatGPT among language learners. Kostka and Toncelli (2023) targeted international students in a pathways programme from both an undergraduate public speaking course and a graduate academic listening and speaking course. They shed light on the use of the tool in an academic context. Shaikh et al. (2023) engaged with 10 students from various departments and offered diverse participant profiles. Xiao and Zhi (2023) included five undergraduate students from an English-medium international university to provide insights into the student experience. Yan (2023) investigated the behaviours and reflections of eight undergraduate students majoring in EFL in response to their exposure to ChatGPT in writing classrooms. Young and Shishido (2023) analysed 450 dialogue samples in their research to demonstrate ChatGPT's potential in generating language learning content. The final study in this context by Li et al. (2023) analysed 45 YouTube videos. It signified the influence of AI-driven content in language learning.

Research Methods

The research methods used in these studies demonstrated a blend of qualitative and quantitative approaches, reflecting the multidimensional nature of this field. On the qualitative front, Ahmed (2023) employed a qualitative design focusing on EFL learners' satisfaction with teacher-mediated versus ChatGPT-assisted writing opportunities. Bin-Hady et al. (2023) employed a qualitative study based on grounded theory to explore the dimensions of ChatGPT in language learning. Using qualitative content analysis, Mohamed (2023) delved into faculty members' perceptions and suggested a focus on detailed examination. Alexander et al. (2023) conducted a qualitative study to evaluate academic essays for AI-generated content. They pointed out its exploratory nature. Similarly, Xiao and Zhi (2023) and Yan (2023) adopted qualitative exploratory approaches to assess the impact of ChatGPT on learners in a second language writing practicum.

Li et al. (2023) adopted the inductive content analysis method, while Kostka and Toncelli (2023) included qualitative student quotations about the use of ChatGPT. Conversely, the studies by Guo and Wang (2023), Shaikh et al. (2023) and Young and Shishido (2023) applied quantitative approaches. Their studies reflected an interest in gathering numerical data to assess the potential of ChatGPT in supporting teacher feedback in EFL writing and generating dialogue materials for EFL learners, respectively. Similarly, Liu and Ma (2023) utilised a quantitative cross-sectional survey design to examine users' perceptions and acceptance of ChatGPT in informal English language learning. The versatility in research methods in this domain accommodated both the intricate exploration of participants' experiences and the quantitative measurement of the impact of ChatGPT in language education.

Data Collection Tools

The research data collection tools used in these journal articles reflected the diversity of approaches and underscored the adaptability of methodologies to explore the multifaceted role of ChatGPT in language education. Liu and Ma (2023) employed online surveys, in line with the digital nature of the use of ChatGPT. Mohamed (2023) conducted in-depth interviews with EFL faculty members. Although conducted via email, the interviews allowed for extensive exploration of their perceptions. Xiao and Zhi (2023) employed semi-structured interviews to investigate students' experiences with ChatGPT and its role in language learning. Ahmed (2023) relied on interviews to gather qualitative data when engaging directly with university freshman EFL students, while Yan (2023) utilised observation and in-depth interviews to assess the impact of ChatGPT in a second language writing practicum, with a focus on experiential data. Similarly, Kostka and Toncelli (2023) utilised student quotations and incorporated them in their study, emphasising participant engagement and perspectives in pathways programmes.

In contrast, Alexander et al. (2023) combined various methods such as essay sample preparation, AI detectors and the analysis of texts by ESL lecturers to examine AI-generated content in academic essays. Guo and Wang (2023) used a combination of ChatGPT, EFL teachers' feedback on students' writing and questionnaires answered by EFL teachers to evaluate the potential of ChatGPT in supporting teacher feedback. Shaikh et al. (2023) also adopted questionnaires to collect data, while data for Bin-Hady et al. (2023) was collected through discussions. Li et al. (2023) uniquely collected primary data from videos on YouTube and supplemented their findings with secondary data from the associated comments on the videos. Young and Shishido (2023) adopted established readability assessment tools such as Flesch Reading Ease, McAlpine EFLAW and Dale-Chall to evaluate the effectiveness of ChatGPT in generating dialogue materials for EFL students.

Impacts of the Integration of ChatGPT in Language Education

The selected journal articles reflected a keen interest in integrating ChatGPT into language education. They underscored ChatGPT's applications and potential in teaching and learning languages. The exploration of both learners' and academics' experiences with ChatGPT addressed its benefits and challenges, highlighting its role in the ongoing evolution of language education.

Benefits of Using ChatGPT

Several major themes emerged regarding the benefits of using ChatGPT. The first theme highlighted ChatGPT's effectiveness in enhancing learning. The use of ChatGPT was also linked to learners' attitudes towards ChatGPT and their engagement levels. In addition, ChatGPT served a dual role as both a source of valuable feedback and a personal tutor, assisting with various language-related tasks. Furthermore, ChatGPT was recognised as a valuable tool in supporting teachers' efforts in education.

Language Learning

The contributions of various authors underscored the substantial role of ChatGPT in facilitating language learning across various dimensions. Shaikh et al. (2023) emphasised how ChatGPT expanded vocabulary, improved grammatical and syntactical structures, and enhanced written and conversational skills. Similarly, Bin-Hady et al. (2023) discovered that ChatGPT offered five subcategories of language skill development, including enhancing EFL conversation practice, reading and writing skills, grammar mastery, vocabulary and pronunciation. Yan (2023) underscored the significance of ChatGPT in assisting L2 writing when students interacted with the system.

Also with a focus on writing, Xiao and Zhi (2023) reported on improved textual quality and language competence with the assistance of ChatGPT. Moreover, they asserted that ChatGPT aided language proficiency when students employed critical thinking skills to modify prompts, trained the model and selectively accepted outputs. Young and Shishido (2023) suggested that the dialogues created by ChatGPT were well-suited for students at level A2 (elementary level) of the Common European Framework of Reference (CEFR) for Languages and B1 (intermediate level) for learning new words. They provided comprehensible content and stimulated vocabulary acquisition. Mohamed (2023) highlighted the advantages of ChatGPT in EFL learning, such as real-time feedback, personalised instruction, a vast knowledge base, natural language processing, human-like responses and cost-effectiveness.

Student Attitude

The integration of ChatGPT in language learning and its impact on student attitude was a key focus in the examined studies. Two studies highlighted the significance of student attitude in influencing the adoption and acceptance of ChatGPT for language learning. Liu and Ma (2023) found that learners with a positive view of ChatGPT's usefulness were more likely to intend to use it, a tendency that was strongly linked to their actual English learning outside the classroom. In addition, their research indicated that even EFL learners who initially found ChatGPT challenging could gradually develop a positive attitude and interest in the technology as they recognised its benefits.

In a similar vein, Xiao and Zhi (2023) reported that students in their study displayed a positive attitude towards using ChatGPT, overwhelmingly supporting its adoption in universities instead of its prohibition. Students' acknowledgement of ChatGPT's significant benefits seemed to mitigate concerns about its potential drawbacks, reflecting a favourable view of its integration. Shaikh et al. (2023) further emphasised the effortless and friendly interface of the tool, which greatly enhanced user experience. The high satisfaction ratings and positive student feedback regarding the acceptance of ChatGPT underscored its promising and practical value for language learners.

Engagement

The findings of multiple authors demonstrated the positive impact of ChatGPT on student academic engagement. Kostka and Toncelli (2023) observed an increase in student engagement with both course materials and their interactions with peers after integrating ChatGPT into classes. This heightened engagement led to a more enthusiastic approach to learning content and a deeper interest in critically analysing the output generated by ChatGPT. Similarly, Liu and Ma (2023) found a general consensus among participants regarding the usefulness of ChatGPT in various English learning activities. Particularly noteworthy was ChatGPT's role as a creative tool that effectively enhanced engagement in independent learning activities outside the classroom.

The positive engagement fostered by ChatGPT effectively impacted learning, enhancing student autonomy, boosting independent learning and encouraging critical evaluation of AI-generated information. Xiao and Zhi (2023) highlighted that an engaging learning process not only enhanced language skills but also promoted student autonomy. Learners actively engaged in self-revision, based on the suggestions provided by the system. In this sense, their findings echoed those of Liu and Ma (2023), who also noted the promotion of more active and independent language learning experiences through independent learning activities. Also according to Xiao and Zhi (2023), the involvement of students in modifying prompts, training the system and critically evaluating the output showed a remarkable capacity for critical thinking. Students developed a critical stance towards the role of ChatGPT in English language learning, consistently critiquing its limitations in various learning aspects. They emphasised the importance of evaluating the usability of the information generated.

Feedback

Recognised as a tool for scaffolding learning, ChatGPT emphasised its capabilities in offering students feedback, as highlighted by Bin-Hady et al. (2023). In line with this, Shaikh et al. (2023) argued that ChatGPT acted as a support tool for practising a foreign language. Furthermore, ChatGPT served as a personalised learning partner or personal tutor, delivering easily accessible and adaptive feedback (Xiao & Zhi, 2023). It had the capacity to review writing and speaking assignments, offer corrections for grammar, vocabulary and pronunciation errors and suggest improvements, including alternative word choices, sentence structures and pronunciation techniques (Ahmed, 2023).

However, some distinctions between ChatGPT and teacher feedback in their approach to evaluating student writing were noted. ChatGPT typically provided feedback more quickly and in larger quantities, whereas teachers needed more time to evaluate student essays and provide feedback. In addition, the nature of the feedback differed. ChatGPT offered more directive feedback, whereas teachers typically employed informative and query-based feedback, especially when assessing content and language aspects of student essays. Moreover, ChatGPT tended to provide more praise when evaluating the content of student essays and offered more summaries regarding the organisational aspect. This demonstrated unique characteristics compared to traditional teacher feedback (Guo & Wang, 2023).

Personal Tutor

ChatGPT effectively fulfilled the role of a personal tutor. This innovative tool provided learners with a dynamic platform for engaging in various linguistic exercises, including asking questions, discussing diverse topics, and simulating real-life dialogues. Such interactive features proved instrumental in enhancing motivation among learners, particularly in the context of foreign language learning, as noted by Shaikh et al. (2023). Further emphasising ChatGPT's role as a personal tutor, Xiao and Zhi (2023) conducted research demonstrating how participants extensively used ChatGPT for various educational tasks. One significant use case was text revision, in which learners sought ChatGPT's assistance for structural and content suggestions in their essays. In addition, ChatGPT proved helpful in providing examples and ideas to strengthen the arguments in written work. This capability became especially beneficial in larger classroom settings, where the number of students might limit individual attention from teachers. As noted by Xiao and Zhi (2023), the assistance offered by ChatGPT extended beyond mere language practice; it encompassed a more comprehensive approach to language skill development. By offering personalised feedback and suggestions, ChatGPT enhanced learners' understanding of language nuances and improved their ability to construct coherent and sophisticated texts. This personalisation was particularly crucial in language learning, where the needs and learning paces of students could vary significantly.

Teachers' Aid

The question of whether ChatGPT could entirely replace human language teachers led to a consensus that it cannot fully serve as a substitute. This consensus primarily arose from the understanding that certain aspects of human interaction, such as humour, wit and empathy, could not be replicated or programmed into AI technology (Li et al., 2023). However, ChatGPT exhibited characteristics of a knowledgeable native speaker and proved useful in extended conversations, avoiding language fatigue (Li et al., 2023). It demonstrated the ability to understand essay content, offer relevant revision suggestions, use praise for student achievements and employ flexible language in feedback (Guo & Wang, 2023). Academics viewed ChatGPT as a collaborator and a valuable source of learning, leading them to use it for generating feedback on student writing. As a result, there was a prevailing view that a combination of AI and human interaction represented a promising approach for enhancing language learning experiences (Li et al., 2023).

ChatGPT demonstrated the capacity to effectively assist educators in automating mechanical tasks, such as assigning grades and evaluating assignments based on criteria like grammar accuracy, vocabulary usage and syntax correctness, thereby saving time and effort (Ahmed, 2023). Furthermore, ChatGPT played an integrative role alongside teachers in contributing to language learning (Bin-Hady et al., 2023). Research highlighted the potential of ChatGPT to enhance the efficiency of EFL teachers by complementing traditional teaching methods, thereby improving student language proficiency and success (Mohamed, 2023). In addition, Xiao and Zhi (2023) emphasised the importance of teachers embracing this AI tool and providing appropriate guidance to students. They underlined the need for educators to adapt and effectively integrate ChatGPT in the teaching process.

Challenges Related to the Use of ChatGPT

Despite the multifaceted benefits of ChatGPT in language education, several challenges were presented. These included inaccessibility, inaccuracy of information, inappropriate feedback and responses, and inappropriate language levels produced by ChatGPT. Learners' ethical and privacy concerns and the potential replacement of humans also posed significant challenges.

In their study, Guo and Wang (2023) emphasised the negative impact of inaccessibility, highlighting how it prevented teachers in certain countries or regions from using ChatGPT as an educational tool. This gap in accessibility limited the widespread availability of this powerful resource to educators and deprived students of its potential benefits. Furthermore, Mohamed (2023) pointed out that AI-powered language learning tools might not suit those without access to necessary technology. Despite its advanced capabilities, ChatGPT was still susceptible to errors or deviations from correct language use. In their research, Li et al. (2023) observed that these inaccuracies posed challenges in crafting accurate and effective prompts. Similarly, Mohamed (2023) expressed concerns about ChatGPT's precision, particularly with idiomatic expressions, cultural references and other nuanced aspects of human language.

The tendency of ChatGPT to produce inappropriate feedback was a concern for educators. For instance, Guo and Wang (2023) observed that ChatGPT occasionally deviated from the expected feedback focus, providing off-task feedback. In contrast, EFL teachers in the same study consistently provided on-task feedback, highlighting a significant discrepancy between ChatGPT and human instructors. Furthermore, teachers expressed concerns about aligning ChatGPT's evaluation criteria with their own. The lack of in-depth knowledge about the class and individual students further compounded this issue. Echoing this concern, Mohamed (2023) emphasised the limitations of ChatGPT, including generating inappropriate responses and facing challenges in adequately addressing critical language components.

The suitability of the materials generated by ChatGPT for language learners at all levels was a complex issue. Li et al. (2023) pointed to a contradiction in this regard. They implied that ChatGPT may not cater to the diverse proficiency levels of language learners. As Young and Shishido (2023) suggested, the dialogues produced were well-suited for students with CEFR A2 proficiency, enabling them to comprehend most of the words used. However, creating content for students at higher CEFR levels had its limitations. While dialogues intended for CEFR B1 students benefited those at the A2 level by exposing them to new vocabulary, the need for more advanced content, tailored specifically for higher-level learners, remained. Consequently, ChatGPT's potential to provide valuable resources and its alignment with the varied needs and abilities of learners across different proficiency levels may not be consistently effective.

The adoption of ChatGPT raised several ethical and privacy concerns. Mohamed (2023) emphasised the urgency to address these issues. The primary ethical concerns centred around the risk of perpetuating language biases and stereotypes. In addition, there were substantial privacy and data protection concerns, especially in safeguarding student data during interactions with the technology. The research also highlighted apprehensions about ChatGPT potentially replacing human roles. According to Kostka and Toncelli (2023), some students recognised the need for human intervention when using ChatGPT, acknowledging that, while beneficial, technology cannot fully replace human guidance and expertise. Yan (2023) further revealed the concerns about the unrestricted use of ChatGPT in L2 writing. Participants in the study demonstrated more concern than satisfaction when it came to the fully automated workflow of ChatGPT. Undergraduate EFL learners, particularly those with limited exposure to the latest technologies, were uneasy about the potential displacement of human educators in L2 writing pedagogy.

Bridging Findings and Literature

The findings have effectively demonstrated the connection between empirical evidence on ChatGPT's role in language education and existing academic discourse. This connection is particularly evident in the authentic learning contexts enabled by integrating ChatGPT, a conclusion supported by literature from Baskara and Mukarto (2023), Cai (2023), Hong (2023) and Kohnke et al. (2023). This integration is evident in the learning content created by ChatGPT and its dual roles as both a feedback provider and a personal tutor. A profound impact of ChatGPT on language learning is its ability to enhance various aspects of the learning process, such as improving conversational skills, reading, writing, grammar and pronunciation. Designed for diverse groups of participants, ChatGPT offers personalised instruction, thereby enriching the learning experience, although its effectiveness may currently vary across different proficiency levels. Its capability to provide language learning content tailored to different learners and skills mirrors real-world scenarios. This particular aspect is emphasised in the research by Baskara and Mukarto (2023) and Cai (2023). Moreover, in line with the findings of Baskara and Mukarto (2023), Cai (2023) and Hong (2023), ChatGPT's provision of personalised and adaptive feedback is highlighted as a unique characteristic that sets it apart from traditional teacher feedback in language education. As a personal tutor, ChatGPT facilitates language learning by engaging in questions, discussions and simulated dialogues that resemble human-like responses. This approach aligns with the assertions of Kohnke et al. (2023), Baskara and Mukarto (2023) and Hong (2023), who praise ChatGPT's interactive and personalised teaching capabilities, as well as those of Cai (2023), who emphasises its adaptability to each learner's unique requirements.

Another significant aspect of the findings is ChatGPT's role in empowering students to actively engage in their learning process. Several impactful areas have been identified. The findings indicate that ChatGPT, serving as a personal tutor, plays a crucial role in enhancing learner motivation, making learning materials more appealing and interactive. Its personalised interactions with learners ensure that they remain engaged and motivated, as emphasised by Cai (2023). ChatGPT's ability to function as a personalised tool also allows learners to engage with the AI's output and explore topics more independently. Students with favourable perceptions of ChatGPT's effectiveness are more inclined to use it, leading to a significant increase in their independent learning outside the classroom environment. This level of engagement is crucial for developing self-directed learners who can navigate and assimilate information without direct supervision from teachers. This resonates with the literature's focus on learner-driven control and engagement (Cai, 2023). These findings not only validate the existing literature but also add depth by detailing specific instances of increased student enthusiasm and active participation in learning activities.

The integration of ChatGPT in language education requires careful consideration of educators' input, a factor that is prominently emphasised in the findings. On one hand, the findings indicate that, while ChatGPT cannot replace human language teachers, its role as a knowledgeable assistant is significantly valuable. Academics regard ChatGPT as a collaborator that, when combined with educators' involvement, enhances the teaching and learning process. Serving as an effective support tool, it aids in extended conversations and tasks such as grading and assignment evaluation. This synergy points to a promising future for AI-augmented language education. The roles of ChatGPT, in line with its characterisation as teachers' aid (Cai, 2023; Hong, 2023), contribute to reducing their workloads. On the other hand, there are notable concerns, such as the potential of ChatGPT replacing human roles in teaching. These apprehensions, as echoed by Baskara and Mukarto (2023), reflect broader scepticism about the role of

AI in education. Therefore, it is crucial to strike a balance between technological advancements and the essential role of human oversight and interaction within the educational process.

Echoing the study of Kohnke et al. (2023), the findings emphasise the challenge of ensuring accurate responses and alignment with educational standards. They also highlight the challenges educators face, such as ChatGPT's occasional delivery of inappropriate feedback and its difficulty in understanding students' specific needs. These issues correspond to identified limitations of ChatGPT, such as its tendency to produce factually incorrect or irrelevant outputs, as noted by Cai (2023) and Kukulska-Hulme et al. (2023). Furthermore, the integration raises ethical considerations, particularly concerning adaptability and data privacy. This reflects concerns about cultural and social biases in the source database and algorithms, as discussed by Cai (2023), Kohnke et al. (2023) and Kukulska-Hulme et al. (2023).

Notable differences between the two sources include the emphasis in the literature on ChatGPT's role in creating a comfortable and safe learning environment. This aspect, highlighted by Cai (2023), enhances learner confidence and encourages participation, yet it is not specifically addressed in the findings of this research. While this study aligns with the existing body of knowledge, it also expands upon it. It offers new insights, such as the challenges in accessing AI tools like ChatGPT in less advantaged regions and the generally positive attitude of students towards ChatGPT in facilitating the learning process. Students appreciate ChatGPT's ease of use and effectiveness in language learning, leading to increased acceptance and high satisfaction scores. They also favour integrating ChatGPT into educational settings, recognising its significant benefits. In addition, the findings reveal that students generally view ChatGPT positively in the context of language learning, appreciating its practicality and accessibility, and recognising its potential to facilitate more effective and engaging learning processes. Moreover, the findings suggest that ChatGPT encourages critical thinking in students, prompting them to modify prompts, train the system, and selectively accept information. This helps students to evaluate the usability of generated information and develop a critical stance towards the role of AI in language learning, an aspect not exclusively highlighted in the existing literature.

IMPLICATIONS

The significant outcomes of this project also lie in the implications that it carries. These implications are not just about technological advancements but also include pedagogical and ethical considerations that can shape a more effective and responsible approach to language teaching and learning.

Technological Implications

As the landscape of language education progresses, the necessity for AI technologies like ChatGPT to undergo regular updates and monitoring becomes increasingly apparent. More than just enhancing the learning experience, these efforts are crucial for aligning educational journeys with the rapid pace of technological advancements. A key aspect of this evolution involves integrating AI tools like ChatGPT into educational platforms. This necessitates a design that is not only compatible with existing digital tools and learning management systems but also user-friendly and intuitive. This ensures their relevance and effectiveness in an evolving educational environment. Central to this process is the continuous professional development and support extended to educators. It is essential that educators are trained not only in the technical aspects of AI tools but also in effectively integrating these tools into their teaching practices. An example of this is the revision of assessment policies and the development of suitable rubrics and criteria, as suggested by Alexander et al. (2023).

Moreover, educators should explore strategies that facilitate the integration of AI tools into language education, adopting effective pedagogical frameworks. In this context, Xiao and Zhi (2023) highlight the benefits of integrating tools like ChatGPT in language classrooms. They propose strategies that enable students to use these tools legitimately and productively. Complementing this, Tseng and Warschauer (2023) present a comprehensive five-part pedagogical framework (understand, access, prompt, corroborate and incorporate), specifically designed to support second language learners. Such frameworks are instrumental in helping both educators and students to understand how to effectively collaborate with AI technologies. This prepares them for a future increasingly intertwined with technological advancements, both within the educational sphere and beyond.

Pedagogical Implications

As AI technologies continue to advance, their impact on language education is set to grow, transforming the ways in which languages are taught and learnt. Among the pedagogical implications, a significant aspect is the role of ChatGPT as teachers' aid. This involves the substantial role of AI in augmenting educators' capabilities, as demonstrated by this project. By handling routine tasks, AI technologies enable educators to focus on more personalised, adaptive and authentic aspects of teaching. This includes monitoring AI's interactions with students and the feedback it provides. Ensuring that AI serves as a reliable and effective tool is essential for students engaging with it in language learning, and it also enriches the overall teaching experience. Educators are thus encouraged to deliberately integrate AI-driven tools into their teaching practices.

Moreover, AI technologies like ChatGPT act as personalised tutors, offering valuable feedback to students. This capability plays a crucial role in student learning, particularly in fostering independent learning opportunities outside of the classroom where teachers are not present. This underscores the need to adapt language education methods to integrate such pedagogical advancements. On another level, this development calls for educators to re-evaluate the significance of students' contributions to their learning processes. Leveraging the supportive role of AI technologies, educators should encourage students to engage in collaborative and reflective interactions with AI. This approach may involve incorporating students' input into the learning process. In addition, educational institutions should initiate open dialogues with students, educating them about the responsible use of AI tools and informing them about their limitations, biases, inaccuracies, and the ethical considerations involved. As Mills et al. (2023) suggest, engaging students in such a collaborative manner fosters emergent, student-centred and student-guided methods of exploring AI, contributing to broader societal discussions about its future role.

Ethical Implications

One crucial ethical implication is addressing bias in AI algorithms. Therefore, educators are responsible for preventing the reinforcement of prejudices through these AI models. This ensures that the language and content generated by AI tools, particularly for teaching purposes, are as unbiased as possible, reflecting the utmost efforts of educators. Equally important is safeguarding students' privacy. Considering the need for ethical use of student data, it is imperative that educators establish and strictly adhere to rigorous protocols and policies. This step is crucial in ensuring the protection of student privacy and in guaranteeing responsible and ethical handling of their data.

In addition, educators must ensure the appropriate and judicious use of AI to avoid the risk of becoming overly reliant on it for educational purposes and potentially diminishing the value of human input and interaction in the learning process. Therefore, it is essential for educators to strike a balance between leveraging AI for its advantages and preserving the irreplaceable human elements of teaching languages. Moreover, AI has the potential to bridge accessibility gaps in language education. Educators need to ensure that all students, particularly those in resource-limited areas, have equitable access to the necessary technology for using AI tools. Implementing such practices not only enriches learning environments but also helps to create a more diverse and technologically inclusive educational landscape.

CONCLUSION

This chapter has comprehensively reviewed research from various geographies and online platforms, uncovering a significant global interest in integrating ChatGPT in language education. The inclusion of diverse participant groups, such as educators, researchers, and learners, has offered deep insights into the complex implications of ChatGPT in this field. The use of both qualitative and quantitative research methods has highlighted the multifaceted nature of this dynamic educational technology. In addition, the chapter has emphasised the considerable benefits, challenges and broader implications of ChatGPT within the educational context.

However, this chapter is not without its limitations. The relatively small sample size of 12 selected articles may limit the generalisability of the findings. In addition, the inclusion criteria, which required articles to be in English, could have introduced language bias and possibly excluded valuable non-English language research. Moreover, relying primarily on the Scopus and Web of Science databases for article identification might have overlooked relevant articles from other databases, potentially leading to selection bias. Although forward citation search was conducted to identify additional articles, the chosen timeframe for article inclusion, ending in September 2023, may have excluded newer research pertinent to the topic.

Despite these limitations, the chapter provides valuable insights into AI-driven projects in various educational settings, as exemplified by ChatGPT. It highlights the technology's impact from the perspectives of both students and educators. The chapter's significance lies in its thorough exploration of AI's role in language education, demonstrating its potential to shape the future of this field. This analysis equips educators, researchers and policymakers with insights to guide their strategies for effectively integrating AI in language education. It advocates for leveraging the benefits of AI tools like ChatGPT while thoughtfully addressing the challenges and ethical considerations inherent in their use. As language education continues to evolve, understanding and adapting to AI technologies will be crucial in enhancing learning experiences and outcomes.

REFERENCES

Ahmed, M. A. (2023). ChatGPT and the EFL classroom: Supplement or substitute in Saudi Arabia's eastern region. *Information Sciences Letters*, *12*(7), 2727–2734. doi:10.18576/isl/120704

Alexander, K., Savvidou, C., & Alexander, C. (2023). Who wrote this essay? Detecting AI-generated writing in second language education in higher education. *Teaching English with Technology*, *23*(2), 25–43. doi:10.56297/BUKA4060/XHLD5365

Auer, M. E., Pester, A., & May, D. (Eds.). (2022). *Learning with Technologies and Technologies in Learning: Experience, Trends and Challenges in Higher Education* (Vol. 456). Springer International Publishing. https://link.springer.com/10.1007/978-3-031-04286-7

Baïdoo-Anu, D., & Ansah, L. O. (2023). Education in the era of generative artificial intelligence (AI): Understanding the potential benefits of ChatGPT in promoting teaching and learning. *Journal of AI*, *7*(1), 52–62. doi:10.61969/jai.1337500

Baskara, R., & Mukarto. (2023). Exploring the implications of ChatGPT for language learning in higher education. *Indonesian Journal of English Language Teaching and Applied Linguistics, 7*(2), 343–358. https://eric.ed.gov/?id=EJ1391490

Bin-Hady, W. R. A., Al-Kadi, A., Hazaea, A., & Ali, J. K. M. (2023). Exploring the dimensions of ChatGPT in English language learning: A global perspective. *Library Hi Tech*. Advance online publication. doi:10.1108/LHT-05-2023-0200

Cai, W. (2023, February 24). ChatGPT can be powerful tool for language learning: The innovation offers multiple opportunities for language teaching and learning. *University Affairs*. https://www.universityaffairs.ca/career-advice/career-advice-article/chatgpt-can-be-powerful-tool-for-language-learning/

Crompton, H., & Burke, D. (2023). Artificial intelligence in higher education: The state of the field. *International Journal of Educational Technology in Higher Education*, *20*(1), 22. doi:10.1186/s41239-023-00392-8

Golonka, E. M., Bowles, A. R., Frank, V. M., Richardson, D. L., & Freynik, S. (2014). Technologies for foreign language learning: A review of technology types and their effectiveness. *Computer Assisted Language Learning*, *27*(1), 70–105. doi:10.1080/09588221.2012.700315

Guo, K., & Wang, D. (2023). To resist it or to embrace it? Examining ChatGPT's potential to support teacher feedback in EFL writing. *Education and Information Technologies*. Advance online publication. doi:10.1007/s10639-023-12146-0

Hong, W. C. H. (2023). The impact of ChatGPT on foreign language teaching and learning: Opportunities in education and research. *Journal of Educational Technology and Innovation*, *5*(1). https://jeti.thewsu.org/index.php/cieti/article/view/103

Huang, X., Zou, D., Cheng, G., Chen, X., & Xie, H. (2023). Trends, research issues and applications of artificial intelligence in language education. *Journal of Educational Technology & Society*, *26*(1), 112–131. https://www.jstor.org/stable/48707971

Kasneci, E., Sessler, K., Küchemann, S., Bannert, M., Dementieva, D., Fischer, F., Gasser, U., Groh, G., Günnemann, S., Hüllermeier, E., Krusche, S., Kutyniok, G., Michaeli, T., Nerdel, C., Pfeffer, J., Poquet, O., Sailer, M., Schmidt, A., Seidel, T., ... Kasneci, G. (2023). ChatGPT for good? On opportunities and challenges of large language models for education. *Learning and Individual Differences*, *103*, 102274. doi:10.1016/j.lindif.2023.102274

Kohnke, L., Moorhouse, B. L., & Zou, D. (2023). ChatGPT for language teaching and learning. *RELC Journal*, *54*(2), 537–550. doi:10.1177/00336882231162868

Kostka, I., & Toncelli, R. (2023). Exploring applications of ChatGPT to English language teaching: Opportunities, challenges, and recommendations. *TESL-EJ*, *27*(3). Advance online publication. doi:10.55593/ej.27107int

Kukulska-Hulme, A., Bossu, C., Charitonos, K., Coughlan, T., Deacon, A., Deane, N., Ferguson, R., Herodotou, C., Huang, C.-W., Mayisela, T., Rets, I., Sargent, J., Scanlon, E., Small, J., Walji, S., Weller, M., & Whitelock, D. (2023). *Innovating Pedagogy 2023: Open University Innovation Report 11*. The Open University.

Li, B., Bonk, C. J., & Kou, X. (2023). Exploring the multilingual applications of ChatGPT: Uncovering language learning affordances in YouTuber videos. *International Journal of Computer-Assisted Language Learning and Teaching*, *13*(1), 1–22. Advance online publication. doi:10.4018/IJCALLT.326135

Liu, G., & Ma, C. (2023). Measuring EFL learners' use of ChatGPT in informal digital learning of English based on the technology acceptance model. *Innovation in Language Learning and Teaching*, *0*(0), 1–14. doi:10.1080/17501229.2023.2240316

Mills, A., Bali, M., & Eaton, L. (2023). How do we respond to generative AI in education? Open educational practices give us a framework for an ongoing process. *Journal of Applied Learning and Teaching*, *6*(1), 16–30. doi:10.37074/jalt.2023.6.1.34

Moeller, A., & Catalano, T. (2015). Foreign language teaching and learning. In J. D. Wright (Ed.), *International Encyclopedia of the Social & Behavioral Sciences* (2nd ed., Vol. 9, pp. 327–332). Elsevier. doi:10.1016/B978-0-08-097086-8.92082-8

Mohamed, A. M. (2023). Exploring the potential of an AI-based Chatbot (ChatGPT) in enhancing English as a foreign language (EFL) teaching: Perceptions of EFL faculty members. *Education and Information Technologies*. Advance online publication. doi:10.1007/s10639-023-11917-z

Rebolledo Font De La Vall, R., & González Araya, F. (2023). Exploring the benefits and challenges of AI-language learning tools. *International Journal of Social Sciences and Humanities Invention*, *10*(01), 7569–7576. doi:10.18535/ijsshi/v10i01.02

Roumeliotis, K. I., & Tselikas, N. D. (2023). ChatGPT and open-AI models: A preliminary review. *Future Internet*, *15*(6), 192. doi:10.3390/fi15060192

Shadiev, R., & Yang, M. (2020). Review of studies on technology-enhanced language learning and teaching. *Sustainability (Basel)*, *12*(2), 524. doi:10.3390/su12020524

Shaikh, S., Yayilgan, S. Y., Klimova, B., & Pikhart, M. (2023). Assessing the usability of ChatGPT for formal English language learning. *European Journal of Investigation in Health, Psychology and Education*, *13*(9), 1937–1960. doi:10.3390/ejihpe13090140 PMID:37754479

Tseng, W., & Warschauer, M. (2023). AI-writing tools in education: If you can't beat them, join them. *Journal of China Computer-Assisted Language Learning*, *3*(2), 258–262. Advance online publication. doi:10.1515/jccall-2023-0008

Xiao, Y., & Zhi, Y. (2023). An exploratory study of EFL learners' use of ChatGPT for language learning tasks: Experience and perceptions. *Languages (Basel, Switzerland)*, *8*(3), 212. Advance online publication. doi:10.3390/languages8030212

Yan, D. (2023). Impact of ChatGPT on learners in a L2 writing practicum: An exploratory investigation. *Education and Information Technologies*, *28*(11), 13943–13967. Advance online publication. doi:10.1007/s10639-023-11742-4

Young, J. C., & Shishido, M. (2023). Investigating OpenAI's ChatGPT potentials in generating chatbot's dialogue for English as a foreign language learning. *International Journal of Advanced Computer Science and Applications*, *14*(6), 65–72. doi:10.14569/IJACSA.2023.0140607

Ziegler, N., & González-Lloret, M. (2022). *The Routledge Handbook of Second Language Acquisition and Technology* (1st ed.). Routledge. doi:10.4324/9781351117586

KEY TERMS AND DEFINITIONS

AI: Or Artificial Intelligence, is a system that simulates human intelligence and can perform tasks traditionally carried out by humans.

AI Technologies: Refer to systems that utilise principles and techniques of AI to carry out various tasks.

ChatGPT: Is a prominent AI language model developed by OpenAI. The remarkable ability of ChatGPT to handle complex tasks has received significant attention in the field of language education.

Language Education: Aims to foster effective communication and meaningful interaction in different linguistic and cultural contexts. It provides learners with skills to overcome linguistic barriers and collaborate across diverse geographical boundaries.

Language Learning: Is a process through which learners immerse themselves in a new language, developing proficiency in its linguistic components, language learning skills and cultural awareness. This comprehensive development contributes to their ability to effectively use the language for communication and understanding in real-world contexts.

Language Teaching: Is a process through which teachers aim to enhance learners' linguistic proficiency, develop their language learning skills, foster their cultural awareness and enable learners to use the language effectively for communication and understanding in real-world contexts.

Learner Attitude: Refers to the emotions, thoughts and actions of learners towards their learning process.

Learner Engagement: Is characterised by the extent of involvement and enthusiasm displayed by learners as they participate in their learning process, impacting their learning outcomes.

APPENDIX

Table 4. Summary of the selected journal articles

	Authors	Publication Year	Title of Publication	Number of Participants	Participants	Research Site	Research Design	Data Collection Tools
1	Ahmed	2023	ChatGPT and the EFL classroom: Supplement or substitute in Saudi Arabia's eastern region	64	First-year university EFL students	Saudi Arabia	Qualitative design	Interviews
2	Alexander et al.	2023	Who wrote this essay? Detecting AI-generated writing in second language education in higher education	6	ESL lecturers (C1 level English academic writing)	Cyprus	Exploratory qualitative study	Essay sample preparation; AI detector analysis of essays; ESL lecturer text analysis
3	Bin-Hady et al.	2023	Exploring the dimensions of ChatGPT in English language learning: A global perspective	20	ResearchGate researchers in technology-based language learning and teaching	ResearchGate	Grounded theory-based qualitative study	Discussion data collection
4	Guo and Wang	2023	To resist it or to embrace it? Examining ChatGPT's potential to support teacher feedback in EFL writing	5	Chinese EFL teachers	China	Exploratory study	ChatGPT feedback; EFL teacher feedback; EFL teacher questionnaires
5	Kostka and Toncelli	2023	Exploring applications of ChatGPT to English language teaching: Opportunities, challenges, and recommendations	n/a	International students in a pathways programme	USA	Qualitative student quotations	Student quotations
6	Li et al.	2023	Exploring the multilingual applications of ChatGPT: Uncovering language learning affordances in YouTuber videos	45	YouTube video content	YouTube	Inductive content analysis	YouTube videos (primary data) and comments (secondary data)
7	Liu and Ma	2023	Measuring EFL learners' use of ChatGPT in informal digital learning of English based on the technology acceptance model	405	EFL learners	China, the United States, Other Anglophone countries	Quantitative cross-sectional survey	Online survey

continues on following page

Table 4. Continued

	Authors	Publication Year	Title of Publication	Number of Participants	Participants	Research Site	Research Design	Data Collection Tools
8	Mohamed	2023	Exploring the potential of an AI-based Chatbot (ChatGPT) in enhancing English as a foreign language (EFL) teaching: Perceptions of EFL faculty members	10	EFL faculty members	Saudi Arabia	Qualitative content analysis	Email interviews
9	Shaikh et al.	2023	Assessing the usability of ChatGPT for formal English language learning	10	Students from various departments of a university	Norway	Quantitative exploratory study	Questionnaires
10	Xiao and Zhi	2023	An exploratory study of EFL learners' use of ChatGPT for language learning tasks: Experience and perceptions	5	Undergraduate students (English-medium international university)	China	Qualitative exploratory study	Semi-structured interviews
11	Yan	2023	Impact of ChatGPT on learners in a L2 writing practicum: An exploratory investigation	8	Undergraduate EFL majors	China	Qualitative exploratory approach	Observations; In-depth interviews
12	Young and Shishido	2023	Investigating OpenAI's ChatGPT potentials in generating Chatbot's dialogue for English as a foreign language learning	450	ChatGPT-generated dialogues	Japan	Quantitative study	Flesch reading ease analysis; McAlpine EFLAW analysis; Dale-Chall analysis

Chapter 2
Enhancing Language Teaching Materials Through Artificial Intelligence:
Opportunities and Challenges

Surjit Singha
https://orcid.org/0000-0002-5730-8677
Kristu Jayanti College (Autonomous), India

Ranjit Singha
https://orcid.org/0000-0002-3541-8752
Christ University, India

Elizabeth Jasmine
Indian Institute of Psychology and Research, India

ABSTRACT

Incorporating artificial intelligence (AI) into language education signifies a paradigm shift that promotes originality and inclusiveness. The partnership between AI developers and educators effectively tackles obstacles and establishes a foundation for continuous progress. Anticipating the future, the progression of AI holds the potential to deliver intricate customization, customizing educational encounters to suit the unique requirements of each individual. Responsible incorporation of AI into teaching methodologies transforms them into a collaborative model that empowers educators to engage in individualized interactions. Ethics remain of the utmost importance, encompassing bias mitigation and privacy. In essence, the integration of AI into language education signifies an impending era in which the combined powers of technology and human proficiency foster the development of capable individuals who are prepared to navigate an interconnected, digitally globalized society.

DOI: 10.4018/979-8-3693-0872-1.ch002

INTRODUCTION

AI revolutionizes language education, offering interactive content, chatbots, and intelligent tutors for personalized and adaptive learning experiences, transforming traditional approaches. (Li & Yu, 2021). Implementing artificial intelligence (AI) in language learning platforms has profoundly impacted user experiences and learning outcomes, representing a paradigm shift in education. Prominent media, including Duolingo, Rosetta Stone, Babbel, Lingodeer, ChatGPT Language Tutor, and Memrise, have effectively utilized artificial intelligence (AI) to deliver customized lessons, modify instructional materials, and augment user involvement. These technological advancements deliver immediate feedback, accommodate unique learning preferences, and provide unprecedented personalization. AI transforms language assessments, offering adaptive learning, real-time analytics, and automated evaluations for precise insights. Collaboration ensures ethical and effective AI integration (Akgün & Greenhow, 2021). Advancing technology allows educators to integrate AI for dynamic, individualized language learning, fostering inclusivity, innovation, and educational evolution. This chapter examines the convergence of artificial intelligence (AI) and language teaching materials, investigating novel approaches to utilizing AI to enhance and supplement the materials employed in language classrooms.

AI transforms language education by offering adaptive, personalized resources and customizing material for varied linguistic proficiencies, preferences, and cultural backgrounds. (Towle & Halm, 2006). AI-driven language education employs interactive platforms, tutoring systems, and chatbots for real-time assessment, offering immediate feedback and tailored assistance to foster interactive education with adaptive pathways, tailoring lessons based on individual progress, ensuring inclusivity, and enhancing cultural relevance (Roche et al., 2022). By employing this tool, the cultural sensitivity of language education materials is elevated. The purpose of this chapter is to present a thorough examination of the potential benefits AI can bring to improve language teaching materials. AI in language education spans interactive platforms and intelligent tutors. Ethical considerations and teacher preparedness are vital for successful integration (Meng et al., 2022). Understanding AI in language education involves exploring fundamental theories and contextual frameworks to develop effective instructional materials.

LITERATURE REVIEW

The concept of cognitive load theory, initially introduced by John Sweller, centres on the degree of cognitive exertion required during the learning process (Sweller, 2012). It is proposed that the design of instructional materials should regulate cognitive burden to maximize learning outcomes efficiently. AI can assist in customizing language teaching materials for individual students by regulating and modifying the difficulty level following their cognitive abilities. This customization is consistent with the tenets of Cognitive Load Theory, given that artificial intelligence can analyze real-time data on student performance, identify problem areas, and adapt learning materials dynamically (Gandhi et al., 2023; Zhao et al., 2022). Furthermore, artificial intelligence (AI) can utilize tactics such as chunking information into more manageable segments, thereby reducing the cognitive burden on learners. Artificial intelligence can augment comprehension and retention by deconstructing and presenting intricate linguistic concepts sequentially. It is consistent with cognitive load theory principles, which advocate reducing unnecessary cognitive load and enhancing relevant cognitive load. As a result, language learners can concentrate on comprehending and utilizing newly acquired skills. Adaptive learning pathways may also be incorporated into AI-powered language instructional materials, following the Cognitive Load Theory's suggestion that personalized instruction is optimal (Sweller et al., 2022; Zhao et al., 2022). By dynamically adapting these pathways following the learners' progress, it is possible to maintain a challenging yet optimally designed curriculum that promotes effective learning. The capacity for adaptation mitigates cognitive excess and guarantees that learners can effectively process and assimilate language concepts. Fundamentally, incorporating artificial intelligence (AI) into language instructional resources exemplifies a beneficial implementation of cognitive load theory. Anger management, adaptive learning experiences, and the personalization of content are a few of the functionalities of artificial intelligence that educators can utilize to improve the efficacy and efficiency of language instruction (Sweller et al., 2022; Paas & Van Merriënboer, 2020). By adhering to the principles of Cognitive Load Theory, this language learning environment becomes more learner-centric and optimized from a cognitive standpoint.

Building upon the research of Jean Piaget and Lev Vygotsky, constructivism places significant emphasis on the active engagement of learners as they construct their understanding of knowledge. The social process of learning is characterized by collaboration and interaction. Language-teaching materials propelled by AI have the potential to foster collaborative and interactive learning environments. The constructivist approach is compatible with chatbots, virtual language exchange platforms, and AI-driven discussion forums, enabling students to participate in language learning actively. Within the constructivist paradigm, learners are perceived as engaged contributors who construct knowledge utilizing practical experiences and interpersonal engagements. Some theories say that AI tools, including chatbots, facilitate learners' active application of language skills through the simulation of real-world conversations. Assisting learners in dialogues while providing immediate corrections and feedback, these interactive conversational agents support the constructivist principle of learning through reflection and feedback. An additional implementation of AI in language education is virtual language exchange platforms, which link students with native speakers or peers from around the globe (Behrens, 2021; Kaufman, 2004). Implementing virtual language exchange platforms facilitates this engaging and cooperative linguistic setting. These platforms serve as spaces where students actively partake in authentic dialogues, cultural interchanges, and collaborative language exercises. The constructivist principle is upheld, emphasizing that the most efficient learning occurs within social and meaningful environments. In addition, discussion forums powered by artificial intelligence can strengthen collaborative learning by providing a venue for students to exchange thoughts, pose inquiries, and work together on projects about language. AI can facilitate these forums to guarantee that discussions follow language learning objectives and encourage constructive interactions among learners (Cohen & Téllez, 1994; Bruffee, 1984). By actively participating in discussions, learners can exchange their unique viewpoints and collaboratively develop an understanding of language usage, grammar, and cultural subtleties. Language instructional materials powered by artificial intelligence facilitate a constructivist approach to language education. AI aligns with the constructivist philosophy by providing collaborative and interactive learning experiences via discussion forums, chatbots, and virtual language exchange platforms (Kaufman, 2004). For example, a language-learning application powered by artificial intelligence could incorporate chatbots that engage learners in simulated conversations, offering immediate feedback and corrections. A virtual language exchange platform could connect students with native speakers or peers globally, enabling authentic dialogues and cultural exchanges. Through these AI-driven tools, students actively participate in constructing their understanding of language, aligning with the constructivist approach to education. This philosophy underscores the significance of active participation, social interaction, and collective knowledge construction as critical components of the language learning journey. Incorporating artificial intelligence (AI) into language education improves its efficacy by providing learners with dynamic and interactive learning experiences.

Adaptive Learning Theory (Towle & Halm, 2006) is predicated on the customization of instruction to the specific requirements of each learner. Utilizing technology facilitates individualized learning experiences by adapting the material, speed, and evaluations to the learner's progress. By analyzing learner data, AI technologies can dynamically adapt language instructional materials. The ability to adjust ensures that educational materials align with students' individual learning patterns, preferences, and proficiency levels, promoting a more efficient and tailored educational experience. The impact of AI's adaptive learning capabilities in language education is especially significant. By continuously analyzing learner interactions, AI algorithms can detect patterns, strengths, and areas that require refinement. By leveraging data, this methodology permits the adaptation of language instructional resources to cater to the unique requirements of each learner. For example, suppose a student excels at specific language abilities while encountering difficulties with others. In that case, artificial intelligence can adapt the level of difficulty and emphasis of lessons in real time to deliver specific assistance where it is required most. Moreover, the adaptability of AI surpasses mere content customization and encompasses personalized cadence as well. Language learners advance individually, guaranteeing adequate time to comprehend concepts and solidify their comprehension before proceeding.

Adaptive pacing accommodates a wide range of learning rates, including those who progress quickly and those who benefit more from a deliberate and comprehensive approach. Providing targeted and immediate feedback is an additional crucial element of AI-powered adaptive learning. AI can give instantaneous feedback on language usage, pronunciation, and comprehension based on real-time analysis of learner responses. Implementing this immediate feedback loop is crucial in expeditiously rectifying errors, reinforcing proper usage, and augmenting overall language proficiency. The incorporation of AI into language education perfectly matches the tenets of Adaptive Learning Theory (Jiang, 2022; Seo et al., 2021). Using artificial intelligence (AI) to analyze learner data and dynamically adapt instructional materials enhances language education's responsiveness, personalization, and efficacy (Seo et al., 2021). By implementing this adaptive methodology, students are guaranteed personalized assistance, the ability to advance at their rates, and the advantage of prompt evaluation, all of which contribute to a more captivating and fruitful language-learning encounter.

A subfield of artificial intelligence (AI), Natural Language Processing (NLP), examines the relationship between computers and human language (Kaddari et al., 2020). It entails the creation of models and algorithms that empower machines to comprehend, interpret, and produce text that resembles that of humans. NLP is paramount in developing intelligent tutors, chatbots, and language assessment tools for language instructional materials. These applications facilitate language acquisition through immediate feedback, the simulation of authentic language usage, and the delivery of customized language practice. An essential impact of natural language processing (NLP) on language education has been the development of intelligent language instructors (Tafazoli et al., 2019). By utilizing NLP algorithms, these instructors analyze students' responses to determine their level of language proficiency and subsequently customize instruction. These competent instructors create a dynamic and engaging learning environment by simulating interactive conversations and replicating real-life language interactions closely. Using NLP-powered instructors facilitates immediate correction for students and reinforces adherence to correct language usage. NLP-powered chatbots are an additional asset that can be added to language-teaching materials. By engaging learners in text or voice conversations, these chatbots simulate the learning environment and facilitate the practice of language skills. NLP empowers chatbots to comprehend input in natural language, provide contextually relevant responses, and adjust the level of complexity of conversations following the learner's proficiency (Jeon & Lee, 2023; Belda-Medina & Calvo-Ferrer, 2022). By giving hands-on and immersive experiences, this conversational and interactive method enhances language acquisition. In addition, NLP makes a substantial contribution to language assessment instruments. Utilizing NLP algorithms, automated language assessment systems are capable of real-time evaluation of learners' language proficiency. The evaluations encompass various topics, such as pronunciation, vocabulary, and grammar. Using NLP-based assessments enables learners to monitor their progress, pinpoint areas that require refinement, and obtain focused guidance to enhance their skills through immediate feedback. NLP is critically important in creating language instruction materials powered by AI. NLP enhances language education by utilizing intelligent instructors, chatbots, and assessment tools, all of which facilitate dynamic, interactive, and personalized learning experiences. The ongoing progression of technology presents an opportunity to enhance language learning experiences by incorporating natural language processing (NLP) into instructional materials (Baha et al., 2023; Kurni et al., 2023). This integration could result in more effective, engaging, and individualized language learning journeys for students.

Lev Vygotsky's sociocultural theory significantly emphasizes the influence of cultural context and social interactions on forming cognitive processes (Eun, 2010). The learning process is socially mediated; AI can facilitate sociocultural interactions in language learning by enabling collaborative initiatives, language exchange platforms, and virtual language communities. These technological advancements transcend the confines of the traditional classroom setting, fostering connections between students and culturally and linguistically diverse environments. AI-enabled virtual language communities offer a platform for language learners to participate in collaborative language activities. These communities can replicate authentic language usage by integrating chatbots, virtual tutors, and peer interactions. Students can cultivate a sense of community and engage in collective learning experiences by honing their language abilities in a social setting. AI-powered language exchange platforms facilitate connections between language learners, language enthusiasts and native speakers worldwide. These platforms pair language learners according to their shared interests, proficiency levels, and language objectives. Through active participation in language exchanges, students not only enhance their linguistic proficiency but also acquire a deeper understanding of diverse cultures, dialects, and modes of communication. AI-supported collaborative projects enable students to join efforts to complete language-related assignments. AI can support group endeavours by offering necessary resources, constructive criticism, and coordination instruments. Collaborative initiatives furnish learners with prospects to collectively resolve challenges, exchange insights, and investigate linguistic variety (Zou et al., 2023; Machwate et al., 2021). An example of a community facilitating collaborative language projects with AI support is "Tandem." Tandem is a language exchange app that connects users with language learners worldwide for virtual language exchange. In this community, learners can collaborate on language-related assignments, engage in conversation, and provide feedback to each other, enhancing their linguistic skills and cultural understanding. The platform utilizes AI to suggest conversation topics, match language exchange partners, and provide language resources, contributing to a collaborative and enriching language learning experience.

Moreover, language learning platforms propelled by AI can expose students to authentic materials, traditions, and customs by integrating cultural elements into lessons. Through a greater comprehension of the cultural milieu in which the language is utilized, this integration enhances the educational experience. AI promotes collaborative and culturally diverse learning environments in language education, contributing to sociocultural theory (Li & Yu, 2021). By facilitating sociocultural exchanges facilitated by AI, language learners can engage with a worldwide community and gain first-hand knowledge of various linguistic and cultural milieus. Incorporating artificial intelligence (AI) into sociocultural language learning can augment the depth and genuineness of language instruction as technology progresses. AI language platforms integrate authentic materials, traditions, and customs, enhancing cultural understanding. Learners experience a personalized, culturally diverse education using multimedia content and adaptive algorithms aligning with sociocultural theory.

Concerning algorithmic bias, privacy, and data security, implementing AI in education raises ethical issues. It is imperative to comprehend the ethical ramifications to guarantee the responsible and equitable implementation of artificial intelligence in language instructional resources. In language education, developers and educators must be conscious of and address ethical concerns associated with AI applications. It encompasses measures to safeguard data privacy, reduce biases in artificial intelligence models, and promote transparency regarding the implementation of AI technologies. Data privacy is of the utmost importance in language education powered by AI. Because these systems amass and analyze enormous quantities of learner data, it is critical to implement stringent safeguards to secure sensitive information (Nguyen et al., 2022; Akgün & Greenhow, 2021). To protect learners' privacy, it is imperative to implement explicit policies and procedures that guarantee data is utilized exclusively for educational intentions and remains invulnerable to unauthorized access or exploitation. Addressing biases in AI models constitutes an additional pivotal element of ethical AI integration. It is incumbent on developers to consistently assess and rectify any biases that might unintentionally manifest in language teaching materials, algorithms, or datasets. It is critical to understand cultural, linguistic, and gender biases to guarantee that AI technologies foster inclusiveness rather than perpetuate prejudice or discrimination. Integrity is crucial for establishing confidence in AI applications (Holmes et al., 2021; Akgün & Greenhow, 2021). Singha and Singha (2023) suggest safeguarding sensitive data and user privacy in organizations through encryption, access controls, threat detection mechanisms, and privacy protection measures. Developers and educators must communicate transparently regarding how AI is incorporated into language learning materials, including the algorithms employed, data categories gathered, and the integration process. Transparent communication assures accountability in utilizing these technologies and aids stakeholders, learners, and educators in comprehending the function of AI in the learning process. Educators and developers can strategically incorporate AI into language teaching materials by considering these ethical principles. It would ensure that technology remains in line with established educational principles and ultimately improve the quality of the language learning experience (Klímová et al., 2023; Akgün & Greenhow, 2021). By employing this methodology, the advantages of AI in language instruction are optimized, while possible hazards and ethical considerations are reduced. In the ongoing evolution of AI in education, it is critical to establish and uphold a robust ethical framework to foster an environment that is secure, responsible, and inclusive.

CURRENT LANDSCAPE OF AI IN LANGUAGE TEACHING

This wide range of AI-driven instructional tools not only exemplifies the cutting-edge technologies that are reshaping the field of language education but also underscores the dynamic and comprehensive learning opportunities accessible to students. Automated language instructors, furnished with sophisticated machine learning and natural language processing (NLP) algorithms, are a prime illustration of AI-powered education's individualized and flexible characteristics (Eguchi, 2021; Chaudhry & Kazim,

2021). For example, the conversational practice on Duolingo and Microsoft Xiaoice can be customized to suit the proficiency levels of individual users, thereby establishing a dynamic and captivating atmosphere for language acquisition. Incorporating AI into language learning applications like Babbel surpasses a simple examination of user interactions. The learning paths are proactively customized according to individual performance and preferences, guaranteeing a customized and productive educational experience. Platforms like Tandem utilize artificial intelligence to connect learners with native speakers, facilitating collaborative and interactive language practice in the real world (App Store, 2015). Knewton's demonstration of the adaptability of content and curriculum platforms guarantees that educational materials are consistently modified to cater to each learner's unique requirements, providing a flexible and personalized learning experience (El-Sabagh, 2021). By adjusting content in response to user performance, gamified language learning applications, such as Memrise, demonstrate how artificial intelligence can augment motivation and engagement, rendering language acquisition interactive and pleasurable. Rosetta Stone's multimodal language learning platforms exemplify artificial intelligence's (AI) adaptability in handling diverse input formats, furnishing students with an all-encompassing and immersive language acquisition encounter. The investigation into these AI-driven instructional tools highlights their capacity for profound change and the learner-centred and interactive characteristics that characterize contemporary language instruction (Tan, 2023; Yeşilyurt, 2023). As these technologies progress, individuals pursuing language acquisition can anticipate an ever-expanding selection of practical, interactive, and personalized resources that accommodate their specific learning inclinations. It will create a dynamic and captivating educational experience.

Integrating AI applications in language education represents a paradigm shift in pedagogy, establishing an interdependent ecosystem that enhances learning. Integrating diverse AI-powered tools creates a unified and ever-changing educational setting, facilitating a more individualized and efficient learning experience. Apps for personalized learning, intelligent language tutors, and adaptive chatbots are examples of how AI integrates seamlessly with conventional teaching methods. Language instructors enhance learners' progress by implementing targeted feedback and personalized instruction via machine learning algorithms and natural language processing (Zhu, 2020). Practical communication skills are enhanced through chatbots such as Microsoft's Xiaoice, which facilitate immersive conversations and provide learners with simulated real-world language practice. Language learning applications showcase how AI analysis of user interactions and progress monitoring customizes learning trajectories according to personal preferences—providing a more captivating and individualized language learning encounter—with Babbel serving as an illustrative case. As exemplified by ETS's SpeechRater, automatic language assessment systems demonstrate the efficacy that artificial intelligence (AI) imparts to education by providing immediate evaluations of spoken competence. The combined influence of these artificial intelligence technologies in language education is readily apparent, establishing a pathway towards a revolutionary, student-focused, and interrelated process of acquiring a language (Hou, 2020; Zhu, 2020). With the ongoing development of these technologies, students can expect an educational voyage that is progressively more immersive and dynamic. Throughout this process, artificial intelligence (AI) will seamlessly integrate into the language learning framework, enhancing each aspect of the journey.

PERSONALIZED LEARNING: REDEFINING LANGUAGE ACQUISITION

Powered by Artificial Intelligence (AI), adaptive learning pathways have ushered in a paradigm shift in language education, fundamentally reshaping traditional instructional approaches. This innovative application of artificial intelligence entails customizing the educational experience to precisely align with every learner's requirements, speed, and inclinations. AI algorithms, which frequently integrate Natural Language Processing (NLP) and machine learning, form the basis of this innovation. These algorithms consistently evaluate and analyze the progress of every learner. Dynamic personalization facilitates the instantaneous modification of lesson sequences, content, and difficulty levels, following the learner's learning style and level of proficiency. By utilizing real-time assessment and promptly modifying the learning pathway, this approach guarantees that areas of improvement are attended to, deficiencies are rectified, and students' progress to more complex concepts when suitable.

AI-driven adaptive learning pathways provide individualized scheduling that surpasses the constraints of conventional education models, thereby accommodating learners with varying rates of progress. The ability to adapt enables individuals to make progress at a personalized pace, granting them the flexibility to explore ideas in greater depth or rapidly advance. The system's proficiency in discerning particular language abilities that require enhancement guarantees focused skill development, concentrating on each individual's strengths and limitations. As individuals improve their linguistic skills, AI-powered trajectories consistently adjust to guarantee that the educational process remains pertinent and thought-provoking, fostering enduring interest and development. In brief, artificial intelligence-driven adaptive learning pathways signify a fundamental change in language acquisition by providing a customized, adaptable, and data-informed learning experience that accommodates individual students' distinct requirements and inclinations (Karoui et al., 2022). By employing this revolutionary methodology, acquiring language skills is optimized, and AI is also positioned as a fundamental element in moulding the trajectory of education in the coming years.

A paradigm shift in language education is exemplified by the use of Artificial Intelligence (AI) to facilitate personalized content delivery and learner engagement. AI's significant impact on transforming how content is delivered, and learners engage with it represents a fundamental change toward a more individualized and effective educational environment. Through analyzing user interactions and learning preferences, language learning platforms powered by artificial intelligence have been at the forefront of providing content tailored to each individual's proficiency level. This individualized methodology also encompasses adaptive learning materials, in which AI algorithms consistently evaluate the aptitudes and deficiencies of learners, dynamically modifying the level of difficulty of the material in real-time to guarantee an ideal equilibrium between problem and involvement. AI-driven content delivery enables an inherent level of personalization that surpasses simple customization and significantly enhances learner engagement. By integrating gamification components, interactive activities, and practical situations, acquiring language skills is transformed into something both pleasurable and highly applicable.

Artificial intelligence's prompt and specific feedback functionalities foster a nurturing educational setting, enabling students to promptly remedy errors and solidify accurate language applications. Incorporating AI into interactive learning platforms enhances the language-learning experience by incorporating chatbots and virtual language exchanges, among other features. AI customizes content and entire learning paths by offering recommendations for specific modules and activities that align with the individual's objectives and advancement (Karoui et al., 2022). Fundamentally, this innovative and learner-focused methodology for language instruction, facilitated by artificial intelligence, represents a substantial deviation from conventional frameworks. It guarantees students encounter individualized material and participate actively in a gratifying and customized educational experience.

INNOVATIVE ASSESSMENT METHODS: AI'S ROLE

The implementation of AI-powered real-time performance analytics in language education brings about a significant transformation through the provision of instantaneous insights, flexible teaching methodologies, and a data-centric approach that ultimately improves the efficacy and learner-centric nature of language learning experiences (Salas-Pilco et al., 2022; Khan et al., 2021). With the continuous progression of technology, the incorporation of real-time analytics holds significant potential as a determining factor in the trajectory of language education itself. Integrating automated assessment and feedback systems powered by Artificial Intelligence (AI) capabilities represents a paradigm shift in language education. By implementing sophisticated natural language processing (NLP) algorithms, these systems have significantly transformed the evaluation procedure by furnishing learners with prompt, focused feedback. The utmost importance is placed on the effectiveness and promptness of automated assessment, as AI algorithms rapidly scrutinize written assignments and oral responses, assessing aspects such as pronunciation, vocabulary utilization, and grammar. Educators can provide timely feedback by automating the assessment process, promoting an ongoing learning cycle. Automated grading guarantees a consistent and unbiased evaluation by consistently implementing pre-established criteria and reducing the influence of subjective biases in the assessment process. The feedback produced by these systems is tailored to individual needs, enabling learners to obtain precise evaluations of their performance that direct them towards their most substantial areas and those that necessitate enhancement. In addition, the flexibility of automated grading systems facilitates the development of adaptive learning environments by customizing subsequent assignments per each student's unique abilities and deficiencies, thus maximizing their educational experience.

Grading systems propelled by AI are invaluable in educational environments with many students due to their scalability. Finally, educators are equipped with valuable information regarding overall class performance trends and individual student progress through the data-driven insights produced by these systems (Xi, 2010). It empowers them to customize instructional strategies following empirical evidence. Automated evaluation and feedback systems powered by artificial intelligence are of utmost importance in improving the effectiveness and responsiveness of language education assessments through the facilitation of consistency, personalization, and efficiency.

A frontier of revolution in language education is being traversed with the assistance of Artificial Intelligence (AI) in real-time performance evaluation and analytics. This innovative methodology entails the ongoing surveillance and evaluation of students' engagement with language resources, delivering immediate and dynamic feedback. AI algorithms efficiently evaluate written and spoken responses, continuously monitoring learners' pronunciation, vocabulary comprehension, and grammar usage. It provides educators with instantaneous insights into the proficiency levels of their students. In addition to conventional evaluation methods, real-time performance analytics provide continuous assessments of student engagement, enabling instructors to modify their instructional approaches following changing demands. The ongoing assessment of adaptability guarantees that the learning process remains precisely calibrated to confront obstacles promptly (Roll & Wylie, 2016). In addition, real-time analytics empowers instructors to deliver immediate and customized feedback, cultivating a nurturing educational setting where students actively pursue language proficiency. The abundance of data produced by these analytics facilitates improved decision-making based on data, allowing educators to discern recurring obstacles, customize instructional approaches, and efficiently distribute resources. Constant tracking of the progress of individual students enables educators to gain a more comprehensive comprehension of their learning trajectories, providing them with invaluable information to tailor assistance accordingly.

ETHICAL CONSIDERATIONS AND CHALLENGES

Amidst the emergence of AI-mediated learning environments, the imperative to uphold the utmost ethical standards in education becomes more apparent: the need to safeguard academic integrity and combat plagiarism. Incorporating Artificial Intelligence (AI) into educational platforms offers both a prospect and a hurdle in fostering an equitable and truthful academic environment. One advantage is the possibility of real-time detection via sophisticated plagiarism tools that employ advanced algorithms. It enables prompt identification of instances of academic dishonesty and facilitates immediate intervention. Student consciousness is considerably increased through integrating integrity-focused educational modules into AI-mediated platforms; these modules inform users of the significance of generating original content and the repercussions associated with plagiarism. AI's distinctive capability to deliver immediate feedback strengthens adherence to ethical writing standards, thereby establishing a proactive stance towards upholding academic integrity.

AI plays a role in providing personalized guidance to students, aiding them in comprehending appropriate paraphrasing techniques and citation standards. In addition to preventing plagiarism, this promotes academic integrity by providing students with the necessary understanding to conduct themselves ethically as scholars. Nevertheless, obstacles continue to endure, specifically in light of the rise of advanced plagiarism methods that exploit developing AI capabilities. It emphasizes the sustained importance of privacy and ethical considerations in learning environments mediated by AI. To adequately confront these challenges, education and awareness continue to be crucial. Under its ability to provide reminders and contextualized information, AI has the potential to significantly contribute to the ongoing reinforcement of students regarding the critical nature of academic integrity. Mitigation strategies include implementing thorough institutional policies, routine audits of artificial intelligence (AI) tools to verify their effectiveness and impartiality, and fostering a culture of integrity by acknowledging and commemorating innovative contributions. To ensure academic integrity in AI-mediated learning, adopt a comprehensive and multifaceted strategy incorporating technological advancements, educational programs, and solid institutional structures (Foltýnek et al., 2023). Integrating these components establishes an environment that promotes ethical behaviour and actively safeguards it. It fosters a culture that emphasizes and adheres to the tenets of academic integrity.

The imperative to guarantee AI-generated materials are devoid of bias is paramount in educational content creation and distribution. The growing incorporation of Artificial Intelligence (AI) into educational platforms requires an increased recognition of the possible inadvertent biases that may enter datasets and algorithms. The onus is on those who conscientiously conceive and curate educational resources, which include evaluations, tasks, and instructional material. To establish an AI-driven educational environment devoid of bias, it is imperative that both developers and educators proactively participate in the detection and rectification of preferences that may arise from cultural stereotypes or historical data. Adopting this proactive stance is crucial for guaranteeing that the artificial intelligence algorithms utilized in educational technology are not only technologically sophisticated but also intrinsically equitable, inclusive, and reflective of a wide range of viewpoints. It is critical to prioritize integrating diversity and inclusivity principles into AI-driven educational materials to cultivate honest learning experiences. Singha & Singha (2023a) argue that sustaining artificial intelligence (AI) and machine learning (ML) necessitates both human diversity and mindfulness.

The dedication to reducing bias goes beyond the preliminary design stage. Consistent audits and continuous surveillance of AI-generated content are fundamental elements of a holistic approach to identifying and rectifying potential biases that may develop gradually. Utilizing this dynamic and iterative procedure, educational content is consistently synchronized with the ever-changing benchmarks of equity and inclusiveness. To develop AI-driven educational materials that are devoid of bias, it is imperative to balance technological proficiency and an unwavering dedication to inclusiveness (Akter et al., 2021; Loder et al., 2019). Through proactive measures to mitigate biases during all stages of development, implementation, and upkeep, the academic community can cultivate an environment conducive to learning in which AI-powered resources function as impartial, fair, and enlightening instruments that enhance the educational experience in its entirety and breadth.

SUCCESSFUL CASES OF AI INTEGRATION IN LANGUAGE EDUCATION

Language learning platforms incorporating artificial intelligence (AI) symbolize a substantial advancement in educational technology by presenting novel methods for acquiring a second language. Numerous prominent platforms exemplify the effective incorporation of artificial intelligence, thereby showcasing the capacity for individualized, adaptable, and captivating language instruction. As an industry-leading AI-enhanced language learning platform, Duolingo is distinguished. By utilizing AI-driven algorithms and a gamified interface, Duolingo customizes lessons to suit the unique proficiency levels of its users. Chatbots on the platform provide interactive conversational practice and alter the difficulty level based on the user's performance, resulting in effective language acquisition.

AI is utilized by Rosetta Stone, a renowned provider of immersive language learning experiences, to improve user engagement and outcomes. The platform offers immediate feedback on pronunciation through AI-powered speech recognition. Rosetta Stone ensures effective and individualized language instruction by modifying content following student development.

By utilizing AI, Babbel optimizes users' language learning paths. The platform analyses user interactions and customizes courses to suit users' requirements and preferences. Babbel's AI-powered methodology prioritizes pragmatic language proficiencies, delivering an individualized and adaptable educational encounter that strongly connects with students.

As an illustration of the incorporation of AI into language education, Lingodeer provides individualized learning trajectories. The platform modifies the content by customizing the learning experience according to an individual's assets and weaknesses. Lingodeer implements AI-powered interactive exercises and lexical drills to augment user engagement and language proficiency.

ChatGPT Language Tutor and other AI-powered language tutoring applications offer users conversational and interactive language practice. By simulating real-life dialogues with natural language processing (NLP) algorithms, these platforms provide language learners with an immersive and interactive experience.

AI is integrated into the language learning platform Memrise to increase user engagement. The platform generates an engaging and interactive learning environment by incorporating gamification elements and adjusting content in response to user performance. The methodology employed by Memrise exemplifies how AI can render language instruction both productive and enjoyable. These illustrations showcase the wide-ranging implementations of artificial intelligence in language learning, encompassing interactive conversational practice and personalized content delivery. By utilizing artificial intelligence, these platforms provide students with a personalized and dynamic method for acquiring proficiency in foreign languages, ultimately enhancing the efficacy and appeal of language learning.

The utilization of AI in personalized learning paths guarantees that students are provided with material customized to their specific requirements and levels of expertise. Implementing AI algorithms, such as those found in the chatbots of Duolingo or the speech recognition system of Rosetta Stone, enables instantaneous corrections and enhancements in language usage and pronunciation. Implementing dynamic adaptation leads to improved learning outcomes, as it ensures that learners receive focused assistance exactly where they require it, thereby expediting the development of their language proficiency.

The integration of artificial intelligence has fundamentally transformed how language learners interact. Duolingo and Memrise exemplify that gamified interfaces introduce interactivity and enjoyment into the learning process. AI-powered personalization implemented in platforms such as Lingodeer and Babbel fosters a user-centric atmosphere by ensuring that teachings correspond to individual progress and preferences. By replicating authentic language exchanges, the incorporation of natural language processing into ChatGPT Language Tutor facilitates conversational practice that is both realistic and responsive.

These platforms' ability to accommodate their users' strengths and limitations cultivates a feeling of achievement and encouragement. Incorporating AI into interactive exercises, vocabulary lessons, and content adaptation makes language learning more dynamic and engaging. Consequently, individuals are more inclined to maintain their motivation and dedication towards pursuing language acquisition, fostering favourable user experiences. AI integration in language learning platforms has initiated a paradigm shift towards individualized and captivating instruction. The influence on educational achievements is demonstrated in the expedited growth of linguistic competence, while user engagement is enhanced via interactive interfaces, personalized material, and prompt corrections. These developments collectively improve the quality and appeal of language education, demonstrating the revolutionary capacity of artificial intelligence to shape the future learning trajectory.

FUTURE HORIZONS: AI'S EVOLUTION IN LANGUAGE EDUCATION

The evolution of Artificial Intelligence (AI) is poised to revolutionize language education, ushering in a new era of personalized, adaptable, and multimodal learning experiences. The rapid advancements in AI promise not only to transform instructional resources but also to reshape the educational landscape. Language education is poised to undergo a significant paradigm shift shortly, propelled by the swift progressions in Artificial Intelligence (AI). These advancements have the potential to not only revolutionize instructional resources but also transform the overall educational environment (Roll & Wylie, 2016). The forthcoming improvement in artificial intelligence holds the potential to introduce a novel epoch characterized by learning pathways that are exceptionally personalized and adaptable. Sophisticated algorithms, equipped with a profound comprehension of personal learning styles, preferences, and proficiency levels, are poised to bring about a paradigm shift in instructional materials by precisely customizing them to suit the distinct requirements of every learner. It is anticipated that the impact of AI will not be limited to simple customization but will also encompass content production autonomously. It implies that instructional resources will adapt dynamically and immediately in response to student progress and performance, guaranteeing that students remain consistently engaged and suitably stimulated throughout their academic trajectory. An imminent development is incorporating multimodal learning resources, including augmented reality applications, virtual reality experiences, and interactive videos. It indicates a transition towards a more all-encompassing and captivating educational encounter, which caters to the varied inclinations of students and promotes a more profound comprehension of the content (De Oliveira et al., 2019). With the ongoing progress in Natural Language Processing (NLP), individuals learning the language can expect significant improvements in the precision of language evaluations, instantaneous feedback systems, and conversational language resources that imitate human interactions almost precisely. In addition, forthcoming developments can incorporate gamification and interactive components into educational resources, bolstering motivation and maintaining long-term engagement. The expected progressions in artificial intelligence (AI) possess the capacity to enhance and fundamentally transform the language education field (Jiang, 2022). By utilizing teaching resources that are highly personalized, adaptable, and multimodal, students can anticipate a future in which education is more effective, immersive, and dynamic. The aforementioned transformative capacity establishes the foundation for an educational encounter that is not solely technologically sophisticated but also profoundly tailored to every learner's specific requirements and inclinations.

The investigation into teaching resources generated by artificial intelligence signals the beginning of a paradigm shift in language education, as AI is poised to reshape how educational materials are produced and distributed. One fundamental aspect of this paradigm shift resides in the capacity of artificial intelligence to customize the development of educational materials independently to suit the distinct characteristics of every learner. By harnessing sophisticated algorithms, artificial intelligence (AI) evaluates learners' strengths, weaknesses, and preferences to generate tailored materials that effectively target their requirements. Doing so guarantees that educational materials are pertinent and their difficulty is maximized, promoting a more streamlined and individualized learning experience. One crucial element concerning the potential of teaching resources generated by AI is their ability to alter in real time in response to dynamic learner interactions. As students interact with the resources, artificial intelligence algorithms evaluate their progress and modify the material to correspond with their reading speed and level of understanding. The capacity to adapt ensures that instructional materials remain sensitive to changing learning requirements, resulting in a personalized and productive educational experience (Holmes, 2019). By integrating diverse modalities, including interactive videos, virtual reality scenarios, and augmented reality applications, artificial intelligence demonstrates its capacity to generate multimodal learning experiences. AI extends the learning experience by incorporating multimedia components, increasing engagement and immersion, accommodating a wide range of learning preferences, and substantially influencing comprehension.

The potential for language education to be substantially scaled up is heightened by the efficacy of AI resource generation. By eliminating the need for educators to allocate time and resources towards material development, automated content creation allows them to focus on more strategic facets of instruction. This enhanced efficacy enables a broader and more readily available dissemination of superior educational content produced by artificial intelligence. An essential element that significantly contributes to the transformative capacity of teaching resources generated by AI is the ongoing enhancement achieved via machine learning algorithms. Over time, content generation processes are refined as AI systems learn and adapt in response to learner feedback and material interaction. By implementing this iterative development process, instructional materials are continuously updated to align with students' evolving needs and preferences, augmenting language education's overall efficacy. Investigating instructional materials produced by artificial intelligence (AI) portends a forthcoming era in which technology dominates the creation of adaptive, individualized, and multimodal learning encounters. The potential for a paradigm shift in language education exists due to AI's increasing efficiency in generating and improving instructional materials. It could offer students a more individualized, captivating, and productive journey towards language proficiency.

The forthcoming developments in AI hold the potential to customize dynamically and autonomously produce instructional materials, leading to a paradigm shift in language education. With personalized, adaptive, and multimodal learning experiences on the horizon, students can anticipate a more effective, immersive, and tailored educational journey towards language proficiency. The transformative capacity of AI-generated teaching resources signals a shift towards a technologically sophisticated and highly individualized approach to language education.

COLLABORATION AND MITIGATION OF AI'S DRAWBACKS

Effective collaboration between educators and AI developers is crucial for realizing the complete potential of AI in education while efficiently addressing its limitations. Such cooperation is not only beneficial but essential. A symbiotic relationship is established through this collaborative synergy; educators contribute their profound pedagogical knowledge, comprehension of student requirements, and insights into efficacious teaching approaches. AI developers have the technical proficiency to seamlessly integrate AI systems into educational settings. Educators' contributions to this collaborative partnership are of immense value as they influence the development of AI-powered tools. Educators guarantee that the technology is advanced and grounded in effective pedagogy by ensuring that these tools align with educational goals and curricular objectives. Implementing this co-design process is critical to developing AI applications that integrate seamlessly into the educational experience, improving overall academic performance (Kim, 2023; Kasepalu et al., 2022). AI developers contribute their technical proficiency, guaranteeing that the deployed AI systems adhere to the utmost operation, security, and effectiveness criteria. Their function is of the utmost importance in connecting educational theory with technological application, thereby enabling the development of AI tools that are efficient and flexible enough to accommodate the ever-changing educational environment. Consistent and transparent lines of communication between developers and educators are critical for fostering a dynamic feedback loop. The ongoing exchange of knowledge and experiences facilitates the iterative enhancement of AI applications in response to user feedback and classroom requirements. Utilizing collective improvement, AI-powered instruments can be customized to tackle particular obstacles, improve usability, and more effectively cater to the varied needs of the academic community. The foundation of an effective incorporation of AI in education is the fruitful partnership between educators and AI developers (Kim et al., 2022). By utilizing this collaborative model, the advantages of AI are optimized, and potential disadvantages are proactively recognized and resolved. As a result, a profoundly transformative educational environment is created, as it maximizes artificial intelligence's (AI) capabilities to enhance students' and instructors' learning and teaching processes.

To adequately address the limitations of AI in language education, it is critical to adopt a proactive and all-encompassing strategy. It requires aggressive implementation of strategies to mitigate potential ethical, privacy, and bias concerns to prevent their escalation into significant issues. Transparency becomes a fundamental aspect of this undertaking, requiring unambiguous and candid communication regarding the operational complexities of AI systems, the data they employ, and the algorithms that govern their operation. Educators and AI developers contribute significantly to establishing comprehensive guidelines and ethical frameworks governing the ethical application of AI in educational settings through their collaborative efforts (Akgün & Greenhow, 2021; Holmes et al., 2021). Moreover, because education is an ever-changing and dynamic domain, educators must engage in continuous professional development about AI-related subjects. This practice guarantees that individuals teaching languages remain abreast of the most recent developments, possible obstacles, and ethical implications of artificial intelligence in the field. With this understanding, educators can actively participate in the responsible implementation of AI technologies, promoting a culture that values ethical and well-informed usage. Systematic evaluations and routine audits constitute a pivotal component of the proactive mitigation approach. Through the systematic assessment of AI applications, educators and developers can detect and address any potential biases or ethical issues that may develop gradually. The aforementioned iterative procedure substantially contributes to the overall reliability of AI applications in language education, assuring stakeholders regarding the honest and impartial implementation of these technologies. A solid groundwork for the responsible incorporation of AI in language education is established upon the collaboration between educators and AI developers, supplemented by proactive measures to mitigate concerns (Gartner & Krašna, 2023; Nguyen et al., 2022). By adopting this cooperative and foresee methodology, we guarantee that AI technologies augment the educational process and are dedicated to mitigating possible disadvantages. In essence, this cultivates an educational setting that is equitable and efficient, wherein the revolutionary capabilities of artificial intelligence are judiciously utilized for the advantage of both students and instructors.

DISCUSSION

The discourse thoroughly analyzes the significant ramifications of incorporating Artificial Intelligence (AI) into language instruction, emphasizing the mutually beneficial association between human proficiency and technological advancement. A compelling future vision arises wherein artificial intelligence (AI) surpasses its present capabilities and develops the ability to comprehend and address the intricate requirements of individual learners. Ongoing enhancements to AI algorithms hold the potential for ever more intricate customization, dynamically adjusting to a wide range of learning styles and preferences to optimize the process of language acquisition in a manner that is distinct for every student. The transformative capacity of artificial intelligence (AI) encompasses a fundamental change in pedagogical approaches, wherein AI-generated materials supplement educators rather than replace them. This collaborative framework enables educators to allocate additional time for personalized engagements, guidance, and the cultivation of critical thinking abilities. Ethical considerations are emphasized, focusing on addressing biases, safeguarding privacy, and maintaining academic integrity. The discourse emphasizes the need for AI developers and educators to establish comprehensive ethical frameworks to navigate the intricacies associated with the responsible incorporation of AI in language education.

The future depicted in the envisioned era of AI-integrated language education is characterized by its inclusiveness and dynamism, as it anticipates a seamless collaboration between human expertise and technology. The potential benefits of this collaborative interaction extend beyond the development of skilled language learners; it also cultivates self-assured and flexible individuals prepared to flourish in an increasingly interconnected digital and global society. Collaboration between educators and AI developers is crucial for ongoing progress, as it resolves present obstacles and promotes sustained innovation in language education. The pivotal role of the dynamic and evolving relationship between human expertise and AI in this transformative endeavour is to guarantee that AI enriches the educational experience while maintaining the utmost ethical principles. The conclusion and subsequent discussion collectively construct an all-encompassing account of a future in which language education is transformed into a dynamic, inclusive, and ethically guided domain through the fusion of human ingenuity and technological understanding.

A proactive and all-encompassing strategy is necessary to mitigate the adverse effects of AI in language education. It entails recognizing and proactively addressing potential ethical, privacy, and bias issues. Ensuring stakeholders are well-informed regarding AI system operations, data usage, and algorithms is considered crucial, and this is facilitated by transparent communication. Educators and AI developers lead collaborative initiatives to establish ethical frameworks and guidelines, which demonstrate a steadfast dedication to the responsible utilization of AI in educational environments. Aware of the ever-changing nature of education, educators must engage in continuous professional development concerning AI-related subjects. It guarantees that educators are adequately prepared to navigate the ever-changing environment, actively participating in the responsible implementation of AI technologies. Systematic evaluations and audits of AI systems regularly function as preventative actions, scrutinizing applications to detect and address potential biases or ethical issues. This iterative procedure contributes substantially to developing confidence in AI applications for language education. A solid groundwork for the responsible incorporation of AI in language education is established upon the collaboration between educators and AI developers, supplemented by proactive measures to mitigate concerns. By adopting this cooperative and foreseeing methodology, we guarantee that AI technologies augment the educational process and are dedicated to mitigating possible disadvantages. In essence, this cultivates an educational setting that is equitable and efficient, wherein the revolutionary capabilities of artificial intelligence are judiciously utilized for the advantage of both students and instructors.

CONCLUSION

Integrating artificial intelligence (AI) into language education marks a transformative moment in academia, heralding an era where technological prowess and human insight synergize. This paradigm shift promises a future where personalized, adaptive learning environments optimize language acquisition. As this collaborative journey progresses, ethical considerations such as correcting biases and protecting privacy are critical. Educators can enhance their roles by responsibly integrating AI, fostering critical thinking and personalized engagements. This fundamental intersection of AI and human expertise cultivates literate individuals and nurtures self-assured, versatile beings poised to thrive in an interconnected, digitally globalized society.

REFERENCES

Akgün, S., & Greenhow, C. (2021). Artificial intelligence in education: Addressing ethical challenges in K-12 settings. *AI and Ethics*, *2*(3), 431–440. doi:10.1007/s43681-021-00096-7 PMID:34790956

Akter, S., McCarthy, G., Sajib, S., Michael, K., Dwivedi, Y. K., D'Ambra, J., & Shen, K. N. (2021). Algorithmic bias in data-driven innovation in the age of AI. *International Journal of Information Management*, *60*, 102387. doi:10.1016/j.ijinfomgt.2021.102387

App Store. (2015). *Tandem: Language exchange*. https://apps.apple.com/us/app/tandem-language-exchange/id959001619

Baha, T. A., Hajji, M. E., Es-Saady, Y., & Fadili, H. (2023). The impact of educational chatbot on student learning experience. *Education and Information Technologies*. Advance online publication. doi:10.1007/s10639-023-12166-w

Behrens, H. (2021). Constructivist approaches to first language acquisition. *Journal of Child Language*, *48*(5), 959–983. doi:10.1017/S0305000921000556 PMID:34382923

Belda-Medina, J., & Calvo-Ferrer, J. R. (2022). Using chatbots as AI conversational partners in language learning. *Applied Sciences (Basel, Switzerland)*, *12*(17), 8427. doi:10.3390/app12178427

Bruffee, K. A. (1984). Collaborative learning and the "Conversation of Mankind.". *College English*, *46*(7), 635. doi:10.2307/376924

Chaudhry, M., & Kazim, E. (2021). Artificial intelligence in education (AIEd): A high-level academic and industry note 2021. *AI and Ethics*, *2*(1), 157–165. doi:10.1007/s43681-021-00074-z PMID:34790953

Cohen, M. D., & Téllez, K. (1994). Implementing cooperative learning for language minority students. *Bilingual Research Journal*, *18*(1–2), 1–19. doi:10.1080/15235882.1994.10162655

De Oliveira, L. C., Jones, L., & Smith, S. L. (2019). Multimodal literacies in the english language arts classroom for english language learners. In English language education (pp. 21–31). doi:10.1007/978-3-030-02245-7_2

Eguchi, A. (2021). AI-powered educational robotics as a learning tool to promote artificial intelligence and computer science education. In Advances in intelligent systems and computing (pp. 279–287). doi:10.1007/978-3-030-82544-7_26

El-Sabagh, H. A. (2021). Adaptive e-learning environment based on learning styles and its impact on development students' engagement. *International Journal of Educational Technology in Higher Education*, *18*(1), 53. Advance online publication. doi:10.1186/s41239-021-00289-4

Eun, B. (2010). From learning to development: A sociocultural approach to instruction. *Cambridge Journal of Education*, *40*(4), 401–418. doi:10.1080/0305764X.2010.526593

Foltýnek, T., Bjelobaba, S., Glendinning, I., Khan, Z. R., Santos, R., Pavletic, P., & Kravjar, J. (2023). ENAI Recommendations on the Ethical Use of Artificial Intelligence in Education. *International Journal for Educational Integrity*, *19*(1), 12. Advance online publication. doi:10.1007/s40979-023-00133-4

Gandhi, T. K., Classen, D. C., Sinsky, C. A., Rhew, D. C., Garde, N. V., Roberts, A., & Federico, F. (2023). How can artificial intelligence decrease cognitive and work burden for front line practitioners? *JAMIA Open*, *6*(3), ooad079. Advance online publication. doi:10.1093/jamiaopen/ooad079 PMID:37655124

Gartner, S., & Krašna, M. (2023). Artificial intelligence in education - Ethical framework. In *12th Mediterranean Conference on Embedded Computing (MECO)* (pp. 1-7). 10.1109/MECO58584.2023.10155012

Holmes, W., Porayska-Pomsta, K., Holstein, K., Sutherland, E., Baker, T. T., Shum, S. B., Santos, O. C., Rodrigo, M. M. T., Cukurova, M., Bittencourt, I. I., & Koedinger, K. R. (2021). Ethics of AI in education: Towards a community-wide framework. *International Journal of Artificial Intelligence in Education*, *32*(3), 504–526. doi:10.1007/s40593-021-00239-1

Hou, Y. (2020). Foreign language education in the era of artificial intelligence. In Advances in Intelligent Systems and Computing (pp. 937–944). doi:10.1007/978-981-15-2568-1_128

Jeon, J. H., & Lee, S. (2023). Large language models in education: A focus on the complementary relationship between human teachers and ChatGPT. *Education and Information Technologies*, *28*(12), 15873–15892. doi:10.1007/s10639-023-11834-1

Jiang, R. (2022). How does artificial intelligence empower EFL teaching and learning nowadays? A review on artificial intelligence in the EFL context. *Frontiers in Psychology*, *13*, 1049401. Advance online publication. doi:10.3389/fpsyg.2022.1049401 PMID:36467167

Kaddari, Z., Mellah, Y., Berrich, J., Belkasmi, M. G., & Bouchentouf, T. (2020). Natural language processing: Challenges and future directions. In Lecture Notes in Networks and Systems (pp. 236–246). doi:10.1007/978-3-030-53970-2_22

Karoui, A., Alvarez, L., Geoffre, T., Guin, N., Lefèvre, M., Lachand, V., & Ramalho, M. (2022). Towards an automated adaptive learning web platform through personalization of language learning pathways. In Lecture Notes in Computer Science (pp. 448–454). doi:10.1007/978-3-031-16290-9_35

Kasepalu, R., Prieto, L. P., Ley, T., & Chejara, P. (2022). Teacher artificial intelligence-supported pedagogical actions in collaborative learning coregulation: A wizard-of-oz study. *Frontiers in Education*, *7*, 736194. Advance online publication. doi:10.3389/feduc.2022.736194

Kaufman, D. (2004). Constructivist issues in language learning and teaching. *Annual Review of Applied Linguistics*, *24*. Advance online publication. doi:10.1017/S0267190504000121

Khan, I., Ahmad, A. R., Jabeur, N., & Mahdi, M. N. (2021). An artificial intelligence approach to monitor student performance and devise preventive measures. *Smart Learning Environments*, *8*(1), 17. Advance online publication. doi:10.1186/s40561-021-00161-y

Kim, J. (2023). Leading teachers' perspective on teacher-AI collaboration in education. *Education and Information Technologies*. Advance online publication. doi:10.1007/s10639-023-12109-5

Klímová, B., Pikhart, M., & Kacetl, J. (2023). Ethical issues of the use of AI-driven mobile apps for education. *Frontiers in Public Health*, *10*, 1118116. Advance online publication. doi:10.3389/fpubh.2022.1118116 PMID:36711343

Kurni, M., Mohammed, M. S., & Srinivasa, K. G. (2023). Natural language processing for education. In Springer eBooks (pp. 45–54). doi:10.1007/978-3-031-32653-0_3

Li, P., & Yu, L. (2021). Digital Language Learning (DLL): Insights from behavior, cognition, and the brain. *Bilingualism: Language and Cognition*, *25*(3), 361–378. doi:10.1017/S1366728921000353 PMID:35669733

Loder, C., Minadeo, L., Jiménez, L. E. C., Luna, Z., Ross, L. J., Rosenbloom, N., Stalburg, C. M., & Harris, L. H. (2019). Bridging the expertise of advocates and academics to identify reproductive justice learning outcomes. *Teaching and Learning in Medicine*, *32*(1), 11–22. doi:10.1080/10401334.2019.1631168 PMID:31293184

Machwate, S., Bendaoud, R., Henze, J., Berrada, K., & Burgos, D. (2021). Virtual exchange to develop cultural, language, and digital competencies. *Sustainability (Basel)*, *13*(11), 5926. doi:10.3390/su13115926

Meng, N., Dhimolea, T. K., & Ali, Z. (2022). AI-enhanced education: Teaching and learning reimagined. In *Educational Communications and Technology* (pp. 107–124). Issues and Innovations. doi:10.1007/978-3-030-84729-6_7

Nguyen, A., Ngo, H. N., Hong, Y., Dang, B., & Nguyen, B. T. (2022). Ethical principles for artificial intelligence in education. *Education and Information Technologies*, *28*(4), 4221–4241. doi:10.1007/s10639-022-11316-w PMID:36254344

Paas, F., & Van Merriënboer, J. J. G. (2020). Cognitive-load theory: Methods to manage working memory load in the learning of complex tasks. *Current Directions in Psychological Science*, *29*(4), 394–398. doi:10.1177/0963721420922183

Roche, C., Wall, P. J., & Lewis, D. (2022). Ethics and diversity in artificial intelligence policies, strategies and initiatives. *AI and Ethics*, *3*(4), 1095–1115. doi:10.1007/s43681-022-00218-9 PMID:36246014

Roll, I., & Wylie, R. (2016). Evolution and revolution in artificial intelligence in education. *International Journal of Artificial Intelligence in Education*, *26*(2), 582–599. doi:10.1007/s40593-016-0110-3

Salas-Pilco, S. Z., Xiao, K., & Hu, X. (2022). Artificial intelligence and learning analytics in teacher education: A systematic review. *Education Sciences*, *12*(8), 569. doi:10.3390/educsci12080569

Seo, K., Tang, J., Roll, I., Fels, S., & Yoon, D. (2021). The impact of artificial intelligence on learner–instructor interaction in online learning. *International Journal of Educational Technology in Higher Education*, *18*(1), 54. Advance online publication. doi:10.1186/s41239-021-00292-9 PMID:34778540

Singha, R., & Singha, S. (2023a). Economic sustainability, mindfulness, and diversity in the age of artificial intelligence and machine learning. In P. Raj, P. B. Soundarabai, & P. Augustine (Eds.), *Machine Intelligence: Computer Vision and Natural Language Processing* (pp. 273–285). Taylor & Francis Group. doi:10.1201/9781003424550-15

Singha, S., & Singha, R. (2023). Protecting data and privacy: Cloud-based solutions for intelligent transportation applications. *Scalable Computing: Practice and Experience*, *24*(3), 257–276. doi:10.12694/scpe.v24i3.2381

Sweller, J. (2012). Cognitive load theory. In Springer eBooks (pp. 601–605). doi:10.1007/978-1-4419-1428-6_446

Tafazoli, D., María, E. G., & Abril, C. H. (2019). Intelligent language tutoring system. *International Journal of Information and Communication Technology Education*, *15*(3), 60–74. doi:10.4018/IJICTE.2019070105

Tan, S. (2023). Harnessing artificial intelligence for innovation in education. In *Learning Intelligence* (pp. 335–363). Innovative and Digital Transformative Learning Strategies. doi:10.1007/978-981-19-9201-8_8

Towle, B., & Halm, M. J. (2006). Designing adaptive learning environments with learning design. In Springer eBooks (pp. 215–226). doi:10.1007/3-540-27360-3_12

Xi, X. (2010). Automated scoring and feedback systems: Where are we and where are we heading? *Language Testing*, *27*(3), 291–300. doi:10.1177/0265532210364643

Yeşilyurt, Y. E. (2023). AI-enabled assessment and feedback mechanisms for language learning. In Advances in Educational Technologies and Instructional Design book series (pp. 25–43). doi:10.4018/978-1-6684-9893-4.ch002

Zhao, J., Wu, M., Zhou, L., Wang, X., & Jia, J. (2022). Cognitive psychology-based artificial intelligence review. *Frontiers in Neuroscience*, *16*, 1024316. Advance online publication. doi:10.3389/fnins.2022.1024316 PMID:36278021

Zhu, Y. (2020). The application of artificial intelligence in foreign language teaching. *2020 International Conference on Artificial Intelligence and Education (ICAIE)*. 10.1109/ICAIE50891.2020.00024

Zou, B., Guan, X., Shao, Y., & Chen, P. (2023). Supporting speaking practice by social network-based interaction in artificial intelligence (ai)-assisted language learning. *Sustainability (Basel)*, *15*(4), 2872. doi:10.3390/su15042872

KEY TERMS AND DEFINITIONS

Adaptive Assessment: Evaluation methods that dynamically adapt in response to the performance of individual learners, utilizing artificial intelligence to deliver immediate feedback and streamline language assessment procedures.

AI (Artificial Intelligence): An intelligent behaviour simulation technological system that enhances personalized learning experiences and adaptive assessment in language education.

Challenges: The integration of AI into language education is accompanied by various hindrances and obstacles, including but not limited to ethical concerns, biases, and privacy considerations, all of which necessitate a cautious approach when navigating.

Integration: Learning outcomes can be improved by integrating artificial intelligence (AI) into language education, which entails a smooth synergy between conventional pedagogical approaches and technological systems.

Language Acquisition: Language learning necessitates the development of linguistic proficiency and cultural awareness, which are frequently improved by AI-integrated instructional materials.

Language Teaching Materials: Educational materials specifically developed to support the progress of language learners, including textbooks, multimedia materials, and interactive tools that aid in the acquisition of the target language.

Personalized Learning: Optimizing language acquisition outcomes by customizing educational experiences to suit the needs, preferences, and proficiency levels of individual learners, frequently with the assistance of AI.

Chapter 3
The Reality of Artificiality: The Impact of Artificial Intelligence on Language and Culture Course Assessments and Rubrics

Teresa Lobalsamo
https://orcid.org/0009-0008-6807-4862
University of Toronto Mississauga, Canada

Dellannia Segreti
https://orcid.org/0009-0007-7320-9808
University of Toronto Mississauga, Canada

Mohammad J. Jamali
University of Toronto, Canada

Sylvia Gaspari
University of Toronto, Canada

ABSTRACT

As artificial intelligence (AI) continues to increase its presence and accessibility within education, the need to address AI's impact on assignment design and the production of original coursework is heightened. Within the context of an undergraduate language and culture course, this chapter thus offers reflections on the integration of AI tools and their effect on shaping assessment methods. The authors also highlight that there indeed remains a great need for continued research in the realm of AI and education going forward, especially where enhanced AI-detection technologies, institutional policies, academic rigour, and learner expressiveness are concerned.

DOI: 10.4018/979-8-3693-0872-1.ch003

INTRODUCTION

Artificial Intelligence (AI) has been in steady development in information technology and other industry sectors for several decades. However, recent developments in Generative AI and the unprecedented accessibility of tools such as ChatGPT have heightened the need for critical discussion on AI and the ways in which they will inevitably affect the education sector. In an effort to contribute to this evolving discussion, this chapter reflects on the recent implementation of Generative AI on methods of assessments assigned and completed for an undergraduate Italian Language and Culture course (University of Toronto Mississauga). The course is structured around 12 thematic units; weekly to bi-weekly assessments chart learning progress through formative pieces of work related to each [unit]. For students who undertake the course to fulfill an Italian language requirement as part of their program of study, select assignments are completed in Italian. By outlining how generative AI tools were integrated within the context of Italian Language and Culture, we will consider how modifications made to the course's syllabus, assessments, and rubrics reveal new opportunities and potential pitfalls that instructors will want to consider--and quickly--so that course delivery, academic rigour and integrity can remain impactful in this new reality. In sharing our preliminary reflections, we hope to offer some pathways toward navigating such technological advancements, today and in future.

CURRENT DEBATE SURROUNDING AI

Current hesitations around the use of AI in education are simply the next phase of a decades-long discussion on the feasibility and necessity of bringing new technologies into the classroom which, in recent years, has also engaged topics such as text messaging (Carrington, 2005) and machine translation (Urlaub & Dessein, 2022).

With regards to the language classroom, Urlaub and Dessein (2022) diffuse the perceived disruption caused by machine translation, such as Google Translate, to the acquisition of language-learning outcomes by drawing an intriguing comparison with pocket calculators in Mathematics classrooms, which became a widespread practice in schools only once the S.A.T. permitted their use in 1994. Initial debates in the 1970s hinged upon whether the availability of pocket calculators in the mathematics classroom would lead to a loss of basic arithmetic skills among students. Urlaub and Dessein (2022) point to a shift in instructor perception of the pocket calculator, as it went from being considered an impediment to a learning tool that could optimize learning outcomes. Analogously, they argue that a targeted and thoughtful approach toward machine translation in the language classroom could enhance learning outcomes. The prevailing concern is that the frequent use of machine translation could prevent students from accumulating the skills necessary to produce written communication in the target language without the support of aids (51). Urlaub and Dessein (2022) admit that there is a real danger that tools such as Google Translate can contribute to a reductionistic perception of language and language learning. They underscore that if language proficiency is "treated as a tool, it reduces human beings to speakers exchanging messages in crude manners that are agnostic of the sociocultural embeddedness of message and speaker" (p. 57). Naturally, this concern has implications for oral and written communication across academic disciplines. However, the possibility that communication in a foreign language could be reduced to mere "translation" particularly stands out in the language classroom. In order to combat this outcome, Urlaub and Dessein (2022) argue that we must understand language proficiency as a nuanced and context-sensitive form of communication that reflects and represents the individual within society. Moreover, machine translations' inability to harness cultural nuance (through, for example, idiomatic expressions)[1] in fact limits the depths to which it is beneficial in achieving language competence.

Rather than fleeing from this danger, Urlaub and Dessein (2022) recommend introducing tools such as Google Translate into the classroom in a thoughtful and goal-oriented way. They cite several studies from the past two decades in which students have been observed to "develop higher levels of linguistic awareness through the use of online translators by using the technology to elicit feedback on both their written and spoken language" (p. 51). The authors also suggest that prohibiting Google Translate in the classroom will not impede the "proliferation of increasingly sophisticated online translators in the 'real world' and the impact of this technology on human communicative behaviour in general and our students' and society's perceptions of the purpose of language education" (p. 53). They propose that language instructors instead consider the gradual integration of machine translators into the classroom by designing tasks that (1) require students to recognize instances where the use of online translation tools can enhance the learning process; (2) train students to use these machine translators as study aids rather than a default "go-to" resource for completing assignments (Urlaub & Dessein, 2022, p. 54). There remains another major hurdle to overcome with regards to intentionally using Large Language Model-based tools such as Google Translate in the classroom: the difficulty in implementing a systemic approach to their integration at all educational levels (Urlaub & Dessein, 2022). Urlaub and Dessein (2022) highlight the importance of sharing a consensus around how tools such as chatbots can and should be used at all teaching, learning, and assessment levels; otherwise, without an overarching model for their integration, such tools will not be maximized beyond their dictionary-like uses.

While the pocket calculator and Google Translate present unique challenges to overcome for educators, the most challenging of any new technology yet is undoubtedly the introduction of LLM-based chatbots. Chatbots like ChatGPT, Bard, and Ernie are conversational artificial intelligence models designed to generate text that resembles natural, human-like writing based on prompts they receive from the user. As their utilization has increased, these tools have exponentially augmented the importance of refining our teaching, learning, and assessment practices. In an opinion piece published in June 2023, Hao Yu, a Professor in the Faculty of Education at the Shaanxi Normal University (Xi'an, Shaanxi, China), debates the pros and cons of banning ChatGPT from academia, whether it is a useful approach, and whether it is even possible to eliminate it at this stage. Based on recent surveys, Hao Yu finds that a growing number of students in American colleges are using ChatGPT for a variety of purposes, such as to complete homework tasks (89% of students in American colleges), write papers (53%), exams (48%), and generate essay outlines (22%) (McGee, 2023). Major concerns surround student use of LLMs in the completion of exams and other academic tasks meant to function as objective evaluations of students' understanding of the material taught in class (Yu, 2023). Similarly, students may depend on AI in lieu of engaging in critical thinking on assignments, negatively impacting their ability to actively explore, verify, and summarize sources (Yu, 2023). Further concerns are expressed regarding the knowledge provided by these tools, as it is viewed by many educators as superficial and mechanized, "which cannot help students deeply understand the surrounding world and operate effectively in it" (Yu, 2023, p. 7). In addition, the use of ChatGPT has also raised ethical and legal questions. Many educators view its use in examinations and written assignments as academic plagiarism. Since the very function of these LLMs is based on data from sources available on the Internet, their usage in an academic setting prompts further inquiry into the nature of intellectual theft and artistic and academic integrity (Kitamura, 2023). These concerns lead scholars and educators to the same question: How should we view the use of AI in the classroom? Many scholars tread a fine line between acceptance of and weariness towards this technology.

Maureen Walsh brings an optimistic perspective to the potential benefit of using tools such as ChatGPT in the classroom. She describes how the definition of literacy has changed from merely reading and writing to now encompassing a broad range of skills that students hone by using technology regularly outside of school (Walsh, 2017). For Walsh (2017), the changing definition of literacy goes together with many students developing a higher level of digital literacy outside the classroom. Technology has changed the nature of communication, directly impacting the definition of "literacy," especially as it pertains to the classroom. Nowadays, students require a repertoire of "print and digital literacy practices for their future workplace and life" (Walsh, 2017, p. 21). Traditional writing assignments (on paper) have given way to multi-modal approaches - students can still incorporate traditional skills such as style, vocabulary, and sentence structure, but this is now paired with the added potential offered by digital media (Walsh, 2017). Literacy as a multimodal skill also requires that students be given multiple literacies to be able to work with different forms of media and curriculum content; as Walsh emphasizes, digital technology can be used as an inclusive tool in developing literacy (Walsh, 2017).

It has also been argued that the decision by institutions and instructors to ignore or dismiss AI inadvertently creates space for its unwarranted use, which could be a detriment to student learning. On the topic of AI regulation for classroom assignments, Aikens and Kuo (2023) and Fulford (2023) both point to the fact that, like it or not, AI has arrived, and educators need to find a way to cope with it because the technology is here to stay. Aikens and Kuo interviewed a small sample of 30 students at an unnamed private university who used LLMs such as ChatGPT in their academic work. Their research revealed that an ever-growing number of students are "turning to AI as a first resort for almost everything." Students believe that AI provides them with better tools than traditional learning for their postgraduate careers, and they tend to value AI-aware class environments that permit the use of these tools more than those that do not. Especially in mathematical and statistical fields, students "praised the democratizing effect of on-call and accurate code checking as a "game-changer," with ChatGPT being a nimbler learning resource than static course materials or discussion boards" (Aikens & Kuo, 2023, para. 8). Aikens and Kuo conclude that while "AI by no means obviates the need for human help - which students said was still situationally preferable - its availability seems a helpful antidote to last-minute despair, especially during exam periods, when tutoring appointments may be scarce" (Aikens & Kuo, 2023, para. 9).

Fulford (2023) further suggests that, by not incorporating AI into their classroom or intentionally using ChatGPT on assignment design, teachers will spend an abundance of their time trying to detect cheating and uninvited AI usage instead of focusing on their students' learning progress and knowledge gains. He argues that perspectives surrounding the use of AI must necessarily shift away from assumptions of plagiarism. Instead, educators should focus on specific learning objectives related to reading and writing assessments (Fulford, 2023). In his own experience, time spent determining whether students used AI ends up taking over the grading process instead of looking at what the students are writing. Fulford (2023) shares that he finally began to look at the ideas the students were presenting as opposed to how much AI they were using, which, in turn, proved to be an effective detection method due to the generally poor quality of AI writing. This shift in perception of the use of AI allowed Fulford to focus on creativity in research and writing more than simply regurgitating ideas. Further, he is confident that, if the technology is employed appropriately, more space will be left open for students to engage in creative thinking. With this in mind, some scholars see the possibility for tools like ChatGPT to reduce researchers' workloads, allowing them to devote their time and energy to conducting new experiments

(Fulford, 2023). However, van Dis et al. (2023) acknowledge that AI indeed faces many obstacles that need to be addressed, namely issues of bias, provenance, and accuracy, before it can be implemented and accepted fully in the workplace and, inevitably, in the classroom as well.

While the AI debate in the education sector and other fields is ongoing, the growing body of literature already available provides a valuable foundation for beginning to incorporate AI into the classroom. In the sections that follow, we will consider how the ongoing debate has supported the Humanities faculty in navigating the abrupt introduction of AI technologies into Higher Education and guided a successful implementation of AI into the language and culture course in focus here.

CONSIDERATIONS ON INSTITUTIONAL POLICY

Technological advancements should continue to be approached as an opportunity for education administrators to reflect upon and audit instructor teaching practices and student learning behaviours to ensure that academic integrity, learning outcomes, and institutional visions are in seamless alignment. Growth is an essential component of education. As practices are revisited and revised to respond to societal changes and needs, pedagogies are improved, and students' learning experiences are enhanced.

The inclusion of clear institutional policies where AI use is concerned can provide valuable support to students and teachers alike. Formal policies promote a standardized approach to the integration of AI in education, which can, in turn, create opportunities for students to utilize it properly and effectively across their university experience. Many post-secondary institutions have left the decision to allow the use of ChatGPT in the classroom to departments and their course instructors. Institutional policies do, however, differ from one university to another. In North America, the Higher Education sector has spent the last 12 months pre-empting the potential impact that this technology may have on teaching and learning, developing resources and policies on how to navigate student engagement with generative AI, particularly concerning academic integrity at course (Indiana University, 2023; Harvard Business School, 2023), program (University of British Columbia, 2023), or university (University of Toronto, 2023; University of Wisconsin–Madison, 2023) levels. While one (University of Toronto) gives each instructor the autonomy to identify authorized and unauthorized aids for their specific course, it also guides the effort by providing suggested wording for course syllabi. Similarly, the University of Hong Kong requires students to obtain written permission from their professors to use AI in their coursework; otherwise, its use will be considered plagiarism.[2]

To get ahead of the inevitable increase in student engagement with and reliance upon AI, several institutions have indeed started to publish best practices and guidelines for instructors and students engaging with AI in the classroom. We highlight, in particular, the University of Toronto's resource on "Using ChatGPT or other generative AI tools on a marked assessment," which provides students with detailed scenarios of and strategies around AI use and potential consequences associated with using it outside of suggested boundaries (University of Toronto, n.d.b). McGill University Library's guide on AI literacy provides students with the foundational knowledge needed to understand the complexity of AI and provides them with tangible tests (such as the ROBOT test) to evaluate the legitimacy of the produced results (McGill Library, 2023). The University of British Columbia (UBC, n.d.) shares Generative AI Resources from various sources that aim to provide education surrounding effective AI use in a variety of contexts. With clearly stipulated policies and supportive resources in place, and by engaging in open conversations around the ethical use of AI in academia, institutions foster a strong commitment to academic responsibility and integrity while highlighting boundaries, insights, and acceptable uses.

AI'S ACKNOWLEDGEMENT AND INCORPORATION INTO AN UNDERGRADUATE LANGUAGE AND CULTURE COURSE

In an effort to analyze the role that AI can play in the language-culture classroom, we will now examine a 12-week undergraduate course offered at the University of Toronto Mississauga. The course is unique in the way that it brings together students from various disciplines, bridging academic backgrounds by being taught in English and providing all members of the class, regardless of program of study, with opportunities to engage in multimodal and experiential learning activities in order to work towards achieving a series of learning outcomes. All learners acquire and recognize the language of Italian cultural currency either in the classroom or through experiential learning, thereby connecting how and why the practical learning experience applies to course content; they gain an appreciation of the Italian language and culture in authentic environments and, overall, seek to recognize the relevance of Italian culture. More specifically, students are well positioned to assess how history has shaped various aspects of culture - art, fashion, cinema, cuisine, and how each of those intersects with politics, socio-economics, economics, migration, gender, and self-expression. Learners also trace the impact of Italian immigration and the development of diaspora in international contexts and are encouraged to discover the links between course content and their own histories, cultures, and identities. In order to develop such outcomes and to help students identify course-based connections for in-class discussions and as features of their assignment submissions, Experiential Learning is a cornerstone of this course's pedagogy. As such, numerous immersive opportunities are available to students, including local and international field trips and virtual walking tours of cultural heritage sites. For students who are part of an Italian-Language Program (Minor, Major, or Specialist), language proficiency ranges from beginner to beginner-intermediate, having undertaken one year of formal academic preparation in the language of study, and they may opt to use the course to fulfill the Program's language requirements. For Italian-program students, then, the course provides them with opportunities to employ spoken and written Italian with ease, spontaneity, and organically in both personal and professional contexts; they also recognize the relevance and inextricable links between the Italian language and culture.

Since the inception of the course in 2014, assignments have been intentionally curated to prompt students to extend their learning beyond the classroom, fostering their critical thinking skills and self-reflection to personally connect their lived experiences with course concepts in the language - Italian or English - best suited to their respective program. In particular, methods of assessment centre on weekly and bi-weekly assignments which incorporate logic-, fact-, and opinion-based (personal) reflections into multiple choice, true/false, written and/or recorded responses. Each assignment is intentionally designed and structured in its multimodal format to reflect a variety of learning styles and to maximize course goals, learning outcomes, and student success. Before the widespread availability of AI and its capabilities were readily known, student engagement with lecture content and experiential learning opportunities was evaluated mainly through written and/or audiovisual, essay-style assignments that sought a balance of personal anecdotes and academic reflections on scholarly and popular articles. Responses were evaluated according to a standardized course rubric, composed in alignment with the institution's grading scheme, that considered the following three key areas of assessment: (1) content, (2) sources, (3) language, organization, style. Specifically, coursework content was assessed based on its quality and the extent to which it addressed all aspects of the assignment question(s), whether it contained meaningful and detailed personal and academic reflections, and whether it was connected to the course's learning objectives. "Sources" were evaluated based on, for example, their relevance to the topic at the core of the paper and the judiciousness students exercised when citing from such sources. "Language, organization, style" looked at, among other factors, the overall progression or sequence of arguments and the clarity of the writing style employed. The rubric and its adjacent criteria were in place to support students in approaching their work holistically and in a manner that encouraged them to draw close connections to their learning experiences, and they [the rubric and criteria] ensured that as instructors and assistants graded such work, we approached evaluations with the same goals in mind.

The necessary decision to incorporate AI into course assessments came ahead of the Summer (May-June) 2023 iteration of the course when generative tools, such as ChatGPT, were quickly gaining momentum. Based on institutional policies released at the same time (May 2023), adjustments were made to coursework expectations and rubrics accordingly. The University presented instructors with descriptions to include in course syllabi according to how they intended to engage with Generative AI tools in their courses: (1) Can Use Generative AI Tools, (2) Can Use Generative AI in Certain Instances or Specific Ways, and (3) Cannot Use Generative AI ("U of T Syllabus Language - Use of Generative AI in Assignments," Spring/Summer 2023). For courses in which Generative AI use would be permitted--that is, (1) and (2)--the description acknowledged and outlined flexible parameters to promote an open dialogue around ethical AI use and its capabilities for learning. The language-culture course, in particular, opted to use descriptions (1) and (2), permitting students to use AI for specific, reflective written and/or audio-visual submissions. Students were also invited to submit an optional "AI Appendix" with their assignments outlining if and how they had used Generative AI tools in completing the assessment and including a screenshot of the generated response, if applicable. Furthermore, the course's experiential learning opportunities and accompanying reflection questions lent themselves well to limiting the presence of AI use, given that assessments emphasized personal experiences and required references from select sources. The flexibility of multimodal submissions and the personal nature of the assignments left us cautiously optimistic that with a few tweaks, such as adding the AI Appendix and an increased emphasis in the rubric on students' use of explicit sources, we might outwit and stave off any unwarranted AI uses.

AI's adoption into the course for Summer 2023 was slow as Generative AI had only recently made an incursion into academia. The course's stance on AI use acknowledged its presence and welcomed it in ways that did not impede or infiltrate students' personal and academic reflections while also operating on an expectation of student understanding and honesty. Students were advised against using AI for large components of their coursework submissions, and the importance of ethical AI use was stressed. Authentic academic processes and benefits of self-generated work were shared, and students were asked to confirm their understanding of the information and tools they were given. During the Summer course offering, only 1 of 115 students used AI on 5 of 7 written reflections. The student's use of AI was limited to including 1-2 generated paragraphs on each submission, but the grading team noted that personal contributions were either missing or minimal. Beyond online dictionaries, students specifically enrolled in an Italian program did not rely on a generative AI tool to complete their assignments.

As generative AI tools grew in sophistication[3] and their implications continued to dominate public discourse over the summer, this group of instructors and assistants was keenly sensitive to the fact that the course would need to re-address appropriate AI usage ahead of its Fall 2023 offering.[4] The AI Appendix was made into a mandatory declaration that all students appended to each assignment, lest their submission be considered incomplete and their mark temporarily withheld. Taking into consideration the data collected during the Summer 2023 term and the limited reliability of self-reported data (Mensah et al., 2018; Yang et al., 2017), it was apparent that this declaration, whether optional or required, would not be enough to sustain academic rigour throughout the Fall iteration of the course. It was necessary to make further modifications to course assignments and rubrics.

The teaching team continued to refine its approach to embedding AI into coursework. While detecting AI usage is becoming easier, it is not yet an exact science, and, importantly, there are ethical and privacy issues concerning detection software. Our practices are, therefore, in part informed by Fulford (2023), who argues that AI use must not be treated as plagiarism but as an opportunity for assignment reform, which begins with explicitly drawing the line between using AI as a research and writing aid rather than a cheating tool. Select assessments were designed to encourage learners to engage firsthand with AI tools and assess the language of AI-generated responses by judging the accuracy of the grammatical concepts employed, vocabulary appropriateness, and the general tone of the Italian produced. Students were also invited to adjudicate the quality of the content generated by corroborating or debunking its claims with information procured from primary and secondary sources (e.g., scholarly articles and course textbooks) and personal anecdotes. Reflective assignments, in other words, necessarily underwent a series of modifications, from asking students to draw tighter connections between their in-class learning, accompanying readings, and course objectives to asking students to evaluate the accuracy, or otherwise, of AI-generated responses. Entirely new assessments were also created that did not require and/or would not be well-served by AI tools, leveraging multimodal frameworks such as live discussions, improvised elevator-pitch-style presentations, and audiovisual social media posts. This approach has the added benefit of reducing the gap between the tools available to some students by bringing a wide variety of multimodal literacy tools to classroom learning and practice and supporting creative reflections on student participation in experiential learning opportunities. We also harkened back, on some assignments, to traditional multiple choice and true or false-style questions.

Within the updated rubric, parameters for evaluating content were expanded to include further considerations on originality and innovation, including whether the response offered new interpretations of primary and secondary sources. As both a deterrent for a heavy reliance on AI and a way to better evaluate the students and not ChatGPT, the rubric considered how much and for what purposes AI was employed. Further, the rubric stated that responses should be well-substantiated and demonstrate sufficient depth and innovation with minimal to no use of AI. The rubric's criteria for sources assessed their quality and the extent to which referenced materials were used accurately and effectively. Evaluations of language, organization, and style continued to esteem work that was presented diligently and which showed evidence of self-editing prior to submitting a final copy of any coursework, including the extent to which learners exercised care in elevating the language produced by AI and transforming it into a clearer, more concise response. For Italian-program students specifically, a language analysis was embedded into their assignment which asked them to compare the language level of the AI-generated answer against their own preparation by identifying, for example, the verb tenses, syntactic structures, and academic conjunctions present in the response.

REFLECTING ON THE USE OF AI IN COURSEWORK DESIGN

In the Fall 2023 term, we noted a gradual increase in the number of students who confirmed using AI. The first two assignments had an identical number of confirmed generative AI uses; however, starting from Assignment 3 onward, the number significantly rose, and by Assignment 5, the number had risen by 100% (compared to Assignment 1). This growth can be attributed to the fact that course content became more complex as the term progressed and that, perhaps, external factors, such as elevated amounts of work in other courses, prompted learners to seek out ChatGPT as an aid more frequently than before.

In most instances, students who answered positively to the AI Appendix shared that they used such systems to brush up on their original composition's language (Italian or English) or to provide correct formatting for in-text citations and reference lists. Using AI tools also proved advantageous for some students who, for example, benefitted from it to gain feedback on their composition skills. Moreover, given how these platforms tend to generate responses by pulling information from the vast amounts of data accessible online, they provided strong starting points for generating ideas into which students then investigated topics further on their own. This allowed the students to engage in fact-checking exercises, upon which they elaborated their additional research findings. Other uses, however, did seem to bring with them a few caveats, namely an over-reliance on the AI system, which impeded students from developing self-directed learning techniques, critical thinking, and research skills.

Among students who acknowledged at least some measure of reliance on generative AI in their assignments, submissions, by and large, continued to leave out the personal reflections outlined and expected by the assessment questions and adjacent rubrics. In extreme cases of an over-reliance on technology, students turned to ChatGPT for assignments that sought to connect their personal lives and/or experiences on field trips to topics in the course. The chatbot provided responses written in the first person, but again, they contained no personal opinions. AI-generated responses also frequently exhibited an unnatural use of the English or Italian language. In the case of Italian, specifically, the language presented complex grammatical structures and advanced vocabulary beyond students' beginner-intermediate preparation. Moreover, the ability to compose complex texts with advanced words is different across all languages, as AI machines rely on the number of tokens available to them in a given language. Similar to other LLMs, ChatGPT is trained on a mix of data from multiple languages; however, since the vast majority of data to which they have access is in English, generative AI tools are not, as of now, able to adequately evaluate texts that exhibit complex language proficiency (Lai et al., 2023) in most languages outside of English. Therefore, the community lacks a comprehensive, public, and independent evaluation of ChatGPT in various non-English languages for diverse natural-language processing tasks to provide proper perspectives for this research application. What the authors have noted to date is that due to this inefficiency with translation and multilingual data, some students resorted to using multiple tools to translate into English the prompt they wanted to give the AI machine and then, at most, paraphrased the response received without sufficiently editing the entire response. Students sometimes used these tools multiple times for one assignment to achieve their desired content. For instance, for a text that was to be written in Italian, a student declared having (1) used Google Translate to translate their prompt from Mandarin (native language) to English, (2) fed the English translation of the prompt to ChatGPT, (3) used Google Translate again to translate ChatGPT's response to Italian (target language) in an effort to arrive at a text with minimal errors. Unsurprisingly, this machine-driven game of broken telephone resulted in the final text exhibiting language structures beyond the expected level of proficiency and containing errors in otherwise simple grammatical concepts.

A second significant caveat to AI usage is the potential hindrance it may cause to developing research skills. When students excessively rely on AI systems for information retrieval and quality control, they may miss the opportunity to develop and practice the critical thinking skills required for research proficiency. As with all university courses, students were provided with the course syllabus at the beginning of the term, and the instructor reviewed course expectations during the first lecture, one of which was the exclusive use of APA style for reflective essays. To aid with citation style and formatting, students also participated in research-related workshops on navigating online resources and where to find detailed guides for the APA citation format. While most students effectively applied their workshop learnings and online resources for sound research and to compose proper citations, there remained a few students who continued to struggle with standardized APA guidelines and turned to AI tools to check the quality of their citations for them. Unfortunately, in those instances, the AI system failed to provide the correct formatting style, underscoring the importance of fostering a comprehensive understanding of citation formats beyond automated tools and emphasizing the necessity to cross-verify one's work against the exemplars and guidelines provided in course materials.

The process of manually researching, critically evaluating, and synthesizing knowledge is integral to fostering intellectual autonomy and analytical thinking. By delegating these tasks to AI systems, students may miss the opportunity to develop a deeper understanding of their research subjects and refine their academic productions. We observed that students who declared having used AI tools to paraphrase paragraphs, which they themselves composed, to improve their language and style, or to make their paragraphs more succinct in order to meet the required word count, are overly trusting of the chatbot's diligence and language skills. Thus, oftentimes, passages omitted a keyword or a critical component of the original passage written by the student and left key words or phrases untranslated in instances where those expressions were original and specific to lecture content. The capacity to critically evaluate and rectify discrepancies in AI-generated content requires a foundational proficiency in writing and a keen understanding of the subject matter. Indeed, this course permits the use of AI tools to support the refinement of one's work, but a combination of efforts - both human and technologically-generated - should be employed if a response is to be optimized. To maximize the use of AI, the integration of technology into the writing process should be a supplementary measure, complementing rather than replacing the core skills that students possess.

As AI tools become more diverse and polyvalent in what content they can generate, older systems will lose users. Regardless of the number of online dictionaries available, some students, particularly those composing a text in their non-native language, tend to seek assistance from LLM-based translators like Google Translate. The AI Appendix exercise in this course revealed that, in some instances, students used systems such as ChatGPT to seek the meaning of words or, at other times, ask for synonyms and related terminology of words that they intended to use in their long answers. When it comes to language, be it looking for a simple word or paraphrasing a passage, AI tools are faced with the shortcoming that they cannot accurately assess the context in which words appear, as their LLMs are served by what is available in their databases and elsewhere on the Internet. Furthermore, texts generated by these systems do not (and cannot) anticipate the user's language level. Therefore, it is relatively easy to detect whether a student who does not possess advanced knowledge of the language—Italian, in our case—has used generative AI tools in their compositions due to abrupt shifts in language complexity, the use of advanced vocabulary, or the incorporation of complex syntactic structures that deviate from the student's beginner-intermediate language proficiency.

When used effectively, however, AI machines can be valuable learning tools. If a student has already developed composition skills and knowledge of grammar, then AI tools, such as *Grammarly* for learners completing their work in English, or *Word Reference* or *Google Translate* for Italian program students, can be used as time-efficient mechanisms in place to provide feedback on grammar, awkward phrasing, verbosity, and overall coherence in a text. In other words, again, users must be encouraged to review AI's suggestions and revise their writing as necessary. With the help of AI tools, the student can identify their weaknesses, if any, and, through suggested instructions provided by the software, identify ways to improve their writing skills for future assignments. In addition, the availability of such tools can help the student to foster a habit of revision and editing, thereby elevating the quality of the work submitted, as working through feedback received from AI tools mirrors the real-life iterative learning process wherein professional writers will undergo multiple rounds of editing to refine their composition. The feedback and editing loop can teach students that it is okay to make mistakes, helping them to develop autonomy in their writing and self-correct their future compositions, according to the feedback received from the AI.

FUTURE CONSIDERATIONS

For the Fall 2023 iteration of the course in focus, the teaching team was able to leverage data collected during its Summer 2023 offering to improve the implementation of AI tools. Moving forward, the teaching team will continue to improve this aspect of the course and engage in important discussions on the role of AI in education. Reflecting on the efforts made over the past two terms, the AI Appendix will be further amended to include a space in which students can describe their thoughts on AI (in relation to, for example, its reliability and how it affects their claim to intellectual property), assignment rubrics will undergo additional updates that directly address and account for the use of AI tools, and select future assessments will ask learners to address in more depth the language and content of an AI-generated response, at times provided for them and at other times produced by their prompts. Specifically, students will continue to analyze a response's accuracy, corroborating and/or debunking, as needed and as determined by the students themselves, any AI-generated information with the support of different pedagogical materials (e.g. scholarly articles, the course textbook) and personal anecdotes. We will also continue to create new assessments that do not require and/or would not benefit from AI use. Such advancements in the course's assessment methods require that the capabilities of AI be explored more and understood better by the teaching team. Ultimately, we will reimagine assessments at their core to more precisely centre the learner and course concepts, further calling upon students' active engagement in all aspects of the course.

In terms of large language models, specifically within this language-culture course, we noted that students spent significant time using copy-and-paste functions from Google Translate to adopt the vocabulary and grammatical structures necessary to continue their learning. In future studies, we intend to work with students to parse out the differences between AI tools (e.g. ChatGPT vs. *Google Translate*) to reach a common understanding of the use and impact on learning of various technologies. Following Bonner et al. (2023), we will redesign methods of assessment in ways that call upon generative AI to facilitate certain dimensions of language teaching and learning, such as using it to reinterpret texts, to write using level-appropriate grammar and vocabulary, including academic conjunctions, idiomatic expressions, etc. In sum, we will develop assessments that consider the language level of each learner to co-construct appropriate AI usages and better support students' language-learning journeys.

CONCLUSION

In this self-reflective effort, we highlight the importance of constantly evolving our assessment design practices and maintaining a good grasp, as instructors, of the capabilities and limitations of generative AI. For all learners, coursework perhaps fell short of encouraging autonomous critical production, and, for Italian-program students specifically, they were perhaps insufficiently structured around the language abilities and tools with which learners have the most practice. Nonetheless, it is the ongoing work of any instructor to try to be ahead of the technological curve as much as possible and/or address the inevitable changes it actualizes in a timely fashion. With that, assignment design gaps will be considered and reworked into new assessments that will be first piloted among focus groups before their implementation in future course iterations.

The introduction of generative AI into various contexts has impacted education systems worldwide, and it is an important leap forward in technological advancements. AI will inevitably continue to grow and increase its presence in various contexts, but in our course alone, we did not consider its employment to have drastically improved student performance. The skills students bring to the classroom, and the knowledge gains they achieve on their own far surpass the production capabilities of ChatGPT. When AI-produced responses are correctly cited, we may see the fruits of an effective collaboration if instructors and students utilize AI as a tool to support learning in a way that does not override the human element and contribution. In that case, AI can allow us all to promote and engage with course concepts differently and develop new skills. To emphasize the inevitable interconnectivity of human and machine future, we end this chapter in collaboration with ChatGPT. Prompt: "How should a chapter on 'The Reality of Artificiality: Artificial Intelligence in the Language-Culture Classroom' conclude?" Generated Response: In conclusion, the integration of artificial intelligence into the cultural classroom is a multi-faceted journey that holds both promises and challenges. As we navigate this intersection of technology and education, it becomes crucial to foster a balanced approach that leverages AI's capabilities while preserving the essential human elements of cultural competence, understanding, and interpretation. In essence, the convergence of artificial intelligence and language-cultural education offers an opportunity for innovation, collaboration, and the cultivation of a global perspective. By navigating the challenges thoughtfully and ethically, we can pave the way for a future where AI contributes positively to the classroom, enhancing our understanding of diverse societies and fostering a more interconnected world. (Paraphrased by the authors; response curated by ChatGPT, 2023a)

REFERENCES

Academic Integrity at UBC. (2023). *CHATGPT Q&A*. https://academicintegrity.ubc.ca/chatgpt-faq/

Aikins, R., & Kuo, A. (2023). *What Students Said About the Spring of ChatGPT*. Inside Higher Ed. https://www.insidehighered.com/opinion/views/2023/09/07/what-students-said-about-spring-chatgpt-opinion?fbclid=IwAR0vUM4HY5ideFrvGVABp2sz8MZGuzEss4EH-YiXtaUZZ1_UsZA0xKar8kk_aem_AaflEki-AJcqt065wZj0M4DpuY4xmlkyGMnz6JBFWzOh8ZjZMuKvLmriGOa6Cr1rHDho&mibextid=Zxz2cZ

Azzo, A. (2023). *Teaching Artificial Intelligence Literacy: 'AI Is for Everyone.'* Artificial Intelligence at Northwestern. https://ai.northwestern.edu/news-events/articles/2023/teaching-artificial-intelligence-literacy-ai-is-for-everyone.html

Bonner, E., Lege, R., & Frazier, E. (2023). Large Language Model-Based Artificial Intelligence in the Language Classroom: Practical Ideas for Teaching. *Teaching English with Technology*, *2023*(1). doi:10.56297/BKAM1691/WIEO1749

Carrington, V. (2005). Txting: The end of civilization (again)? *Cambridge Journal of Education*, *35*(2), 161–175. doi:10.1080/03057640500146799

Dreibelbis, E. (2023). *Google Translate vs. ChatGPT: Which One Is the Best Language Translator?* PC-Mag UK. https://uk.pcmag.com/ai/147242/google-translate-vs-chatgpt-which-one-is-the-best-language-translator#:~:text=AI Will Level Up Web Translation&text=But as we saw with,Translate's capabilities across the board.

Font de la Vall, R., González Araya, F. (2022). Exploring the Benefits and Challenges of AI-Language Learning Tools. *The International Journal of Social Sciences and Humanities Invention*. doi:10.18535/ijsshi/v10i01.02

Fulford, M. (2023). *In the AI age, it's time to change how we teach and grade writing: If we continue to treat the use of AI as plagiarism, we're doomed to fail. Here's what we should be doing instead.* Chalkbeat Colorado. https://co.chalkbeat.org/2023/8/4/23820783/ai-chat-gpt-teaching-writing-grading?fbclid=IwAR2IuQa23f0M6dxmfay5nB_DlQgrJfMfPmm9hMbrWYVMW3WKAaruL3XrNKE

Harvard Business School. (2023). *2.1 Academic Standards of Conduct.* Harvard Business School MBA. https://www.hbs.edu/mba/handbook/standards-of-conduct/academic/Pages/chatgpt-and-ai.aspx

Indiana University Knowledge Base. (2023). *Acceptable uses of generative AI services at IU.* https://kb.iu.edu/d/biit

Kitamura, F. C. (2023). ChatGPT Is Shaping the future of medical writing but still requires human judgment. *Radiology*, *230171*(2). Advance online publication. doi:10.1148/radiol.230171 PMID:36728749

Lai, V. D., Ngo, N. T., Veyseh, A. P. B., Man, H., Dernoncourt, F., Bui, T., & Nguyen, T. H. (2023). *ChatGPT Beyond English: Towards a Comprehensive Evaluation of Large Language Models in Multilingual Learning.* /arxiv.2304.05613 doi:10.18653/v1/2023.findings-emnlp.878

Lee, H., Ahn, H., Nguyen, T. G., Choi, S. M., & Kim, D. J. (2017). Comparing the Self-Report and Measured Smartphone Usage of College Students: A Pilot Study. *Psychiatry Investigation*, *14*(2), 198–204. doi:10.4306/pi.2017.14.2.198 PMID:28326119

Liang, W., Yuksekgonul, M., Mao, Y., Wu, E., & Zou, J. (2023). GPT detectors are biased against non-native English writers. *A Cell Press Journal*, *4*(7). doi:10.1016/j.patter.2023.100779

Lin, Z., Zhang, D., Tao, Q., Shi, D., Haffari, G., Wu, Q., He, M., & Ge, Z. (2023). Medical visual question answering: A survey. *Artificial Intelligence in Medicine*, *143*, 102611. Advance online publication. doi:10.1016/j.artmed.2023.102611 PMID:37673579

McGee, R. W. (2023). Is Chat Gpt biased against conservatives? An empirical study. SSRN *Electron. J.* doi:10.2139/ssrn.4359405

McGill Library. (2023). *AI Literacy Guide.* https://libraryguides.mcgill.ca/ai/literacy

Mensah, C., Azila-Gbettor, E. M., & Asimah, V. (2018). Self-Reported Examination Cheating of Alumni and Enrolled Students: Evidence from Ghana. *Journal of Academic Ethics*, 89-102. doi:10.1007/s10805-017-9286-x

Mohan, D. D., Jawade, B., Setlur, S., & Govindaraju, V. (2023) Chapter 4 - Deep metric learning for computer vision: A brief overview. Handbook of Statistics, 48, 59–79. doi:10.1016/bs.host.2023.01.003

OpenA. I. (2023a). *ChatGPT.* https://chat.openai.com/c/02af3cf9-1598-4fa1-882b-f543a27b21cc

Open, A. I. (2023b). *ChatGPT - Release Notes*. OpenAI. https://help.openai.com/en/articles/6825453-chatgpt-release-notes

Schiff, D. (2021) Out of the laboratory and into the classroom: the future of artificial intelligence in education. *AI & Soc*, 331–348. doi:10.1007/s00146-020-01033-8

Southern, M. G. (2023, February 8). Google Launches Ai-Powered Contextual Translations. *Search Engine Journal.* https://www.searchenginejournal.com/google-launches-ai-powered-contextual-translations/478863/#close

UBC. (n.d.). *Generative AI Resources*. The University of British Columbia: Generative AI. https://genai.ubc.ca/resources/

UNESCO. (2023). *UNESCO survey: Less than 10% of schools and universities have formal guidance on AI.* UNESCO. https://www.unesco.org/en/articles/unesco-survey-less-10-schools-and-universities-have-formal-guidance-ai

University of Toronto. (n.d.a). *ChatGPT and Generative AI in the Classroom.* Office of the Vice-Provost, Innovations in Undergraduate Education. https://www.viceprovostundergrad.utoronto.ca/strategic-priorities/digital-learning/special-initiative-artificial-intelligence/

University of Toronto. (n.d.b). *Using ChatGPT or Other Generative AI Tools on a Marked Assessment.* https://www.academicintegrity.utoronto.ca/perils-and-pitfalls/using-chatgpt-or-other-ai-tool-on-a-marked-assessment/

Urlaub, P., & Dessein, E. (2022). From Disrupted Classrooms to Human-Machine Collaboration? The Pocket Calculator, Google Translate, and the Future of Language Education. *Journal of Linguistics and Language Teaching*, *14*(1). Advance online publication. doi:10.5070/L214151790

UW–Madison Information Technology. (2023, August 24). *Generative AI @ uw–madison: Use & policies*. https://it.wisc.edu/generative-ai-uw-madison-use-policies/

van Dis, E. A., Bollen, J., Zuidema, W., van Rooij, R., & Bockting, C. L. (2023). ChatGPT: five priorities for research. *Nature, 614*, 224–226. doi: m10.1038/d41586-023-00288-7

Walsh, M. (2017). Multiliteracies, Multimodality, New Literacies and.... What Do These Mean for Literacy Education? *Inclusive Principles and Practices in Literacy Education*, *11*, 19–33. doi:10.1108/S1479-363620170000011002

Yu, H. (2023). Reflection on whether Chat GPT should be banned by academia from the perspective of education and teaching. *Frontiers in Psychology*, *14*, 1181712. doi:10.3389/fpsyg.2023.1181712 PMID:37325766

KEY TERMS AND DEFINITIONS

Cultural Competence: Increasing individuals' cross-cultural awareness and appreciation. Achieving cultural competence is seen as inextricably linked to language proficiency.

Digital Literacy: Honing the skills needed to effectively navigate today's technology-drive world.

Experiential Learning: Hands-on learning and reflection through direct contact with the subject matter.

Generative AI: Artificial Intelligence technologies that generate responses based on inputted prompts.

Italian Cultural Studies: Examining various aspects of Italian culture (art, fashion, cinema, cuisine, etc.) within historical context.

LLMs: Large Language Models (LLMs) are sophisticated AI systems trained on vast amounts of textual data, allowing them to learn complex linguistic patterns. The versatility of LLMS makes them useful tools that could be applied to language processing tasks such as translation, answering questions, and providing summaries. Within the umbrella of Generative AI tools available to the public, ChatGPT, developed by OpenAI, falls under the category of an LLM-based chatbot. Other LLM-based chatbots include Bard, developed by Google, and Ernie, developed by Baidu. While Google Translate is an LLM, it is not an LLM-based chatbot.

Multimodal: Coursework or activities which are enhanced through a variety of formats (e.g. audio-visual assignments, in-person and virtual delivery of lecture content).

Reflective Assignments: We define reflective assignments as a blend of students' considerations on the ways in which their in-class and lived experiences intersect with their academic research and analyses of scholarly sources.

ENDNOTES

1. See also Font de la Vall and González Araya (2022) on generative AI's limited abilities in creative expression and in producing natural-sounding language or replicating "cultural and contextual nuances of language, such as idioms, colloquialisms" (Font de la Vall, R., González Araya, 2022, p. 7573).
2. Despite the progress that has been made in devising policies at an increasing number of institutions, according to a recent (2023) UNESCO global survey of over 450 schools and universities, "approximately 13% of the universities reported having institutional policies and/or some formal guidance concerning the use of generative AI applications guidance, while only 7% of schools did" (UNESCO survey, 2023).
3. ChatGPT first launched on November 30, 2022 and 27 subsequent updates, with 26 of them occurring from January 2023 to November 2023 (Open AI, 2023b).
4. See Appendix (T. Lobalsamo_Supplemental Teaching Notes) for a sample Style Guide, AI Appendix/Declaration, Rubric, Essay-Style Reflection Question.

APPENDIX

Teaching Notes

STYLE AND RESOURCE GUIDE

The course's dedicated research page contains a detailed style guide (APA) and several course-related resources (books, articles, etc.).

APA

a. In-text citations &
b. Reference list

Work submitted in this course follows APA GUIDELINES.

- **APA citation has two parts:** an in-text citation for each source used or paraphrased AND a complete citation in a reference list in alphabetical order at the end of the paper.
- **Academic Integrity:** Work submitted which - to any extent - is not your original work, does not adequately/accurately cite sources, demonstrates the University's Code of Behaviour on Academic

AI

Generative Artificial Intelligence (AI) Applications

- Any content produced by an AI tool must be cited appropriately, in text, as indicated by the APA.
- For each assignment, complete/include an AI Appendix. See below.
- When coursework demonstrates the use of AI, but a student has not completed the Appendix, a meeting with the professor is required.
- Even when an AI appendix is provided and the AI tool is cited, the use of AI may result in a lower score on relative assignments when, for example, responses do not align with assignment requirements, when information is not from course materials and/or personal

AI Appendix/Declaration - *Did you use a generative AI tool?*
Indicate Yes or No. If yes, attach a screenshot of the response generated and complete the following fields:
Website/Source Information (e.g. ChatGPT 3.5, OpenAI):
Date accessed:
Prompt used/inputted in AI generator:
Citation used within submission:

RUBRIC

Inline with the University's grading scheme, the following rubrics are considered when evaluating coursework.

Evaluations are based on the quality of the coursework submitted; that is, the extent to which the work met, did not meet, and/or exceeded the following thresholds:

CONTENT

- All aspects of the assigned question(s) was (were) addressed.
- The response(s) contained both personal and academic reflections (based on course materials and required sources).
- The response(s) connected to the course's learning objectives.
- The argument and/or approach to the response(s) was substantiated.
- The response(s) was (were) innovative (original, minimal to no use of AI).

Points removed if the above criteria are not met.

SOURCES

- The minimum number of sources were consulted/ accessed and cited, according to the question(s).
- Response(s) incorporated information presented in lecture (student's attendance in relevant lectures is taken into consideration).
- Sources were used accurately.
- Sources were used effectively: the most pertinent aspects of the sources were used, research supported and elevated the information presented (and the response(s), overall).
- (If applicable) An AI appendix was included in the submission.

Points removed if the above criteria are not met.

LANGUAGE, ORGANIZATION, STYLE

- The writing style was clear and concise (within allotted word count).
- Language was natural; vocabulary and grammar were appropriate (according to the topics and to the learner's language proficiency).
- The response was organized systematically and/or logically, according to the question(s).

Points removed if the above criteria are not met.

Sample Essay-Style Reflection Question (with Integration of AI)

(Total word count: - - - words)

Content:

- Using an AI tool of your choice, generate a response to the following prompt: "- - -."
- In separate paragraphs, assess/describe the truths and falsities of the AI-generated response. If you believe that AI's response provides NO false statements, express that; amplify any information that you felt AI did not delve into deeply enough with your own knowledge, experiences, and research.

Italian-Program Students

- Add the following details to the same prompt used above: "Generate this response in A1-level Italian..."
- Based on your familiarity with Italian (e.g. the grammar, vocabulary to which you have been exposed thus far), provide a brief language analysis in reference to the generated response. In point and/or chart form, indicate:
  - All of the verb tenses used and whether or not each tense is A1-level appropriate (i.e. have you learned them/when will you learn them?).
  - The academic conjunctions used. Next to each one, provide an alternative expression/synonym.
  - 3 new learnings (anything which which you were unfamiliar before; e.g., a verb tense, syntactic structure, vocabulary).

Required with Your Response:

✓ AI Appendix/Declaration, including a screenshot of the generated response

✓ citations from/references to 2 lectures

✓ citations from/references to 1 course reading (scholarly or popular)

✓ citations from/references to 1 additional scholarly reference

✓ citations from/references to 1 additional popular reference

Section 2

Perspectives: What People Say About AI

Chapter 4
Enriching the Teaching-Learning Experience by Using AI Tools in the L2 Classroom

Dimaris Barrios-Beltran
Mount Holyoke College, USA

ABSTRACT

Artificial intelligence (AI) has emerged as a transformative force in second language (L2) education, reshaping teaching and learning methodologies. This chapter explores AI's impact on L2 educators and learners through insights from questionnaires and a follow-up conversation. Initial apprehension towards AI is counterbalanced by curiosity about its potential to enhance educational practices. The chapter provides practical guidance, showcasing how AI tools can be aligned with key language learning skills and offering structured examples of activities to enhance these skills. It highlights AI's role in providing immediate feedback, simplifying complex concepts, and creating inclusive classrooms tailored to individual learning styles and needs. The discussion also addresses educators' recognition of AI's potential and underscores the need for clear guidelines and training in ethical AI implementation. As AI technology evolves, it promises a more personalized, dynamic educational journey, enriching the L2 learning process.

INTRODUCTION

The integration of Artificial Intelligence (AI) in educational settings is a burgeoning discourse, particularly in the United States, where educators express a mix of doubt, insecurity, and skepticism about this emerging technology. Concerns range from viewing AI as a potential threat to student cognition to an under-recognition of its nuanced intelligence applications. Some institutions are banning AI use due to concerns over facilitating plagiarism, while others emphasize responsible usage but struggle to define and clarify its ethical boundaries (Singer, 2023). Conversely, higher education institutions in Asia and Europe are increasingly adopting AI, not only in remote learning platforms (Adipat et al., 2022) but also

DOI: 10.4018/979-8-3693-0872-1.ch004

in administrative systems (Sellar & Gulson, 2019), fostering innovative pedagogies like flipped learning and universal design teaching.

Recent studies, focusing on the need for regulatory frameworks and examining AI's impact on learning outcomes and classroom integration (Zheng et al., 2021), have yet to fully uncover AI's potential in education. Specifically, in second language (L2) classrooms, there are many doubts about how this technology can truly enhance learners' linguistic skills without doing the work for them. Questions arise about the extent to which these tools might minimize effort but jeopardize learning, or conversely, support the language learning process. Furthermore, most studies focus on perceptions of current AI tool users, such as those using ChatGPT and Grammarly, leaving the actual improvement in their performance largely unassessed.

Additionally, many technology experts are still learning about the capabilities of these new tools and are tasked with guiding educators on their usage. This leads to the central challenge: exploring how to ethically incorporate these tools in the classroom, ensuring they fulfill their intended purposes. A pivotal question emerges: How can educators be best prepared, through targeted training or orientation, to navigate a future increasingly intertwined with AI? This chapter contributes to the ongoing dialogue about AI in higher education by presenting an in-depth analysis of second language (L2) educators' and learners' perceptions, with a focus on face-to-face learning environments. It examines their readiness to adopt AI tools for diverse linguistic needs, specifically in areas such as time management and planning, memorization, interpersonal communication, presentation, and creative and critical thinking – all crucial for mastering a second language. Furthermore, the chapter offers practical insights, aligning specific AI tools with these key language skills and providing structured activity examples. This approach demonstrates how AI can be effectively integrated into classroom activities and pedagogical practices, enhancing the language learning experience.

LITERATURE REVIEW

Previous research on AI in language education spans a diverse range of areas, from ethical considerations to the facilitation and personalization of learning experiences. This body of work converges on a key consensus: the integration of AI necessitates a deep ethical awareness and a nuanced understanding of its implications for learners. Highlighting this, studies emphasize fostering critical thinking in learners, enabling them to navigate the ethical dimensions inherent in the use of AI in education.

This integration of AI use into the curriculum assumes a role of preponderant significance, not only in fostering a futuristic pedagogical outlook but also in nurturing the professional mindset of potential developers and consumers of this emerging technology (Borenstein & Howard, 2021). Emphasis on AI ethical use in education is exemplified in Sabuncuoglu (2020) which demonstrates how incorporating AI into curricula can enhance not just subject knowledge, like mathematics and science, but also students' understanding of AI's ethical implications. Building on this, a novel area of exploration is AI's application in classroom teaching analysis. Roschelle et al. (2020) and Sun et al. (2023) illustrate how AI can meticulously scrutinize classroom dynamics, behavior patterns, and knowledge representation. This multidimensional assessment serves to refine classroom management and enhance teaching and learning practices. By recognizing and deciphering behavioral trends, educators can optimize their teaching methodologies, aligning with data-informed pedagogical movements and equipping them to tailor learning experiences.

In line with these ethical considerations, Roe et al. (2023) emphasizes the need for clear guidelines and transparent rules regarding the use of technology in the classroom. Their analysis extends to the advantages and disadvantages of three common tools: Machine Translation services (MTs), Digital Writing Assistants (DWAs), and Academic Plagiarism Trackers (APTs). Unlike tools like ChatGPT that generate original content, these technologies provide support in translation, grammar, vocabulary, sentence structure, and plagiarism detection. However, Roe et al. (2023) also highlights a critical concern: students often lack clarity on what constitutes a violation of academic honor codes versus proper AI use in academia. This finding underscores the necessity for educational institutions to develop explicit guidelines to help students navigate the ethical use of AI tools in their academic pursuits.

Further research efforts have been directed towards leveraging AI for various educational purposes, such as student tutoring, writing assistance, immersive virtual reality settings, chatbot dialogues, and adaptive learning experiences (Samea Qoura & Moustafa Elmansi, 2023; Zawacki-Richter et al., 2019). AI's most compelling attribute in this domain is its ability to craft personalized learning experiences by adapting teaching materials to students' proficiency levels and reconfiguring learning paths. Extending its capabilities, AI now includes immediate feedback provision, translation assistance, error identification, and support in pronunciation and grammatical reflections (Dodigovic, 2009; Miller, 2019; Samea Qoura & Moustafa Elmansi, 2023), highlighting its role as a versatile tool in enhancing language proficiency.

The impact of AI on writing skills, in particular, has attracted considerable interest. Gayed et al. (2022) examined the use of predictive text tools, focusing on a study with Japanese students learning English. Their AI-assisted app improved syntactic complexity but not lexical diversity or production rates. In contrast, Abdul Rahman et al. (2022) observed substantial improvement in writing scores through Grammarly use, indicating its effectiveness in detecting grammatical errors. Nonetheless, they recognize that such technology alone cannot replace the critical role of instructors in guiding high-quality writing.

Although a significant majority of second language acquisition studies predominantly focus on English, there is a noticeable dearth of research on other languages. Among the limited studies in this under-researched area, the work of Li et al. (2023) is particularly notable. Assessing the impact of ChatGPT in Chinese L2 classrooms, their research targeted low-income Hispanic students in New York City. The study revealed improvements in writing skills and increased empowerment among students, highlighting AI's potential to equalize educational opportunities. However, it also underscored the importance of ethical integration strategies, emphasizing the role of AI as a supportive tool rather than a replacement in the learning process.

Delving into instructor perspectives, Marzuki et al. (2023) analyzed how AI tools are perceived in Indonesian classrooms. While recognizing AI's benefits in improving writing skills, concerns arose about students using complex vocabulary without full comprehension, potentially affecting their creativity and critical thinking. This underscores the necessity for balanced and informed use of AI in teaching practices.

Kohnke (2023) and similar studies (Wahyuni, 2022; Fryer et al., 2019) illustrate the growing acceptance of AI among learners for its role in facilitating independent learning and providing accessible, enjoyable experiences. Additionally, these technologies are being employed to support inclusive and equitable practices, particularly for individuals facing language, mental, emotional, or physical challenges (Mohato, 2023). AI serves as a transformative tool within classrooms, offering opportunities for students with disabilities to remain integrated in standard courses.

Despite the predominantly positive reception of AI in language learning, challenges regarding interaction authenticity, dehumanization, privacy issues, and technological barriers persist. Furthermore, it is important to note that most studies focus on the opinions or perceptions of learners and educators who are already engaging with these technologies, predominantly in online learning environments. The actual impact of AI on linguistic skills remains unclear, as much of the existing data do not evaluate tangible performance outcomes. Additionally, not every educator feels confident incorporating AI into their teaching practices and student evaluations. Alharbi (2023) advocates for increasing familiarity with these technologies among educators and students. This involves enhancing digital literacy and developing a deeper understanding of how AI can support and enhance the teaching-learning process.

Therefore, this chapter aims to delve into technology usage in the second language classroom, examining perceptions of AI integration and pinpointing specific educational needs that technology can address. It also seeks to bridge the gap in existing literature by providing explicit examples of AI-enhanced activities and tasks. This approach is intended to equip educators and learners to navigate and thrive in the changing terrain of learning and digital advancements.

THE PERCEPTION OF AI IN THE L2 CLASSROOM

The integration of artificial intelligence into educational settings, particularly in today's digital era, represents a complex and evolving area of inquiry. In education, the harnessing of a diverse array of technological tools – from computers, tablets, and smartphones to projectors, VR headsets, and smart whiteboards – has created dynamic learning experiences. This technological shift has transformed classroom interactions, dynamics, and access to information, marking a new era in teaching and learning methodologies. AI, with its distinct capabilities, adds a new dimension to this transformation. Its integration into educational tools and platforms signifies a paradigm shift, prompting a reassessment of its role in equipping students to navigate and contribute to a world that is continually evolving in terms of communication, learning, and information acquisition.

The incorporation of AI in the second language classroom, however, has been met with diverse perspectives. While AI offers unique interactive capabilities that differ from conventional tech tools, there are concerns about its potential impact on language proficiency. This is especially pertinent in second language acquisition, where the focus is on developing the ability to express thoughts and ideas in the target language. In the United States, there exists a notable degree of reluctance among educators and administrators regarding the implementation of AI in the curriculum and its impact on students' learning experiences. These apprehensions are more pronounced in L2 learning due to the emphasis on preparing students for real-world interactions in the target language. Key questions emerge: To what extent can AI assistance improve students' linguistic skills? Can AI act as an interactive tool that not only assists but also promotes reflection on the learning process and language-related errors? Despite these concerns, various studies have acknowledged AI's potential in offering personalized learning experiences, providing immediate feedback, and exposing learners to a diverse range of linguistic content, at least from the perspective of current users of these technologies.

Before delving into these complexities, it is vital to understand the current perceptions and potential misconceptions surrounding the use of AI and technology in the L2 classroom, particularly in higher education in the United States. Familiarity with AI's capabilities and limitations could significantly shape this discourse.

To contribute to this ongoing discussion, this study surveyed L2 educators and L2 learners at a higher education institution in the United States, focusing on the following research questions:

RQ1. *Do educators and learners integrate technology into their daily lives?*
RQ2. *Do they consider technology an essential aspect of the L2 learning process?*
RQ3. *Are they familiar with the application of AI in the L2 classroom?*
RQ4. *Do they believe AI should be integrated into the L2 classroom?*

METHODOLOGY

This study adopted a mixed-methods approach to comprehensively explore the perceptions of AI in second language education. The data collection process involved administering a structured questionnaire to both educators and learners, which comprised both open and closed questions. The closed questions were designed to gather quantitative data, while the open questions aimed to elicit more in-depth qualitative responses. In addition to the questionnaire, follow-up open-ended conversations with educators were conducted to delve deeper into the preliminary findings and discuss potential strategies for AI implementation in the second language classroom.

For the analysis, the quantitative data derived from the closed questions were processed using independent samples t-tests and descriptive statistics. This approach facilitated the examination of patterns and differences in the responses. The qualitative data, sourced from the open-ended questions in the questionnaire and the post-study conversations with educators, were analyzed through a thematic approach. This method aligned with the research questions and enabled a nuanced exploration of the themes and insights emerging from participants' responses.

Context and Participants

This study was conducted at Mount Holyoke College (MHC), a private liberal arts institution known for its diverse language program and emphasis on global citizenship. The study involved a total of fifty participants (N=50), comprising twelve educators (N=12) teaching second language courses and thirty-eight students (N=38) enrolled in these courses.

MHC offers an extensive range of language courses, including Arabic, Chinese, French, German, Hebrew, Italian, Japanese, Korean, Russian, and Spanish. These courses range from introductory levels to advanced literature and research-focused studies. Language learning is a curricular requirement at MHC, underscoring the institution's commitment to fostering multicultural understanding and global engagement. The most populous language departments at MHC are Spanish, Latino/a, and Latin American Studies, and French. However, a significant number of students also enroll in other language classes. Additionally, the college participates in the Five College interchange program with Amherst College, Hampshire College, Smith College, and the University of Massachusetts Amherst, allowing students to take courses across these institutions. For this study, only students enrolled in language courses at MHC were considered for participation.

Regarding the demographic composition of the participants, the majority identified as White (52%), followed by Hispanic/Latino (28%). More detailed demographic information is presented in Table 1.

The educator group in this study included twelve individuals: 8 females, 3 males, and 1 person who preferred not to disclose their gender. A significant majority of these educators, 83.3%, had over 21 years of experience in teaching second language courses. There was a notable preference for in-person instruction among them, with 91.7% favoring this mode of teaching. In terms of languages taught, Spanish was the most common (41.7%), followed by French and Italian (each at 16.7%).

The learner group comprised thirty-eight students with diverse gender identities: 25 females, 7 identifying as non-binary/non-conforming, 2 as transgender, and 4 who chose not to disclose their gender. The majority of these students were in the early stages of their college education, with first-year students making up 39.5% and sophomores 34.2%. Like the educators, these learners showed a strong preference for in-person courses (97.4%). Spanish was the most commonly studied language (76.3%), followed by Italian (10.5%) and French (5.3%).

Table 1. Ethnicity of participants by profession

	Ethnicity						
Profession	**Asian**	**Black or African American**	**Hispanic or Latino**	**White**	**Prefer Not to Say**	**POC, Do Not Identify With Any Race or Ethnicity**	**Total**
Educator	1	0	4	6	1	0	12
Learner	2	2	10	20	3	1	38
Total	3	2	14	26	4	1	50

Materials and Procedures

The study's participants were drawn from the academic community of Mount Holyoke College. Recruitment began with initial contact via email, facilitated by the Academic Department Coordinators of the language departments who had access to the email lists of both L2 educators and learners. Comprehensive information about the research, including its objectives, participant involvement, and data confidentiality, was provided to potential participants. Emphasis was placed on the voluntary nature of participation, with informed consent required from all participants.

Data collection was primarily conducted using a structured questionnaire distributed through Google Forms. This questionnaire consisted of 22 questions, designed to explore participants' daily interactions with technology and their perceptions of its relevance in educational settings. Questions also probed familiarity with AI tools and attitudes towards integrating these tools in second language education. The primary format of the questionnaire was a 5-point Likert scale, ranging from 1 (strongly agree) to 5 (strongly disagree), allowing participants to express their level of agreement with various statements (see Example 1 below). In addition to the Likert scale items, the questionnaire featured multiple-choice and open-ended questions to capture a wider range of responses.

Example 1. *Likert Scale Question Format in the Questionnaire*

Statement #12: *I understand what artificial intelligence (AI) tools/platforms are.*

1 - Strongly agree
2 - Agree
3 - Neither agree nor disagree
4 - Disagree

5 - Strongly disagree

A demographic section with six questions was included in the questionnaire to collect essential participant information. This section asked about ethnicity, gender identity, teaching experience (for educators) or academic year (for learners), language of instruction or study, and preferred mode of instruction. The questionnaire aimed to assess attitudes towards technology, capture current usage patterns, evaluate familiarity with AI tools, and determine openness to incorporating AI into language learning experiences.

Following the analysis and interpretation of the data collected from the questionnaire, language educators at MHC were invited to engage in a follow-up conversation. This gathering served as a platform to present the general results of the study, allowing participants to ask questions, share their experiences, and discuss various activities that could enhance the teaching-learning process. Approximately 15 educators attended this session. Among them were some who had completed the questionnaire, as well as others who joined the conversation to gain deeper insights into the implications of AI in higher education, specifically in the context of in-person teaching.

This interactive session provided an opportunity for educators to reflect on the study's findings and explore practical ways of integrating AI tools in their teaching methodologies. It also allowed for an exchange of ideas and perspectives, enriching the study's overall understanding of AI's role in language education.

Results and Discussion

The findings of this study offer valuable insights into the role of technology in language education and the potential benefits of integrating AI tools. The discussion is structured thematically, aligned with the research questions, to facilitate a clear understanding and interpretation of the results.

Role of Technology in the Daily Lives of Educators and Learners (RQ1)

To address RQ1, responses to three specific statements in the questionnaire were analyzed. As indicated in Table 2, the data predominantly underscore the integral role of technology in the daily lives of participants and its influence on their teaching and learning experiences. The majority of participants (98%) affirmed the significance of technology in their lives, with no statistical difference between educators and learners, $t(48) = -.902$, $p > 0.05$. Furthermore, 72% recognized technology's potential to enhance the teaching-learning experience, with no significant difference between the groups in this regard, $t(30.267) = 1.587$, $p > 0.05$.

However, perspectives varied regarding technology's role in easing tasks. While 44% of participants agreed that technology makes everything easier, a notable 46% remained neutral. This pattern of neutrality was consistent across both groups, $t(48) = .179$, $p > 0.05$, indicating no significant statistical difference. This lack of a strong consensus suggests a varied perception of technology's practical utility. One possible interpretation is that participants' digital literacy levels may influence their recognition of technology's ease-of-use. Those more familiar with technology may more readily acknowledge its facilitative role in completing regular tasks, while those with less experience might not perceive the same level of ease.

Given the lack of statistical significance observed across all analyses, the remainder of the quantitative data discussion will primarily focus on descriptive statistics rather than inferential ones.

Table 2. Importance of technology in the daily lives of participants

Profession	Strongly Agree	Agree	Neutral	Disagree	Strongly Disagree
Statement #1: *Technology is an important aspect of my life.*					
Educator	5	7	0	0	0
Learner	23	14	1	0	0
Total	28	21	1	0	0
Statement #2: *Technology makes everything easier.*					
Educator	0	6	5	1	0
Learner	3	13	18	3	1
Total	3	19	23	4	1
Statement #3: *Technology improves the teaching-learning experience.*					
Educator	1	10	1	0	0
Learner	4	21	12	1	0
Total	5	31	13	1	0

Essential Use of Technology for Teaching and Learning (RQ2)

This part of the study explored whether educators and learners view technology as indispensable in teaching and learning contexts. Analysis mainly focused on two statements, as detailed in Table 3. When considering whether teaching and learning are possible without technology, the responses varied. A majority of learners (66%) disagreed with the notion that learning is impossible without technology, suggesting a recognition of the value of non-technological learning methods. In contrast, half of the educators felt that teaching is not feasible without technology, possibly reflecting their reliance on technological tools such as audio and video resources, computer and projector use, and online platforms for homework assignments.

Table 3. Essential use of technology for teaching and learning

Profession	Strongly Agree	Agree	Neutral	Disagree	Strongly Disagree
Statement #4: *Teaching is not possible without technology (educators). Learning is not possible without technology (learners).*					
Educator	1	5	3	1	2
Learner	0	1	4	20	13
Total	1	5	7	21	15
Statement #5: *Students cannot learn a second language without technology.*					
Educator	2	4	1	2	3
Learner	0	7	6	15	10
Total	2	11	7	17	13

Further, when asked about the necessity of technology in learning a second language, 63.1% of learners disagreed with its indispensability, compared to 41.7% of educators. This difference might indicate a divergence in perspectives based on roles. Historical evidence suggests substantial contributions to society in eras before advanced technology, supporting the learners' views. However, the responses may also be influenced by students' perceptions of expected or appropriate answers in an academic setting, though no specific evidence was found to support this hypothesis.

Additional statements in the questionnaire addressed the role of technology in the L2 classroom. A notable 76% of participants reported using digital online platforms in their language classes, yet only 30% did not see the benefits of such platforms for completing homework assignments. Interestingly, 64% of both educators and learners expressed a preference for hard copy textbooks over digital versions. This preference, spanning generations, challenges the assumption that younger 'digital natives' would favor digital materials. The coexistence of this preference with an acknowledgment of digital platforms' advantages illustrates a balanced approach to learning resources.

Regarding the usage of cellphones, tablets, and laptops/computers, all educators noted their students' use of these devices for in-class activities or note-taking. This observation aligns with the majority of learners' responses, though eight disagreed. At MHC, the use of technological devices in the classroom is common, with students permitted to use them for note-taking and class activities. The preference for notebooks among some students reflects individual differences in learning styles.

In addition to exploring the perceived essentiality of technology in teaching and learning, the study also assessed participants' familiarity with various educational platforms, such as Edmodo, Moodle, Google Classroom, and Blackboard. A striking 94% of participants demonstrated a high degree of comfort and confidence in using these platforms for educational purposes. This widespread proficiency underscores the integral role these digital tools play in the current educational landscape at MHC.

The participants' familiarity and ease with these platforms further reinforce the findings that, despite some reservations about the indispensability of technology for learning, there is a significant acceptance and utilization of digital tools in educational settings. This comfort level with educational platforms is indicative of a broader trend towards integrating technology into the teaching and learning process, aligning with the institution's commitment to leveraging digital advancements in education.

Familiarity With AI Tools in the L2 Classroom (RQ3)

To assess participants' familiarity with AI tools and their implementation in the second language classroom, responses to three specific statements were analyzed, as shown in Table 4. Additionally, participants were asked multiple-choice and open-ended questions about popular AI tools. The data indicate that a majority of participants (76%) are confident in their understanding of what AI tools/platforms are. However, their responses regarding the actual application of AI in the L2 classroom showed considerable variation. Only four educators reported integrating AI into their teaching, and eleven learners indicated using AI to aid their language learning, suggesting that a significant 70% of participants have not actively experienced AI in the classroom setting. Furthermore, when it comes to using AI tools for completing assignments, only seven learners (18%) and two educators (16%) acknowledged its utilization.

The responses were even more varied when participants were asked about AI's effectiveness in enhancing language comprehension. The majority showed neutrality (34%) or disagreement (40%), with only 26% agreeing that AI helps students better understand the language they are learning.

In exploring specific AI tools, participants chose from a list that included Brainly, ChatGPT, ChatPDF, Grammarly, Scite.ai, Quillbot, and others, indicating their familiarity and usage. The most recognized tools among both educators and learners were ChatGPT and Grammarly. However, a striking 83% of educators reported not using any of these tools in their L2 classrooms. This contrasts with learners, where 44.7% reported using Grammarly and 28.9% using ChatGPT. This discrepancy suggests that while educators are aware of AI tools, their actual usage in teaching is limited. On the other hand, learners, despite a lower self-reported use of AI for assignments, have been using these tools more frequently than indicated, with many acknowledging the use of at least two AI tools.

Table 4. Participant's familiarity with the use of AI in the L2 classroom

Profession	Strongly Agree	Agree	Neutral	Disagree	Strongly Disagree
Statement #12: *I understand what artificial intelligence (AI) tools/platforms are.*					
Educator	5	5	2	0	0
Learner	12	16	7	3	0
Total	17	21	9	3	0
Statement #13: *I have used AI tools in my second language classroom (educators). I have used AI tools to clarify doubts about the L2 language I am learning (learners).*					
Educator	1	3	2	4	2
Learner	5	6	3	10	14
Total	6	9	5	14	16
Statement #14: *My students have used AI tools to complete assignments for my class (educators). I have used AI tools to complete assignments in my L2 language class (learners)*					
Educator	2	0	5	3	2
Learner	4	3	3	11	17
Total	6	3	8	14	19
Statement #15: *AI helps students better understand the language they are learning.*					
Educator	0	4	7	0	1
Learner	4	5	10	7	12
Total	4	9	17	7	13

The Need for AI to Be Integrated in the L2 Classroom (RQ4)

This subsection examines participants' perspectives on the necessity of integrating AI in second language education. The analysis was based on responses to three statements (illustrated in Table 5) and a multiple-choice question regarding various descriptions of AI tools. This approach was designed to assess if perceptions differed when considering the potential of AI tools to enhance linguistic skills and performance.

Table 5. The need for using AI in the L2 classroom

Profession	Strongly Agree	Agree	Neutral	Disagree	Strongly Disagree
Statement #16: *Students should be trained on how to use AI tools for academic purposes.*					
Educator	4	6	2	0	0
Learner	7	9	10	6	6
Total	11	15	12	6	6
Statement #17: *Instructors should use AI tools in the second language classroom.*					
Educator	2	3	4	1	2
Learner	0	8	11	13	6
Total	2	11	15	14	8
Statement #18: *Instructors should allow students who are learning a second language to use AI tools.*					
Educator	1	6	2	2	1
Learner	2	6	11	10	9
Total	3	12	13	12	10

Regarding the need for AI tool training for academic purposes, over half of the participants (52%) expressed some agreement. Specifically, 10 educators and 17 learners viewed such training positively, while a smaller number remained neutral. This result suggests a general consensus on the importance of educating both educators and learners about AI tools.

Curiously, 41.7% of educators and 28.9% of learners agreed that AI should be integrated into the L2 classroom. This indicates a disparity in perceptions, with educators showing a slightly higher inclination toward AI integration, possibly due to their recognition of the evolving technological landscape. However, learners displayed a more hesitant stance, potentially reflecting concerns about the diminishing role of the educator in a tech-driven learning environment.

The need for AI integration becomes more evident when considering attitudes towards allowing AI tool usage for language learning. A majority of educators (58%) agreed with this, compared to only 21% of learners. This difference may stem from concerns about AI's ethical implications or its potential impact on the learning experience. Educators might perceive training as a means to instruct students in the ethical use of AI, while learners may fear a reduced human interaction in their language education.

To further probe into misconceptions and interest in AI tools, participants were asked to select from descriptions of various AI functionalities without knowing their commercial names. The top choices for educators included tools for memorization, live speech transcription, grammar checking, learning progress tracking, and literature mapping. These preferences align with functionalities of tools like Anki, Otter.ai, Grammarly, Knowji, and Research Rabbit. Learners showed similar interests, with their top choices encompassing tools for memorization, grammar checking, live speech transcription, intelligent tutoring, and generating human-like responses. This mirrors functionalities of Anki, Grammarly, Otter.ai, Scite.ai, and ChatGPT.

The findings from the questionnaire underscore the significant role of technology in both educators' and learners' lives. Educators generally acknowledge the importance of technology in second language teaching, while learners do not view it as indispensable for learning. There's a notable awareness of AI among participants, but its actual implementation in the classroom is limited. Educators, more than learners, recognize the need for training in the ethical use of AI tools. Despite some initial apprehension, learners showed interest in AI tools that could support their language learning through personalized experiences and assist in completing assignments.

These insights affirm the integral role of technology and the emerging interest in AI within second language classrooms. While debates continue over the necessity of technology in language learning, there's a shared curiosity about how AI might enhance language proficiency.

Follow-Up Conversation with Educators

The follow-up conversation with educators sought to deepen the understanding of AI implementation in L2 education. Focusing on fundamental skills necessary for language learning success, the discussion explored AI tools that could aid their development. Educators, showing a strong interest in AI functionalities from the questionnaire, engaged in an in-depth dialogue about specific learning skills crucial for linguistic proficiency. They considered how various AI tools might support or enhance these skills, aiming to reconcile the potential of AI with its practical application in the classroom. This conversation also served as a forum for educators to voice their concerns and explore practical integration strategies for AI in their teaching.

The discussion began by acknowledging the diversity in pedagogical approaches, assessment tools, and classroom activities, underscoring the individuality of each learner's language learning journey. Educators noted that students often face unique challenges, leading to varied error patterns. Recent research, such as Zablotsky et al. (2019), highlights a rise in learning disabilities among students, presenting additional challenges in language education. Howard (2023) further emphasizes the need to recognize and value the linguistic diversity these students bring to the classroom.

A major motif became apparent around the need for personalized instruction. Educators expressed difficulties in creating individualized learning experiences due to time and resource constraints. Current accommodations in classrooms are often reactive rather than proactive, focusing on immediate solutions like extending deadlines rather than anticipating and addressing potential learning barriers. There was consensus on the need for more comprehensive, universally designed teaching frameworks that adapt flexibly to diverse learning needs.

The conversation then shifted to identifying key skills essential for L2 success: time management and strategic planning, memorization, interpersonal communication, presentation skills, creative thinking, and critical and reflective thinking. While recognizing the importance of these skills, educators expressed uncertainty about integrating AI tools without undermining the value of human interaction and instructor guidance. To bridge this gap, examples of AI tools corresponding to each skill were presented, helping educators visualize how AI could complement traditional teaching methods (see Table 6 for details).

The discussion about essential language learning skills and the potential support of AI tools was enlightening, especially when contextualized with example activities. Some educators realized that they were already using AI in their classrooms, unaware that certain tools and methods they employed were AI-based. This realization led to a deeper exploration into the broader perception of AI among educators. It became apparent that many primarily associated AI with ChatGPT, not recognizing the full spectrum of AI technologies already integrated into educational platforms, emails, and other applications. Their main concern was ChatGPT's potential use in completing assignments, which posed a risk of academic dishonesty.

Table 6. AI tools and their corresponding support for key language learning skills

Language Learning Skill	Skill Description	AI Tools for Skill Enhancement	Example Activity #1 Using AI	Example Activity #2 Using AI
Time Management and Planning	Effective time management is essential for punctual assignment completion, enhanced focus, and improved learning.	Click Up, Clockwise, and Motion can analyze calendars to highlight tasks and assignments requiring immediate or prompt attention. They also recommend optimal time slots for completing specific tasks.	*Creating a Schedule*: Students consult the syllabus, academic calendar, class schedule, assignment list, and personal events. Using AI tools, they then create a weekly or monthly schedule to effectively manage their time and ensure timely completion of assignments.	*Solving Scheduling Conflicts*: Students analyze the schedule of a real or fictional character using AI tools. They identify priority tasks, potential conflicts, assess AI tool recommendations, and devise creative solutions to enhance overall time management and scheduling.
Memorization	Memorization is a key skill essential for everyday tasks, complex work, and academic requirements. It entails the ability to retain and store information, thus demanding considerable capacity from the brain's memory storage.	Generative Flashcard tools such as Limbiks and Quizlet can create flashcards from diverse sources like study guides, online textbooks, and multimedia content. These tools feature organizational capabilities, enabling users to create folders, study sets, and personalized study plans. Additionally, they provide various options for testing and reinforcing learning of challenging material.	*Generating Flashcards*: In group collaborations, students use AI tools to create flashcard sets for reviewing specific topics. These sets are shared with the class, facilitating peer-to-peer learning and aiding in the memorization of relevant vocabulary, grammar, and other content.	*Error Identification Task*: Educators utilize AI tools to develop flashcard sets containing intentional errors. Students work in groups to spot and correct these inaccuracies, thereby deepening their understanding of proper language usage.
Interpersonal Communication	Interpersonal Communication involves exchanging information, thoughts, ideas, feelings, and emotions among individuals. This exchange can occur face-to-face or through written and digital channels such as phone calls, chat applications, emails, and letters.	AI tools like Small Talk and ChatGPT serve as linguistic tutors by creating a simulated, pressure-free conversational environment, ideal for practicing language skills without fear of judgment.	*Oral Interview Practice*: Students utilize AI tutors to practice oral interviews outside the classroom. These tools dynamically adjust to the conversation's focus and topics, generating relevant questions, responding to inquiries, and offering hints and constructive feedback.	*Interpersonal Written Communication*: Students use ChatGPT for written dialogues on specific topics, providing detailed prompts to guide the conversation. Additionally, they can conduct interviews with the AI, instructing it to emulate a historical figure or personality.
Presentation	Presentation skills involve delivering a one-way message to an audience, which may consist of readers, listeners, or viewers. These skills are crucial in formal contexts where the aim is to inform or persuade, and presentations are often well-rehearsed.	AI tools, including chatbots like ChatGPT and Jasper, and voice bots like Small Talk, assist in various presentation-related tasks. Additionally, tools such as Sendsteps, SlidesAI, and Haiku Deck can automate the creation of visually appealing slides, enhancing visual storytelling.	*Brainstorming Presentation Ideas*: Students utilize ChatGPT to brainstorm and generate potential topics for their presentations, tapping into the AI's ability to suggest diverse and relevant ideas.	*Structuring Presentation Ideas*: Students use AI tools to obtain examples and guidance on effectively structuring their presentations, ensuring coherent organization and adequate support for their ideas.
Creative Thinking	Creative Thinking is characterized by flexibility, originality, and realism. This skill enables individuals to generate innovative ideas and devise novel solutions to complex problems.	Chatbots such as ChatGPT and Jasper aid students in brainstorming sessions and creating engaging content. For visual creativity, AI-driven tools like DALL-E, Canvas, and Adobe Firefly add a visual dimension, enriching creative language usage.	*Pictionary-Like Game*: In this activity, students are given a word or phrase and must describe it effectively using AI tools to generate a corresponding image. This task enhances descriptive language skills and fosters creative expression.	*Develop a Short Story or Dialogue*: Students craft a story or dialogue related to a specific topic or vocabulary. Following brainstorming, character development, and dialogue creation, they utilize AI comic generator tools to either use predefined templates or create original comics, incorporating their written dialogues.
Critical and Reflective Thinking	Critical and Reflective Thinking empowers students to analyze, compare, contrast, and challenge encountered knowledge. This process enables them to construct new meanings, engage in meaningful discourse, and contribute to academic dialogue with unique insights and perspectives.	Perplexity aids in identifying relevant sources, while ChatPDF and Humata help pinpoint key topics and address specific reading questions. Scholarcy and Scite.ai engage students critically with the literature. ChatGPT and Quillbot are instrumental in enhancing writing skills.	*Summary Task*: Students read a text or article and summarize its main points. Subsequently, they use ChatPDF to obtain automated highlights of key information. This enables them to compare and contrast their summaries with AI-generated ones, fostering critical evaluation.	*Structuring a Research Paper*: Students choose a research topic, formulate a thesis statement, and outline their paper. They then consult ChatGPT for structural suggestions and critically assess these against their initial ideas, refining their approach. Tools like Scite.ai are used to gather pertinent information from various sources.

However, the dialogue effectively helped to dispel these misconceptions. Educators began to see ChatGPT not merely as a tool that could be misused but as a potential tutor capable of providing substantial learning assistance. Despite this progress in understanding AI among educators, three attendees noted a reluctance among Mount Holyoke College students to use AI tools due to fears of plagiarism and cheating. This observation in their own classrooms and interactions with their students underscores the need for enhanced training and clearer communication about AI use in educational settings. Attendees called for more explicit guidelines from the administration on AI's role in higher education and effective ways to inform students about ethically using AI in their coursework.

In addition to addressing misconceptions about AI, the conversation also delved into the educators' interest in fostering inclusivity within the classroom. Attendees were introduced to a variety of AI-powered tools designed to create more inclusive learning environments. These tools, including Curipod, Education Copilot, and Yippity, aid in the design of class and course materials while offering progress analysis and feedback. Platforms like Quizlet, Mango Languages, and Duolingo are renowned for providing personalized learning experiences that cater to individual student needs, thus enabling educators to support diverse learning styles. They can be integrated seamlessly into classrooms, allowing students to progress at their own pace and focus on areas needing improvement, with real-time progress monitoring by instructors.

Beyond classroom instruction, Text-to-Speech (TTS) tools like Google Cloud Speech-to-Text and IBM Watson Speech to Text enhance pronunciation practice and intonation understanding by converting text into audio. Video captioning and subtitling tools, such as YouTube, Amara, and Subtitle Edit, improve accessibility, while applications like InVideo, Lumen5, and Raw Shorts enrich lessons with dynamic visuals and voiceovers. AI's role extends to critical areas such as pronunciation, writing, listening, and speaking, providing immediate feedback and tailored learning experiences. These tools are crucial in helping students enhance their language skills, boost confidence, and deepen cultural understanding.

This follow-up conversation illuminated key insights, clarifying misconceptions about AI in education and offering practical ideas for its integration in L2 classrooms to foster inclusivity. It highlighted how AI tools could transform the classroom into a multidimensional and engaging space, accommodating and inspiring students from diverse backgrounds and learning needs.

CONCLUSION AND FUTURE DIRECTIONS

Emerging technologies, particularly artificial intelligence, have become a pivotal part of daily life, revolutionizing the educational landscape. While AI has rendered learning more interactive, engaging, and dynamic, research gaps remain, particularly concerning non-English language learning and in-person instruction contexts outside of Asia and Europe. These gaps are most pronounced in empirical research assessing AI's impact on performance in L2 classroom activities.

This study explored the perceptions of L2 educators and learners in the United States regarding technology and AI adoption in education. It aimed to clarify misconceptions about AI and highlight the need for more comprehensive understanding and implementation strategies in L2 classrooms. The findings indicate that technology is an essential component of both life and education. Despite initial reservations, there is a growing curiosity among educators and learners about how AI can enhance language learning experiences. The study underscored the potential of AI to make classrooms more dynamic and tailored to learners' needs. Traditional classrooms face challenges such as limited access to authentic resources and constraints in creating personalized learning environments. AI offers a solution to these challenges, providing opportunities for tailored language learning and preparing learners for a technology-centric world.

AI tools support the development of essential language skills such as time management, memorization, interpersonal communication, presentation, creative and critical thinking, and also play a key role in creating inclusive classrooms. They enable a shift from generic teaching methods to individualized learning trajectories, addressing diverse student needs. As education evolves, it's crucial to recognize AI's applicability and adapt teaching practices accordingly. Ethical use of AI, coupled with training for educators and students, can enhance the teaching-learning experience and maximize academic success. AI should be seen as an opportunity to unlock each student's potential, creating dynamic, inclusive, and effective language learning environments.

Future research should focus on evaluating the tangible impact of AI tools by analyzing learners' progress and outcomes before and after using these technologies. Such studies would help correlate positive perceptions with actual improvements in language proficiency, applicable to both online and in-person instruction. Embracing AI as an ally in language education offers a comprehensive, integrative approach to academic experiences, paving the way for more universal and effective language learning strategies.

REFERENCES

Abdul Rahman, N. A., Zulkornain, L. H., & Hamzah, N. H. (2022). Exploring artificial intelligence using automated writing evaluation for writing skills. *Environment-Behaviour Proceedings Journal, 7*(SI9), 547–553. doi:10.21834/ebpj.v7iSI9.4304

Adipat, S., Laksana, K., Busayanon, K., Piatanom, P., Mahamarn, Y., Pakapol, P., & Ausawasowan, A. (2022). The world of technology: Artificial intelligence in education. *Special Education, 2*(43), 2142–2146.

Alharbi, W. (2023). AI in the foreign language classroom: A pedagogical overview of automated writing assistance tools. *Education Research International, 2023*, 1–15. doi:10.1155/2023/4253331

Aziz, R. (2023). Creativity in higher education: The effect of personality on students' creative thinking skills. *Thinking Skills and Creativity Journal, 6*(1), 44–51. doi:10.23887/tscj.v6i1.54916

Borenstein, J., & Howard, A. (2021). Emerging challenges in AI and the need for AI ethics education. *AI and Ethics, 1*(1), 61–65. doi:10.1007/s43681-020-00002-7

Dodigovic, M. (2007). Artificial intelligence and second language learning: An efficient approach to error remediation. *Language Awareness, 16*(2), 99–113. doi:10.2167/la416.0

Ennis, R. H. (2015). Critical thinking: A streamlined conception. In M. Davies & R. Barnett (Eds.), *The Palgrave Handbook of Critical Thinking in Higher Education.* doi:10.1057/9781137378057_2

Fryer, L. K., Nakao, K., & Thompson, A. (2019). Chatbot learning partners: Connecting learning experiences, interest and competence. *Computers in Human Behavior, 93*, 279–289. doi:10.1016/j.chb.2018.12.023

Gayed, J. M., Carlon, M. K. J., Oriola, A. M., & Cross, J. S. (2022). Exploring an AI-based writing assistant's impact on English language learners. *Computers and Education: Artificial Intelligence*, *3*(100055), 100055. Advance online publication. doi:10.1016/j.caeai.2022.100055

Howard, K. B. (2023). Supporting learners with special educational needs and disabilities in the foreign languages classroom. *Support for Learning*, *38*(3), 154–161. doi:10.1111/1467-9604.12449

Kohnke, L. (2023). L2 Learners' perception of a chatbot as a potential independent language learning tool. *Int. J. Mobile Learning and Organization*, *17*(1/2), 214–226. doi:10.1504/IJMLO.2023.128339

Li, X., Li, B., & Cho, S. J. (2023). Empowering Chinese language learners from low-income families to improve their Chinese writing with ChatGPT's assistance afterschool. *Languages (Basel, Switzerland)*, *8*(4), 238. doi:10.3390/languages8040238

Marzuki, W., Widiati, U., Rusdin, D., Darwin, & Indrawati, I. (2023). The impact of AI writing tools on the content and organization of students' writing: EFL teachers' perspective. *Cogent Education*, *10*(2), 2236469. Advance online publication. doi:10.1080/2331186X.2023.2236469

Miller, T. (2019). Explanation in artificial intelligence: Insights from the social sciences. *Artificial Intelligence*, *267*, 1–38. doi:10.1016/j.artint.2018.07.007

Roe, J., Renandya, W. A., & Jacobs, G. M. (2023). A review of AI-powered writing tools and their implications for academic integrity in the language classroom. *Journal of English and Applied Linguistics*, *2*(1), 22–30. doi:10.59588/2961-3094.1035

Roschelle, J., Lester, J., & Fusco, J. (Eds.). (2020). AI and the future of learning: Expert panel report [Report]. *Digital Promise*. https://circls.org/reports/ai-report

Sabuncuoglu, A. (2020). Designing one year curriculum to teach artificial intelligence for middle school. In *Proceedings of the 2020 ACM Conference on Innovation and Technology in Computer Science Education (ITiCSE '20)*. Association for Computing Machinery. 10.1145/3341525.3387364

Samea Qoura, A., & Moustafa Elmansi, H. (2023). *Artificial intelligence in language education: Implementations and policies required* [Conference presentation]. The first national conference for the educational studies sector. 10.21608/foej.2022.180319.1169

Sellar, S., & Gulson, K. N. (2021). Becoming information centric: The emergence of new cognitive infrastructures in education policy. *Journal of Education Policy*, *36*(3), 309–326. doi:10.1080/02680939.2019.1678766

Singer, N. (2023). Ban or embrace? Colleges wrestle with A.I.-generated admissions essays. *The New York Times*. https://www.nytimes.com/2023/09/01/business/college-admissions-essay-ai-chatbots.html

Sun, Z., Yu, Z. C., & Xu, F. Y. (2023). Analysis and improvement of classroom teaching based on artificial intelligence. In H. Niemi, R. D. Pea, & Y. Lu (Eds.), *AI in Learning: Designing the Future*. Springer. doi:10.1007/978-3-031-09687-7_7

Wahyuni, D. S. (2022). Integrated classroom-chatbot experience: An alternative solution for English as foreign language learners. *English Language Education and Current Trends*, *1*(1), 63–68. doi:10.37301/elect.v1i1.36

Zablotsky, B., Black, L. I., Maenner, M. J.; Schieve, L. A., Danielson M. L., Bitsko, R. H., Blumberg, S. J., Kogan, M. D. & Boyle C. A. (2019). Prevalence and trends of developmental disabilities among children in the United States: 2009–2017. *Pediatrics 144*(4). doi:10.1542/peds.2019-0811

Zawacki-Richter, O., Marín, V. I., Bondand, F., & Gouverneur, M. (2019). Systematic review of research on artificial intelligence applications in higher education–Where are the educators? *International Journal of Educational Technology in Higher Education, 16*(39), 39. Advance online publication. doi:10.1186/s41239-019-0171-0

Zheng, L., Niu, J., Zhong, L., & Gyasi, J. F. (2021). The effectiveness of artificial intelligence on learning achievement and learning perception: A meta-analysis. *Interactive Learning Environments*, 1–15. doi:10.1080/10494820.2021.2015693

KEY TERMS AND DEFINITIONS

AI Tools: Software programs equipped with artificial intelligence, designed to perform specific tasks by learning and adapting based on the information and user interactions.

Enriching: Improving or enhancing the quality of something.

Higher Education: Level of schooling that follows secondary education, such as college, university, or vocational training, where students pursue specialized studies and advanced degrees.

Inclusive Education: An educational approach that aims to ensure all students, regardless of their backgrounds, abilities, or challenges, have equal access to learning opportunities.

Innovative Pedagogies: Teaching methods that introduce new ideas, creative approaches, or novel techniques to enhance the learning experience.

Innovative Technology: Advanced or novel technological developments that introduce new methods, ideas, or products.

Integration: The process of combining or incorporating different elements, systems, or groups to work together effectively as a whole.

L2 Classroom: A learning environment where students are taught a second language that is not their native tongue.

Language Acquisition: The process through which individuals learn a language, whether it be their native tongue (first language acquisition) or an additional language (second language acquisition).

Language Learning Skills: Abilities and techniques used to effectively acquire language.

Linguistic Needs: Specific areas or aspects of language learning that require focused attention or improvement, such as vocabulary, grammar, pronunciation, listening, speaking, reading, or writing skills.

Multidimensional Tools: Tools or resources that offer multiple features or capabilities, addressing various aspects or needs within a single platform or system.

Chapter 5
A Qualitative Journey on Instructors' Perceptions of Artificial Intelligence in EFL Education

Nazmi Dincer
https://orcid.org/0000-0002-2901-5367
Turkish Air Force Academy, Turkey

Samet Bal
Turkish Airlines, Turkey

ABSTRACT

Artificial intelligence influences education, particularly language instruction. Despite its expanding attention, few studies have examined teachers' views on AI in education. This qualitative study explores EFL teachers' AI-related views and insights. The study uses semi-structured interviews with 21 instructors from diverse universities to uncover complex attitudes toward AI, pedagogical ideologies, perceived benefits and drawbacks of AI, and privacy concerns. The study highlights four main themes: AI's capacity to adapt to individual learning needs, its influence on pedagogical dynamics, the need for technical proficiency to integrate AI, and ethical and security issues related to AI use. These results highlight the perceived benefits and challenges educators face when using AI and emphasize the need for continued research to develop successful AI integration techniques for language instruction.

INTRODUCTION

The technological advancements of the digital era have catalyzed a significant metamorphosis across different sectors of society, not least within the labor market, and more pointedly in education (Kannan & Munday, 2018). The surge in Artificial Intelligence (AI) technologies, and their potential impact on education, has captured the attention of both researchers and practitioners, provoking intriguing debates

DOI: 10.4018/979-8-3693-0872-1.ch005

and explorations (Popenici & Kerr, 2017). AI's remarkable capacity for adaptive learning, bespoke instruction, and student engagement presents a plethora of unexplored opportunities within modern education (Chen et al., 2020). Simultaneously, it poses new challenges that necessitate a comprehensive understanding of the real-world intricacies involved in its integration (Knox, 2020).

At the heart of this pedagogical metamorphosis, the teachers are the key actors harnessing these innovative technologies to enrich students' learning experiences. Yet, a gap exists in the current research landscape, with limited studies focusing on teachers' perceptions towards AI integration in education and specifically language classrooms (Haristiani, 2019). The attitudes, beliefs, and experiences of instructors constitute a crucial determinant of the successful realization of AI-driven instruction and, consequently, its impact on learner outcomes (Celik, 2017; Malik et al., 2022).

Examining the perspectives of EFL teachers warrants special attention due to the inherent complexities of language instruction. Beyond the confines of subject-specific knowledge, language learning extends into a wider ambit, including linguistic proficiency, cultural appreciation, and communicative skills (Dodigovic, 2009). The incorporation of AI in this sensitive instructional ecosystem thus calls for a more profound exploration of language teachers' viewpoints and their interactions with these emerging technologies.

While AI is not an unfamiliar concept in educational technology discourse, its accelerating advancements and expanding influence warrant a refreshed and more focused scrutiny (Holmes et al., 2019). Considering the broad spectrum of AI's potential applications in language instruction, coupled with a wide variety of teacher perspectives, the narrative surrounding AI integration is multifaceted and complex.

This qualitative study endeavors to unearth these narratives by probing the beliefs and insights of EFL teachers concerning AI's integration into language instruction. By broadening our comprehension of teacher perspectives, this study aims to underpin more effective AI implementation strategies, thereby enhancing language learning experiences and equipping teachers to adeptly navigate the ever-evolving educational landscape. In this respect, this study seeks answers to the following questions:

1. How do EFL teachers perceive the use of AI in language classrooms?
2. What are the perceived benefits and challenges of AI in the language learning and teaching process from the perspective of EFL teachers?
3. What concerns do EFL teachers have about the impact of AI on teaching and learning?

ARTIFICIAL INTELLIGENCE AND EDUCATION

Artificial Intelligence (AI), as a discipline, falls within the purview of computer science, specifically dedicated to the design and development of software and hardware systems capable of mirroring facets of human intelligence. The scope of these capabilities is quite expansive, including the ability to learn from experiences and surroundings, apply gained knowledge to troubleshoot issues, comprehend and process complex content, and refine performance continually through self-assessment and rectification of errors (Clark, 2020). AI fundamentally aims at fabricating machines that can emulate human cognition and learning patterns.

The genesis of the term 'Artificial Intelligence' can be traced back to 1956 when John McCarthy introduced it at the Dartmouth Conference, thereby marking the inception of AI as an independent academic discipline. The journey of AI has been characterized by alternating periods of intense enthusiasm and 'AI Winters' - phases marked by diminished funding and interest due to inflated expectations and consequent disappointments (Haenlein & Kaplan, 2019). However, the past two decades have witnessed a consistent surge in AI interest and developments, catalyzed by exponential growth in computational power, availability of vast datasets or 'big data', and advancements in learning algorithms, particularly those associated with deep learning.

With its widespread applications across diverse sectors, including healthcare, transportation, and finance, education has not remained untouched. The application of artificial intelligence to education, known as AIEd, has been a topic of academic research for over three decades. This field explores learning in various settings, such as traditional classrooms and workplaces, with the aim of supporting formal education and lifelong learning. AIEd combines interdisciplinary fields like AI, education, psychology, neuroscience, linguistics, sociology, and anthropology to create adaptive learning environments and other AIEd tools (Clark, 2020). These tools are designed to be flexible, inclusive, personalized, engaging, and effective. The core objective of AIEd is to make educational, psychological, and social knowledge explicit and precise, which is often left implicit (Self, 1998). In simpler terms, AIEd goes beyond being a driving force behind smart educational technology; it also helps us gain deeper insights into the process of learning (Luckin et al., 2016). For instance, it reveals how learning is influenced by factors like socioeconomic context, physical environment, and technology. These insights can guide the development of future AIEd software and enhance non-technological approaches to learning. AIEd enables us to observe and understand the small steps learners take when acquiring knowledge in subjects like physics, as well as identify common misconceptions (Lameras & Arnab, 2021). Teachers can then apply this understanding in their classrooms. AI relies on computer software programmed to interact intelligently with the world, requiring both knowledge about the world and algorithms for processing that knowledge effectively.

The dynamic growth and widespread application of artificial intelligence across diverse sectors find a mirrored reflection in the sphere of education. As of 2020, the global AI market boasted a valuation of approximately $62.35 billion, demonstrating an expected compound annual growth rate (CAGR) of 40.2% from 2021 through to 2028, a testament to the expanding demand and assimilation of AI in various industries (Cardano et al., 2023). In the educational domain, this growth trajectory is even more striking. The value of AI within the education sector stood at $1.1 billion in 2019 and is projected to reach $8.0 billion by 2024, indicative of an astounding CAGR of 47.0% (Cardano et al., 2023). This rapid growth underscores the acknowledged capacity of AI to revolutionize personalized learning, amplify learner engagement, and optimize educational outcomes. The steady increase in AI investments in the educational sector heralds a paradigm shift towards technologically enriched, individualized learning environments. However, the swift integration of AI also highlights the essentiality of continuous research to effectively understand and address associated challenges.

Artificial Intelligence (AI) finds its applications in the field of education in a myriad of ways, significantly contributing to the technological advancement of learning processes. Examples of such integration include the use of AI in instructional technologies like intelligent tutoring systems, automated grading mechanisms, and chatbots (Clark, 2020; Heffernan & Heffernan, 2014). These AI-facilitated systems offer extensive opportunities for all parties involved in the education process, as noted by Chen et al., (2020).

Historical examinations of AI's educational usage have highlighted the system's capabilities to enhance student collaboration and tailor learning experiences to individual student's needs (Luckin et al., 2016). Furthermore, AI plays a vital role in organizing learning activities, offering adaptive feedback on learning progress (Koedinger et al., 2012), alleviating teachers' workload in collaborative knowledge creation

(Roll & Wylie, 2016), and even predicting students' academic trajectory, such as potential dropout risks or admission possibilities (Popenici & Kerr, 2017).

AI also enables comprehensive profiling of students' backgrounds (Cohen et al., 2017), consistent monitoring of students' academic progression (Swiecki et al., 2019; Gaudioso et al., 2012), and summative assessments, as observed in the case of automated essay grading (Vij et al., 2020; Yuan et al., 2020; Okada et al., 2019). However, the current utilization of AI in education has yet to reach the levels of adoption and integration seen in other sectors, like finance and health.

A successful transition to AI-based educational systems mandates the active involvement of all stakeholders, particularly teachers, in the stages of AI development, from conception to integration (Langran et al., 2020; Qin et al., 2020). The role of teachers remains pivotal to ensuring the effective and seamless inclusion of AI into the educational landscape, a factor crucial for maximizing the benefits that AI promises to deliver in the realm of education (Malik et al., 2022).

ARTIFICIAL INTELLIGENCE IN EFL EDUCATION

Given the multifaceted nature of EFL learning, which involves gaining linguistic competence, promoting communicative skills, and understanding cultural nuances, AI can play a critical role. The application of AI within the realm of EFL teaching shows remarkable potential (AbdAlgane & Othman, 2023). Through intelligent tutoring systems, adaptive learning platforms, and AI-powered language learning applications, AI can address this diverse range of learning requirements. Yet, there has been a disagreement among academics and educators over the use of AI technology in language learning environments (Alshumaimeri & Alshememry, 2023).

Numerous studies highlight the advantages of AI in language acquisition since it offers the prospect of personalized instruction. For instance, it has been discovered that AI systems can analyze learner input (Alhalangy & AbdAlgane, 2023), evaluate the grammar skills of learners and offer advanced feedback (Koraishi, 2023), and provide more useful grammatical review (Nagata, 1996). The majority of early AI research focused on sentence structure, while more recent work demonstrates that AI can do more as a result of advancements in computer technology. For example, the use of AI in language classrooms has been shown to assist students in a number of ways, including by facilitating genuine interaction (Lu, 2018), supporting cooperative responsibilities (Jiang, 2022), strengthening reading comprehension (Bailey et al., 2021), developing oral performance (Jeon, 2021), and boosting inspiration (Yin et al., 2021). AI-powered educational systems can customize learning materials to align with each student's learning pace and language proficiency. This individualized approach to instruction, which can be challenging to implement in traditional classroom environments, is facilitated by AI (Chen et al., 2020). AI allows learners to receive immediate, tailored feedback on aspects of language use, including pronunciation and grammar, promoting real-time language practice and enhancement. Furthermore, AI can simulate conversational scenarios, offering EFL learners a non-judgmental environment to practice their English skills. Such AI conversational platforms can be specifically designed to cater to learners' unique interests or needs, thereby boosting motivation and engagement (Coniam, 2014).

Notwithstanding these favorable arguments, other research had conflicting outcomes. Early on in its development, the optimistic perspectives on artificial intelligence in the study of language were seen as exaggerated (O'Brien, 1993) and misinterpreted (Last, 1989). In addition, while considering the potential of AI in the course of the 90s, Salaberry (1996) expressed skepticism about its usefulness in acquiring languages and instruction. Hu and Cooper (2014) propose that AI has little effect on students' learning, while other contemporary research argues that AI is not a valid means of instruction (Gallacher et al., 2018). Additionally, AI-generated language is often unnatural and inappropriate (Sigge & Sumakul, 2021) and lacks contextual relevance (Wilson et al., 2021). Concerning the use of AI in classrooms, the difficulties may stem from the constrained educational structure of AI applications (Zawacki-Richter, 2019) or the insufficient instructional knowledge of instructors (Sumakul, 2019).

It is a well-known fact that enriching EFL with AI is not devoid of hurdles. Debates surrounding the AI's capacity to interpret and teach cultural subtleties, the potential decrease in face-to-face human interactions, privacy and security concerns related to student data, and the evolving role of the teacher in an AI-empowered classroom persist (Langran et al., 2020; Luckin et al, 2016).

Despite these challenges, the promise that AI holds for EFL learning contexts is compelling and continues to kindle interest among educators and technologists. As this dynamic field continues to evolve, the need to explore EFL teachers' experiences and perceptions of AI grows, holding the potential to guide the course of future AI integration strategies in language classrooms.

METHODOLOGY

In order to gain a rich and comprehensive understanding of teachers' perceptions and experiences concerning the application of Artificial Intelligence (AI) in English as a Foreign Language (EFL) teaching settings, this study employed a qualitative research methodology. This approach was chosen due to its suitability for exploratory research, as it enables the researcher to delve deeper into personal experiences, perceptions, motivations, and emotions, which are often essential in understanding complex phenomena such as the integration of AI in teaching.

An integral component of our qualitative approach was the utilization of semi-structured interviews. Semi-structured interviews, by virtue of their flexible and open-ended nature, allowed the researchers to gather detailed and nuanced data directly from the participants in their own words. Each interview was conducted individually, spanned approximately 30 minutes, and was audio-recorded, subject to the participant's consent. The interview guide comprised a series of broad, open-ended questions pertaining to their experiences and perceptions of AI tools, but the interviewers were also free to explore emerging themes and unexpected responses in depth. This approach not only ensured that the key research questions were addressed but also allowed new ideas and perspectives to surface during the discussion.

In terms of data analysis, thematic analysis was used to interpret the interview transcripts. This involved several steps: (1) transcribing the interviews, (2) getting familiar with the data, (3) identifying and coding potential themes, (4) reviewing and refining the themes, and finally (5) defining and naming the themes (Braun & Clarke, 2006). This rigorous process ensured a thorough and systematic analysis of the data.

The trustworthiness of the study was also considered. Techniques such as member checking, where participants were given the opportunity to review and confirm the accuracy of their responses, and peer debriefing, in which the research team collectively reviewed and discussed the findings, were conducted to increase the validity and reliability of the results.

This qualitative research methodology, with its focus on capturing rich, detailed, and complex data, was crucial in enabling a deep and holistic understanding of how EFL instructors perceive and experience the integration of AI in their teaching practices.

PARTICIPANTS

Table 1 illustrates that the study includes a total of 21 instructors, out of which approximately 57% are female (12 instructors) and the remaining 43% are male (9 instructors). The average age for female instructors is approximately 36 years, while for male instructors; it's about 35 years, signifying proximity in age demographics between the genders. Considering their professional experience, the average years of teaching for female instructors is about 9 years, with a range from 1 to 22 years. Similarly, the male instructors have an average of about 9 years of experience, ranging from 4 to 18 years, suggesting a comparable level of professional experience across both genders in the study.

It is noteworthy to highlight that institutional disparities may have a substantial impact on instructors' viewpoints about the integration of artificial intelligence in EFL instruction. Variables such as the presence of resources, the characteristics of the student population, and the objectives of the institution might influence their experiences and attitudes toward the incorporation of artificial intelligence. Teachers at well-endowed private institutions may have more favorable perspectives as a result of their superior access to artificial intelligence (AI) technologies, while educators in underprivileged public schools may encounter difficulties in using such technology. Furthermore, the perspectives of teachers regarding AI in EFL instruction might be influenced by their level of experience. Experienced instructors who have been in the profession for a long time may exhibit greater skepticism or want more persuasion when it comes to embracing new technology, due to their well-established teaching approaches. Conversely, recently hired educators, who are often better acquainted with digital resources, may exhibit more receptiveness and flexibility in incorporating artificial intelligence into their instructional methods.

In this study, purposeful sampling was implemented to gather information-rich cases that provide in-depth insight into the integration of AI-supported applications in teaching EFL. This technique was particularly suited for this study because it enabled the selection of instructors who have substantial experience with the use of these AI tools in their teaching practices.

First, the initial candidate pool was identified from various foreign language schools across different universities in Turkey. These were EFL instructors who were known, either through professional networks, previous research, or institutional records, to have some level of engagement with AI applications in their pedagogy. To refine this list, the researchers sent out an initial survey or conducted preliminary interviews to gauge the extent of each instructor's experience with the AI tools and their general tech-savviness. This assisted researchers in determining whether they had 'hands-on experience', as highlighted in our selection criteria. Next, researchers anayzed the specific AI applications the instructors used, focusing on those who utilized a diverse range of tools. This ensured that the sample represented a wide spectrum of AI applications in the classroom.

In addition to the profile of the instructors, Table 2 also provides an interesting snapshot of their technological utilization in response to the question about their familiarity with AI-supported educational applications. Instructors used these applications once or more than once for instructional purposes. The most widely adopted application among the instructors is Duolingo, a language learning platform used by 20 instructors. Grammarly, a writing assistant enhancing clarity and checking for plagiarism, is the next most prevalent tool, being used by 19 instructors. Other notable applications include ChatGPT, an AI chatbot used as a tutoring tool by 16 instructors, and Turnitin, a plagiarism detection tool, used by 15 instructors. Further down the list, Canva, Quillbot, and Achieve3000 are used by 12, 8, and 8 instructors respectively, signifying their importance in content creation and improving reading comprehension. Transcription service Otter.ai and voiceover platform Murf.ai are used by 7 and 6 instructors respectively.

Video creation platforms Vyond and Synthesia are used by 5 instructors each. Lastly, the less prevalent applications include Slide.ai for presentation generation, Knowji for vocabulary learning, ChatYoutube for interactive video engagement, and Copilot for AI-assisted lesson plan generation, used by 3, 3, 2, and 1 instructor(s) respectively. This diversity of tools illustrates the wide range of digital resources being harnessed by the participants in the teaching environment.

Table 1. Participants

Instructors	Gender	Age	Years of Exp.
Instructor 1	Female	27	**1**
Instructor 2	Female	31	**3**
Instructor 3	Female	28	**3**
Instructor 4	Female	29	**4**
Instructor 5	Female	35	**7**
Instructor 6	Female	34	**7**
Instructor 7	Female	45	**12**
Instructor 8	Female	39	**14**
Instructor 9	Female	42	**15**
Instructor 10	Female	43	**16**
Instructor 11	Female	47	**20**
Instructor 12	Female	50	**22**
Instructor 13	Male	30	**4**
Instructor 14	Male	32	**5**
Instructor 15	Male	33	**6**
Instructor 16	Male	35	**8**
Instructor 17	Male	36	**9**
Instructor 18	Male	36	**10**
Instructor 19	Male	40	**11**
Instructor 20	Male	42	**17**
Instructor 21	Male	40	**18**

FINDINGS

This section illustrates the primary findings derived from the semi-structured interviews with 21 EFL instructors with regard to their experiences and perceptions of Artificial Intelligence (AI) integration in the classroom. The insights gathered have been arranged under four major themes: AI Adaptability, Influence on Pedagogical Dynamics, Technological Proficiency, and Ethical and Security Concerns. Each theme is further subdivided into several subthemes, allowing for a comprehensive exploration of the many aspects of AI usage in the EFL teaching environment. The interview data has been analyzed and is presented in a way that provides an in-depth understanding of the nuances and complexities of AI in the educational realm while keeping the focus on the voices and lived experiences of the educators themselves. The findings aim to offer a detailed picture of the current state of AI in EFL classrooms, shedding light on both its potential advantages and the challenges it may pose.

Table 2. AI-supported applications

Application	Information	Number of Instruction
Duolingo	To provide lessons in multiple languages, using a variety of interactive exercises	20
Grammarly	Writing assistant that helps users correct grammatical errors, enhance clarity and engagement, and check for plagiarism	19
Chatgpt	A chatbot that acts as a tutor	16
Turnitin	To detect potential plagiarism	15
Canva	To generate content	12
Quillbot	A writing tool that improves the quality of written text	8
Achieve3000	To improve reading comprehension, vocabulary, and writing proficiency by providing leveled reading materials tailored to individual skill levels.	8
Otter.ai	To convert spoken language into written text, enabling real-time transcriptions, and note-taking	7
Murf.ai	To convert text into lifelike speech using customizable voiceovers, enhancing the auditory experience of digital content.	6
Vyond	To create grade animated videos	5
Synthesia	To create synthetic videos, enabling the generation of personalized video content without traditional filming.	5
Slide.ai	To generate presentation	3
Knowji	To learn vocabulary	3
ChatYoutube	To chat with YouTube videos by asking questions	2
Copilot	To generate lesson plans with AI-generated templates	1

AI Adaptability

The first emergent theme was the adaptability of AI in EFL classrooms. This theme embodies sub-themes such as personalization of learning, reinforcement of learning, supplementation in teaching, and accessibility of instruction. Teachers largely recognized the value of AI in tailoring learning to individual needs. "*AI allows me to tailor the learning experience to each student's unique needs and progress*," shared one participant. The potential for AI to reinforce learning also emerged. Another teacher explained, "*AI tools provide additional practice opportunities, reinforcing the knowledge acquired during lessons*." The instructors also viewed AI as a supplement to traditional teaching, "*AI can handle aspects such as grammar checks, freeing me up for more interactive teaching*," revealed one participant. Lastly, instructors valued the increase in instructional accessibility provided by AI, with one teacher noting, "*AI enables students to continue their language practice outside the classroom, fostering a continuous learning environment.*"

Table 3. The thematic framework of the data

Theme	Subtheme	Sample Codes
Adaptability	Personalization	**Customized lesson plans, Adaptive learning exercises Specific learning goals**
	Reinforcement	**Additional practice, Reinforcing classroom lessons Progress tracking**
	Teaching Supplementation	**Grammar checks, Pronunciation correction Automated writing check Real-time error detection**
	Accessibility	**Anytime availability, Off-classroom language practice Compatibility Mobile**
Impact on Pedagogy	Shifting role of educators	**Facilitator role, Content curator role Guide role Support role**
	Influence on teaching strategies	**Integration of AI tools, Modifying lesson plans, Personalized feedback Interactive teaching**
	Alteration of assessment methods	**Automated grading, Real-time performance tracking Formative assessment Predictive analytics**
	Change in student engagement patterns	**Increased self-learning, Greater student participation**
Technological Proficiency	Teacher tech-savviness	**Comfort with tech tools, Previous experience with Edtech**
	Familiarity with AI	**Understanding AI functionality, Confidence in utilizing AI tools**
	Professional development	**Training in AI tools, Tech support requirements**
	Adoption barriers	**Technological glitches, Difficulty in integrating AI tools**
Ethical and Security Concerns	Privacy issues	**Protection of student data, Confidentiality of learner information Anonymity concerns**
	Misuse apprehensions	**Fear of AI misuse, Unethical AI applications**
	Trust in AI	**Reliability of AI-generated results, Accuracy of AI language feedback**
	Policies and regulations	**Need for robust tech policies, Adherence to AI usage regulations**

Influence on Pedagogical Dynamics

The second emergent theme encapsulated the impact of AI on teaching dynamics. This theme was classified into sub-themes like the evolving role of teachers, alteration of teaching strategies, modification of assessment methods, and changes in student engagement. The role of teachers is seen to be shifting in the face of AI integration, as one participant stated, "*With AI, I've transitioned from being a mere deliverer of information to more of a guide and facilitator in the learning process.*" The influence on teaching strategies was another prominent sub-theme. "Incorporating AI necessitated a revision of my teaching approaches," mentioned one teacher. Changes in assessment methodology were another facet, "*The use of AI tools for grading and providing immediate feedback has revolutionized our assessment methods*," another participant highlighted. Teachers also noted a difference in student engagement after the introduction of AI, with one stating, "*The use of AI tools has sparked higher student involvement and proactive participation.*"

Technological Proficiency

The third theme, technological proficiency, was further categorized into teacher's comfort with technology, familiarity with AI, need for professional development, and barriers to AI adoption. Teachers' comfort levels with technology generally influenced their stance toward AI. One participant confessed, "*While I'm adept with tech tools in general, AI does pose a new learning curve.*" The necessity for professional development to fully harness AI was another key insight, "*To use AI to its full potential in our classrooms, more targeted training is required*," revealed another teacher. Several participants also discussed hurdles they experienced while adopting AI, "*Despite my competence with technology, integrating AI tools into my curriculum has its challenges*," shared one participant.

Ethical and Security Concerns

The final theme encompassed ethical and security concerns related to AI usage in classrooms. This theme is divided into sub-themes such as potential privacy issues, fear of misuse, trust in AI, and the need for robust policies and regulations. Teachers expressed concern over data privacy, "*While AI has potential, the security of our students' information is a crucial factor*," voiced one participant. Another echoed similar sentiments regarding misuse, "*AI is a powerful tool but could lead to problems if misused or if it provides inaccurate feedback.*" The reliability of AI also emerged as a concern, "*How can we ensure the AI's outputs are consistently accurate and reliable?*" questioned one educator. Lastly, participants underscored the importance of firm policies and regulations, "*Clear guidelines and regulatory policies are necessary to ensure ethical application and prevent misuse of AI in classrooms*," shared another participant.

In sum, these findings reveal the multifaceted perspectives of teachers toward the incorporation of AI in EFL classrooms. The identified themes encompassed the practical applications and potential challenges of AI, indicating a need for comprehensive training for teachers, strategic integration of AI into curriculum planning, careful attention to data security, and the development of robust policies for AI use in educational settings. The nuanced insights gathered from the teachers' experiences can contribute to shaping more informed, effective, and ethical practices for the integration of AI in language education moving forward.

PRACTICAL APPLICATIONS OF AI IN EFL EDUCATION

As for the practical implementation of AI in EFL Education, it is crucial to acknowledge that the subsequent case studies are directly based on the experiences of the interviewed instructors in the present investigation. These real-world instances exemplify a wide array of inventive ideas and tactics that these educators have used in their classrooms. Every example demonstrates the use of AI technologies in real-world scenarios, providing significant insights into their practical effectiveness and influence. These tales not only demonstrate the adaptability of AI in language education but also provide specific instances of its implementation, as described by the instructors themselves. Our objective is to narrow the divide between theoretical comprehension and actual execution by illustrating the concrete advantages and difficulties of incorporating AI into EFL teaching methods via the presentation of these scenarios.

Case: Implementing AI Chatbot for Interactive Language Practice in a Flight School

A renowned aviation university in Turkey has included an AI-driven chatbot, known as "Sky Tutor", into its English language instruction program. The chatbot may be accessed using the following link: https://chat.openai.com/g/g-hgsIGvQci-sky-tutor. The program's objective was to improve the aviation English proficiency of student pilots, a crucial competency for conducting international flight operations. The institution's classroom management system included Sky Tutor. The trainee pilots utilized the chatbot to participate in regular practice sessions, specifically targeting aviation-specific vocabulary and phraseology, in addition to enhancing their overall English proficiency. The chatbot's artificial intelligence was optimized to prioritize aircraft communication protocols and international radiotelephony expressions. The trainees exhibited significant progress in their skills in aviation English, displaying a clear increase in their capacity to successfully communicate in simulated international flight settings. The AI chatbot offered personalized attention and prompt feedback, which were crucial elements in the trainees' advancement. This instance serves as a prime example of the effective implementation of an AI chatbot in the realm of specialized language instruction. The AI's capacity to adjust to the precise language requirements of aviation, along with the ease of online accessibility, made Sky Tutor an indispensable tool in the trainees' educational progression.

Figure 1. Customized GPT for aviation training

Case: Implementing AI for Vocabulary Practice

An instructor at a public university's English language school included ChatGPT into the curriculum to augment vocabulary acquisition. The approach included the instructor formulating precise prompts pertaining to vocabulary subjects and instructing students on how to engage using ChatGPT. Students used the AI technology to engage in exercises including new vocabulary within different scenarios, receiving instant feedback on their usage and grammar. They participated in activities such as phrase construction, synonym/antonym identification, and simulated contextual conversations. Each week, pupils in the classroom were assigned distinct vocabulary subjects. Utilizing ChatGPT, individuals participated in focused activities that included formulating sentences using unfamiliar terms, investigating alternative words with similar or opposite meanings, and participating in simulated dialogues specifically designed to enhance their vocabulary. For example, when studying weather-related vocabulary, students might request ChatGPT to generate phrases including these words, and thereafter construct their own sentences for evaluation. During simulated dialogues, students engaged with ChatGPT in a manner resembling real-life conversations, where they discussed the weather. This provided them with an opportunity to learn vocabulary in a contextual manner. The practical and engaging method, along with instant AI feedback, enhanced students' comprehension and application of new terminology in real-life situations. The AI's flexibility allowed a customized educational encounter, accommodating the distinct requirements and speed of each learner. This approach offered a more captivating and dynamic means of acquiring language, surpassing conventional methods of rote memorizing. The constant availability of ChatGPT allowed students to engage in language practice at any time, resulting in a more regular and engaging learning experience. This instance emphasizes the significant impact of AI on language teaching, namely in improving the extent and efficacy of vocabulary acquisition.

Case: Implementing AI-Based Text-to-Speech to Generate Listening Materials

At a higher education institution, an English teacher employed an innovative language learning method by utilizing MURF.AI, an advanced text-to-speech technology, to produce realistic podcasts and audio resources for classroom instruction. She understood the need to include relevant and practical material, so she created scripts covering a wide range of subjects, including casual chats and in-depth debates on contemporary global issues. These scripts were customized to suit the specific interests and educational levels of her pupils. Utilizing MURF.AI's technology, she was able to convert these texts into podcasts that showcased a diverse array of authentic voices. The presence of many accents and speaking styles was crucial since it provided students with exposure to the abundant range of English speech they would experience in authentic scenarios. Every podcast was meticulously constructed to include aspects of narrative, conversation, and informative material, making them not only instructive but also interesting for the students. The listening sessions in the classroom were organized based on these podcasts that were created by artificial intelligence. Following each session, the instructor organized activities like group discussions, vocabulary assessments, and comprehension drills. The purpose of these exercises was to strengthen listening comprehension skills and promote active involvement with the topic. Students often engaged in activities that required them to contemplate the material, articulate their viewpoints, and generate replies or alternative conclusions to the podcast tales, augmenting their abilities in critical thinking and creative language use. The use of AI technology in language instruction has shown remarkable efficacy. Students indicated greater involvement and enhanced auditory understanding. The users valued the podcasts' authenticity, as it facilitated their adaptation to different English accents and colloquial expressions. This greatly improved their comprehension of real-life language and boosted their confidence in using English. Overall, this study illustrates the capacity of AI to transform language learning by showcasing how technology can provide immersive, tailored, and very efficient learning situations.

Figure 2. Text-to-speech application

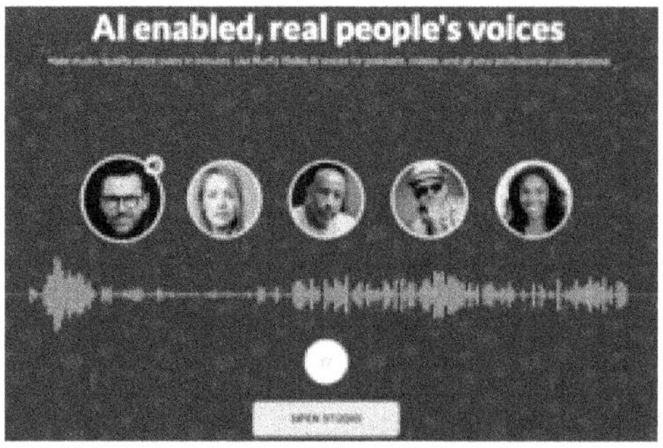

DISCUSSION

The discussions that arise from this study provide significant insights into the complex perceptions and attitudes of EFL teachers toward the integration of AI in language classrooms. Four main themes emerged from the qualitative analysis, each revealing intricate dimensions of teachers' experiences and beliefs. These themes, in turn, were classified into multiple sub-themes that further nuanced our understanding of the dynamics at play. Each theme is discussed below, drawing connections with existing literature and reflecting on the implications of the findings.

Adaptability of AI

The theme of "Adaptability of AI in EFL Teaching" emerged as a core concept in teachers' perceptions of AI, revealing their recognition of AI's potential to significantly enhance language teaching and learning. First, a key advantage perceived by teachers regarding AI was its ability to foster "Personalization of Learning". This was characterized by AI's ability to align instruction to each learner's pace, ability, and learning style. For example, one participant noted, "*With AI, every student gets a unique learning experience tailored to their strengths and weaknesses*." This perspective aligns with Chen et al.'s (2020) findings, which highlighted the ability of AI-driven adaptive learning environments to offer individualized education that caters to the diverse learning needs of students. Yet, as Clark (2020) cautions, while personalization is a significant asset of AI, there is a need for educators to carefully balance personalized learning with collaborative learning experiences that can foster social and communication skills.

"Reinforcement of Learning" emerged as another sub-theme, emphasizing the unique role of AI in providing learners with additional practice opportunities outside formal classroom settings. One teacher expressed, "*AI-based tools enable students to practice their language skills. They provide that extra practice that is often needed to truly master a foreign language*." This reflects Kannan and Munday's (2018) assertions, which lauded the reinforcement potential of AI in facilitating continuous practice for students, thereby improving language acquisition. However, Holmes et al. (2019) advised that while reinforcement is important, it should not be devoid of critical and creative thinking skills, which are equally vital for comprehensive language learning.

"Supplementation in Teaching" was observed in teachers' narratives which affirmed AI's role in aiding their instructional efforts. A teacher mentioned, "*AI tools are not replacing us; they are supporting us, helping us teach more effectively. They handle routine tasks, giving us more time to engage with students on a deeper level.*" This aligns with Edwards and Cheok's (2018) perspective, which depicted AI as a tool to support and supplement human instruction, allowing teachers to focus more on fostering student engagement and less on administrative tasks. Additionally, Scholars such as Chin, Wu, and Hong (2011), Lee et al. (2008), and You et al. (2006) argue against the possibility or feasibility of artificial intelligence assuming the role of teachers. They contend that AI lacks the necessary capabilities to fully replace human educators in the classroom. Nonetheless, Lameras and Arnab (2021) have suggested that while AI can supplement teaching, ongoing professional development for teachers is necessary to ensure the effective implementation and use of AI tools in classrooms.

Lastly, "Accessibility of Instruction" underpinned the potential of AI in extending the reach of language instruction beyond classroom boundaries. Teachers were appreciative of how AI-enabled learning to happen anywhere, any time. One teacher shared: "*AI breaks down walls; it allows learning to happen everywhere. The classroom is not confined to four walls anymore.*" This sentiment echoes Wang and Chen's (2020) research, which emphasized AI's role in supporting continuous and ubiquitous learning, thus increasing the accessibility of language instruction.

Impact on Pedagogy

The second central theme that emerged from the teachers' perceptions was the "Impact on pedagogy", indicating their cognizance of the substantial implications of AI integration on their instructional practices. This theme encompassed four critical sub-themes: Shifting Role of Educators, Influence on Teaching Strategies, Alteration of Assessment Methods, and Change in Student Engagement Patterns. First, the 'Shifting Role of Educators' sub-theme was evident in teachers' insights about how the integration of AI is revolutionizing their roles within the classroom. As one teacher expressed, "*With AI, our role is changing from a knowledge provider to a learning facilitator.*" This sentiment is congruent with the findings of Holmes et al. (2019), who argued that the introduction of AI is transforming the traditional role of teachers, moving them towards a more facilitative, guiding role. However, Cook (2020) advises that in this transformative phase, educators must not lose sight of their crucial humanistic role in fostering emotional and social learning, which is something AI cannot replace.

Teachers also highlighted the "Influence on Teaching Strategies" brought about by AI technologies. One teacher noted, "*AI has changed my teaching strategies; it enables me to use more interactive and learner-centered methods.*" This statement corroborates Bostrom and his colleagues' (2014) research, emphasizing that AI's capabilities can lead to more student-centered pedagogical strategies, enhancing both learning effectiveness and engagement. Yet, Larsen-Freeman (2019) warns of the need for pedagogical balance; while AI encourages innovative teaching strategies and traditional methods, emphasizing direct teacher-student interaction, the sharing of knowledge and experiences, and real-time adjustment to the learning flow according to student responses, still hold merit and can be effective in certain learning scenarios. These methods allow for a high degree of emotional, cultural, and contextual nuance that AI, despite its many benefits, currently cannot fully replicate (Buckingham, 2019). For instance, in teaching language, nuances such as idiomatic expressions, cultural references, and the subtleties of verbal and non-verbal communication can be better explained and modeled by human teachers. Moreover, traditional methods like cooperative learning, group discussions, role-playing, storytelling, and many more, play an essential role in promoting critical thinking, creativity, teamwork, and social skills among students (Johnson & Johnson, 2009). These are competencies that an AI-driven pedagogical approach may not be able to cultivate as effectively due to its algorithmic nature.

Another sub-theme of "Alteration of Assessment Methods' emerged from teachers" perceptions about the potential of AI to revolutionize assessment in the language classroom. An instructor stated, "*AI provides real-time feedback and can assist in regular assessments, making it easier for us to track and measure students' progress*." This echoes Hooda and his colleagues' (2022) work, which highlighted the potential of AI in providing immediate, personalized feedback, thereby enhancing formative assessment processes. Nonetheless, as Griffin and Care (2014) point out, while computer-based assessments offer promising advancements in assessment, human judgment and interpretation remain essential, particularly in complex language assessments requiring nuanced evaluation. For example, evaluating a learner's proficiency in pragmatic skills, such as the appropriate use of language in various social contexts, or assessing a learner's ability to communicate creatively and effectively, require nuanced understanding and interpretation that AI systems, as of now, cannot fully replicate. That's to say; AI can efficiently evaluate language learners' vocabulary usage, grammatical structures, and pronunciation patterns, which are largely rule-based aspects of language learning (Chen et al., 2020). It's also worth noting that language is not merely a system of rules; it is also a medium for expressing thoughts, emotions, and cultural nuances, which may not always adhere strictly to predefined linguistic structures (Larsen-Freeman, 2019).

Lastly, the "Change in Student Engagement Patterns" sub-theme arose from teachers observing alterations in how students interact and engage with the learning material due to AI. One teacher remarked, "AI-based tools have brought about new engagement patterns. Students now spend more time learning interactively rather than passively receiving information." This aligns with Zheng et al.'s (2020) study, which noted the transformative effect of AI on student engagement, encouraging active learning. However, Alam (2021) reminds us that while AI can foster increased engagement, a one-size-fits-all approach is insufficient, as different students engage differently with AI tools.

Technological Proficiency

In the theme of "Technological Proficiency", the sub-themes of "Teacher tech-savviness", "Familiarity with AI", "Professional development needs", and "Adoption barriers" collectively address the competencies and challenges teachers face while incorporating AI in EFL instruction. First, "Teacher tech-savviness" is a crucial aspect that influences the effectiveness of AI implementation in the language classroom. A high degree of competency and proficiency with technology among teachers can translate into more seamless integration and better utilization of AI tools (Pilco et al., 2022). For example, a teacher who is comfortable with technology is likely to exploit the benefits of AI-driven personalized learning more effectively, creating adaptive learning paths for their students. On the other hand, the sub-theme "Familiarity with AI" suggests the necessity of understanding specific AI functionalities, its capabilities, and its limitations. This knowledge goes beyond general tech-savviness. Without this familiarity, teachers may either underutilize the potential of AI or over-rely on it, ignoring areas where human instruction is irreplaceable (Lameras & Arnab, 2021).

Addressing the "Professional development needs," many teachers highlighted the need for appropriate training to successfully integrate AI into their teaching. Research by Avci et al. (2020) has already demonstrated that professional development programs that provide hands-on, context-specific training in technology use significantly enhance teachers' self-efficacy and willingness to integrate technology. In the case of AI, such training would be beneficial not only in using AI tools but also in understanding how these tools can be pedagogically integrated to improve language learning outcomes (Kannan & Munday, 2018).

Finally, the sub-theme "Adoption barriers" brings attention to the practical challenges teachers face, which include lack of time, resources, or institutional support. These barriers are consistent with those found in previous research on educational technology integration (Malik et al., 2022). Addressing these barriers would require systemic efforts at the school or district level to ensure adequate resources, including time for teachers to learn and experiment with AI tools, technical support, and integration of AI technologies into the curriculum and assessment methods.

Ethical and Security Concerns

The final theme of "Ethical and Security Concerns" encapsulates several pressing issues associated with the increasing use of AI in educational settings, particularly within the EFL classroom. This includes "Privacy Issues", "Misuse Apprehensions", "Trust in AI", and the necessity for "Policies and Regulations". Starting with "Privacy Issues", participants shared concerns regarding data collection, storage, and potential misuse, echoing the broader societal concerns about AI and data privacy. These worries are not unfounded; AI-driven educational tools collect vast amounts of data about learners to function effectively (Clark, 2020). This data, if mishandled or misused, could potentially lead to privacy violations. This concern aligns with similar findings from Qin et al. (2020), emphasizing the need for stringent data privacy measures when implementing AI in education.

"Misuse Apprehensions" refer to fears that AI technology could be misused either by students, who might rely excessively on AI for learning tasks thereby undermining their learning process, or by entities for commercial exploitation. As stated by Cardano et al. (2023), ensuring the ethical usage of AI in education is a collective responsibility involving teachers, students, and AI tool developers.

Trust in AI" emerged as another sub-theme, reflecting teachers' concerns about the accuracy and reliability of AI tools. Indeed, the credibility of AI systems plays a significant role in their acceptance and effectiveness in education. As Bostrom and Yudkowsky (2014) pointed out, trust in AI systems, especially in their ability to aid learning without causing harm, is vital to the successful integration of AI into the classroom.

The need for "Policies and Regulations" was a recurring concern among teachers. They noted the absence of clear guidelines about the use of AI in education, particularly in relation to data privacy and ethical usage. These findings are congruent with those of Luan et. al (2020), who highlighted the need for appropriate regulation and governance mechanisms to address ethical and security issues related to AI use in education.

CONCLUSION

The advent of AI presents a transformative potential in various sectors, and its implications for education, particularly language teaching, are immense. Through this qualitative study, we sought to explore and understand the perceptions of EFL teachers towards the incorporation of AI in language classrooms.

The study has revealed that EFL teachers hold multifaceted beliefs about AI integration into their pedagogical practice. Broadly, these beliefs coalesce around four major themes, including the adaptability of AI to individual learning needs, the impact of AI on teaching dynamics, the technological proficiency needed for effective AI integration, and the ethical and security concerns associated with AI use.

Our findings underscore that AI, with its ability to provide personalized learning, reinforcement, and accessible resources, offers significant potential to support language learning. However, AI's influence on teaching dynamics also necessitates a shift in teachers' roles, strategies, and assessment methods, and a change in student engagement patterns, further underscoring the need for professional development and the cultivation of teachers' tech-savviness and familiarity with AI. Moreover, the study also highlighted the importance of addressing teachers' concerns around privacy, misuse, trust, and the need for clear policies and regulations related to AI use in education.

The insights derived from this study contribute to the evolving narrative around the integration of AI in language education. They shed light on the complex dynamics that educators navigate in their attempt to incorporate AI technologies into their classrooms. The responses also elucidate some of the potential hurdles that need to be overcome, such as barriers to adoption, professional development needs, and the necessity for policies and regulations governing AI use.

As we advance further into the digital era, the integration of AI into language classrooms will become increasingly crucial. It is, therefore, of paramount importance that we continue to explore and understand the nuances of this integration from the teachers' perspectives. Such an understanding will guide the development of more informed strategies for AI implementation, ultimately enriching language learning experiences for students and empowering teachers in the evolving educational landscape. The study's findings, while illuminating, are also a launchpad for further inquiry. Additional research is needed to explore these themes in different contexts, with varied student populations, and over an extended period to fully comprehend the long-term implications of AI use in language teaching.

In conclusion, while AI offers exciting possibilities for language teaching, it also presents unique challenges. Addressing these challenges requires an informed, nuanced approach that balances the potential benefits of AI with a commitment to ethical, pedagogically sound practices. As educators, policymakers, and researchers, we are all stakeholders in this endeavor. The future of language teaching is undoubtedly intertwined with AI, and it is our shared responsibility to navigate this path effectively and responsibly.

REFERENCES

AbdAlgane, M., & Othman, K. A. J. (2023). Utilizing artificial intelligence technologies in Saudi EFL tertiary level classrooms. *Journal of Intercultural Communication*, *23*(1), 92–99. Advance online publication. doi:10.36923/jicc.v23i1.124

Alam, A. (2021, November). Possibilities and apprehensions in the landscape of artificial intelligence in education. In *2021 International Conference on Computational Intelligence and Computing Applications (ICCICA)* (pp. 1-8). IEEE. https://doi.org/10.1109/ICCICA52458.2021.9697272

Alhalangy, A., & AbdAlgane, M. (2023). Exploring the impact of AI on the EFL context: A case study of Saudi universities. *Journal of Intercultural Communication*, *23*(2), 41–49. doi:10.36923/jicc.v23i2.125

Alshumaimeri, Y. A., & Alshememry, A. K. (2023). The extent of AI applications in EFL learning and teaching. *IEEE Transactions on Learning Technologies*. Advance online publication. doi:10.1109/TLT.2023.3322128

Bailey, D., Southam, A., & Costley, J. (2021). Digital storytelling with chatbots: Mapping L2 participation and perception patterns. *Interactive Technology and Smart Education*, *18*(1), 85–103. doi:10.1108/ITSE-08-2020-0170

Bostrom, N., Yudkowsky, E., & Frankish, K. (2014). The Cambridge handbook of artificial intelligence. In K. Frankish & W. M. Ramsey (Eds.), *The ethics of artificial intelligence* (Vol. 316, p. 334). Cambridge University Press.

Braun, V., & Clarke, V. (2006). Using thematic analysis in psychology. *Qualitative Research in Psychology*, *3*(2), 77–101. doi:10.1191/1478088706qp063oa

Cardona, M. A., Rodríguez, R. J., & Ishmael, K. (2023). *Artificial Intelligence and the Future of Teaching and Learning: Insights and Recommendations*. U.S. Department of Education, Office of Educational Technology. https://policycommons.net/artifacts/3854312/ai-report/4660267/

Celik, I., Dindar, M., Muukkonen, H., & Järvelä, S. (2022). The promises and challenges of artificial intelligence for teachers: A systematic review of research. *TechTrends*, *66*(4), 616–630. doi:10.1007/s11528-022-00715-y

Chen, L., Chen, P., & Lin, Z. (2020). Artificial intelligence in education: A review. *IEEE Access : Practical Innovations, Open Solutions*, *8*, 75264–75278. doi:10.1109/ACCESS.2020.2988510

Chin, K. Y., Wu, C. H., & Hong, Z. W. (2011). A humanoid robot as a teaching assistant for primary education. In *2011 Fifth International Conference on Genetic and Evolutionary Computing* (pp. 21-24). IEEE. 10.1109/ICGEC.2011.13

Clark, D. (2020). *Artificial intelligence for learning: How to use AI to support employee development.* Kogan Page Publishers.

Cohen, I. L., Liu, X., Hudson, M., Gillis, J., Cavalari, R. N., Romanczyk, R. G., Karmel, B. Z., & Gardner, J. M. (2017). Level 2 Screening With the PDD Behavior Inventory: Subgroup Profiles and Implications for Differential Diagnosis. *Canadian Journal of School Psychology*, *32*(3-4), 299–315. doi:10.1177/0829573517721127

Coniam, D. (2014). The linguistic accuracy of chatbots: Usability from an ESL perspective. *Text & Talk*, *34*(5), 545–567. doi:10.1515/text-2014-0018

Dodigovic, M. (2007). Artificial intelligence and second language learning: An efficient approach to error remediation. *Language Awareness*, *16*(2), 99–113. doi:10.2167/la416.0

Edwards, B. I., & Cheok, A. D. (2018). Why not robot teachers: Artificial intelligence for addressing teacher shortage. *Applied Artificial Intelligence*, *32*(4), 345–360. doi:10.1080/08839514.2018.1464286

Gallacher, A., Thompson, A., Howarth, M., Taalas, P., Jalkanen, J., Bradley, L., & Thouësny, S. (2018). "My robot is an idiot!"–Students' perceptions of AI in the L2 classroom. *Future-proof CALL: language learning as exploration and encounters–short papers from EUROCALL*, 70-76.

Gaudioso, E., Montero, M., & Hernandez-del-Olmo, F. (2012). Supporting teachers in adaptive educational systems through predictive models: A proof of concept. *Expert Systems with Applications*, *39*(1), 621–625. doi:10.1016/j.eswa.2011.07.052

Griffin, P., & Care, E. (Eds.). (2014). *Assessment and teaching of 21st-century skills: Methods and approach*. Springer. doi:10.1007/978-94-017-9395-7

Haenlein, M., & Kaplan, A. (2019). A brief history of artificial intelligence: On the past, present, and future of artificial intelligence. *California Management Review*, *61*(4), 5–14. doi:10.1177/0008125619864925

Haristiani, N. (2019). Artificial Intelligence (AI) chatbot as language learning medium: An inquiry. In Journal of Physics: Conference Series (Vol. 1387, No. 1, p. 012020). IOP Publishing. doi:10.1088/1742-6596/1387/1/012020

Heffernan, N. T., & Heffernan, C. L. (2014). The ASSISTments ecosystem: Building a platform that brings scientists and teachers together for minimally invasive research on human learning and teaching. *International Journal of Artificial Intelligence in Education*, *24*(4), 470–497. doi:10.1007/s40593-014-0024-x

Hooda, M., Rana, C., Dahiya, O., Rizwan, A., & Hossain, M. S. (2022). Artificial intelligence for assessment and feedback to enhance student success in higher education. *Mathematical Problems in Engineering*, *2022*, 1–19. Advance online publication. doi:10.1155/2022/5215722

Jeon, J. (2021). Exploring AI chatbot affordances in the EFL classroom: Young learners' experiences and perspectives. *Computer Assisted Language Learning*, 1–26. doi:10.1080/09588221.2021.2021241

Jiang, R. (2022). How does artificial intelligence empower EFL teaching and learning nowadays? A review on artificial intelligence in the EFL context. *Frontiers in Psychology*, *13*, 1049401. doi:10.3389/fpsyg.2022.1049401 PMID:36467167

Kannan, J., & Munday, P. (2018). New trends in second language learning and teaching through the lens of ICT, networked learning, and artificial intelligence. *Círculo de Lingüística Aplicada a la Comunicación*, *76*, 13–30. doi:10.5209/CLAC.62495

Knox, J. (2020). Artificial intelligence and education in China. *Learning, Media and Technology*, *45*(3), 298–311. doi:10.1080/17439884.2020.1754236

Koedinger, K. R., Corbett, A. T., & Perfetti, C. (2012). The Knowledge-Learning-Instruction framework: Bridging the science-practice chasm to enhance robust student learning. *Cognitive Science*, *36*(5), 757–798. doi:10.1111/j.1551-6709.2012.01245.x PMID:22486653

Koraishi, O. (2023). Teaching English in the age of AI: Embracing ChatGPT to optimize EFL materials and assessment. *Language Education and Technology, 3*(1).

Lameras, P., & Arnab, S. (2021). Power to the teachers: An exploratory review on artificial intelligence in education. *Information (Basel)*, *13*(1), 14. doi:10.3390/info13010014

Langran, E., Searson, M., Knezek, G., & Christensen, R. (2020, April). AI in teacher education. In *Society for Information Technology & Teacher Education International Conference* (pp. 751-756). Association for the Advancement of Computing in Education (AACE).

Larsen-Freeman, D., & DeCarrico, J. (2019). Grammar. In *An introduction to applied linguistics* (pp. 19–34). Routledge. doi:10.4324/9780429424465-2

Last, R. W. (1989). *Artificial intelligence techniques in language learning*. Halsted Press.

Lee, E., Lee, Y., Kye, B., & Ko, B. (2008). Elementary and middle school teachers', students', and parents' perception of robot-aided education in Korea. In EdMedia+ Innovate Learning (pp. 175-183). Association for the Advancement of Computing in Education (AACE).

Lu, X. (2018). Natural Language processing and intelligent computer-assisted language learning (ICALL). *The TESOL encyclopedia of English language teaching*, 1-6. doi:10.1002/9781118784235.eelt0422

Luan, H., Geczy, P., Lai, H., Gobert, J., Yang, S. J., Ogata, H., Baltes, J., Guerra, R., Li, P., & Tsai, C. C. (2020). Challenges and future directions of big data and artificial intelligence in education. *Frontiers in Psychology*, *11*, 580820. doi:10.3389/fpsyg.2020.580820 PMID:33192896

Luckin, R., Holmes, W., Griffiths, M., & Forcier, L. B. (2016). *Intelligence unleashed: An argument for AI in education*. Pearson Education.

Malik, G., Tayal, D. K., & Vij, S. (2019). An analysis of the role of artificial intelligence in education and teaching. In *Recent Findings in Intelligent Computing Techniques: Proceedings of the 5th ICACNI 2017,* Volume 1 (pp. 407-417). Springer Singapore. 10.1007/978-981-10-8639-7_42

Nagata, N. (1996). Computer vs. workbook instruction in second language acquisition. *CALICO Journal*, 53–75.

O'Brien, P. (1993). eL: AI in CALL. In M. Yazdani (Ed.), Multilingual multimedia. Bridging the language barrier with intelligent systems (pp. 85–139). Intellect.

Okada, A., Whitelock, D., Holmes, W., & Edwards, C. (2019). e-Authentication for online assessment: A mixed-method study. *British Journal of Educational Technology*, *50*(2), 861–875. doi:10.1111/bjet.12608

Pace-Sigge, M., & Sumakul, D. T. (2021). What teaching an algorithm teaches when teaching students how to write academic texts. *Linguistic, Educational and Intercultural Research 2021 (LEIC Research 2021)*, 78.

Qin, F., Li, K., & Yan, J. (2020). Understanding user trust in artificial intelligence-based educational systems: Evidence from China. *British Journal of Educational Technology*, *51*(5), 1693–1710. doi:10.1111/bjet.12994

Roll, I., & Wylie, R. (2016). Evolution and revolution in artificial intelligence in education. *International Journal of Artificial Intelligence in Education*, *26*(2), 582–599. doi:10.1007/s40593-016-0110-3

Salaberry, M. R. (1996). A theoretical foundation for the development of pedagogical tasks in computer-mediated communication. *CALICO Journal*, *14*(1), 5–34. doi:10.1558/cj.v14i1.5-34

Salas-Pilco, S. Z., Xiao, K., & Hu, X. (2022). Artificial intelligence and learning analytics in teacher education: A systematic review. *Education Sciences*, *12*(8), 569. doi:10.3390/educsci12080569

Self, J. (1998). The defining characteristics of intelligent tutoring systems research: ITSs care, precisely. *International Journal of Artificial Intelligence in Education*, *10*, 350–364.

Selwyn, N. (2019). *Should robots replace teachers?: AI and the future of education*. John Wiley & Sons.

Steenbergen-Hu, S., & Cooper, H. (2014). A meta-analysis of the effectiveness of intelligent tutoring systems on college students' academic learning. *Journal of Educational Psychology*, *106*(2), 331–347. doi:10.1037/a0034752

Sumakul, D. T. (2019). When robots enter the classrooms: Implications for teachers. In *International Conference on Embedding Artificial Intelligence (AI) in Educational Policy and Practice for Southeast Asia, Jakarta, Indonesia*. SEAMEO SEAMOLEC.

Swiecki, Z., Ruis, A. R., Gautam, D., Rus, V., & Williamson Shaffer, D. (2019). Understanding when students are active-in-thinking through modeling-in-context. *British Journal of Educational Technology*, *50*(5), 2346–2364. doi:10.1111/bjet.12869

Vij, S., Tayal, D., & Jain, A. (2020). A machine learning approach for automated evaluation of short answers using text similarity based on WordNet graphs. *Wireless Personal Communications*, *111*(2), 1271–1282. doi:10.1007/s11277-019-06913-x

Wilson, J., Ahrendt, C., Fudge, E. A., Raiche, A., Beard, G., & MacArthur, C. (2021). Elementary teachers' perceptions of automated feedback and automated scoring: Transforming the teaching and learning of writing using automated writing evaluation. *Computers & Education*, *168*, 104208. doi:10.1016/j.compedu.2021.104208

Yin, J., Goh, T. T., Yang, B., & Xiaobin, Y. (2021). Conversation technology with micro-learning: The impact of chatbot-based learning on students' learning motivation and performance. *Journal of Educational Computing Research*, *59*(1), 154–177. doi:10.1177/0735633120952067

You, Z. J., Shen, C. Y., Chang, C. W., Liu, B. J., & Chen, G. D. (2006). A robot as a teaching assistant in an English class. In *Sixth IEEE International Conference on advanced learning technologies (ICALT'06)* (pp. 87-91). 10.1109/ICALT.2006.1652373

Yuan, S., He, T., Huang, H., Hou, R., & Wang, M. (2020). Automated Chinese essay scoring based on deep learning. *CMC-Computers Materials & Continua, 65*(1), 817-833. https://doi.org/.2020.010471 doi:10.32604/cmc

Yurtseven Avci, Z., O'Dwyer, L. M., & Lawson, J. (2020). Designing effective professional development for technology integration in schools. *Journal of Computer Assisted Learning*, *36*(2), 160–177. doi:10.1111/jcal.12394

Zawacki-Richter, O., Marín, V. I., Bond, M., & Gouverneur, F. (2019). Systematic review of research on artificial intelligence applications in higher education–where are the educators? *International Journal of Educational Technology in Higher Education, 16*(1), 16–39. doi:10.1186/s41239-019-0171-0

KEY TERMS AND DEFINITIONS

Artificial Intelligence: A digital realm where machines mimic human cognition to solve tasks.

Artificial Intelligence in Education: Infusing smart algorithms into learning environments to enhance teaching and student performance.

CAGR: CAGR stands for Compound Annual Growth Rate, which is a measure used to express the mean annual growth rate of an investment over a specified time period longer than one year.

EFL: It stands for "English as a Foreign Language" which refers to the study or learning of English by speakers with different native languages.

Generative Artificial Intelligence: The branch of AI that crafts new content based on patterns from data.

Large Language Models: Massive digital libraries trained on vast text data to predict and produce language.

Technological Proficiency: It refers to teachers' ability to effectively use and integrate technology in their teaching practices.

APPENDIX

Interview Questions

1. What are your initial thoughts about the integration of Artificial Intelligence (AI) in language teaching?
2. Can you describe any past experiences you have had with using technology, particularly AI, in your classroom?
3. How do you perceive AI could assist your language classroom?
4. Do you think AI could be a useful tool to facilitate language practice for your students? Could you provide some examples?
5. In what ways do you believe AI could enhance learner motivation in language learning?
6. Do you have any concerns about the impact of AI on your role as a teacher? Could you elaborate?
7. How do you think AI could affect student-teacher interactions?
8. What are your thoughts on the potential benefits and drawbacks of using AI in the classroom?
9. Do you have any privacy concerns related to the use of AI in the classroom?
10. How confident do you feel about your competency in using AI effectively for language teaching?
11. Can you comment on the availability and effectiveness of technical support for AI integration in your school?
12. How have your pedagogical beliefs shaped your perspectives on AI integration in language education?
13. What kind of changes do you foresee in the teaching and learning process with AI integration in the future?
14. How would you like to be supported as a teacher in order to enhance the use of AI in your classroom?

Chapter 6
AI-Powered Lesson Planning:
Insights From Future EFL Teachers

Banu Çiçek Başaran Uysal
https://orcid.org/0000-0002-4978-0891
Eskisehir Osmangazi University, Turkey

İlknur Yüksel
Eskisehir Osmangazi University, Turkey

ABSTRACT

This chapter explores the integration of artificial intelligence (AI) into language education, focusing on the perspectives of pre-service English as a foreign language (EFL) teachers. Employing a mixed-methods approach, the study investigates the effectiveness of AI-powered lesson plans, specifically designed for teaching writing to 5th-grade students. Through a comprehensive evaluation rubric and qualitative analysis, the research identifies strengths, areas for improvement, and suggested changes in AI-generated lesson plans. Findings highlight the tool's success in engagement, appropriateness, and overall structure, while indicating challenges in differentiation and assessment. The chapter concludes with implications for teacher training in AI literacy, emphasizing the need for educators equipped to harness the potential of AI in diverse language teaching settings.

INTRODUCTION

In the dynamic domain of technology, it is rare for a groundbreaking advancement to get noticed and exert impact as fast as ChatGPT has. Recently, this AI-powered language model has rapidly received global appeal, captivating both experts and casual internet users with its remarkable powers. Generative AI has been applied in various ways to support language education. It has the potential to revolutionize language education by providing innovative tools and approaches to enhance language learning and teaching. These tools can provide more interactive and personalized language learning experiences for students (Lee et al., 2022); immediate feedback on learners' language (Fu et al., 2020); and authentic

DOI: 10.4018/979-8-3693-0872-1.ch006

language practice (Bibauw et al., 2019). While AI has been increasingly incorporated into K–12 education, little research has been conducted on the trust and attitudes of teachers towards the use and adoption of AI-powered educational technology (Nazaretsky et al., 2022).

Teachers' perspectives and conceptions of employing AI in schools are also crucial to consider when understanding how generative AI influences pedagogy and learning. Analyzing and comprehending the adoption of AI is of great significance but challenging (Pedró et al., 2019). As with most new technology, teachers need to be equipped with AI literacy such as providing hands-on activities (Lee & Perret, 2022) to provide an understanding of the benefits and challenges of using AI in language teaching and learning. Thus, integration of AI to teacher education is of great importance. The pre-service teachers should be trained how and when to use AI, and how to improve their teaching performance with AI-powered applications.

Lesson planning is one of the crucial steps where teachers will decide on the technology integration to enhance the overall quality of teaching (Kehoe, 2023). Lesson planning is a roadmap for teachers to address the diverse needs and preferences of learners, promoting inclusive and equitable education. Additionally, for pre-service teachers, lesson planning is a critical component in the development of pedagogical competence, as it enables them to reflect on, modify and implement lesson plans, assess student learning, and create effective learning media and select and apply effective learning techniques and tools. (König, Bremerich-Vos, Buchholtz, Fladung, & Glutsch, 2019). AI integration starts at lesson planning where teachers decide on where, how, and why to use AI (Kehoe, 2023).

Additionally, AI could help teachers to design effective lessons at the first step of lesson preparation. It has the capacity to greatly revolutionize the process of lesson planning in education. First, AI systems can scan massive volumes of educational data to detect student learning patterns, strengths, and weaknesses, helping teachers create more personalized and engaging classes. AI can anticipate student concerns and help teachers address them by using predictive analytics (Yildirim, Arslan, Yildirim, & Bisen, 2021). AI-powered systems may also select and recommend instructional articles, videos, and interactive materials, saving teachers' time. AI-driven evaluation technologies can also provide real-time feedback on student achievement, allowing teachers tailor lessons to specific learning needs. In the end, AI can help teachers improve lesson planning, engage students, and create more inclusive learning environments (Kehoe, 2023). However, the studies on what teachers think about AI-powered lesson planning are scarce in literature. In fact, it is crucial to investigate teachers', especially pre-service teachers' views on the benefits or hinders of AI in lesson planning process as they are the ones who will or will not use AI in lesson planning and their perspectives could reveal what they need to use AI in the process and how AI could be use more effectively in learning and teaching process.

Addressing this need, this chapter aims to show how future EFL teachers perceive the integration of AI technologies like ChatGPT in their lesson planning process. Pre-service teachers' views on AI-powered lesson planning can help create targeted professional development programmes that give pre-service teachers the skills and expertise to use these technologies effectively, to explore the problems and ethical dilemmas of AI integration in education, preparing future educators to handle complex technology issues in the classroom. AI-powered lesson planning from the perspective of pre-service teachers can help stakeholders improve digital teacher training by being more informed, flexible, and responsive. Thus, it can be claimed that exploring the evaluations and beliefs of future teachers using AI for their teaching preparation, could shed light on the effectiveness and practicality of in such tools in educational settings. Additionally, this research can inform the development of training programs that specifically address the needs and concerns of EFL teachers incorporating AI into their teaching practices.

This chapter investigates the evaluations and beliefs of English as a Foreign Language (EFL) pre-service teachers who explored the potential of ChatGPT for creating lesson plans for young learners. After discussing the AI technologies in language teaching and teacher education, the results are presented and discussed accordingly.

LITERATURE REVIEW

AI in Language Teaching

The increasing use of Artificial intelligence (AI) in education (i.e., machine learning, adaptive learning, natural language processing, and data mining (Pokrivčáková, 2019)) highlights AI's potential to revolutionize learning and teaching. The incorporation of AI in language education has resulted in the creation of AI-powered digital learning applications that aid in language acquisition. For example, Ghali et al. (2018) examined the efficacy of an artificial intelligence tool known as the Intelligent Tutoring System in the context of grammar instruction. The study found that by giving students individualized instruction based on student performance data and quick feedback on their responses, this application enhanced learner's comprehension of grammar. In a similar vein, Dewi et al. (2021) investigated AI-powered platforms like Duolingo, Google Translate, and Grammarly to validate whether they improve language proficiency. The study's findings suggest that AI has a positive impact on English language learning and should be included to improve student learning outcomes. Moreover, Fitria (2021) recommended the use of Grammarly, an AI-powered software, to enhance students' writing proficiency. In addition, Toncic (2020) proposed that AI grammar checkers provide significant benefits to instructors by minimizing their workload when grading students' papers. Some of these applications utilize AI-enabled automatic scoring systems, which have been shown to enhance learners' motivation to continue studying (Fu et al., 2020).

In addition to these AI-powered platforms, chatbots have been popular as innovative tools in language teaching, offering unique opportunities to enhance language learning experiences. For example, ChatGPT can be used by learners in text-based tasks ranging from simple inquiries to more complex assignments. Kasneci et al. (2023) investigated the efficacy of ChatGPT in assisting university students with research and writing assignments and detected that ChatGPT improves students' abilities in critical thinking and problem-solving.

Critical viewpoints on AI's use in education highlight its potential to revolutionize education by enhancing efficiency and customizing learning experiences. However, concerns include incorrect use of AI technology, changing roles of instructors and students, and social and ethical issues. It is crucial to approach AI with caution, avoiding its default supremacy. The integration of AI brings unprecedented potential but also presents complex obstacles, causing a paradigm change in teaching and learning. Ethical implications include widespread acceptability and substantial difficulties, economic injustice, transparency, speed, and a human-centered approach (Verdegem, 2021). The use of AI in education also raises issues regarding fair access to computing infrastructure and equipment, transparency, and speed. Ultimately, it is essential to take a cautious and deliberate approach to AI integration, addressing the accompanying obstacles, ethical concerns, and providing fair access to its advantages (Williamson, Eynon, Knox, & Davies, 2023).

Teachers' Perspectives on AI

As Yau et al. (2022) highlighted, there is a need to take teachers' perspectives into account when designing ecologically valid AI education programs. In line with this argument, several studies have been carried out to explore teachers' viewpoints on the use of AI-powered tools in educational settings (Al Darayseh, 2023; Kuleto et al., 2023). The majority of these studies affirm that teachers hold favorable attitudes towards integrating chatbots into language learning and teaching (An et al., 2023; Pokrivčáková, 2019; Sütçü & Sütçü, 2023). Multiple studies on ChatGPT have demonstrated positive attitudes among educators toward its application in education (Limna et al., 2023; Rudolph et al., 2023), despite notable ethical concerns and limitations (Willems, 2023; Zhai, 2022).

The tech-savvy students appreciate its impressive functionalities, while teachers are both astonished and concerned. Teachers' main concerns about ChatGPT is its potential for academic misconduct, particularly regarding cheating (Willems, 2023) The AI-powered chatbot is capable of engaging in complex discussions based on human input, and it can also do diverse jobs like composing essays or finishing examinations. There is a possibility that students may exploit the chatbot to plagiarize replies or seek assistance in completing tasks, potentially engaging in cheating. Furthermore, there is apprehension regarding the potential adverse effects of employing ChatGPT on students' educational encounters (Zhai, 2022). The AI-powered tool has the capability to produce conversational replies based on user input, but it lacks the ability to instruct students on critical thinking or the cultivation of original ideas. There is concern that students may excessively depend on the chatbot and rely on it for problem-solving instead of cultivating their own ideas, perhaps leading to a significant deterioration in the quality of learning results.

Rudolph et al. (2023) proposed that learners may get advantages from experiential learning by using the potential of ChatGPT to provide diverse problem-solving situations. ChatGPT offers the option for students to have individualized training sessions. Hence, AI-marking may reduce the burden of marking for instructors, enabling them to allocate more time towards class preparation. ChatGTP provides significant benefits specifically tailored for learners.

Baskara and Mukarto (2023) conducted a study that revealed the efficacy of ChatGPT in reducing the workload of instructors. The authors highlighted the utility of ChatGPT in supporting educators with tasks such as designing lesson plans, creating educational resources, and facilitating classroom activities. Similarly, Kasneci et al. (2023) supported this assertion by stating that ChatGPT has the potential to reduce the workload of instructors by providing personalized resources and feedback. This allows them to focus on other important aspects of teaching, such as offering captivating and interactive sessions. Zhai (2022) verified the significance of ChatGPT in evaluating the academic achievements of students. According to the study, the tool can provide students with automated assessment and feedback, as well as assistance in proofreading and modifying their written assignments. The study conducted by Moore et al. (2022) provided more support for this assertion by demonstrating that ChatGPT can aid instructors in evaluating students' answers. Rudolph et. al. (2023) highlighted the substantial assistance provided by ChatGPT in analyzing and evaluating student performance. This includes generating tasks, quizzes, and assignments, assessing student work, and offering valuable comments tailored to individual students.

AI in Teacher Education

Several studies have discussed the benefits of generative AI technologies like ChatGPT, to help teachers/ instructors prepare for their teaching. Van der Berg & du Plessis (2023) outline the use of ChatGPT to create customized scenarios for assessing and critically evaluating lesson plans. Aldeman et al. (2021) show how generative AI technologies can foster inspiration and encourage self-reflection in teachers. Huang et al. (2023) emphasize how AI can enhance professional development through teaching assessment models and recommendations for better teaching methods. Finally, Liu et al. (2020) show that AI can provide automated language project assessment and individualized multimodal feedback.

In order to fully benefit from generative AI technologies, however, teachers require effective training to understand what such tools offer and how best they can be used to help prepare for teaching and learning. Dincer (2018) shows how instructors feel challenged when trying to incorporate technology into their teaching and concludes that they require training to properly deploy instructional technology. Similarly, Liden and Nilros (2020) argue that teachers need to be provided with detailed instruction such as the effective use of chatbots, how to integrate them into existing lesson plans, and how to monitor student engagement and achievement to effectively integrate chatbots into pedagogical methodologies. Adding such training into teacher education, especially into pre-service education, is thus critical to ensure a competent use of AI-powered tools in language learning and teaching. As such training is fairly new and improvement is crucial, the study described in this chapter examines the critical evaluation of AI-powered lesson plans by pre-service EFL teachers.

As the first step to improve teacher education programs with training on the use of AI-powered tools, pre-service teachers' perspectives and evaluations of AI-powered ramifications should be examined. Addressing this, the study investigating the EFL future teachers' critical evaluations of AI-powered lesson plans is presented in the following sections.

RESEARCH METHODOLOGY

This study used a mixed-methods approach, which allows simultaneous collection and analysis of both quantitative and qualitative data. This research methodology is in line with the study's objective, which is to extensively investigate the lived experiences and perspectives of pre-service teachers in the context of language instruction. Additionally, the use of a mixed-methods design derives from its adaptability, which permits the incorporation of various data sources to obtain a broader understanding of the research inquiries (Creswell, 2012). This methodology is especially useful for researching complex phenomena, such as the incorporation of artificial intelligence into language instruction, for which a single approach could not adequately capture the complexity and breadth of the phenomenon. This design made it possible to provide a comprehensive and complementary analysis of the various facets of AI integration in language instruction.

The Aim of the Study

This study aims to explore and understand how pre-service English as a Foreign Language (EFL) teachers assess the effectiveness of lesson plans powered by AI, specifically ChatGPT. The primary focus is on gaining insights into the perspectives, criteria, and judgments employed by pre-service EFL teachers when evaluating the impact and appropriateness of AI-generated lesson plans. Through a comprehensive examination of their assessments, the research seeks to contribute valuable insights into integrating AI in educational practices, particularly within the context of language education. Accordingly, the following research question has been asked within the scope of the study:

- How do pre-service English as a Foreign Language (EFL) teachers assess the effectiveness of lesson plans powered by artificial intelligence (AI)?

Participants of the Study

The study involved a diverse group of 43 college students who were actively engaged in a comprehensive training program to become proficient English as a Foreign Language (EFL) teachers. The participants, aged between 21 and 23, were selected from the third year of the undergraduate program. Of the 43 participants, 17 were male and 26 were female, contributing to a balanced sample. Convenience sampling was chosen as the selection process to accommodate the participants' availability and willingness to participate in the study. This diverse group of college students provided valuable insights into the integration of AI in language instruction, considering their current training and future career aspirations as EFL teachers.

The participants were enrolled in two key English Language Teaching (ELT) methodology courses, specifically "Teaching Language Skills" and "Teaching English to Young Learners." These courses played a fundamental role in their professional development as they inquired into both the theoretical foundations and practical aspects of teaching English. The curriculum of these courses included careful exploration of pedagogical theories and methodologies, preparing the participants with a solid understanding of the complexities of language teaching. Additionally, these courses incorporated theory with in-class demonstrations, where the prospective teachers actively applied theoretical knowledge to real classroom scenarios. Additionally, as a requirement of these courses, the participants were expected to write ELT lesson plans to accompany the in-class teaching demonstrations. The participants not only learned about effective teaching strategies but also had the opportunity to enhance their teaching practice through hands-on experience.

Data Collection Procedures and Tools

The authors employed a three-step data collection process to unravel the beliefs of future EFL teachers concerning the use of artificial intelligence in lesson planning. In the initial phase, participants engaged in the creation of AI-powered EFL lesson plans, specifically designed for teaching writing to 5th-grade students. As illustrated in Figure 1, the prompt used to generate lesson plans was as follows: *"Write me a lesson plan for Turkish learners of English in 5th grade to improve their writing skills. The topic of the lesson is superheroes, and the duration is 90 minutes."* All of the participants used the same prompt to create AI-powered lesson plans. This immersive experience aimed not only to familiarize the participants with ChatGPT but also to evaluate its practical utility in the pedagogical context.

Figure 1. Screenshot of the prompt for AI-generated writing lesson plan for 5th graders

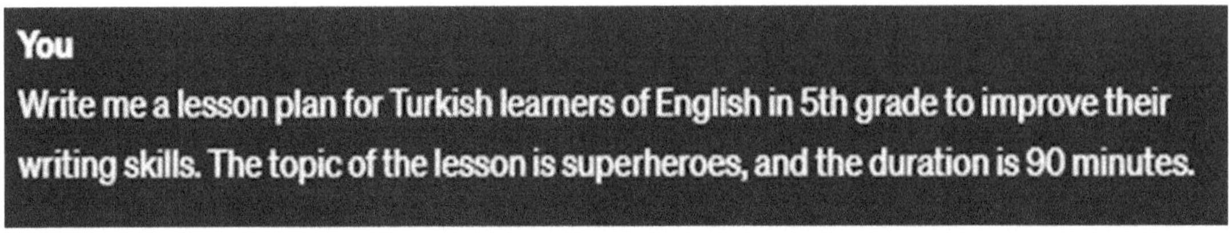

As participants explored the hands-on lesson planning facilitated by ChatGPT, the subsequent phase involved a comprehensive assessment of the effectiveness of the generated lesson plans (Figure 10 and Figure 11 in the Appendix). The authors decided to employ an AI-powered rubric for evaluating the AI-generated lesson plans (Table 3 in the Appendix). The reason was the inherent alignment between the tool's capabilities and the nature of the study. GPT, or Generative Pre-trained Transformer, is a language model designed to generate coherent and contextually relevant text based on the input it receives. Given the complexity of language and the pedagogical considerations involved in crafting a rubric for an AI-generated educational resource, utilizing a rubric generated by the same AI system provided a harmonious and contextually appropriate framework. This approach aimed to maintain consistency in linguistic patterns, educational terminology, and evaluative criteria, thereby enhancing the rubric's relevance to the specific characteristics of the GPT-generated lesson plans.

The AI-written rubric was then reviewed and edited by the authors based on the literature (Carlson et al., 2023; Dwivedi et al., 2023). After the designing process, the final tool emerged as a structured 5-point evaluation rubric, comprising 30 items and 10 sub-dimensions. The internal consistency of the rubric, as measured by Cronbach's alpha, was found to be .875, indicating high internal consistency (Creswell, 2012). This high level of internal consistency suggests that the evaluation rubric is reliable and consistent in measuring the effectiveness of the generated lesson plans. Additionally, the use of a structured 5-point evaluation rubric with 30 items allows for a comprehensive assessment of various aspects of the lesson plans, ensuring a thorough evaluation process. By employing the rubric, the participants were asked to examine the AI tool's capacity to yield desired learning outcomes, construct coherent lesson structures, present meaningful content, and ensure the overall appropriateness of the lesson plans for the specified student profile.

Following the quantitative assessment, participants were prompted to articulate their evaluations in a qualitative format. This crucial step aimed to unearth the underlying rationale behind their rubric scores. Participants were encouraged to provide detailed justifications, offering insights into the specific aspects of the AI-generated lesson plans that influenced their scoring. This qualitative layer added depth to the evaluation process, enriching the understanding of the participants' perceptions and preferences. The final phase of data collection inquired into the participants' beliefs about the integration of AI in language teaching and its potential impact on their professional development. For this phase, a series of probing questions were addressed to the participants. The participants were asked to report on the prospect of incorporating ChatGPT into their future professional endeavors, to reflect on alternative applications of the tool in language teaching, and to consider how they could leverage the AI tool for their personal growth as English language teachers. Questions such as "Do you think you will use this tool in your professional life?" inquired about the participants' inclination toward practical adoption. The inquiry into other potential uses of ChatGPT for language teaching aimed to uncover innovative perspectives and applications beyond the immediate context of lesson planning. Meanwhile, questions like "How can you use this tool for improving yourselves as English language teachers?" examined the participants' introspective analysis, encouraging them to envision the tool as a catalyst for continuous professional development. An overview of the data collection procedures can be viewed in Figure 2 below.

This triangulation of data—quantitative evaluation scores, qualitative justifications, and beliefs expressed through open-ended questions—enabled the researcher to gain a comprehensive understanding of participants' experiences and perspectives. The data collected from the participants allowed the researcher to explore the tool's effectiveness not only in lesson planning but also in broader educational contexts. The participants' reflections on AI written lesson planning would reveal their teaching philosophies, priorities and beliefs. By considering both quantitative evaluation scores and qualitative justifications, the researcher gained a holistic understanding of the participants' experiences and perspectives, ultimately providing a rich foundation for future research and implementation of the tool.

Figure 2. Overview of the data collection procedures

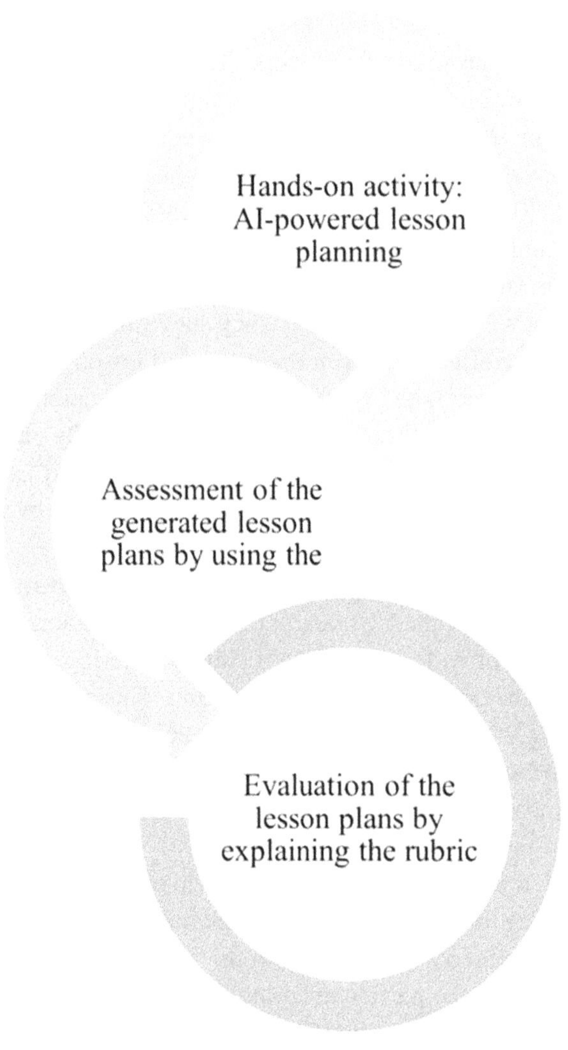

Data Analysis

To investigate the insights garnered from the evaluation rubric, the researchers employed a descriptive statistical approach. The primary aim was to probe into the assessments provided by 43 prospective EFL teachers regarding AI-powered lesson plans. This involved computing total ratings on the rubric, not only for an overall assessment but also for each sub-category presented within the rubric. In addition, the researchers incorporated qualitative data to enhance the quantitative findings with a deeper level of comprehension. This holistic approach sought to illuminate the reasons behind the scores assigned in the rubric, aiming for a comprehensive grasp of the participants' evaluations of AI-generated lesson plans.

In the qualitative analysis phase, the researchers initiated an in-depth exploration of the data. By utilizing memoing techniques, they established associations among emerging concepts, facilitating a sophisticated comprehension of the qualitative components of the evaluations. Memoing is a key technique in qualitative research, where researchers write down their thoughts, insights, and interpretations of the data throughout the research process. Memoing can help to deepen the analysis, generate new ideas, and communicate the findings (Birks, Chapman, & Francis, 2008). Following this exploration, the research team convened for collective negotiation to establish a common coding scheme. This method, a critical component of qualitative analysis, laid the foundation for rendering qualitative insights into structured and analyzable data.

To maintain uniformity among the two raters, the researchers coded 10% of the data, namely selecting five files randomly. Thorough coding and analysis of these data were conducted to evaluate and confirm the consistency amongst different raters. In the coding process, each selected file was carefully examined, and relevant themes, patterns, or categories were identified and labeled. This involved a line-by-line analysis of the content, with careful consideration given to the context of the data. The researchers engaged in a collaborative discussion to ensure a shared understanding of the coding criteria and to resolve any discrepancies that arose during the process. Afterward, the researchers gathered again to utilize the percentage of agreement as a standard for inter-rater reliability. The results showed 83% consensus among the researchers, emphasizing the credibility of the qualitative analysis process (Graham et al., 2012). Subsequently, the research team directed their focus to the remaining dataset. The following phase involved an in-depth coding process and a thorough analysis. Once the coding was completed, the researchers gathered once more to collectively identify and garner the primary findings, ensuring a holistic synthesis of both quantitative and qualitative dimensions.

RESULTS

This part presents the results of the study in a detailed manner, specifically addressing the research issues at hand. By methodically analyzing the collected data, the following sections provide a thorough examination of important themes and trends.

Before presenting the findings of the study, it is worth mentioning how the generated lesson plans were formatted. When asked, ChatGPT started by writing a title for the lesson and then produced the outcomes (objectives) of the lesson. The materials to be used in the class were the following section of the lesson plan and the stages of the writing class were as follows: (i) introduction (15 minutes), (ii) vocabulary building (10 minutes), (iii) warm-up activity (10 minutes), (iv) main writing activity (30 minutes), (v) peer review (15 minutes), (vi) class discussion and reflection (15 minutes) and (vii) closure (no time specification).

Evaluating AI-Powered Lesson Plans

The first research question was, *"How do pre-service English as a Foreign Language (EFL) teachers assess the effectiveness of lesson plans powered by artificial intelligence (AI)?"* To answer this question, the researchers first employed descriptive statistics for the rubric. In the rubric, the scores ranges from the lowest score for the criteria as 1 (very poor) to the highest score 5 (very good). The overall mean score of the whole rubric was 3.54 (SD =.45), which indicated positive evaluations for the AI-generated lesson plans. For further exploration, the sub-dimensions of the rubric were also analyzed in the same manner.

The scores obtained from the rubric suggest high evaluations for some aspects of AI-powered lesson plans, such as engagement and student interaction (M = 4.11, SD =.65), appropriateness (M = 4.05, SD =.78), and lesson structure and organization (M = 3.89, SD =.52). For example, for student interaction, the lesson plan provided several discussion opportunities for the learners at the beginning of the writing class related with the topic of the lesson. Figure 3 illustrates the introduction stage of the lesson. Since the prompt asked to design a writing lesson based on superheroes, the AI tool suggested opening the lesson with a brief discussion about superheroes. Later, the tool integrated another discussion activity around the key characteristics of superheroes. In other words, the tool followed communicative activities to activate the existing schemata of the learners about superheroes.

Figure 3. The introduction stage of the AI-generated lesson plan

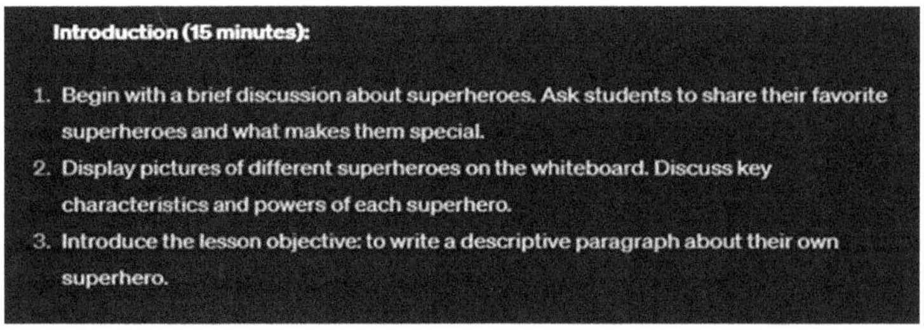

Introduction (15 minutes):

1. Begin with a brief discussion about superheroes. Ask students to share their favorite superheroes and what makes them special.
2. Display pictures of different superheroes on the whiteboard. Discuss key characteristics and powers of each superhero.
3. Introduce the lesson objective: to write a descriptive paragraph about their own superhero.

On a similar note, the activities provided in the lesson were also considered appropriate for the age (5th graders) and language proficiency (A1) (MoNE, 2018) of the learners. Similarly, the lesson structure and organization of the AI-powered writing lesson also scored high on the rubric. Figure 4 presents the main writing activities of the lesson. The AI tool included a template for the writing activity (step 1), asked students to use the newly studied vocabulary items in a meaningful way (step 2), enhanced creative writing (step 3), and added monitoring of the teacher (step 4).

Figure 4. The writing stage of the AI-generated lesson plan

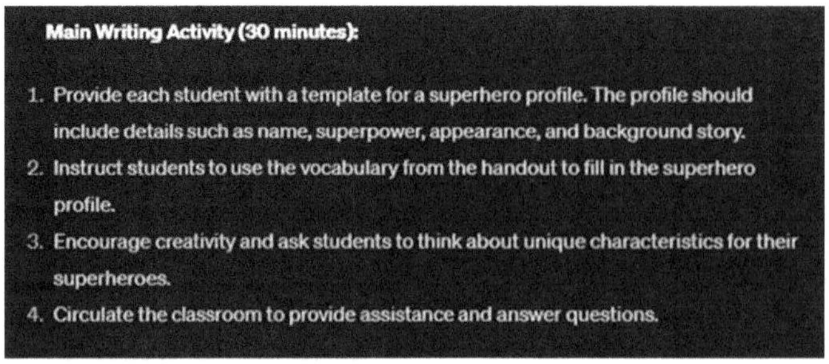

Main Writing Activity (30 minutes):

1. Provide each student with a template for a superhero profile. The profile should include details such as name, superpower, appearance, and background story.
2. Instruct students to use the vocabulary from the handout to fill in the superhero profile.
3. Encourage creativity and ask students to think about unique characteristics for their superheroes.
4. Circulate the classroom to provide assistance and answer questions.

On the other hand, for differentiation and adaptation (M = 2.71, SD =.77) and assessment and feedback (M = 2.98, SD =.85), the same lesson plans were scored below average. To give an example, for differentiation and adaptation, ChatGPT suggested that the participants could change the lesson plan "based on the specific needs and dynamics" of their classes; they felt the lesson was not satisfying in this regard. S3 (Student/participant 3) stated that the lesson plan lacked specific assessment criteria for the students' written work and suggested that the lesson plan needed improvements in terms of *"incorporating differentiation measures, such as modified activities or supplemental materials, would help meet the unique requirements of students and providing them with suitable challenges and assistance"*. Furthermore, for assessment and feedback, the AI-generated lesson plan included a separate stage in the lesson after the main writing activity called "peer review". Figure 5 below presents this stage of the lesson. Although the procedure of this stage was presented, future EFL teachers pointed out the need for a rubric.

Figure 5. The peer-review stage of the AI-generated writing lesson

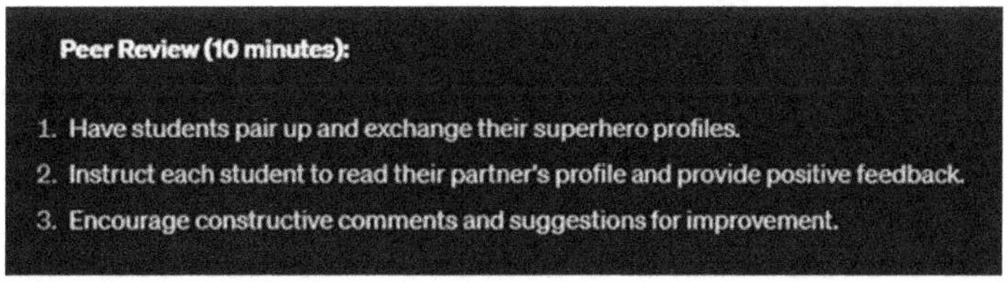

One of the pre-service teachers, S25 wrote *"specific criteria or rubric should be provided for assessing student work"* while S7 underlined that in this stage the teacher needs to give a *"checklist or rubric to the students and they give feedback based on the criteria in the rubric"*. Some participants also observed that there should be a rubric for the main writing task and another one for the speaking activities in the lesson.

These results indicate that AI-powered lesson plans excel in areas such as engagement and student interaction, as well as appropriateness and lesson structure. However, they appear to struggle with differentiation and adaptation, as well as assessment and feedback. This suggests a need for improvement in these specific areas to enhance the overall effectiveness of AI-generated lesson plans. The results can be seen in Table 1 below.

To gain a better understanding of the scores given to the generated lesson plans and to explore the participants' reasoning for those scores, qualitative analysis was conducted as a follow-up. The findings revealed that the participants were generally content with the ELT lesson planning of the AI tool but had some reservations. The emerged themes can be grouped as follows: strengths of the AI-powered lesson plan, areas for improvement, and suggested changes.

*Table 1. Results obtained from the evaluation rubric**

Sub-Dimension	M	*SD*
Engagement and Student Interaction	4.11	.65
Appropriateness	4.05	.78
Lesson Structure and Organization	3.89	.52
Overall Effectiveness	3.73	.58
Learning outcomes	3.62	.93
Content and Resources	3.60	.71
Time Management	3.53	.89
Reflection and Extension	3.24	.86
Assessment and Feedback	2.98	.85
Differentiation and Adaptation	2.71	.77
Overall score	**3.54**	**.45**

*The rubric ranged from 1 (very poor) to 5 (very good).

Table 2. Frequency of the themes emerged for evaluating the AI-powered lesson plans

Themes and Codes	Frequency
Strengths	**232**
Engaging Introduction	43
Clear Outcomes	39
Vocabulary Building	34
Creativity and Collaboration	38
Variety of Activities	41
Reflective closure	37
Areas for Improvement	**111**
Measurable Outcomes	29
Detailed Instructions	32
Time Management	26
Assessment Criteria	24
Suggested Changes	**344**
Enhanced Warm-up	33
Interactive Vocabulary Activities	30
Activity Examples	32
Context Development	28
Clear Instructions	31
Assessment Clarity	29
Optimized Time Management	25
Extension Activities	25

Strengths of AI-Powered Lesson Plans

As illustrated in Table 2, the participants mentioned quite a few strengths of AI-generated ELT lesson plans for teaching writing to 5th graders by using the topic of superheroes. Firstly, the engaging introduction is a positive aspect as it utilizes visuals of superheroes, effectively capturing students' attention and creating an engaging atmosphere. This engagement strategy plays a crucial role in generating interest and establishing a positive tone for the entire lesson. For example, the lesson plan included a description of how the visuals of superheroes are incorporated into an interactive activity where students must identify and name the superheroes. This activity not only grabs students' attention but also activates their prior knowledge and builds anticipation for the rest of the lesson.

Secondly, the lesson plan demonstrates clarity in its outcomes, which are generally clear and specific, providing a well-defined roadmap for both teachers and students. Clear outcomes contribute significantly to effective lesson planning, guiding participants throughout the learning process. In that sense, the participants reported that

Lesson plan the AI created has clear objectives. The objectives of the lesson are well-defined and focused on developing students' writing skills. (S9)

The learning objectives that AI plan consists of are fully clear, specific, and aligned with the activities as well as measurable, and achievable. (S14)

Moreover, the incorporation of vocabulary building was recognized as a strength, employing diverse techniques such as visuals, matching exercises, and sentence usage. Vocabulary building is crucial in this lesson plan because it helps students expand their language skills and enhances their ability to comprehend and express ideas related to superheroes. By introducing new vocabulary through visuals, matching exercises, and sentence usage, students not only learn new words but also gain the confidence to use them effectively in their own writing and communication. This multifaceted approach ensures that different learning styles are accommodated, reinforcing the understanding of newly introduced vocabulary. Figure 6 shows the suggested pre-teaching vocabulary stage of the lesson.

Figure 6. Pre-teaching vocabulary stage of the AI-generated writing lesson

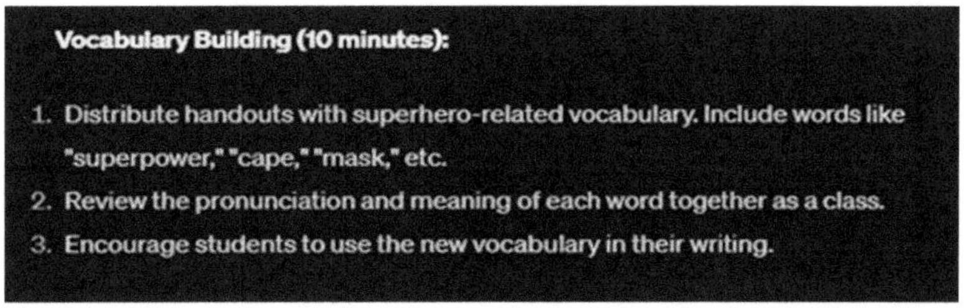

Vocabulary Building (10 minutes):

1. Distribute handouts with superhero-related vocabulary. Include words like "superpower," "cape," "mask," etc.
2. Review the pronunciation and meaning of each word together as a class.
3. Encourage students to use the new vocabulary in their writing.

The results revealed that the AI-powered lesson plan also excels at fostering creativity and collaboration through a writing activity that encourages students to imagine and describe their own superheroes, with an emphasis on peer feedback and collaboration. This approach not only stimulates creativity but also contributes to a supportive classroom environment. Furthermore, the inclusion of a variety of activities, ranging from brainstorming to writing, peer review, and a concluding stage, is a commendable aspect. This diversity caters to different learning preferences, maintaining student interest throughout the lesson. For instance, the brainstorming activity appeals to students who prefer collaborative and interactive learning, as they can engage in discussions and share ideas with their peers. On the other hand, the writing activity caters to students who excel in individual expression and prefer reflective learning. By including both collaborative and individual activities, the lesson plan accommodates a range of learning preferences and ensures that all students can actively participate and contribute. The participants commented as follows:

Students will love to work with the superheroes; the lesson will spark the creativity of the students by making them imagine and write a plot for their superheroes, and peer feedback is also a great way to encourage teamwork and collaboration. (S6)

By providing superhero-themed writing prompts, like imagining a superpower or designing a superhero character, it sparks students' creativity and critical thinking. (P35)

The opportunity for expressing their creativity and practicing their writing skills independently is provided by the individual writing tasks. Engaging in the peer feedback activity encourages collaboration and aids students in cultivating their critical thinking and communication skills. (P40)

Lastly, as another positive aspect, the lesson plan concludes with a reflective stage, allowing students to summarize and share their achievements. This reflective closure promotes metacognition and reinforces key takeaways from the lesson. For instance, as part of the reflective closure, students could be asked to write a short reflection on what they learned during the lesson and how they can apply their new knowledge in real-life situations. This activity prompts students to think metacognitively about their learning process, encouraging them to evaluate their progress and make connections between the lesson content and their own experiences. The screenshot of suggested reflection stage in AI-powered lesson plan is given in Figure 7:

Figure 7. Post-lesson reflection stage of the AI-generated writing lesson

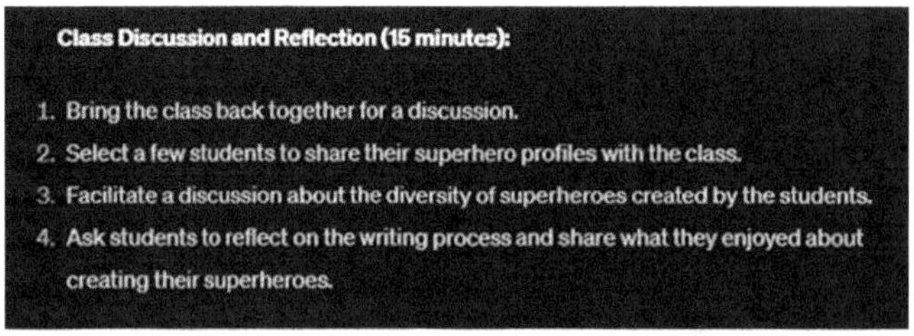

Class Discussion and Reflection (15 minutes):

1. Bring the class back together for a discussion.
2. Select a few students to share their superhero profiles with the class.
3. Facilitate a discussion about the diversity of superheroes created by the students.
4. Ask students to reflect on the writing process and share what they enjoyed about creating their superheroes.

Concerning this theme, the pre-service teachers underlined the importance of reflection for improving the target language skills and stated:

The wrap-up and reflection stages allow students to reflect on their learning and celebrate their accomplishments, instilling a sense of satisfaction and success. (S13)

In this way, the lesson plan gives an opportunity for students to reflect on their own learning and make advancements on their writing. (S20)

In summary, the strengths observed in the lesson plan, including the engaging introduction, clear outcomes, vocabulary building, creativity and collaboration, variety of activities, and reflective closure, collectively contribute to a well-structured and effective learning experience.

Areas for Improvement

In addition to the strengths mentioned above, the prospective EFL teachers also identified some areas for improvement in the generated lesson plans. Firstly, the need for measurable outcomes is highlighted, as some outcomes lack specificity, posing challenges in assessing their achievement. To address this, it is recommended that outcomes be clearly stated using measurable and observable language, ensuring a more accurate evaluation of student progress. For example, instead of stating an outcome as "Students will understand the concept of present simple tense," a more measurable and observable outcome could be "Students will be able to demonstrate their knowledge of the present simple tense by verbally expressing their daily routines." Figure 8 illustrates the outcomes generated by ChatGPT.

Figure 8. The outcomes of the AI-generated writing lesson

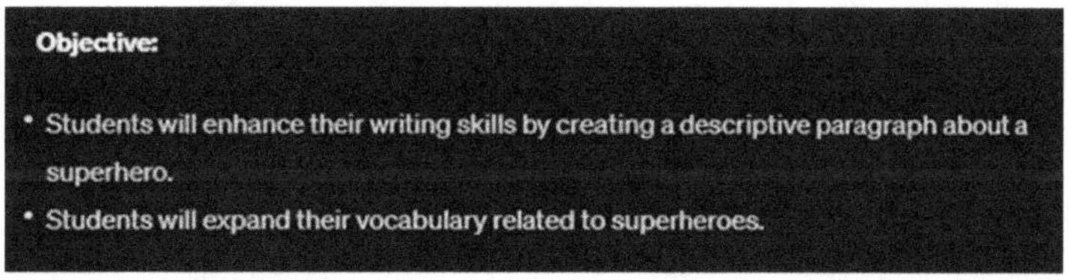

Objective:

- Students will enhance their writing skills by creating a descriptive paragraph about a superhero.
- Students will expand their vocabulary related to superheroes.

Related to the problems about the learning outcomes the participants observed that not every learning activity had an outcome, they were not specific, and detailed. Although in the rubric the score for learning outcomes was high (M=3.62, SD=.93), the specificity and the measurability of the generated outcomes were identified as problematic by the participants.

Firstly, there should be an outcome for each activity, but this lesson plan just gives an objective for the during-stage activity. (S4)

To begin with, the objectives of the plan, not each outcome line, are specific and align with the purpose of the activities. (S11)

Especially for the outcome, it should be more detailed. It says that students will work in pairs or small groups. There should not be an uncertainty like this. Is it in pairs or small groups? If it is in small groups, how many students will be in groups? (S17)

Secondly, the instructions for certain activities, notably the post-writing activity and peer review, were identified as lacking specificity and clarity. To enhance the overall execution of the lesson, it is suggested that detailed instructions be provided for each activity. To give an example, proper instruction needs to have step-by-step guidance, level- and age-appropriate language use, and a time limit. This ensures a smoother and more effective implementation of the lesson plan. For example, S8 indicated that "*the lesson plan could benefit from providing more explicit and detailed instructions for each activity or task.*" *since clear instructions "help students understand what is expected of them and minimize confusion*" (S19). Additionally, about this point, one of the participants observed that the lesson plan did not have instruction-checking questions (ICQs).

Another thing to improve is ICQs and clear instructions in the classroom. Young learners lose their attention easily and if your instructions are not clear or if you do not check whether they understand you or not, you are not going to have a fruitful class, even if it is perfect in every aspect of the paper. ICQs are a must-have in the lesson plan of teachers who are teaching young learners, and this lesson plan does not have them. (S1)

Thirdly, a notable area for improvement is identified in the domain of time management. The allocation of time for certain activities, particularly the introduction stage, is deemed excessive. To prevent students from losing focus, the suggestion is made to adjust time allocations based on the nature of each activity, promoting optimal engagement throughout the lesson. As S26 observed, "*the time limit could be edited to match with young learners' attributes and eased to execute more successful lesson.*" For example, for the introduction stage, the lesson plan could allocate 10 minutes for brainstorming. This would provide a clearer guideline for teachers to follow.

Lastly, the absence of explicit assessment criteria or rubrics for evaluating student work is recognized as a deficiency in the lesson plan. S15 indicated that the *"plan could be evolved to a better version by adding a rubric for feedback."* To address this, it is recommended that clear assessment criteria be incorporated, guiding both teachers and students in understanding expectations and facilitating a more transparent evaluation process.

Suggested Changes for the AI-Generated Lesson Plans

Another recurring theme was how to enhance the generated lesson plans. The participants in the study provided several suggestions for the tool and the lesson plans to improve their quality. Firstly, to enhance the warm-up, it is suggested to infuse more creativity by having the teacher dress as a superhero. This engaging approach, coupled with a context related to a recent superhero movie, can significantly elevate student interest and set a positive tone for the lesson. For example, the teacher could dress as a well-known superhero character like Spiderman or Wonder Woman. They could wear a costume complete with a cape, mask, and emblem. Alternatively, the teacher could create their own superhero persona and design a unique costume that reflects their personality and teaching style.

Secondly, for interactive vocabulary activities, the recommendation is to introduce engaging elements such as word search maps and crossword clues. These interactive tools can reinforce vocabulary understanding in a more enjoyable manner, catering to diverse learning styles. For example, word search maps can help students visually identify and recognize the spelling and meaning of vocabulary words. By searching for words hidden in a grid, students are actively engaging with the vocabulary, which can aid in memorization and comprehension. Crossword clues, on the other hand, require students to think critically about the definitions and connections between words, helping them to understand and apply the vocabulary in context.

Thirdly, to support students in the writing activity, it is proposed to provide examples of the expected paragraph or story beforehand. This addition aims to guide students, ensuring a better understanding of the task and fostering more confident and effective participation. By providing examples, the students can better understand the task requirements and expectations. This can help them develop a clearer idea of the structure, language, and content needed for their own writing. Additionally, seeing examples can boost students' confidence and reduce anxiety, as they have a model to follow and can better envision what a successful piece of writing looks like.

Additionally, to strengthen the context, the proposed change suggests incorporating elements from popular culture, such as discussing a recent Avengers movie. This adjustment aims to make the topic more relatable and engaging for students, connecting the lesson to their real-life experiences. For example, the teacher could start the lesson by asking students if they have seen the recent Avengers movie and what they think about it. This can generate excitement and encourage students to actively participate in the discussion. The teacher could also relate the topic of the lesson to themes or characters from the movie, making connections between the fictional world and the lesson content.

Moreover, in terms of clear instructions, the recommendation is to add explicit guidance, especially for post-writing activities. This change aims to eliminate uncertainties and ensure a smoother flow of the lesson, contributing to a more seamless learning experience. For example, the teacher could provide a set of questions or prompts for students to consider when sharing their work. These questions could ask students to explain their thought processes, justify their choices, or reflect on what they learned from the activity. Additionally, the teacher could model effective sharing techniques, such as active listening and constructive feedback, to ensure a productive and inclusive sharing session.

Furthermore, to address the absence of clear assessment criteria, the proposed change suggests including specific assessment criteria or rubrics. This addition aims to provide transparency and clarity on how student work will be evaluated, facilitating a more structured assessment process. The lesson plans should include evaluation criteria for student work as appendices. Also, to optimize time management, the suggestion is to adjust time allocations for activities based on the attention span of the students. This change aims to ensure optimal engagement throughout the lesson, preventing potential lapses in focus or off-task behavior.

Lastly, the recommendation includes integrating extension activities for students who finish early. This addition aims to provide additional challenges and opportunities for exploration, catering to the varying pace of student learning and promoting continuous engagement. Additionally, the recommendation suggests incorporating regular breaks into the lesson plan to allow students to recharge and maintain their focus. These short breaks can help prevent fatigue and increase productivity during the lesson. Moreover, it is important to create a healthy learning environment by minimizing distractions and providing the necessary resources for students to complete their work effectively. By implementing these strategies, educators can ensure that students are actively engaged and motivated to participate in the lesson.

Synthesizing Quantitative and Qualitative Findings

To answer the research question, which probes into the future teachers' assessments of AI-powered lesson plans, the researchers collated the findings obtained from the evaluation rubric and the qualitative data. As can be seen in Figure 9, the findings revealed that the AI-powered lesson plan demonstrates notable strengths in the domains of engagement and student interaction, appropriateness, and overall lesson structure and organization. Qualitative analysis reveals a consensus among participants, acknowledging the lesson plan's engaging nature, particularly in the warm-up and writing activities. This result aligns with the quantitative analysis, where rubric scores affirm high evaluations for engagement and student interaction (M = 4.11, SD =.65). Additionally, the appropriateness of the lesson plan, characterized by its alignment with 5th-grade students and improved instructions, is supported by both qualitative recognition and high rubric scores (M = 4.05, SD =.78) The well-structured nature of the lesson plan, with commendable transitions between stages and activities, is echoed in qualitative analysis and corroborated by high rubric scores for lesson structure and organization (M = 3.89, SD =.52).

Figure 9. Overview of the evaluation of AI-powered lesson plans

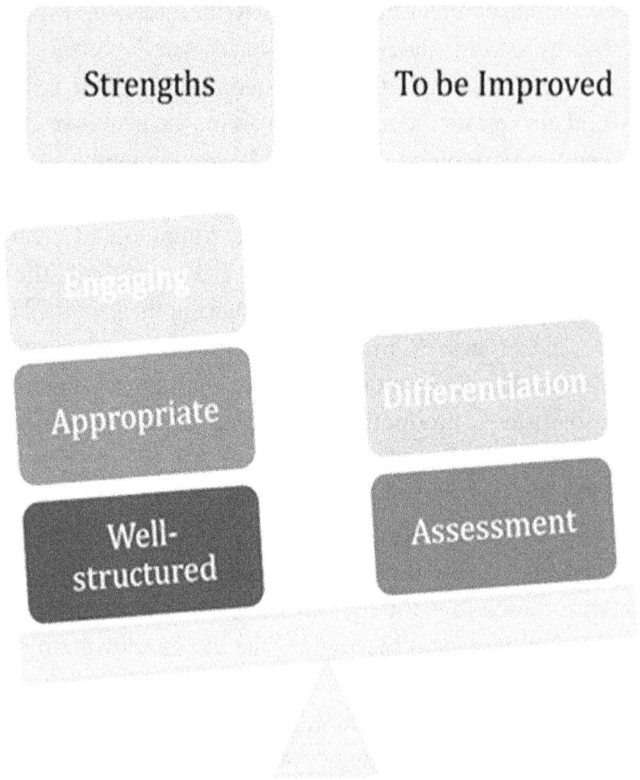

However, the lesson plan also exhibits areas for improvement, particularly in differentiation and adaptation, as identified in both qualitative feedback and low rubric scores (M = 2.71, SD =.77). Participants expressed concerns about the inadequacy of differentiation, advocating for more tailored activities to address varying proficiency levels and cultural relevance. Similarly, deficiencies in feedback and assessment criteria were identified, impacting the overall evaluation process. The quantitative analysis further underscores these concerns, with below-average scores for assessment and feedback (M = 2.98, SD =.85).

To address these areas for improvement, proposed changes focus on enhancing differentiation strategies, refining assessment methods, and introducing diverse language practice activities. These changes aim to elevate the overall quality and effectiveness of the lesson plan by accommodating diverse learning needs, providing clearer assessment criteria, and enriching language practice opportunities.

All in all, the AI-powered lesson plan has been praised for its engagement, student interaction, appropriateness, and overall structure and organization. Participants acknowledged its engaging nature, particularly in warm-up and writing activities. The plan's alignment with 5th-grade students and clear instructions were also praised. However, there are areas for improvement, particularly in differentiation and adaptation. Participants criticized the inadequacy of differentiation and the lack of feedback and assessment criteria. The quantitative analysis also showed below-average scores for assessment and feedback. To address these issues, proposed changes include enhancing differentiation strategies, refining assessment methods, and introducing diverse language practice activities. These changes aim to improve the lesson plan's overall effectiveness by accommodating diverse learning needs, providing clearer assessment criteria, and enriching language practice opportunities. In conclusion, while the lesson plan has strengths, addressing these areas is crucial for optimizing its effectiveness in a diverse classroom setting.

DISCUSSION

The findings of this study provide an in-depth analysis of how pre-service English as a Foreign Language (EFL) instructors evaluate the efficacy of AI-powered lesson plans. The study's goal was to identify differences in numerous areas of artificial intelligence-generated lesson plans and contextualize the findings within the larger framework of the research objectives. By integrating quantitative and qualitative data, this work provides significant contributions to the field of language instruction by highlighting the benefits and limitations of AI-powered lesson design.

In terms of the benefits of lesson plans, the results reveal several notable benefits of AI-generated lesson plans, particularly in terms of student involvement and interaction, overall class structure and organization, and propriety. Higher rubric scores, which indicate positive ratings, are consistent with the participants' qualitative comments. A diversity of activities, a thought-provoking introduction, clear objectives, vocabulary growth, cooperation and creativity, and a reflective conclusion all help to create a cohesive and effective educational experience for the future teachers participating in the study. These findings comply with related studies on the merits of AI in language teaching such as Baskara and Mukarto (2023) and Kasneci et al. (2023), which indicated that ChatGPT provided significant support in reducing teachers' workload, saving time and energy in creating learning materials, and designing learning activities.

Participants in the study questioned the use of AI-powered lesson plans, and for areas for improvement, they identified differentiation and adaptability, evaluation and feedback, and defined assessment criteria. Participants reported some concerns about the lack of differentiation, emphasizing the necessity for activities that are more adaptable to varied skill levels and cultural significance. Furthermore, weaknesses in the criteria for delivering feedback and grading performance were discovered, affecting the overall evaluation process. These findings are supported by quantitative data, which reveals that differentiation and adaptation, as well as assessment and feedback, received below-average scores. The proposed changes aim to address these concerns by including more student-centered activities, creating clear and explicit evaluation criteria, and improving assessment methodologies to respond to students' diverse learning needs while simultaneously ensuring a clear and effective evaluation approach. These results point out the similar apprehension commonly mentioned in the related literature. For instance, Zhai (2022) underlined the fact that AI lacks the emotional support and the interpersonal connection necessary for effective teaching despite its huge potential to deliver specific and pertinent information. Thus, as the participants reported, ChatGPT possesses remarkable qualities in generating educational resources including lesson plans, visual presentations, worksheets, and assessment assignments, nonetheless, it cannot replace teachers.

Participants make useful suggestions for increasing the quality of artificial intelligence-generated lesson plans. Among the suggested measures are increasing the amount of creativity in warm-up activities, including interactive vocabulary exercises, giving visuals for writing tasks, strengthening the contextual framework through its relationship to popular culture, and streamlining time management. Participants suggested adjustments to activity time allotment, clear instructions, and straightforward evaluation methods. The modifications are intended to remove ambiguity, provide more clear work instructions, and ensure maximum involvement throughout the educational session.

While the transition from positive evaluations to effective classroom implementation requires careful consideration of pedagogical strategies, teacher roles, and student engagement, the preliminary results of the study suggest advantageous uses of AI in education. The findings underscore that ChatGPT can be a valuable tool for English language teachers in generating lesson plans and providing a wide range of ideas and activities. Its flexibility allows for personalized lesson plans based on individual student needs and interests, saving time and effort for teachers seeking inspiration and diversifying teaching strategies. As for teacher professional development, the data suggests that ChatGPT can serve as a resource for teachers, helping them stay updated on language teaching advancements and providing insights into different approaches and methodologies. It can assist teachers in designing materials, activities, and resources for language teaching. Additionally, the participants indicated that ChatGPT can be utilized to improve their problem-solving skills, self-evaluate, and assess their teaching practices, and assist in overcoming challenges such as student engagement and time management.

The clarity in outcomes and vocabulary building received commendations, aligning with the literature's emphasis on the importance of clear learning objectives and effective vocabulary instruction (Ghali et al., 2018; Dewi et al., 2021). The study's participants recognized the significance of well-defined outcomes and diverse vocabulary-building techniques, such as visuals, matching exercises, and sentence usage, in facilitating language acquisition.

The study's focus on creativity and collaboration in writing activities draws parallels with the literature's exploration of the benefits of AI tools in promoting critical thinking and problem-solving (Kasneci et al., 2023). The participants acknowledged the AI-powered lesson plans for fostering creativity through activities that encourage students to imagine and describe their own superheroes, emphasizing the positive impact on students' creative expression and collaboration.

The variety of activities and reflective closure received positive feedback, reinforcing the literature's recognition of diverse instructional strategies and the importance of metacognition in learning (Toncic, 2020; Liu et al., 2020). The study's participants appreciated the inclusion of activities ranging from brainstorming to writing, peer review, and reflective closure, catering to different learning preferences and promoting reflective thinking.

Despite the strengths identified, the study revealed areas for improvement, particularly in differentiation and adaptation, and assessment and feedback. The participants expressed concerns about the need for more tailored activities to address varying proficiency levels and cultural relevance, aligning with literature that highlights the challenges of effectively integrating AI tools into diverse classroom settings (Dincer, 2018).

The deficiency in explicit assessment criteria and feedback, as identified in both qualitative feedback and low rubric scores (M = 2.98, SD =.85), supports existing literature emphasizing the importance of clear assessment methods and criteria (Meyer et al., 2023). The study's participants recognized the need for measurable outcomes, detailed instructions, and explicit assessment criteria to enhance the overall execution of the lesson plans. In addition, the results support the literature's emphasis on the need for effective differentiation strategies, clear assessment criteria, and diverse language practice activities (Liden & Nilros, 2020).

CONCLUSION

In conclusion, this study contributes valuable insights into the evolving role of teachers in an AI-augmented educational landscape. It is crucial to comprehend not only AI's technical functionalities but also educators' perceptions and experiences as tools like ChatGPT become potential ultimate lesson planners. By bridging the gap between generative AI and the social dynamics of language education, this research opens avenues for informed integration, ensuring that AI serves as a supportive ally in shaping the future of language learning and teaching.

This chapter investigated the assessment of AI-powered lesson plans by pre-service EFL teachers, offering valuable insights into both the strengths and areas for improvement in integrating artificial intelligence into language education. The findings underscore the positive impact of AI on aspects such as engagement, clarity of outcomes, vocabulary building, creativity, and collaboration, while also identifying specific challenges related to differentiation, adaptation, and assessment practices. Still keeping in mind that the paramount role of teachers to have effective and successful lesson as they implement the lesson plans, AI is accepted by the participants in the study as an effective tool that can scaffold teachers with good lesson planning components and ideas.

Implications

The implications of this study extend to both practitioners and researchers in the field of language education. For educators, the identified strengths of AI-powered lesson plans highlight the potential for enhancing student engagement, language acquisition, and collaborative learning experiences. The study's recommendations for improvement, particularly in the areas of differentiation and assessment, provide practical insights for educators seeking to optimize the use of AI tools in diverse classroom settings. Additionally, the study emphasizes the importance of clear communication of learning objectives, explicit assessment criteria, and the need for tailored activities to address students' varying proficiency levels. For practice, the teachers could ask ChatGPT to propose specific assessment criteria or rubrics, differentiated learning tasks, and better learning outcomes based on their context of teaching. To achieve this, the teachers need AI literacy and competency.

In the rapidly evolving landscape of educational technology, the role of teachers becomes pivotal in ensuring the effective integration and utilization of AI-powered tools. As this study underscores the benefits and challenges associated with AI-powered lesson planning, it becomes evident that preparing teachers to harness the potential of artificial intelligence is crucial for maximizing its impact in the classroom. Training AI-ready teachers involves more than just technical proficiency; it encompasses developing a practical understanding of AI's capabilities, limitations, and its pedagogical implications. Educators need to be equipped with the skills to navigate AI-powered environments, interpret data-driven insights, and tailor their instructional approaches to complement the capabilities of AI tools. In other words, the teachers need to have AI literacy skills and AI competency to productively use generative chatbots for educational purposes. Moreover, fostering a mindset of adaptability and continuous learning is essential, considering the dynamic nature of technological advancements. By investing in comprehensive training programs, educational institutions can empower teachers to leverage AI not as a replacement but as a powerful ally, enhancing their capacity to create innovative and personalized learning experiences for their students. As we move towards an AI-augmented educational future, nurturing a team of AI-ready teachers is not merely advantageous but imperative for ensuring the transformative potential of technology in the hands of skilled and informed educators.

For researchers, the understanding of AI's role in language education contributes to the ongoing discourse on technology-enhanced pedagogy. The study suggests that while AI holds promise in certain aspects of lesson planning, addressing specific challenges is imperative for its effective integration. Future research endeavors could focus on refining AI algorithms to better cater to diverse learning needs, exploring innovative strategies for adapting AI-powered lesson plans to different cultural contexts, and developing comprehensive frameworks for assessing student performance in AI-powered language learning environments.

Suggestions for Future Research

The study points towards several promising avenues for future research. Although the present study implemented a hands-on approach for AI lesson planning, future research could focus on the implementation of AI-powered lessons in real classrooms. It would be interesting to observe and investigate if AI lesson plans can accommodate the diverse language teaching settings and/or how the teachers evaluate them after actual implementation in the class. Furthermore, exploring the long-term impact of AI integration in language education, both on student outcomes and teacher practices, presents an intriguing area for future inquiry. Longitudinal studies could provide insights into the sustainability of positive effects and the potential adaptations required over time. Additionally, comparative studies across different AI platforms and tools could offer a comprehensive understanding of the strengths and limitations inherent in various AI-powered approaches.

Limitations of the Study

Despite the valuable insights gained, this study is not without limitations. Firstly, the sample primarily consisted of 43 pre-service EFL teachers, potentially limiting the generalizability of the findings to experienced educators. Future research could benefit from a more diverse participant pool, including in-service teachers with varied levels of technological proficiency. Secondly, the study focused on a specific context and topic (teaching writing to 5th graders using the theme of superheroes). While this specificity allowed for a detailed examination, it may restrict the broader applicability of the findings. Replicating the study across different language skills, grade levels, and topics could provide a more comprehensive understanding of AI's effectiveness in diverse educational settings. Lastly, the study employed a single AI tool for lesson plan generation (ChatGPT). While this allowed for a focused investigation, different AI tools may yield varied results. Comparative studies involving multiple AI platforms could offer a nuanced understanding of the strengths and limitations inherent in each tool.

In conclusion, this study contributes to the growing body of research on AI in language education, offering practical insights for educators and valuable considerations for future research endeavors. As technology continues to evolve, understanding the intricacies of AI's role in language teaching becomes increasingly critical. By addressing the identified limitations and building on the implications and future research directions outlined in this study, educators and researchers can collectively contribute to the refinement and effective integration of AI into language education, ultimately enhancing the learning experiences of students in an ever-evolving educational landscape.

REFERENCES

Al Darayseh, A. (2023). Acceptance of artificial intelligence in teaching science: Science teachers' perspective. *Computers and Education: Artificial Intelligence*, *4*, 100–132. doi:10.1016/j.caeai.2023.100132

Aldeman, N. L. S., Aita, K., Machado, V. P., da Mata Sousa, L. C. D., Coelho, A. G. B., da Silva, A. S., Mendes, A. P. D., Neres, F. J. D., & do Monte, S. J. H. (2021). Smartpath (k): A platform for teaching glomerulopathies using machine learning. *BMC Medical Education*, *21*(1), 248. doi:10.1186/s12909-021-02680-1 PMID:33926437

Almutairi, A., Gegov, A., Adda, M., & Arabikhan, F. (2020). Conceptual artificial intelligence framework to improving English as second language. *WSEAS Transactions on Advances in Engineering Education*, *17*, 87–91. doi:10.37394/232010.2020.17.11

An, X., Chai, C. S., Li, Y., Zhou, Y., Shen, X., Zheng, C., & Chen, M. (2023). Modeling English teachers' behavioral intention to use artificial intelligence in middle schools. *Education and Information Technologies*, *28*(5), 5187–5208. doi:10.1007/s10639-022-11286-z

Baskara, R. (2023). Exploring the implications of ChatGPT for language learning in higher education. *Indonesian Journal of English Language Teaching and Applied Linguistics*, *7*(2), 343–358.

Bibauw, S., François, T., & Desmet, P. (2019). Discussing with a computer to practice a foreign language: Research synthesis and conceptual framework of dialogue-based call. *Computer Assisted Language Learning*, *32*(8), 827–877. doi:10.1080/09588221.2018.1535508

Birks, M., Chapman, Y., & Francis, K. (2008). Memoing in qualitative research: Probing data and processes. *Journal of Research in Nursing*, *13*(1), 68–75. doi:10.1177/1744987107081254

Carlson, M., Pack, A., & Escalante, J. (2023). Utilizing OpenAI's GPT-4 for written feedback. *TESOL Journal*, *759*, e759. Advance online publication. doi:10.1002/tesj.759

Chen, L., Chen, P., & Lin, Z. (2020). Artificial Intelligence in Education: A Review. *IEEE Access : Practical Innovations, Open Solutions*, *8*, 75264–75278. doi:10.1109/ACCESS.2020.2988510

Creswell, J. W. (2012). *Educational research.* Pearson.

Dewi, H. K., Putri, R. E., Rahim, N. A., Wardani, T. I., & Pandin, M. G. R. (2021). *The use of AI (artificial intelligence) in English learning among university student: Case study in English Department, Universitas Airlangga.* https://doi.org/ doi:10.31235/osf.io/x3qr6

Dincer, S. (2018). Are preservice teachers really literate enough to integrate technology in their classroom practice? Determining the technology literacy level of preservice teachers. *Education and Information Technologies*, *23*(6), 2699–2718. doi:10.1007/s10639-018-9737-z

Dwivedi, Y. K., Kshetri, N., Hughes, L., Slade, E. L., Jeyaraj, A., Kar, A. K., Baabdullah, A. M., Koohang, A., Raghavan, V., Ahuja, M., Albanna, H., Albashrawi, M. A., Al-Busaidi, A. S., Balakrishnan, J., Barlette, Y., Basu, S., Bose, I., Brooks, L., Buhalis, D., ... Wright, R. (2023). Opinion Paper: "So what if ChatGPT wrote it?" Multidisciplinary perspectives on opportunities, challenges and implications of generative conversational AI for research, practice and policy. *International Journal of Information Management*, *71*, 102642. doi:10.1016/j.ijinfomgt.2023.102642

Fitria, T. N. (2021). Grammarly" as AI-powered English Writing Assistant. *Journal of English Language Literature and Teaching, 5*(1), 65-78.

Fu, S., Gu, H., & Yang, B. (2020). The affordances of AI-enabled automatic scoring applications on learners' continuous learning intention: An empirical study in China. *British Journal of Educational Technology*, *51*(5), 1674–1692. doi:10.1111/bjet.12995

Ghali, M. A., Ayyad, A. A., Abu-Naser, S. S., & Abu, M. (2018). An Intelligent Tutoring System for Teaching English Grammar. *International Journal of Academic Engineering Research*, *2*(2), 1–6.

Graham, M., Milanowski, A., & Miller, J. (2012). *Measuring and Promoting Inter-Rater Agreement of Teacher and Principal Performance Ratings*. Online Submission.

Hang, N. T. T. (2023). EFL Teachers' Perspectives toward the Use of ChatGPT in Writing Classes: A Case Study at Van Lang University. *International Journal of Language Instruction*, *2*(3), 1–47. doi:10.54855/ijli.23231

Hong, W. C. H. (2023). The impact of ChatGPT on foreign language teaching and learning: Opportunities in education and research. *Journal of Educ. Technol. Innov.*, *5*, 37–45.

Huang, W., Hew, K. F., & Fryer, L. K. (2022). Chatbots for language learning – are they really useful? A systematic review of chatbot-supported language learning. *Journal of Computer Assisted Learning*, *38*(1), 237–257. doi:10.1111/jcal.12610

Jaiswal, A., & Arun, C. J. (2021). Potential of artificial intelligence for transformation of the education system in India. *International Journal of Education and Development Using Information and Communication Technology*, *17*(1), 142–158.

Kannan, J., & Munday, P. (2018). New trends in second language learning and teaching through the lens of ICT, networked learning, and artificial intelligence. *Círculo de Lingüística Aplicada a la Comunicación*, *76*, 13–30. doi:10.5209/CLAC.62495

KasneciE.SeßlerK.KüchemannS.BannertM.DementievaD.FischerF.NerdelC. (2023). Chatgpt for good? on opportunities and challenges of large language models for education. https://doi.org/ doi:10.35542/osf.io/5er8f

Kehoe, F. (2023). Leveraging generative ai tools for enhanced lesson planning in initial teacher education at post primary. *Irish Journal of Technology Enhanced Learning*, *7*(2), 172–182. doi:10.22554/ijtel.v7i2.124

König, J., Bremerich-Vos, A., Buchholtz, C., Fladung, I., & Glutsch, N. (2019). Pre–service teachers' generic and subject-specific lesson-planning skills: On learning adaptive teaching during initial teacher education. *European Journal of Teacher Education*, *43*(2), 131–150. doi:10.1080/02619768.2019.1679115

Kuleto, V., Ilić, M. P., Bucea-Manea-Ţoniş, R., Ciocodeică, D. F., Mihălcescu, H., & Mindrescu, V. (2022). The Attitudes of K–12 Schools' Teachers in Serbia towards the Potential of Artificial Intelligence. *Sustainability (Basel)*, *14*(14), 8636. doi:10.3390/su14148636

Lee, D., Kim, H., & Sung, S. (2022). Development research on an AI English learning support system to facilitate learner-generated-context-based learning. *Educational Technology Research and Development*, *71*(2), 629–666. doi:10.1007/s11423-022-10172-2 PMID:36533222

Lee, I., & Perret, B. (2022). Preparing high school teachers to integrate AI methods into STEM classrooms. *Proceedings of the AAAI Conference on Artificial Intelligence*, *36*(11), 12783–12791. doi:10.1609/aaai.v36i11.21557

Li, R. (2020). Using artificial intelligence in learning English as a foreign language: An examination of IELTS Liulishuo as an online platform. *Journal of Higher Education Research*, *1*(2). Advance online publication. doi:10.32629/jher.v1i2.178

Lidén, A., & Nilros, K. (2020). *Perceived benefits and limitations of chatbots in higher education* (Dissertation). Retrieved from https://urn.kb.se/resolve?urn=urn:nbn:se:lnu:diva-96327

Limna, P., Kraiwanit, T., Jangjarat, K., Klayklung, P., & Chocksathaporn, P. (2023). The use of ChatGPT in the digital era: Perspectives on chatbot implementation. *Journal of Applied Learning and Teaching*, *6*(1).

Meyer, J. G., Urbanowicz, R. J., Martin, P. C. N., O'Connor, K., Li, R., Peng, P.-C., Bright, T. J., Tatonetti, N., Won, K. J., Gonzalez-Hernandez, G., & Moore, J. H. (2023). ChatGPT and large language models in academia: Opportunities and challenges. *BioData Mining*, *16*(20), 20. Advance online publication. doi:10.1186/s13040-023-00339-9 PMID:37443040

Ministry of National Education. (2018). *Ortaöğretim İngilizce dersi (9, 10, 11 ve 12. sınıflar) öğretim programı* [Secondary school English course (grades 9, 10, 11 and 12) curriculum]. http://mufredat.meb.gov.tr/ProgramDetay.aspx?PID=342

Nazaretsky, T., Ariely, M., Cukurova, M., & Alexandron, G. (2022). Teachers' trust in AI-powered educational technology and a professional development program to improve it. *British Journal of Educational Technology*, *53*(4), 914–931. doi:10.1111/bjet.13232

Öztürk, G., & Aydin, B. (2019). English language teacher education in turkey: Why do we fail and what policy reforms are needed? *Anadolu Journal of Educational Sciences International*, *9*(1), 181–213. doi:10.18039/ajesi.520842

Pack, A., & Maloney, J. (2023). Using generative artificial intelligence for language education research: Insights from using OpenAI's ChatGPT. *TESOL Quarterly*, *57*(4), 1571–1582. doi:10.1002/tesq.3253

Pedró, F., Subosa, M., Rivas, A., & Valverde, P. (2019). *Artificial intelligence in education: Challenges and opportunities for sustainable development*. UNESCO.

Pokrivčáková, S. (2019). Preparing teachers for the application of ai-powered technologies in foreign language education. *Journal of Language and Cultural Education*, *7*(3), 135–153. doi:10.2478/jolace-2019-0025

Republic of Türkiye Ministry of National Education. (2018). *English Curriculum for Primary and Secondary Schools*. Retrieved from: https://mufredat.meb.gov.tr/Dosyalar/201812411191321-%C4%B0NG%C4%B0L%C4%B0ZCE%20%C3%96%C4%9ERET%C4%B0M%20PROGRAMI%20Klas%C3%B6r%C3%BC.pdf

Rudolph, J., Tan, S., & Tan, S. (2023). ChatGPT: Bullshit spewer or the end of traditional assessments in higher education? *Journal of Applied Learning and Teaching*, *6*(1).

Schuengel, C., & van Heerden, A. (2023). Editorial: Generative artificial intelligence and the ecology of human development. *Journal of Child Psychology and Psychiatry, and Allied Disciplines*, *64*(9), 1261–1263. doi:10.1111/jcpp.13860 PMID:37528517

SlimiZ. (2021). The impact of AI implementation in higher education on educational process future: A systematic review, Research Square. doi:10.21203/rs.3.rs-1081043/v1

Sun, Z., Anbarasan, M., & Kumar, D. (2020). Design of online intelligent English teaching platform based on artificial intelligence techniques. *Computational Intelligence*, *37*(3), 1166–1180. doi:10.1111/coin.12351

Sütçü, S. S., & Sütçü, E. (2023). English Teachers' Attitudes and Opinions Towards Artificial Intelligence. *International Journal of Research in Teacher Education*, *14*(3).

Toncic, J. (2020). Teachers, AI Grammar Checkers, and the Newest Literacies: Emending Writing Pedagogy. *Digital Culture & Education*, *12*(1), 26–51.

Vall, R., & Araya, F. (2023). Exploring the benefits and challenges of ai-language learning tools. *The International Journal of Social Sciences and Humanities Invention*, *10*(01), 7569–7576. doi:10.18535/ijsshi/v10i01.02

van den Berg, G., & du Plessis, E. (2023). ChatGPT and Generative AI: Possibilities for Its Contribution to Lesson Planning, Critical Thinking and Openness in Teacher Education. *Education Sciences*, *13*(10), 998. doi:10.3390/educsci13100998

Verdegem, P. (2021). Introduction: Why We Need Critical Perspectives on AI. In P. Verdegem (Ed.), *AI for Everyone?: Critical Perspectives* (pp. 1–18). University of Westminster Press. doi:10.16997/book55.a

Willems, J. (2023). *ChatGPT at Universities – The Least of Our Concerns* (*SSRN* Scholarly Paper No. 4334162). doi:10.2139/ssrn.4334162

Williamson, B., Eynon, R., Knox, J., & Davies, H. C. (2023). Critical perspectives on AI in education: Political economy, discrimination, commercialization, governance and ethics. In B. du Boulay, A. Mitrovic, & K. Yacef (Eds.), *The handbook of artificial intelligence in education* (pp. 555–573). Edward Elgar Publishing Ltd. doi:10.4337/9781800375413.00037

Yang, H., & Kyun, S. (2022). The current research trend of artificial intelligence in language learning: A systematic empirical literature review from an activity theory perspective. *Australasian Journal of Educational Technology*, *38*(5), 180–210. doi:10.14742/ajet.7492

Yau, K., Chai, C., Chiu, T., Meng, H., King, I., & Yam, Y. (2022). A phenomenographic approach on teacher conceptions of teaching artificial intelligence (AI) in K-12 schools. *Education and Information Technologies*, *28*(1), 1041–1064. doi:10.1007/s10639-022-11161-x

Yildirim, Y., Arslan, E. A., Yildirim, K., & Bisen, I. E. (2021). Reimagining education with artificial intelligence. *Eurasian Journal of Higher Education*, *2*(4), 32–46. doi:10.31039/ejohe.2021.4.52

Zhai, X. (2022). *ChatGPT User Experience: Implications for Education* (*SSRN* Scholarly Paper No. 4312418). doi:10.2139/ssrn.4312418

ADDITIONAL READING

Boubker, O. (2024). From chatting to self-educating: Can AI tools boost student learning outcomes? *Expert Systems with Applications*, *238*, 121820. doi:10.1016/j.eswa.2023.121820

Cotton, D., Cotton, P. A., & Shipway, J. R. (2023). Chatting and cheating: Ensuring academic integrity in the era of ChatGPT. *Innovations in Education and Teaching International*, 1–12. doi:10.1080/14703297.2023.2190148

Fütterer, T., Fischer, C., Alekseeva, A., Chen, X., Tate, T., Warschauer, M., & Gerjets, P. (2023). ChatGPT in education: Global reactions to AI innovations. *Scientific Reports*, *13*(1), 15310. Advance online publication. doi:10.1038/s41598-023-42227-6 PMID:37714915

Hashem, R., Ali, N., El Zein, F., Fidalgo, P., & Abu Khurma, O. (2023). Ai to the rescue: exploring the potential of ChatGPT as a teacher ally for workload relief and burnout prevention. *Research and Practice in Technology Enhanced Learning, 19*, 23. doi:10.58459/rptel.2024.19023

Javier, D. R. C., & Moorhouse, B. L. (2023). Developing secondary school English language learners' productive and critical use of ChatGPT. *TESOL Journal*, *00*, e755. doi:10.1002/tesj.755

Rudolph, J., Tan, S. & Tan, S. (2023). *War of the chatbots: Bard, Bing chat, ChatGPT, Ernie and beyond: The new AI gold rush and its impact on higher education.* doi:10.37074/jalt.2023.6.1.23

Tlili, A., Shehata, B., Adarkwah, M. A., Bozkurt, A., Hickey, D. T., Huang, R., & Agyemang, B. (2023). What if the devil is my guardian angel: ChatGPT as a case study of using chatbots in education. *Smart Learning Environments*, *10*(1), 15. Advance online publication. doi:10.1186/s40561-023-00237-x

KEY TERMS AND DEFINITIONS

AI Competence: The collective set of skills, knowledge, and attitudes required for effectively understanding, implementing, and navigating the use of artificial intelligence in educational settings.

AI Literacy: The set of skills covering understanding, utilizing, and critically evaluating artificial intelligence technologies.

Generative AI: A wing of artificial intelligence (AI) that focuses on creating systems capable of producing human-like outputs, such as language, images, or other forms of content.

Lesson Planning: The systematic process of designing and organizing instructional activities, materials, and assessments to achieve specific learning objectives within a given timeframe.

Pedagogical Context: The specific teaching and learning conditions, including instructional methods, classroom dynamics, and educational objectives, within which a particular educational intervention or tool, such as ChatGPT, is implemented.

Rubric Assessment: A systematic and structured evaluation process that utilizes a rubric with predefined criteria and scales to assign numerical scores, providing a quantitative measure.

APPENDIX

Figure 10 and Figure 11 Screenshots of an Example AI-generated Writing Lesson Plan

Figure 10. Examples of AI-generated writing lesson plan

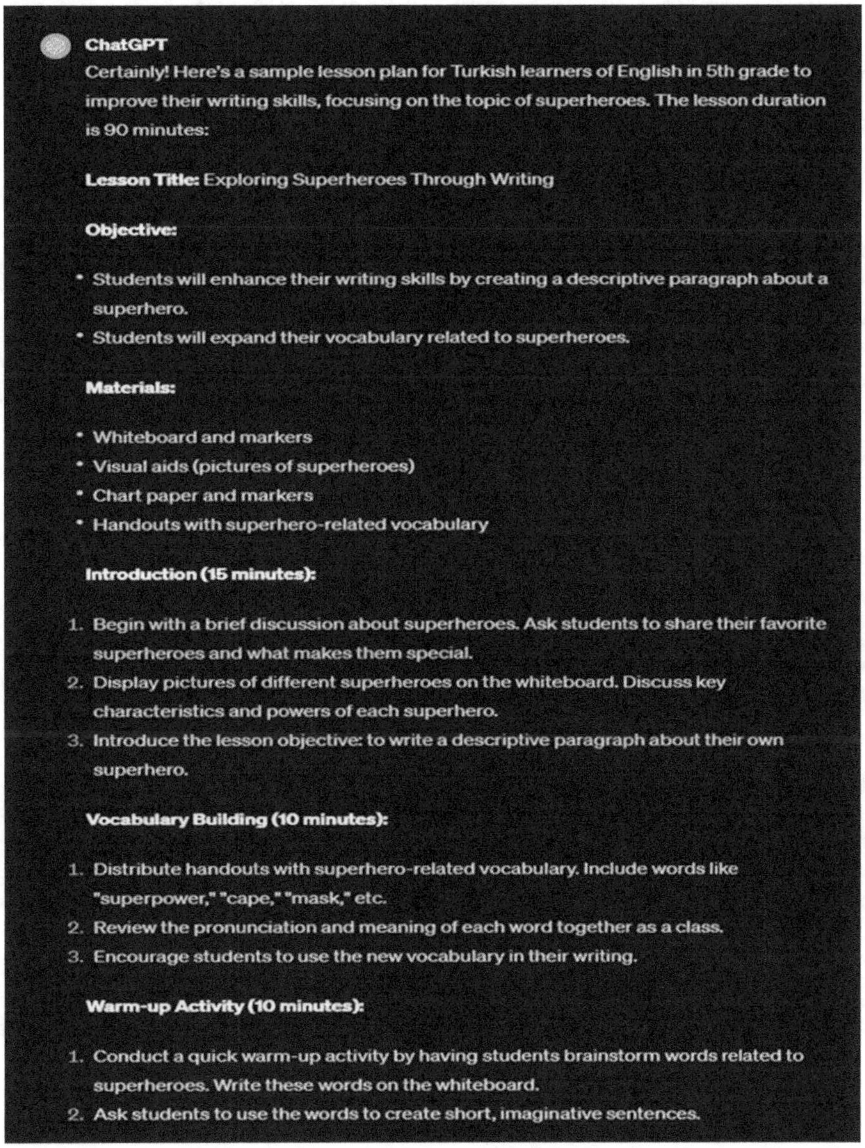

ChatGPT

Certainly! Here's a sample lesson plan for Turkish learners of English in 5th grade to improve their writing skills, focusing on the topic of superheroes. The lesson duration is 90 minutes:

Lesson Title: Exploring Superheroes Through Writing

Objective:

- Students will enhance their writing skills by creating a descriptive paragraph about a superhero.
- Students will expand their vocabulary related to superheroes.

Materials:

- Whiteboard and markers
- Visual aids (pictures of superheroes)
- Chart paper and markers
- Handouts with superhero-related vocabulary

Introduction (15 minutes):

1. Begin with a brief discussion about superheroes. Ask students to share their favorite superheroes and what makes them special.
2. Display pictures of different superheroes on the whiteboard. Discuss key characteristics and powers of each superhero.
3. Introduce the lesson objective: to write a descriptive paragraph about their own superhero.

Vocabulary Building (10 minutes):

1. Distribute handouts with superhero-related vocabulary. Include words like "superpower," "cape," "mask," etc.
2. Review the pronunciation and meaning of each word together as a class.
3. Encourage students to use the new vocabulary in their writing.

Warm-up Activity (10 minutes):

1. Conduct a quick warm-up activity by having students brainstorm words related to superheroes. Write these words on the whiteboard.
2. Ask students to use the words to create short, imaginative sentences.

Figure 11. Examples of AI-generated writing lesson plan

Main Writing Activity (30 minutes):

1. Provide each student with a template for a superhero profile. The profile should include details such as name, superpower, appearance, and background story.
2. Instruct students to use the vocabulary from the handout to fill in the superhero profile.
3. Encourage creativity and ask students to think about unique characteristics for their superheroes.
4. Circulate the classroom to provide assistance and answer questions.

Peer Review (10 minutes):

1. Have students pair up and exchange their superhero profiles.
2. Instruct each student to read their partner's profile and provide positive feedback.
3. Encourage constructive comments and suggestions for improvement.

Class Discussion and Reflection (15 minutes):

1. Bring the class back together for a discussion.
2. Select a few students to share their superhero profiles with the class.
3. Facilitate a discussion about the diversity of superheroes created by the students.
4. Ask students to reflect on the writing process and share what they enjoyed about creating their superheroes.

Closure:

- Summarize the key points of the lesson.
- Assign homework for students to write a short paragraph about how their superhero helps others.

This lesson plan aims to engage students with the topic of superheroes while providing opportunities for vocabulary expansion and creative writing. Feel free to adjust the activities based on the specific needs and dynamics of your classroom.

Table 3. AI-generated lesson plan evaluation rubric

Criteria	1 Very Poor	2 Poor	3 Average	4 Good	5 Very Good
A. Learning outcomes:					
1. Are the outcomes clear, specific, and aligned with the activities in the lesson?					
2. Do the outcomes cover the necessary knowledge, skills, and understanding?					
3. Are the outcomes measurable and achievable?					
B. Content and Resources:					
4. Is the content relevant for the target audience?					
5. Are the resources well-selected and effectively utilized to support the lesson?					
6. Are there multiple modalities or resources used to accommodate different learning styles?					
C. Lesson Structure and Organization:					
7. Is there a clear and logical sequence of activities or steps?					
8. Is the lesson organized in a way that promotes engagement and understanding?					
9. Are the instructions for each activity or task clear and easy to follow?					
D. Differentiation and Adaptation:					
10. Does the lesson plan provide strategies for differentiating instruction to meet the needs of diverse learners?					
11. Are accommodations or modifications suggested for students with special needs or English language learners?					
12. Does the lesson plan provide flexibility for the teacher to adapt it for different topics?					
E. Assessment and Feedback:					
13. Are there appropriate methods or tools for assessing student learning during and at the end of the lesson?					
14. Does the lesson plan include opportunities for providing timely and constructive feedback to students?					
15. Are there specific criteria or rubrics provided for assessing student work or participation?					
F. Engagement and Student Interaction:					
16. Does the lesson plan include strategies to engage students actively in the learning process?					
17. Are there opportunities for student collaboration, discussion, or hands-on activities?					
18. Does the lesson plan promote student interaction and participation?					
G. Time Management:					
19. Is the lesson plan realistically designed to fit within the available class time?					
20. Are time estimates provided for each activity, allowing for smooth transitions?					
21. Does the lesson plan allocate sufficient time for important components of the lesson?					
H. Reflection and Extension:					
22. Does the lesson plan include opportunities for students to reflect on their learning?					
23. Are extension activities or suggestions provided to deepen students' understanding or to challenge advanced learners?					
24. Does the lesson plan encourage connections to real-life situations or other subjects?					

continues on following page

Table 3. Continued

Criteria	1 Very Poor	2 Poor	3 Average	4 Good	5 Very Good
I. Appropriateness:					
25. Is the lesson plan appropriate for the level of the students?					
26. Is the lesson plan suitable for the age of the learners?					
27. Is the lesson plan appropriate for the EFL context?					
J. Overall Effectiveness:					
28. Does the lesson plan demonstrate coherence and alignment with instructional goals?					
29. Does the lesson plan provide a clear roadmap for teachers to implement the lesson effectively?					
30. Does the lesson plan seem engaging, innovative, and likely to meet the needs of the students?					

Chapter 7
Discussions of Using AI in Language Education in Hong Kong

Siu-lun Lee
https://orcid.org/0000-0002-2306-9217
The Chinese University of Hong Kong, Hong Kong

Yongyin Chen
Independent Researcher, Hong Kong

ABSTRACT

This chapter sets out to investigate the discussions of using AI in language education in Chinese press in Hong Kong. From 2018-2023, there are news articles showcasing the AI tools and potential use of AI in language education in Hong Kong. This chapter discusses the debates on the use of artificial intelligence in language education and analyses newspaper discourse to investigate the different views of stakeholders in language education including students, teachers, educators, and policymakers in Hong Kong. A corpus containing Hong Kong newspaper articles discussing and debating the effectiveness and challenges of applying artificial intelligence in language education in Hong Kong has been constructed and analysed.

INTRODUCTION

Artificial intelligence has an impact on different aspects of human life. The use of artificial intelligence has been actively discussed in the educational field. There are studies discussing the use of conversational artificial intelligence in language classrooms (Jeon, 2022; Ji et al., 2023). Some research explores how artificial intelligence and chatbot technology can shape future language learning and teaching (Kim et al., 2019). The discussion about the development and impact of artificial intelligence as well as its use in education has been a topic receiving the attention of linguists, educators, policymakers, and the public in recent years (Chen et al., 2022; Zai et al., 2021). Topics relating to the use of artificial intelligence in education have been widely discussed in Hong Kong's public media (Chen, 2023) and there

DOI: 10.4018/979-8-3693-0872-1.ch007

are ongoing debates on these topics in Hong Kong press. Some newspaper articles suggest that the use of artificial intelligence is effective in language learning in Hong Kong schools (Yeung, 2019). On the other hand, some articles voice out that the students and the educational field are not benefiting from artificial intelligence (Liu & Yau, 2023). This paper sets out to discuss the debates on the use of artificial intelligence in language education and investigate the different views of the stakeholders in language education including students, teachers, educators, and policymakers expressed in Hong Kong newspapers. A corpus containing Hong Kong newspaper articles discussing and debating the effectiveness and challenges of applying artificial intelligence in language education in Hong Kong has been constructed and analysed. The research questions are set as follows: (i) to investigate the extent to which the Hong Kong press expressed arguments in favour of the use of artificial intelligence in language education in Hong Kong; and (ii) to analyse the range of arguments to oppose the use of artificial intelligence. This is the first systematic investigation of opinions in Hong Kong's public opinions expressed in printed media concerning the use of artificial intelligence in language education in Hong Kong. This study will shed some light on the discussions of the use of artificial intelligence in language education in the Hong Kong context.

ARTIFICIAL INTELLIGENCE AND LANGUAGE LEARNING

It has been a long history of computer-assisted language learning (CALL). There have been some discussions about the use of artificial intelligence (AI) in language education since OpenAI laid the groundwork with GPT-1 on 11 June 2018 and marked the advancement of a natural language processing model that can produce a coherent and contextually relevant response to a particular prompt. Then, AI has been adopted and used in education in different forms. AI initially took the form of computer and computer-related technologies, transitioning to web-based and online intelligent education systems, and ultimately with the use of embedded computer systems, together with other technologies, the use of humanoid robots and web-based chatbots to perform instructors' duties and functions independently or with teachers (Chassignol, et al., 2018; Pedró et al., 2019; Chen et al., 2020). These platforms can help teachers review and grade students' assignments more effectively and efficiently to achieve higher quality in their teaching activities. There was also research demonstrating the design of AI applications in language education (Sun et al., 2021), discussing how AI can change students' learning styles and habits (Kang & Kang, 2020), and modeling the role of teachers in the AI era (Cope et al., 2021; Schmidt & Strasser, 2022). There was also a bibliometric analysis to study the research literature relating to the use of AI in language education (Huang et al., 2023). This research reviewed 516 papers published from 2000 to 2019 relating to the theme and summarised the 10 most popular topics related to AI in language education were, (1) automated writing evaluation, (2) intelligent tutoring systems for reading and writing, (3) automated error detection, (4) computer-mediated communication, (5) personalized systems for language learning, (6) natural language and vocabulary learning, (7) web-resources and web-based systems for language learning, (8) intelligent tutoring systems for writing in English for specific purposes, (9) intelligent tutoring systems for pronunciation and speech training, and (10) affective states and emotions (Huang et al., 2023). Given the rapid development of AI and its use in education, UNESCO urged stakeholders to deal with ethics and transparency in data collection, use, and dissemination, to develop a comprehensive view of public policy on AI for sustainable development, to develop quality and inclusive data systems, to ensure inclusion and equity for AI in education, to enhance research on AI in education, and to prepare teachers for an AI-powered education (Pedró et al., 2019).

The official launch of ChatGPT on 30 November 2022 took the world by surprise with its sophisticated capacity. ChatGPT, a large language model-based chatbot developed by OpenAI, enables users to refine and steer a conversation towards a desired length, format, style, level of detail, and language. Microsoft announced that ChatGPT-powered features were coming to Bing on 7 February 2023. The access of Bing and ChatGPT is free at the time when the author is writing this chapter. Research has been done to identify opportunities and challenges of implementing generative AI chatbots in language education (Rudolph, et al., 2023; Ng et al., 2023). Moorhouse, et al. (2023) suggested that language teaching pedagogies have been reconceptualised after the global pandemic period and the use of technology in language teaching and learning has increased and 'seems to be the norm' in the post-pandemic age and generative AI tools have the potential to offer new and innovative ways to support both teaching and self-directed language learning. Kohnke et al. (2023) studied the use of ChatGPT for language teaching and learning and suggested that ChatGPT can help explain vocabulary, create vocabulary lists, and provide sample sentences and sample texts in different genres. They demonstrated that ChatGPT can also create grammar exercises and comprehension exercises and adjust difficulties according to learners' needs. On the contrary, there were also studies iterating the concerns of language educators, such as biases in data training, wrong information provided by the Chatbots, and privacy issues (Baidoo-Anu & Owusu Ansah, 2023; Chan, 2023).

TECHNOLOGY IN LANGUAGE LEARNING IN HONG KONG

The research literature on language education in Hong Kong tells us that universities have experience using online teaching and learning materials to supplement their formal classes (Chin, 2023; Kataoka, 2023; Lee, 2011, 2016, 2018). Since 2009, universities in Hong Kong have encouraged and implemented e-learning in undergraduate language courses (King, 2016). Because of the implementation of these e-learning projects, universities have produced online materials to supplement face-to-face language courses. The implementation of computer-assisted learning was also promoted in primary and secondary education in Hong Kong (Bai et. al., 2021). Lee (2016) discusses the implementation of e-learning components in traditional face-to-face Cantonese classrooms, as well as the normalization process of such implementation. During the Covid pandemic period, the demand for online learning materials was particularly high (Yaacob, & Saad, 2020). Studies are showing that artificial intelligence, augmented reality, big data, and social media, can enhance language learning by providing authentic, contextualised, and collaborative learning experiences (Kessler, 2017). The results of a study by Lee (2022) suggested that students' acceptance of blended teaching and learning models has grown substantially throughout the pandemic period. The global pandemic not only moved educational institutions throughout the world to implement various forms of online teaching but also increased the value of virtually available resources for self-learners as well as students taking formal language courses.

After the launch of ChatGPT in November 2022, the discussions on using AI in education and language education in Hong Kong's news media have been growing. There are diverse views among these news articles. Yeung, (2019) suggests that the use of generative artificial intelligence is effective in language learning in Hong Kong schools. On the other hand, Liu and Yau (2023) voice out that the students and the educational field are not benefiting from artificial intelligence. Chan (2023) collected survey data from students and teachers in Hong Kong universities and urged universities to develop AI education policies for higher education, focusing on governance, operational and pedagogical dimensions, based on the perceptions and implications of text-generative AI technologies. This chapter sets out to study the diverse public views and debates about the use of AI in language education in Hong Kong.

THE STUDY

Data Collection and Methodology

An extensive corpus of Chinese-language newspaper articles concerning the use of artificial intelligence in language education in Hong Kong has been compiled. More specifically, this database has focused on press articles discussing the use of artificial intelligence in education which has drawn comments and commentaries from members of the public as well as professional journalists. Newspaper articles were retrieved from a number of sources, including the WiseOne (formerly WiseNews) database for the Hong Kong press, as well as individual searches of fourteen leading Chinese newspapers, namely *AM730*, *Headline Daily* (頭條日報), *HK01* (香港01), *Hong Kong Commercial Daily* (香港商報), *Hong Kong Economic Journal* (信報財經新聞), *Hong Kong Economic Times* (香港經濟日報), *Master Insight* (灼見名家), *Mingpao Daily* (明報), *Oriental Daily* (東方日報), *Sing Pao* (成報), *Sing Tao Daily* (星島日報), *Sky Post* (晴報), *Ta Kung Pao* (大公報), and *Wen Wei Po* (文匯報) in Hong Kong. The research issues in investigating newspaper articles on discussions and comments relating to the use of artificial intelligence in language education in Hong Kong were as follows: (i) to investigate the extent to which the Hong Kong Chinese press expressed arguments in favour of the use of artificial intelligence in language education in Hong Kong; and (ii) to analyse the range of argumentation to oppose the use of artificial intelligence.

The data collection took place from March 2023 to September 2023, a total of 299 newspaper articles were downloaded from the internet, and the text was then entered into the database. These articles were initially searched using such terms 人工智能 'artificial intelligence', 電腦輔助語言教學 'computer-assisted language teaching and learning', 電腦輔助語言學習 'computer-assisted language learning', 網上語言學習 'online language learning', and closely related terms, as well as English terms as they also appear in Chinese texts, such as 'artificial intelligence', 'AI', 'generative AI', and 'ChatGPT'. Before inclusion in the database, the articles were briefly reviewed to determine their relevance to the use of AI in the language education in question and were grouped by the time of publication. These articles were grouped before and after the launching time of ChatGPT, November 2023, to understand public views and discussions before and after the official launch of generative AI and chatbots. Later, a further round of filtering took place, after the researcher decided to categorise such data into clusters related to these topics: (1) showcasing AI applications for language education, (2) arguments supporting the use of AI in language education, and (3) views against the promotion of AI in language education. After classifying the data according to the above incidents in terms of topic and timeline, there is a total of 259 articles related specifically to these three topics discussed in the past five years (2018-2023).

RESULTS

Quantitative Results

To carry out a broad quantitative analysis of the opinions expressed by news reporters and columnists in the newspapers investigated, the articles in our dataset have been grouped into three categories: (1) showcasing AI applications for language education, (2) arguments supporting the use of AI in language education, and (3) views against the promotion of AI in language education. This study was centrally concerned with discussions, where public opinions on the use of AI in language education were explicitly expressed. The limitations of adopting such an approach may be obvious, as, the subjective methodology used by the investigator in deciding and identifying the main discussions in a particular newspaper text. Two raters were recruited to review and verify the investigator's categorisations and judgment on these newspaper texts. Despite some inevitable subjectivity in making such decisions, given the familiarity of the researcher with language pedagogies and the language education issues of society, the methodology adopted was appropriate and effective in the qualitative analysis of texts.

Table 1 below shows that a total of 259 articles fall into three categories: (1) showcasing AI applications for language education, (2) arguments supporting the use of AI in language education (pro-AI arguments), and (3) views against the promotion of AI in language education (anti-AI arguments).

Table 1. Discussions in the press relating to the use of AI in language education in Hong Kong, 2018-2023

Date	Showcasing AI Applications	Pro-AI Arguments	Anti-AI Arguments
January 2018 – October 2022	32 (33%)	49 (43.7%)	3 (6%)
November 2022 – August 2023	65 (67%)	63 (56.3%)	47 (94%)
Total	97 (37.5%)	112 (43.2%)	50 (19.3%)

As can be seen from the above table, 37.5% of the articles in the dataset showcased the use of AI in language education in Hong Kong. The number of these demonstrations doubled after November 2022 since the launch of generative AI ChatGPT. In the meantime, there are a number of articles (43.2%) presenting arguments to support the use of AI in language education in Hong Kong. The distribution of these arguments is quite even before the official launch of generative AI (43.7%, January 2018 - October 2022) and after the official launch of ChatGPT (56.3%, since November 2022). In the dataset, there are 19.3% of the articles express views against the promotion of AI in language education. However, this kind of discussion and concern increased rapidly from 6% (January 2018 - October 2022) to 94% (November 2022 - August 2023). This indicates that many of the discussions against the use of AI in language education were started after the official launch of the generative AI, ChatGPT.

In the discursive presentation of the qualitative data, which is presented a little later in this chapter, the results of our analysis have been grouped according to those topics that emerged from this analysis and illustrated by translated quotations from the Chinese newspaper articles in question. Here again, however, there were limitations to the method of classification used in arriving at these results, as in many cases more than one argument was present in any given text. The task for the researcher and raters, therefore, was to make a judgment as to which argument was most salient in any given text, and this we attempted to do, as accurately and consistently as possible.

Qualitative Results

The qualitative methodology employed by the researcher was used at many levels of analysis. First, each of the articles in the database was carefully read to identify the major arguments presented in each article, and to decide which of these arguments was most salient in a particular text. This then provided the basis for the quantitative analysis of arguments as presented in Table 1. Following this, at a narrower level of examination, the researchers were then able to examine individual articles in order to determine how particular arguments were realised. One overarching result that emerged from this next level of analysis was that reference to or presentation of 'major arguments' overlapped within individual newspaper articles, contributing very often to a multi-layered discourse where a range of closely related arguments find expression. This multilayering of argumentation can be seen in many of the excerpts presented below. We shall first consider those arguments most frequently made in support of the use of AI in language education in Hong Kong, before moving on to a discussion of arguments against such use. The texts presented below were extracted from articles representing different styles or genres of journalism, including opinion columns, feature articles, and news reports.

Showcasing the Use of AI in Language Education in News Media

In recent decades, the Hong Kong SAR government has promoted 'trilingualism and biliteracy', that is the use of three spoken languages, Cantonese, Putonghua, and English, and two written codes, standard written Chinese and written English, in official settings (Bacon-Shone et al., 2015; Bolton et al., 2020; Bolton & Lee, 2020). Cantonese, English, and Putonghua are three major languages used in Hong Kong, and both written Chinese and English are used in government announcements, in the education domain, and in business sectors. As may be seen in Table 1, there were some cases of AI applications in language education during 2018-2023. Before the official launch of generative AI in November 2022, there were already some demonstrations of the use of AI in language teaching and learning. Articles in *Ta Kung Pao* and *Sing Tao Daily* showcased the use of tools and applications to help students learn English vocabulary and improve English reading skills, as in excerpts (1) and (2).

(1) An AI learning-oriented intelligent hardware product, "Xunfei Scanning Dictionary Pen," has been released. The core function of this dictionary pen is to scan and look up words, and it also has corresponding innovative functions designed for listening, speaking, reading, and memorizing English vocabulary. (*Ta Kung Pao*, 27/10/2020)

(2) *Microsoft Teams* recently launched the 'Reading Progress' feature, which introduces an English article about 'Food & Drink' and distributes it to children at home to practise reading along with. The AI function built into 'Reading Progress' automatically analyzes most of the students' pronunciation accuracy, helping teachers to understand which words are commonly misread by everyone and to grasp the different learning situations of the whole class and individual students through the teacher interface on Teams. This helps teachers and schools to further improve students' learning efficiency in limited face-to-face or online course hours according to different learning needs. (*Sing Tao Daily*, 21/06/2022)

There were also AI applications that helped analyse Chinese sentences and morphological structures to assist ethnic minority students learning Chinese as a second language in Hong Kong, as shown in excerpt (3) below.

(3) Chinese words have a large variety of combinations, and 'how to split Chinese sentences' is a complex problem. After years of research, he developed an analysis tool called *HanMosaic*, which can split Chinese characters, sentences, and paragraphs, and distinguish between words and single characters. People generally think that this requires a huge database to assist, but it turns out that it only needs artificial intelligence that can learn on its own. The research results have been transformed into an online dictionary designed for non-Chinese-speaking students. It automatically dissects Chinese sentences into words, analyzes them one by one, and teaches stroke order and radicals. It has already begun to be used in schools. (*Hong Kong Economic Journal*, 25/01/2019)

There were also discussions about using AI technology and applications to arouse students' interest in learning Chinese literature, as in excerpt (4) below.

(4) Students enjoy using AI to enhance their learning interests. Some students have even been simulated by Li Bai's *Thoughts in the Silent Night* and interacting with ancient people in the AI system in their Chinese reading classes. (*Hong Kong Economic Times*, 13/04/2021)

In the dataset, there were also displays that AI can change students' language learning styles. Excerpt (5) shows that AI-based gamified applications changed students' learning habits outside the language classrooms.

(5) This application encourages children to learn through gamified experiences. The children receive immediate feedback after practice and record poorly pronounced words to help improve them in the future. It's worth noting that the app also provides multiple scenario choices, such as school, restaurant, airport, and hospital, among other daily situations. After selecting a scenario, an AI robot will play different roles with children to practise English conversation in the form of sentences or dialogues. (*Sky Post*, 08/03/2022)

There are news articles promoting the use of AI technology to match students' language learning needs to language schools and tutors, as shown in the excerpt (6).

(6) *FluentUp*, a local online language learning platform, uses its 'efficient learning management system' to analyze users' preferences and needs through artificial intelligence, and then matches them with language schools around the world in real-time. (*Hong Kong Economic Times*, 22/01/2019)

After the official launch of generative AI in November 2022, more varieties of applications used in language education were demonstrated. Excerpts (7) and (8) illustrate using ChatGPT to help students' English grammar and writing in English.

(7) Children can now learn English through the internet and smart devices, and ChatGPT can be a useful tool to help them learn the tenses of English. (*Sing Tao Daily*, 21/07/2023)

(8) ChatGPT can help to improve English grammar. First, write the composition, and then give ChatGPT the command 'Please correct my English composition and correct my grammar errors'. A student shared that ChatGPT can present grammar errors and improvement suggestions in a list, which is more convenient. (*Hong Kong Economic Times*, 17/04/2023)

Excerpts (9) and (10) below demonstrate two mobile applications, *SpokenBot* and *ReadOutLoud.* These two applications were developed by the Hang Seng University of Hong Kong. These applications made use of generative AI technology to help students improve English and Putonghua pronunciation and students' accuracy in speaking English and Putonghua. *SpokenBot* helps students practise English and Chinese vocabulary, assesses pronunciation when students read these vocabulary items in English and in Putonghua, and assesses pronunciation on the sentence level. This application contains 100 scenarios with 3 levels of difficulties for students to practise. *ReadOutLoud* is a learning system that downloads news from radio channels and government websites and generates English and Putonghua speech samples. Students can record their reading of these pieces of news in English or Putonghua. The systems can assess students' English and Putonghua pronunciation.

(9) A team has successfully developed two free mobile applications, *SpokenBot* and *ReadOutLoud*, for students and citizens to learn languages. These apps use artificial intelligence engines and chatbot technology to help users improve their accuracy in English and Mandarin Chinese. (*Wen Wei Po*, 08/06/2023)

(10) The English and Mandarin Chinese learning program *ReadOutLoud* downloads news content from radio stations and government news websites every day. Users first listen to AI-read Mandarin Chinese or English news content, then record themselves reading the content. The AI engine will analyze the recording in real-time, score it, and point out vocabulary that can be improved for pronunciation. (*Sing Tao Daily*, 07/06/2023)

The advancement of linguistic research to predict child language development using AI technology is also reported in the news media, shown in excerpt (11).

(11) Using electroencephalogram (EEG) test to collect data on 300 healthy Hong Kong children as a benchmark, and then using artificial intelligence computing programs to predict their future language development. (*HK01*, 13/07/2023)

The development of this electroencephalography test was a joint project led by a linguist, Patrick Wong, who collaborated with Paediatrics doctors to construct a predictive algorithm to forecast language development in individual children. With early intervention strategies, it could reduce the severity of potential language impairment as well as optimise language learning for children, in particular Cantonese and Mandarin pronunciation, at the earliest possible time. The research team thinks that it is important to screen out children who may suffer from a developmental language disorder so that parents can act and provide appropriate intervention and training as early as possible (The Chinese University of Hong Kong, 2021).

'Pro-AI' Arguments

As may be seen in Table 1, 43.2% of the arguments in the newspaper texts were identifiable as 'Pro-AI', in the sense that these produced arguments in favour of the use of AI in language education in Hong Kong. These articles emphasized that the use of AI in language education can provide personalised support for students, offer real-time assistance to students, and create an extended language classroom. This section of the article presents a detailed account of the arguments that have been deployed in recent debates in the Hong Kong Chinese press. These arguments clustered in three areas focusing on the use of AI in language education can provide personalise teaching and support to students, offer real-time assistance to students, and encourage students to learn anywhere.

Providing personalised teaching and support to students. The Chinese press emphasized a lot on personalised language teaching and support to students. As AI systems become more mature, they can make use of complex sets of data to understand students' learning styles and needs and, in turn, adjust course content according to students' abilities and provide each student with the most appropriate learning materials, as shown in excerpts (12), (13) and (14).

(12) The integration of big data with technologies such as speech recognition and image recognition has led to interdisciplinary and cross-domain development. The 'smart adaptive learning' technology that simulates the one-on-one teaching process between teachers and students and gives personalised teaching to the learning system has been widely used in the field of language education. (*Wen Wei Po*, 18/11/2019)

(13) AI language translation has a significant impact on human language learning. In recent years, students' extracurricular English tutoring has been changed. (*Ta Kung Pao*, 22/12/2022)

(14) AI applications have already become trendy tutors in the field of language education. They can not only impart knowledge to learners but also adjust teaching styles and progress according to their needs, rhythm, and preferences. For example, the *Duolingo* language learning application can not only teach you fluent French but also has an AI system that adjusts according to your learning progress, strengthens your weak areas in learning, and reminds you to practise regularly. (*AM730*, 18/08/2023)

Offering real-time assistance to students. In addition, commentaries in the Chinese press suggested that when students face learning difficulties after school and seek support, AI and generative AI can offer real-time assistance to their learning difficulties. When AI systems can provide language support and assistance at school and after school, the workload of teachers can be reduced and teachers can devote more time and resources to take care of students' psychological needs, as presented in excerpt (15) below.

(15) Using AI to provide students with learning, assessment, and feedback, as well as providing them with appropriate learning progress and challenges, and switching to the next learning topic at the appropriate time. As AI technology matures, machines can read students' facial expressions to determine their learning pace and to provide each student with the most appropriate learning materials. After-school language tutoring and learning plans will also become more advanced, permeating different learning methods in the learning process. When students are struggling with

homework or exam preparation at home, AI will be a great help to them. This will reduce the teaching workload of teachers and free up more time to take care of students' spiritual needs. (*Sing Tao Daily*, 08/03/2021)

Learning anywhere and arousing students' interest. The implementation of computer-assisted language learning can break the limitations of time and space. This can be proved in the global pandemic period, where various types of synchronous and asynchronous online language teaching attempts have been made to solve the social distancing issues (Lee, 2022). There are arguments in the Hong Kong Chinese press showing support that students can learn and practice anytime and anywhere with AI and generative AI technology. Excerpt (16) below shows this view.

(16) From a student's perspective, ChatGPT can provide personalised support and answer individual questions. ChatGPT breaks the limitations of time and space, allowing students to use it anytime, anywhere. Furthermore, ChatGPT can provide real-time language assistance to students, whether it is after class, when teachers are busy, or even late at night. This greatly enhances their learning efficiency. ChatGPT also allows students to explore different fields through real-time interactive feedback and dialogue, making language learning more attractive and interactive, while also helping to increase their interest in learning. (*Sing Tao Daily*, 07/04/2023)

'Anti-AI' Arguments

The major debates that emerged in the Chinese press revolved around a number of interlocking and overlapping issues and themes. Those articles that were judged to present strong arguments 'against the use of AI in language education' formed a small but significant minority, accounting for a total of 19.3% of all the articles in the database. It was nevertheless considered important to give these 'anti-AI' arguments close examination. The major arguments and themes in articles against AI were identified as an infringement of intellectual property, stakeholders' questions about the accuracy of answers provided by generative AI, and challenges to teachers' roles.

Infringing intellectual property and plagiarism. A major comment, among the articles in the dataset, on the use of AI and generative AI in language teaching is the infringement of intellectual property and the issues of plagiarism. Commentaries raised the issues about ethics, ghostwriting, and cheating issues, as in excerpts (17) and (18) below.

(17) Artificial intelligence also involves a series of issues such as ethics, morality, intellectual property rights, scientific research plagiarism, and cheating in exams. (*HK01*, 07/03/2023)

(18) If students violate the rules and use AI tools such as ChatGPT without the consent of others, it is equivalent to using their works without permission, which involves an element of 'deception'. If relevant AI tools are used without exemption, they also meet the relevant definition. Therefore, the school will treat such cases as 'potential plagiarism'. (*Headline Daily*, 18/02/2023)

Questioning the accuracy of answers provided by generative AI. Some commentaries also questioned the accuracy and credibility of the answers and suggestions provided by AI, as shown in the excerpt (19).

(19) The answers provided by ChatGPT are too generalized, inaccurate, low credibility, and outdated. All these defects greatly affect the practicality of ChatGPT. (*Master Insight*, 20/02/2023)

Challenging teachers' role. Some comments focused on the negative impact on human teachers once AI applications were implemented in language education. An article in *Sing Tao Daily* worried generative AI can damage the status of teachers and weaken students' attention in class, as shown in excerpt (20).

(20) Although ChatGPT can help with natural language generation, it should be noted that it may have some negative effects on the work of some teachers, such as damage to the power and status of teachers and weakening of students' passion and attention for teachers. (*Sing Tao Daily*, 2023-02-16)

DISCUSSION

The debate relating to the implementation of AI applications in language education shows the merits of using AI, as well as the worries about this technological innovation towards language education, in particular, and education, in general.

Generative AI is a new global trend that changes the way of searching for information. The good side of using generative AI as a teaching tool is that it can cultivate students' use of information technology and enhance their information literacy. Generative AI can also do one-on-one tutoring, provide personalised teaching and support to students, offer real-time support to students, and allow students to learn language skills and study on their own. There is research aiming at setting up an AI curriculum framework for secondary schools in Hong Kong to promote the use of AI in pre-tertiary classrooms (Chiu et al., 2022).

The opposite side raised their concerns that students may use generative AI to complete their homework, which does not help them grow and hinders the development of their critical thinking and problem-solving skills. Commentaries on the 'anti-AI' side worried that the use of generative AI encourages students to cheat and copy which, in a way, encourages academic dishonesty. The 'anti-AI' arguments also emphasize generative AI's errors and inaccuracy. Some articles echoed UNESCO's suggestions and urged setting up rules and regulations for the use of generative AI in education. Although universities have started to set policies and guidelines on the use of artificial intelligence in tertiary education, some of these guidelines are very preliminary, for example, permission must be granted before using AI in in-class exercises and assignments, the use of AI should be fully acknowledged similar to citation of other sources, and encourage students to use AI ethically (The Chinese University of Hong Kong, 2023; The Hong Kong Polytechnic University, 2023). It is clear that more work is needed to deal with the ethical issues relating to the use of AI in language education.

The data in this study also shows language teachers' worries relating to their role in the teaching process. To some extent, this is due to both teachers and learners lacking digital competencies to use generative chatbots ethically and effectively to support language learning. Research on teachers' and students' attitudes can be done in institutions to understand the needs of both teachers and students so that institutions can plan adequate training on digital proficiency and ethics of using generative AI technology in teaching and learning (Kohnke et al., 2023).

IMPLICATION

From the debate on the use of generative AI in language education, the impact brought about by generative AI on language education can be very prominent. The data in this study shows that issues concerning the ethical use of generative AI are of primary concern to many stakeholders, research on these ethical issues and setting precise and agreeable guidelines are of foremost importance to many educators, language teachers, parents as well as students.

The dataset in this study shows that the number of 'Pro-AI' arguments (119 articles, 43.2%) is double that of the 'Anti-AI' arguments (50 articles, 19.3%). The situation, in general, is more favourable to the development and use of AI in language education. However, the barriers to the use of generative AI in education cannot be neglected (Wang & Cheng, 2021). It is worth noting that in computer-assisted language learning (CALL) literature, for effective implementation of innovative pedagogical technology, not only do teachers need adjustments and training, but students also need training in terms of computer efficacy, motivation for using the new technology, ethics and learning habits, and culture to naturalise or normalise the use of such innovation in their academic life. Lee (2016) studied the normalisation process of technological innovation in language education. This study compared students' expectations of technological innovation with institutional targets. The result showed that the characteristics, habits, and expectations of students, though may be subject to change with the advancement of computer technologies, may not always match with the pedagogical beliefs of the institution as well as teachers' expectations. If such a mismatch happens, institutions/teachers need to understand students' learning habits and expectations, on the one hand; and on the other hand, instructional strategies, and training for teachers and students need to be developed to smooth the normalisation process.

For sure, the technology of generative AI will continue to be advanced and more widely applied in more aspects of human life. Language teaching pedagogy relating to the use of AI also needs to be closely followed. This is a preliminary study about using AI in language education in Hong Kong. More research on such use, including the development in curriculum design, change in teaching and learning mode, extension of language classrooms, as well as language assessment, are needed to look at the different applications and effectiveness of this cutting-edge technology in the field of language education.

CONCLUSION

This chapter discusses the debates on the use of artificial intelligence in language education and analyse Chinese newspaper discourse to investigate the different views of the stakeholders in language education including students, teachers, educators, and policymakers in Hong Kong. A corpus containing Hong Kong newspaper articles discussing and debating the effectiveness and challenges of applying artificial intelligence in language education in Hong Kong has been constructed and analysed. From 2018-2023, there are news articles showcasing the AI tools and potential use of AI in language education in Hong Kong. In the meantime, there are debates about the use of AI in education and language education, in particular. The 'pro-AI' arguments emphasized that the use of AI in language education can provide personalised support for students, offer real-time assistance to students, and create an extended language classroom, while the 'anti-AI' views concern the infringement of intellectual property, the accuracy of answers provided by generative AI, and challenges to teachers' roles if AI and generative AI technology is implemented in language education. Studies on students' learning habits, and expectations, as well as readiness, will be important for administrators to investigate implementation plans and effectiveness. On the pedagogical side, more research is needed to investigate language teaching approaches and assessments incorporating AI technologies. Given the importance of artificial intelligence and related technology in the age of the Internet, the popularity and research of such technology are likely to further increase in the years to come.

REFERENCES

Bacon-Shone, J., Bolton, K., & Luke, K. K. (2015). *Language use, proficiency and attitudes in Hong Kong*. Social Sciences Research Centre, HKU.

Bai, B., Wang, J., & Zhou, H. (2020). An intervention study to improve primary school students' self-regulated strategy use in English writing through e-learning in Hong Kong. *Computer Assisted Language Learning*, *35*(9), 2265–2290. doi:10.1080/09588221.2020.1871030

Baidoo-Anu, D., & Owusu Ansah, L. (2023). Education in the Era of Generative Artificial Intelligence (AI): Understanding the Potential Benefits of ChatGPT in Promoting Teaching and Learning. *Journal of AI*, *7*(1), 52–62. doi:10.61969/jai.1337500

Bolton, K., Bacon-Shone, J., & Lee, S.-l. (2020). Societal multilingualism in Hong Kong. In P. Siemund & J. Leimgruber (Eds.), *Multilingual global cities: Dubai, Hong Kong and Singapore* (pp. 160–184). Routledge. doi:10.4324/9780429463860-12

Bolton, K., & Lee, S.-l. (2020). A socio-historical approach to multilingualism in Hong Kong. In P. Siemund & J. Leimgruber (Eds.), *Multilingual global cities: Hong Kong, Singapore, and Dubai* (pp. 38–62). Routledge. doi:10.4324/9780429463860-4

Chan, C. K. Y. (2023). A comprehensive AI policy education framework for university teaching and learning. *International Journal of Educational Technology in Higher Education*, *2023*(20), 38. doi:10.1186/s41239-023-00408-3

Chassignol, M., Khoroshavin, A., Klimova, A., & Bilyatdinova, A. (2018). Artificial Intelligence trends in education: A narrative overview. *Procedia Computer Science*, *136*, 16–24. doi:10.1016/j.procs.2018.08.233

Chen, L. (2023, June 23). Hong Kong rolls out first AI curriculum for junior secondary students, including lessons on ChatGPT, with 'lives definitely affected by artificial intelligence'. *South China Morning Post*.

Chen, L., Chen, P., & Lin, Z. (2020). Artificial intelligence in education: A review. *IEEE Access: Practical Innovations, Open Solutions*, *8*, 75264–75278. doi:10.1109/ACCESS.2020.2988510

Chen, X., Zhou, D., Xie, H., Cheng, G., & Liu, C. (2022). Two decades of artificial intelligence in education: Contributors, collaborations, research topics, challenges, and future directions. *Journal of Educational Technology & Society*, *25*(1), 28–47.

Chin, A. C. (2023). A corpus-based approach to learning and teaching Cantonese. In S. L. Lee (Ed.), The learning and teaching of Cantonese as a second language (pp. 184–195). Routledge.

Chiu, T. K. F., Meng, H., Chai, C.-S., King, I., Wong, S., & Yam, Y. (2022). Creation and Evaluation of a Pretertiary Artificial Intelligence (AI) Curriculum. *IEEE Transactions on Education*, *65*(1), 30–39. doi:10.1109/TE.2021.3085878

Cope, B., Kalantzis, M., & Searsmith, D. (2021). Artificial intelligence for education: Knowledge and its assessment in AI-enabled learning ecologies. *Educational Philosophy and Theory*, *53*(12), 1229–1245. doi:10.1080/00131857.2020.1728732

Huang, X., Zou, D., Cheng, G., Chen, X., & Xie, H. (2023). Trends, Research Issues and Applications of Artificial Intelligence in Language Education. *Journal of Educational Technology & Society*, *26*(1), 112–131.

Jeon, J. (2022). Exploring AI chatbot affordances in the EFL classroom: Young learners' experiences and perspectives. *Computer Assisted Language Learning*, 1–26. Advance online publication. doi:10.1080/09588221.2021.2021241

Ji, H., Han, I., & Ko, Y. (2023). A systematic review of conversational AI in language education: Focusing on the collaboration with human teachers. *Journal of Research on Technology in Education*, *55*(1), 48–63. doi:10.1080/15391523.2022.2142873

Kang, B., & Kang, S. (2022). Construction of Chinese Language Teaching System Model Based on Deep Learning under the Background of Artificial Intelligence. *Scientific Programming*, *2022*, 1–10. doi:10.1155/2022/3960023

Kataoka, S. (2023). Textbook Cantonese romanization. In S. L. Lee (Ed.), *The learning and teaching of Cantonese as a second language* (pp. 196–216). Routledge.

Kessler, G. (2017). Technology and the future of language teaching. *Foreign Language Annals*, *2018*(51), 205–218.

Kim, N.-Y., Cha, Y., & Kim, H.-S. (2019). Future English learning: Chatbots and artificial intelligence. *Multimedia-Assisted Language Learning*, *22*(3), 32–53.

King, I. (2016, July 29). E-learning is the way forward for quality education. *South China Morning Post*.

Kohnke, L., Moorhouse, B. L., & Zou, D. (2023). ChatGPT for Language Teaching and Learning. *RELC Journal*, *54*(2), 537–550. doi:10.1177/00336882231162868

Lee, S. L. (2011). 高班閱讀課的網上課件 [Online components for advanced Chinese reading classes]. *Journal of Technology and Chinese Language Teaching*, *2*, 1–22.

Lee, S. L. (2016). E-Learning Readiness in Language Learning: Students' Readiness Survey and Normalization Process. *Journal of Technology and Chinese Language Teaching*, *7*(2), 23–37.

Lee, S. L. (2018). Modular approaches in eLearning design. *Journal of Technology and Chinese Language Teaching*, *9*, 48–61.

Lee, S. L. (2022). Synchronous online language teaching: a reflection from Hong Kong. In S. Liu (Ed.), *Teaching the Chinese language remotely: Global cases and perspectives* (pp. 235–251). Palgrave Macmillan. doi:10.1007/978-3-030-87055-3_10

Liu, O., & Yau, C. (2023, March 22). Who needs a teacher? As ChatGPT takes off in Hong Kong, educationists worry about impact on teaching, learning. *South China Morning Post.*

Moorhouse, B. L., Wong, K. M., & Li, L. (2023). Teaching with Technology in the Post-Pandemic Digital Age: Technological Normalisation and AI-Induced Disruptions. *RELC Journal*, *54*(2), 311–320. doi:10.1177/00336882231176929

Ng, D. T. K., Lee, M., Tan, R. J. Y., Downie, J. S., & Chu, S. K. W. (2023). A review of AI teaching and learning from 2000 to 2020. *Education and Information Technologies*, *2023*(28), 8445–8501. doi:10.1007/s10639-022-11491-w

Pedró, F., Subosa, M., Rivas, A., & Valverde, P. (2019). *Artificial Intelligence and Language Learning: Opportunities and Challenges*. Working Paper on Language Policy. UNESCO. Retrieved from https:// unesdoc.unesco.org/ark:/ 48223/pf0000366994

Rudolph, J., Tan, S., & Tan, S. (2023). ChatGPT: Bullshit spewer or the end of traditional assessments in higher education? *Journal of Applied Learning & Teaching*, *6*(1), 342–363.

Schmidt, T., & Strasser, T. (2022). Artificial Intelligence in Foreign Language Learning and Teaching: A CALL for Intelligent Practice. *Anglistik: International Journal of English Studies*, *33*(1), 165–184. doi:10.33675/ANGL/2022/1/14

Sun, Z., Anbarasan, M., & Kumar, D. P. (2021). Design of online intelligent English teaching platform based on artificial intelligence techniques. *Computational Intelligence*, *2021*(37), 1166–1180. doi:10.1111/ coin.12351

The Chinese University of Hong Kong. (2021, 24 August). A 30-minute EEG Test Forecasts Children's Language Development. *CUHK in Touch*. Retrieved from https://cuhkintouch.cpr.cuhk.edu.hk/2021/08/7463/

The Chinese University of Hong Kong. (2023). *Use of Artificial Intelligence Tools in Teaching, Learning and Assessments: A Guide for Students*. Hong Kong: The Chinese University of Hong Kong. Retrieved from https://www.aqs.cuhk.edu.hk/documents/A-guide-for-students_use-of-AI-tools.pdf

The Hong Kong Polytechnic University. (2023). *Guidelines for Students on the Use of Generative Artificial Intelligence*. Hong Kong: The Hong Kong Polytechnic University of Hong Kong. Retrieved from https://www.polyu.edu.hk/ar/ docdrive/polyu-students/Student-guide-on-the-use-GenAI.pdf

Wang, T., & Cheng, E. C. K. (2021). An investigation of barriers to Hong Kong K-12 schools incorporating Artificial Intelligence in education. *Computers and Education: Artificial Intelligence, 2.*

Yaacob, Z., & Saad, N. H. M. (2020). Acceptance of YouTube as a learning platform during the Covid-19 pandemic: The moderating effect of subscription status. *TEM Journal*, *4*, 1732–1739. doi:10.18421/ TEM94-54

Yueng, P. (2019, 31 January). AI will be a game changer for Hong Kong education. *China Daily Hong Kong*.

Zai, X., Chu, X., Chai, C. S., Jong, M. S. Y., Istenic, A., & Spector, M. (2021). A review of artificial intelligence (AI) in education from 2010 to 2020. *Complexity*, *2021*, 1–18. Advance online publication. doi:10.1155/2021/8812542

KEY TERMS AND DEFINITIONS

Blended Teaching and Learning: Blended teaching and learning or hybrid learning in this chapter is defined as an educational model that combines classroom face-to-face learning experiences with online learning experiences.

Cantonese: The term 'Cantonese' refers to the language varieties used by immigrants who came to Hong Kong from various districts in Guangdong province, including Macau, Panyu, Taishan, Xinhui, and Zhongshan. Over time, their speech coalesced into the contemporary variety of Cantonese used in Hong Kong from the late nineteenth century onwards. Cantonese is often used to refer to the entire Yue subgroup of Chinese, which includes varieties of Cantonese spoken in southern China, Hong Kong, Macau, Malaysia, Singapore, and among overseas Chinese in North America, Europe, and Australia. It is currently estimated that there are about 70 million Cantonese speakers in the world. Cantonese has been and is a major language variety used by people in daily life in Hong Kong.

Computer-Assisted Language Learning (CALL): Computer-assisted language learning (CALL) or Computer-aided instruction (CAI) is briefly defined as the search for and study of applications of the computer in language teaching and learning. CALL includes a wide range of information and communications technology applications and approaches to teaching and learning foreign languages.

Normalization Process: Normalization refers to a social process through which ideas and actions come to be seen as 'normal' and 'natural' in everyday life. The normalization process refers to a social organization that brings practice or practices into action.

Putonghua: Putonghua is the official language of the People's Republic of China. It serves as the common national language of the PRC. Under Hong Kong's Basic Law and the promotion of trilingualism and biliteracy, Putonghua has an official status in Hong Hong.

Standard Written Chinese: A *baihua yundong* 白話運動 ('vernacular language movement') was started in 1917 by the scholar *Hu Shi* 胡適. This *baihua* literary movement advocated adopting the *baihua* 白話('vernacular') style of Chinese as a written language to revitalize the Classical Chinese literary language and make it more accessible to the common people. *Baihua* is the form of written Chinese based on the varieties of Chinese spoken throughout China, in contrast to *wenyan* 文言('classical Chinese') or ('literary speech') used in Imperial China up to the early twentieth century. This movement succeeded in making *baihua* the language of textbooks, periodicals, newspapers, and public documents. *Baihua* now commonly refers to the standard written Chinese or modern written Chinese. Since the early 1920s, this modern vernacular form has been the standard style of writing for speakers of all varieties of Chinese throughout mainland China, Taiwan, Malaysia, and Singapore as written form of modern standard Chinese. Standard written Chinese (presented in traditional characters) is used in all official and educational contexts in Hong Kong.

Trilingualism and Biliteracy: Since the 1990s, the Hong Kong government has promoted 'trilingualism and biliteracy', which refers to the spoken command of Cantonese, Putonghua, and English, and literacy in written Chinese and English.

Chapter 8
What Are Students Saying About AI as an Academic Tool

Lee Luan Ng
https://orcid.org/0000-0001-6741-6201
Universiti Malaya, Malaysia

Venosha Ravana
https://orcid.org/0000-0002-4941-5309
Tunku Abdul Rahman University of Management and Technology, Malaysia

ABSTRACT

The introduction of artificial intelligence, ChatGPT, and other machine learning technologies has shaken up numerous industries across the globe. The World Economic Forum Future of Jobs Report 2023 predicts that due to a combination of macro trends and technology adoption, over the next five years jobs in the education industry are expected to grow at least by 10%. Many learners in higher education are integrating the use of AI when attending to their academic work, yet there is not much investigation exploring how they plan and perceive the use of AI whilst completing their academic tasks. Therefore, this chapter aims to (1) explore how learners' intention of using AI affects their language learning behavior and (2) uncover the factors that influence the learners' perceptions toward the usefulness of AI as an academic support. Grounded in the theory of planned behavior (TPB), students from two tertiary education institutions in Malaysia were asked to respond to a series of questions that explored their perspectives on utilizing AI-powered tools to aid their academic writing.

INTRODUCTION

The Status Quo of AI in the Academia

AI-powered tools such as ChatGPT, Google Bard, Bing, QuillBot and Gradescope, to name a few, have gained global attention as the new fad in the education sector (Lim et al., 2023). Reiss (2021) had anticipated that AI was going to transform education, and those who would benefit the most were

DOI: 10.4018/979-8-3693-0872-1.ch008

students with special and differentiated needs. In fact, Haleem et al. (2023) made a case that students could potentially utilize AI tools in their academic works without the teacher ever knowing, i.e. to check grammar or sentence structures. Simultaneously, as indicated in Figure 1, there has been press coverage that highlighted the potential issues that are linked to the emergence of AI in the education context.

Figure 1. Excerpts extracted from the websites of different newspaper related to the influence of AI on the instructors and learners.
Last retrieved from The New Straits Times online on 31/08/2023

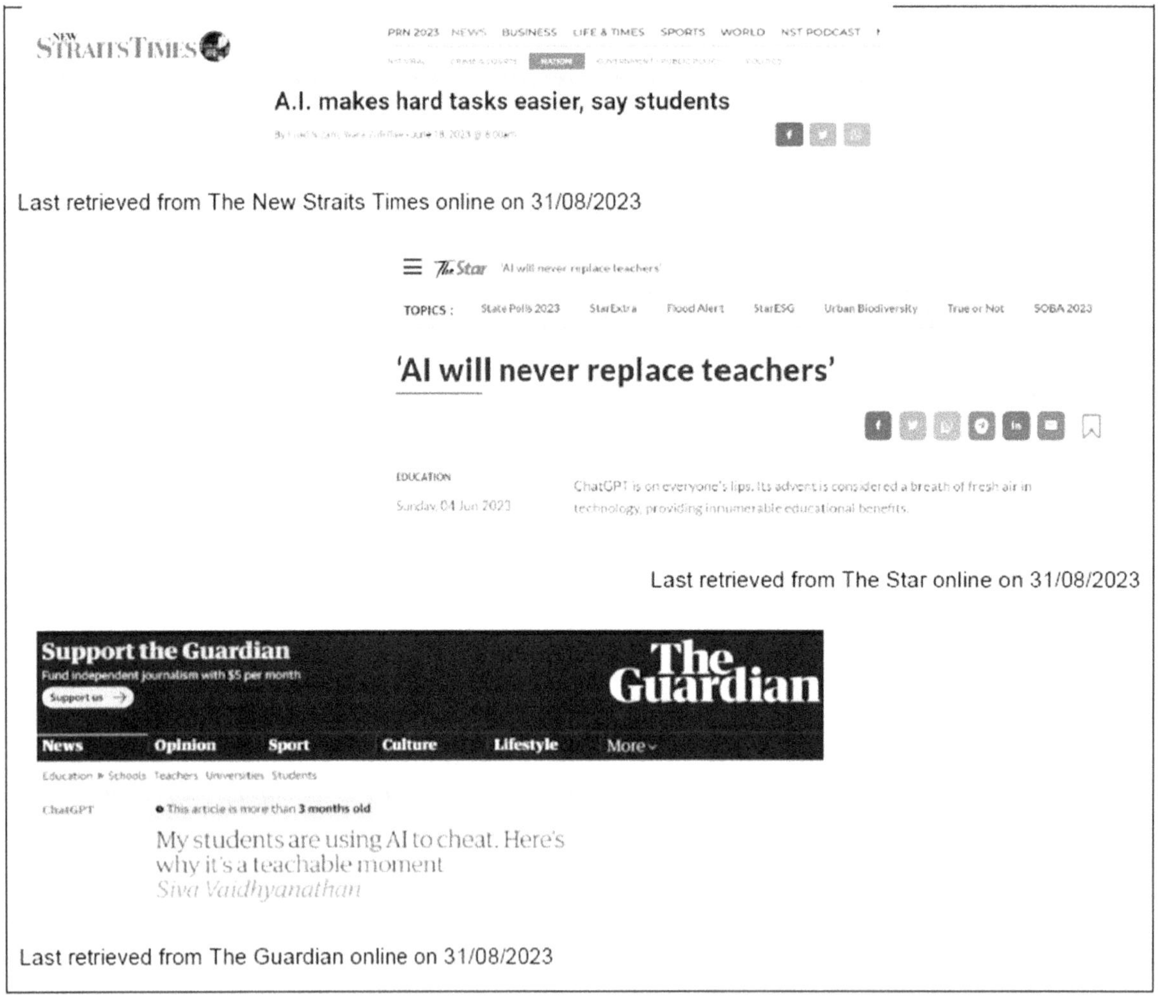

Due to this, various universities worldwide have developed guides or policies related to students' use of AI tools in academic works to delimit potential issues concerning academic integrity and assessment. Table 1 presents some noteworthy excerpts from three different university guidelines that can be found publicly online.

Table 1. Selected university guidelines on AI usage

Topic/Source	The Chinese University of Hong Kong	Heriot Watt University United Kingdom	University of Western Australia
1. Published online in	March 2023	February 2023	February 2023
2. Definition of AI tools and examples according to the institution	*"… There are different types of AI tools, for instance generative AI tools (e.g., Chat GPT) which can be easily instructed using ordinary human language to generate various formats of texts. Some AI tools facilitate the creation of 'original' artwork (e.g. DALL·E 2), translated text (e.g. Google Translate), formulas (e.g. Sheet+), and computer code (e.g. OpenAI Codex), etc. applicable to a great variety of use."*	*"… Artificial intelligence (AI) content creation tools cover a range of skills e.g., writing, art / design, computer coding. They create content based on questions that the user inputs to the tool. There is a wide range of AI content creation tools, you may have heard of some of them e.g., ChatGPT, OpenArt, Dalle-2, Hugging Face. You have probably already used some of these tools without even realising, e.g., Microsoft Editor."*	*"… Artificial intelligence tools have been used to support learning at universities for many years. Spell-checkers, email spam filters, search engines, speech-to-text tools and recommendation systems all use AI algorithms to help us get things done at uni. Recently some generative artificial intelligence tools, such as ChatGPT and Bing, have become prominent."*
3. Reminder for students	*"…AI is a double-edged sword; we should use but not abuse it, use it as research but not cheating tool, and most importantly, use AI to think with you, but not for you."*	*"…Think carefully and critically about the risks, benefits and ethics before you make use of any technology, including AI content creation tools."*	*"… UWA's Academic Integrity Policy allows for the limited use of AI in research, study and assessment. The policy permits you to use AI as educational and study tools."*
4. Regulations on the use of AI tools	*"…Students are prohibited from using any AI tools in their assignments and assessments that count towards students' final grade of the course, or for evaluating their attainment of the desired learning outcomes." "…In courses where students are allowed or expected to collaborate with or use AI tools, students may use these tools for in-class learning activities, exercises or assignments as long as they explicitly cite or acknowledge the use of these tools."*	*"…If you were to use an AI content tool to draft / write your assessment, then the assessment would not be your own work. If you do use an AI tool in any way, ensure that you clearly identify any work in an assessment which is not your own work e.g. if you ask questions of an AI tool and use the answers, then this would not be wholly your own work and should be identified and referenced appropriately."*	*"…these tools must not be used as a replacement of your critical thinking and analysis skills. AI tools may only be used in an assessment where it is explicitly permitted by your Unit Coordinator. Where it is permitted by your Unit Coordinator to use AI, you must always cite and reference your uses of it."*
5. Possible repercussions of undeclared use of AI	*"… Similar to other serious cases of academic dishonesty, penalties for improper/unauthorized use of AI tools in assignments/assessments may include reviewable/permanent demerit(s), failure grade for the course concerned, suspension from the University."*	*"… The Heriot-Watt Student Discipline Policy clearly states that submitting work which is not your own is academic misconduct and a form of cheating. Being found to have committed academic misconduct has potentially severe consequences for your studies and future employment."*	*"…Improper use of AI-generated material in assignments for assessment is grounds for academic misconduct. Remember, there is no time limit on when an occurrence of academic misconduct can be detected. This means that even if improper use of AI is not detected at the time of submission, it can be in the future, and misconduct penalties can be applied retrospectively, including after you graduate."*

Generally, these tertiary learning institutions have acknowledged that the usage of AI tools among students for academic-related tasks cannot be monitored or regulated fully at any given point. Based on the definitions of AI given in the guidelines, universities also accept the existence of various AI-powered tools that serve different purposes and highlight the multifaceted nature of AI support in academia. Interestingly, the use of tools like Microsoft Editor suggests that some students may have already unknowingly utilized AI-powered features, highlighting the seamless integration of AI into academic workflows.

The increased media discourse regarding the ethics related to using AI to produce written products by students has indirectly coerce universities to alert as well as remind students about the ethical, critical, and balanced use of AI in academia. The idea of AI as a "double-edged sword" is introduced, emphasizing that AI should be used judiciously and responsibly. Students are advised to use AI as an aid in their academic pursuits, helping them with problem-solving tasks, but not as a substitute for their own intellectual efforts. Many institutions of higher learning began to come to terms on the importance of promoting a balanced approach to AI usage in education.

While threats of disciplinary action may be apparent in the guidelines, it is still unclear to many as to what extent are students willing to take the risk in getting some extra support for their assignments or tests. It is an interesting premise worth exploring; that is to look at how students make sense of the disruptive technology of AI in education while still adhering to rules, policies and guidelines set by their respective higher learning institutions.

AI in English Language Teaching and Learning

In the context of English language teaching and learning, Ray (2023) had found AI-powered tools to enhance students' productivity in various proficiency-based tasks. In more specific instances, Lakkala et al. (2022) had shown that Poetry Machine helped students to develop and revise poems written during literature class while Su et al. (2023) claim that digital story writing (DSW) turned out to be an effective and meaningful inquiry-based pedagogical approach in teaching writing to EFL students.

Some common areas that language instructors integrate AI into teaching and learning are assessment and feedback, translation support and content creation. In terms of assessment and feedback, Duolingo offers a wide range of language courses which can be personalized according to students' starting proficiency levels and provides instant feedback based on the listening, speaking, reading and writing exercises performed (Maria et al., 2018). LanguageTool has also been recently added as an extension to Microsoft Word and Google Docs as an official grammar and style checker (Puspitasari et al., 2022). Secondly, there are recent developments for translation support that particularly helps EFL students apart from ESL students. Other than Google Translate which offers text translation, voice translation, and image translation, Deep Learning approach of AI can also be utilized for high-quality machine translations (Birdsell, 2022) which allows EFL students to learn English using authentic materials. While content creation is also fast becoming a blooming area with AI's intervention as language exercises, quizzes, and testable content like reading passages or audio materials can be created and tailored to students' varied proficiencies and needs. Tools like ChatCPT and Articoolo support these functions well and are available for free at the time being (Lim et al., 2023).

However, just like everyone else, language scholars seem to be concerned that AI-powered tools could end up as a double-edged sword in the context of language teaching and learning. These concerns revolve around the transformative impact of AI on education and its implications for students, educators, and society as a whole. The first concern relates to the increasing personalization in education using new technologies; Chen et al. (2020) shared an alarming prediction where AI-powered tools could end up further dividing students from their peers, teachers and the society as students may become dependent on AI for tutoring. This overreliance on AI could result in the fragmentation of the learning experience, isolating students from the rich social and collaborative aspects of education. Secondly, Carvalho et al. (2022) also highlighted their concern on how practitioners may still not have figured out the ways to support the young generation of learners to develop the skills that they will need to adapt to and innovate with AI. This includes prompting skills (Mackenzie, 2023) and academic integrity of using AI-generated knowledge and information (Lim et al., 2023). It is a great fear that when students use AI tools with inadequate awareness, it may lead to a generation of learners who are highly proficient in navigating AI-driven educational environments but lack essential interpersonal and critical thinking skills.

Therefore, there is a pressing need to gather a comprehensive understanding of university students' lived experiences and perceptions when utilizing AI-powered tools in English language learning based on qualitative data. As urged by researchers Bilquise and Shaalan (2022), this would greatly help to shed light on the potential benefits and challenges students encounter, with a particular emphasis on how these tools may enhance or hinder students' language skills. These insights are particularly vital in informing educators and tertiary level institutions about the best practices in integrating AI into language education. Insights from qualitative data may provide more substantial evidence and support for AI-related policies in the education sector.

The Theory Behind It All: Quick Dive Into the Theory of Planned Behavior (TPB)

In order to explore how students perceive and use the existing AI, this chapter aims to capture students' viewpoints towards the emergence of AI in education and the ways to go forward. To provide a more meaningful analysis of students' perspectives and expectations of AI-powered tools in day-to-day language learning activities, the authors have decided to explore the data using the Theory of Planned Behavior (TPB).

TPB is a psychological theory that provides insights into how individuals' attitudes, subjective norms, and perceived behavioral control influence their intentions and behaviors (Ajzen, 1991). It posits that individuals' intentions to engage in a specific behavior are influenced by three main constructs: attitudinal behavior (AB), subjective norms (SN), and perceived behavioral control (PBC). These three constructs collectively shape an individual's behavioral intentions. Higher positive attitudes, perceived social support (subjective norms), and a stronger belief in their ability to control the behavior led to a greater intention to engage in that behavior. TPB advocates that behavioral intentions are the immediate antecedents of actual behavior. In other words, stronger intentions are more likely to result in the desired behavior. TPB has been applied across various domains, including health psychology, marketing, environmental behavior, and social sciences, to explain and predict human actions. It has proven to be a useful framework of reference for behavioral related studies such those related to intervention for desirable behaviors. In his study, Ajzen (1991) utilized TPB to examine how beliefs and attitudes influence the adoption of environmentally friendly behaviors. The findings revealed that individuals with more favorable attitudes and subjective norms were more likely to engage in performing the intended actions.

Similarly, in exploring the students' intention toward the inclusion of AI in their academic work process, it will be important to understand if the students' attitudinal behavior (AB), subjective norms (SN), and perceived behavioral control (PBC) affect their perceptions and usage of AI in attending to their academic tasks. As shown in the study of Chai et al. (2023), TPB is also helpful to understand students' intentions to use AI as academic support, and this in turn, sheds light on their decision-making process. In the context of the current study, TPB can be applied in the ways shown in Figure 2.

Figure 2. Theory of planned behavior in context

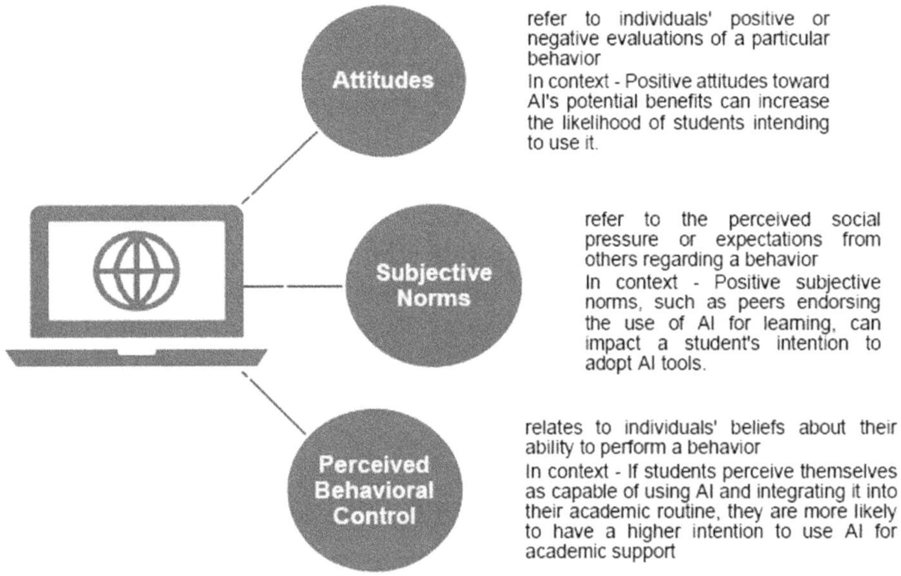

In summary, the TPB framework is well-suited to analyze university-level students' usage of AI-powered tools for academic support because it provides a comprehensive model that incorporates intentions, attitudes, subjective norms, and perceived behavioral control. Its well-established predictive power and practical applications make it a valuable tool for understanding the factors influencing AI tool adoption in educational contexts.

THE STUDY: UNVEILING STUDENT PERSPECTIVES

Methodology of the Current Study

This research uses a qualitative approach that involves conducting semi-structured interviews with participants who had experienced using AI in attending to their academic work. 8 students enrolled in 2 different tertiary learning institutions in Malaysia were selected based on convenience-based non-probability sampling method. 4 students were diploma level students at a private university while another 4 were postgraduate level students at a public university. All students were well briefed about the study in prior to engaging them in individual semi-structured interview sessions.

The interviews were recorded using audio recording devices and later on be transcribed. The qualitative approach offers an in-depth understanding of complex phenomena by exploring nuances, contexts, and subjective experiences. Whilst semi-structured interviews, a key qualitative tool, enabled the researchers to ensure that the interview questions posed during the interviews address the key dimensions of TPB, as well as foster rich insights and accommodate individual perspectives. Table 2 presents a validated semi-structured interview protocol used in the current investigation.

Table 2. Proposed semi-structured interview protocol

Domain	Attitude	Subjective Norms	Perceived Behavior Control	Others
Questions*	a. What are your initial thoughts or feelings about using AI tools for academic assistance? b. What specific academic tasks do you believe AI tools could help you with?	c. Have you observed other students using AI tools for their studies? How has that impacted your perception of these tools? d. Have you discussed AI tools with your peers or lecturers? If yes, what were their opinions?	e. Have you already used AI tools such as ChatGPT or Google Bard for academic purposes? f. If yes, how often and for what tasks? g. What factors might influence your decision to continue or discontinue using AI tools?	h. Based on your previous experiences, how satisfied are you with the performance and results of AI tools? i. In your experience, what are the weaknesses of AI tools for academic support? j. Are there any specific features or improvements you would like to see in AI tools to better support your academic needs?
**Questions developed based on literature on AI tools for education and the Theory of Planned Behavior. Questions have been loosely adapted from the qualitative instruments and findings from the studies of Sumakul et al. (2022) and (Burkhard, 2022).*				

In terms of data analysis, the analysis of the transcribed interview data basically involved the use of content and thematic analysis. Content analysis plays a key role in enabling a systematic examination of data. It involves the labeling of condensed meaning units by formulating codes and then grouping these codes into categories (Erlingsson & Brysiewicz, 2017).

Thematic analysis, on the other hand, focuses on identifying, analyzing, and reporting patterns (themes) within the interview data. As stated by Braun & Clarke (2006), themes capture a prominent aspect of the data in a patterned way. Not only thematic analysis offers flexibility in terms identifying trends, it also promotes interpretive depth and helps to uncover complex interrelationships between themes (Braun et al., 2020). Both methods provide rigor for uncovering insights and understanding the underlying meanings and nuances.

Background of Study Participants' Usage of AI in Language Classrooms

According to Xuan et al. (2023), a majority of tertiary level learners in Malaysia have started using AI-powered tools in their classrooms in 2023. To exemplify, in a Malaysian private university, diploma level students from various faculties are allowed to use AI-powered tools such as ChatGPT for one of their coursework for the language course, Academic English. The coursework is referred to as a 'Grammar Project' which constitutes 30% of their overall coursework grade. The instruction for the coursework is as follows:

Box 1.

Coursework 3: Grammar Project (30%) Week 6

Description
This is a group project consisting between 3 and 4 students. Students are tasked to prepare an activity in presenting a grammatical item assigned to them. Subsequently, students have to present the grammar activity in the class. Each group is given 20-30 minutes to present. Students may use online materials or AI-powered tools approved by their tutor at all stages of this activity.

Assessment Criteria
Students will be assessed on the following:

- The ability to write a feasible plan outlining the materials, timelines and description of the grammar project.
- The ability to contribute to the grammar activities
- The ability to present appropriate grammatical item in a creative way
- The ability to cooperate in group activities
- The ability to answer questions about the grammar activities presented

Marking Criteria

- Outline: 5 marks
- Language: 30 marks
- Content: 30 marks
- Delivery: 30 marks
- Q & A: 5 marks

Total: 100 marks
This coursework supports Quality Education under the 17 groups of the Sustainable Development Goals.

For this project, students are required to prepare an activity which allows the whole class to revise various grammatical items using interesting activities such as games, quizzes and more. At the planning stage, tutors allow students to utilize search engines and AI-powered tools such as ChatGPT, Bing or Bard to gather ideas on the kinds of classroom activities they can do for topics such as tenses, sentence structures, active-passive sentences, direct and indirect speeches, prepositions and adjectives and adverbs.

A sample query performed on ChatGPT by one of the groups is presented in Figure 3 along with response. The grammar topic assigned to them was Adjectives and Adverbs.

Using this guide, the students then adapted this activity with some changes and submitted an outline to the tutor to be approved. The tutor also provides some feedback to the students. A sample is shown in Table 3.

Using this example, it can be understood that while students may turn to AI-powered tools to help them with their language assignments, they also have the opportunities to infuse their own creativity and ideas into the suggestions provided by the AI tools. Unfortunately, some tutors have reported whereby students were found to copy-paste Chat-GPT's suggestion of activities directly into the outline of grammar project and submit as their own. The tutors found themselves in a tricky situation to award marks for outline in this case as nowhere in the coursework brief it was mentioned that students cannot copy directly from AI sources. The course coordinator of Academic English subject at this particular university has been alerted to update the coursework brief to reflect ethical use of AI-powered tools.

To further expand on this phenomenon, this study has conducted interviews with selected diploma and postgraduate students from two universities in Malaysia. Findings are presented in the next section.

Figure 3. Sample response from ChatGPT for a query from students
Last retrieved on 31/12/2023 at https://chat.openai.com/c/32226718-e31f-4c5d-bd43-957f147bf67b

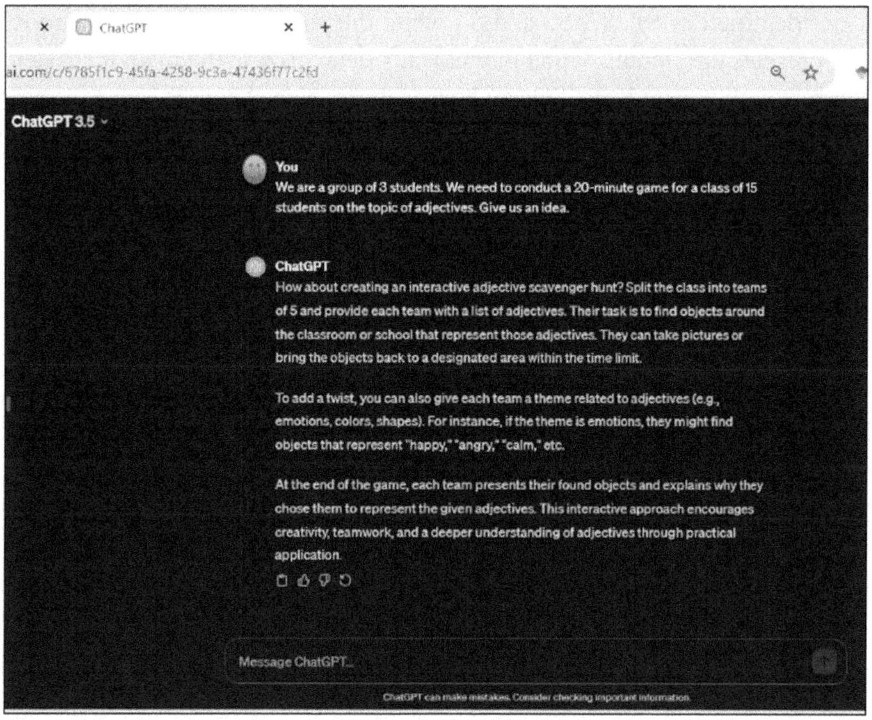

Table 3. Sample grammar project outline submitted for tutor's approval

Topic	Adjectives and Adverbs
Members in the group	3
Activity Description	First, we will introduce different types of adjectives and their uses using a short presentation on Canva. Next, we will divide the class into 3 groups and each of us will be in charge for a group. We will then provide each group with some photos that we have taken from around the campus. Photos will be taken from canteen, indoor and outdoor events and general outings of our classmates. They then need to create as many sentences as they can based on the theme given. The themes we have selected for the groups are "feelings", "colors" and "numbers". They are given only 10 minutes for this. The group with the most number of sentences that match the theme given, wins the game. To show our own understanding of adjectives, once the groups have completed, the three of us will explain the types and uses of the adjectives found in their sentences.
Materials	Canva presentation, printed photos on A4 papers, more papers, candies as rewards
Other Remarks	This activity has been improvised from a Chat-GPT suggestion on 20th December 2023.
Tutor's Feedback	*Good plan! Please make sure they do not take more than 10 minutes to write sentences, or else you will not be able to complete this activity within 20 minutes. Secondly, since you have already explained different types of adjectives and uses in the introduction, it may be redundant to do that again with the students' sentences. I would suggest you to try change the adjectives identified into adverbs (if possible) to demonstrate the relationship between adjectives and adverbs. This may give you better roles to play for this activity, and I will have more substance to grant you marks out of 95.*
Marks given for this outline	4/5 marks

FINDINGS AND DISCUSSION

To maintain anonymity of the students for ethical purposes, in the presentation of findings, the diploma level students are identified as S1, S2, S3 and S4 while the postgraduate students are R1, R2, R3 and R4. This section presents the findings upon thematically categorizing the main ideas detected from the interview responses of all the students. Selected excerpts are also shown for illustration purposes. It is to be noted while section 2.2 shows how students have specifically used ChatGPT for the preparation of Grammar Project, this section presents findings from their general and overall usage of AI-powered tools throughout their semester.

The Role of Intention in Perceiving AI as a Companion

From the lens of TPB, to understand students' intention to use AI for language learning, it is important to first understand their initial thoughts on AI. Responses for the question on initial reaction show that students perceived AI as a tool for improvement and enhancement in various academic tasks, as an advanced and amazing technology, and also as a tool worth cautioning.

Using AI as a Tool for Enhancement of Academic Work

As simplified in Table 4, all the postgraduate participants were found to use various AI tools to improve their academic work in terms of rephrasing, replacing words, double rephrasing, summarizing, and researching.

AI Is Viewed as an Advanced and Amazing Technology

Students such as S2 expressed a sense of wonder and amazement about the rapid and sudden advanced nature of AI tools, suggesting that university students may be impressed by the capabilities of AI technology, possibly implying a willingness to explore it.

Similarly, R2 seemed to be impressed with AI's capabilities as well when she said:

"My classmates' use of AI tools actually made me look highly of AI tools, because I found that they would ask AI tools about some very basic questions like what was definition of 'foregrounding', and the AI tools could provide some straightforward explanations." (R2)

On the other hand, some participants perceive AI in a less favourable manner, whereby the students felt that it's not all about AI is "hunky-dory" in nature. The next section depicts some of the students' views on the hidden risks of AI.

AI Is a Tool That Should Be Used With Caution

S3's response reflects a more cautious perspective, influenced by depictions of AI in movies as potentially harmful or destructive to humanity. This alludes that some students may approach AI with caution for its potentially negative consequences. He stated:

Table 4. Academic tasks participants performed using AI tools

Task	Description	Excerpt From Interviews
Rephrasing	AI tools can use advanced natural language processing algorithms to generate alternative versions of a given sentence while preserving the original meaning. This can be particularly useful when trying to rephrase information from existing sources or when attempting to avoid repetitive language in academic writing.	"...I feel that AI is an exceedingly valuable tool to be used as an academic assistance, specifically in sentence paraphrasing" (R3)
Replacing Words	It is also understood that AI tools can provide suggestions for synonyms or alternative word choices that are contextually appropriate for academic writing. This feature can help students improve the variety and precision of their vocabulary, making their writing more sophisticated and effective.	"...mostly for proofreading and give me suggestions on how to improve my writing and make my writing more "academic". (R4) The same participant also stated that: "It can give me advice from various perspectives like clarity, consistency, grammar, transitions, etc."
Double Paraphrasing	Double paraphrasing involves using AI tools to generate a paraphrased version of a sentence or paragraph and then applying another AI tool for further paraphrasing. This iterative process can help refine and enhance the clarity, coherence, and originality of the written content.	"Double paraphrasing (i.e., using ChatGPT to generate a paraphrased academic sentence or paragraph from past studies, and use Quillbot to paraphrase the same sentence/paragraph the second time). AI tools can also help with widening one's academic vocabulary and aid in filtering relevance studies for academic use..." (R3)
Summarizing journal articles	AI tools can automatically extract key information and main points from lengthy journal articles, providing concise summaries that capture the essence of the original content. This enables researchers to quickly grasp the main findings and implications of a study without having to read the entire article, as pointed out by one of the participants.	"...I have used AI tools such as ChatPDF to efficiently summarize relevance journal articles" (R3)
Researching	Students seem to use ChatGPT to gather information on topics easily. Instead of browsing multiple websites or articles, they seem to appreciate that they can find concise information at a one-stop ChatGPT.	"I try to search on Google for some information, which I can't get, so then I use ChatGPT to get the information instead." (S1)
For Daily use outside of Academic Work	Some students seemed to have familiarized themselves with AI-powered tools in daily life activities outside of academic work way long before they started using it in classrooms.	"I now use it as a starting point for my assignments, but I also already AI tools like SIRI with my daily activities such as to wake up on time. For the easy things, such as calling somebody or setting alarm" (S4)

"I think, before the AI thing really came out, I thought it is something that could destroy humanity, based on the movies that we have watched before. So, we should be careful with it." (S2)

It's important to note that while AI tools can be valuable for these specific tasks, some postgraduate students also mentioned that they should be used judiciously and in conjunction with human judgment. Students and researchers should critically evaluate the output generated by AI tools, verify the accuracy of information, and exercise caution to avoid potential issues such as plagiarism or overreliance on automated processes. As pointed out by a participant (R1):

"It might lead to overreliance and hinder genuine academic progress. This concern is particularly relevant for non-native English speakers, as GPT's direct translation feature could make one lazy and impede real academic improvement."

Emphasizing on the enabling factors, the students generally demonstrated a positive attitude towards using AI tools for various academic tasks. A majority of them mentioned using AI, like ChatGPT, to assist with paraphrasing, editing and proofreading, locating appropriate research articles and summarization. This suggests that they see AI as a helpful and effective tool for improving their academic work. Their intention to use AI for these tasks is influenced by their positive attitude towards its potential benefits. In fact, S4 mentions using AI tools like Siri for daily tasks, which indicates a general acceptance of AI technology.

S2, S3 and R1, on the other hand, did not express a positive attitude towards using AI for academic tasks; which implies a lack of interest or enthusiasm. This can be attributed as a cautionary factor among the students interviewed.

In summary, the students' responses reflect varying attitudes and perceived behavioral control when it comes to using AI for academic tasks. Attitude, as demonstrated by their views on the usefulness of AI, plays a significant role in shaping their intentions.

Social and Contextual Factors Shaping Student Perceptions

2 questions were formulated to dive into the various social or contextual factors that affect how students perceive AI in language learning. The first is, have you observed other students using AI tools for their studies and the second is, have you discussed AI tools with your peers or lecturers? If yes, what were their opinions?

In short, the responses to Question 3 and Question 4 highlight the significant role of subjective norms, including peer behavior and opinions of authority figures (teachers/lecturers), in shaping students' perceptions and intentions related to AI tools for academic purposes. Mostly students' decision to use AI to a certain extent is influenced by the individuals such as friends, classmates.

Friends and Lecturers Use AI Tools Openly

S1 observed other students using AI tools and saw it as a positive influence. The student noticed that others were benefiting from AI, which encouraged him to try it himself. In another similar situation, S4 saw most of his classmates using AI tools and felt left out because he thought that he was not thinking as creatively. He admitted to have started using AI for academic tasks in order to appear to be more creative. On the other hand, S2 also observed his classmates using AI tools but had a negative perception of it. He mentioned that the answers generated by AI felt artificial and not genuine.

When asked if they discussed AI with their peers or lecturers, S1 answered that peer discussion likely reinforced his positive perception of AI tools and his intention to use them for academic purposes. S2 mentioned that some lecturers allow the use of AI tools in classrooms. This suggests that there is some level of acceptance by authority figures (lecturers), which can positively influence students' perceptions and intentions to use AI in academic settings.

In another interesting instance, R3 also noted about peers who used AI-powered tools openly for classwork:

"A friend of mine used AI tools for double paraphrasing purposes. The AI tools have helped her to complete tasks efficiently and produce quality academic writeups. This completely changed my perception towards AI tools and since then, I have started using them as academic support for my PhD thesis writeup."

Some Parties Are Not in Favor of AI Tools

S4, on the other hand, mentioned that using AI in university is discouraged, and lecturers deem students as lazy when they use it. This negative view expressed by lecturers likely had a discouraging effect on students' intentions to openly discuss and use AI. S4 confessed that he still uses AI, but without declaring it to anyone around him, especially to his lecturers.

R1 also shared similar views whereby she said:

"I have discussed it with my peers. Most of them are not good at using it. One of my peers told me that she doesn't think GPT is very useful, perhaps GPT plugins are more useful." (R1)

Thus, one can conclude that due to the influence of individuals in their social circles, some of these students do think of AI in a less favourable manner.

Social Factors Shaping Student Perceptions

It can be concluded that positive peer behavior and support from teachers can encourage the use of AI, while negative peer perceptions and discouragement from lecturers can deter its adoption. These findings align with the principles of the Theory of Planned Behavior, where subjective norms play a crucial role in shaping intentions and behaviors.

It is important to note that subjective norms refer to the perceived social pressure to perform or not perform a behavior. If students' peers or professors have a strong opinion against using AI for academic tasks, this could potentially influence their intention not to use AI.

Students' Perceived Control Matters When Dealing With AI

Based on the interview data, due to the varying experience in incorporating AI as a tool when attending to their academic tasks, whereby a number of students even admitted that they only begun to explore the use of AI in aiding their academic work, the data that relates to students' view on how much control they feel they possess in terms of integrating data was very limited. Therefore, the findings that relates to the perceived behavioral control are presented in a single paragraph.

In general, when the participants were asked to share what factors would help them decide if they would continue or discontinue using AI tools for academic purposes. Some students expressed the intention to continue using AI, citing the busy schedule and the need for efficiency in completing tasks. This response seems to align with a perception of high control, as AI is seen as a practical tool that helps manage time and workload effectively. It is to be noted that participants like S1 and R1 were consistent in expressing a positive attitude toward AI, viewing it as a tool for improvement. Similarly, S2 mentioned turning to AI for help when struggling with assignments, especially when his friends are not helpful or do not contribute to the generation of ideas. This indicates a perceived level of control over the decision to use AI in specific situations where personal resources (ideas from friends) are limited. On the contrary, S3 mentioned a condition under which he would discontinue using AI if it becomes too smart and scares him. This indicates a perception of potential risks associated with AI becoming too advanced. It appeared to be that his decision was influenced by perceived risks and a lack of control over potential negative outcomes. In short, students' perceptions of control may be influenced by factors such as the perceived efficiency and time-saving benefits of AI, the availability of alternative resources (like friends for ideas), concerns about potential risks, and considerations about the impact on cognitive processes.

As stated by Gado et. al (2022), the results in their study showed that apart from perceived usefulness of AI, attitude towards AI, perceived social norm regarding AI; student's perceived knowledge of AI turned out to be important predictors of individuals' intention to use AI. In the context of the present study, many of these students seem to have very limited experience in using AI when dealing with the various learning tasks, thus it is not surprising that many of them did not revealed much about their views regarding how much behavioural control they possess when dealing with AI.

Incidentally, based on the interviews carried out with the diploma level students, the findings revealed that the students' English language proficiency does play a role in shaping their views regarding the roles and usefulness of AI.

Perception Shaped by Language Proficiency of Students

Interestingly, the participants responses to questions related to perception also differed based on their ESL proficiency levels. It is to be noted that S1, S2, S3 and all postgraduate participants were intermediate to advanced users of ESL while S4 was a beginner level user.

S1, who had an intermediate to advanced level of ESL proficiency, did not mention any weaknesses other than the potential issue of plagiarism. This response indicates a generally positive view of AI tools, with a specific concern related to academic integrity. S2, with intermediate to advanced ESL proficiency, identified a weakness related to the artificial sound of some answers. Similarly, S3, with intermediate to advanced ESL proficiency, highlighted a weakness related to the depth of information provided by AI. He said:

"Sometimes, the information provided is too deep for our knowledge. Some assignments just want simple and basic answers but the AI's answers are too deep for me to understand. So, even if we use it in assignment, it won't be useful for us." (S3)

Some students' proficiency level likely contributes to recognizing the challenge of aligning AI-generated content with their own comprehension levels. On the contrary, S4, who is a beginner level ESL user, mentioned a weakness related to students becoming lazier and dependent on AI. His response suggests a broader concern about the impact of AI on student behavior and work ethic.

In general, students with higher ESL proficiency levels might be more attuned to language-related weaknesses, such as the artificiality of responses or the complexity of information provided by AI. On the other hand, students with lower ESL proficiency levels might focus on broader concerns about the impact of AI on learning habits rather than specific linguistic aspects. This can be seen in the differences of responses of the diploma level students who were more general in their responses and the postgraduate students who mentioned very specific linguistic aspects. One main takeaway from this finding is that the language proficiency of students can shape how they utilize AI and in their daily academic tasks understand the strengths and weaknesses of AI tools. This insight can be valuable for educators and researchers aiming to implement or study the impact of AI tools in diverse language learning environments.

AI USAGE AMONG STUDENTS FROM THE LENS OF THEORY OF PLANNED BEHAVIOUR

Based on the findings presented, it is very clear that intentions matter, perceptions are complex, and student voices are crucial. One of the major findings from this study is that, intention does matter in the context of students' usage of AI-powered tools for academic support. As agreed by Choi and Suh (2022), intention acts as a crucial factor to consider when analyzing students' behavior and attitudes for learning. The Theory of Planned Behavior (TPB) emphasizes the significance of intention in predicting and understanding behavior (Niepel et al., 2018).

Intention should be part of needs assessment moving forward for adds predictive power. Ajzen (1991) asserts that intention serves as a strong predictor of actual behavior. In the TPB, intention is a key determinant of whether an individual will engage in a specific behavior, such as using AI-powered tools for academic support. Students' intentions to use or not use these tools can provide insights into their likely behavior. Also relating the current findings to studies by Prasad and Jaheer (2023) and Tuomi (2018), students' intentions may be influenced by their attitudes (whether they see AI tools as beneficial), subjective norms (what their peers and professors think), and perceived behavioral control (how easy they perceive it to use AI tools) as well.

Acknowledging that individuals' attitudes and beliefs are multifaceted is vital in accepting the complex views presented by students. As supported by Soomro et al. (2015) students performing academic tasks in English may come from diverse backgrounds and have unique educational experiences. Due to this, their prior exposure to AI, technology, and academic environments can vary significantly. This diversity leads to a wide range of perceptions about AI tools. Some students may be highly familiar with AI and embrace it, while others may be less experienced and more apprehensive. Furthermore, perceptions are also influenced by subjective norms, which according to Ajzen (1991), represent the perceived social pressure or expectations of others. Students may be influenced by the attitudes and behaviors of their peers, instructors, and the wider academic community. As proven in a similar study by Ramirez-Anormaliza et al. (2015), these external influences can contribute to the complexity of students' perceptions about their learning environments.

This is related to the final point, where students' voices are crucial in understanding their changing views and multi-faceted concerns regarding AI's influence in the education sector. According to Ajit et al. (2022), student voices can be instrumental in tailoring support services and interventions. In the context of the current study, if the students express concerns about AI making them lazier, institutions can use their voices to design interventions that promote responsible and effective AI use. This is to ascertain that as students' perceptions evolve, their feedback can drive ongoing enhancements to AI tools, ensuring that the tools remain relevant and effective over time.

In line with what has been proposed by Ajit et al. (2022) regarding the significance of student voices or opinions in the endeavour to enhance the usefulness of AI, the present investigation also asked these students for suggestions pertaining to the weaknesses of AI tools for academic support, as well as if there any specific features or improvements AI tools that they opine will better support their academic needs. The suggestions given are presented in the next section.

WHAT STUDENTS WANT: SUGGESTIONS FOR THE FUTURE

Pertaining to the last question of the interview protocol, "Are there any specific features or improvements you would like to see in AI tools to better support your academic needs?". Overall, the diploma-level students' responses indicate a mix of contentment, recognition of limitations in suggesting improvements, and specific requests for features that align with their individual preferences and needs.

AI Tools Are Good as They Are

S1 expresses satisfaction with the current state of AI tools, indicating that he does not have any specific features or improvements in mind. This might suggest contentment with the existing functionalities, possibly reflecting a positive overall experience with AI tools. S2 too perceives the current tools as effective and sufficient for his needs.

Adding Voice Features to AI Tools

S3 and S4 actually offered some useful suggestions. S3 suggested the addition of voice features to AI tools. He mentioned that listening would be preferable to reading, indicating a preference for auditory learning. This request for voice features aligns with a specific learning preference, possibly influenced by his personal learning style. S3 was interviewed in September 2023, and perhaps he was not aware of the voice command features that were being integrated into many popular AI tools. However, by October 2023, many AI tools have published guides in activating voice commands to generate response.

Figure 4. Bing's voice command feature published in June 2023

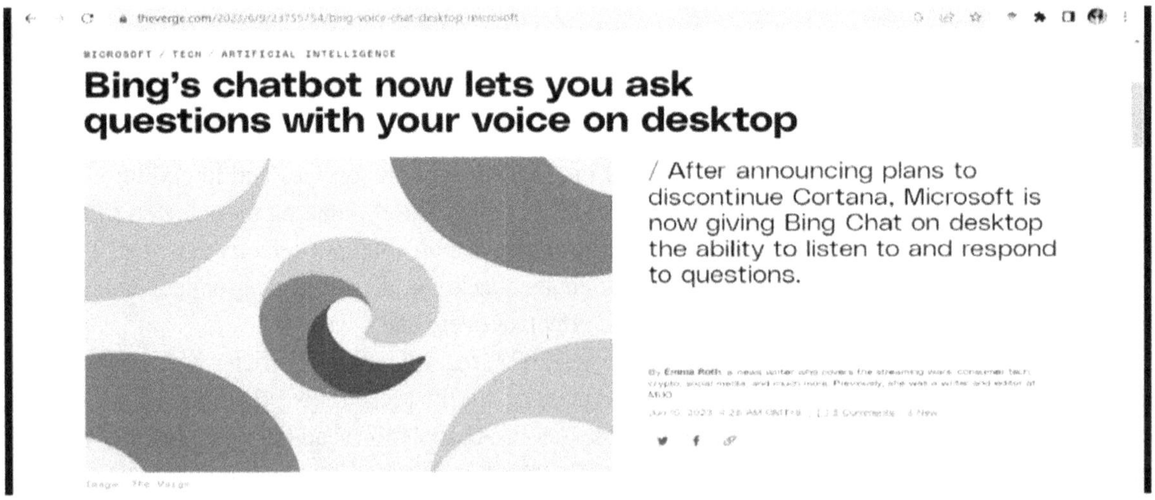
MICROSOFT / TECH / ARTIFICIAL INTELLIGENCE

Bing's chatbot now lets you ask questions with your voice on desktop

/ After announcing plans to discontinue Cortana, Microsoft is now giving Bing Chat on desktop the ability to listen to and respond to questions.

More Self-Learning Support From AI Tools

In another interesting sharing, S4 expressed a desire for AI tools to facilitate studying at home without the need to come to school. He specifically mentioned the wish for classes, mini lessons, or tutorials from AI tools. This request implies a desire for more comprehensive educational support beyond information retrieval, possibly reflecting a preference for a more structured and guided learning experience. Recognizing individual learning preferences is crucial when designing or improving AI tools for academic support. Features such as voice support or structured learning modules might enhance the overall user experience for some students.

FINAL THOUGHTS

Learning Together in the Age of AI

Whether individuals such as students or instructors embrace AI or not, AI and AI-related tools are already a part the academic life and are here to stay. Henceforth, it is the responsibility of learners and instructors alike to learn what they are and how to harness AI potentials (Esplugas, 2023).

An ideal AI-powered language learning tool, based on the students' input for the current study and aligned with the Theory of Planned Behavior (TPB), should prioritize positive attitudes, social influence, perceived behavioral control, and seamless integration with academic tasks. Customization options, feedback mechanisms, and features addressing specific concerns contribute to a well-rounded language learning experience that caters to the diverse needs and preferences of students. In visualizing an AI-powered tool that can support language learners, attention should be given to adaptive learning paths (Kularbphettong et al., 2015), feedback (Butow & Hoque, 2020), cultural context integration (Tuomi, 2018), interactive conversations (Ligorio, 2022), offline learning support (Radha et al., 2020) and multilingual support (Tamim, 2021).

At this juncture, it is important to encouraging ongoing dialogue between students, educators, and developers as it is pivotal for the effective and inclusive integration of AI in educational settings. As suggested by Reiss (2021), the authors of this chapter too strongly believe that continuous dialogue among stakeholders ensures that AI tools are developed in a user-centered manner. By actively engaging students, educators, and developers in discussions, the tools can be tailored to meet the diverse needs and preferences of the users, resulting in more effective and relevant solutions for 21st century education and beyond.

REFERENCES

Ajit, G., Lucas, T., & Kanyan, R. (2022). Design and Technology in Malaysian Secondary Schools: A Perspective on Challenges. *Malaysian Journal of Social Sciences and Humanities*, *7*(1), 335–351. doi:10.47405/mjssh.v7i1.1219

Ajzen, I. (1991). The theory of planned behavior. *Organizational Behavior and Human Decision Processes*, *50*(2), 179–211. doi:10.1016/0749-5978(91)90020-T

Bilquise, G., & Shaalan, K. (2022). AI-based Academic Advising Framework: A Knowledge Management Perspective. *International Journal of Advanced Computer Science and Applications, 13*(8), 193–203. doi:10.14569/IJACSA.2022.0130823

Birdsell, B. (2022). Student Writings with DeepL: Teacher Evaluations and Implications for Teaching. *JALT Postconference Publication, 2021*(1), 117. doi:10.37546/JALTPCP2021-14

Braun, V., Clarke, V., Boulton, E., Davey, L., & McEvoy, C. (2020). The online survey as a qualitative research tool. *International Journal of Social Research Methodology, 00*(00), 1–14. doi:10.1080/13645579.2020.1805550

Burkhard, M. (2022). Student Perceptions of Ai-Powered Writing Tools: Towards Individualized Teaching Strategies. *Proceedings of the 19th International Conference on Cognition and Exploratory Learning in the Digital Age, CELDA 2022, Celda*, 73–81. 10.33965/CELDA2022_202207L010

Carvalho, L., Martinez-maldonado, R., Tsai, Y., & Markauskaite, L. (2022). Computers and Education : Artificial Intelligence How can we design for learning in an AI world ? *Computers and Education: Artificial Intelligence, 3*(July), 100053. doi:10.1016/j.caeai.2022.100053

Chen, X., Xie, H., & Hwang, G. J. (2020). A multi-perspective study on Artificial Intelligence in Education: Grants, conferences, journals, software tools, institutions, and researchers. *Computers and Education: Artificial Intelligence, 1*(October), 100005. doi:10.1016/j.caeai.2020.100005

Choi, Y., & Suh, K. H. (2022). Verifying the usefulness of the theory of planned behavior model for predicting illegal use of online content: The role of outcome expectancies and social loafing. *BMC Psychology, 10*(1), 1–12. doi:10.1186/s40359-022-00978-3 PMID:36371253

Esplugas, M. (2023). The use of artificial intelligence (AI) to enhance academic communication, education and research: A balanced approach. *The Journal of Hand Surgery, 48*(8), 819–822. doi:10.1177/17531934231185746 PMID:37417005

Gado, S., Kempen, R., Lingelbach, K., & Bipp, T. (2022). Artificial intelligence in Psychology: How can we enable psychology students to accept and use artificial intelligence? *Psychology Learning & Teaching, 21*(1), 37–56. doi:10.1177/14757257211037149

Haleem, A., Javaid, M., & Pratap, R. (2023). BenchCouncil Transactions on Benchmarks, Standards and Evaluations An era of ChatGPT as a significant futuristic support tool : A study on features, abilities, and challenges. *BenchCouncil Transactions on Benchmarks. Standards and Evaluations, 2*(4), 100089. doi:10.1016/j.tbench.2023.100089

Lakkala, M., Toom, A., Kangasharju, A., & Ilom, L. (2022). *Computers and Education : Artificial Intelligence Lower secondary students ' poetry writing with the AI-based Poetry Machine.* doi:10.1016/j.caeai.2022.100048

Lim, W. M., Gunasekara, A., Pallant, J. L., Pallant, J. I., & Pechenkina, E. (2023). Generative AI and the future of education: Ragnarök or reformation? A paradoxical perspective from management educators. *International Journal of Management Education, 21*(2), 100790. doi:10.1016/j.ijme.2023.100790

Mackenzie, D. (2023). Surprising Advances in Generative Artificial Intelligence Prompt Amazement — And Worries. *Engineering (Beijing)*, *xxxx*, 4–6. doi:10.1016/j.eng.2023.04.004

Maria, G., Sousa, B. De, Cardoso, L., & Toassi, P. (2018). *Duolingo As a Tool to Improve Vocabulary Writing in English as a No Inglês Como Língua Estrangeira*. Academic Press.

Niepel, C., Burrus, J., Greiff, S., Lipnevich, A. A., Brenneman, M. W., & Roberts, R. D. (2018). Students' beliefs and attitudes toward mathematics across time: A longitudinal examination of the theory of planned behavior. *Learning and Individual Differences, 63*(June), 24–33. doi:10.1016/j.lindif.2018.02.010

Prasad, B. N., & Jaheer, B. (2023). The Use of AI (artificial Intelligence) in English Learning Among Engineering Students: A Case Study. *International Journal of English Learning & Teaching Skills*, *5*(4), 3500–3508. doi:10.15864/ijelts.5410

Puspitasari, E., & Tsara, E. (2022). Learning Tools for EFL Writing: What and How based on Upper Secondary School Students' Perspectives. *VELES: Voices of English Language Education Society*, *6*(2), 488–499. doi:10.29408/veles.v6i2.5878

Ramirez-Anormaliza, R., Sabaté, F., & Guevara-Viejo, F. (2015). Evaluating Student Acceptance Level of E-Learning Systems. *8th Annual International Conference of Education, Research and Innovation*, 2393–2399. https://library.iated.org/view/RAMIREZANORMALIZA2015EVA

Ray, P. P. (2023). ChatGPT: A comprehensive review on background, applications, key challenges, bias, ethics, limitations and future scope. *Internet of Things and Cyber-Physical Systems*, *3*(March), 121–154. doi:10.1016/j.iotcps.2023.04.003

Reiss, M. J. (2021). The use of AI in education: Practicalities and ethical considerations. *London Review of Education, 19*(1). doi:10.14324/LRE.19.1.05

Soomro, S. A., Kazemian, B., & Mahar, I. H. (2015). The Importance of Culture in Second and Foreign Language Learning. SSRN *Electronic Journal, 15*(1), 1–10. doi:10.2139/ssrn.2656713

Su, J., Tsz, D., Ng, K., Kai, S., & Chu, W. (2023). Computers and Education : Artificial Intelligence Artificial Intelligence (AI) Literacy in Early Childhood Education : The Challenges and Opportunities. *Computers and Education: Artificial Intelligence*, *4*(January), 100124. doi:10.1016/j.caeai.2023.100124

Tuomi, I. (2018). The Impact of Artificial Intelligence on Learning, Teaching, and Education Policies. Science for Policy. doi:10.2760/12297

KEY TERMS AND DEFINITIONS

21st Century Education: 21st-century education is an adaptive, technology-driven approach (Turiman et al., 2012). In this chapter, this term mainly refers to the adoption of digital literacy into English language-based courses that prepares students for an ever-evolving global landscape.

Academic Integrity: Academic integrity refers to the ethical foundation of honesty, responsibility, and trustworthiness in scholarly pursuits (Lim et al., 2023). In this chapter, this term is referred to the values of originality, proper citation, and the avoidance of plagiarism or cheating in classroom activities and assignments.

Artificial Intelligence (AI): Artificial intelligence in education refers to the utilization of technology and algorithms to enhance and personalize learning experiences (Haleem et al., 2023). In this chapter, AI is explored from the angles of content creation, student assessment, and personalized tutoring.

Attitude: Attitude in this chapter refers to the disposition, mindset, and emotional stance a student holds towards their learning process, encompassing their beliefs, motivations, perseverance, and receptiveness towards existing and new knowledge (Gu & Wu, 2019).

Behavior: Behavior refers to the actions, conduct, and responses exhibited by an individual or a group in various situations (Boguszewicz-Kreft et al., 2020). In this chapter, this term encompasses how students engage, participate, and react within the learning environment.

Language Education: Language education involves the structured teaching and learning of a language, encompassing its grammar, vocabulary, pronunciation, and cultural context (Kazakov, 2021). In this chapter, language education specifically refers to language courses that are taught in English, focusing on reading, writing, listening, speaking skills and grammar acquisition.

Machine Learning: In the context of language education, machine learning refers to the application of artificial intelligence techniques and algorithms to enhance language learning experiences (Godwin-Jones, 2022). This chapter briefly visits the development of systems that optimize and customize the language learning process for students.

Perception: Perception encompasses the way students receive, process, and understand knowledge, influenced by their prior experiences, beliefs, attitudes, and cognitive abilities (Chai et al., 2023). In this chapter, this term refers to how students engage with AI-powered tools to construct their understanding of academic content.

Plagiarism: Plagiarism is the act of using someone else's ideas, words, or work without proper acknowledgment or attribution, presenting them as one's own (Khan, 2016). In this chapter, this term is referred to students' actions of copying or closely imitating content from AI-powered sources.

APPENDIX: CASE SUPPORT MATERIALS

Questions and Answers

1. What is the overall problem presented in this case?
   The overarching problem presented in this case is the lack of understanding and exploration regarding how learners intend to use AI in their academic tasks, particularly in the context of language education.

2. How does this case help to address the gap in the problem presented?
   The study aims to address this gap by investigating how students' intentions to use AI impact their language learning behaviour and by identifying the factors influencing their perceptions of AI's usefulness as an academic support tool. This lack of exploration in the current literature hinders the optimization of AI integration in language education and may limit its effective utilization in enhancing academic tasks for students.

3. What are the factors affecting the problem(s) related to this case?
   The factors are: perceived usefulness of AI, ease of use, social influence, attitudes towards AI and subjective norms. These factors collectively influence students' intentions and perceptions regarding the utilization of AI in language education, ultimately impacting their adoption and integration of these technologies into their academic pursuits.

4. Discuss managerial, organizational, and technological issues and resources related to this case.
   Managerial issues addressed are: Effective guidance on AI integration, training for educators, and policies ensuring responsible AI use. Next, the main organizational issue addressed is, establishing support structures for students. Finally, in terms of technological issues, infrastructure for seamless integration, and continuous technological advancements for educational purposes are explored.

5. What is the final solution that can be recommended to the management of the organization described in the case? Provide your arguments in support of the recommended solution.
   It is suggested for relevant education stakeholders to offer educator training, ensure accessible AI tools, and develop guidelines for responsible AI use. This holistic approach fosters responsible adoption, empowers educators, and optimizes AI's academic benefits, enhancing student learning experiences and outcomes in language education.

Epilogue and Lessons Learned

Tailoring learning experiences to individual students' interests, abilities, knowledge levels, and talents fosters greater engagement, thereby enhancing motivation and success while also amplifying their voices and choices. This makes personalized learning a prominent trend in education. Thanks to artificial intelligence, students now could benefit from customized learning process that align with their unique experiences and preferences. Additionally, individuals can receive enhanced support through personalized AI-based recommendations, surpassing the attention teachers can provide. The personalized integration of AI stands also out as a major milestone in education, making learning more seamless, comfortable, and adaptable to individual knowledge levels.

From this case study, we, the researchers have developed a better understanding of what AI is and what roles it plays in the Malaysian teaching and learning context. Hereby, this section is presented to encapsulate the key insights garnered from this study, offering a concise overview of the lessons learned and their implications for the field of AI in language education, particularly within the Malaysian context.

Lesson 1: Students' Conservative Use of AI Tools

Contrary to prevalent assumptions, our study uncovered a surprising trend: students demonstrated a judicious approach towards AI integration in their academic endeavours. Despite initial concerns among educators regarding potential overreliance, the reality reflected a cautious and selective utilization of AI-powered tools. Students appeared to harness these resources as supplementary aids rather than primary solutions, showcasing a balanced integration into their academic workflow. This unexpected revelation challenges conventional presumptions, highlighting the need for a nuanced understanding of students' actual usage patterns and the dynamic roles AI plays in their learning journey.

Lesson 2: Collaborative Development for Targeted AI Solutions

The study underscored the necessity for interdisciplinary collaboration between AI developers and social science researchers. Bridging these domains becomes imperative to tailor AI tools effectively for educational contexts. Our findings emphasized that developers must engage with insights from social sciences, incorporating pedagogical theories and methodologies into the design and refinement of AI-based educational tools. This synergy holds the potential to yield more targeted, impactful, and contextually relevant solutions, aligning technological advancements with the intricate nuances of learning and teaching processes.

Lesson 3: Strengthening Expertise and Global Competitiveness

The study illuminated an area demanding greater attention within the Malaysian academic landscape: the cultivation of expertise in AI integration for educational purposes. Recognizing the pivotal role AI plays in shaping the future of education, there arises an urgency to bolster local expertise. Building a robust knowledge base and skill set within this domain not only enriches the quality of educational practices but also positions Malaysian researchers competitively on the global stage. This imperative emphasizes the significance of investing in specialized training, research initiatives, and collaborative efforts to fortify Malaysia's standing in the rapidly evolving landscape of AI-driven education.

While we are excited to further explore this topic using various other theories, we also hope that more researchers from around the world can work with AI-developers to personalize teaching and learning for the 21st century. We are looking forward to the interesting developments that AI could bring to the education landscape in 2024 and beyond!

List of Additional Sources

Ministry of Science, T. & I. (MOSTI). (2021). *Malaysia National Artificial Intelligence Roadmap 2021-2025 (Ai-Rmap)*. https://airmap.my/apps

Dewan Rakyat Malaysia. (2019). *Penyata Rasmi Parlimen: Kamar Khas Parlimen ke-14, penggal ke-2, mesyuarat ke-2*. 8. https://www.parlimen.gov.my/files/hindex/pdf/KKDR-15072019.pdf

Section 3

Practice: Use of AI in Language Education

Chapter 9
Integrating ChatGPT Into a Culture-Focused Flipped Curriculum for Chinese as a Foreign Language:
Experiments and Implications

Jianfen Wang
https://orcid.org/0000-0003-0890-5253
Berea College, USA

ABSTRACT

This chapter explores ChatGPT's potential for assisting in a culture-focused flipped curriculum to facilitate the development of intercultural communicative competence, a core value of foreign language education in the 21st century. Three experiments assess ChatGPT's performance in generating scenarios and performance scripts for practicing intercultural communication in Chinese-speaking contexts. While ChatGPT demonstrates remarkable linguistic accuracy and comprehension abilities, it struggles to generate scripts that reflect communicative strategies specific to Chinese-speaking contexts, especially when the prompt lacks explicit instructions about Chinese cultural expectations. The limitation can be rooted in ChatGPT's training and the user's ineffective prompting. The findings suggest that ChatGPT is better suited as a reference tool than a primary learning resource in the curriculum. The implications for foreign language education and the integration of AI are also discussed.

A core value of foreign language education in the 21st century is the development of intercultural communicative competence (ICC), the ability to interact effectively and appropriately with people from other linguistic and cultural backgrounds (American Council on the Teaching of Foreign Languages [ACTFL], 2017). Compared with "communicative competence," ICC adds an emphasis on the ability to take up the perspectives of the listener or reader in intercultural communication (Byram, 2020). This emphasis necessitates a more effective integration of language and culture in foreign language instruction. To

DOI: 10.4018/979-8-3693-0872-1.ch009

meet this challenge, proponents of the Performed Culture Approach (PCA) (Walker, 2010; Wang &Jia, 2023; Yu, 2021) propose a shift to a culture-focused framework characterized by performance-based instruction and assessment. For example, by enacting various scenarios that simulate interactions between individuals of different social hierarchies in Chinese-speaking contexts and receiving feedback from a Chinese perspective, students develop a concrete understanding of how hierarchy plays out in Chinese-speaking contexts while developing proficiency in the language. Such experiential knowledge is more easily registered and more readily accessible than what is gleaned merely from cultural notes. It equips students with the flexibility to effectively navigate similar situations, whether in life or in reading.

In lower-level foreign language courses, the development of ICC can be greatly facilitated by a culture-focused flipped curriculum, which dedicates classroom instruction to enactments of intercultural scenarios. Effective implementation of the curriculum requires students to teach themselves the language before class and demonstrate their knowledge in class to receive feedback. The instructor's preparation for class centers on creating a range of meaningful scenarios that enhance cultural understanding while facilitating language practice. Both the students and the instructor may benefit greatly from the assistance of ChatGPT, a remarkable achievement in the realm of artificial intelligence (AI). Equipped with a transformer architecture and trained on extensive datasets, ChatGPT has demonstrated excellence in swiftly generating realistic texts of various forms and providing detailed responses to factual and conceptual queries (Hong, 2023; Kasneci et al., 2023). This chapter explores ChatGPT's potential for assisting in a culture-focused flipped curriculum.

In the forthcoming sections, I first offer a brief description of the culture-focused flipped curriculum, highlighting how it may incorporate ChatGPT while upholding academic integrity and depth of learning. I then review current discussions among educators about ChatGPT's capabilities and limitations for language education. Furthermore, I report findings from three experiments that I conducted with ChatGPT3.5, assessing its performance in one of the most demanding lesson-planning tasks faced by human instructors implementing the culture-focused flipped curriculum, namely, generating a variety of context-specific performance scripts for practicing intercultural communication. The chapter concludes with implications for language educators aspiring to harness ChatGPT's potential to enhance the effectiveness of language education for cultivating ICC.

THE CULTURE-FOCUSED FLIPPED CURRICULUM

The culture-focused flipped curriculum is an application of the Performed Culture Approach (PCA) (Walker, 2010), specially developed to help learners participate effectively in cultures that are fundamentally different from their own. PCA, informed by sociocultural theories and recent developments in cognitive science, pioneers a culture-focused framework, where the goal of foreign language education is to enable learners to function effectively in the target culture (Wang & Jia, 2023). It emphasizes the learning of behavioral culture in all levels of language classes for long-term benefits. Behavioral culture is the tacit knowledge of effective (re)actions in specific contexts. It is embodied in the dynamic processes that frame the behavior of its members and give them the means to recognize the behaviors of their own and others in specific contexts (Walker, 2021). The emphasis on behavioral culture is achieved by using performance as a unifying framework for language and culture.

Performance, in this context, refers to a situated communicative event specified by five basic elements of human behavior, namely time, place, roles, audience, and script (Noda, 2007; Walker, 2010; Walker

& Noda, 2010). The script, specifying both verbal and nonverbal communicative behavior, is always specific to the sociocultural context. Therefore, in the culture-focused curriculum, learners' language use is evaluated primarily for effectiveness and appropriateness within the specific target-culture context, rather than solely for linguistic accuracy and fluency. For example, a student's creative use of "*Wǒ xǐhuan nǐde màozi* (I like your hat)" to compliment a Chinese friend's new hat will be corrected because, in a Chinese-speaking context, such a comment is often interpreted as an implication of wanting the hat. As part of the correction, the instructor would typically model appropriate compliments, such as, "*Nǐde màozi hěn hǎokàn* (Your hat looks nice)" or "*Màozi hěn shìhe nǐ* (The hat fits you well)."

By consistently emphasizing performance as the basic unit of instruction and assessment, the curriculum allows students to study language and culture as an integrated whole. It does not only respect the holistic nature of human behavior (Pike, 1967) but also emphasizes effective and appropriate interaction with people from other cultural backgrounds – the essence of ICC. Enacting intercultural scenarios in class allows students to expose their misconceptions about the target culture and receive immediate feedback, facilitating the learning of target-culture perspectives. Furthermore, practicing the language in realistic intercultural scenarios helps students develop visions of their Chinese-speaking selves, a crucial factor in maintaining long-term motivation to learn the language (Dörnyei & Ushioda, 2009; Wang & Jia, 2023).

The flipped aspect of the curriculum promotes autonomous learning and a sense of ownership in the achievements. It requires students to study substantially before class and be ready to enact simulated real-life scenarios in class. Classroom instruction is dedicated to rehearsing sociocultural scenarios, offering students ample opportunities to experiment with language usage in target-culture contexts. In the scenarios, the teacher plays various roles of Chinese speakers, providing feedback primarily as an interlocutor and offering explicit correction or modeling when needed. The flipped curriculum combines self-directed independent learning with in-class experiential learning. Such hybrid learning environments align well with the preferences of Gen-Z learners, who value personalized and on-demand experiences and benefit from opportunities for independent learning before joining other learners (Seemiller & Grace, 2019). Moreover, with ChatGPT being "a free and more efficient alternative to human tutors" (Hong, 2023, p.40), flipped classrooms emerge as a natural direction for educational innovation, taking full advantage of ChatGPT for pre-class learning and allowing more hands-on collaborative activities during class.

The curriculum, respecting language's nature as being "primarily oral" (Hammerley, 1986, p.34), uses conversation as a primary assessment tool. Here, the term "conversation" broadly refers to any spontaneous interaction involving two or more participants collaborating toward a shared goal in a specific context, with or without the assistance of external media (such as a writing system) (Wang, 2016). A conversation may be as simple and brief as mutual nods to acknowledge one another in the elevator, or as sophisticated and extensive as discussing a novel to gain a deeper understanding of the themes. The essence lies in an awareness of and genuine respect for the perspectives of the other participant(s) in the specific context. Since both the pronunciation and the writing system of the Chinese language are highly challenging for learners, the beginning-level curriculum distinguishes speaking-focused and reading-focused classes to focus on one challenge at a time without breaking the unity of language and culture.

The two types of classes use different prompting strategies to elicit conversations. The prompts in speaking-focused classes only assume aural-oral knowledge of the assigned script, whereas those in the subsequent reading-focused classes will require knowledge of the assigned character text. For example, if a speaking-focused class engages students in performing various scenarios involving discussions about one's schedule for an appointment. One activity in the subsequent reading-focused class may put students in a scenario where they receive an email about the cancellation of an appointment and need to relay it to another person who is also impacted by the cancellation. Their comprehension of the email is demonstrated by the simulated conversation. Since the roles of the email sender, the reader (i.e., the student), and the other person (acted either by the teacher or another student) are specified, the way the students talk during the conversation reflects their sociocultural knowledge.

In this curriculum, students are required to demonstrate their learning in person, so they must personalize and internalize the content. However, they may employ ChatGPT as an accessible and versatile learning companion during self-directed learning. At the beginning level, where pre-class learning involves mostly basic and physical tasks, such as repeating aloud after audio samples and manually tracing characters, students may only occasionally turn to ChatGPT to satisfy their curiosity about the language and the culture. However, as they progress, their pre-class learning tasks will gradually align with what the teacher does for lower-level learners, such as brainstorming intercultural scenarios and creating conversation or narrative scripts for class performance. ChatGPT's assistance in these tasks will benefit both the learners and the teacher, further enhancing the curriculum's effectiveness.

CHATGPT AS A TOOL FOR LANGUAGE TEACHING AND LEARNING: A REVIEW

Numerous educators have explored ChatGPT's capabilities and limitations for language teaching and learning. Some share their speculations about ChatGPT's potential for language education based on its advanced technology (e.g., Baskara & Mukarto, 2023; Hong, 2023), while others test the tool with concrete language learning tasks (e.g., Kohnke, Moorhouse &Zou, 2023). They generally acknowledge ChatGPT's potential as an efficient tool for language teaching and learning, albeit with a notable need for human oversight to counter biases and inaccuracies. This section focuses on reviewing ChatGPT's performance in language-learning tasks reported in the existing literature to understand the tool's potential for serving in the culture-focused curriculum.

Most of the experiments with ChatGPT have focused on how language learners may use it. Their results confirm the tool's versatile capabilities while revealing its inconsistent performance. For instance, Pasden (2023) demonstrates ChatGPT's capability of performing a variety of Chinese language learning tasks, including translating between English and Chinese, providing vocabulary lists, generating Chinese texts, and responding to chat prompts in Chinese, but it tends to make factual errors. For example, when asked about the Chinese novelist Ba Jin's most famous work, ChatGPT initially mistakenly presented the novel's name as "The Family (Jiājiào, 家教)" while the Chinese title should actually be "Jiā, 家." ChatGPT self-corrects the mistake when asked, "Are you sure that's the correct Chinese name of Ba Jin's novel 'Family'?" The self-correction is unusual because, in Wang's (2023a) experiment, where ChatGPT wrongly states that the verb occurs before the 把*ba* particle, a similar rhetorical question fails to trigger a self-correction. When asked, "Are you sure that in a 把 sentence, the verb is placed before the 把 particle?" ChatGPT ignores the implication and continues to assert that "the verbs *indeed* precede the 把 particle (italics added)." Such factual errors, especially when presented with a self-asserted tone, can be confusing and misleading for learners who are not proficient enough in the target language to discern the errors. Therefore, learners would be running a risk if they relied on ChatGPT to gain new knowledge.

Some educators have explored ways that ChatGPT can assist language teachers, using tasks typically associated with language-focused approaches (Buchanan-Shrader, 2023; Kohnke, Moorhouse & Zou, 2023). For example, Kohnke, Moorhouse, and Zou (2023) demonstrate how ChatGPT can support English language teachers in various capacities, such as explaining difficult terms and providing sample sentences, generating texts of various genres (e.g., dialogs, emails, stories) relating to a single topic, rewriting a text in another language, adjusting the complexity of the dialog, preparing vocabulary notes, and generating comprehension or expansion questions to accompany reading tasks. However, the authors' evaluation of ChatGPT's performance focuses on linguistic and factual accuracy, neglecting sociocultural appropriateness. They point out the wordiness and inaccuracies in ChatGPT's explanations of grammatical errors but not its poor context-awareness in the dialog creation task.

In the dialog creation task, Kohnke, Moorhouse, and Zou (2023) instruct ChatGPT to "write a dialog between Amy and Jane about rising electricity prices." Despite not knowing who Amy and Jane are, ChatGPT immediately produces a dialog script instead of requesting more information about the context. While the script is content-rich and linguistically accurate, it suffers from lengthy and overly formal sentences that do not sound conversational. The longest line in the script starts with a complex preposition phrase ("with the hot weather coming up") and ends with a subordinate clause ("which will probably drive the bill even higher"). When further prompted to adjust the complexity for beginner or advanced learners, ChatGPT maintains the length of the initial version and the complex sentences, merely replacing words or phrases. This results in dialog versions that, despite differing in vocabulary, maintain similar levels of complexity and formality, failing to reflect the intended simplicity for beginners and the sophistication for advanced learners. In fact, all three versions resemble the decontextualized dialogs often found in traditional textbooks for English language learners.

The decontextualized dialog script is most likely due to the generic prompt. ChatGPT does not ask follow-up questions despite its seemingly powerful comprehension and synthesis abilities. What it does is comparing existing data "to draw the most likely (e.g., the most frequent and relevant) responses" (Hong, 2023, p.28), functioning more like a smart search tool. According to prompt-engineering guides, the precision of ChatGPT's responses can be significantly enhanced by being specific, descriptive, and detailed about the context, expected outcome, length, format, style, or providing examples (Mittal, 2023; Schulhoff, Khan & Yanni, 2023). Therefore, prompts that specify the sociocultural context are more likely to yield realistic conversation scripts, and this is evident in Zeng's (2023) experiment, which instructed ChatGPT to generate conversation scripts for an elevator scenario in a Chinese-speaking context.

In Zeng's (2023) experiment, the prompt provides a detailed scenario description in English, specifying the roles (i.e., a new employee comes across the company's HR manager Mr. Zhang whom she met during the job interview), the place and time of the interaction (i.e., in the elevator on the new employee's first day of work) and the new employee's intention (i.e., to take the opportunity to thank the HR manager for the interview). ChatGPT's immediate response appropriately addresses the social context, providing a seven-line exchange in Chinese suitable for an elevator conversation. Throughout the script, the new employee sounds polite and grateful while the manager sounds friendly and encouraging. Although some of the expressions bear traces of English influence, the overall script serves as a decent starting point for thoughtful language learners and teachers.

ChatGPT's impressive performance in Zeng's (2023) experiment is a result of effective prompting and can be expected even when instructions are provided in Chinese, showcasing its excellent comprehension ability in Chinese. Figure 1 is a screenshot of Wang's (2023b) interaction with ChatGPT, where ChatGPT responds to a prompt provided in Chinese. The prompt translates as follows:

Please create a dialog script for beginner learners based on the following description: It's a little after eight in the evening. An American student and his friend have finished dinner at a restaurant near campus. They walk out of the restaurant and are about to leave.

Figure 1. Conversation script generated by ChatGPT

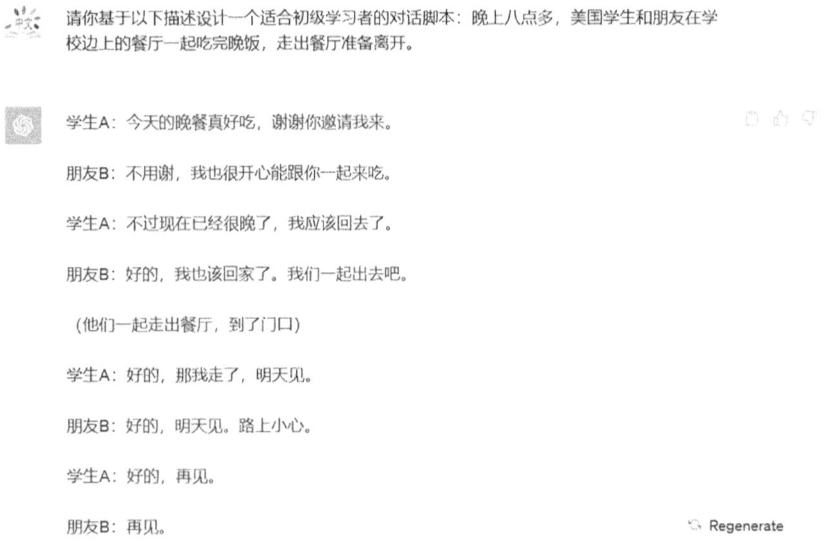

The script ChatGPT generates in response is highly usable. Although the first four lines carry a subtle hint of English influence, the last four lines sound surprisingly natural for a parting scene in Chinese: one person announces his departure and bids goodbye, the other person echoes it and reminds him to stay safe on the way, the first speaker bids goodbye again using a different phrase, and the second speaker echoes it. The script serves as a reminder that real-life partings between friends involve a more elaborate and varied exchange than the simplistic phrase "*Zàijiàn* (See you again)" commonly found in textbooks.

Zeng's (2023) and Wang's (2023b) experiments demonstrate ChatGPT's ability to consider social contexts and create realistic scripts when prompted effectively. Integrating such realistic scripts into the curriculum can allow students to see a more diverse range of performance scripts. However, the tasks that Zeng and Wang use do not require strategies specific to Chinese-speaking contexts, so ChatGPT's performance on these tasks may not reflect its grasp of cultural nuances. Moreover, these tasks only require ChatGPT to generate scripts for predefined scenarios, whereas generating intercultural scenarios is a more demanding part of developing and implementing a culture-focused curriculum. Therefore, ChatGPT's potential for culture-focused curriculums remains to be assessed through more culture-focused tasks.

ASSESSING CHATGPT'S INTERCULTURAL SKILLS: THREE EXPERIMENTS

In communication, a shared understanding of the cultural context is primary because more information comes from the cultural context than the linguistic codes, whose meaning is subject to the users' interpretation of the context. When the users are from different cultural backgrounds, a shared understanding of the context may not always be assumed. For instance, in Chinese culture, it is perfectly acceptable to decline an offer with a simple "*Bú yòng* (No need)" without saying "*Xièxie* (Thanks)," but in an English context, such brevity is often perceived as rude. Similarly, responding to an offer with "I'm fine" in English can be confusing for a Chinese speaker as it does not clearly indicate acceptance or refusal.

Miscommunications are common in intercultural scenarios but often remain unnoticed until relationships between parties begin to deteriorate. Therefore, a culture-focused curriculum strives to acquaint students with situations and expected reactions specific to the target culture and help them practice useful scripts to improve effectiveness when communicating with people from the target culture. The range of intercultural scenarios an individual instructor can conceive is inherently constrained by their experience. Here, ChatGPT's extensive knowledge base and remarkable search capabilities offer a potential solution. In this section, I detail three experiments that I conducted with ChatGPT3.5 in the summer of 2023 to explore the free AI tool's capability of brainstorming intercultural scenarios and generating performance scripts for practicing intercultural strategies in Chinese-speaking contexts.

Each experiment employs a different prompting strategy inspired by PCA's model of cultural knowledge compilation. In this model, personal memories of performances constitute categories of "cases" (memories related to tasks and functions), "sagas" (memories related to specific people or places), and "themes" (memories related to a culture-specific concept that underlies a wide range of behaviors) (Noda, 2007; Walker & Noda, 2000). These categories are interconnected. For example, performances about meeting new friends at parties and those about meeting potential business partners at professional conferences may all fall into a "first encounter" case or an "introduction" case, while the former will be part of a "friend" or a "party" saga and the latter a "business partner" or a "professional conference" saga. Depending on how the performances unfold, they may relate to other memories by the "face-saving" or "hierarchy" theme. Each of the three categories serves as the objective for the scenario-brainstorming tasks.

While a culture-focused curriculum encompasses various types of performances, the experiments will focus on generating conversational scripts because performing conversations is the most fundamental and productive for learners' literacy development (Keating & Egbert, 2004; Schieffelin & Ochs, 1986; Wang, 2016). Conversations engage the learner's entire body and allow them to gain concrete experiences of the target culture. Personal stories accumulated from the conversational performances will facilitate comprehension and performance of narrative texts, which constitute most of the higher-level courses. The ChatGPT-generated scenarios and scripts are analyzed for linguistic accuracy and suitability for teaching intercultural strategies in Chinese-speaking contexts.

Experiment 1. Creating Materials for Teaching the Case of Complimenting

The first experiment tests ChatGPT's ability to brainstorm scenarios and scripts that illustrate how cultural differences influence expected reactions in specific situations. I use the case of complimenting in the United States versus in China as an example. Table 1 shows the interaction. While the response contains mostly relevant information free of linguistic errors, its explanations about the differences in each situation tend to be overly general, and some are ambiguous or even nonsensical. For instance, Situation 8 suggests that one should avoid sounding insincere or overly familiar when giving compliments to elders; however, this advice, especially the sounding overly familiar part, will not apply if the elders are family members. Situation 4 states that the Chinese might offer small gifts in return for compliments but does not mention the types of compliments that may prompt such a reaction. Situations 2 and 5 contain incorrect statements, which I have marked with strikethroughs. These statements mistakenly attribute the Chinese indirectness in expressing compliments to the cultural value of modesty, whereas in fact, openly praising individual achievements, while less common than in the United States, is not considered immodest in China.

Table 1. Interaction with ChatGPT about compliments (Part 1)

Prompt:	Can you brainstorm situations where cultural context might lead to different reactions to compliments in the USA versus in China?
ChatGPT:	Certainly! Cultural context can indeed lead to different reactions to compliments in the USA and China. Here are some situations where compliments might be perceived differently due to cultural nuances: **1. Accepting Compliments: USA:** In the USA, it's generally expected that individuals accept compliments graciously with a simple "Thank you" or a positive acknowledgment of the compliment. **China:** In China, it's common for individuals to downplay compliments to demonstrate humility and modesty. A response might involve a polite refusal or a self-effacing comment. **2. Personal Achievements: USA:** Praising individual achievements, even in public settings, is common and encouraged. It's a way to acknowledge personal success and hard work. **China:** ~~Praising individual achievements too openly might be seen as immodest~~. In China, a more collective-oriented approach might involve attributing success to the support of others or the circumstances. **3. Appearance Compliments: USA:** Complimenting someone's appearance, clothing, or hairstyle is often seen as a friendly gesture in the USA. **China:** Compliments about personal appearance might be received with more reserve in China, as humility and not drawing attention to oneself are valued. **4. Gift-Giving and Reciprocation: USA:** In the USA, receiving compliments might be met with a smile or a thank you. Gift-giving might not always be a direct response to compliments. **China:** In China, receiving compliments might prompt the individual to offer a small gift or token of appreciation in return, as a way to show gratitude and maintain harmony. **5. Compliments in Professional Settings: USA:** In professional settings in the USA, compliments about someone's work, presentation, or accomplishments are encouraged as a form of recognition. **China:** In professional settings in China, ~~compliments might be more reserved and expressed indirectly to maintain a level of modesty and not appear boastful~~. **6. Compliments in Social Gatherings: USA:** Compliments about the event, food, or arrangements at a social gathering are common in the USA and contribute to the overall positive atmosphere. **China:** In China, compliments about the host's efforts might be expected, but they might be given more subtly, as openly expressing praise could be seen as excessive. **7. Cultural Differences in Language and Expressions: USA:** Expressing compliments using direct and positive language is typical in the USA. **China:** In China, expressions might be more indirect and nuanced, involving the use of comparative phrases or metaphors to convey compliments. **8. Giving Compliments to Elders: USA:** Complimenting elders is generally well-received and a sign of respect in the USA. **China:** In China, while showing respect to elders is crucial, compliments might be offered more cautiously to avoid sounding insincere or overly familiar. These examples illustrate how cultural differences can lead to variations in the reception and expression of compliments in the USA and China. Understanding these differences can help foster effective communication and relationships in cross-cultural interactions.

Imperfection aside, the response provides useful information and serves as a strong starting point for exploring the cultural differences associated with the case of complimenting. Firstly, the response aptly captures the Chinese tendency toward reservation and indirect expressions when giving compliments. It also highlights how they tend to downgrade or attribute success to collective efforts when responding to compliments. Secondly, the explanations show how the acts of expressing and responding to compliments align with the cultural values of modesty, sincerity, and social harmony. ChatGPT also makes useful connections to other cases where the cultural context may significantly influence expected reactions. For example, Situation 4 connects complimenting with the case of gift-giving. Situation 8 suggests that respect for elders is expressed in different ways in China than in the USA. These connections inspire the user to brainstorm additional intercultural scenarios.

Among the situations provided by ChatGPT, the sixth one, labeled as "Compliments in Social Gathering," potentially encompasses a variety of role relationships and occasions. To delve deeper into this, I instruct ChatGPT to provide scripts that illustrate the cultural differences in social gatherings. Table 2 shows this interaction. ChatGPT uses the scenario of a guest complimenting the host's cooking at a dinner party as an example and provides a two-line exchange for this scenario in both the United States and China. While the guest's message remains the same in both languages, the hosts' responses appropriately differ. In the Chinese context, the host modestly downplays their cooking skills by saying, "只是一些

家常小菜而已*zhīshì yìxiē jiācháng xiǎocài éryǐ* (These are just some simple home-cooking)," but such modesty is not featured in the American context. In the subsequent comment, ChatGPT attributes this difference to the value of humility in Chinese culture, which is insightful.

Table 2. Interaction with ChatGPT about compliments (Part 2)

Prompt	Can you provide scripts to illustrate how different reactions to compliments in social gathering might play out in conversations in the USA and in China?
ChatGPT	Certainly! Let's explore how different reactions to compliments in the context of social gatherings might play out in conversations in both the USA and China. **Situation: Compliments in Social Gatherings** **USA:** *Context: A guest compliments the host's cooking at a dinner party.* Guest: "The food is absolutely delicious! You're an amazing cook." Host: "Thank you so much! I'm glad you're enjoying it." **China:** *Context: A guest compliments the host's cooking at a dinner party.* Guest: "这些菜真好吃!您的厨艺真厉害。" Host: "谢谢夸奖,只是一些家常小菜而已。" In the USA, the host responds with appreciation for the compliment. In China, the host responds modestly, attributing the quality of the food to simple home-cooking skills, in line with the value of humility. These scripts highlight how cultural norms influence the way compliments are received and acknowledged in the context of social gatherings. Keep in mind that individual personalities and relationships can also impact these conversations.

ChatGPT thoughtfully concludes the response by emphasizing the impact of individual personalities and relationships, so my follow-up prompt requests ChatGPT to provide scripts that illustrate how different relationships may impact the conversations. Table 3 shows the interaction. This time, the response contains three different scenarios, featuring conversations between close friends, acquaintances, and family members with generational differences. Each scenario is furnished with a two-line exchange, featuring the same compliment in both cultural contexts but different response strategies, followed by a brief comment about the differences.

The sample scripts and comments for the first two scenarios are coherent, but those for Scenario 3 are problematic. The comment marked with a strikethrough in Scenario 3 is nonsensical because the elder in the Chinese script does not "respond with appreciation" and "the cultural value of showing respect to elders" does not apply in this context. The scripts for the Chinese context are unnatural because elders do not typically respond humbly to a younger person's compliment, although such humility may be expected if the younger person were an international guest and the elder intended to indicate her pride in Chinese cuisine. Usually, the elder might simply encourage the younger to eat more or promise to cook the food again in the future, saying something like "*xǐhuan chī jiù duō chī yìdiǎn* (If you like it, then eat more)" or "*xiàhuí hái gěi nǐ zuò* (I'll make it for you again)." The unexpected modest response of the Chinese elder in Scenario 3 may reflect ChatGPT's tendency to overgeneralize. Nonetheless, ChatGPT rightly reminds us at the end of the response that "personal dynamics, familiarity, and cultural norms all play a role in shaping the interactions." Discerning such nuances, however, requires thorough immersion in social life, which is beyond ChatGPT's capacity and will thus rely on human instructors.

Table 3. Interaction with ChatGPT about compliments (Part 3)

Prompt	Can you provide scripts to illustrate how different relationships between the speakers may impact reactions to compliments in social gatherings in the USA and in China?
ChatGPT	Certainly! The nature of the relationship between speakers can have a significant impact on how compliments are given and received in social gatherings. Let's explore how different relationships might influence reactions to compliments in both the USA and China. **Situation: Compliments in Social Gatherings** **Scenario 1: Close Friends** **USA:** *Context: Close friends at a gathering.* Friend A: "Your new hairstyle looks fantastic!" Friend B: "Thank you! I'm so glad you like it." **China:** *Context: Close friends at a gathering.* Friend A: "你的新发型很棒!" Friend B: "哈哈,谢谢,我觉得还行吧。" In both cultures, close friends might respond more openly and lightheartedly to compliments, but in the Chinese context, there might be a bit of playful modesty. **Scenario 2: Acquaintances** **USA:** *Context: Acquaintances at a gathering.* Acquaintance A: "You have a great sense of humor!" Acquaintance B: "Thank you! That's really kind of you to say." **China:** *Context: Acquaintances at a gathering.* Acquaintance A: "你的幽默感真不错!" Acquaintance B: "哪里哪里,其实还好啦。" In both cultures, acquaintances might respond with gratitude, but in the Chinese context, there might be a touch of modesty even in the response to a compliment. **Scenario 3: Generational Difference** **USA:** *Context: A younger person compliments an elder at a family gathering.* Younger Person: "Grandma, you always make the best pies!" Elder: "Thank you, dear. I'm glad you enjoy them." **China:** *Context: A younger person compliments an elder at a family gathering.* Younger Person: "奶奶,您做的派真好吃!" Elder: "哪里哪里,我这点手艺还差得远呢。" ~~In both cultures, the elder responds with appreciation for the compliment, but in the Chinese context, there might be more humility expressed due to the cultural value of showing respect to elders.~~ These scripts demonstrate how different relationships can influence the way compliments are given and received, even within the same cultural context. Personal dynamics, familiarity, and cultural norms all play a role in shaping these interactions.

To assess the consistency of ChatGPT's performance in brainstorming scenarios, I used the prompt "Can you provide more scenarios?" four times, yielding 12 more scenarios. The first six scenarios are mostly sensible with feasible scripts and relevant comments. These scenarios feature colleagues at an office party, siblings at a family gathering, boss and employee at a company celebration, childhood friends at a reunion, teacher and student at a school event, and in-laws at a family gathering, However, when the prompt is used the third time, ChatGPT begins to reveal inconsistencies in its work. The Chinese script starts to include literal translations from English that make little sense in Chinese, such as "你真是有绿手指*Nǐ zhēn shì yǒu lǜ shǒu zhǐ*," which is a literal translation of "You really have a green thumb." Moreover, the comment starts to mention differences that are not reflected in the corresponding scripts. Without pointing out the mistakes, I used the prompt one more time. In the final response, all three scenarios – "Mentors and mentees," "Extended family members," and "Service providers and customers" – have Chinese scripts that are equivalents to the English ones and reflect no difference in the complimenting and responding strategies in the Chinese-speaking context. While the same strategies do apply to both contexts, ChatGPT still states a fabricated difference in the Chinese context. These irrelevant comments confirm ChatGPT's tendency to overgeneralize when prompted to compare cultural differences.

This experiment shows that ChatGPT can gather useful information about cultural differences, brainstorm scenarios, and, to some extent, generate feasible performance scripts. However, it tends to overgeneralize the differences and rely on translating from English scripts. While the overgeneralization or fabrication of cultural differences may be triggered by the words "different reactions" in the initial prompt, the reliance on translation is likely innate. ChatGPT is trained on English-language sources, and its multilingual capability derives from a translation mechanism (Rettberg, 2022). Another observation from this experiment is that ChatGPT does not always remember the context provided in earlier prompts, and once its response starts to go off track, it tends to go further off if the mistake is not corrected in time. Therefore, ChatGPT's performance is highly dependent on timely, effective feedback.

Experiment 2: Creating Performance Scripts for Practicing Face-Saving Strategies

The second experiment explores ChatGPT's ability to generate scenarios that illustrate a value unique to Chinese culture. I first ask ChatGPT about the Chinese cultural themes or values that a foreign person needs to be aware of to communicate effectively with Chinese speakers. In response, ChatGPT provides a list of 15 Chinese cultural themes in bullet points, each accompanied by a brief explanation of why or how the value should be observed. Figure 2 is a screenshot of the first part of ChatGPT's response, showing the first four bullet points.

Figure 2. Screenshot of part of a ChatGPT-generated text

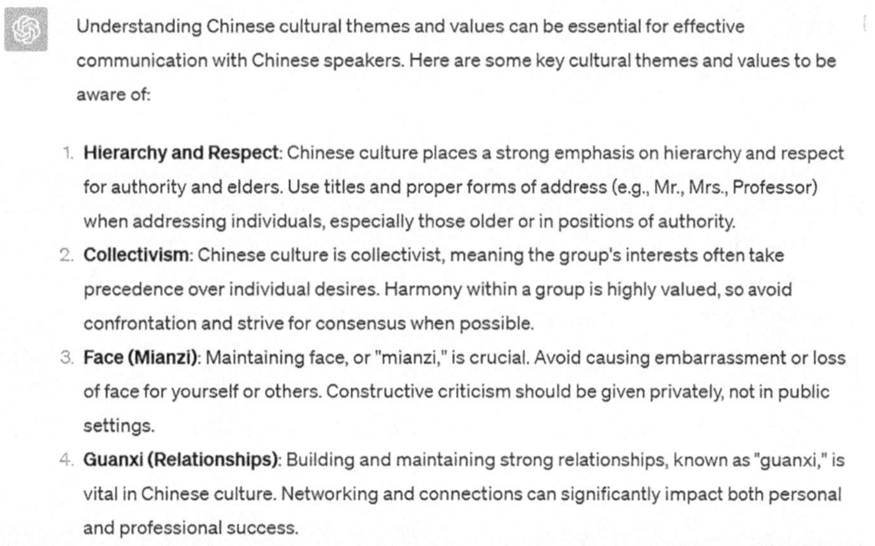

Understanding Chinese cultural themes and values can be essential for effective communication with Chinese speakers. Here are some key cultural themes and values to be aware of:

1. **Hierarchy and Respect**: Chinese culture places a strong emphasis on hierarchy and respect for authority and elders. Use titles and proper forms of address (e.g., Mr., Mrs., Professor) when addressing individuals, especially those older or in positions of authority.
2. **Collectivism**: Chinese culture is collectivist, meaning the group's interests often take precedence over individual desires. Harmony within a group is highly valued, so avoid confrontation and strive for consensus when possible.
3. **Face (Mianzi)**: Maintaining face, or "mianzi," is crucial. Avoid causing embarrassment or loss of face for yourself or others. Constructive criticism should be given privately, not in public settings.
4. **Guanxi (Relationships)**: Building and maintaining strong relationships, known as "guanxi," is vital in Chinese culture. Networking and connections can significantly impact both personal and professional success.

All fifteen themes are pertinent, with accurate explanations and valuable advice. Notably, the concept of "face" appears twice – first by itself and then in "Face saving," emphasizing the importance of avoiding direct refusals or negative responses. Curious about ChatGPT's practical knowledge in this area, I request it to create scenarios and performance scripts for beginner learners of the Chinese language to practice face-saving strategies in Chinese-speaking contexts. In response, ChatGPT provides five scenarios with scripts, collected in Table 4. However, the quality of the scenarios is inconsistent.

Table 4. ChatGPT-generated scenarios and scripts illustrating face-saving strategies

Scenario 1: Receiving an Invitation *Context*: You've been invited to a social event, but you're not sure if you can attend due to a prior commitment. *Script:* Host (in Chinese): 你能来参加我的生日聚会吗?(Nǐ néng lái cānjiā wǒ de shēngrì jùhuì ma?) - "Can you come to my birthday party?" You (in Chinese): 嗯,我会尽量安排时间的。(Ēn, wǒ huì jìnliàng ānpái shíjiān de.) - "Well, I'll try to arrange my schedule."
Scenario 2: Declining **a Gift Politely** *Context*: Someone is offering you a gift, but you're unsure if you should accept it. *Script:* Gift Giver (in Chinese): 这是一份小礼物,送给你的。(Zhè shì yī fèn xiǎo lǐwù, sòng gěi nǐ de.) - "This is a small gift for you." You (in Chinese): 太客气了,真不好意思。(Tài kèqì le, zhēn bù hǎoyìsi.) - "You're too kind, I'm really embarrassed."
Scenario 3: Responding to a Compliment *Context*: You've received a compliment on your Chinese language skills. *Script:* Complimenter (in Chinese): 你的中文说得真好!(Nǐ de zhōngwén shuō de zhēn hǎo!) - "You speak Chinese really well!" You (in Chinese): 哪里,还差得远呢。(Nǎlǐ, hái chà de yuǎn ne.) - "Not at all, I still have a long way to go."
Scenario 4: Being Offered More Food at a Meal *Context*: You're full at a dinner party, but your host offers you more food. *Script:* Host (in Chinese): 再来一些吧,这是我的招待。(Zài lái yīxiē ba, zhè shì wǒ de zhāodài.) - "Have some more; it's my treat." You (in Chinese): 太客气了,我真的吃不下了。(Tài kèqì le, wǒ zhēn de chī bùxià le.) - "You're too kind, I really can't eat anymore."
Scenario 5: Politely Declining an Invitation *Context*: You've been invited to an event, but you genuinely cannot attend. *Script:* Friend (in Chinese): 下个周末我们去爬山,你要一起来吗?(Xià ge zhōumò wǒmen qù páshān, nǐ yào yīqǐ lái ma?) - "Next weekend, we're going hiking. Do you want to come?" You (in Chinese): 我真的想去,可是下周末我有别的安排了。(Wǒ zhēn de xiǎng qù, kěshì xià zhōumò wǒ yǒu bié de ānpái le.) - "I really want to go, but I have other plans next weekend."

Scenarios 2 and 4 contain glaring mistakes, which are marked with strikethroughs in Table 4. Scenario 2 should be labeled "Accepting" instead of "Declining" a gift politely because "*Tài kèqì le, zhēn bù hǎoyìsi* (You're too kind. I'm really embarrassed)" is typically used when accepting a gift. To politely decline a gift, one might say something like "*Nǐ de xīnyì wǒ lǐng le, dàn lǐwù wǒ zhēnde bùnéng shōu* (I appreciate your kindness, but I really can't accept the gift)." Scenario 4 features the typical Chinese hosting practice of offering more food to the guest, and the suggested response is acceptable. The problem lies with "*zhè shì wǒde zhāodài*" in the host's line, which is a direct translation from the English expression "It's my treat." Although it makes sense, it sounds uncomfortable to the Chinese. To encourage someone to have more food, the Chinese would typically say something to emphasize how special the food is or how much more they have.

Besides the glaring mistakes, a closer examination of the scripts for teaching Chinese behavioral culture reveals subtler issues in Scenarios 1 and 5. Scenario 1 presents "*wǒ huì jìnliàng ānpái shíjiān de* (I'll try to make time for it)" as a way to respond to an invitation with uncertainty. However, in the Chinese-speaking context, such ambiguity is usually intended to decline the invitation. While Scenario 5 appears to be perfect, the scenario and the strategy are not unique to Chinese-speaking contexts and are thus less valuable for teaching Chinese behavioral culture.

Scenario 3 stands out as perfect in terms of accuracy and relevance, presenting a strategy unique to Chinese culture, namely, responding to compliments with modesty. While this might not immediately seem related to face-saving, in Chinese culture where modesty is highly valued and outright acceptance of compliments is discouraged, the responding line here effectively avoids accepting the compliment without direct refusal, saving the face of both parties. Unsurprisingly, this strategy is featured in three of the ten scenarios generated by ChatGPT in response to my subsequent requests for more scenarios.

In the remaining seven scenarios generated in the subsequent interactions, all but one feature generally applicable situations and strategies that resemble those in Scenario 5. For example, there is a scenario labeled "Politely declining an offer to pay for your transportation," and ChatGPT rightly suggests "*Fēicháng gǎnxiè, dàn wǒ háishì zìjǐ fù ba* (Thank you very much, but I'd prefer to pay for it myself)." The one scenario that stands out to be distinctively Chinese involves the common Chinese practice of offering to pay at the restaurant. Figure 3 is a screenshot of the scenario. Although this scenario also involves responding to an offer to pay, ChatGPT aptly suggests a different strategy, "*Tài kèqì le, wǒmen xià cì lún dào wǒ qǐng* (You're too kind; it's my turn to treat next time)," which indicates acceptance. This strategy is expected here but not necessarily in the previous scenario because, in Chinese culture, taking turns to pay for meals is commonly used as a way to nurture relationships. The linguistic structures in the script, while not perfect, are acceptable for the conversational context. The major flaw lies with the scenario label. ChatGPT repeats the same mistake it made in Scenario 2 by mislabeling an indirect acceptance as declining, which reveals its inability to discern this cultural nuance.

Figure 3. ChatGPT-generated script for a restaurant scenario

Scenario 9: Politely Declining an Offer to Pay at a Restaurant

Context: You're dining with friends, and someone offers to pay for your meal.

Script:

Friend (in Chinese): 我请客今天。(Wǒ qǐngkè jīntiān.) - "I'm treating today."

You (in Chinese): 太客气了，我们下次轮到我请。(Tài kèqì le, wǒmen xià cì lún dào wǒ qǐng.) - "You're too kind; it's my turn to treat next time."

Focusing on the concepts specific to Chinese culture may have helped prime ChatGPT for producing more scenarios and scripts specific to Chinese-speaking contexts. Scenarios 2, 3, 4, and the one featuring an offer to pay at a restaurant are more likely to be observed in Chinese-speaking contexts than in English-speaking ones. However, the inaccurate scenario labels that confuse "declining" with "accepting" reveal ChatGPT's weakness in grasping the cultural nuances. Furthermore, the inaccurate labeling and unnatural expressions confirm its reliance on translation. The acceptability of most scripts in this experiment likely reflects ChatGPT's improved translation accuracy, as most of the situations and strategies apply to both English and Chinese contexts, and the few Chinese-specific scenarios have labels that indicate misinterpreted intention.

Experiment 3: Creating a Guest-at-a-Chinese-Home Saga

The third experiment assesses ChatGPT's ability to generate a series of scenarios and scripts for learners to practice acting appropriately in a particular role in Chinese-speaking contexts, in this case, the role of a guest at a Chinese home. This saga is selected because the Chinese have unique expectations for a good guest, particularly the expectation that "the guest should allow the host to make decisions" (Jian et al., 2016, p. 94), which contrasts with the expectations of most English speakers who often prefer to assert their own preferences.

The prompt goes, "Can you create a series of scenarios and performance scripts for beginner learners of the Chinese language to practice acting in the role of a guest at a Chinese home?" ChatGPT immediately provides five scenarios with scripts in Chinese characters, *pinyin*, and English. These scenarios constitute a simplified but coherent story of visiting a Chinese home, including greeting the host, complementing the home, offering to help with preparation, discussing food preferences, and expressing gratitude and enjoyment. When asked for more scenarios, ChatGPT provides five more scenarios that complement the initial ones. These include complimenting the host's cooking, bringing a small gift, engaging in conversation, offering to help with cleanup, and saying goodbye.

While the scenarios align well with the intended saga, and the scripts are linguistically accurate, not all of them are useful for enhancing ICC because they do not consistently reflect typical Chinese cultural expectations. The scripts of Scenarios 4, 7, and 10 stand out as the least useful for Chinese-speaking contexts. Figure 4 is a screenshot of Scenario 4. In the script, the guest's line, *Wǒ bù chī làde shíwù, bù zhīdào jīntiān yǒu shénme càiyáo* (I don't eat spicy food. I wonder what dishes you have today), sounds quite blunt in a Chinese context. In Chinese culture, it is generally considered impolite for a guest to directly inquire about what dishes the host has prepared. Even when the host asks about food preferences, a polite response should convey a willingness to defer to the host's choices, saying something like "*Wǒ bù tiāoshí, zhīshì bútài néng chī làde* (I'm not picky about food; I just can't handle spicy food very well)." Also, both the underlined words *shíwù* (food) and *càiyáo* (dishes) are too formal and unnecessary for a casual conversation.

Figure 5 is a screenshot of Scenarios 6 and 7. Both scenarios involve the host readily accepting the guest's offer, a compliment in the former and a gift in the latter. Readily accepting compliments on the cooking is non-traditional but increasingly accepted in Chinese culture, especially among the younger generations influenced by Western cultures. However, such an accepting approach is less common when the offer is a gift. Practicing such scripts misleads learners to expect the Chinese to accept gifts as readily as Westerners and feel confused or even offended when their Chinese friend in real life does not do so. A more useful script should feature the host saying something to indicate their reluctance or embarrassment about accepting it, such as "*Zěnme hái dài dōngxi lái? Zhè ràng wǒmen duō bù hǎo yìsī ā* (You shouldn't have brought anything. This is really embarrassing for us)." The guest should then encourage the host to accept the gift by saying something like "*Zhè shì wǒde yìdiǎn xīnyì, nín yídìng yào shōuxià* (This is a token of my appreciation. Please accept it)." A Chinese person's polite reaction to the gift may appear as a complaint to someone unfamiliar with the culture, so it is important for learners to understand the host's real intention and practice the strategies for insisting on the offer.

Figure 4. ChatGPT-generated scenario for discussing food preferences

Scenario 4: Discussing Food Preferences

Script:

Guest (you): 我不吃辣的食物，不知道今天有什么菜肴?

(Wǒ bù chī là de shíwù, bù zhīdào jīntiān yǒu shénme càiyáo?)

I don't eat spicy food. Do you have any non-spicy dishes today?

Host: 当然，我们有一些不辣的选项，你不用担心。

(Dāngrán, wǒmen yǒu yīxiē bù là de xuǎnxiàng, nǐ bùyòng dānxīn.)

Of course, we have some non-spicy options. You don't need to worry.

Figure 5. GhatGPT-generated scripts for complimenting the food and presenting a gift

Scenario 6: Complimenting the Host's Cooking

Script:

Guest (you): 这道菜真的很好吃，你做得很棒。

(Zhè dào cài zhēn de hěn hào chī, nǐ zuò dé hěn bàng.)

This dish is really delicious; you cooked it wonderfully.

Host: 谢谢夸奖，我很高兴你喜欢。

(Xièxiè kuājiǎng, wǒ hěn gāoxìng nǐ xǐhuān.)

Thank you for the compliment; I'm glad you like it.

Scenario 7: Bringing a Small Gift

Script:

Guest (you): 这是小小的礼物，希望你们喜欢。

(Zhè shì xiǎoxiǎo de lǐwù, xīwàng nǐmen xǐhuān.)

This is a small gift; I hope you like it.

Host: 谢谢你的礼物，我们非常喜欢。

(Xièxiè nǐ de lǐwù, wǒmen fēicháng xǐhuān.)

Thank you for the gift; we really like it.

The script of Scenario 10 "Saying Goodbye," despite being accurate, misses unique Chinese practices that lack counterparts in English-speaking contexts. Figure 6 is a screenshot of the script. In Chinese culture, it is customary for a hospitable host to escort the guest to the door, and a polite guest would decline the offer by saying "*Qǐng liú bù* (Please save your steps)." As they part ways, the host would say "*Màn zǒu* (Walk slowly)," which means "Take care." These interactions are commonly observed in Chinese-speaking contexts when a host sees their guest off. Therefore, understanding these customary practices is crucial for learners to appear polite as a guest in Chinese-speaking contexts.

Figure 6. ChatGPT-generated scenario for departing a Chinese home

Scenario 10: Saying Goodbye

Script:

Guest (you): 谢谢你们的款待，我过得很愉快。

(Xièxiè nǐmen de kuǎndài, wǒ guò dé hěn yúkuài.)

Thank you for your hospitality; I had a great time.

Host: 非常高兴你能来，下次再见。

(Fēicháng gāoxìng nǐ néng lái, xiàcì zàijiàn.)

We're very glad you came; see you again next time.

The scripts generated in this experiment miss crucial teaching points associated with host-guest practice specific to Chinese-speaking contexts, suggesting they might be meant for general use. To test whether ChatGPT considered the Chinese cultural context when creating the scripts, I request ChatGPT to "create a series of scenarios and performance scripts for beginner learners of the *English* language to practice acting in the role of a guest at an *American* home." Disappointingly, it immediately provides the same ten scenarios in the exact same sequence, merely replacing the Chinese characters and *pinyin* with English. Consequently, each exchange in the conversation features the same English sentence twice. It is evident that ChatGPT does not account for the distinct expectations in the specific cultural context when producing the scenarios and scripts.

Given ChatGPT's demonstrated knowledge of situations and strategies unique to Chinese culture in the previous two experiments, the failure here is likely due to ineffective prompting. The prompt does not explicitly instruct ChatGPT to generate interactions unique to Chinese-speaking contexts. However, to provide such instructions and evaluate ChatGPT's response, one must have clear ideas of the Chinese-specific cultural practices to be included in the script. Therefore, ChatGPT is good for concretizing or elaborating on the ideas that human instructors conceptualize but cannot substitute for their creative thinking and cultural expertise.

CHATGPT'S PERFORMANCE AND LIMITATIONS IN A CULTURE-FOCUSED CURRICULUM

In all three experiments, ChatGPT exhibited remarkable linguistic accuracy and comprehension abilities. Its responses were highly relevant to the given prompts, demonstrating its prowess in comprehending and translating content between English and Chinese. While linguistic accuracy is valuable, it alone does not suffice to meet the culture-focused curriculum's goal of fostering ICC, which emphasizes the ability to take up target-culture perspectives. While ChatGPT generated scenarios that are inspirational, a closer examination revealed that only a few of the Chinese scripts contained communicative strategies typical of Chinese-speaking contexts. This limitation arises because ChatGPT's dataset lacks situations and strategies that are unique to Chinese culture. ChatGPT has been trained to align with the values of its initial trainers who are all English speakers (Lowe & Leike, 2022), so even when Chinese-specific scenarios and scripts are generated in Experiments 1 and 2, they often lack an accurate grasp of cultural nuances and sometimes misinterpret the speaker's real intentions. The user needs to know the Chinese culture enough to discern useful content.

ChatGPT's performance in grasping the cultural context may be dependent on explicit instruction. In Experiments 1 and 2, where ChatGPT received explicit instructions to compare communicative strategies in different cultural contexts or was primed by Chinese cultural values, it generated a few Chinese-specific scenarios and scripts. However, in Experiment 3, where such explicit instructions were absent, ChatGPT's responses lacked Chinese-specific interactions. Moreover, while all three experiments produced scenarios and scripts that feature receiving compliments or gifts, only those in the first two experiments had the receiver respond modestly to compliments and embarrassedly to the gift, which are expected reactions in Chinese cultural contexts. In Experiment 3, such scenarios featured the receiver readily accepting the compliment and the gift, a practice more likely to be observed in English-speaking contexts. These findings highlight the significance of prompt design when using AI tools like ChatGPT to generate content for teaching intercultural communication.

To yield the most cost-effective, accurate, useful, and safe outputs, the prompt must contain explicit, precise, and detailed instructions. Creating such prompts requires (a) an understanding of how ChatGPT interprets input; (b) adequate knowledge of the inquired domain; and (c) a tedious trial-error process (Mittal, 2023). Designing a prompt to produce a script for practicing intercultural communicative strategies would require knowledge of both the learner's base culture and the target culture. Therefore, ChatGPT's capability in responding to inquiries does not readily translate into convenience for language teachers and students in the culture-focused curriculum. Teachers and students need substantial training to be able to really harness ChatGPT's power.

ChatGPT's responses in all three experiments consisted of generic scenarios and brief two-turn scripts, many of which were not readily usable as they contained expressions that were accurate but unnatural for Chinese conversational contexts. The brevity of scripts was likely due to ineffective prompting. Instructing ChatGPT to brainstorm scenarios and scripts might have made it focus more on the number of scenarios than the details of the scripts. To generate more elaborate performance scripts, ChatGPT may need prompts that resemble those used in Zeng's (2023) and Wang's (2023b) queries, providing specific descriptions of the roles and their intentions. Yet, creating such prompts requires much imagination and creativity. Therefore, ChatGPT's creative capabilities appear limited for culture-focused tasks, often requiring human instructors to carry out the real creative work.

In sum, ChatGPT's prowess in comprehension and translation makes it a valuable tool for various language learning tasks, but its performance in the context of a culture-focused curriculum reveals notable limitations. While ChatGPT can generate relevant and linguistically accurate content for reference, the scenarios and scripts often need much scrutiny for cultural representativeness and appropriateness. Therefore, human instructors remain essential in selecting useful scenarios and creating culturally rich scripts to help learners develop effective strategies for intercultural communication.

THE IMPLICATIONS FOR FOREIGN LANGUAGE EDUCATION AND THE INTEGRATION OF AI

Foreign language education in the AI era can thrive by harnessing ChatGPT's remarkable linguistic abilities and complementing their weaknesses in intercultural awareness and skills. Compared with human instructors, ChatGPT can offer cheaper, more accessible, and more personalized instruction for enhancing linguistic accuracy and fluency, threatening the sustainability of foreign language classes that are solely driven by language-focused goals. However, it cannot teach learners practical strategies for negotiating expectations and intentions with members of the target culture. Therefore, foreign language instruction should shift its focus toward the more practical and cultural aspects of language learning to maintain its vigor in the AI era.

Culture-focused, flipped curricula like the one described at the beginning of this chapter prove to integrate AI while preserving academic integrity and the depth of learning. Such curricula are characterized by the enactment of scenarios where non-native speakers may inadvertently misrepresent or misinterpret intentions. This performance-based approach integrates culture into language application. It compels students to personally demonstrate their language knowledge in real-life situations, exposing their misconceptions about target-culture expectations and receiving feedback from the instructor. To succeed in such curricula, students must go beyond mere memorization or translation and develop the ability to assess the situation and adjust their communicative strategies on the fly, leaving little room for students to have ChatGPT do their work. In such culture-focused curricula, ChatGPT's role becomes one of a reference tool rather than a primary learning resource. It can facilitate learning and teaching, but not substitute for them.

While incorporating ChatGPT into language education can benefit teachers and learners in many ways, it is not without its challenges and consequences. Using ChatGPT in a cost-effective way requires us to learn to play its language-game, which is very different from the one we play daily with fellow beings. In our daily language-game, "the meaning of a word is in its use in the language" (Wittgenstein, 1958, p.20), so words can take on different meanings depending on the activity that employs them. When playing the game, we focus on the communal activity rather than the words. By contrast, in ChatGPT's language-game, a word's meaning is prescribed and finite, so specific keywords or sequences are necessary to trigger certain responses. When playing the game, one must focus on the words and ensure their use aligns with the large language model (LLM) that powers the AI tool. Playing AI's language-game restrains the creativity of human language and stifles human culture, the process of meaning-making that frames our actions and our conceptions of ourselves (Hall, 1996; Street, 1993). Overreliance on ChatGPT runs the risk of eroding our proficiency in playing the human language-game and leading to social challenges and hardships.

Finally, foreign language instructors and learners must understand that achieving ICC primarily involves creative and culturally responsive work, for which ChatGPT's capabilities may not align. While AI tools can provide valuable support, the true development of ICC requires the guidance of human instructors. Therefore, foreign language educators should place increased emphasis on broadening their intercultural experiences and enhancing their sensitivity to cultural differences to complement AI tools and keep enriching the human language-game.

REFERENCES

American Council on the Teaching of Foreign Languages (ACTFL). (2017). *NCSSFL-ACTFL Can-Do Statements*. Retrieved from https://www.actfl.org/resources/ncssfl-actfl-can-do-statements

Baskara, R., & Mukarto, M. (2023). Exploring the implications of ChatGPT for language learning in higher education. *Indonesian Journal of English Language Teaching and Applied Linguistics*, *7*(2), 343–358. doi:10.21093/ijeltal.v7i2.1387

Buchanan-Shrader, H. (2023). Top 8 *Ways Chinese Teachers Can Use ChatGPT to Create Lesson Plans*. https://www.thechairmansbao.com/blog/chatgpt-teach-chinese/

Byram, M. (2020). *Teaching and assessing intercultural communicative competence: Revisited*. Multilingual Matters. doi:10.21832/BYRAM0244

Dörnyei, Z., & Ushioda, E. (Eds.). (2009). *Motivation, language identity and the L2 self*. Multilingual Matters. doi:10.21832/9781847691293

Hall, S. (1996). Introduction: Who needs "identity"? In S. Hall & P. Du Gay (Eds.), *Questions of Cultural Identity* (pp. 1–17). Sage.

Hammerly, H. (1986). *Synthesis in language teaching: An introduction to languistics*. Second Language Publications.

Hong, W. (2023). The impact of ChatGPT on foreign language teaching and learning: Opportunities in education and research. *Journal of Educational Technology and Innovation*, *5*(1), 37–45.

Jian, X., Wang, J., Jia, J., & Feng, C. (2016). *Perform Suzhou: A course in intermediate to advanced spoken Mandarin*. Soochow University Press.

Kasneci, E., Sessler, K., Küchemann, S., Bannert, M., Dementieva, D., Fischer, F., Gasser, U., Groh, G., Günnemann, S., Hüllermeier, E., Krusche, S., Kutyniok, G., Michaeli, T., Nerdel, C., Pfeffer, J., Poquet, O., Sailer, M., Schmidt, A., Seidel, T., ... Kasneci, G. (2023). ChatGPT for good? On opportunities and challenges of large language models for education. *Learning and Individual Differences*, *103*, 1–9. doi:10.1016/j.lindif.2023.102274

Keating, E., & Egbert, M. (2004). Conversation as a cultural activity. In A. Duranti (Ed.), *A companion to linguistic anthropology* (pp. 169–188). Blackwell Publishing Ltd.

Kohnke, L., Moorhouse, B. L., & Zou, D. (2023). ChatGPT for Language Teaching and Learning. *RELC Journal*, *0*(0), 537–550. Advance online publication. doi:10.1177/00336882231162868

Lowe, R., & Leike, J. (2022). *Aligning language models to follow instructions*. OpenAI. https://openai.com/research/instruction-following

Mittal, A. (2023, July 26). *The essential guide to prompt engineering in ChatGPT* [Blog post] Retrieved from https://www.unite.ai/prompt-engineering-in-chatgpt/

Noda, M. (2007). Performed culture: Cataloguing culture gains during study abroad. *Japanese Language and Literature*, *41*(2), 297–314.

Pasden, J. (2023). *Using ChatGPT to learn Chinese* [Blog post]. Retrieved from https://www.sinosplice.com/life/archives/2023/02/03/using-chatgpt-to-learn-chinese

Pike, K. L. (1967). Language in relation to a unified theory of the structure of human behavior (2nd, revised edition). Mouton & Co., Publishers.

Rettberg, J. W. (2022, December 6). *ChatGPT is multilingual but monocultural, and it's learning your values* [Blog post]. https://jilltxt.net/right-now-chatgpt-is-multilingual-but-monocultural-but-its-learning-your-values/

Schieffelin, B. B., & Ochs, E. (Eds.) (1986). *Language socialization across cultures: Studies in the social and cultural foundations of language*. Cambridge University Press.

Schulhoff, S., Khan, A., & Yanni, F. (2023). *Your guide to communicating with artificial intelligence.* Retrieved from https://learnprompting.org/

Seemiller, C., & Grace, M. (2019). *Generation Z: A century in the making*. Routledge.

Street, B. V. (1993). Culture is a verb: Anthropological aspects of language and cultural process. In D. Graddol, L. Thompson, & M. Byran (Eds.), *Language and Culture* (pp. 23–44). BAAL and Multiple Matters.

Walker, G. (2010). Performed culture: Learning to participate in another culture. In G. Walker (Ed.), *The pedagogy of performing a culture* (pp. 1–21). National East Asian Languages Resource Center.

Walker, G. (2021). Why we perform. In X. Zhang & X. Jian (Eds.), *The third space and Chinese language pedagogy: Negotiating intentions and expectations in another culture* (pp. 139–158). Routledge.

Walker, G., & Noda, M. (2010). Remembering the future: Compiling knowledge of another culture. In G. Walker (Ed.), *The pedagogy of performing a culture* (pp. 22–48). National East Asian Languages Resource Center.

Wang, J. (2016). *Ecology of literacy: A context-based inter-disciplinary curriculum for Chinese as a foreign language* (Doctoral dissertation). Retrieved from https://rave.ohiolink.edu/etdc/view?acc_num=osu1461251633

Wang, J. (2023a, March 25). *Xiang ChatGPT qingjiao "ba" zi ju – xisijikong de liangge quehan*向ChatGPT请教"把"字句——细思极恐的两个缺憾 [Consulting ChatGPT on the "ba" sentence – Two terrifying deficiencies upon careful reflection] [Blog post]. Retrieved from https://mp.weixin.qq.com/s/dXvedrVHrdtJKJ9Yda6qpQ

Wang, J. (2023b, March 18). *ChatGPT neng fou zhuli tiyan wenhua chuji xuecai zhizuo? ChatGPT能否助力体演文化初级学材制作?* [Can ChatGPT assist in creating beginner-level learning materials for performing the culture?] [Blog post]. Retrieved from https://mp.weixin.qq.com/s/rY4GkQYw7umEqR-fEQVepmQ

Wang, J., & Jia, J. (Eds.). (2022). *Performed Culture in action to teach Chinese as a FL: Integrating PCA in curriculum, pedagogy, and assessment*. Routledge.

Wittgenstein, L. (1958). *Philosophical investigations* (3rd ed.; G. E. M. Anscombe, Trans.). Prentice Hall. (Original work published 1953)

Yu, L. (2021). The Performed Culture Approach. In Z. Ye (Ed.), New trends in teaching Chinese as a foreign language (pp.1–34). Singapore: Palgrave Macmillan. doi:10.1007/978-981-13-6844-8_7-1

Zeng, Z. (2023, February 25). *Yu ChatGPT zuo pengyou!与ChatGPT做朋友!* [Befriending ChatGPT] [Blog post]. Retrieved from https://mp.weixin.qq.com/s/LLruwI7bWpSuCkAUx5BkiA

KEY TERMS AND DEFINITIONS

Behavioral Culture: The tacit knowledge of effective (re)actions in specific contexts. It is embodied in the dynamic processes that frame the behavior of its members and give them the means to recognize the behaviors of their own and others in specific contexts.

Conversation: Any spontaneous interaction involving two or more participants collaborating toward a shared goal in a specific context, with or without the assistance of external media (such as a writing system). The essence lies in an awareness of and genuine respect for the perspectives of the other participant(s) in the specific context.

Cultural Knowledge Compilation: The conceptualization of memory processes in the Performed Cultural Approach. In this conceptualization, personal memories of performances constitute categories of "cases" (memories related to tasks and functions), "sagas" (memories related to specific people or places), and "themes" (memories related to a culture-specific concept that underlies a wide range of behaviors).

Culture-Focused: A framework for developing and implementing foreign language curricula where the goal is to enable learners to function effectively in the target culture. Within a culture-focused framework, linguistic codes are both a product and an integral part of communicative behavior. Their significance relies on individual speakers' interpretation of communicative intentions, which are determined by communicative situations. Personal perception of situations is constrained by one's cultural experiences. Hence, the primary goal of language learning within a culture-focused framework is to accumulate experiences in communication within the target culture and acquire the ability to accurately identify one's own and others' behavioral intentions in specific situations.

Flipped Curriculum: A curriculum designed for implementing the flipped classroom strategy. It combines self-directed independent pre-class learning with in-class experiential learning to enhance the effectiveness of language acquisition.

Intercultural Communicative Competence (ICC): The ability to interact effectively and appropriately with people from other linguistic and cultural backgrounds. Compared with "communicative competence," this concept emphasizes the ability to take up the perspectives of the listener or reader in intercultural communication.

Performance: A situated communicative event specified by five basic elements of human behavior, namely time, place, roles, audience, and script. It is the basic unit of culture-focused foreign language instruction and assessment.

Performed Culture Approach (PCA): An innovative approach to foreign language education founded by Dr. Galal Walker and his colleagues at The Ohio State University. It is rooted in the Confucian concept of "*Zhixing heyi* (Knowing and doing as one and the same process)" and informed by sociocultural theories and the latest developments in cognitive science. This language-teaching approach pioneers a culture-focused framework characterized by performance-based instruction and assessment.

Prompting Strategies: Deliberate approaches or techniques employed by users to elicit specific, desired responses from large language models (LLMs). Users may structure their input, question wording, or context in a way that guides the model to generate information, ideas, or answers aligned with their preferences or objectives. These strategies aim to influence the output by shaping the conversation through thoughtful prompts.

Chapter 10
Redefining Traditional Pedagogy:
The Integration of Machine Learning in the Contemporary Language Education Classroom

Géraldine Bengsch
University of York, UK

ABSTRACT

The digital transformation of education, accelerated by unforeseen global events like the COVID-19 pandemic, has ushered in a new era in pedagogy, including in language instruction. While the shift to online platforms has been swift, the evolution of content from static digital forms to dynamic, interactive experiences driven by artificial intelligence (AI) is still emerging. This chapter explores the transformative potential of machine learning (ML) in redefining traditional language learning materials into adaptive, responsive, and personalised educational experiences. The chapter outlines theoretical applications and presents a prototype app, "TalkToMe," designed to boost speaking practice in the target language. Additionally, it addresses ethical concerns surrounding ML integration in education, ensuring the preservation of academic integrity. This chapter aims to bridge the gap between traditional methodologies and cutting-edge technology, offering a roadmap for the future of language instruction through collaboration between pedagogy and technology.

INTRODUCTION

The onset of the 21st century has begun to integrate an unparalleled fusion of technology and education. Never before have educators had access to such a broad array of tools, designed not just to inform, but to reshape instruction (Dalton-Puffer, 2011; Hussherr & Hussherr, 2017; Warschauer & Healey, 1998). The use of technology in the classroom was accelerated to an unforeseen pace through the advent of global events, especially the Covid-19 pandemic, forcing education to adapt, reinvent, and move predominantly

DOI: 10.4018/979-8-3693-0872-1.ch010

to online platforms in the provision of emergency teaching (Hodges et al., 2020; Klimova, 2021; W. Li et al., 2021). This digital transformation, while swift, carried with it remnants of traditional pedagogy, often translating physical materials directly into their digital counterparts without harnessing the full potential of the digital medium (Radić et al., 2021). However, now that the pandemic and emergency teaching provisions have become a thing of the past, educators may be considered to contemplate new ways of utilising technology in their everyday practice (Korkmaz & Toraman, 2020).

In the realm of language education, this dynamic is particularly salient. The rich concept of language, with its nuances, cultural contexts, and multifaceted layers of comprehension, presents both challenges and opportunities when integrated with technology (Arnó-Macià & Barés, 2015; Misiejuk et al., 2023). Traditional methods, ranging from vocabulary lists to static grammar exercises, while effective to an extent, often lack the adaptability and responsiveness that the digital age promises (Arnó-Macià & Barés, 2015). It is here, at the intersection of traditional language instruction and cutting-edge technological potential, that Machine Learning (ML) emerges as a potential tool of transformation and extension of traditional methods (Briggs, 2018).

The subsequent sections aim to show some of the ways in which ML, particularly through tools like Large Language Models (LLMs), can redefine the landscape of language education (Jeon & Lee, 2023). By transferring static resources into dynamic, responsive, and tailored experiences, ML is set to change how educators can approach and leverage language instruction and how learners engage with (Bonner et al., 2023). This chapter will address both the potential of this connection between pedagogy and technology, as well as the challenges and ethical considerations it brings forth.

It is important to note that the main argument of this chapter is on utilising machine learning as a tool to enhance traditional teaching methods. It is argued that the future of language instruction is not about replacing the human touch, but about amplifying it (Selwyn, 2019). It is about harnessing the power of ML to complement, enrich, and diversify the learning experience, ensuring that every student not only learns a language but has an opportunity to immerse themselves in it (Kharb & Singh, 2021; Zou et al., 2018).

BACKGROUND

In the heart of every classroom lies a microcosm of the world outside – one that reflects broader trends, attitudes, and shifts. Over the last decade, educators have observed the ebb and flow of students' engagement with language learning, their aspirations mingling with their apprehensions, crafting a complex landscape of challenges and potential (Asiksoy, 2018).

Static Digital Forms vs. Dynamic ML-Powered Experiences

Traditionally, language instruction has been rooted in fixed formats. Be it textbooks, flashcards, or worksheets, these static methods have been the bedrock of foundational language learning (Preis et al., 2023). While effective to a certain extent, they come with inherent limitations. This chapter is inspired by the author's decade long experiences of teaching German at a university in England. Recollecting an instance from the classroom, a group of beginner-level students grappled with the intricacies of the German language. Their primary struggle? Engaging authentically with the language. Static tools offered them limited, often repetitive experiences, which, over time, diminished their enthusiasm. However, for beginners to pre-intermediate learners of a language, it often remains difficult to find material that is suitable for their level (Gilmore, 2007; Nikitina, 2011; Shadiev et al., 2020).

Enter the world of Machine Learning. What if these students had access to dynamic platforms that adjusted in real-time to their responses? Tools that could simulate real-world interactions, adapt to their learning curve, and offer personalised feedback. Such tools would allow even beginners to engage meaningfully with their target language, without the steep learning curve that traditionally exists to interacting with authentic material or native speakers. The transition from static digital forms to ML-powered experiences is not just about innovation; instead, it invites practitioners to consider reimagining the very essence of language engagement (Preis et al., 2023).

The Gap Between Traditional Pedagogies and Technological Potential

The divide between what traditional pedagogies offer and what technology promises is vast. As an educator, some of the most poignant feedback received revolves around the limitations of conventional tools. Over the years, the author noticed that students become frustrated with the lack of scalable resources that can adjust to their unique pace. Others expressed apprehension about communicating with native speakers, fearing the loss of face due to potential mistakes (Ryan & Viete, 2009; Shumin, 2002).

Moreover, the challenges extend beyond the classroom. Many students seek immersive experiences outside formal instruction, attempting to engage with authentic material like newspapers or movies. But here lies the dilemma: the absence of real-time feedback and guidance often leaves them feeling overwhelmed and lost (Lochtman, 2002; Sari & Aminatun, 2021). However, post the Covid-19 era, there appears to be a change in students' attitude towards language learning and the use of technology within it. The behavioural patterns of learners have undergone a noticeable shift. Digital platforms, once viewed with scepticism and a burden, are now embraced with a somewhat more open mindset (Toquero, 2020). The remote working culture further accentuates this, leading to a dispersed learner base, more inclined to experiment with digital tools (Moser et al., 2021).

Navigating the New Normal

The world post-Covid has evolved in ways beyond what could have been imagined at the beginning stages of the pandemic. For language education, this meant a drastic transformation in how students perceive and interact with digital tools (Son et al., 2020). Returning to the classroom then, makes the use of static grammar exercises from often outdated textbooks seem even more jarring (Dooly, 2023). Today's learner seeks engagement, real-time feedback, and, most importantly, a touch of fun (Pujiani et al., 2022). The lack in engagement that once was so dominant in digital interactions appears to gradually be giving way to a more open, experimental mindset, showing the readiness of a new era in language instruction (Ironsi, 2022; Pujiani et al., 2022).

The current landscape of language education is witnessing a shift from static digital forms to dynamic ML-powered experiences. Traditional pedagogies are being challenged by the potential of technology, and educators are recognising the need to bridge the gap between the two.. It is noted that learners have become used to the ever increasing availability of dedicated apps and websites that promote language learning outside of the classroom (Heil et al., 2016; Pikhart, 2020). This is not a particularly new notion (Gilakjani, 2012), but the current direction of the use of technology in language learning that is not restrained to the classroom can be potentially utilised to increase grit and learner motivation in the classroom as well (Hejazi & Sadoughi, 2023; Lai et al., 2022).

MACHINE LEARNING AND LANGUAGE LEARNING

Introduction to Machine Learning and Its Significance

Machine Learning (ML) – a phrase that has echoed across various industries, has shaped most of everything in day-to-day activities, from e-commerce to medical diagnostics. At its core, ML enables computers to learn from and make decisions based on data. Unlike traditional algorithms that operate under explicitly programmed instructions, ML systems can fine-tune their operations based on patterns they identify. However, what sets ML apart from traditional computer programs is its ability to learn and adapt without being explicitly programmed with step-by-step instructions (Hopkins, 2022).

In the realm of language education, Machine Learning has found various applications that have shaped the field. Early iterations of ML in language learning focused on basic pattern recognition in linguistic data, laying the foundation for more sophisticated tools that combine language acquisition with computational algorithms These tools leverage ML's ability to learn from data and make decisions based on identified patterns (Sutton & Barto, 1998). Reinforcement learning, a subfield of ML, has been applied to language education to improve the quality of language literacy. By using ML algorithms, the effectiveness and readability of teaching materials can be enhanced, leading to better interactions in the classroom (Jatzlau et al., 2019). These applications highlight the potential of ML to improve language instruction and create more personalised and effective learning experiences which will be discussed in future sections.

The Gamification Wave: Duolingo and Its Kin

Duolingo stands out as a prominent example of Machine Learning's impact on language education, characterised by its innovative integration of gamification elements into language instruction. The platform's appeal lies in its ability to transform language learning from a passive endeavour into an interactive and engaging journey. Duolingo's gamified approach presents learners with bite-sized lessons, encouraging them to maintain streaks, and offering rewards for consistent progress. This approach capitalizes on the principles of active engagement and motivation, aligning with contemporary educational theories that emphasize learner involvement (Shortt et al., 2023). The gamification features employed by Duolingo, such as points, leaderboards, and achievements, foster competition and motivation among learners. This engagement is particularly beneficial for self-paced learners who require intrinsic motivation to stay committed to their language learning journey. Duolingo's approach not only caters to diverse learning styles but also resonates with learners after a pandemic, who are accustomed to interactive and rewarding online experiences (Ünal & Güngör, 2021).

One noteworthy critique revolves around Duolingo's treatment of grammar. The platform's implicit approach to grammar instruction, although effective for certain learners, can pose challenges when merging with traditional classroom instruction, where explicit grammar teaching remains an important concept, not only for ensuring learning progress, but also to ensure a common language for teachers to talk to students to about their target language (Jiang et al., 2021). Striking a balance between the advantages of gamified language learning and the necessity of explicit grammar instruction remains an ongoing challenge in the field. In this chapter, some suggestions are made to create apps that embrace technology but are targeted to complement existing teaching practices in the language classroom.

The Google Translate Conundrum

Google Translate stands as an important tool in breaking down language barriers in real-time, offering a lifeline to many learners navigating unfamiliar linguistic terrains. Its convenience and accessibility make it an indispensable resource for quick translations, especially in today's globalised world.

One of the primary limitations of Google Translate in the context of language education is its tendency to overlook granular details such as grammar, nuances, and context. Learner dictionaries, which are pivotal in language acquisition, excel in providing these finer points (Lew, 2004). While Google Translate excels in bridging communication gaps, its reliance on machine-driven translation algorithms can occasionally result in translations that lack cultural sensitivity or context appropriateness. This limitation can hinder learners striving for cultural and contextual fluency in addition to linguistic competence (Tumbal et al., 2021). Language educators and learners need to be mindful of these constraints and consider supplementary resources to achieve a more holistic language learning experience. The suggestions in this chapter aim to use technology in a manner that is meaningful to language learners and provides them with an option to obtain useful feedback that they can implement into their learning goals.

The Evolution: Transformers, Generative AI, and LLMs

The rapid advancement of Machine Learning (ML), including the advent of the transformer architecture, reshaped the landscape of natural language processing (NLP) and have since become instrumental in enhancing language instruction.

Transformers, as architectural innovations, stand as a testament to the power of deep learning. They introduced a novel way of processing sequential data, allowing for more efficient and context-aware language modelling (Vaswani et al., 2017). Their ability to capture long-range dependencies within text highly improved the quality of machine-generated text, enabling applications ranging from chatbots to language translation systems. This breakthrough has had a profound impact on language education, enhancing the development of more advanced and contextually aware language learning tools (Kim et al., 2023; Suresh et al., 2021). For instance, it has enabled the development of chatbots and virtual language tutors capable of engaging in natural language conversations with learners, thereby providing them with a realistic language practice environment (Baidoo-Anu & Ansah, 2023; Baskara, 2023; Su & Yang, 2023). In this strand of ML fall Large Language Models (LLMs) and Generative AI. These models, such as GPT-3 and 4 (Generative Pre-trained Transformer 3 and 4), exhibit an unprecedented capacity to comprehend and generate human language with remarkable accuracy. LLMs have shown great impact on many areas of society and are more than likely to shape a future where language instruction is not just tailored to individual learners but is deeply personalised, contextual, and dynamically adaptive (Bozkurt, 2023; Pérez-Núñez, 2023). LLMs have the capability to make language instruction more effective and accessible to learners of all backgrounds, especially with limited contact hours in the classroom (Baidoo-Anu & Ansah, 2023; Pérez-Núñez, 2023).

However, it is imperative to keep mindful while exploring this promising yet evolving landscape. Challenges related to privacy, bias in training data, and the ethical use of AI in education must be addressed as we harness the potential of LLMs for language learning (Lee, 2018). Furthermore, the integration of LLMs into educational environments requires thoughtful pedagogical considerations to ensure that they enhance, rather than replace, the vital role of human educators.

TRANSFORMATIONAL CAPACITY OF ML IN LANGUAGE INSTRUCTION

The very essence of language learning is transformative. It is not just mere acquisition of vocabulary and grammar rules, but a personal journey that encompasses culture, cognition, and communication. With the infusion of Machine Learning (ML) into this intricate landscape, the process of transformation takes on an even more profound resonance. The potential of ML within language instruction is extensive, and while this chapter will delve into pivotal aspects such as vocabulary acquisition, pronunciation improvement, reading comprehension enhancement, cultural immersion, and speaking proficiency, it is crucial to recognise that these represent just the tip of the iceberg (Su & Yang, 2023).

However, it is important to emphasise that while ML offers immense potential, it should complement, not replace, the role of human educators. Cultural insights, and nuanced guidance provided by teachers remain indispensable in language instruction. The following sections discuss some of the areas in which ML can offer avenues into personalised learner journeys.

Vocabulary Acquisition: Unlocking the Power of Personalisation

Vocabulary acquisition is undeniably central to language learning. In traditional language instruction, the emphasis has often been on memorisation and repetition, where learners are tasked with committing an extensive list of words to memory through sheer repetition and static activities (Paribakht & Wesche, 1997). Rather than subjecting all learners to the same list of words and the same pace, ML systems tailor the vocabulary learning experience to the individual.

Consider a student who is grappling with certain words in the language they are learning. In a traditional setting, these challenging words might be presented once, and the student is left to memorize them through repetition. ML changes this paradigm. When a learner struggles with specific words, ML algorithms ensure that these words are revisited in subsequent exercises, ensuring consistent reinforcement until mastery is achieved. This approach is akin to a personal language coach who identifies the learner's areas of difficulty and provides targeted support, thereby optimising the learning trajectory. Rather than presenting words in isolation, these systems can introduce vocabulary within the context of sentences or real-world scenarios. This contextual learning not only aids in better comprehension but also facilitates the application of newly acquired vocabulary in practical situations, which is essential for language proficiency (Ehara, 2023; Ginn et al., 2021).

Pronunciation: Precision Through ML-Powered Feedback

Pronunciation serves as the vital bridge that connects the knowledge of words to their effective use in communication. Traditional methods for improving pronunciation, such as listening to model recordings or relying on textbook guidelines, have played essential roles in language learning. However, these approaches have inherent limitations in providing real-time, personalised feedback and analysis. This is where Machine Learning (ML)-powered tools can step in, ushering in a new era of precision and efficiency in pronunciation enhancement.

ML-driven pronunciation tools offer a dynamic and responsive learning experience. Instead of merely listening to model recordings, learners can engage in real-time speech exercises with ML-powered systems. As learners speak, the ML algorithms instantly evaluate their pronunciation against native or ideal speech patterns. This immediate feedback is invaluable as it allows learners to make corrections and improvements on the spot, helping them develop an authentic and fluent speaking style (Liu & Quan, 2022; Piotrowska et al., 2021).

Reading Comprehension: Interactive Mastery With ML

Reading comprehension stands as a vital test for language proficiency, representing the ability to not just recognise words but to understand their context and meaning within sentences and passages. Traditional methods for enhancing reading comprehension often involve static exercises where learners read predefined passages followed by a set of questions. However, the advent of Machine Learning has opened exciting possibilities to transform this conventional approach into a dynamic and interactive learning experience.

ML-powered reading comprehension tools excel in making the process of understanding and absorbing written content highly engaging and informative. One of the most significant transformations is the ability to click on any word within the text to instantly access a wealth of information. ML also enhances reading comprehension by offering context-rich content. Traditional exercises often involve isolated passages, lacking the real-world context that learners encounter in their everyday language usage. ML-powered tools can provide learners with articles, news stories, or literary excerpts that mirror real-life situations and offer a deeper understanding of the language in its natural context. This exposure not only improves comprehension but also cultivates cultural awareness and contextual fluency (Chen et al., 2021; Hassan Taj et al., 2017).

Cultural Immersion: Enriching Language Learning Through ML-Enhanced Experiences

Language is not merely a collection of words and grammar rules; it is interwoven with culture, history, and societal nuances. Traditional language learning methods have often attempted to provide glimpses into cultural contexts through supplementary notes or additional readings. Rather than presenting learners with static descriptions or explanations of cultural elements, ML can enable them to step into these cultural contexts, fostering a truly immersive and enriching experience. ML can provide learners with insights into cultural nuances and comparisons between their native culture and the culture associated with the language they are learning. This transformational approach to cultural immersion not only enhances language learning but also cultivates a deeper appreciation and respect for the cultural diversity that language embodies. ML can analyse a learner's native cultural context and draw parallels or contrasts with the culture of the target language. Such comparative insights help in developing a nuanced understanding of cultural differences and similarities. This perspective is vital in cultivating empathy and respect for diversity, an essential component of global citizenship. It enables learners to understand the cultural contexts in which languages thrive, fostering a more profound connection with the language and the communities that speak it. They do not just learn to communicate; they learn to connect, appreciate, and engage with a different culture on a profound level. This not only enhances their language skills but also broadens their worldview, preparing them to navigate and contribute positively in a globally interconnected world. (Kolovou, 2021).

Speaking: Unlocking Fluency Through ML-Enhanced Interactions

Speaking is one of the most challenging and crucial facets of language learning. It represents the juncture where knowledge meets real-world application, where learners transform their understanding of words and grammar into effective communication. Traditional language classrooms, while essential, often provide limited opportunities for speaking practice, and learners may not feel ready to speak in front of their peers. However, Machine Learning has emerged as a potential bridge to overcome these limitations, offering innovative solutions that enable learners to enhance their speaking skills and achieve fluency more effectively. ML's speech recognition capabilities are continually evolving, enabling systems to understand various accents, dialects, and speaking styles. This adaptability ensures that learners from diverse linguistic backgrounds receive accurate feedback and can practice speaking in a way that aligns with their target language's native speakers. ML leverages Natural Language Processing (NLP) to understand and respond to learners' spoken language. This technology allows learners to engage in open-ended conversations, ask questions, and receive detailed responses, simulating real-life interactions (Brena et al., 2021).

CONCEPTUAL EXPLORATION: FROM STATIC TO DYNAMIC

So far, it has been discussed that in the ever-evolving landscape of the digital age, the conventional methods of language learning often fall short of meeting the dynamic demands and aspirations of modern learners. These traditional tools and approaches, while valuable in their own right, frequently leave learners desiring more engaging and personalised experiences. In this section, various aspects of a potential the fusion of pedagogy and technology, through the lens of ML, are explored with more specific examples of how ML could be incorporated into applications useful to enhance traditional language learning. The concepts introduced earlier are revisited and imagined as apps that could be incorporated into the traditional language learning classroom.

Adaptive Vocabulary Quizzes: Personalised Reinforcement Through ML

Traditional vocabulary learning methods, often centred around static vocabulary lists or flashcards, have long been employed in language education. However, these conventional approaches tend to adopt a one-size-fits-all strategy, where all learners are presented with the same set of words and exercises, regardless of their individual proficiency levels or learning paces. In contrast, Machine Learning can introduce the concept of adaptive vocabulary quizzes to optimise vocabulary acquisition. Let's delve into the potential of this ML-driven approach and outline an example app for language learning, both inside and outside the classroom.

App Concept Outline: DynamicVocaLearn

Features and Functionality of an app to increase the interactivity of vocabulary are outlined below.

- Adaptive Quizzes: The core feature of DynamicVocaLearn is its adaptive quizzes. Learners begin with a quick assessment to gauge their current vocabulary proficiency level. Based on this initial evaluation, the app tailors vocabulary quizzes to each learner's unique needs and performance.
- Progress Tracking: The app provides real-time feedback and tracks learners' progress. It offers insights into areas of improvement, words frequently missed, and overall vocabulary growth.
- Personalised Vocabulary Sets: DynamicVocaLearn utilises ML algorithms to curate vocabulary sets for each learner. The system considers the learner's strengths and weaknesses, ensuring that challenging words are revisited for reinforcement, while familiar words are introduced less frequently.
- Difficulty Adjustment: The app dynamically adjusts the difficulty of quizzes based on the learner's performance. Learners are consistently challenged without feeling overwhelmed.
- Real-Life Context: Vocabulary is presented in context, with sentences and examples that mimic real-life language use. This contextual learning aids comprehension and retention.
- Spaced Repetition: ML-driven spaced repetition techniques are employed to optimise long-term retention. Words are reintroduced at strategic intervals to reinforce memory.

Pronunciation Corrector

While traditional methods rely on model audio recordings, ML provides real-time feedback. By analysing the learner's pitch, stress, and pronunciation against a vast database, instant corrections can be suggested, aiding in quicker and more accurate mastery.

App Concept Outline: PronunCheck

Features and Functionality of an app to increase the interactivity of pronunciation improvement are outlined below.

- Real-Time Pronunciation Assessment: PronunCheck's core feature is its real-time pronunciation assessment tool. Learners can speak into the app, and ML algorithms instantly evaluate their pronunciation against native or ideal speech patterns.
- Pitch and Stress Analysis: The app meticulously analyses aspects such as pitch, stress, intonation, and phonetic accuracy. It provides learners with feedback on these crucial elements of pronunciation.
- Immediate Corrections: Learners receive instant feedback and suggested corrections. If a learner mispronounces a word or phrase, the app offers guidance on how to improve.
- Adaptive Exercises: PronunCheck offers adaptive exercises to target specific pronunciation challenges. Learners can focus on vowel sounds, consonant clusters, or other areas requiring improvement.
- Voice Recognition: The app employs advanced voice recognition technology to accurately assess spoken language. It adapts to various accents and speaking styles.
- Personalisation: The app personalises pronunciation exercises based on the learner's individual needs, accent, and progress, offering a tailored learning experience.
- Real Life Context: Pronunciation exercises and examples are presented in real-life contexts, such as conversations and speeches, enhancing practical language skills.

Grammar Checker

Beyond fill-in-the-blanks or sentence correction exercises, ML offers a more in-depth approach. Students can input sentences, receiving feedback not only on errors but also suggestions and hints, moving from mere correction to true understanding.

App Concept Outline: GrammaWise

Features and Functionality of an app to increase the interactivity of practising grammar are outlined below.

- Contextual Grammar Analysis: GrammaWise goes beyond traditional sentence correction exercises. Learners can input sentences or passages, and the app provides detailed feedback on errors, suggestions for improvements, and hints on grammar rules.
- Grammar Proficiency Assessment: The app assesses learners' current grammar proficiency levels through an initial assessment. It then customizes grammar exercises and feedback based on individual needs.
- Hints and Explanations: GrammaWise offers hints and explanations alongside error corrections, fostering a deeper understanding of grammar rules and usage.
- Interactive Exercises: Interactive exercises allow learners to practice applying grammar rules in real-world sentences. These exercises adapt in difficulty as learners progress.
- Adaptive Learning Paths: The app adjusts the complexity of grammar exercises based on learners' performance, ensuring continuous challenge and growth.
- Real Life Context: Grammar exercises are framed within real-life scenarios and contexts, such as emails, conversations, and articles, providing practical language usage.

Reading Comprehension Enhancer

Traditional reading passages are complemented with questions. ML tools elevate this process: students can interact with texts, receiving definitions, context, and even quizzes on-demand, enhancing depth and breadth of understanding. Moreover, ML can facilitate interactive exercises within the reading material. For instance, learners can answer comprehension questions, engage in discussions, or participate in quizzes directly within the text. These interactive elements promote active engagement, reinforce understanding, and enhance the overall learning experience.

App Concept Outline: ReadSmart

Features and Functionality of an app to increase the interactivity of reading comprehension are outlined below.

- Interactive Reading Materials: ReadSmart offers a library of interactive reading materials enriched with ML-driven features. Learners can engage with texts in a dynamic and immersive way.
- On-Demand Definitions and Context: ML algorithms provide on-demand definitions and contextual explanations. Learners can simply tap on a word or phrase to access its meaning and usage in context.

- Comprehension Quizzes: Within the text, learners can access comprehension quizzes tailored to the content they are reading. These quizzes reinforce understanding and measure comprehension.
- Personalisation: ReadSmart personalises the reading experience by recommending texts and quizzes based on the learner's interests and reading level, facilitating a more engaging and effective learning process.
- Real Life Application: Texts and reading materials include real-life scenarios, news articles, and practical dialogues to help learners apply their comprehension skills in everyday situations.

Writing Assistant

Instead of waiting for teacher feedback on essays, ML provides an interactive platform for real-time feedback on vocabulary, grammar, and coherence, refining the writing process as it unfolds.

App Concept Outline: WriteWise

Features and Functionality of an app to increase the interactivity of written mastery are outlined below.

- Real-Time Interactive Writing Platform: WriteWise offers a dynamic writing platform where learners can compose essays, articles, and compositions. ML algorithms provide real-time feedback on vocabulary, grammar, coherence, and other writing aspects.
- Instant Feedback: As learners write, WriteWise offers instant feedback on vocabulary usage, grammar errors, sentence structure, and coherence. Suggestions for improvements are provided as they type.
- Grammar and Vocabulary Suggestions: ML algorithms identify and highlight grammar mistakes and suggest alternative vocabulary choices to enhance writing quality.
- Coherence and Structure Analysis: WriteWise assesses the coherence and overall structure of the text, offering suggestions for improving the flow and organization of ideas.
- Real-Time Editing Assistance: Learners can edit and revise their writing within the app, implementing suggested changes with a simple click.
- Personalisation: WriteWise personaliwes feedback and suggestions based on the learner's writing style, skill level, and progress, offering a tailored writing improvement experience.
- Real Life Context: Writing prompts and exercises are based on real-life scenarios and contexts, helping learners to apply their writing skills in practical situations.

Cultural Contextualiser

Moving beyond mere notes on cultural contexts, ML and Augmented Reality (AR) provide immersive experiences. As learners engage with content, they can visualise and interact with cultural phenomena, with ML offering real-time insights.

App Concept Outline: CultureConnect

Features and Functionality of an app to increase the interactivity of engaging with cultural concepts are outlined below.

- Immersive Cultural Experiences: CultureConnect provides learners with immersive experiences that allow them to explore and interact with cultural phenomena associated with the language they are studying.
- Augmented Reality Integration: The app integrates Augmented Reality to bring cultural elements to life. Learners can use their device's camera to visualize and interact with cultural objects, landmarks, and events.
- Real-Time Cultural Insights: ML algorithms provide real-time insights and information about the cultural elements learners encounter. This includes historical facts, cultural significance, and contemporary relevance. By integrating real-life cultural scenarios, learners can better grasp the practical application of cultural knowledge in real-world situations, enhancing their ability to navigate and appreciate different cultures.
- Interactive Cultural Exercises: Within the cultural experiences, learners can engage in interactive exercises such as quizzes, challenges, and discussions to deepen their cultural understanding.
- Personalisation: CultureConnect personalises the cultural learning experience by recommending content and activities based on the learner's interests, prior knowledge, and learning goals. This feature ensures that each learner receives a customised experience that caters to their unique cultural interests and educational needs.

These are merely some starting ideas on what could be created using ML to feature in the contemporary language education classroom. As becomes evident, the examples all follow a similar formula, routed in traditional activities featured in language learning. They aim to not fundamentally change what research has shown to be conducive to a learner's journey towards fluency. Instead, they extend static concepts to incorporate modern tools, so that they can serve today's learner better, both inside and outside the classroom. The human educator stays at the forefront of connecting the learner with their target language. The following section presents a high-level walkthrough of how a ML-powered app can be created.

FROM CONCEPT TO CREATION: CRAFTING ML-POWERED APPS

So, how might one convert these conceptual tools into tangible applications? It begins with ideation—identifying gaps in traditional tools and envisioning how ML can bridge these. Once the concept is clear, considerations of tools to use and data collection becomes pivotal; ML thrives on data. With a robust dataset or adjacent technology in place, such as existing APIs, the design phase begins, considering user experience and interface. Then comes the development phase, where ML algorithms are integrated. Iterative testing ensures the app's efficacy and user-friendliness. Throughout this process, feedback loops are essential: from educators, learners, and tech experts. Lastly, once deployed, constant updates and refinements ensure the tool's relevance and impact. While technology is changing and evolving quickly, the basic steps remain the same. Here, the chapter will use the example of an app the author had built previously.

TalkToMe: A Prototype Case Study

Recognising the ubiquitous issue of speaking in the classroom and the inherent limitations of traditional classroom conversation dynamics, the author created a working prototype for a dedicated app, titled "TalkToMe"[1]. The app was entered into the 2023 Streamlit hackathon and was one of the winners in its technology category.

Problem Statement

Students, especially those new or returning to learning a language, frequently exhibit reluctance to vocalise their thoughts in the classroom. This hesitation is further accentuated by the traditional pedagogic approach, where instructors, though well-intentioned, frequently interrupt students to provide immediate feedback on their speech. While this technique has its merits, it does quite emulate real-world conversations where constant interruption is not only uncommon but often deemed rude (Kasper, 2006; Wong & Waring, 2020). The need, therefore, was to devise an instrument where learners could simulate realistic conversational scenarios and have control over the feedback they receive. This is not only related to the level of corrections they obtain, but also related to how the bot response to them. In a purely auditory context, it can often be challenging to not only understand what is being said, but to also learn new vocabulary from the interaction. Creating an opportunity for students to add a form of subtitles to the output to aid with comprehension and learning (Danan, 2004; Kanellopoulou, 2019).

Introducing TalkToMe

"TalkToMe" is a proposed language learning app designed to bridge the gap between classroom instruction and real-world application. It embodies the principles of Dynamic Learning, offers Holistic Feedback, and champions a Goal-Oriented approach. At its core, "TalkToMe" recognises the diverse needs of its users, offering them the autonomy to tailor their learning experience.

Features of the App

Dynamic Learning: Instead of static revision modules, students have the option to integrate vocabulary they are keen to practice, making their learning journey interactive and personal. This feature can help students prepare for exams. In addition, it can aid learners in practicing for specific interactional concepts, such as ordering in a restaurant, before they proceed with the conversation either in the classroom or in a real-world environment (Van Dijk, 1977).

Figure 1 shows a screenshot of the app's interface and highlights its features. These are further described below. Note that the individual features are based on existing language learning pedagogy and accompanying research.

- Holistic Feedback: Recognising the varied comfort levels among learners, "TalkToMe" offers a unique feature that lets users select their desired feedback intensity. Whether they seek constant guidance or periodic pointers, the choice is theirs (S. Li, 2010).

Figure 1. Screenshot of TalkToMe's user interface

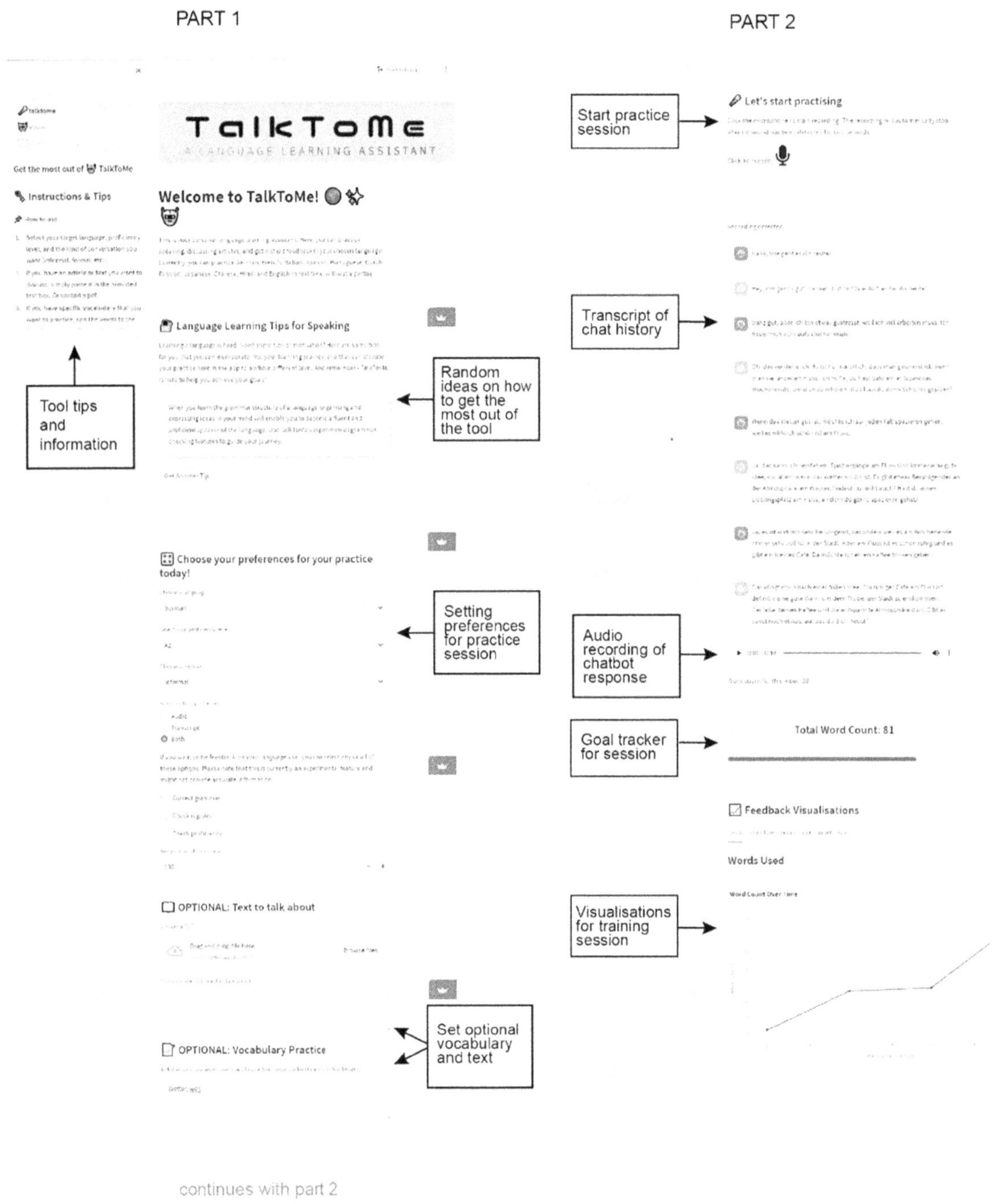

- Goal-Oriented Approach: With a focus on real-world applications, students can incorporate texts or subjects they wish to discuss. Be it prepping for an academic presentation or an upcoming exam, "TalkToMe" caters to these targeted needs. The implementation is deliberately flexible to cater for students with diverse needs and language learning goals. While a similar concept to choosing specific vocabulary to practice, being able to provide a target text as input allows students to test their comprehension of the material and to anticipate questions when discussing the text in the classroom (O'Malley et al., 1989).
- Visualisations: The app contains visual feedback for the learner. This includes a bar that counts the words they have spoken during their session. It also visualises the individual turn length of the utterances a learner produces. This can be an important part for students to move from simple yes/no responses to confident and longer utterances (Seedhouse, 2004). Additional feedback is provided on the most common words a learner is using to help them diversify their vocabulary (Huttenlocher et al., 1991). It also provides visual feedback on how often a learner has used their set vocabulary, so that they can keep track of how often they have practiced a word in context (Sternberg, 2014; Webb, 2007).

Direct Application in a Classroom Setting

The versatility of "TalkToMe" ensures it is not just a tool for individual learners but also an asset in the classroom. Educators can utilise it to complement their teaching methods, allowing students to practice outside of class hours and come prepared, thus maximising classroom interactions. Students can upload class materials to the app to practice and revise it. This allows students to create a learning environment suitable for their own personal interests and aims. One feature that has not been mentioned so far is the integration of general speaking tips and specific ideas for novel ways to utilise the app and to diversify the user's learning experience.

Building TalkToMe: Behind the Scenes

Constructing an app that seamlessly integrates language learning with AI might seem like a daunting endeavour. But, with the right tools and a clear vision, it becomes a journey of connecting the dots. Below, the author outlines the building blocks of "TalkToMe", in creating an ML-powered app.

1. Choosing the Right Language: Python

"TalkToMe" was programmed in Python. Its extensive libraries for various aspects, including machine learning and the supportive community make it a good choice for developing applications, especially when working with AI.

2. Crafting the User Interface: Streamlit

One of the significant challenges when building an app is designing an intuitive and responsive user interface. Streamlit is a free and open-source app framework based on React, but specifically crafted for Python. It allowed to transform the Python scripts into interactive web applications without the added complexities of web development.

3. Conversing with the Machine: Integrating APIs

APIs, or Application Programming Interfaces, are like bridges connecting the app to vast reservoirs of functionalities. For "TalkToMe", several APIs were used to harness pre-built ML tools:

- AssemblyAI: Once a student records their speech, AssemblyAI translates this audio into text. This "speech-to-text" capability is crucial as it translates human speech, with all its nuances, into a format that machines can understand.
- OpenAI: To make the app conversational, OpenAI's GPT-3.5 model is utilised. By sending custom prompts to OpenAI, the platform crafts coherent and contextually relevant responses. Think of it like feeding a sentence to a knowledgeable assistant and receiving an insightful reply. The model used is likely to be known to readers in OpenAI's ChatGPT tool.
- Google's TTS (Text-to-Speech): The conversation comes full circle with Google's TTS. It translates the machine's text response back into human-like speech, providing an auditory feedback to the learner.

4. Budgetary Considerations: Building an app, especially one that relies on state-of-the-art technologies, might raise concerns regarding costs. While many tools and libraries available are free, some specialised services, like certain APIs, come with associated costs. It's essential to be mindful of these expenses, especially when relying on third-party tools. Fortunately, many providers offer tiered pricing or usage-based costs, allowing developers to scale their expenses based on actual usage. While the app itself has been built keeping future scaling in mind, some of the functionalities could be improved further by making more dedicated calls to the APIs at hand, or the integration of other APIs. However, given that this project has not been further funded, a balance had to be found to ensure that the app would be useable, while keeping costs down.

In essence, creating "TalkToMe" combines various technologies. But at its core, it is about simplifying complex AI processes into an easy-to-use tool, making language learning more engaging and effective for all.

Ethical Considerations in ML-Powered Education

The integration of machine learning (ML) into education, particularly in language learning, promises significant benefits. However, with the great potential of ML also come profound ethical dilemmas that must be carefully addressed. It is crucial that we approach this fusion of technology and education with caution, responsibility, and ethical discernment (Paschal & Melly, 2023).

Figure 3 demonstrates the connection between value creation and constraints, including some of the central ethical concerns. So far, the chapter has focused on the benefits that implementing ML applications into the classroom might bring. The following sections will focus on the constraints of the new technology and provide some suggestions of how to navigate them.

Figure 2. Technical flow of information through TalkToMe

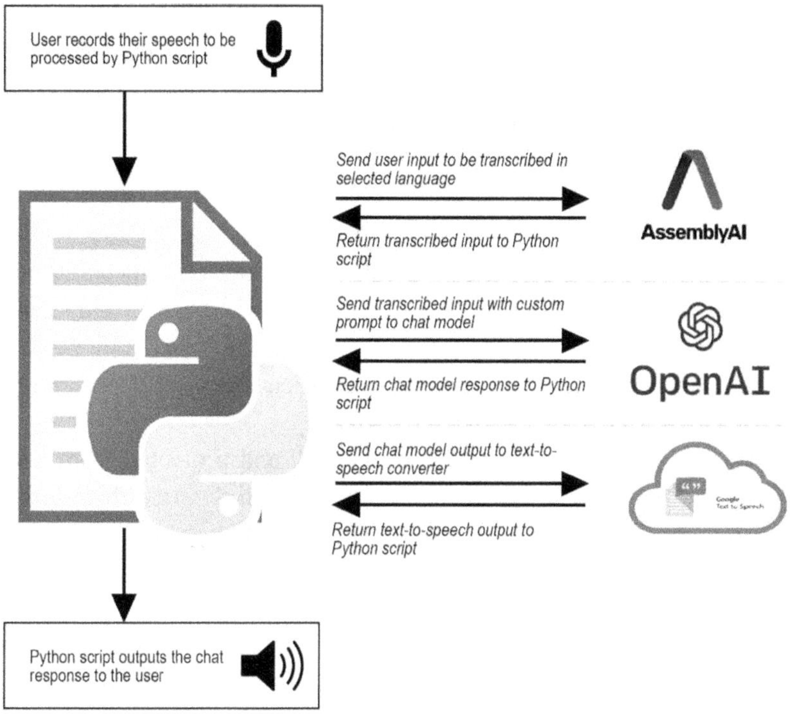

Figure 3. Value and constraints of ML applications

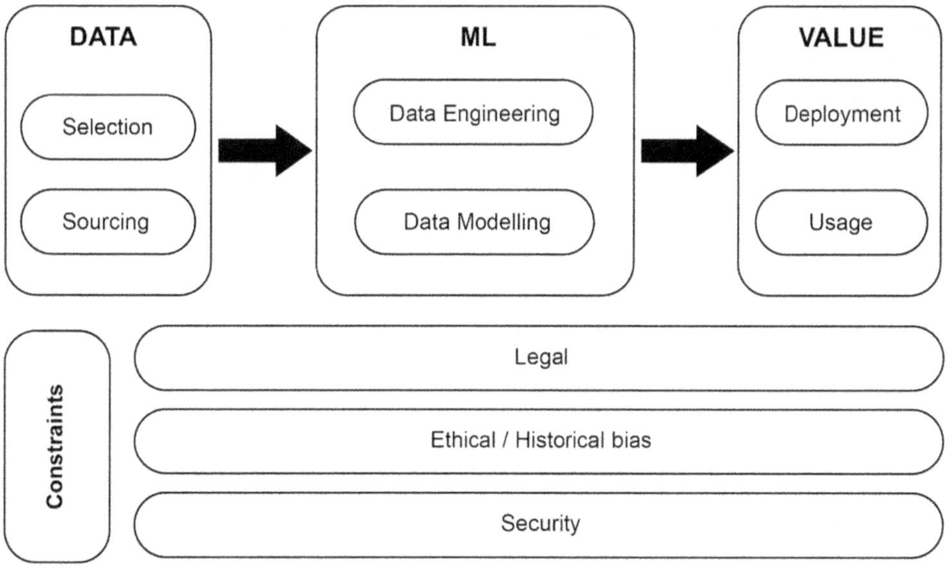

Data Privacy and Security

One of the foremost ethical concerns in ML-powered education is data privacy and security. As learners engage with ML-driven language learning apps and platforms, their data, including personal information and learning progress, is collected and processed. Protecting this data from breaches and ensuring learners' privacy is paramount (Kamarinou et al., 2017).

Suggestions:

Transparency: Educational institutions and app developers should be transparent about the data they collect, how it is used, and who has access to it. Learners should have a clear understanding of their data's journey.

Consent: Learners should provide informed consent before their data is collected and processed. Consent forms should be easily accessible and understandable.

Secure Storage: Data should be securely stored, encrypted, and protected from unauthorised access. Regular security audits should be conducted to identify and rectify vulnerabilities.

Bias and Fairness

ML algorithms can inadvertently perpetuate biases present in training data. This bias can manifest in the content, examples, or assessments provided to learners, affecting their language learning experience and reinforcing stereotypes (Leavy et al., 2020; Lee, 2018).

Suggestions:

Diverse Training Data: Ensure that ML models are trained on diverse and representative datasets that encompass various cultures, languages, and backgrounds to mitigate bias.

Bias Audits: Regularly assess ML algorithms for bias and take measures to correct it. Employ fairness-aware techniques to reduce bias in recommendations and content.

Ethical Review Boards: Establish ethical review boards or committees to scrutinise the content and recommendations provided by ML-powered systems for potential bias.

Accessibility

While ML can enhance language learning experiences, it may inadvertently create barriers for learners with disabilities if not designed with accessibility in mind (Sahami, 1999).

Suggestions:

Universal Design: Ensure that ML-powered educational tools are designed with universal accessibility in mind, incorporating features like screen readers, text-to-speech, and alternative navigation methods.

Accessibility Testing: Regularly test educational apps and platforms for accessibility with input from users with disabilities to identify and address any shortcomings.

Equity and Inclusivity

ML-powered language learning tools should not exacerbate existing disparities in education. There is a risk that learners without access to advanced technology or high-speed internet may be left behind (Lobel, 2022; Stephenson & Harvey, 2022).

Suggestions:

Equity Initiatives: Implement initiatives to provide access to ML-powered language learning tools for underserved communities, including schools and learners in remote or low-income areas.

Low-Tech Alternatives: Develop low-tech or offline versions of ML-powered tools to ensure that learners without high-speed internet can still benefit from technology-assisted language learning.

Ethical Use of AI Tutors

The use of AI-powered tutors in language learning raises ethical questions about the potential for learners to become emotionally detached from the learning process or for AI tutors to replace human educators entirely (Ifelebuegu et al., 2023).

Suggestions:

Complementing Human Teachers: Emphasise that AI tutors should complement human teachers, not replace them. Human educators play a vital role in providing emotional support and personalized guidance.

Ethical Guidelines: Develop and adhere to ethical guidelines for the use of AI tutors, including limitations on the emotional involvement of learners with AI entities.

In conclusion, the integration of ML in language education is a double-edged sword. While it holds immense promise, it also presents ethical challenges that require careful consideration. To harness the full potential of ML while upholding ethical standards, educators, developers, policymakers, and learners must work together to establish clear guidelines, promote transparency, and prioritise the well-being, privacy, and inclusivity of all learners. By doing so, it can be ensured that the fusion of technology and education serves as a force for positive transformation in language learning.

SOLUTIONS AND RECOMMENDATIONS

The digital age brings with it boundless potential to redefine the landscape of language education. Educators, technologists, and lifelong learners, stand at the crossroads of pedagogy and technology, seeking the best way to bridge the two realms. This chapter has underscored the transformative potential that machine learning brings to language education. From adaptive learning experiences to real-time feedback, the promise is undeniable. But with great potential comes the imperative to exercise caution and educators should remain mindful of the challenges and navigate them with foresight.

The main recommendation for this chapter is the encouragement of collaborations between educators and ML experts. The integration of ML into language education goes beyond algorithms and datasets; it embodies a shared vision where technologists appreciate the nuances of language pedagogy, and educators comprehend the capabilities and limitations of ML. Collaborative workshops, joint research endeavours and interdisciplinary projects serve as vehicles for fostering this inclusive approach, ensuring that ML-powered language learning solutions genuinely meet educational needs while avoiding potential pitfalls.

FUTURE DIRECTIONS

This chapter has shown some of the potential for integrating technology, especially ML into the traditional language learning classroom to present one possible vision of a technologically enhanced language learning future:

- Personalised Learning Journeys: The idea that language learners can embark on a journey tailored specifically to their needs, where learning pace, content, and feedback adapt in real-time based on learner inputs and performance has been a central point in this chapter.
- Bridging the Gap: With the confluence of pedagogy and technology, the divide between traditional teaching methods and the technological potential diminishes. Future classrooms might seamlessly blend face-to-face interactions with digital experiences, ensuring learners get the best of both worlds.
- Embracing the Global Village: As technology breaks down barriers, language learners can engage in authentic, culturally rich experiences, virtually traveling to distant lands, interacting with native speakers, and immersing themselves in foreign cultures, all from the comfort of their classrooms or homes.

In conclusion, while the path to integrating ML into language education comes with challenges, the potential should guide the development. By fostering collaborations, maintaining an ethical stance, and keeping the learners' needs at the centre of future pedagogies, practitioners and researchers can craft a future where technology and pedagogy harmoniously work together, creating opportunities for language learning experiences fit for the twenty-first century.

CONCLUSION

This chapter has aimed to show the profound transformative potential of machine learning. It explored just some of the myriad ways in which this dynamic technology can augment traditional teaching methods, making learning more adaptive, interactive, and engaging.

It was shown that a potential evolution of language education is not just about integrating the latest technological advancements; it is about reshaping our pedagogical approaches to fully leverage these tools. Machine learning, with its capability to process vast amounts of data and provide personalised experiences, promises a future where every learner can have a tailored educational journey. However, with great power comes great responsibility. The integration of ML into classrooms needs to ensure that it enhances rather than hampers the learning experience. It is vital to consider the ethical implications, the challenges of maintaining academic integrity, and the importance of ensuring that technology serves as an aid, not a crutch.

Thus, this chapter concludes with a call to action for educators, technologists, policymakers, and learners alike. The future of language education is not preordained. It is ready for a holistic evolution, where pedagogical methods and technological innovations converge harmoniously. The aim is to strive for a future where technology not only complements but elevates the human touch, making language learning more meaningful, accessible, and effective for all. In the end, the goal remains unchanged: to equip learners with the tools and skills they need to navigate our interconnected world confidently.

REFERENCES

Arnó-Macià, E., & Barés, G. M. (2015). The Role of Content and Language in Content and Language Integrated Learning (CLIL) at University: Challenges and Implications for ESP. *English for Specific Purposes*, *37*, 63–73. Advance online publication. doi:10.1016/j.esp.2014.06.007

Asiksoy, G. (2018). ELT students' attitudes and awareness towards the use of Web 2.0 technologies for language learning. *Journal of Language and Linguistic Studies*, *14*(2), 240–251.

Baidoo-Anu, D., & Ansah, L. O. (2023). Education in the era of generative artificial intelligence (AI): Understanding the potential benefits of ChatGPT in promoting teaching and learning. *Journal of AI*, *7*(1), 52–62. doi:10.61969/jai.1337500

Baskara, R. (2023). Exploring the implications of ChatGPT for language learning in higher education. *Indonesian Journal of English Language Teaching and Applied Linguistics*, *7*(2), 343–358.

Bonner, E., Lege, R., & Frazier, E. (2023). Large language model-based artificial intelligence in the language classroom: Practical ideas for teaching. *Teaching English with Technology, 23*(1).

Bozkurt, A. (2023). Generative artificial intelligence (AI) powered conversational educational agents: The inevitable paradigm shift. *Asian Journal of Distance Education*, *18*(1).

Brena, R. F., Zuvirie, E., Preciado, A., Valdiviezo, A., Gonzalez-Mendoza, M., & Zozaya-Gorostiza, C. (2021). Automated evaluation of foreign language speaking performance with machine learning. [IJIDeM]. *International Journal on Interactive Design and Manufacturing*, *15*(2–3), 317–331. doi:10.1007/s12008-021-00759-z

Briggs, N. (2018). Neural Machine Translation Tools in the Language Learning Classroom: Students' Use, Perceptions, and Analyses. *The JALT CALL Journal*, *14*(1), 3–24. Advance online publication. doi:10.29140/jaltcall.v14n1.221

Chen, X., Zou, D., Xie, H., & Cheng, G. (2021). Twenty years of personalized language learning. *Journal of Educational Technology & Society*, *24*(1), 205–222.

Dalton-Puffer, C. (2011). Content-and-Language Integrated Learning: From Practice to Principles? *Annual Review of Applied Linguistics*, *31*, 182–204. Advance online publication. doi:10.1017/S0267190511000092

Danan, M. (2004). Captioning and subtitling: Undervalued language learning strategies. *Meta*, *49*(1), 67–77. doi:10.7202/009021ar

Dooly, M. (2023). Moving Back into the Classroom while Moving beyond Current Paradigms: Lessons for Post-Covid Language Education. *Technology-Enhanced Language Teaching and Learning: Lessons from the Covid-19 Pandemic*, 213.

Ehara, Y. (2023). *Innovative Software to Efficiently Learn English Through Extensive Reading and Personalized Vocabulary Acquisition*. Academic Press.

Gilakjani, A. P. (2012). The significant role of multimedia in motivating EFL learners' interest in English language learning. *International Journal of Modern Education and Computer Science*, *4*(4), 57–66. doi:10.5815/ijmecs.2012.04.08

Gilmore, A. (2007). Authentic materials and authenticity in foreign language learning. *Language Teaching*, *40*(2), 97–118. doi:10.1017/S0261444807004144

Ginn, J., Salas, C. B., Barlowe, S., & Lehman, W. (2021). A novel framework for integrating mobile machine learning and L2 vocabulary acquisition. *Journal of Computing Sciences in Colleges*, *36*(5), 47–56.

Hassan Taj, I., Ali, F., Sipra, M., & Ahmad, W. (2017). *Effect of technology enhanced language learning on EFL reading comprehension at tertiary level. Arab World English Journal*, 8.

Heil, C. R., Wu, J. S., Lee, J. J., & Schmidt, T. (2016). A review of mobile language learning applications: Trends, challenges, and opportunities. *The EuroCALL Review*, *24*(2), 32–50. doi:10.4995/eurocall.2016.6402

Hejazi, S. Y., & Sadoughi, M. (2023). How does teacher support contribute to learners' grit? The role of learning enjoyment. *Innovation in Language Learning and Teaching*, *17*(3), 593–606. doi:10.1080/17501229.2022.2098961

Hodges, C. B., Moore, S., Lockee, B. B., Trust, T., & Bond, M. A. (2020). *The difference between emergency remote teaching and online learning*. Academic Press.

Hopkins, E. (2022). Machine learning tools, algorithms, and techniques. *Journal of Self-Governance and Management Economics*, *10*(1), 43–55.

Hussherr, F.-X., & Hussherr, C. (2017). *Construire le modèle éducatif du 21e siècle-Les promesses de la digitalisation et les nouveaux modes d'apprentissage*. FYP éditions.

Huttenlocher, J., Haight, W., Bryk, A., Seltzer, M., & Lyons, T. (1991). Early vocabulary growth: Relation to language input and gender. *Developmental Psychology*, *27*(2), 236–248. doi:10.1037/0012-1649.27.2.236

Ifelebuegu, A. O., Kulume, P., & Cherukut, P. (2023). Chatbots and AI in Education (AIEd) tools: The good, the bad, and the ugly. *Journal of Applied Learning and Teaching*, *6*(2).

Ironsi, C. S. (2022). Navigating learners towards technology-enhanced learning during post COVID-19 semesters. *Trends in Neuroscience and Education*, *29*, 100189. doi:10.1016/j.tine.2022.100189 PMID:36470617

Jatzlau, S., Michaeli, T., Seegerer, S., & Romeike, R. (2019). *It's not magic after all–machine learning in snap! Using reinforcement learning*. Academic Press.

Jeon, J., & Lee, S. (2023). Large language models in education: A focus on the complementary relationship between human teachers and ChatGPT. *Education and Information Technologies*, *28*(12), 1–20. doi:10.1007/s10639-023-11834-1 PMID:37361830

Jiang, X., Rollinson, J., Plonsky, L., Gustafson, E., & Pajak, B. (2021). Evaluating the reading and listening outcomes of beginning-level Duolingo courses. *Foreign Language Annals*, *54*(4), 974–1002. doi:10.1111/flan.12600

Kamarinou, D., Millard, C., Singh, J., & Leenes, R. (2017). Machine learning with personal data. In *Data protection and privacy: The age of intelligent machines*. Hart Publishing.

Kanellopoulou, C. (2019). Film subtitles as a successful vocabulary learning tool. *Open Journal of Modern Linguistics*, *9*(02), 145–152. doi:10.4236/ojml.2019.92014

Kasper, G. (2006). Beyond Repair: Conversation Analysis as an Approach to SLA. *AILA Review*, *19*, 83–99. doi:10.1075/aila.19.07kas

Kharb, L., & Singh, P. (2021). Role of machine learning in modern education and teaching. In Impact of AI Technologies on Teaching, Learning, and Research in Higher Education (pp. 99–123). IGI Global. doi:10.4018/978-1-7998-4763-2.ch006

Kim, D.-E., Hong, C., & Kim, W. H. (2023). *Efficient Transformer-based Knowledge Tracing for a Personalized Language Education Application*. Academic Press.

Klimova, B. (2021). An insight into online foreign language learning and teaching in the era of COVID-19 pandemic. *Procedia Computer Science*, *192*, 1787–1794. doi:10.1016/j.procs.2021.08.183 PMID:34630743

Kolovou, T. A. (2021). Recreating Cultural Immersion in an Online Environment. *Journal of Teaching and Learning with Technology*, *10*, 408–413.

Korkmaz, G., & Toraman, Ç. (2020). Are we ready for the post-COVID-19 educational practice? An investigation into what educators think as to online learning. *International Journal of Technology in Education and Science*, *4*(4), 293–309. doi:10.46328/ijtes.v4i4.110

Lai, Y., Saab, N., & Admiraal, W. (2022). University students' use of mobile technology in self-directed language learning: Using the integrative model of behavior prediction. *Computers & Education*, *179*, 104413. doi:10.1016/j.compedu.2021.104413

Leavy, S., Meaney, G., Wade, K., & Greene, D. (2020). Mitigating gender bias in machine learning data sets. *Bias and Social Aspects in Search and Recommendation: First International Workshop, BIAS 2020, Lisbon, Portugal, April 14. Proceedings*, *1*, 12–26.

Lee, N. T. (2018). Detecting racial bias in algorithms and machine learning. *Journal of Information. Communication and Ethics in Society*, *16*(3), 252–260. doi:10.1108/JICES-06-2018-0056

Lew, R. (2004). *Which dictionary for whom? Receptive use of bilingual, monolingual and semi-bilingual dictionaries by Polish learners of English*. Robert Lew.

Li, S. (2010). The effectiveness of corrective feedback in SLA: A meta-analysis. *Language Learning*, *60*(2), 309–365. doi:10.1111/j.1467-9922.2010.00561.x

Li, W., Zhang, H., Zhang, C., Luo, J., Wang, H., Wang, H., Zhu, Y., Cui, H., Wang, J., Li, H., Zhu, Z., Xu, Y., & Li, C. (2021). The Prevalence of Psychological Status During the COVID-19 Epidemic in China: A Systemic Review and Meta-Analysis. *Frontiers in Psychology*, *12*, 614964. Advance online publication. doi:10.3389/fpsyg.2021.614964 PMID:34017278

Liu, Y., & Quan, Q. (2022). AI recognition method of pronunciation errors in oral English speech with the help of big data for personalized learning. *Journal of Information & Knowledge Management*, *21*(Supp02), 2240028. doi:10.1142/S0219649222400287

Lobel, O. (2022). The equality machine: Harnessing digital technology for a brighter, more inclusive future. Hachette UK.

Lochtman, K. (2002). Oral corrective feedback in the foreign language classroom: How it affects interaction in analytic foreign language teaching. *International Journal of Educational Research*, *37*(3–4), 271–283. doi:10.1016/S0883-0355(03)00005-3

Misiejuk, K., Ness, I. J., Gray, R. M., & Wasson, B. (2023). Changes in Online Course Designs: Before, During, and After the Pandemic. *Frontiers in Education*, *7*, 996006. Advance online publication. doi:10.3389/feduc.2022.996006

Moser, K. M., Wei, T., & Brenner, D. (2021). Remote teaching during COVID-19: Implications from a national survey of language educators. *System*, *97*, 102431. doi:10.1016/j.system.2020.102431

Nikitina, L. (2011). Creating an authentic learning environment in the foreign language classroom. *International Journal of Instruction*, *4*(1).

O'Malley, J. M., Chamot, A. U., & Küpper, L. (1989). Listening comprehension strategies in second language acquisition. *Applied Linguistics*, *10*(4), 418–437. doi:10.1093/applin/10.4.418

Paribakht, T. S., & Wesche, M. (1997). Vocabulary enhancement activities and reading for meaning in second language vocabulary acquisition. *Second Language Vocabulary Acquisition: A Rationale for Pedagogy, 55*(4), 174–200.

Paschal, M. J., & Melly, I. K. (2023). Ethical Guidelines on the Use of AI in Education. In *Creative AI Tools and Ethical Implications in Teaching and Learning* (pp. 230–245). IGI Global. doi:10.4018/979-8-3693-0205-7.ch013

Pérez-Núñez, A. (2023). Exploring the Potential of Generative AI (ChatGPT) for Foreign Language Instruction: Applications and Challenges. *Hispania*, *106*(3), 355–362. doi:10.1353/hpn.2023.a906568

Pikhart, M. (2020). Intelligent information processing for language education: The use of artificial intelligence in language learning apps. *Procedia Computer Science*, *176*, 1412–1419. doi:10.1016/j.procs.2020.09.151 PMID:33042299

Piotrowska, M., Czyżewski, A., Ciszewski, T., Korvel, G., Kurowski, A., & Kostek, B. (2021). Evaluation of aspiration problems in L2 English pronunciation employing machine learning. *The Journal of the Acoustical Society of America*, *150*(1), 120–132. doi:10.1121/10.0005480 PMID:34340465

Preis, R., Bećirović, S., & Geyer, B. (2023). EFL Teaching in a Digital Environment. *Map Education and Humanities*. doi:10.53880/2744-2373.2023.3.1.56

Pujiani, T., Sukmawati, I. D., & Indrasari, N. (2022). Teachers' Readiness Toward the New Paradigm of English Language Teaching: A Narrative Inquiry. *Uc Journal Elt Linguistics and Literature Journal*. doi:10.24071/uc.v3i2.5363

Radić, N., Atabekova, A., Freddi, M., & Schmied, J. (2021). *The world universities' response to COVID-19: Remote online language teaching*. Research-publishing. net.

Ryan, J., & Viete, R. (2009). Respectful interactions: Learning with international students in the English-speaking academy. *Teaching in Higher Education*, *14*(3), 303–314. doi:10.1080/13562510902898866

Sahami, M. (1999). *Using machine learning to improve information access*. Stanford University.

Sari, S. N., & Aminatun, D. (2021). Students' perception on the use of English movies to improve vocabulary mastery. *Journal of English Language Teaching and Learning*, *2*(1), 16–22. doi:10.33365/jeltl.v2i1.757

Seedhouse, P. (2004). The organization of turn taking and sequence in language classrooms. *Language Learning: A Journal of Research in Language Studies*.

Selwyn, N. (2019). *Should robots replace teachers? AI and the future of education*. John Wiley & Sons.

Shadiev, R., Liu, T., & Hwang, W. (2020). Review of research on mobile-assisted language learning in familiar, authentic environments. *British Journal of Educational Technology*, *51*(3), 709–720. doi:10.1111/bjet.12839

Shortt, M., Tilak, S., Kuznetcova, I., Martens, B., & Akinkuolie, B. (2023). Gamification in mobile-assisted language learning: A systematic review of Duolingo literature from public release of 2012 to early 2020. *Computer Assisted Language Learning*, *36*(3), 517–554. doi:10.1080/09588221.2021.1933540

Shumin, K. (2002). Factors to consider: Developing adult EFL students' speaking abilities. *Methodology in Language Teaching: An Anthology of Current Practice*, *12*(35), 204–211. doi:10.1017/CBO9780511667190.028

Stephenson, B., & Harvey, A. (2022). Student equity in the age of AI-enabled assessment: Towards a politics of inclusion. In *Assessment for Inclusion in Higher Education* (pp. 120–130). Routledge. doi:10.4324/9781003293101-14

Sternberg, R. J. (2014). Most vocabulary is learned from context. In *The nature of vocabulary acquisition* (pp. 89–105). Psychology Press.

Su, J., & Yang, W. (2023). Unlocking the power of ChatGPT: A framework for applying generative AI in education. *ECNU Review of Education*.

Suresh, A., Jacobs, J., Lai, V., Tan, C., Ward, W., Martin, J. H., & Sumner, T. (2021). Using transformers to provide teachers with personalized feedback on their classroom discourse: The TalkMoves application. *arXiv Preprint arXiv:2105.07949*.

Sutton, R. S., & Barto, A. (1998). Reinforcement Learning: An Introduction. *IEEE Transactions on Neural Networks*, *9*(5), 1054. Advance online publication. doi:10.1109/TNN.1998.712192

Toquero, C. M. D. (2020). *Challenges and Opportunities for Higher Education Amid the COVID-19 Pandemic: The Philippine Context*. Pedagogical Research. doi:10.29333/pr/7947

Tumbal, S., Liando, N. V., & Olii, S. T. (2021). Students' perceptions toward the use of Google Translate in translating. *Kompetensi*, *1*(02), 313–320. doi:10.53682/kompetensi.v1i02.1853

Ünal, E., & Güngör, F. (2021). The continuance intention of users toward mobile assisted language learning: The case of DuoLingo. *Asian Journal of Distance Education*, *16*(2).

Van Dijk, T. A. (1977). Context and cognition: Knowledge frames and speech act comprehension. *Journal of Pragmatics*, *1*(3), 211–231. doi:10.1016/0378-2166(77)90035-2

Vaswani, A., Shazeer, N., Parmar, N., Uszkoreit, J., Jones, L., Gomez, A. N., Kaiser, L., & Polosukhin, I. (2017). *Attention Is All You Need*. https://doi.org//arxiv.1706.03762 doi:10.48550

Warschauer, M., & Healey, D. (1998). Computers and language learning: An overview. *Language Teaching*, *31*(2), 57–71. doi:10.1017/S0261444800012970

Webb, S. (2007). The effects of repetition on vocabulary knowledge. *Applied Linguistics*, *28*(1), 46–65. doi:10.1093/applin/aml048

Wong, J., & Waring, H. Z. (2020). *Conversation analysis and second language pedagogy: A guide for ESL/EFL teachers*. Routledge. https://books.google.com/books?hl=en&lr=&id=fybxDwAAQBAJ&oi=fnd&pg=PP11&dq=conversation+analysis+language+teaching+correction&ots=5gbus7JfWb&sig=-mgbXRuvOTp4vHDNcMaVDgQTAcs

Zou, D., Xie, H., & Wang, F. L. (2018). Future trends and research issues of technology-enhanced language learning: A technological perspective. *Knowledge Management & E-Learning*, *10*(4), 426–440.

KEY TERMS AND DEFINITIONS

Application, App: Here, computer or software application. A computer program to carry out a specific task for a specific purpose. Designed for an end user.

Application Programming Interface (API): A software service that allows two programmes to transmit data between each other. Allows to access other company's data or software to enhance functionality and features in another app without having to create it from scratch.

Deployment: Here: software deployment. Activities that make software available to use on a device. Low and no code environments often have integrated deployment solutions. Other free services include Netlify and Heroku.

Generative AI: A subset of artificial intelligence (AI) that focuses on developing models and algorithms capable of generating content, such as text, images, or even videos, in a way that appears to be created by humans.

Graphical User Interface (GUI): A form of user interface using graphical icons and menus.

Large Language Models (LLM): Advanced machine learning models that are particularly designed for natural language understanding and generation tasks.

Machine Learning (ML): Computer algorithms which improve through the use of data, without following explicit instructions. Part of artificial intelligence.

Natural Language Processing (NLP): A subfield of artificial intelligence (AI) that focuses on enabling computers to understand, interpret, and generate human language. NLP involves tasks such as language translation, sentiment analysis, and speech recognition.

ENDNOTE

1 The app can be accessed here: https://talktomelanguagelearning.streamlit.app/

Chapter 11
Creating Stories:
Generative Artificial Intelligence Tools as Writing Tutors

Franziska Lys
https://orcid.org/0000-0001-8979-5601
Northwestern University, USA

ABSTRACT

This chapter focuses on examining the strengths and limitations of prompt-driven ChatGPT for a creative writing task using German as a foreign language. College students of German at the advanced level were asked to develop, write, and illustrate a unique children's story using ChatGPT as a thinking partner. Interacting with ChatGPT in German, students engaged in informal and low-stakes writing-to-learn activities that could help them think through ideas and key concepts for their stories, as well as learn new vocabulary, expressions, and language patterns. Answering to learner-produced prompts, ChatGPT provided both explicit and implicit learning situations that focused on vocabulary development and grammar in a meaning-focused context, creating conditions in which learners could learn according to their current language proficiency. The author discusses how they set up the project, what tasks and prompts they used to elicit content, and how they prepared illustrations using an artificial intelligence image generator.

Writing is an important and necessary skill to communicate with others effectively. It can be challenging, however, to be able to express oneself accurately and convincingly, especially for learners of a second or foreign language. Achieving a high level of proficiency, that is, effectiveness of meaning, structure, tone, and mood of one's writing, presupposes a good understanding of grammatical features as well as a large vocabulary. The question of how to best help a group of college students learning German at a university in the Midwest in the U.S. improve their writing and grammar skills surfaced during the preparation of one of the author's latest teaching assignments, a class on advanced German grammar. The author had taught this course before, using a grammar book for speakers at the C1 level. Although students seemed to be satisfied with the course material and grammar assignments and thought they had

DOI: 10.4018/979-8-3693-0872-1.ch011

learned a reasonable amount, in-class writing tasks, homework assignments, and quiz results suggested otherwise. Overall, students were able to solve grammar exercises such as fill-in-the-blanks and short rewrites when presented with rules and examples but failed to use or understand the same structures in more contextualized and meaning-driven contexts. For example, students were able to fill in past tense forms in prepared sentences, but unable to explain the usage and meaning of the following verb forms found in a children's book *Die Kleine Hexe: Ausflug mit Abraxas* (Preussler et al., 2017):

- *Das hätte ihm höchstens die kleine Hexe erklären können. Aber die hatte sich längst mit Abraxas davongeschlichen* (Only the little witch could have explained that to him. But she had long since sneaked away with Abraxas).
- *Als sie auch noch ihren Besen Purzelbäume schlagen ließ, unterbrach sie Abraxas (*As she was also making her broom do somersaults, Abraxas interrupted her).

A further conundrum concerned the grammar points to present and practice. As experience had shown, many of the explanations and exercises that the grammar book offered were beyond students' active language use. The students could translate expressions such as *angesichts des schlechten Wetters* (given the bad weather), *kraft ihres Amtes* (by virtue of their office), *ungeachtet der Warnungen* (regardless of the warnings), as well as reflexive verbs such as *sich ins Zeug legen* (to do your best) and they could also use these expressions in full sentences, but they could not use them clearly and correctly in different contexts. Similarly, most students struggled to see the relevance to their learning of sentences such as the ones below, either because of the complexity of the grammar (subjunctive and passive) or the strange context:

- *Wenn die Deiche nicht ausgebaut worden wären, hätte es zu grösseren Überschwemmungen kommen können* (If the dikes had not been expanded, major flooding could have occurred).
- *Je mehr Schokolade eine Frau ißt, je besser ist sie vor Schlaganfällen geschützt* (The more chocolate a woman eats, the better protected she is against strokes).

Chavez (2016, 2017) investigated what grammar points college learners of German (1st through 4th year) found to be the most difficult to learn as well as the least relevant for self-expression. Third-year college learners of German listed adjective endings and noun gender as the most difficult, and fourth-year college learners mentioned cases, noun gender, and adjective endings. The forms third-year learners listed as the least relevant for self-expression for them were passive and subjunctive. Some of the reasons the students gave for the abovementioned difficulties were the complexity and opacity of rules, the number of rules, and the infrequent occurrence of certain forms in the material they encountered. There was a disconnect between what the grammar book provided (i.e., the forms that the book's author felt needed to be practiced as well as how to practice them) and what the learners perceived as difficult and worthy of reviewing and practicing.

In order to provide a more engaging and effective learning environment, the author added a task-based writing project that involved the creative use of ChatGPT (https://chat.openai.com) to the class syllabus: The instructor asked the students to develop, write, and illustrate a unique children's story using ChatGPT as a thinking partner. Interacting with ChatGPT in German via its Web-based interface, the students developed their story by weaving together ChatGPT's suggestions to text prompts eliciting cultural and linguistic information. The instructor chose a task-based approach because of its focus on meaning and form, which presents language in context and promotes incidental grammar and vocabulary learning. Prewriting learning tasks included the reading and analysis of a set of children's books to present new vocabulary and language forms in context and occasional explicit grammar lessons followed by structural exercises.

In this chapter, the author discusses ChatGPT's potential as an innovative learning and teaching tool for students of German as a second language. The goal of the project is to provide a better understanding of the issues involved, to uncover the strengths and limitations of prompt-driven uses of ChatGPT for developing writing in a foreign language including the development of grammar, and to design a roadmap for instructors on the most effective use and integration of ChatGPT. The chapter is structured as follows: The background section provides an overview of the theoretical and pedagogical underpinnings of the project, such as explicit and implicit learning, and explains how writing-to-learn tasks can potentially improve language learning. Furthermore, the section presents the pedagogical implications of reading and analyzing children's books as a precursor or preparatory task to the writing of the students' own stories. The methodology section provides information on how the author set up the project, the participants in the project, and the material the author collected to evaluate the use of ChatGPT. The author adopted an explorative approach to evaluate the effectiveness of ChatGPT. The researcher collected qualitative data from observations, unstructured focus group discussions, personal interviews with students, and the analysis of ChatGPT's discussion protocols. The discussion and implementation section illustrates the author's findings and offers suggestions on how to best integrate ChatGPT to ensure a successful experience.

BACKGROUND

Theoretical Underpinnings

Grammar knowledge is important for language learners to improve proficiency, but how grammar learning fits into the overall learning of a second language is an unresolved question. Some language learners find studying and memorizing grammar rules and doing isolated skill drills frustrating and exhausting since they often fail to improve meaning-focused writing or speaking skills. Other learners, however, think of it as giving reassurance that their writing or speaking will become clear and effective. Research has shown that it is not uncommon for students and instructors to have mixed feelings about grammar instruction. Several study results (Incecay & Dollar, 2011; Jean & Simard, 2011; Loewen et al., 2009) have shown that instructors and students perceive grammar as important and necessary to improve language proficiency, but, at the same time, not as something desirable and enjoyable. They considered communicative activities, authentic materials, and real-world tasks as more effective and sought-after learning activities. This makes teaching grammar unnecessarily complex.

In this section, the author elaborates on two theoretical underpinnings that support the incorporation of ChatGPT-driven learning tasks as described in this chapter. First, the author will highlight the distinction between explicit and implicit learning and how focus on form (FonF) can support incidental learning and promote the acquisition of grammar (Pouresmaeil & Vali, 2023). Task-based language teaching as an effective, form-focused, learner-centered, and experiential approach that fosters language use in meaningful contexts is within this framework (Byrnes & Manchón, 2014; East, 2015). Second, while writing (or learning-to-write) is often seen as an assessment tool to ascertain how well language has been learned, writing-to-learn tasks can play a facilitative role for language acquisition, as the relatively slow-paced activity and the resulting written record encourage increased reflection and monitoring (Williams, 2012).

Explicit or Implicit Grammar Teaching and Focus on Form

The question of how best to teach grammar plays a central role in the field of second language teaching. The distinction between explicit teaching of grammar, in which the learner is taught grammar rules and explanations, and implicit teaching of grammar, where learning happens experientially through meaning-focused communications in the target language, is important and has drawn much attention in the literature (Basturkmen, 2023). There is ample debate on these two approaches and how much explicit or implicit grammar teaching contributes to the overall language proficiency, and the results are mixed. For example, after synthesizing much of the research on explicit instruction over the last 35 years, Leow (2019) concluded that explicit instruction was better than implicit instruction. Sok et al. (2019), on the other hand, found little difference between the success of explicit and implicit grammar teaching, except that implicit teaching had a longer-lasting effect. Lys (2013a) reported the results of a year-long empirical investigation of the effectiveness of extended explicit grammar practice (i.e., grammar explanations and controlled exercises) on the overall language development of learners of German. Her results suggested that prolonged grammar practice on discrete grammar items translated into higher gain scores on quiz questions (i.e., explicit knowledge), but did not influence the quality of two open-ended meaning-focused tasks (i.e., implicit knowledge). In a follow-up study, Lys (2013b) investigated how the use of meaningful, purposeful, and goal-directed discourse affected the development of students' oral proficiency. In this empirical study, students were asked to chat once a week with a partner online on a variety of cultural topics and then record a short video containing spontaneous reactions to a set of questions on the topic. The results showed that, despite the lack of explicit grammar instruction, the language students produced in the videos became more complex as learners gained more experience using their L2 in the meaning-focused chats. The learner-centered and task-based language learning approach facilitated interactions and provided scaffolded assistance.

Ellis (2009) suggested that a more nuanced understanding of explicit and implicit learning may be helpful and that some degree of attention to form may be necessary for learners to develop high levels of proficiency. First introduced by Long (1991), and cited by Ellis (2016), two forms of attention have received considerable recognition in the literature: Focus on forms (FonFs) and FonF. Ellis pointed out that the understanding of these terms has considerably changed since they were first introduced, and he uses the terms not to describe teaching approaches, but different teaching techniques:

Focus on form entails various techniques designed to attract learners' attention to form while they are using the L2 as a tool for communicating. In contrast, focus on forms entails various devices (such as "exercises") designed to direct learners' attention to specific forms that are to be studied and learned as objects. (Ellis, 2016, p. 409)

Given the need for a communicative context, FonF can successfully be introduced in task-based learning where the focus is on meaning and form. While there are proponents of both forms of teaching, Ellis (2016) points out that current research has not been able to tease out which approach is more effective. However, some data suggest, according to Ellis (2016), that FonF interactions are more meaningful and result in incidental acquisition of language, especially through implicit corrective feedback such as recasts. Pouresmaeil and Vali (2023) reviewed several studies on the effectiveness of incidental FonF and concluded that incidental FonF facilitates the development of learners' new language, and that this technique may benefit learners with a higher level of proficiency more than learners with a lower level of proficiency. The results of their study revealed that incidental FonF helped develop learners' language knowledge across different linguistic categories, including vocabulary, pronunciation, and grammar.

Writing-to-Learn Activities

In many teaching environments, writing in a foreign language largely serves as a tool for instructors to assess the quality of student writing, often a final product of a class. While writing is a very complex process that encompasses "cognitive and linguistic processes and resources, conscious problem solving, and efficient self-regulation strategies" (Kormos, 2023, p. 622), it can also play a facilitative role in learning a language, as the relatively slow-paced task and the resulting written record encourage increased reflection and monitoring, as well as thinking through evaluative feedback (Williams, 2012). As such, writing is understood as a tool to promote learning, hence the term "writing-to-learn." Proponents of writing-to-learn activities believe in the process of writing and not in the outcome. For them, composing and producing a text opens various avenues for exploration and critical reflection on the content as well as on the language used, and such explorations foster critical thinking and learning (Chmarkh, 2021). The idea that writing promotes learning is not new, as Langer and Applebee had already described it in 1987: "There is clear evidence that activities involving writing lead to better learning than activities involving reading and studying only. Writing assists learning" (as cited in Chmarkh, 2021, p. 92). However, research into writing-to-learn practices, in which researchers looked for effective strategies that make use of the unique properties of writing to help learning, has only recently figured prominently in the literature, and many of the processes are not clearly understood yet. Summarizing the results of empirical research on the concept and practice of writing-to-learn research between 2004 and 2019, Chmarkh's (2021) concludes that "… implementing writing to learn tasks result in notable learning benefits in language and content area classrooms" (p. 93) and therefore should be included as a possible learning strategy: "Informal, ungraded, writing activities such as learning journals, reflections, and online discussions are viable avenues for students not only to negotiate and construct their understanding of content but also to develop their critical thinking skills" (p. 93).

Task Design

Reading as a Prewriting Task

The importance of reading for the development of writing is well established, whether it is in the native language or in a second language. The more people read, the more familiar they become with the structure of a text, the development of a character, the description of a setting, unfamiliar words and expressions, and different writing styles. In the author's class, the students read several German children's books during the first five weeks of the quarter as a prewriting exploration: The students learned how to analyze children's stories by discussing topics, themes, characters, and storylines, as well as the language used. These texts served as models and inspirations for the students.

The idea to explore children's books with adult learners who are normally accustomed to moving to more advanced books may seem for some a bit questionable, at first glance. However, Rundell (2019, 2023) pointed out that adults reading stories they enjoyed as children will find them still interesting because they remember what made these stories so precious: Learning about shared experiences, customs and norms, struggles and adversities, and family and community life. More importantly, research has shown (Nation et al., 2022) that the variety, depth, and sophistication of the language (i.e., words and syntactic constructions found in the narratives are normally not used in speech) in children's books help develop social, emotional, and verbal skills. Children who read much showed improved sentence comprehension and grammaticality judgment and were more likely to use difficult grammatical patterns in their speech.

The author selected the children's books for this class not only for the quality of the language, but for the themes and illustrations which could speak to the varied interests of the students in class. *Der Struwwelpeter* (Hoffmann, 2005) and *Max und Moritz* (Busch, 2015) contain stories in which children often suffer drastic consequences because they behave recklessly. While students were horrified by some of the consequences the children in the stories suffered, they were interested in the teaching aspect of these two books. *Die kleine Hexe: Ausflug mit Abraxas* (Preussler et al., 2017), the second volume of the trilogy of a little witch developing self-confidence and strength to be able to exist in the adult world, provided complex language and ample material for grammatical analysis. The author chose the famous biblical story of *Die Arche Noah* (Janisch & Zwerger, 2008) because of its relevance today, namely the question of whether life on Earth is threatened. In addition to connecting the theme to current environmental issues, this story gave the learners the opportunity to analyze particularly expressive and thoughtful illustrations. The author chose *Zwei Papas für Tango* (Schreiber-Wicke & Holland, 2017) because it dealt sensitively with the topics of homosexuality and rainbow families, and it showed students that real-life stories could easily become topics of a children's book. *Zarah und Zottel* (Birck, 2017) is a magical story of a child longing for acceptance among a group of children who are different from who she is. Moving with her mother to a new neighborhood where she initially is told "to go back to where she came from," Zarah wants to be like her father, an American Indian, who, in her imagination, rides a horse all day long. This makes her special.

The analysis and discussion of the language in the stories the students read was based on a set of questions the author adapted from *Reading and Writing Haven: A Blog for Educators* (https://www.readingandwritinghaven.com/), and included the following:

- Is the author using specific nouns, verbs, adjectives, and adverbs? How do they contribute to the meaning of the story? Does the author use words with multiple meanings? What is the effect of this wordplay?
- What punctuation does the author use in the text and in the dialogues? What effect do punctuation marks such as ellipses, dashes, and colons have on the reading experience? Are there parts without proper punctuation and what effect does the lack of punctuation have on the reader?
- What grammar features or topics can you recognize? How do these elements contribute to the meaning, overall tone, or mood of the story?

Setting up the Writing Task

The creative task for this class was to write a children's story including illustrations using generative artificial intelligence (AI) tools. When developing the frame of the story, the students followed these guidelines:

- The topic of the story should interest and inspire children (and adults, too). Think of stories from everyday life, fantasy stories or stories from the distant world.
- The place and time of the story could include the realistic world, the fairy tale world detached from time and space, as well as futuristic places. Consider these questions: What does the place look like? What is the weather like and how does it smell? What can you discover there? Who lives in the world you created? How is the social structure and are there any rules in this world?
- Interesting characters can draw the reader into the story. What does your protagonist look like? How can you describe the character of your protagonist? How does your protagonist act?
- Find a goal for your character to pursue. Include at least three turning points (i.e., the triggering event, the character's journey, and the final event). Consider these questions: What is your character's goal? What motivates your character to achieve this goal? Who is stopping your character? Who will help your character? What hurdles does your character have to overcome along the way? What insights does your character gain from the journey?

Incorporating ChatGPT

Discussing and analyzing the children's stories during the first five weeks of the quarter gave the students a chance to start storyboarding their story by developing the topic, theme, setting, storyline, and plot, as well as main characters (e.g., protagonists, heroes, and villains). During the second five weeks of the quarter, the students began to further develop their ideas with the help of ChatGPT. They interacted conversationally by writing prompts in German and by evaluating and responding to the answers ChatGPT provided. The idea of using ChatGPT as a model for effective writing in a second language is not completely new. For example, Kwon et al. (2023) studied the effect of chatbot-based writing practices on Korean elementary school students learning English as a second language. In this study, the results of the posttest showed that the experimental group had learned more than the control group, suggesting that the writing practice with a chatbot facilitated language acquisition.

The goal of the author's study on the incorporation of ChatGPT was to try to understand the strengths and limitations of various prompt-driven language exchanges. What could a learner reasonably expect from the dialogue format of ChatGPT? Would it be possible to get answers to questions on vocabulary, idiomatic expressions, and grammar issues, to get help in rewriting a short text with a different focus including corrections or explanations of mistakes, and to get descriptions or short conversations? How sensitive was ChatGTP to input or queries that were written in less-than-perfect German? Because recognizing and learning new German language patterns was an important part of their intellectual growth, the students evaluated ChatGPT's output not only for its cultural significance (i.e., focus on meaning), but also for its linguistic value (i.e., focus on meaning and form). The instructor asked the students to pay attention to new words, expressions, and idiomatic phrasing, and to specific grammatical forms (i.e., use of simple past and past perfect tenses, imperatives, relative clauses, present and past participles as adjectival forms; subjunctive and passive sentences, onomatopoeic expressions, and alliterations) in their queries.

METHODOLOGY

Study Design

In this study, the author adopted an explorative approach to investigate the experiences of the students using ChatGPT for a creative writing assignment, and to design a roadmap for instructors on the most effective use and integration of ChatGPT. The researcher collected qualitative data through observations, unstructured focus group discussions, personal interviews with the students, and ChatGPT discussion protocols or queries. The author chose this research method as a viable approach to determine the nature of the integration of ChatGPT (i.e., what, why, and how) and to provide a better understanding of how the students learned with it. The students interacted with ChatGPT via the Web-based interface: They wrote text prompts in German as input and evaluated and answered ChatGPT's output. The goal of the study was to explore the following:

- What can ChatGPT offer to language students developing a creative writing project? What are some of the limitations?
- What are effective language prompts and why? What are effective rewrites or follow-up prompts?
- How well can ChatGPT understand input that is less than perfect in grammar and vocabulary?
- While the writing task was a meaning-focused activity, did the students also pay attention to the form of the language? What kind of help did ChatGPT provide?

Participants

A group of 10 college students from a private university in the Midwest of the U.S., five males and five females, all learners of German as a second language, took part in the study. The students were enrolled in an advanced grammar class during the Spring quarter of 2023. The prerequisite for the class was a proficiency level in German of B1/B2 on the Common European Framework of Reference for Languages (Council of Europe, n.d.) scale or Intermediate High/Advanced Low on the ACTFL scale (ACTFL Performance Descriptors for Language Learners, 2024). As is typical of advanced classes, the proficiency levels of the students in the class varied, a result of aptitude and language learning background (i.e., taking various German classes in high school and/or college and study abroad experiences). All students showed a high interest in learning German: Two of the students were majoring and six were minoring in German.

Data Collection

The class met twice a week for 80 minutes over 10 weeks of instruction. During the first five weeks of instruction, the students read and analyzed a series of children's books and reviewed several grammar chapters using a grammar book at the C1 level. Topics covered ranged from a quick review of verb tenses, subjunctive mode, passive construction, to adjectives and adverbs and declension and comparisons. During the second five weeks of instruction, the students began to use ChatGPT productively through in-class instructional units targeting the creative use of prompts. The instructor gave them several homework assignments where they were encouraged to use similar prompt sequences to help them write and design their own children's book. They continued to review grammar using the grammar book as well as examples taken from the readings. Topics covered ranged from the use of conjunctions (i.e., "and" and "but") and conjunctive adverbs (i.e., "however" and "at the same time") to appositions (e.g., "Leo, the neighbor's dog, is destroying my backyard"), relative clauses, participial clauses (e.g., "waiting for my neighbor, I prepared some tea"), and infinitival constructions.

The students interacted with ChatGPT in class during four 40-minute sessions. During these interactions, the instructor observed the students and took notes on their reactions, questions, and comments. Each class session concluded with a brief unstructured focus group discussion on how the session had gone and what might have been helpful as input for their own project.

All the students presented their final story, including comments on how they had used ChatGPT, to the class, at the end of the 10 weeks. The author encouraged each student to meet for a personal interview to discuss the use of ChatGPT, but only a handful of students found time. The instructor asked the students to hand in examples of their ChatGPT discussion protocols at the end of the quarter.

ANALYSIS

In this section, the author analyzes samples of ChatGPT queries in German to understand how students interacted conversationally with the chatbot. The author selected the sample queries from personal student ChatGPT protocols and from the protocols generated during class sessions.

Writing a Full Story

One of the first in-class tasks the author assigned to the students was to ask ChatGPT to write a brief story about two fictional main characters. The prompt was quite nonspecific (i.e., "write a brief children's story about a friendship between two main characters"). Then, the participants shared and discussed the resulting stories in class. Since the students needed to write a unique story with twists and turns, there was general disappointment about the simple and cliché-like stories that ChatGPT had created, often with happy fairy-tale endings like "and if they have not died, they are still alive today." The students immediately recognized the inability of a chatbot to create an intricate story with twists and turns with a simple straightforward request. They realized that they would need to work with smaller parts of the story, be more precise, and create successive follow-up prompts.

Finding Appropriate Names

Developing a description for the protagonist in the story as well as other characters began with the search for appropriate names. The students did not have much experience with German names and ChatGPT was fully capable of providing a list. Below is an example of an initial exchange the instructor and the learners developed together in class:

You: *Ich schreibe ein Kinderbuch. Finde einen Namen für die Hauptperson, ein Kranich.* (I am writing a children's book. Find a name for the main character, a crane.)

ChatGPT: *Wie wäre es mit dem Namen "Karl" für deinen Hauptcharakter Kranich? Andere Optionen könnten "Kiki," "Krümel," "Kasimir" oder "Kira" sein.* (How about the name "Karl" for your main character Crane? Other options could be "Kiki," "Krümel," "Kasimir" or "Kira".)

You: *"Krümel" gefällt mir. Krümel hat einen Freund, einen roten Frosch, der am Ufer des Teiches wohnt. Wähle einen Namen für den Frosch.* (I like "Krümel." Krümel has a friend, a red frog, who lives on the banks of the pond. Choose a name for the frog.)

ChatGPT: *Ein süßer Name für den roten Frosch könnte "Felix" sein. Andere Optionen könnten "Fridolin," "Finn," "Florian" oder "Ferdinand" sein.* (A cute name for the red frog could be "Felix." Other options could be "Fridolin," "Finn," "Florian" or "Ferdinand".)

You: *Finde einen Namen für den Frosch, der zu der roten Farbe passt.* (Find a name for the frog that matches the red color.)

ChatGPT: *Ein passender Name für einen roten Frosch könnte beispielsweise "Rubin" sein, da dieser Edelstein ebenfalls eine rötliche Farbe hat.* (A fitting name for a red frog could be "Rubin" as this gemstone is also reddish in color.)

You: *Keiner dieser Namen gefällt mir. Was könnte es noch sein?* (I don't like any of those names. What else could it be?)

ChatGPT: *Wie wäre es mit dem Namen "Rufio"?* (How about the name "Rufio"?)

Working With Descriptions

A third task the author developed as a class project was asking ChatGPT to help write a character description. The students had already prepared a simple description of their main character: *Krümel ist ein majestätischer Vogel mit einem langen, schlanken Hals, einem rötlichen Kopf, und einem langen spitzen Schnabel* (Krümel is a majestic bird with a long, slender neck, a reddish head, and a long, pointed beak). They asked ChatGPT for suggestions on what they could improve, including a short rewrite. ChatGPT suggested that they should add details about the feathers (are they grey or white?), the color of the eyes, and the size of Krümel. Then, ChatGPT offered the following rewrite:

ChatGPT: *Krümel ist ein majestätischer Vogel von mittlerer Größe mit einem schlanken, langen Hals und einem wohlgeformten rötlich gefärbten Kopf. Sein langer, spitzer Schnabel ist perfekt geformt zum Fischen und Jagen von Beute. Seine Federn sind weiß und grau mit auffälligen schwarzen Mustern auf den Flügeln. Krümels Augen sind groß und bernsteinfarben und glänzen in der Sonne.* (Krümel is a majestic bird of medium size with a slender, long neck and a well-shaped reddish-colored head. Its long, pointed beak is perfectly shaped for fishing and hunting prey. Its feathers are white and gray with striking black patterns on the wings. Krümel's eyes are large and amber and shine in the sun.)

The students felt the paragraph was too stilted. They asked ChatGPT to rewrite it in a simpler version that would be better suited for a children's book and would contain information on what the crane was doing during the day. ChatGPT's next suggestion read:

ChatGPT: *Krümel ist ein schöner Vogel mit einem langen Hals und einem spitz zulaufenden Schnabel. Er hat ein rotes Köpfchen und graue, weiche Federn, die ihn warm halten. Krümel liebt es, im Sumpfgebiet zu leben und im Teich nach Fischen zu suchen. Er ist ein sehr geschickter Jäger und ein lustiger kleiner Vogel zum Beobachten.* (Krümel is a beautiful bird with a long neck and a pointed beak. It has a small red head and grey, soft feathers that keep it warm. Krümel loves to live in the swamp area and look for fish in the pond. He is a very skilled hunter and a fun little bird to watch.)

The instructor used these two rewrites as a writing exercise for the students to come up with a third description considering information from both paragraphs and adding additional material, if appropriate.

The students also used ChatGPT to generate ideas for describing the place where the two main characters lived. They asked for a list of things Krümel and Rufio would see walking along the edge of the pond, and ChatGPT offered several examples with appropriate explanations. The first two were as follows:

ChatGPT: *Wasserlilien: Sie sehen wunderschöne Wasserlilien, die auf der Oberfläche des Teiches schwimmen. Die bunten Blütenblätter der Lilien öffnen sich der Sonne entgegen.* (Water Lilies: They see beautiful water lilies floating on the surface of the pond. The colorful petals of the lilies open towards the sun.)

ChatGPT: *Libellen: Über dem Wasser tanzen bunte Libellen mit glänzenden Flügeln. Sie fliegen elegant von Blatt zu Blatt und jagen nach Insekten.* (Dragonflies: Colorful dragonflies with shiny wings dance above the water. They fly elegantly from leaf to leaf and hunt for insects.)

ChatGTP was also able to give accurate descriptions of what a frog in a children's story might do, distinguishing between appropriate activities for a shy and quiet female frog and for a boyish and confident female frog. The activities suggested for Lilya, the shy frog, were: Counting water lilies, watching the fish in the pond, sunbathing on a sea leaf (but not for too long), and helping the mother look for insects. The activities suggested for Lilly, the boyish, bold, and confident frog, were: Jumping, diving, chasing insects, and discovering new things, among others. This was an excellent description, as the frogs in this story had human qualities; yet ChatGPT described activities appropriate to the environment in which the two characters lived (i.e., in and around a pond).

Developing a Larger Vocabulary

One of the most powerful learning activities was the development of unfamiliar language such as searching for words or phrases including definitions and translations. The students were still using online dictionaries and translation programs they had used before. They soon realized that dictionaries were limited in what they could provide, when compared to the powerful language ChatGTP presented them. One of the students developed a children's story about her service dog, a diabetic alert dog. She checked in Google Translate for "service dog" and was presented with the word "Servicehund," not an expression that is used very much in German. ChatGPT, however, provided a much more helpful and more accurate learning sequence:

You: *Wie nennt man einen Hund, der Menschen hilft*? (What do you call a dog that helps people?)

ChatGPT: *Ein Hund, der Menschen in verschiedenen Aspekten unterstützt, wird oft als "Therapiehund" oder "Servicehund" bezeichnet.* (A dog that assists people in various aspects is often referred to as a "therapy dog" or "service dog".)

ChatGPT then provided a list of specific names with accompanying definitions. Some examples are:

- *Blindenhund: Unterstützt Menschen mit Sehbehinderungen oder Blindheit.* (Guide Dog: Supports people with visual impairments or blindness.)

- *Mobilitätshund: Hilft Menschen mit eingeschränkter Mobilität, indem er Gegenstände aufhebt, Türen öffnet und andere unterstützende Aufgaben erledigt.* (Mobility Dog: Helps people with limited mobility by picking up objects, opening doors, and performing other supportive tasks.)
- *PTSD-Begleithund: Speziell ausgebildet, um Menschen mit posttraumatischer Belastungsstörung zu unterstützen.* (PTSD Service Dog: Specially trained to support people with post-traumatic stress disorder.)
- *Diabetikerwarnhund: Riecht Veränderungen im Blutzuckerspiegel und warnt seinen Besitzer vor einem möglichen Anfall.* (Diabetic alert dog: Smells changes in blood sugar levels and warns its owner of a possible seizure.)
- *Rollstuhlbegleithund: Speziell ausgebildet, um Menschen im Rollstuhl zu unterstützen, indem er Türen öffnet, Gegenstände aufhebt und andere Aufgaben erledigt.* (Wheelchair Service Dog: Specially trained to assist people in wheelchairs by opening doors, picking up objects, and performing other tasks.)
- *Such- und Rettungshund: Wird in Katastrophen- und Suchsituationen eingesetzt, um vermisste Personen zu finden.* (Search & Rescue Dog: Used in disaster and search situations to find missing persons.)

In addition to these translation exercises, students used ChatGPT to find words beyond the ones they already knew to develop a more nuanced language for their stories. For example, to describe the main character as *traurig* (sad), one student wanted a list of synonyms and was presented with *niedergeschlagen, bedrückt, betrübt, melancholisch* (despondent, depressed, unhappy, melancholic). Another requested examples of idiomatic expressions to describe their character as good natured (*Er ist so gutmütig wie ein Lamm*/He is good-natured as a lamb) and as eating super-fast (*Er isst wie ein Scheunendrescher*/He eats like a threshing machine). Other students asked for nouns that expressed various emotions (*Liebe, Hass, Freude, Trauer, Angst, Eifersucht, Hoffnung, Verzweiflung, Glück, Einsamkeit*/love, hate, joy, sorrow, fear, jealousy, hope, despair, happiness, loneliness) and verbs that expressed joy and happiness (*lachen, strahlen, jubeln, hüpfen, tanzen, singen, klatschen, umarmen, küssen*/laugh, beam with you, cheer, jump, dance, sing, clap hug, kiss). One student was interested in an interjection (i.e., a word used to express a feeling or to request something, usually used in dialogues). Asked what a frog would say in certain situations, ChatGPT provided *Boah! Huch! Irre! Mannomann! Unglaublich*! (Wow! Yikes! Crazy! Well! Incredible!). The student asked for German expressions that were frog-like since the list provided did not seem appropriate to her for an animal. ChatGPT presented *Quaak oder Kwaak* (Quaak or Kwaak) as the most used onomatopoeic expression but offered more options: *Krah! Ripp! Kroa! Krick! Brumm! Grummel! Platsch!* The student then wanted to know when and how one would use *Grummel and Platsch*. ChatGPT's answers were:

ChatGPT: *Ein Frosch macht normalerweise "Platsch," wenn er ins Wasser springt.* (A frog usually makes a "splash" when it jumps into the water.)

ChatGPT: *Die Interjektion "Grummel! " wird oft genutzt, um Unzufriedenheit, Verärgerung oder Missfallen auszudrücken.* (The interjection "Grumble!" is often used to express dissatisfaction, annoyance, or displeasure.)

Even alliterations in German (i.e., a literary device that repeats consonant sounds in two or more nearby words), a technique the students had encountered in their readings, became the subject of a prompt. A student asked for language examples that had to do with his protagonist, a monkey, cleaning his room. The student learned the following phrases: *Saubere Socken sortieren* (sorting clean socks) and *Bananenschalen behutsam beseitigen* (carefully removing banana peels).

Developing Grammar Knowledge

Given the large output ChatGPT produced for the prompts the students wrote, the class had much material that they could analyze for specific grammar practice, especially punctuation, inflectional forms, and verb tenses, including word order. The students also used prompts and queries to improve their own grammar skills, such as asking for corresponding past tense forms or asking for grammar feedback on individual sentences. It was most surprising to the students to realize that ChatGPT could even handle a variety of inputs that were lacking accurate spelling, grammar, and even word choices.

You: *Können Sie ein Name, der mit ein "Sch" anfangen, machen?* (Can you make a name that starts with "Sch"?)

ChatGPT: *Natürlich! Hier sind einige Namen, die mit "Sch" beginnen und zu deiner Affen-Hauptfigur passen könnten: Schoko, Schiller, Schröder, Schnufel, Schalko.* (Of course! Here are some names that start with "Sch" that might suit your main monkey character: Schoko, Schiller, Schröder, Schnufel, Schalko.)

You: *Ich wird mein Buch "Schrödi der schelmischer Affe" heißen. Gefällen Sie?* (My book will be called "Schrödi the mischievous monkey." Do you like it?)

ChatGPT: *"Schrödi der schelmische Affe" klingt großartig!* ("Schrödi the mischievous monkey" sounds great!)

You: *Ich will mein Affe weiblich zu sein. Können Sie mein Title verändern?* (I want my monkey to be female. Can you change my title?)

ChatGPT: *"Schrödi, die schelmische Affendame"*. ("Schrödi, the mischievous monkey lady".)

You: *Das Wort "Affendame" gefällt mir nicht. Können sie "Äffin" stattdessen benutzen?* (I don't like the word "monkey lady. " Can you use "monkey" instead?)

ChatGPT: *"Schrödi, die schelmische Äffin"*. ("Schrödi, the mischievous monkey".)

Most useful were the recasts ChatGPT provided. Here is one example that involves the correct use of an adjective ending:

You: *Ich wird mein Buch "Schrödi der schelmischer Affe" heißen. Gefällen Sie?* (My book will be called "Schrödi the mischievous monkey." Do you like it?)

ChatGPT: *"Schrödi der schelmische Affe" klingt großartig!* ("Schrödi the mischievous monkey" sounds great!)

Some students pointed out that they were learning about their mistakes simply by paying attention to the accurate language in ChatGPT's answer.

ChatGPT turned out to be very creative in writing dialogues. Again, as a group project, the students asked ChatGPT to write a dialog between the frog parents forbidding the children to play with Rufio, the red frog, who lived at the edge of the pond. This output provided source material for the students to discuss punctuation rules in German for direct speech as well as conjunctions and word order.

Papa Frosch: *"Kinder, ich möchte nicht, dass ihr mit diesem roten Frosch namens Rufio spielt."* ("Kids, I don't want you to play with that red frog named Rufio.")

Mama Frosch: *"Ja, das stimmt. Rufio ist anders als wir. Er ist rot, nicht grün wie wir. Und wir wissen nicht, woher er kommt oder wer seine Eltern sind."* ("Yes, that's right. Rufio is different from us. He is red, not green like us. And we don't know where he's from or who his parents are.")

Papa Frosch: *"Es ist besser, wenn ihr mit den anderen grünen Fröschen spielt. Sie sind wie wir und ihr wisst, dass ihr mit ihnen sicher spielen könnt."* ("It's better if you play with the other green frogs. They're like us, and you know you can play with them safely.")

Kind 1: *"Aber Papa, Rufio ist nett zu uns und wir mögen ihn. Warum können wir nicht mit ihm spielen?"* ("But Dad, Rufio is nice to us and we like him. Why can't we play with him?")

Mama Frosch: *"Es geht nicht darum, ob er nett ist oder nicht. Es geht darum, dass wir nicht wissen, wer er ist oder woher er kommt. Es ist besser, wenn ihr mit den anderen grünen Fröschen spielt."* ("It's not about whether he's nice or not. The point is that we don't know who he is or where he comes from. It's better if you play with the other green frogs.")

Creating Illustrations Using an Artificial Intelligence Image Generator

Illustrations are a crucial part of a children's book: They help clarify the storyline and unfold visually what the text describes. Beyond simply showing what is expressed in the text, illustrations can add new elements that are not described in the text, therefore providing a fresh viewpoint or narrative. Good illustrations make the reader fall in love with the protagonist or simply draw the reader into the story and keep the reader hooked. In illustrating their books, the students were free to use their drawing talents, take their own photographs, or work with a graphics editor such as Photoshop. Students were introduced in class to the concept of an AI image creator, a program that could create original and realistic images and art by simply understanding a description of the subject matter.

Students experimented with DALL•E (https://labs.openai.com/) and Bing Image Creator (https://bing.com/create). Both AI image generators were able to create fairly accurate pictures, although the learners needed to experiment with the way a prompt was phrased: *Ein Kranich und ein roter Frosch, im Kinderbuchstil* (A crane and a red frog, in children's book style) resulted in more accurate drawings (Figure 1) than *Ein roter Frosch und ein Kranich, im Kinderbuchstil* (a red frog and a crane, in children's book style), where the crane appeared red (Figure 2).

The longer or more complex the input, the more difficult it was for the program to create a true representation. The students experimented with the description *Ein Kranich und ein roter Frosch spazieren am Ufer eines idyllischen Teiches, im Kinderbuchstil* (A crane and a red frog walk on the banks of an idyllic pond, in children's book style), but AI was not able to generate a satisfactory picture (Figure 3).

In some of the stories created, the protagonists were not humans but animals or fantasy characters, while in others the protagonists represented a diverse and inclusive mix of characters, which added to the difficulty of finding the right illustration. Depending on the complexity, the AI generator could not represent the input accurately.

While creating a unique and interesting representation of the protagonist had its difficulties, to make sure that this unique character would appear in all subsequent drawings to represent the story accurately was almost impossible. In the end, the students experimented with other image creators (e.g., NightCafé, https://creator.nightcafe.studio/studio) and other ways of illustrating their storybook: Some searched for appropriate images online, took their own pictures, used their drawing skills, or used image editor software such as Photoshop to manipulate pictures and create appropriate compositions or collages. Figure 4 below is an example of a page of a student-created story book called *Oska, der Ökoheld* (Oska, the Eco-Hero) integrating text and images. The images represent a collage of elements generated by AI.

Figure 1. Ein Kranich und ein roter Frosch, im Kinderbuchstil (A Crane and a Red Frog, in children's book style)
Note. Picture generated using DALL•E.

Figure 2. Ein roter Frosch und ein Kranich, im Kinderbuchstil (A Red Frog and a Crane, in children's book style)
Note. Picture generated using DALL•E.

Figure 3. Ein Kranich und ein roter Frosch spazieren am Ufer eines idyllischen Teiches, im Kinderbuchstil (A Crane and a Red Frog Walk on the Banks of an Idyllic Pond, in children's book style)
Note. Picture generated using DALL•E.

Figure 4. Example page from Oska, der Ökoheld (Oska, the Eco-Hero), a student-created story

Note. Translation of the text: One day, they saw something funny while they were fly fishing. A well-dressed toad, carrying a walking stick and top hat, was walking with a foreman's frog.

"Well," said the wealthy frog, "this is a wonderful place for our landfill."

"Definitely, Count BrightFrog," croaked the foreman.

"Landfill?" asked Oskar. "But you mustn't do that! This pond is our home!"

"Well, Mr. Oscar, I am Count BrightFrog, the richest toad far and wide, and your little pond is mine. This deed states that everything I want to do with this pond is allowed, and you can't do anything about it."

DISCUSSION

The writing of an original children's story was primarily a meaning-focused task. FonF, as the interactions with ChatGPT lay bare, occurred because of lexical, grammatical, and pragmatic questions the students asked in trying to convey accurate meaning. Engaging in the chatbot-mediated writing activities in class and on their own was therefore a welcome addition to the learning environment. The class was taught during Spring 2023, and ChatGPT had been released only a few months before (Open AI released an early version of ChatGPT at the end of 2022). As a result, most of the students were not familiar yet with how to interact with ChatGPT. None of them had used it in German or had entertained the idea that they could work with ChatGPT in a foreign language. They were surprised to learn that ChatGPT could understand and answer in German.

The first exercise in class using ChatGPT turned out to be important. The students discovered immediately that ChatGPT, at this stage, could not provide a full children's story beyond simple cliché-like narratives. This was useful in setting work expectations. Realizing that for a good final project, students would have to actively work on writing and responding to prompts as well as on making critical decisions on what material to use in their final story, legitimized the use of ChatGPT as a German tutor. The students had been told in several other classes that the use of ChatGPT was not allowed because of plagiarism concerns. Understanding that this was not about simply copying output, but that their task included a conversational exchange in German through which their story would take shape, was a relief.

ChatGPT turned out to be a powerful and effective tutor who could answer questions or react to prompts even if they were written in less-than-perfect German. As the author outlined above, the confusing question *Ich wird mein Buch "Schrödi der schelmischer Affe" heißen. Gefällen Sie?* was responded to with a semantically valid answer making meaningful conversations with the learner: *"Schrödi der schelmische Affe" klingt großartig!* This turned out to be important for students, as their questions were often composed hastily without too much concern for the exact grammar.

Where ChatGPT was most helpful was in all areas of language development. The students frequently asked questions about expanding their vocabulary, and the conversations with the chatbot helped the learners solve problems often better than the dictionaries to which they were used. A prime example listed above is the search for the German term for "service dog," where the learner was presented with a list of possible translations including definitions in German. Other excellent examples were the search for synonyms (i.e., what is another word for "sad") or the search for semantic expansions of a category of words (i.e., give me a list of verbs that express "joy"). To mimic the type of language the students had explored in the children's book they read, one student asked for alliterations in German (i.e., *Saubere Socken sortieren*/sorting clean socks) and another for interjections to make the dialog more native-like (i.e., *platsch*/splash). Representing sounds in German was another semantic area that the students explored. One student wanted to know how to say "alarm clock" in German and how to represent the sound it would make. Finally, ChatGPT proved helpful for a student who wanted to use an idiomatic expression to describe the protagonist as good-natured. The chatbot provided *Er ist so gutmütig wie ein Lamm*/He is good-natured as a lamb. To indicate that the protagonist stopped suddenly, the chatbot provided *Er blieb wie angewurzelt stehen*/He stopped in his tracks.

Many students were using ChatGPT to inquire about grammatical information. For example, struggling with the past tense forms of verbs which were important for the stories they wrote, one student asked for a list of verbs indicating "running" and the equivalent forms in the simple past tense. The instructor and the students had previously discussed the possibilities of forming extended participles as adjectival phrases and one student created, using several prompts, the following description: *Eine gut gekleidete, Gehstock und Zylinder tragende Kröte* (A well-dressed toad carrying a cane and top hat). Sometimes, ChatGPT reminded student to check for grammatical accuracy: A student wanted a list of German adjectives that could be alliterative with *Mut* (courage) and could be used to complement someone. After providing examples such as *mutig* (courageous), *majestätisch* (majestic), *mächtig* (mighty), and *mitfühlend* (compassionate), ChatGPT reminded the student to adapt the adjectives to match the gender and number of the person they were complimenting. In some instances, where prompts were less than grammatically perfect, ChatGPT provided recasts to help students onto the right track. One student wanted a name that would start with "Sch," another wanted a list of names that started with "A," and both times ChatGPT answered with the correct grammar.

You: *Können Sie ein Name, der mit ein "Sch" anfangen, machen?* (Can you make a name that starts with an "Sch"?)

ChatGPT: *Natürlich! Hier sind einige Namen, die mit "Sch" beginnen und zu deiner Affen-Hauptfigur passen könnten.* (Of course! Here are some names that start with "Sch" that might suit your main monkey character.)

You: *Können Sie mehr Namen gleich ihnen finden, besonders Namen, die mit ein "A" anfangen?* (Can you find more names like them, especially names that start with an "A"?)

ChatGPT: *Natürlich! Hier sind weitere Namen, die mit dem Buchstaben "A" beginnen und dem Stil der zweiten Liste ähneln.* (Of course! Here are more names that start with the letter "A" and are similar to the style of the second list.)

Quite often recasts involved the correct use of adjective endings, as in this example where a student input *Schrödi der schelmischer Affe* was corrected in ChatGPT's answer with *Schrödi der schelmische Affe* (Schrödi the mischievous monkey). Adjective endings were one of the areas college learners of German found to be the most difficult to learn (Chavez, 2016, 2017). It was very important for the students to have a tutor who would answer their questions at the time when they were most salient, notwithstanding their own language limitations and mistakes in their prompts. ChatGPT did not judge the students, but provided answers with which they could start developing and improving their writing skills.

The class found some limitations when working with ChatGPT. ChatGPT lacked creativity and imagination and was not able to create engaging storylines that included intricate plots or multidimensional characters. It also had considerable difficulties at times to mimic the genre of children's stories, and the descriptions sounded more like an encyclopedic entry, even if asked to rewrite the text for a children's book. At times, there was significant input required in the form of follow-up prompts to develop the storyline, and some students simply gave up relying on their imagination and skills and/or double-checking with a human tutor.

This chapter represents only a snapshot of the work with ChatGPT. Nevertheless, it highlights the endless potential ChatGPT has to engage students in creative writing in a foreign language. Teaching the class, the author learned much about what to do better and what not to do. To ensure a successful experience, the following guidelines could be helpful to make sure that students are prepared:

- **Acquire Strategies for Prompt Design:** One of the first tasks was to model for the students in class how to write a prompt. This allowed everybody to discover the variety of prompts that were possible, such as asking for grammar help, or additional vocabulary and appropriate expressions. Open-ended or vague prompts were not successful in getting good information.
- **Critically Analyze the Prompt Output:** Beginning this project as a collaborative task in class sharing and discussing prompts and corresponding answers was crucial in many ways. Through discussions, the students discovered limitations in terms of the quality of the output (e.g., unsophisticated, cliché-like storylines, a few things were factually wrong) and the lack of nuanced and unique answers.
- **Use Effective Prompt Rewrites to Narrow the Prompt Output:** The students learned to be critical but forgiving. ChatGPT may not get everything right the first time, especially if the prompt is less than specific. Rethinking the output and why it was not what the student was looking for helped refine the prompts to receive the desired output.
- **Focus on Smaller Writing Sections:** Working with individual sections of the full story (e.g., brief descriptions, narrations, and dialogues) was more successful. Examples the students practiced in class were description of a character (mental disposition or physical appearance of the red frog), description of the environment (what the red frog saw when he walked along the pond), and dialogues (what his parents warned him about when swimming in the pond). Asking for too much or overloading a prompt with information overwhelmed the chatbot on occasion.
- **Work Sequentially Throughout the Project:** A story such as a children's book cannot be created through one prompt or in one sitting, especially if the storyline is complex with twists and turns.

The students were most successful when working sequentially through the story, refining each part with well-crafted prompts, and assembling the outputs to create the final story.

- **Keep at It:** On occasion, the students needed encouragement to continue working with ChatGPT. The students who had a particular answer in mind found it sometimes difficult to phrase the prompt in such a way that it would elicit the desired material. However, the more students practiced writing prompts, the better the exchanges.

LIMITATIONS

This project was not intended to show that students using ChatGPT advanced their language proficiency more than students who did not use ChatGPT. The author only had a small group of students involved in the class and not enough to set up a reliable control group. Since the use of ChatGPT to further language proficiency is rather unexplored, the goal of the study was to describe the experiences of language learners using ChatGPT in German and to reflect on the potential for learning grammar and new vocabulary. The author used an explorative approach, collecting ChatGPT protocols (class protocols and individual protocols), detailing observations, and conducting unstructured focus group interviews and personal discussions to gauge students' interaction and satisfaction with ChatGPT. These activities, however, were voluntary and not all the students participated equally.

While many of the observations made on language use, the suggestions provided for how to set up the learning task, and how best to incorporate ChatGPT are valuable contributions to the field of language teaching and learning, more data need to be collected, potentially in different languages, to be able to generalize across all languages. For this project, ChatGPT was an effective tool for engaging students in a variety of language tasks, and the quality of the students' final children's stories showed that they did advance their writing skills substantially, even in areas that were not explicitly discussed or practiced. However, whether learning was the sole result of ChatGPT use is not clear. The students were free to meet with a human tutor to go over their writing, and some took advantage of that offering.

For the interactions with a chatbot, the author used the free version of ChatGPT, version 3.5, to ensure that all the students had equal access. The current version, ChatGPT 4.0, however, is more powerful, and the interactions and results the author presented in this chapter may look different when using ChatGPT 4.0 or a later version.

CONCLUSION

Overall, the learners treated ChatGPT as a valuable addition to their learning tools: They felt that these active, in-time, and student-directed interactions helped them practice their creative thinking and writing skills in fundamentally new ways. There was much they wanted to know and much ChatGPT provided: New vocabulary and expressions such as idiomatic phrases, expansions of semantic and syntactic categories, rewrites, and creative suggestions such as short descriptions or dialogues. Most importantly, the students worked in areas that had relevance to them and that were important for each one at their stage of learning and language development.

It became clear to students that ChatGPT was not a substitute for their engagement, and the more they interacted the more they learned and the better ChatGPT was with providing accurate answers.

They also realized that every learner was bringing a unique perspective and voice to their story and that an overreliance on AI-generated content would not ensure an individual and unique project.

Working with the students on developing and discussing prompts was an effective way of getting them to become familiar with AI. They learned that the interactions were at the level of a conversation with a patient interlocutor whom they could ask follow-up questions and with whom they could disagree at times. Using the language that ChatGPT provided in the output was helpful in forming follow-up questions. The students also realized that their input did not have to be perfect in terms of grammar and vocabulary for ChatGPT to understand, and that ChatGPT's answers quite often contained the correct way of saying or writing something they had attempted.

The exchanges with ChatGPT created conditions in which the learners could learn according to their learning style and their current language proficiency. Grammar was highlighted not according to a prescribed syllabus, but according to the current needs of the learner (Ellis, 2006). The transcripts showed that learning how to write correctly and effectively is a complex undertaking that includes both explicit and implicit learning processes (Ellis, 2015, 2016; Pawlak, 2021). The conversations unfolding between the learners and ChatGPT provided context and various techniques for the students to focus on meaning and on FonF, including incidental FonF, to facilitate the development of learners' second language (Pouresmaeil & Vali, 2023).

REFERENCES

ACTFL. (2024). *ACTFL performance descriptors for language learners*. https://www.actfl.org/educator-resources/actfl-performance-descriptors

Basturkmen, H. (2023). Explicit versus implicit grammar instruction and knowledge. In J. I. Liontas (Ed.), *The TESOL encyclopedia of English language teaching* (pp. 1–7). doi:10.1002/9781118784235.eelt0060

Birck, J. (2017). *Zarah und Zottel: ein Pony auf vier Pfoten*. Fischer Sauerländer Verlag.

Busch, W. (2015). *Max und Moritz: eine Bubengeschichte in Sieben Streichen*. Esslinger Verlag.

Byrnes, H., & Manchón, R. M. (2014). Task-based language learning: Insights from and for L2 writing. An Introduction. In H. Byrnes & R. M. Manchón (Eds.), *Task-based language learning—Insights from and for L2 writing* (pp. 1–23). John Benjamins. doi:10.1075/tblt.7.01byr

Chavez, M. (2016). Students' accounts of grammatical forms of German that are difficult, unattainable, and irrelevant for self-expression. *Language Awareness*, *25*(3), 197–221. doi:10.1080/09658416.2016.1165238

Chavez, M. (2017). Hard rules and bad memories: College learner's accounts of what makes learning German grammar difficult. *Die Unterrichtspraxis*, *50*(1), 1–21. doi:10.1111/tger.12018

Chmarkh, M. (2021). "Writing to learn" research: A synthesis of empirical studies (2004-2019). *European Journal of Educational Research*, *10*(1), 85–96. doi:10.12973/eu-jer.10.1.85

Council of Europe. (n.d.). *Common European Framework of Reference for Languages: Learning, teaching, assessment*. https://www.coe.int/en/web/common-european-framework-reference-languages

East, M. (2015). Task-based teaching and learning: Pedagogical implications. In N. Van Deusen-Scholl & S. May (Eds.), *Second and foreign language education. Encyclopedia of language and education* (pp. 85–95). Springer. doi:10.1007/978-3-319-02323-6_8-1

Ellis, N. C. (2015). Implicit AND explicit learning of language. In P. Rebuschat (Ed.), *Implicit and explicit learning of language* (pp. 3–24). Benjamins. doi:10.1075/sibil.48.01ell

Ellis, R. (2006). Current issue in the teaching of grammar: An SLA perspective. *TESOL Quarterly*, *40*(1), 83–107. doi:10.2307/40264512

Ellis, R. (2009). Implicit and explicit learning, knowledge, and instruction. In R. Ellis, S. Loewen, C. Elder, H. Reinders, R. Erlam, & J. Philp, J. (Eds.), Implicit and explicit knowledge in second language learning, testing, and teaching (pp. 3–26). Multilingual Matters. doi:10.21832/9781847691767-003

Ellis, R. (2016). Focus on form: A critical review. *Language Teaching Research*, *20*(3), 405–428. doi:10.1177/1362168816628627

Hoffmann, H. (2005). *Der Struwwelpeter*. Loewe Verlag GmbH.

Incecay, V., & Dollar, Y. K. (2011). Foreign language learners' beliefs about grammar instruction and error correction. *Procedia: Social and Behavioral Sciences*, *15*, 3394–3398. doi:10.1016/j.sbspro.2011.04.307

Janisch, H., & Zwerger, L. (2008). *Die Arche Noah*. Minedition.

Jean, G., & Simard, D. (2011). Grammar teaching and learning in L2: Necessary, but boring? *Foreign Language Annals*, *44*(3), 467–494. doi:10.1111/j.1944-9720.2011.01143.x

Kormos, J. (2023). The role of cognitive factors in second language writing and writing to learn a second language. *Studies in Second Language Acquisition*, *45*(3), 622–646. doi:10.1017/S0272263122000481

Kwon, S. K., Shin, D., & Lee, Y. (2023). The application of chatbot as an L2 writing practice tool. *Language Learning & Technology*, *27*(1), 1–19.

Leow, R. P. (2019). ISLA: How implicit or how explicit should it be? Theoretical, empirical, and pedagogical/curricular issues. *Language Teaching Research*, *23*(4), 476–493. doi:10.1177/1362168818776674

Loewen, S. (2018). Focus on form versus focus on forms. In J. I. Liontas (Ed.), *The TESOL encyclopedia of English language teaching* (pp. 1–6). doi:10.1002/9781118784235.eelt0062

Loewen, S., Li, S., Fei, F., Thompson, A., Nakatsukasa, K., Ahn, S., & Chen, X. (2009). Second language learners' beliefs about grammar instruction and error correction. *Modern Language Journal*, *93*(1), 91–104. doi:10.1111/j.1540-4781.2009.00830.x

Lys, F. (2013a). Computer-mediated grammar teaching and its effect on different language tasks. In P. Hubbard, M. Schulze, & B. Smith (Eds.), Learner-computer interaction in language education: CALICO Journal: A Festschrift in Honor of Robert Fischer (Vol. 30, pp. 166–186). Academic Press.

Lys, F. (2013b). The development of advanced learner oral proficiency using iPads. *Language Learning & Technology*, *17*(3), 94–116.

Nation, K., Dawson, N. J., & Hsiao, Y. (2022). Book language and its implications for children's language, literacy, and development. *Current Directions in Psychological Science*, *31*(4), 375–380. doi:10.1177/09637214221103264

Pawlak, M. (2021). Implicit versus explicit grammar learning and teaching. In E. Macaro & R. Woore (Eds.), *Debates in second language education* (1st ed., pp. 165–182). Routledge., doi:10.4324/9781003008361-12

Pouresmaeil, A., & Vali, M. (2023). The effects of incidental focus on form on learning vocabulary, grammar, and pronunciation. *Language Teaching Research*, *0*, 1–24. doi:10.1177/13621688231185419

Preussler, O., Preussler-Bitch, S., & Napp, D. (2017). *Die kleine Hexe: Ausflug mit Abraxas*. Thienemann Verlag.

Rundell, K. (2019). *Why you should read children's books, even though you are so old and wise*. Bloomsbury Publishing.

Rundell, K. (2023, July 11). *Why adults should read children's books*. https://www.bbc.com/culture/article/20230711-why-adults-should-read-childrens-books?mibextid=Zxz2cZ

Schreiber-Wicke, E., & Holland, C. (2017). *Zwei Papas für Tango*. Thienemann Verlag.

Sok, S., Kang, E. Y., & Han, Z. (2019). Thirty-five years of ISLA on form-focused instruction: A methodological synthesis. *Language Teaching Research*, *23*(4), 403–427. doi:10.1177/1362168818776673

Williams, J. (2012). The potential role(s) of writing in second language development. *Journal of Second Language Writing*, *21*(4), 321–331. doi:10.1016/j.jslw.2012.09.007

KEY TERMS AND DEFINITIONS

AI Image Generator: An AI-powered tool or software that creates realistic images or art pieces using the information from the description or text prompt the user entered. The images created are entirely new.

ChatGPT Prompt: A statement, a question or instruction written by the user and entered into ChatGPT to generate an answer. A prompt is a request for information or a conversation starter.

Explicit Grammar Learning: Grammar learning that takes place through explicit instruction where the learner is given a grammar explanation or rule.

Focus on Form (FonF): The learning of a foreign language through engagement in meaning-oriented activities that encourage learners to notice various language forms.

Focus on Forms (FonFs): The learning of a foreign language through drills and structured exercises in controlled learning environments.

Implicit Grammar Learning: Grammar learning that takes place through meaning-focused tasks where the learner is not being taught a grammar explanation or rule.

Task-Based Language Teaching: In this approach to second or foreign language teaching, learners are asked to complete a task or tasks using the foreign language which engages their natural abilities for incidental language acquisition.

Writing-to-Learn Activities: Informal and low-stakes writing activities that are designed for the learner to think through key concepts or ideas and to learn how to express, clarify, and organize content.

Chapter 12
Redesigning a Foreign Language Course With the Help of AI:
Benefits and Challenges

Natalie Khazaal
https://orcid.org/0000-0002-7430-9794
Georgia Institute of Technology, USA

ABSTRACT

This chapter evaluates the use of AI for redesigning a foreign (Arabic) language course to significantly incorporate several SDGs. The course provides conditions for experiential learning where students examine their impact on the planet, make meaningful improvements to their lifestyles to lower their carbon footprint, and grow as thoughtful global citizens. It also stimulates students to reflect on the differences between Western and Arab countries' engagement with sustainability goals through real-world scenarios. The analysis focuses on the positive contributions and challenges that AI presents toward the redesigning goal. In particular, it explores how using AI technology in class and for creating course materials affects HIPs elements: significant time on task; frequent, timely feedback; substantive interactions with faculty, peers, and diverse people and ideas; structured reflection and integration of learning; real-world applications; public demonstration of competence; significant learning elements: foundational knowledge, application, integration, human dimension, and learning to learn.

INTRODUCTION

Although the neural networks (transformers) technology used in most recent artificial intelligence (AI)-assisted tools only took off around 2017, AI has spread in healthcare, business, science, entertainment, agriculture, and education, and is expected to eliminate many current jobs as well as create future ones (Samochowiec, 2020; Davenport & Ronanki, 2018; Manyika et al., 2017). In a knowledge-based society,

DOI: 10.4018/979-8-3693-0872-1.ch012

AI is becoming a tool of tremendous importance for students' future careers. And debates about its best uses are becoming more prominent.

Debates around the educational uses of constantly evolving technology more generally have been raging for decades (Zawacki-Richter et al., 2019). While no one questions the need to apply technology in education, debates have turned to the *benefits* and *challenges* of specific technology, especially how different disciplines can best incorporate particular AI tools in the curriculum. Any time educators test latest AI tools in the classroom, students increase their AI literacy (Almelhes, 2023; Educause, 2018; for AI literacy see Burgsteiner, Kandlhofer, & Steinbauer, 2016; Kong, Cheung, & Zhang, 2021; Ng et al., 2021). Soon, classrooms will most likely be unthinkable without some use of AI. According to Xu (2020), instructors who know how to use AI will likely replace those who don't. This prediction captures one of the most significant recent trends in education to orient toward incorporating AI and the increased demand it places on instructors' investment in their own professional development.

But is AI important to the classroom only as a skill set for employment after graduation or for instructors' job security? Why should instructors invest time and effort to research and develop educational curricula that increasingly incorporate AI? Will AI solve important problems in education? Two important problems in education that concern this chapter are first, how to make learning, particularly language learning, *effective* and second, how to make learners' experience *engaging*. Indeed, AI (used together with older technology applications) promises to make the process of learning more effective (Ng et al., 2022; Fan et al., 2021; Arnold & Pistilli, 2012), to improve current learners' experience through greater personalized engagement (Cavalcanti et al., 2021), and to make educators' job more efficient (Vazhayil et al., 2019). As reported in multiple studies, after using AI, learners improve their language abilities and attitudes. They also perceive AI as "effective, efficient, accurate, easy to use, and useful/helpful for language learning," and report "having interesting, enjoyable, and satisfactory experiences with these tools" (Woo & Choi, 2021, p. 1787).

Developers of AI for language learning have invested in tools that bypass in-person human instruction in classroom settings, deploying online AI chatbots and aps like ChatGPT, Bing AI, Bard AI, Duolingo, Rosetta Stone, Phase6, Andy, Lanny (Eggbun), Babbel, Bisuu, Mondly, Memrise, Kommunicate, Na-Takallam, Yalla!, etc. Although Duolingo and Rosetta Stone were built on traditional machine learning (ML) algorithms in natural language processing (NLP) that preexisted large language models (LLMs), recently they have started adding LLM-based assistance. And even the obsolete translation models for language learning on which Dulingo is based (Almelhes, 2023) may offer learners materials tailored to their individual progress as well as personalized conversations that mimic native speech with tips about grammar, vocabulary, and cultural context. Yet, AI chatbots and aps are not sufficiently advanced to guarantee success without human input, which makes them useful as an added bonus to college courses (Almelhes, 2023) instead of replacing such courses.

Instructors remain a main conduit for language learning, with many having a strong desire to adopt AI tools not just as an added bonus but in more integrated ways that address the two issues of effective and engaging language learning experience. However, there is a large gap between instructors' grasp of AI's potential and their understanding of the appropriateness, utility, and limitations of adopting specific AI tools (Almelhes, 2023). Indeed, there may be a single comprehensive review of AI tools for language learning, spanning between 2017 and 2020 (Woo & Choi, 2021). Its authors describe their main concerns about instructors' insufficient knowledge of AI tools and the resulting lack of preparation about how and which tools they can use "to generate personalized and customizable learning experiences for the purposes of optimizing language learning by increasing autonomy, motivation, engagement, and effectiveness" (p. 1784). They also discovered that the majority of research published on how to use AI in foreign language learning took place in Asia, is about learning English, focuses on skills like speaking, listening, writing, and pronunciation, targets university students, and more often explores beginner learners. Given this gap in literature, it is beneficial to explore how AI can be adopted in languages other than English such as Arabic, and for learners beyond the beginner level, which is the focus of this chapter.

In general, when most instructors begin researching the use of AI in foreign language learning, they tend to made little distinction among terms like Intelligent Computer Assisted Language Learning (ICALL), NLP, NNs, chatbots, and intelligent tutoring systems. So where does a foreign language instructor start if they would like to incorporate appropriate AI tools to boost student learning, motivation, and satisfaction with the learning process? What tools are appropriate for elementary versus intermediate versus advanced levels? Are all AI tools as effective for harder languages like Arabic and Russian versus easier languages like Spanish and English for example? What can AI tools do and for what shouldn't they be utilized? What usages will enhance learning outcomes and what might undermine them? And how can AI tools be applied support and advance any number of other goals that instructors might have like framing the learning process around experiential learning, HIPs, or the SDGs?

This chapter is a case study focused on the *experience* of redesigning a language course for university learners of Arabic in the US. It sets out to explore how to integrate AI to make language learning effective, to make learners' experience engaging, and to support and advance other central curricular goals like experiential learning, HIPs, or the SDGs. First, it explores several methodological axes on which the course is structured, starting with the selection, testing, and evaluation of the AI tools. The next three sections explore how AI can aid curricular goals related to experiential learning and High-Impact Practices (HIPs), including UN's Sustainable Development Goals (SDGs) in (language) learning, and goals specific to the field of teaching Arabic. The discussion section analyzes and compares four types of specific examples for engaging the language classroom with AI, while the conclusion section summarizes the benefits and challenges of using AI in the language classroom.

EXPERIENTIAL LEARNING AND HIPS

Experiential learning is learning by doing (Dewey, 2023; Kolb, 1983). According to experiential learning theory, the experience of learning to do something new is an optimal learning strategy. Learners engage in a new experience, reflect on its aspects and meaning, adopt new concepts and methods based on this experience, and apply them to their lives. Experiential learning is beneficial as learners remember new concepts and methods much more vividly and lastingly when they try them out. It typically enhances cooperative attitudes and motivation, and thus better prepares learners for the future. Experiential learning is a type of high-impact practice (HIP). HIPs are program designs and pedagogies that demonstrate great student involvement and success across diverse populations, for example, capstone courses, collaborative projects, first-year seminars, internships, service learning, writing-intensive courses, etc. (Kuh, O'Donnell, & Schneider, 2017; Kuh & O'Donnell, 2013; Kuh, 2008). The benefits are roughly summarized as better grades, higher retention, and higher graduation rates (Brownell & Swaner, 2010). While these are primarily institutional practices (Fink, 2016; see also Fink, 2013), the redesign of this Arabic course required to focus on the following HIPs elements (high-impact *teaching* practices) associated with long projects: significant time on task, frequent, timely feedback, substantive interactions with faculty, peers, and diverse people and ideas, structured reflection and integration of learning, real-world applications, public demonstration of competence, use of AI tools, research on sustainability in understudied areas (Middle East).

AI can play a significant role in enhancing experiential learning by providing personalized, adaptive, and immersive experiences. For instance, AI can also analyze individual learning styles, preferences, and performance data to create personalized learning paths. This ensures that learners engage with content at a pace and in a manner that suits their unique needs. AI-driven tutoring systems can provide real-time feedback and guidance during experiential activities. When such activities involve cross-cultural interactions, AI-powered language translation tools can facilitate communication, contributing to a more inclusive and culturally sensitive learning environment. AI can power interactive learning platforms that simulate real-world situations, allowing learners to apply theoretical knowledge in practical contexts. These platforms often incorporate gamification elements to make experiential learning more engaging.

THE VALUE OF THE SDGS IN (LANGUAGE) LEARNING

In 2015 the UN adopted the *2030 Agenda for Sustainable Development* which lays out the following 17 Sustainable Development Goals (SDGs):

Figure 1. United Nations' Sustainable Development Goals, UNDP

Integrating the SDGs into language education offers students a context-rich learning experience beyond linguistic proficiency that aligns language acquisition with global awareness and social responsibility. This approach fosters critical thinking, empathy, and a sense of responsibility, empowering learners to engage with real-world challenges. This interdisciplinary approach prepares students to be global citizens who can navigate linguistic and cultural diversity while contributing to the broader goals of social and environmental sustainability.

AI-created materials can significantly enhance student engagement with the Sustainable Development Goals (SDGs) in a language class by providing dynamic, interactive, and personalized learning experiences. For example, AI tools can generate diverse learning materials, including videos, podcasts, and infographics, presenting information on the SDGs in various formats. This caters to different learning preferences and enhances engagement by offering a multimedia learning experience. Class work with products created by AI could serve as scaffolding by familiarizing students with the existence and capabilities of AI tools they later use to create their own SDG-related projects. If instructors are comfortable with that, AI can also assist in generating prompts for project-based learning activities that involve researching, presenting, and discussing topics related to the SDGs. This approach encourages collaborative learning and empowers students to apply language skills to solve real-world problems. Infographics or other material created with the help of AI can serve as a base for creating multiple language games, the questions for which could be drafted by chatbots for the instructor to work from (see Alzahrani & Alhalafawy, 2023; Mageira et al., 2022). For advanced learners, AI can simulate virtual language experiences with native speakers discussing sustainability topics. These simulations create a more immersive language learning environment, allowing students to apply their language skills in practical scenarios. Image- and video-based AI-generated content can incorporate cultural nuances and context relevant to the regions associated with the SDGs. This connection to real-world cultural contexts enhances language learning by providing students with a deeper understanding of the global implications of sustainable development.

STATE OF THE FIELD OF TEACHING ARABIC

With over 300 million speakers worldwide, Arabic is the fifth most spoken language in the world and the eighth most commonly-taught language in the US with 31,500 university students (US census).[1] Arabic enrollments jumped 1,600 percent after 9/11, 2001 but started rolling back slowly a decade later (MLA data, see Figure 2), and then plateaued before the COVID 19 pandemic with around 150 US institutions that offer Arabic (Abu Melhim, 2014). According to Awad Awad (2023), director of the Salaam MENA Cultural Center at the University of Illinois, Urbana-Champaign, currently Arabic programs suffer from low student retention beyond the introductory level, low-enrollment class cancelations, low student proficiency, old curricula, and unrealistic expectations.

Figure 2. Arabic language enrollments for 1998, 2009, 2013, and 2016. MLA data.

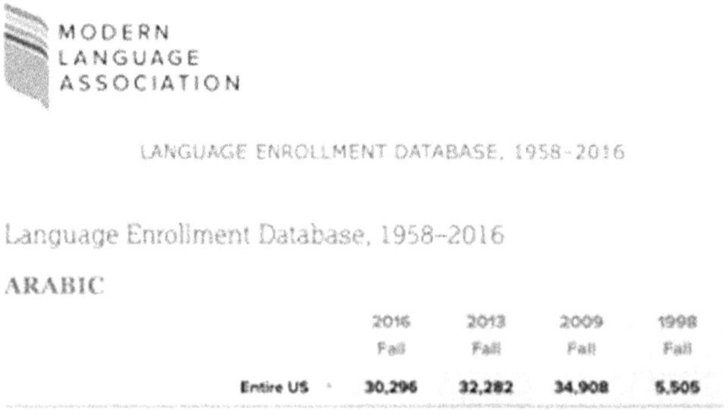

MODERN LANGUAGE ASSOCIATION

LANGUAGE ENROLLMENT DATABASE, 1958-2016

Language Enrollment Database, 1958–2016

ARABIC

	2016 Fall	2013 Fall	2009 Fall	1998 Fall
Entire US	30,296	32,282	34,908	5,505

Indeed, Arabic diglossia (using two varieties, one spoken, one written, simultaneously) has been a serious obstacle to learners. And so has been the lack of multiple, easily accessible authentic materials at the lower competency levels. When available in the future, AI tools can potentially help solve this incurable issue by adapting any written or oral content to a personal or group learner level. AI-powered platforms can adapt content difficulty and learning activities based on the learner's proficiency level, ensuring that the material remains challenging but not overwhelming. AI could also recast content from the spoken variety to the written and vice versa as an essential basis for any Arabic related application in order to help learners improve their weaknesses and develop multiple competencies. And why stop at only 1 Arabic spoken variety rather than include over 20, each associated with a different country? In this sense, AI algorithms, which can analyze individual learning progress and preferences to create personalized learning paths, should potentially strengthen learning effectiveness by focusing on areas where learners need improvement and progress at their own pace and level. AI-driven chatbots can provide tutoring through immersive language experiences by engaging learners in conversations, offering real-time feedback on pronunciation, grammar, and vocabulary usage. AI technologies with voice recognition capabilities can assess and provide feedback on learners' pronunciation, helping them refine their speaking skills and sound more natural.

AI can also gamify language learning, creating interactive and engaging experiences that motivate learners to practice Arabic in a playful and enjoyable way, as this field for Arabic is perhaps among the lowest served fields among all other global and many non-global languages. And last, AI tools can incorporate cultural nuances and context into language lessons, providing learners with a deeper understanding of the cultural aspects of Arabic language and communication.

The options are much more but to sum, the use of AI to revamp Arabic language courses is both innovative and timely, aligning with the increasing interest in technology integration in education. The rest of the chapter offers a valuable overview of various AI tools applicable to language education, benefiting educators seeking to incorporate technology into teaching. The inclusion of a case study on redesigning an Arabic language course provides practical insights, making the concepts discussed more instructive for readers.

METHODOLOGY

In the fall of 2023, a team of a hired student assistant and a faculty member tested a number of AI tools for the college-level Arabic course taught. The course uses *'Arabiyyat al-Naas,* the latest edition of a textbook published by Routledge. There were 18 enrolled students in the course, all in their 20s. Their background ranged from heritage students who had never taken Arabic courses at different skill levels in Arabic, to others with middle and high school Arabic, to Muslim students with some Quranic Arabic, to non-native speakers who had taken all previous courses in the Arabic sequence. None had any previous Arabic courses that incorporated AI tools.

AI tools were selected based on how well they help students develop language proficiency simulating the course materials, particularly reliance on audio-video content and embracing of diglossia as an integral part of learning Arabic (with a practical focus on communication skills through speaking in an Arab dialect and good skills in reading and writing the standard Arabic, Fusha). This led to the narrowing of the tools that were explored to visual tools, such as images and videos, and multimedia tools that incorporate visual elements such as comic strips and again videos. Given the dependence of the redesign of the course on a grant that required a fast turnaround of outcomes, other AI tools were excluded either because they did not offer strong or any visual content (e.g. ChatGPT) or because exploring too many AI tools all at once would have been unfeasible under the stipulations of the grant.

The list of AI tools were tested within minimum basic criteria such as how professional the content they created looked, if it was visually stimulating, and if would be potentially engaging for learners. Another criterium was if the tool handled and produced Arabic script and if it offered voiceover with Lebanese accent (since the textbook is based on Lebanese Arabic and Lebanese culture). One important criterium was the AI tool's cultural sensitivity, for example, if the images of people or the inside and outside environments looked like they came from Lebanon, or if they produced Gulf- or Western-looking options.

Only the tools that produced the best results based on the above criteria were used to create the resulting learning materials. As shown in Table 1 these are: GenCraft for creating AI-generated images, Pictory for creating AI-generated videos, AI Comic Factory (in combination with another tool such as Canva) for creating AI-generated comic strips, MapFight for creating AI-generated geographic comparisons, and Quizlet and Kahoot for learning games and quizzes. These tools are recommended here because they enhanced learning effectiveness student engagement and they also were helpful in addressing goals related to incorporating experiential learning, HIPs, and the SDGs.

Materials generated with these tools were incorporated into the Canvas learning management system (LMS). They were accessible to students on Canvas during class within class activities as well as after class in assignments, projects, or posted keynote presentations.

Table 1. List of AI algorithm/program/tool tested for college-level Arabic

	Name of AI Algorithm/Program	Purpose for Use	Product Created	Time to Accomplish Goal	Recommend? Yes/No Why?
1	MapFight https://mapfight.xyz	Compare sizes of geographic areas	Geometric image	Seconds-minutes	Yes
2	AI Comic Factory, in combination with another tool such as Canva https://huggingface.co/spaces/jbilcke-hf/ai-comic-factory	Illustrate vocabulary, idea, topic, grammar	Comic strips	Hours	Yes Exceptional visual tool
3	GenCraft https://gencraft.com/generate	Text (prompt) to image generator	Image	Seconds	Yes Gives several options and each can be used as another instance/angle for the same entity
4	ArtBreeder https://www.artbreeder.com/	Creative mixer of image and prompt	Image	Seconds	To some degree
5	Quizlet https://quizlet.com	AI-enhanced learning platform	Tests, quizzes, learning tools	Minutes to hours	Yes AI-enhanced personalized quizzes practice tests, expert-written homework solutions, transformative AI study tools
6	Kahoot https://create.kahoot.it	AI-enhanced game-based learning platform	learning games, trivia quizzes	Minutes to hours	Yes AI-enhanced learning games or trivia quizzes
7	Pictory https://pictory.ai/	Text (prompt) to video generator	Video	Hours	Yes, with caution about Western bias

Finally, gathering and analyzing student feedback for the success of the materials created by the AI tools took two approaches. The first was immediate oral feedback solicited from the students by the instructor usually at the end of class or occasionally after the use of the particular tool. This approach was effective in quickly improving materials for the next use of the tool, usually within a class or two. The second approach was a survey administered at the end of the semester. It was used to gain a broader picture of the usefulness of the incorporated AI tools as a group, rather than a singular tool, which is effective in taking stock of the general use of AI in language learning.

DISCUSSION

Four Examples for Learning Effectiveness and Student Engagement in the Foreign Language Classroom With AI

Comparative Map Generators

Foreign (and even many heritage) learners of Arabic often lack a geographical sense of the Arab world, its countries, and their relative prominence be it in terms of land size, population, or economic output. Since there are 22 countries in the League of Arab States, a learner may need visual help to grasp these parameters. One tool is MapFight, which creates maps that compare different geographic areas. For example, when the students in this class learned about SDG 1: No Poverty and reviewed comparative adjectives, an image created by MapFight helped them form a fast, clear, and visceral sense for the relative size difference between a) California and Lebanon, or b) Sham (the Levant) and Sudan, for example. Such sense then helps them become better equipped to understand more qualitative differences between them, such as available arid land, natural resources, population economic opportunities related to land, poverty, etc. It also helps learners practice grammatical structures like comparatives and superlatives in a meaningful way (which depends on the specific class and topic).

Figure 3. MapFight images that visualize the relative size difference between a) California and Lebanon or b) Sham (the Levant) and Sudan

a b

Specific tools like MapChart (https://www.mapchart.net/) allow to create maps for different countries or territories, color them in one or multiple colors, add country names, city names, borders, etc. Any number of Arabic words or names could be added to such maps to respond to specific linguistic and cultural learning goals.

Figure 4. MapChart image of Arab countries and territories

While MapFight and MapChart are free, there are a number of paid map generators that can offer a whole new way of teaching a course from a visual perspective. Those could be used to create or exemplify scenarios, fantasy worlds or living spaces created specifically for the class, or campus or other maps to help with any number of tasks such as giving directions, navigating space, etc.

Figure 5. Images by 3d Map, Inkarnate, and MapMe

https://www.3d-map-generator.com/ https://inkarnate.com https://mapme.com/

Comic-Strips Generators

The tool students liked the most was comic-strips generators. After testing several different tools, AI Comic Factory was selected as the best tool. Three AI-driven art generators were tested before it—Deep-Dream, GenCraft, Runway ML, and Artbreeder—to generate background images or design elements that can be incorporated into comic-strip panels. They were given the same prompt that was developed for the in-person class session, which coincided with Halloween. The prompt built on an activity from an earlier class in which the students were split into teams to role-play a situation with three characters: Rima (a Lebanese heritage student on a year abroad at AUB, Lebanon), her school mate Lina (born and raised in Beirut), and Lina's "tetta" (grandmother) with whom Lina lives. Rima is visiting tetta to talk about moving in with her and Lina. During the role play, the students decided that Rima tattled on the secretly smoking Lina and tetta kicked both of them out, which meant that they would need a new place to live. After class, the following prompt was created to continue developing this story and also make it relevant to the specific cluster of lessons from the textbook that were about apartment hunting and rentals:

Two Lebanese college students Rima and Lina are looking to rent an apartment together. The first apartment they see is too dark because it doesn't have electricity and it's cold in the winter. The second one they check out is on the 10th floor and doesn't have running water or elevator, so they need to lug up bottles of water. The third one is perfect but comes with a ghost called Marwan. Marwan is friendly but can't stop talking. Rima and Lina discuss their options and choose #3. Now they need ghost busters.

The prompt was created in English to test the art with empty speech balloons that would be filled in later with Arabic text. Here are some of the results:

Attempt 1: The first AI tool only generated pictures but not comics when fed in the prompt. As a result, the student assistant split the story into couples of sentences and ran it again. But the tool generated girls that looked like different people in each picture.

Figure 6. Images by DeepDream

Attempt 2: GenCraft and ArtBreeder were then tested with slightly rewritten prompts. While GenCraft's art is most like that of comic-strips, it still generates girls that look like different people in different panels. On the other hand, ArtBreeder's girls looked very consistent but it didn't generate adequate panels with three different apartments and a ghost.

Prompt 3 & 4:

Figure 7. Two Lebanese college girls looking to rent an apartment in Beirut

Figure 8.

Prompt 5: Comic strip showing the apartment, the two Lebanese college girls annoyed by a ghost who talks too much.

Figure 9. Images by GenCraft

Figure 10. Images by GenCraft

Figure 11. Images by ArtBreeder

Figure 12. Images by ArtBreeder

Attempt 3: The last tested AI tool was AI Comic Factory, which proved the winning tool if used in combination with another tool such as Canva to organize the images. AI Comic Factory was consistent, generated our story exactly following the prompt, had great visual appeal, and the panels looked professionally designed.

Figure 13. Images by AI Comic Factory (for individual panels) in combination with Canva (to compile the best matching panels)[2]

Video Generators

The video generators were probably the most challenging tool to use, as a result more options were sought. The first issue was learning how to combine the video images by Pictory with voice over created by a separate tool. Since the video had to be in the Lebanese dialect, which is the basis for the textbook, the two best voice-over choices found proved suboptimal—one was in the standard literary Fusha Arabic with a Lebanese accent (which is different from spoken Lebanese dialect), the other in spoken Syrian (again different from the typical Lebanese). The third option was for the student assistant, who was Lebanese, to record himself narrating the video. While this addressed the issue with the language variety, it created a new issue which many video makers have faced—"the non-professional narrator."

The second issue was that the video generator created scenes with Western-looking characters despite multiple tweaks to the prompts to create "Arab," "Lebanese," "Middle Eastern," etc. spaces and characters. In the end, the AI-generated video footage was cut into inappropriate scenes (which were discarded) and appropriate scenes which were stitched up to outside images or short scenes. That took a lot of time, editing, and generating multiple versions for a less than ideal result. That's why videos that were 5-15 seconds turned out to be much better products than those that were longer (the latter brough in more instances of bias).

Figure 14. Three most important SDGs for Lebanon

Figure 15. The Lebanese cedar and climate change
Videos by Pictory https://pictory.ai/

Image Generators

Images are an important part of illustrating many concepts and vocabulary items not only in the lower but also at higher levels of learning a foreign language. They make cultural specificities easier to grasp. While GenCraft was not first choice as a comic-strip generator, it is an excellent place to generate images for any language classroom and was especially sensitive to cultural differences. In addition, there are a number of other simpler drawing generators that are easy to work with and can serve as a counterbalance to fill in spaces of handouts or presentation slides that are already showcasing more developed images. For example, AutoDraw turns a rough sketch into a technical drawing, while providing multiple suggestions to choose from.

Figure 16. Lebanese grandma

Figure 17. Lebanese college student

Figure 18. AutoDraw
Images by GenCraft

Students were particularly engaged with the AI-generated images of the two "mascots" for the course, one male who was named "Kareem," the other female called "Reema," both engineering students at Georgia Tech, Atlanta. The following prompt was used:

- 2 cartoon characters, male & female
- Lebanese

- 20-25 years old
- Enthusiastic
- Optimistic
- Happy
- One has headphones, loose on the neck
- The other wears a beanie
- One wears glasses
- No religious symbols
- Clothes: for millennials
- Colors for clothes: pastel green, blue, yellow

While the tool never placed the headphones on Kareem's shoulders, or created full body images in different postures by the same characters, the results of front and side faces were very satisfactory. The images were used throughout the semester to engage the students by framing multiple activities such as competitions between "Teem Kareem" and "Team Reema" on topics like "Should the job of househusband become widely acceptable and practiced in the Middle East" (debate between the two teams) or "Which important clean energy sources are currently most in use (choose from wind, water, sunlight, geodesic)" (ranking competition among teams) or "Should Reema live with a Lebanese family during her summer abroad in Beirut, or not—perspectives by Reema and her new boyfriend Kareem" (discussion and persuasion activity among teams), etc.

Figure 19. Mascot images, Kareem

Figure 20. Mascot images, Reema

Other AI tools like Kahoot and Quizlet were also used for multiple purposes like vocabulary review, vocabulary competitions, testing grammar skills (multiple-choice questions, yes/no questions), etc.

Student Feedback

At the end of the semester, the students were administered a written survey regarding their experience with the inclusion of AI, the SDGs, and experiential learning. Here are the results of the survey: The majority of the students described their experience with this course as "enjoyable," satisfactory," engaging," and "positive." They said they enjoyed the AI-generated or AI-assisted materials because they were "original" and provided "substantial amount of learning aid." According to the surveys, the students' preferred tool was the comic strips, the mascots, and the other images, as well as how these were organized within the structured keynote pair, small group, team, and whole class activities. The surveys indicated that the students found the AI tools "helpful" and "effective" as they "enhanced" students' various "skills" in Arabic and the "interesting visual materials" helped visual learning and made for "better class content." This resulted in "satisfaction" with the course, where all but one student "loved" the course, as their comments in the surveys showed. The single student who didn't write they loved the course shared that they felt it was "catering to heritage students" and they had somewhat harder time keeping up. When asked what aided their language acquisition, some students mentioned AI tools, while others related various other aspects of the course, including class activities, the SDGs, projects, emphasis on producing language, and the textbook materials. The student-observed benefits of using AI tools in this course, as demonstrated by the surveys, were confirmed in the regular Course Instructor Opinion Survey (CIOS) comments administered at the end of the semester, e.g.,

Dr. Khazaal has tried some new ways of language learning that I think worked wonderfully. First and foremost, the original resources that Dr. Khazaal created using AI tools were absolutely amazing. I have to say that was my favorite part. The comic strips were fun and engaging because they were made at an appropriate level (challenging but doable) and, of course, they fit well in our class because they were specially made. The emphasis on speaking by doing oral exercises was also very helpful. Lastly, the projects were a good opportunity to practice speaking skills with full length presentations.

The student surveys demonstrate that the incorporation of AI-generated materials aids learning and the acquisition of various language skills, making it a tool for increasing effective learning. The surveys are also a testament to the substantial level of engagement with the learning process that the students attributed to AI tools, especially visual materials and, unanimously, the comic strips. Because of the students diverse background and skill levels, the visual aids including the comic strips provided an engaging outlet for practice. Surveys provide a valuable assessment of the curricular aspects, which instructors and administrators can use to make informed decisions about educational programs. Since surveys can identify what students deem important, they also show where schools should spend their money. In this case, students' surveys can be interpreted as a signal that school investment in instructors' support and professional development in the field of using AI tools can potentially result in greater effectiveness of the learning process and in students' greater engagement with it.

Outcomes Analysis

According to Tom Kashdan (2009), engagement is the first step toward real learning. Three key principles that optimize student engagement are emotions, building a sense of community, and helping students create meaningful and relevant narratives around the content. Emotions are strong motivators because they use neuropathways dedicated to survival, while we learn only things that we care about (Immordino-Yang, 2015). Sarah Rose Cavanagh's (2020) tip on how to harness the power of emotions to produce student engagement is to use emotional hooks such as a relevant controversy, a provocative question, an unsolved mystery, or a humorous meme. Story-telling, as our "most natural form of thought" (Schank & Abelson, 1995), chunks information and optimizes memory space, allowing students to focus their attention on what is important. It also helps them understand better by organizing content into meaning.

A successful Arabic course redesign can benefit greatly from incorporating AI tools as a remarkable vehicle for delivering all the above hard-core principles of engagement. Mascots' images were effective in engaging students in debates relevant to their own lives such as navigating friendships and romance within the specificity of Arab cultures, and appreciating the continuous changes in traditional male and female behaviors and attitudes surrounding household duties and parenting. Comic strips were just as effective in engaging students in story-telling that helped them relate the subject matter to the holiday calendar of their own society as well as to the SDGs and economic realities in the Middle East. In addition, they invited students to identify with the main characters who were of the same age and going through similar student life experiences. This created space to relate their own visions about the comic strips, tell stories from their lives, and deliberate broader social issues creatively applying the textbook's vocabulary and structures in meaning real-world scenarios (albeit imagined).

CONCLUSION

Benefits and Challenges of Using AI in the Language Classroom

This chapter explored a case study of redesigning an Arabic language curriculum to incorporate AI tools in meaningful ways that benefit both the *effectiveness* of the learning process and the *engagement* of the students with the textbook materials and broad issues of importance like sustainability. While this process created many positive outcome, thus offering potential benefits that could be replicated, it also showed areas with challenges that those interested in adopting AI for a language class should heed.

Benefits

Personalization. One of the key benefits of incorporating AI tools in the language classroom for this case has been the personalization of the learning process. We can think of this through multiple perspectives. For example, on an individual basis, tools like ChatGPT can serve as conversation partners and help students practice the new language at their specific level in writing or speaking and adapt to the student's pace and topics of interests. Other tools like Kahoot and Quizlet can serve the student to practice vocabulary displaying flashcard decks in different order and offering practice on grammar in a question format that students can retake in order to learn better. We can also think of personalization on a group basis as well, such as the specific group of students who are taking the class this semester with their interests, levels, and needs. For example, while Kahoot can be a truly individualized tool, it also lends itself well to seeing the strengths and weaknesses of this particular group of students if the tool is used during class. The 2023 Ghaza war took place during this course, which made some of the planned SDGs somewhat irrelevant. Ultimately, it was pivotal to shift toward SDG 16 "Peace, justice, and strong institutions" and use AI tools to imagine scenarios for ending the conflict and establishing lasting peace and justice afterwards. Another way in which AI helped personalize learning for this group was continuing the story lines students created during class into AI products, for example the ghost story created after Reema and Lina were thrown out by grandma (tetta). In this way, every class can have its personal mythology.

Instant feedback. In either case (individual or group), AI tools provide instant feedback. They can assess individual students' language skills in real-time, providing feedback on pronunciation, grammar, and vocabulary. This instant feedback helps students identify and correct errors promptly, enhancing the learning process. AI tools used in class also give the instructor quick statistical information about how many students have grasped or mastered a language item, as we do with Kahoot for instance. Pausing to explain the issue and discuss the correct answer offers students immediate feedback and an opportunity to improve accuracy. It also lets them see that they are not the only student who made this mistake. The non-judgmental nature of AI feedback can create a supportive learning environment when a student works on their own, or when the tool provides anonymous feedback while working in class. As a result, students often feel less anxious about making mistakes, as they know they can receive constructive feedback without judgment, fostering a positive attitude towards language learning.

Redefined instructor role. It is challenging to completely redefine the instructor's role given how time consuming this is and how rooted such role is in current educational settings. However, limited redefinitions may lead to positive outcomes. For example, when it comes to assessment and feedback, typically provided by instructors, AI tools may handle certain aspects, including giving instant feedback. This function is still in its infancy; however, long-term, instructors can shift their focus to more personalized instruction, addressing individual needs, and providing additional support where required. They can also use AI-generated data to identify patterns, assess teaching strategies, and make informed decisions to enhance the overall learning experience for students. This redefined instructor role emphasizes mentorship and guidance.

Instructor creativity enhancement. AI tools can also enhance instructor creativity, which is their most useful function for me as of today. For example, they can assist in creating interactive and adaptive learning materials, such as language games, quizzes, and activities. They can also be utilized to generate visuals, infographics, or animations that help illustrate complex language concepts, which was accomplished in this course with the help of AI Comic Factory, GenCraft, MapFight, Pictory, etc. Visual aids can enhance understanding and retention, making language lessons more accessible and enjoyable. Furthermore, AI tools can curate and analyze current news articles, social media, or other online content in Arabic, allowing teachers to incorporate real-world and culturally relevant materials into lessons. This connection to current issues makes language learning more dynamic and practical. Using AI tools, then, can make language learning more enjoyable and cater to different learning styles, making the classroom experience more engaging.

In sum, incorporating AI tools in the Arabic language classroom has the potential to revolutionize the learning experience, making it more personalized, adaptive, and engaging for students while providing valuable support to teachers in their instructional roles.

Challenges

Today, AI algorithms and programs may be useful teaching and learning tools, however, they also have a number of small and big challenges.

Financial support. On the small side, many of them are associated with costs that allow instructors not only to test them but also to use them continuously. Since each AI tool comes with its own cost, no matter how small, using several tools adds up. New tools or improved versions appear constantly, so the best solution is institutional support for language AI tool use, either covering the costs of individual instructor use or incorporating some of the most useful tools into web-based learning management system (LMS) like Canvas, Moodle, Blackboard, etc.

Time investment. Another challenge that can be tackled relatively painlessly is the lack of instructor familiarity with AI tools that might be useful to language instructors. This requires time investment to explore which AI tools are adequate and effective for which course. Again, the solution to this is better tackled on an institutional level by creating professional development programs involving webinars, group discussions, or sharing best practices by experienced inside or outside practitioners. That could become part of instructors' service load and help lessen the steep learning curve due to the proliferation of different tools and updated version, and to the constant need for instructors to reinvent their teaching with technology.

And then, there are harder challenges to solve.

AI tool performance. Currently, most AI tools are not able to address the long list of learners' and instructors' needs, especially since no one tool can fit all. This case study showed that video and comic-strip editors currently require that many functions be outsourced to other tools and/or to human labor if instructors want to succeed in using them. The solution here is both technical and financial. On the technical side, we expect that with time AI tools will improve, so waiting might be the best strategy. On the financial side, institutions should invest in hiring student assistants to work with instructors on the creation of materials with AI, or giving instructors personal grants or course buy-outs to cover their efforts.

Assignments and assessment. Another serious issue is the ease with which AI tools allow undetectable cheating, avoiding doing homework, and subverting the learning process for the sake of receiving a (good) grade. During this attempt to redesign the Arabic course, it was constantly clear how many students attempted this. Therefore, we need to seriously rethink student assignments and assessment. We are entering a new age of learning.

Boredom/learning preferences. An unexpected problem for this redesign is how quickly students get bored with one particular tool, or how the tool's use may not have matched well their learning preferences. When they were first asked to do a competitive, team Quizlet game on vocabulary, the activity was planned as a single game. However, the students demanded to repeat it four times with different teams for the sake of winning. On subsequent trials, there was considerably less enthusiasm and this tool is now being used once every three-four sessions. The solution here is of course to have more research that results in insights into how technology and its fast-paced innovation affects the expectations of the human brain for engagement, entertainment, and stable attention. This might also indicate general issues of gamification in learning, not so much using a specific tool. According to the narrative presented here, the students don't seem to enjoy, and instructors may need to find out how to avoid the strict "win"/"lose" aspect of the tool to enhance engagement.

Ethics. The last challenge discussed here is lack of appropriate ethical consideration when AI tools are developed for public use. Students frequently fail to notice bias or intellectual property issues (Gong et al., 2020). For example, some suspect that AI can cultivate notions that perpetuate colonialist world views (Williansom & Eynon, 2020). In this case study it was the Western bias of the video generators. In addition, AI may have negative effect on instructors if it is used to measure their performance for punitive purposes (Selwyn & Gasevic, 2020), or on students if it is used to profile or dox them (Selwyn, 2019).

We don't know how AI will ultimately impact education, but we need to pay attention. Instead of just utilizing AI tools to teach foreign languages, we need to critically reflect how inclusive, fair, transparent, and ethical these tools are (Hagendorff, 2021; Zawacki-Richter et al., 2019).

Limitations

While the results in this study clearly show that AI can benefit a foreign language classroom, the small sample size of 18 enrolled students could be a limitation. Most language courses are small, ranging from 5 to 25 students. However, replicating this study by adopting the suggested AI tools in other classrooms could strengthen the study's conclusions.

Furthermore, some courses in languages other than Arabic might have already incorporated more AI tools, perhaps even those proposed here, and thus this chapter would benefit them as a confirmation of the tools' utility, rather than a suggestion for new tools.

Last, AI tools are in constant flux, with new one appearing fast and published ones receiving frequent modifications or new versions. As a result, in addition to relying on this chapter's research, one should also do supplementary exploration of the latest AI tools that might be applicable to the foreign language classroom.

REFERENCES

Abu Melhim, A. (2014). The Status of Arabic in the United States of America post 9/11 and the Impact on Foreign Language Teaching Programs. *Advances in Language and Literary Studies*, *5*(3), 70–81. doi:10.7575/aiac.alls.v.5n.3p.70

Almelhes, S. A. (2023). A Review of Artificial Intelligence Adoption in Second-Language Learning. *Theory and Practice in Language Studies*, *13*(5), 1259–1269. doi:10.17507/tpls.1305.21

Alzahrani, F. K., & Alhalafawy, W. S. (2023). Gamification for Learning Sustainability in the Blackboard System: Motivators and Obstacles from Faculty Members' Perspectives. *Sustainability (Basel)*, *15*(5), 4613. doi:10.3390/su15054613

Arnold, K., & Pistilli, M. (2012). Course signals at Purdue: Using learning analytics to increase student success. *Proceedings of the 2nd international conference on learning analytics and knowledge* (pp. 267–270). New York: ACM. 10.1145/2330601.2330666

Awad, A. (2023). *Interview by author*. MESA.

Brownell, J., & Swaner, L. (2010). *Five High-Impact Practices: Research on Learning Outcomes, Completion, and Quality*. Association of American Colleges and Universities.

Burgsteiner, H., Kandlhofer, M., & Steinbauer, G. (2016). Irobot: Teaching the basics of artificial intelligence in high schools. *Proceedings of the AAAI Conference on Artificial Intelligence*, *30*(1). Advance online publication. doi:10.1609/aaai.v30i1.9864

Cavalcanti, A. P., Diego, A., Carvalho, R., Freitas, F., Tsai, Y. S., Gaˇsevi´c, D., & Mello, R. F. (2021). Automatic feedback in online learning environments: A systematic literature review. *Computers and Education: Artificial Intelligence*, 100027.

Cavanagh, S. R. (2020). How to make your teaching more engaging. *The Chronicle of Higher Education*.

Davenport, T. H., & Ronanki, R. (2018). Artificial intelligence for the real world. *Harvard Business Review*, *96*(1), 108–116.

Dewey, J. (2023). *Experiential Education: Complete Collection: Problem-Based Learning, Pragmatic Philosophy of Scholarship, Democracy & Education*. Sharp Ink Publisher.

Educause. (2018). *Horizon report: 2018 higher education edition*. Author.

Fan, Y., Saint, J., Singh, S., Jovanovic, J., & Gasevic, D. (2021). A learning analytic approach to unveiling self-regulatory processes in learning tactics. *LAK21: 11th international learning analytics and knowledge conference*, 184–195.

Fink, L. D. (2016). *Five High-Impact Teaching practices* (Vol. 9). Collected Essays on Learning and Teaching.

Fink, L. D. (2016). *Creating significant learning experiences: An integrated approach to designing college courses*. John Wiley& Sons.

Gong, X., Tang, Y., Liu, X., Jing, S., Cui, W., Liang, J., & Wang, F. Y. (2020, October). K-9 artificial intelligence education in qingdao: Issues, challenges and suggestions. *IEEE international conference on networking, sensing, and control (ICNSC),* 1–6.

Hagendorff, T. (2020). The ethics of AI ethics: An evaluation of guidelines. *Minds and Machines*, *30*(1), 99–120. doi:10.1007/s11023-020-09517-8

Immordino-Yang, M. T. (2015). *Emotions, Learning, and the Brain: Exploring the Educational Implications of Affective Neuroscience*. Norton Professional Books.

Kashdan, T. (2009). *Curious? Discover the Missing Ingredient to a Fulfilling Life*. Harper Collins.

Kolb, D. (1983). *Experiential Learning: Experience as the Source of Learning and Development*. Prentice Hall.

Kong, S. C., Cheung, W. M. Y., & Zhang, G. (2021). Evaluation of an artificial intelligence literacy course for university students with diverse study backgrounds. *Computers and education. Artificial Intelligence*, 100026.

Kuh, G., O'Donnell, K., & Schneider, C. (2017). HIPs at Ten. *Change*, *49*(5), 8–16. doi:10.1080/00091383.2017.1366805

Kuh, G. D. (2008). High-impact educational practices: What they are, who has access to them, and why they matter. Washington, DC: Association of American Colleges and Universities.

Kuh, G. D., & O'Donnell, K. (2013). Ensuring Quality & Taking High-Impact Practices to Scale. Washington, DC: Association of American Colleges and Universities.

Mageira, K., Pittou, D., Papasalouros, A., Kotis, K., Zangogianni, P., & Daradoumis, A. (2022). Educational AI chatbots for content and language integrated learning. *Applied Sciences (Basel, Switzerland)*, *12*(7), 3239. doi:10.3390/app12073239

Manyika, J., Lund, S., Chui, M., Bughin, J., Woetzel, J., Batra, P., Ko, R., & Sanghvi, S. (2017, December). Jobs lost, jobs gained: Workforce transitions in a time of automation. *McKinsey Global Institute*.

Ng, D. T. K., Leung, J. K. L., Chu, S. K. W., & Qiao, M. S. (2021). Conceptualizing AI literacy: An exploratory review. *Computers and Education: Artificial Intelligence*, *2*, 100041.

Ng, D.T.K., Luo, W., Chan, H.M.Y., & Chu, S.K.W. (2022). Using digital story writing as a pedagogy to develop AI literacy among primary students. *Computers and Education: Artificial Intelligence,* 100054.

Samochowiec, J. (2020). *Future skills: Four scenarios for the world of tomorrow*. Jacobs Foundation. doi:10.59986/WGTT6117

Selwyn, N. (2019). What's the problem with learning analytics? *Journal of Learning Analytics*, *6*(3), 11–19. doi:10.18608/jla.2019.63.3

Selwyn, N., & Gasevic, D. (2020). The datafication of higher education: Discussing the promises and problems. *Teaching in Higher Education*, *25*(4), 527–540. doi:10.1080/13562517.2019.1689388

Vazhayil, A., Shetty, R., Bhavani, R. R., & Akshay, N. (2019, December). Focusing on teacher education to introduce AI in schools: Perspectives and illustrative findings. In *2019 IEEE tenth international conference on technology for education* (pp. 71–77). IEEE.

Williamson, B., & Eynon, R. (2020). Historical threads, missing links, and future directions in AI in education. *Learning, Media and Technology*, *45*(3), 223–235. doi:10.1080/17439884.2020.1798995

Woo, J. H., & Choi, H. (2021). Systematic Review for AI-based Language Learning Tools. *Journal of Digital Contents Society*, *22*(11), 1783–1792. doi:10.9728/dcs.2021.22.11.1783

Xu, L. (2020, December). The dilemma and countermeasures of AI in educational application. In *2020 4th international conference on computer science and artificial intelligence* (pp. 289–294). ACM.

Zawacki-Richter, O., Marín, V. I., Bond, M., & Gouverneur, F. (2019). Systematic review of research on artificial intelligence applications in higher education–where are the educators? *International Journal of Educational Technology in Higher Education*, *16*(1), 1–27. doi:10.1186/s41239-019-0171-0

ADDITIONAL READING

Appleton, J. J., Christenson, S. L., & Furlong, M. J. (2008). Student engagement with school: Critical conceptual and methodological issues of the construct. *Psychology in the Schools*, *45*(5), 369–386. doi:10.1002/pits.20303

Finn, J. D., & Rock, D. A. (1997). Academic success among students at risk for school failure. *The Journal of Applied Psychology*, *82*(2), 221–234. doi:10.1037/0021-9010.82.2.221 PMID:9109280

Fredricks, J. A., Blumenfeld, P. C., & Paris, A. H. (2004). School engagement: Potential of the concept, state of the evidence. *Review of Educational Research*, *74*(1), 59–109. doi:10.3102/00346543074001059

Handelsman, M. M., Briggs, W. L., Sullivan, N., & Towler, A. (2005). A measure of college student course engagement. *The Journal of Educational Research*, *98*(3), 184–192. doi:10.3200/JOER.98.3.184-192

Kahu, E. R. (2013). Framing student engagement in higher education. *Studies in Higher Education*, *38*(5), 758–773. doi:10.1080/03075079.2011.598505

Kuh, G. D. (2009). What student affairs professionals need to know about student engagement. *Journal of College Student Development*, *50*(6), 683–706. doi:10.1353/csd.0.0099

National Survey of Student Engagement (NSSE). (2021). *Documenting Effective Educational Practices*. Indiana University Center for Postsecondary Research.

Schank, R. C., & Abelson, R. P. (1995). Knowledge and memory: The real story. In R. S. Wyer Jr., (Ed.), *Knowledge and memory: The real story* (pp. 1–85). Lawrence Erlbaum Associates, Inc.

Skinner, E. A., & Belmont, M. J. (1993). Motivation in the classroom: Reciprocal effects of teacher behavior and student engagement across the school year. *Journal of Educational Psychology*, *85*(4), 571–581. doi:10.1037/0022-0663.85.4.571

Trowler, V. (2010). *Student engagement literature review*. Higher Education Academy.

Zepke, N., & Leach, L. (2010). Improving student engagement: Ten proposals for action. *Active Learning in Higher Education*, *11*(3), 167–177. doi:10.1177/1469787410379680

KEY TERMS AND DEFINITIONS

AI: Stands for Artificial Intelligence. It is a form of teaching computers to think and make decisions on their own. They can learn from information and do tasks that usually need human intelligence.

Experiential Learning: Is learning by doing. Instead of just reading or listening, you learn better by actively experiencing and practicing things.

HIPs: Are special and effective ways of teaching and learning. They often involve students doing hands-on projects, working in teams, or having experiences that really help them learn deeply.

LLMs: Are big computer programs that are good with language. They can understand, generate, and work with large amounts of text. They're often used for tasks like answering questions or creating content.

NLP: Is a form of teaching computers to understand and use human language. It helps computers read, understand, and respond to what people say or write.

SDGs: Are 17 big goals set by countries around the world to make the planet a better place by 2030. Goals include ending poverty, providing clean water, and taking care of the environment

Student Engagement: Means how much a student is involved, interested, and active in their learning. When students are engaged, they pay attention, participate in class, and enjoy what they're doing in school.

ENDNOTES

1 https://en.wikipedia.org/wiki/List_of_most_commonly_learned_second_languages_in_the_United_States

2 https://huggingface.co/spaces/jbilcke-hf/ai-comic-factory

Chapter 13

Utilizing a ChatGPT Workshop to Foster Ethical Awareness and Enhance L2 English Writing Revision Processes in University Academic Settings:

ChatGPT Workshop for Effective and Ethical L2 English Writing

Sohyeon Lee
https://orcid.org/0009-0008-4945-0965
University of Hawaii at Manoa, USA

ABSTRACT

This chapter explores the design and implementation of a ChatGPT workshop for multilingual university students, focusing on enhancing their L2 English academic writing skills. Utilizing the analyze, design, evaluate (ADE) model, the workshop incorporates practical activities to guide effective, critical, and ethical use of ChatGPT. It addresses challenges faced by L2 learners, emphasizing the tool's role in providing personalized feedback and improving revision processes. Ethical considerations, particularly in maintaining academic integrity, are highlighted. Insights reveal ChatGPT's value as an aid in the writing process, encouraging its use as a facilitator rather than a substitute for students' work. The chapter concludes with recommendations for educators and future research directions in AI and language education.

DOI: 10.4018/979-8-3693-0872-1.ch013

In recent years, the advent of artificial intelligence (AI) has ushered in a transformative wave across various sectors of society, and academia is no exception. One noteworthy AI application that has been making waves in the realm of education is ChatGPT, a powerful language model developed by OpenAI. This AI-driven tool has garnered attention for its potential to enhance educational practices, particularly in the field of academic writing and second language (L2) writing practices (Godwin-Jones, 2022; Grassini, 2023). However, its integration into the classroom is not without its fair share of concerns and challenges.

ChatGPT's entry into academia has ignited discussions about the implications of using AI in educational settings, especially when it comes to the nuanced and complex domain of L2 English writing (Yan, 2023). While its capabilities are impressive, there are genuine apprehensions about the ethical considerations, potential biases, and limitations inherent in large language models like ChatGPT (Barrot, 2023). It is imperative, therefore, that educators and students alike take a proactive approach to understanding these AI tools comprehensively.

This chapter delves into the evolving landscape of AI in education, with a specific focus on how a workshop on ChatGPT for academic writing is being leveraged to foster ethical awareness and enhance the L2 English writing revision processes in university academic settings. I recognize that the road to harnessing AI for pedagogical purposes is not devoid of challenges, but it also presents a plethora of opportunities for students as well as instructors. By examining the responsible use of AI, we can turn these tools into effective instruments for both learning and teaching.

To achieve this balance through the implementation of a workshop to acquaint students with the intricacies of ChatGPT and to cultivate their critical thinking skills in its usage, I designed and conducted a 75-minute instructional workshop for L2 English learners at an American University, focusing on responsible and critical usage of ChatGPT to improve their L2 English academic writing skills. I evaluated the workshop's impact through pre- and post-workshop questionnaires, assessing shifts in students' perceptions of ChatGPT. In my research based on the workshop, I aspired to understand how the perceptions of multilingual university students regarding the use of ChatGPT for academic English writing evolve before and after participating in a 75-minute instructional workshop.

Hopefully, the workshop can serve as a crucial bridge between the potential of AI and its ethical and practical application within the academic context. It may also empower students to navigate the AI landscape with proficiency, enabling them to make informed decisions while composing and revising their academic writing. This study can lead to a significant pedagogical implication as well in that ChatGPT can provide targeted assistance for individual learners with different needs when used responsibly.

Consequently, this chapter aims to shed light on the dual nature of AI in education, acknowledging its transformative potential while addressing concerns that accompany its adoption. Through an exploration of a ChatGPT workshop, I endeavor to provide educators and learners with valuable insights, strategies, and best practices for harnessing the power of AI responsibly and ethically. Ultimately, by embracing AI as a tool for learning and teaching, we can pave the way for a future where academic writing becomes more approachable, meaningful, and effective for students in L2 English language programs within university academic settings.

CHALLENGES OF L2 ENGLISH WRITERS AT AMERICAN UNIVERSITIES

Academic writing, particularly at the university level, is a multifaceted endeavor that demands a high degree of cognitive thinking and language proficiency, which can be one of the fundamental challenges faced by L2 English writers. To elaborate further, the process involves not only linguistic skills and cognitive abilities but also textual and cultural context knowledge such as rhetoric and genre awareness, making it a challenging amalgamation of diverse competencies (Godwin-Jones, 2022; Harklau & Pinnow, 2008). Therefore, academic writing necessitates a structured and systematic approach unlike everyday communication: It demands an intricate interplay of ideas, evidence, and arguments, all intricately woven into a coherent narrative. Attaining such a sophisticated command of language skills, textual understanding, and cultural context knowledge presents a formidable challenge, particularly for students who are in the process of enhancing their language proficiency as L2 learners (Ferris & Hedgcock, 2014). This task is further complicated when the writing conventions in a student's first language (L1) differ markedly from those in their second language (L2), a phenomenon that Kaplan has illustrated through his theory of contrastive rhetoric in relation to English (Connor, 1998). Moreover, academic writing requires a specialized vocabulary and terminology that may be unfamiliar to L2 English learners, further adding to the complexity. For L2 English learners, this journey through the intricate landscape of academic writing can often feel like navigating uncharted waters (Paltridge, 2018; Reichelt et al., 2012).

The varied backgrounds and unique needs of multilingual learners add another layer to the intricacies of achieving proficiency in L2 English writing. These students bring with them a wealth of experiences that significantly shape their approach to learning the language. Some students may have learned English as a foreign language in their home countries and may be categorized as "eye-learners," having acquired their L2 English primarily through visual methods such as studying vocabulary, verb forms, and language rules. Others may have arrived in the USA at an earlier age and received English education in American schools, acquiring the target language more naturally and falling into the "ear-learners" category, learning the language through listening and speaking (Reid, 1998).

Furthermore, multilingual students pursuing their degrees at American universities have diverse academic interests, majoring in various fields ranging from natural sciences to humanities, and the fact that some students are temporarily taking courses for exchange programs, while others are more seriously pursuing their degrees full-time, leads to varied motivations and goals in their writing classes and assignments. Previous L2 writing instruction that these international students have received also plays a significant role, as some students may not have had any experiences with extensive reading or writing in L2 English. These students could easily become overwhelmed by the workload of a composition course, often becoming disengaged and losing their interest. Overall, these multilingual students coming from diverse learning backgrounds, each with unique linguistic strengths and weaknesses can have a tough time making the transition to the specific vocabulary and discourse patterns of academic English (Ferris & Hedgcock, 2014; Paltridge, 2018; Reichelt et al., 2012).

Consequently, multilingual students can benefit from ongoing, timely, and individually targeted feedback on their work. Feedback should not be limited to one-time or specific areas but should be continuous and cover various aspects of writing, recognizing that writing is an iterative process (Ferris & Hedgcock, 2014; Flower & Hayes, 1981; Godwin-Jones, 2022). Nonetheless, providing personalized constructive feedback on student's writing can be a significant challenge for writing instructors as they often face constraints in providing extensive feedback to individual students due to heavy workloads and large class sizes (Ferris & Hedgcock, 2014; Godwin-Jones, 2022). Furthermore, L2 English writers can encompass a broad spectrum of abilities, from those who may require intensive language support to those with advanced language proficiency seeking feedback on more global issues of their writing (Godwin-Jones, 2022; Harklau & Pinnow, 2009). Tailoring instruction to address the varying needs of this diverse student population can be a complex endeavor for educators. Thus. L2 English writers can be left at a disadvantage, as they may not receive the level of feedback and guidance they require to refine their writing skills effectively.

In summary, the challenges faced by L2 English writers at American universities are multifaceted and include the sophisticated aspects of academic writing, the demand for specialized language skills, and the need for personalized feedback. Recognizing and addressing these challenges is essential in ensuring that L2 English learners have the support and resources necessary to excel in the academic writing landscape. It is within this context that the integration of AI tools like ChatGPT and the implementation of targeted workshops can play an essential role in facilitating their academic writing journey.

CHATGPT IN L2 ACADEMIC WRITING

In the context of the challenges faced by L2 English writers in American universities, the emergence of ChatGPT represents a significant technological aid. This AI-driven language model from OpenAI is distinguished by its sophisticated text generation capabilities. It offers nuanced and coherent prose, as a result of its extensive training on diverse datasets (Teubner et al., 2023). By integrating machine learning and deep learning mechanisms with large language data (Dale, 2021; M. Zhang & Li, 2021), Natural Language Processing has become increasingly powerful, effectively handling human languages and providing aid for both global and local issues in human-generated texts (Godwin-Jones, 2022; Yan, 2023). For academic writers, particularly those who are still honing their language skills, ChatGPT can serve as a supportive tool. It assists in crafting content, offering language translation services, proofreading, and much more.

In addition, the user-friendly interface of ChatGPT offers efficient affordances. It is designed to be straightforward, allowing for easy navigation without requiring specialized technological skills from its users (Warschauer et al., 2023; Yan, 2023). Such accessibility is critical, as it ensures that the focus remains on enhancing language proficiency and academic writing skills, without the added challenge of overcoming a steep technological learning curve. This ease of use is particularly beneficial for L2 learners, who may already be facing cognitive overload from mastering a new language and academic content.

The integration of AI tools in education has been met with both enthusiasm and caution. In recent years, AI-based tools have increasingly replaced more conventional linguistic resources (Nazari et al., 2021; Wu et al., 2021). These tools have become a focal point in the pedagogy of L2 writing, falling under the broader category of computer-assisted language learning (Adams & Chuah, 2022; Yan, 2023). Tools like Grammarly, Quillbot, and Google Translate have demonstrated how AI can streamline the writing process; they offer real-time corrections and suggestions that significantly enhance the quality of writing.

More specifically, studies have shown that Grammarly users tend to outperform their peers in L2 writing tasks (Dizon & Gayed, 2021). Additionally, AI-based feedback has been confirmed to positively affect students' motivation and self-efficacy in L2 writing (Nazari et al., 2021). The impact of Automated Writing Evaluation (AWE) on L2 writing is also significant, as it helps multilingual writers practice writing more deliberately (Palermo & Wilson, 2020). This deliberate practice is associated with a positive motivating effect (Camacho et al., 2021; Nunes et al., 2021), especially when users are properly guided in its use (Grimes & Warschauer, 2010; Nunes et al., 2021).

However, it is important to acknowledge that previous AI-based tools have primarily focused on language use and accuracy, mostly being utilized for editing purposes (Ranalli, 2021). These tools often lack the capability to provide feedback on global aspects of writing, such as the strength of argumentation, discourse coherence, or organization (Grimes & Warschauer, 2010; Y. Huang & Wilson, 2021). As a result, they have been mostly integrated into the revision process in classroom contexts (Ranalli, 2021), with a focus-on-form approach targeting specific grammar points (John & Woll, 2020).

Intriguingly, generative AI tools such as ChatGPT have extended the capabilities of previous AI tools, prompting educators to rethink pedagogy in L2 writing. The adaptability and richness of the text generated by ChatGPT hold significant potential to aid learners in developing their writing skills in many different areas. Despite the integration of ChatGPT in education has been explored, with its potential strengths highlighted (Qadir, 2022; Yan, 2023; Zhai, 2022), its adoption raises ethical concerns, including issues of plagiarism and nuanced biases in AI-generated texts (Gao et al., 2022; Godwin-Jones, 2022; Yeadon et al., 2022). The model can sometimes produce biased or inaccurate content, underscoring the need for critical engagement with its output. Educators and students must be vigilant about ethical considerations, such as avoiding plagiarism and ensuring proper attribution of AI-generated content (Borenstein & Howard, 2021). Furthermore, there is the issue of authenticity for the authorship, as ChatGPT can generate text on behalf of the human writer, potentially impacting the creativity and originality of the writing (Godwin-Jones, 2022).

The academic community continues to gauge the impact of tools like ChatGPT on learning outcomes and academic honesty. The challenge involves leveraging ChatGPT's strengths, its comprehensive language understanding and generative capabilities, while mitigating risks associated with its use (Warschauer et al., 2023). As it is reasonable to assume that students across various disciplines are already actively using these tools (Eaton et al., 2021), the critical and judicious use of AI-generated tools should be introduced and taught in classrooms, guided by the instructor's expertise (Godwin-Jones, 2022; Otsuki, 2020).

DESIGNING AND IMPLEMENTING A CHATGPT WORKSHOP

Participants and Context

The English Language Institute Writing Courses at the University of Hawaii at Manoa

The workshop, titled "Promoting Ethical and Critical Use of ChatGPT to Enhance Multilingual University Students' Academic English Writing," is designed for students at the University of Hawaiʻi at Mānoa who are learning English as an additional language. For students who failed to meet the language requirements (neither submitting required English proficiency test scores nor passing the ELI placement tests), enrollment in specific courses is mandated. These courses, provided by the English Language Institute (ELI), are geared towards enhancing the language skills necessary for success in their respective academic disciplines and involve the development of their L2 English proficiency. All ELI courses are offered for both graduate and undergraduate students, catering to intermediate and advanced levels. More specifically, one of the advanced writing classes, 'ELI 83,' consists entirely of graduate students, and another advanced writing class, 'ESL 100,' is only for undergraduate students while the intermediate 'ELI 73' course has mixed groups of undergraduate and graduate students with similar writing abilities.

In my role as a graduate assistant, I was tasked with developing a workshop centered on the use of ChatGPT for academic writing. This initiative followed the success of a similar workshop in 2022, hosted by the ELI department, which focused on Grammarly for academic writing. The success of the previous workshop led to the conception of this year's ChatGPT workshop, designed as a continuation of the department's efforts to provide helpful guidance in the development of writing skills for multilingual writers. Initially designed as a pilot session, the workshop was integrated into the ELI writing course curriculum, with the goal of reaching a broader audience on campus in the following year. It was scheduled to take place during weeks 10 to 15 of the Fall 2023 semester, aligning with the ELI writing instructors' schedule.

Workshop Design Process

Needs Analysis

To lay the groundwork for the workshop, a needs analysis was conducted through a survey distributed to English Language Institute (ELI) instructors (see appendix A.). The purpose of this survey was two-fold: to gather background information on the students' existing L2 English writing competencies and to identify what the instructors would want their students to achieve from the workshop. The survey began by inquiring about the skills students were expected to possess prior to the workshop, such as the ability to craft an outline, organize an academic paper coherently, develop content with clear topic sentences and supporting details, and revise drafts effectively. Following this, instructors were asked to select from a list of potential workshop objectives that they deemed most beneficial for their students. The options included evaluating ChatGPT's utility and limitations in academic writing, using ChatGPT to refine and improve emails, enhancing argumentative essay outlines, obtaining draft feedback, and citing sources properly with ChatGPT's assistance.

Based on the survey results and discussions with ELI writing instructors, it became evident that by the time of the workshop, students should have learned to brainstorm ideas, outline argumentative essays, and prepare initial drafts for final submission. Additionally, there was a consensus among instructors on the need to reduce the workload associated with providing writing feedback. Concerns were also raised about students potentially over-relying on ChatGPT for writing tasks, which might impede their skill development. Lastly, the ELI director who is also my supervisor advised me to incorporate hands-on activities into the workshop to enhance student engagement and improve overall effectiveness.

ADE Approach

In the formulation of the workshop, I was guided by the principles of design-based research, particularly the Analysis, Design, and Evaluation (ADE) model as proposed by Reigeluth and An (2021). The initial step was to pinpoint a performance gap in the English Language Institute (ELI) students' writing abilities and how they are using different AI tools for their writing assignments. From the needs analysis, this gap manifested in various ways: some students write English directly translating phrases and expressions from their first language, leading to unclear communication, while others write in their native language and use AI tools to translate their L1 writing. Meanwhile, advanced students often bypassed tools like ChatGPT entirely, instead seeking extensive individualized feedback, which placed a demand on instructors' time and resources.

To bridge this gap, the workshop was conceived with the goal of equipping ELI students with the skills to utilize ChatGPT effectively, critically, and ethically. The ADE model facilitated a structured approach to this end. In the analysis phase, I examined the specific needs and challenges faced by ELI students in their writing endeavors. The design phase involved creating workshop content that was both responsive to these needs and flexible enough to cater to varying levels of proficiency. The evaluation phase was anticipated to assess the impact of the workshop on students' writing skills, with a focus on their ability to integrate ChatGPT's assistance productively into their writing process.

The workshop design was initiated with a broad, top-level ADE analysis. This initial instructional developmental stage with a general view provided a macroscopic perspective of the instructional content and methods. Subsequently, as the design progressed, finer adjustments were made to align with the nuanced needs of students at different proficiency levels. By iterating through the stages of the ADE model, the workshop was meticulously tailored to foster an environment where students could engage with ChatGPT not just as a tool, but as a means to enhance their academic writing while maintaining the integrity of their work.

Workshop Plan With the Top-Level ADE

In the top-level ADE (Analysis, Design, and Evaluation) stage of the instructional design process (Reigeluth & An, 2021) the objective is to establish a comprehensive vision for the instructional experience. This entails formulating overarching content themes, sequencing, and pedagogical methods. This stage is crucial for delineating what content will be taught and devising the most effective strategies for teaching it. In the context of the ChatGPT workshop, which aims to educate students on the proficient use of ChatGPT for revising their essays, the design was crafted in alignment with the model's guidelines for task expertise. This model is particularly suited for instructional situations where the goal is to equip students with the capability to execute specific tasks or actions. This stands in contrast to topic expertise, which is concerned with cultivating a deep understanding of conceptual knowledge.

The initial step in the top-level design for task expertise is the identification of tasks. These are the distinct, real-world actions students need to complete from start to finish. Subsequently, these tasks are deconstructed into subtasks. This breakdown is essential for structuring the instruction in a way that incrementally builds students' skills. Following the identification and decomposition of tasks, the next critical phase involves sequencing these tasks and subtasks. The sequencing can follow a linear progression, mirroring the real-world order in which the tasks are typically performed. Alternatively, a branching sequence can be employed, offering learners the flexibility to navigate through the task completion sequence. This choice of sequencing is informed by the instructional goals and the learners' needs, aiming to provide an intuitive and effective learning trajectory.

By embracing this methodical approach, I tried to design the ChatGPT workshop ensuring that students not only learn how to use ChatGPT effectively, critically, and ethically but also develop a strategic approach to the task of essay revision, thereby enhancing their overall writing competency. To do so, the workshop's primary objective, 'to equip students with the skills to utilize ChatGPT for effective, critical, and ethical revision of academic writing,' was broken down into three key tasks, each comprising specific subtasks. Initially, participants would be guided to raise their awareness of the ethical implications of AI use in academic writing. For example, participants look at four different scenarios where university students use ChatGPT for their academic writing tasks, and engage in discussions to talk about the right and wrong ways of using AI for academic writing. This session will also involve sharing personal concerns and experiences, followed by collaboratively establishing a set of ethical guidelines for AI utilization. The next focus would be on identifying the strengths and weaknesses of texts generated by ChatGPT. Students use ChatGPT to fix two different emails with errors. One email is for communicating with a professor, while the other is for a friend. This hands-on activity lets students explore ChatGPT and see its strengths and limitations. Participants would compare ChatGPT-generated texts with those of their peers and conduct various inquiries to revise an email, thereby understanding the nuances of AI-generated texts. Finally, the participants would apply their learning to revise their writing with the assistance of ChatGPT. The third part is about students interacting with ChatGPT to get feedback and suggestions for their writing. They chat with ChatGPT using the ChatGPT prompt that I provide in the workshop, ask for feedback, and then change their drafts based on the suggestions. They would request targeted feedback from ChatGPT on specific aspects such as content, organization, and language use. Additionally, they would engage with a feature that suggests academic vocabulary, comparing it with their own words, and then independently revise their drafts based on ChatGPT's suggestions.

With these tasks and subtasks defined, planning for the instructional methods followed. Considering elements such as content mastery, pacing, experiential learning, and delivery methods, a learner-centered approach was adopted. This approach prioritizes learning by doing, an essential strategy given the workshop's focus on practical tool usage. The pacing was set to group pacing, with all participants moving through the learning process collectively, appropriate for a single-session workshop. For delivery, face-to-face instruction was chosen, utilizing electronic forms of prepared writing samples, word processing software like Google Docs or Microsoft Word, the ChatGPT interface, and the student's personal laptop computers. Given the workshop's one-off nature, a mastery approach was deemed unsuitable due to the limited time frame, thus not all tasks could be mastered completely, but substantial exposure to the core concepts was ensured. For more details, please refer to Appendix B, 'Workshop Plan.'

ChatGPT Prompts for Revision Activities

ChatGPT prompts refer to the input or questions that users provide to the ChatGPT model, prompting it to generate responses. During the workshop, students were provided with specific ChatGPT prompts (see Appendix C for the workshop slides) to facilitate their interaction with the AI. These prompts served as a crucial mechanism for obtaining tailored feedback from ChatGPT, and I designed them to assist students in their writing process. For example, a student might have asked ChatGPT: 'Give me feedback on my introductory paragraph based on content, organization, and language use.' ChatGPT then generated suggestions and feedback, offering insights into the strengths and weaknesses of the paragraph without altering the original writing. This exercise was invaluable for L2 English writers, providing direct and specific feedback from ChatGPT to enhance their writing process. Although ChatGPT might provide general feedback if the prompt is not specific enough, students can still utilize this feedback as guidelines or checklists.

The workshop included two main hands-on activities. The first involved students revising emails with pre-identified errors in two scenarios. Email writing was chosen to assess ChatGPT's strengths and weaknesses in generating texts, as it is a primary communication mode in everyday American contexts and poses fewer ethical concerns than academic writing. Students input prompts like 'revise the following email, make it more concise, and use more casual language,' to see how ChatGPT altered the original text. This practice also helped international students adapt to American email writing conventions and etiquette. By comparing ChatGPT's revisions under different scenarios, students evaluated the effectiveness of various prompts. They engaged in peer discussions to identify similarities and differences in the ChatGPT-generated texts, assessing the AI's strengths and weaknesses collectively.

For the second activity, students used ChatGPT to receive feedback and suggestions on their writing drafts. The key prompt word was 'feedback,' ensuring that ChatGPT provided suggestions and explanations, rather than revising the text. For instance, using the prompt 'Can you give me feedback on my language use errors? Are there any specific grammar errors that I should study more?' students received targeted feedback. Another prompt, 'Give me suggestions for word choices to make my writing more academic. Give me a table of words to compare,' resulted in a table comparing their words with suggested academic words.

Importantly, students were guided to make careful decisions when adopting and evaluating ChatGPT's feedback. While ChatGPT can be a valuable tool, it was acknowledged that not all suggestions might be relevant or accurate. Students had the autonomy to select and apply feedback that aligned with their writing goals, which sometimes involved rejecting irrelevant or inaccurate suggestions. Incorporating concrete examples and practical exercises offered participants a hands-on experience, enhancing their understanding of the workshop's objectives and ChatGPT's role as a writing tool.

Workshop Procedure

Five-Week Duration

The study was designed to span five weeks, allowing the workshop to be conducted across multiple classes. This duration was set according to the assigned schedule by the instructors, but it also allowed thorough data collection from multilingual students at varying stages of their academic English writing development. The central element of this research was the 75-minute instructional workshop, which aimed to rigorously evaluate its effectiveness in improving the academic writing skills of multilingual university students. The extended five-week framework (see Table 1), encompassing multiple classes, enhanced the data collection process by accommodating the diverse language proficiencies and academic needs of the students.

Table 1. Schedule for ChatGPT workshops

23 Fall	Week 10	Week 11	Week 12	Week 15
Class	ELI 73-3 Intermediate level Undergrad. + Grad.	ELI 73-1 Intermediate level Undergrad. + Grad.		
	ELI 83 Advanced level Grad.	ESL 100 Advanced level Undergrad.	ESL 100 Advanced level Undergrad.	ESL 100 Advanced level Undergrad.

Data Collection During Workshop

During the workshop, data were collected to ensure research validity and enhance understanding of participants' interactions with ChatGPT. All data collection processes had received approval from the university's Institutional Review Board (IRB) and strictly adhered to ethical standards. Participants were required to provide informed consent for the use of their data in research before any data collection occurred. Data collection within the workshop primarily involved administering pre- and post-workshop questionnaires, monitoring student interactions with ChatGPT, and collecting ChatGPT-generated texts. The questionnaires were distributed via Google Forms to streamline the process, with responses automatically stored on the researcher's Google Drive upon submission. These questionnaires aimed to capture participants' initial perceptions and any shifts in understanding post-workshop. Participants were encouraged to use ChatGPT for feedback and revision of their writing drafts. As part of the data collection, students submitted their ChatGPT chat logs, which contained conversations with the AI platform. These chats, obtained as students worked on revising their drafts, were collected using a digital survey form to ensure security and accessibility for subsequent analysis. Each chat represented a unique engagement between the student and ChatGPT, capturing the student's requests for feedback and ChatGPT's responses. These logs were carefully stored and organized for further examination, forming a critical part of the workshop's data collection process.

WORKSHOP EVALUATION

Methods

Pre-Workshop Questionnaire

The pre-workshop questionnaires were administered before the workshop to establish a foundational understanding of students' awareness and requirements in relation to ChatGPT and the academic writing revision process. These questionnaires consisted of two open-ended questions and 14 items that included multiple-choice questions, options for selecting all that apply, as well as a five-point Likert scale.

The questionnaire was structured into three distinct sections. The initial segment was dedicated to gathering personal background information, delving into aspects such as participants' age and primary language (L1). The subsequent section concentrated on students' writing abilities, assessing factors such as their affinity for writing in both their native and second languages (L1/L2), self-assessed L2 writing proficiency, and their writing habits, including the typical amount of time dedicated to the writing revision process. The final section of the questionnaire delved into ChatGPT usage, seeking to understand the frequency of ChatGPT utilization, specific scenarios in which ChatGPT was employed for writing assignments, awareness of ethical considerations, and students' overall satisfaction levels with their ChatGPT experiences. For additional details, please refer to Appendix D.

Post-Workshop Questionnaire

Following the workshop, participants were asked to complete a post-workshop questionnaire (see Appendix E). This questionnaire aimed to evaluate the workshop's effectiveness in enhancing participants' confidence in using ChatGPT to obtain feedback critically and effectively, all while maintaining ethical standards. Additionally, the questionnaire provided students with the opportunity to offer qualitative feedback on the workshop's content and structure, allowing them to reflect on their learning experiences. The post-workshop questionnaires included a total of 11 questions, encompassing two open-ended questions for suggestions, three multiple-choice questions, and the remaining questions employing a five-point Likert scale. These questions were divided into two sections, with each section focusing on a specific aspect related to the participants' post-workshop experiences and their perception of the workshop's impact.

Findings

Pre-Workshop Questionnaires

The pre-workshop questionnaires were administered before the workshop by providing the instructors with a link to a Google survey form, which the students completed in advance. Among the 55 students who attended the workshop, I analyzed the results from the 46 who submitted their consent forms. The pre-workshop questionnaire results (n=46) provided valuable insights into their comfort levels with various English language skills. Table 2 illustrates that writing was identified as the least comfortable skill, with only 6.5% of the students (three out of 46) considering it their strength. This finding indicates that L2 English writing presents significant challenges for these students, more so than other language skills.

In terms of self-assessment of their L2 English writing abilities, a mere 6.5% of the students considered themselves highly proficient, scoring a 5 on a 5-point Likert scale. A larger segment, 37%, rated their proficiency at 4, while the majority, 43.5%, assigned themselves a moderate score of 3. Notably, 13% of the students rated their writing proficiency at the lower level of 2. It was observed that students enrolled in Advanced writing courses were more likely to select a rating of '4', in contrast to those in lower-level courses.

On average, students reported dedicating approximately two to three hours to revising major writing assignments, such as final papers, as illustrated in Figure 1. Despite this investment of time, the data revealed that students generally lacked confidence in their ability to revise their writing. Remarkably, only one student (2.2%) expressed the highest confidence level, scoring a 5. A quarter of the participants (26.1%) indicated moderate confidence with a score of 4. The largest group, encompassing 45.7%, chose 3, signifying a neutral level of confidence. A considerable minority, 21.7%, reported a lower confidence level of 2. Additionally, 4.3% of the students rated their confidence in revising their writing at the lowest level of 1.

Table 2. Most favored English language skill by student preference

Comfortable Lg. Skill	Count (n)	Percentage (%)
Listening	14	30.4
Reading	14	30.4
Speaking	15	32.6
Writing	3	6.5
total	46	100

The aspect of feedback where students expressed the most concern (see Table 3) was in areas of spelling and grammar correction, word choice for natural language use, and the structure, clarity, and coherence of their writing. These categories were prioritized over content, fluency, and research and citation for desired feedback. This suggests that while students are concerned with the substantive aspects of writing, there is a particular focus on the technical and linguistic accuracy of their work.

Figure 1. A pie chart of students' time investment in assignment revision

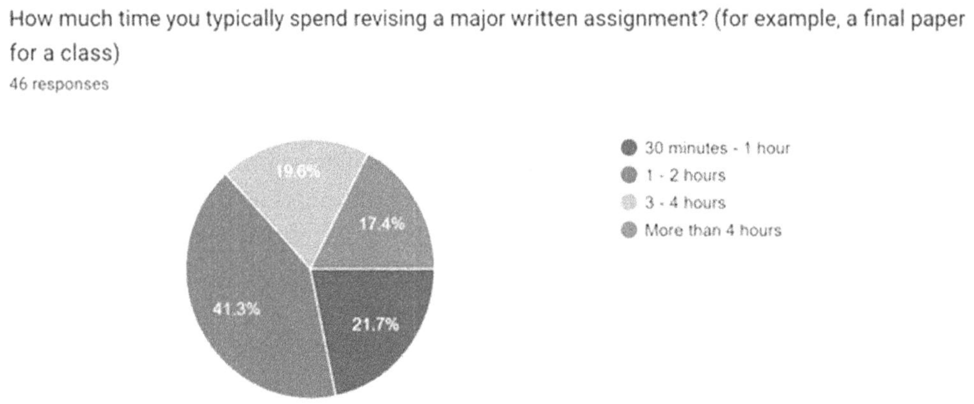

Table 3. Preferred types of writing revision feedback

Feedback Type	Count	Percentage (%)
Spelling/ Grammar correction	28	60.87
Word choice for natural language use (vocabulary, expressions)	32	69.57
Content (ideas)	17	36.96
Structure (organization)	24	52.17
Fluency (writing a lot)	16	34.78
Research and Citations	14	30.43
Clarity and Coherence	23	50

Note. Students could select up to three choices. (n = 46)

In the section addressing ChatGPT usage, the questionnaire data offered insights into the students' engagement with the technology. Of the respondents, a significant majority (65.2%) indicated that they use the free version of ChatGPT, while a small fraction (6.5%) opted for the premium version. Notably, nearly a third of the participants (28.3%) reported no prior experience with ChatGPT. Among the students who had used ChatGPT, approximately half (48.5%) reported utilizing the tool either daily or weekly. This suggests a substantial integration of ChatGPT into their academic routine. Inquiring into the specific academic tasks for which students employ ChatGPT, idea generation or brainstorming emerged as the most common use, selected by 43.5% of users. This was followed by other applications, including proofreading, completing homework assignments, and assisting with research papers and essays.

When leveraging ChatGPT for writing support, students predominantly sought assistance with grammar and punctuation, sentence structure enhancement, and organization of ideas. This trend underscores a focus on the tool's capability to refine the technical elements of writing, suggesting that students primarily view ChatGPT as a means to polish the mechanical aspects of their work (for details, see table 4).

Interestingly, responses illustrated in Figure 2 regarding ethical concerns associated with using ChatGPT revealed a tendency towards fewer worries in this area. A notable number of students did not express significant ethical apprehensions, which could indicate a possible gap in awareness or understanding of the potential ethical issues tied to AI assistance in academic writing. This finding raises questions about students' recognition of the ethical dimensions of using AI tools in academic contexts and suggests a need for more education on this topic.

Table 4. Feedback types multilingual writers look for in ChatGPT

Feedback Type	Count	Percentage (%)
Grammar and punctuation correction	19	57.58
Vocabulary Suggestions	18	54.55
Sentence Structure Improvements	22	66.67
Guidance on organizing ideas	18	54.55
Recommendations for improving clarity and coherence	15	45.45
Assistance with academic style and tone	10	30.30
Help with research and citations	8	24.24
N/A (Never used ChatGPT before)	13	

Note. Students were given the option to select all responses that apply (n = 46). Percentages were calculated based on the number of applicable students, excluding those who selected 'N/A'. For instance, in the case of 'Help with research and citations', 8 responses were divided by 33 (the total of 46 minus the 13 who selected 'N/A'), resulting in a percentage of 24.24%.

Figure 2. A histogram of levels of ethical concern regarding the use of ChatGPT

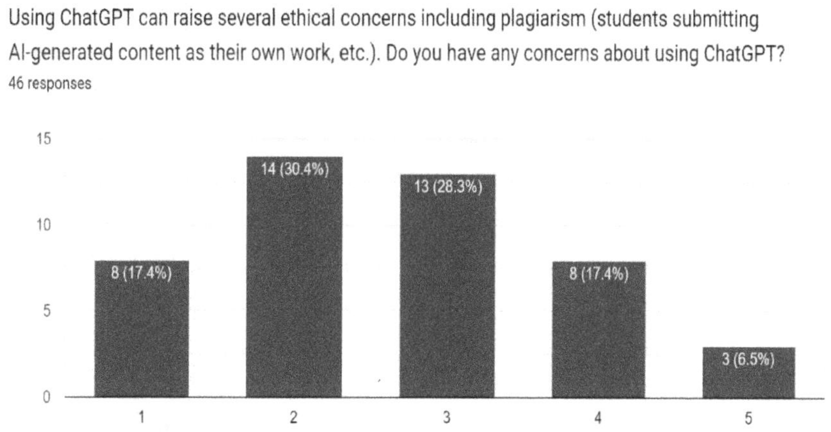

Finally, the question regarding students' satisfaction level with ChatGPT was assessed using a 5-point Likert scale, targeting only those students who had prior experience with ChatGPT. To determine the overall satisfaction with the feedback and suggestions provided by ChatGPT, an average satisfaction score was calculated from the responses. The students rated their satisfaction on a scale from 1 (very dissatisfied) to 5 (very satisfied). The calculation considered the number of responses in each category along with their respective satisfaction ratings: 1 response rated 5 points (very satisfied), 14 responses rated 4 points (somewhat satisfied), 10 responses rated 3 points (neutral), 7 responses rated 2 points (somewhat dissatisfied), and 1 response rated 1 point (very dissatisfied). The resulting average satisfaction score was 3.21, indicating a generally mild positive level of satisfaction among the respondents.

Post-Workshop Questionnaires

The results from the post-workshop questionnaires were gathered from 42 students who provided consent and attended the workshop. Notably, four students who had submitted the pre-workshop questionnaire were absent from the workshop. In the post-workshop questionnaire, the students reflected on their experience and evaluated the effectiveness of the workshop. They highly rated its overall quality, with 45.2% labeling it as 'outstanding' and 54.8% as 'good'. In terms of the content and activities of the workshop, the majority of students felt that no significant changes were required, reflecting high levels of satisfaction. This sentiment was particularly pronounced among those who were new to ChatGPT prior to the workshop, implying that the framework was both accessible and beneficial even for beginners.

The questionnaire further explored changes in students' confidence regarding their English writing revision process and their perceptions of ChatGPT after participating in the workshop. There was a notable increase in confidence in their ability to revise English writing using ChatGPT, with an average rating of 4 out of 5 on the Likert scale. This suggests an enhanced level of confidence in utilizing ChatGPT as well. Additionally, Figures 3 and 4 highlight a significant shift towards higher scores in students' understanding of the strengths and weaknesses of ChatGPT, as well as their awareness of related ethical considerations. This indicates that the workshop effectively increased students' comprehension and critical awareness of these aspects.

Figure 3. A histogram of understanding the strengths and weaknesses of ChatGPT after workshop

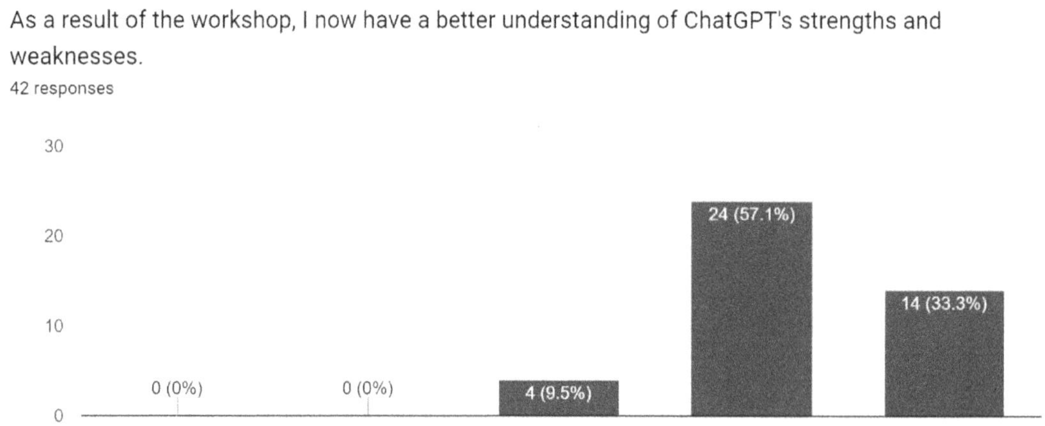

Figure 4. A histogram of understanding ethical issues of ChatGPT after workshop

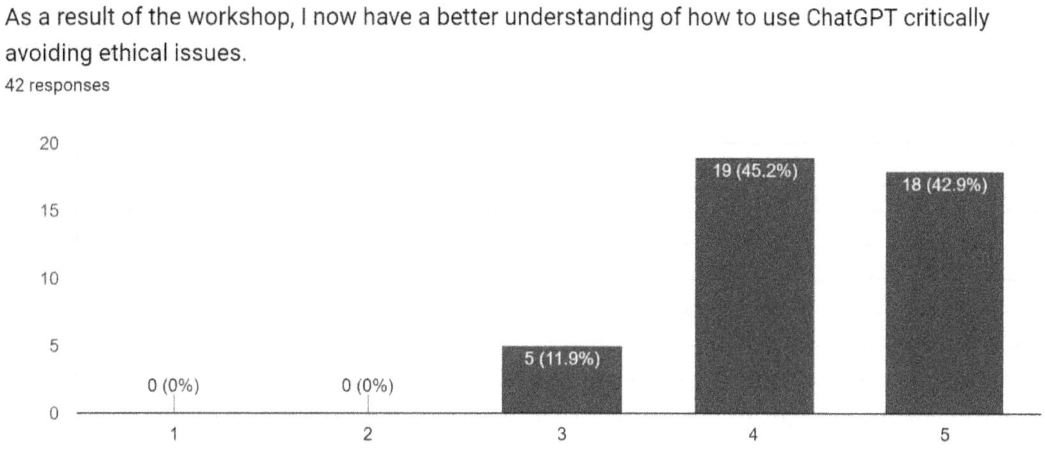

The workshop was highly successful in enhancing students' understanding of ChatGPT. This success was evident as the vast majority of participants, over 90%, rated their comprehension of the strengths, weaknesses, and ethical considerations of using ChatGPT in academic writing as 4 or 5 on a 5-point Likert scale. This high level of rating reflects a significant enhancement in their understanding and critical application of ChatGPT. In terms of feedback from ChatGPT, the aspects most valued by students were its assistance with spelling and grammar, word choice, and organizational structure. For a more comprehensive analysis, please refer to Table 5, which offers a detailed breakdown of these elements.

Table 5. Feedback types multilingual writers appreciated in ChatGPT feedback

Feedback Type	Count	Percentage (%)
Spelling/ Grammar correction	32	76.2
Word choice for natural language use (vocabulary, expressions)	28	66.7
Content (ideas)	17	40.5
Structure (organization)	28	66.7
Fluency (writing a lot)	16	38.1
Research and Citations	5	11.9
Clarity and Coherence	9	21.4
Others (coding, translation, etc.)	1	2.4

Note. Students could select all that apply. (n = 42)

Furthermore, the workshop positively impacted the students' anticipated future use of ChatGPT. A significant 48.6% of the participants planned to use it more frequently, while 45.7% intended to maintain their current usage levels. This inclination towards increased or sustained use correlates with the high levels of satisfaction reported with the workshop, suggesting that the workshop not only met but potentially exceeded its intended goals in terms of enhancing students' proficiency and comfort with the AI tool. In the open-ended comment section of the post-workshop questionnaires, among many positive responses, one particularly intriguing comment stood out: 'I was happy to learn the useful functions of ChatGPT and I think I'm going to be a heavy user of it.' This feedback was from a student who had never used ChatGPT before.

Guidelines and Future Directions

As educators and academic institutions increasingly adopt AI technology, it's essential to establish guidelines for the responsible and ethical use of AI tools like ChatGPT. Based on the insights from my workshop research, this section aims to provide educators with a practical framework for integrating AI-driven writing assistants into their pedagogical approaches. The overarching goal is to employ these tools as supplements that enhance learning, rather than as replacements for writing skills.

Ethical and Responsible Use

The ethical deployment of AI in educational settings must comprehensively address issues of plagiarism, dependency, and the integrity of student work. These concerns were notably underscored by the findings of my workshop. To uphold academic standards, educators should cultivate an environment where AI tools are leveraged to support and refine students' writing skills, rather than supplant them. This approach involves several key strategies:

- Establishing Clear Policies: Implementing explicit guidelines on the appropriate use of AI in academic work helps in setting boundaries and expectations.
- Educating Students: Instructors should inform students about both the potential and the limitations of AI, emphasizing that these tools are aids in the learning process, not definitive solutions.
- Encouraging Critical Engagement: Students should be guided to critically evaluate AI-generated content and understand its proper role in their work.

Additionally, instructors can leverage technology to monitor the development of students' writing skills. By utilizing the version history features in Google Docs or Microsoft Word, both educators and students can track changes, revisions, and improvements in writing assignments over time. Additionally, incorporating occasional paper and pencil writing during class can help instructors gauge students' real-time writing abilities. These practices are valuable for assessing current skill levels and for making informed decisions on how to enhance students' learning and revision processes, while also promoting transparency and accountability in the use of AI tools.

To ensure critical and ethical use of these tools, instructors might consider requiring students to submit their ChatGPT chat logs as well. This would allow for an analysis of how students interact with the technology during their writing process. It is crucial for students to understand the role of AI as a facilitator in their learning journey, rather than mistakenly perceiving it as the author of their work. This distinction is vital to maintain the authenticity and integrity of their academic work.

RECOMMENDATIONS FOR EDUCATORS

Educators should receive comprehensive training to assist students in effectively navigating AI tools, a need underscored by the positive outcomes observed in the workshop. This training should encompass various strategies, including how to integrate AI feedback into the revision process in a manner that enhances rather than overrides students' efforts. Educators must be adept at helping students discern between beneficial and potentially misleading suggestions provided by AI, ensuring that the student's original voice and intent in writing are preserved. Moreover, training should focus on how educators can leverage AI tools to provide more personalized and nuanced feedback. By doing so, they can address specific needs and challenges faced by individual students, thereby substantially improving the efficiency and effectiveness of the writing and revision process. Such personalized attention, facilitated by AI, can lead to better learning outcomes and a more supportive educational environment. In sum, empowering educators with the skills to use AI tools responsibly and effectively is crucial for maximizing the potential of these technologies in educational settings.

CONCLUSION

In this chapter, my objective was to equip educators, researchers, and practitioners in language education with a detailed understanding of how ChatGPT workshops can benefit multilingual students in their academic writing endeavors. By delving into the challenges faced by L2 English learners, exploring the design and implementation of effective workshops, and considering the ethical aspects of AI integration, my aim was to present a comprehensive view of the transformative potential of AI-driven tools in academic writing education at the university level.

During the workshops, it became evident that student engagement in group discussions or class-wide conversations was crucial for fostering critical thinking about ethical issues and understanding the limitations of ChatGPT. Observations also showed that student engagement was highest when their regular instructors participated in the activities and when a positive rapport existed among students and between students and instructors. This highlights the importance of established relationships and expert support in facilitating effective use of AI tools in an educational setting. For my future research, I plan to analyze how students incorporate and modify ChatGPT suggestions in their revision processes and assess the extent to which ChatGPT provides useful feedback, using data from students' ChatGPT chat logs.

Additionally, further research is necessary to comprehend the long-term implications of integrating AI in academic writing. This research should focus on how tools like ChatGPT can aid students with diverse learning needs and backgrounds, how they influence the development of writing skills over time, and how they can be adapted to meet a variety of educational objectives, as indicated by the preliminary outcomes of my workshop.

ACKNOWLEDGMENT

I would like to extend my heartfelt gratitude to Priscilla, my supervisor and the director of the ELI, for her invaluable guidance on this workshop project. My thanks also go to Dan Holden, the education specialist, for his support. I am grateful to Dr. Crowther for encouraging the research aspect of this project and providing helpful feedback. Special appreciation is due to my academic advisor, Dr. Isbell, and to SLS professors Dr. Gilliland and Dr. Zheng, for their significant academic insights. Lastly, I am thankful for the constant encouragement from the supportive SLS ‘ohana. Any oversights in this work are my own responsibility.

REFERENCES

Adams, D., & Chuah, K.-M. (2022). Artificial Intelligence-Based Tools in Research Writing. In P. P. Churi, S. Joshi, M. Elhoseny, & A. Omrane (Eds.), *Artificial Intelligence in Higher Education: A Practical Approach* (pp. 169–184). CRC Press. doi:10.1201/9781003184157-9

Barrot, J. S. (2023). Using ChatGPT for second language writing: Pitfalls and potentials. *Assessing Writing*, *57*, 100745-. doi:10.1016/j.asw.2023.100745

Borenstein, J., & Howard, A. (2021). Emerging challenges in AI and the need for AI ethics education. *AI and Ethics*, *1*(1), 61–65. doi:10.1007/s43681-020-00002-7

Camacho, A., Alves, R. A., & Boscolo, P. (2021). Writing motivation in school: A systematic review of empirical research in the early twenty-first century. *Educational Psychology Review*, *33*(1), 213–247. doi:10.1007/s10648-020-09530-4

Chang, D. H., Lin, M. P.-C., Hajian, S., & Wang, Q. Q. (2023). Educational Design Principles of Using AI Chatbot That Supports Self-Regulated Learning in Education: Goal Setting, Feedback, and Personalization. *Sustainability*, *15*(17), 12921-. doi:10.3390/su151712921

Connor, U. (1998). Contrastive rhetoric: Developments and challenges. *Studia Anglica Posnaniensia*, *33*, 105–116.

Dale, R. (2021). GPT-3: What’s it good for? *Natural Language Engineering*, *27*(1), 113–118. doi:10.1017/S1351324920000601

Dizon, G., & Gayed, J. M. (2021). Examining the Impact of Grammarly on the Quality of Mobile L2 Writing. *The JALT CALL Journal*, *17*(2), 74–92. doi:10.29140/jaltcall.v17n2.336

Ferris, D., & Hedgcock, J. (2014). *Teaching L2 composition: Purpose, process, and practice* (3rd ed.). Routledge.

Flower, L., & Hayes, J. R. (1981). A cognitive process theory of writing. *College Composition and Communication*, *32*(4), 365–387. doi:10.2307/356600

GaoC. A.HowardF. M.MarkovN. S.DyerE. C.RameshS.LuoY.PearsonA. T. (2022). Comparing scientific abstracts generated by ChatGPT to original abstracts using an artificial intelligence output detector, plagiarism detector, and blinded human reviewers. doi:10.1101/2022.12.23.521610

Godwin-Jones, R. (2022). Partnering with AI: Intelligent writing assistance and instructed language learning. *Language Learning & Technology*, *26*(2), 5–24.

Grassini, S. (2023). Shaping the Future of Education: Exploring the Potential and Consequences of AI and ChatGPT in Educational Settings. *Education Sciences*, *13*(7), 692-. doi:10.3390/educsci13070692

Grimes, D., & Warschauer, M. (2010). Utility in a fallible tool: A multi-site case study of automated writing evaluation. Journal of Technology. *Language, and Assessment*, *8*(6), 1–43.

Harklau, L., & Pinnow, R. (2009). Adolescent Second-Language Writing. In L. Christenbury, R. Bomer, & P. Smagorinsky (Eds.), *Handbook of Adolescent Literacy Research* (pp. 126–134). Guilford Publications.

Huang, Y., & Wilson, J. (2021). Using automated feedback to develop writing proficiency. *Computers and Composition*, *62*, 102675. doi:10.1016/j.compcom.2021.102675

John, P., & Woll, N. (2020). Using grammar checkers in an ESL context: An investigation of automatic corrective feedback. *CALICO Journal*, *37*(2), 169–172. doi:10.1558/cj.36523

Kasneci, E., Sessler, K., Küchemann, S., Bannert, M., Dementieva, D., Fischer, F., Gasser, U., Groh, G., Günnemann, S., Hüllermeier, E., Krusche, S., Kutyniok, G., Michaeli, T., Nerdel, C., Pfeffer, J., Poquet, O., Sailer, M., Schmidt, A., Seidel, T., … Kasneci, G. (2023). ChatGPT for good? On opportunities and challenges of large language models for education. *Learning and Individual Differences*, *103*, 102274. doi:10.1016/j.lindif.2023.102274

Nazari, N., Shabbir, M. S., & Setiawan, R. (2021). Application of Artificial Intelligence powered digital writing assistant in higher education: Randomized controlled trial. *Heliyon*, *7*(5), e07014. doi:10.1016/j.heliyon.2021.e07014 PMID:34027198

Nunes, A., Cordeiro, C., Limpo, T., & Castro, S. L. (2021). Effectiveness of automated writing evaluation systems in school settings: A systematic review of studies from 2000 to 2020. *Journal of Computer Assisted Learning*, *38*(2), 599–620. doi:10.1111/jcal.12635

Palermo, C., & Wilson, J. (2020). Implementing automated writing evaluation in different instructional contexts: A mixed-methods study. *Journal of Writing Research*, *12*(1), 63–108. doi:10.17239/jowr-2020.12.01.04

Paltridge, B. (2018). Graduate student writing. In D. Belcher & A. Hirvela (Eds.), *The TESOL Encyclopedia of English Language Teaching* (pp. 1–6). Wiley Blackwell. doi:10.1002/9781118784235.eelt0516

Qadir, J. (2022). *Engineering Education in the Era of ChatGPT: Promise and Pitfalls of Generative AI for Education.* TechRxiv xiv. 21789 434. v1 doi:10. 36227/ techr

Ranalli, J. (2021). L2 student engagement with automated feedback on writing: Potential for learning and issues of trust. *Journal of Second Language Writing*, *52*, 100816. doi:10.1016/j.jslw.2021.100816

Reichelt, M., Lefkowitz, N., Rinnert, C., & Schultz, J. M. (2012). Key issues in foreign language writing. *Foreign Language Annals*, *45*(1), 22–41. doi:10.1111/j.1944-9720.2012.01166.x

Reid, J. (2006). "Eye" learners and "ear" learners: Identifying the language needs of international student and US resident writers. In P. K. Matsuda, M. Cox, J. Jordan, & C. Ortmeier-Hooper (Eds.), *Second-language writing in the composition classroom: A critical sourcebook* (pp. 76–88). St. Martin's.

Reigeluth, C. M., & An, Y. (2019). *Merging the instructional design process with learner-centered theory: The holistic 4d model.* Taylor & Francis Group.

Teubner, T., Flath, C. M., Weinhardt, C., van der Aalst, W., & Hinz, O. (2023). Welcome to the Era of ChatGPT et al. *Business & Information Systems Engineering*, *65*(2), 95–101. doi:10.1007/s12599-023-00795-x

WarschauerM.TsengW.YimS.WebsterT.JacobS.DuQ.TateT. (2023, October 31). *The affordances and contradictions of AI-generated text for writers of English as a second or foreign language*. doi:10.2139/ssrn.4404380

Wu, L., Wu, Y., & Zhang, X. (2021). L2 Learner Cognitive Psychological Factors About Artificial Intelligence Writing Corrective Feedback. *English Language Teaching*, *14*(10), 10. Advance online publication. doi:10.5539/elt.v14n10p70

Yan, D. (2023). Impact of ChatGPT on learners in a L2 writing practicum: An exploratory investigation. *Education and Information Technologies*, *28*(11), 13943–13967. doi:10.1007/s10639-023-11742-4

Yeadon, W., Inyang, O.-O., Mizouri, A., Peach, A., & Testrow, C. (2022). *The Death of the Short-Form Physics Essay in the Coming AI Revolution*. arXiv. . 2212. 11661 doi:10. 48550/arXiv

Zhai, X. (2022). ChatGPT User Experience: Implications for Education. SSRN *Scholarly Paper*. . 43124 18 doi:10. 2139/ ssrn

Zhang, M., & Li, J. (2021). A commentary of GPT-3 in MIT Technology Review 2021. *Fundamental Research*, *1*(6), 831–833. doi:10.1016/j.fmre.2021.11.011

APPENDIX A: Survey for Instructors

1. Instructor's Name
2. What is the name of the ELI writing course you're teaching this semester? (e.g., ELI 73-3)
3. Please provide the course schedule for your ELI writing course (e.g., T/R 1:30-2:45 pm).
4. If you're interested in scheduling a ChatGPT workshop for your ELI writing students, please select a suitable time slot from the schedule in the provided link, ensuring that you avoid the yellow shaded ones. Additionally, kindly provide the name of your course when selecting the time slot. *multiple choice*
    - I want a workshop for my students.
    - I don't want a workshop for my students.
    - Not decided yet.
5. How many students do you have in your class?
6. By Week 10, your students would have learned (and know)... *checkboxes*
    - How to structure and make an outline for an academic paper
    - How to organize academic paper and make it coherent (introduction, body, conclusion)
    - How to develop content with a clear topic sentence and supporting details
    - How to revise drafts (language use, transitional words, etc.)
    - Other…
7. Please select the top three objectives you consider most important for a workshop involving ChatGPT. (Your input will help me prioritize the workshop's focus.) *checkboxes*
    - Evaluate the usefulness and limitations of ChatGPT for academic writing.
    - Revise and improve an email using ChatGPT effectively.
    - Enhance an outline for an argumentative essay with the assistance of ChatGPT.
    - Edit and refine a draft using ChatGPT as a writing tool.
    - Properly cite sources with the guidance of ChatGPT for academic papers.
    - Other
8. What specific improvements do you anticipate for your students' writing skills from this workshop, and in which areas do you believe the workshop can complement and enhance their skills? Please provide detailed explanations. *Open-ended*
9. Have you already taught your students how to utilize ChatGPT in your course? If you have, could you please share your experiences and provide any tips or advice for using ChatGPT in your course? *Open-ended*

APPENDIX B: Workshop Plan

Workshop Description:

In this workshop, students will gain proficiency in utilizing the Large Language Model, ChatGPT, with a critical approach to receive direct feedback during the self-revision process. The session will also involve group discussions to foster awareness of ethical considerations associated with ChatGPT use. Participants will become acquainted with the fundamental features of the ChatGPT platform and explore prompts for sample email revisions, enabling them to identify both the strengths and limitations of ChatGPT-generated text. Subsequently, students will be equipped with strategies for effectively leveraging ChatGPT prompts and will apply this knowledge to revise their own writing drafts, receiving feedback on content, organization, and language usage.

Learning Objectives:

By the end of this workshop, students will be able to:

- Understand the ethical considerations of ChatGPT use.
- Evaluate ChatGPT's strengths and weaknesses as a writing tool.
- Apply ChatGPT for effective feedback and revision in academic writing.

Materials:

Computers or tablets with internet access for each participant
Projector and screen for presentations: slides
Survey forms (Google Survey): Pre-workshop Questionnaire and Post-workshop Questionnaire
Workshop materials for activities (Google Docs)

- Chat GPT Do's and Don'ts
- Email Prompt

Instructor Feedback
Workshop Length: 75 minutes

Before the Workshop:

- Request ELI teachers to provide links to their students' writing drafts (these will be utilized during the workshop; it might be advisable for teachers to discuss how to provide feedback).
- Distribute pre-workshop questionnaires ahead of time to streamline the workshop process (kindly ask ELI teachers to allocate five minutes of class time for students to complete these questionnaires or to assign homework with time expectations).
- Examine students' pre-workshop questionnaire responses to gain insights into their typical Chat GPT usage habits and their perspectives on ethical concerns.

Workshop Procedure:

I. Introduction (3 minutes)

<Teacher>

- Welcome participants to the ChatGPT workshop.
- Introduce the workshop agenda, highlighting the importance of critical and ethical use of ChatGPT for academic writing.
- Explain that the workshop will cover ethical considerations, best practices for effective use, and practical hands-on activities.

<Student>

- Listen to the workshop introduction.

II. Engaging Prior Knowledge (7 minutes)

<Teacher>

- In pairs, have students discuss their prior experiences with ChatGPT.

<Student>

- Engage in partner discussions and share their experiences and perceptions of ChatGPT.

(Students will talk about whether they've used ChatGPT before, how often they've used it, their perceptions of its strengths and weaknesses, and any concerns they might have about using ChatGPT.)

- Share their thoughts and experiences with the class.

III. Ethical Considerations (15 minutes)

<Teacher>

- Discuss ethical considerations when using ChatGPT, including the importance of critical thinking and issues like plagiarism and attribution.
- Introduce ChatGPT Do's and Dont's, encouraging students to express their opinions on ethical use. (Depending on the class level, the number of scenarios can be varied for the discussion.)

<Student>

- Engage in discussions with their partners about ethical considerations using provided scenarios.
- Share their insights with the class.

IV. ChatGPT Walk-Through & Email Revision (15 minutes)

<Teacher>

- Provide a concise overview of ChatGPT, emphasizing its role in natural language understanding and generation.
- Present two scenarios for email writing and demonstrate how ChatGPT can be used for revision.
- Encourage students to share their prompts and revised writings with their partners. (Depending on the class level, the underlined parts can be omitted.)
- Introduce keywords for ChatGPT revision prompts and facilitate discussions on the differences between student revisions and ChatGPT-generated content.

<Student>

- Pay attention to the walk-through and explanations.
- Work in pairs to revise email drafts using ChatGPT.
- Explore ChatGPT's capabilities by using different ChatGPT prompts for the Email revision activity.
- Exchange prompts and revised drafts with their partners.
- Discuss the effectiveness of keywords for ChatGPT prompts and identify differences between their revisions and ChatGPT-generated content. (Depending on the class level, the underlined parts can be omitted.)

V. Feedback from ChatGPT (25 minutes)

<Teacher>:

- Introduce ChatGPT feedback prompts and keywords for feedback.
- Instruct students to use ChatGPT to receive feedback on their writing drafts.
- Encourage students to revise their writing based on ChatGPT feedback and share their experiences.
- Visit different groups to see if students need extra support.

<Student>

- Use ChatGPT feedback prompts and keywords to request feedback on their writing drafts.
- Revise their writing drafts based on ChatGPT feedback.
- Discuss the effectiveness and helpfulness of ChatGPT feedback with their partners.

VI. Post-Workshop (10 minutes)

<Teacher>

- Have students complete post-workshop questionnaires.
- Summarize the key take-home messages of the workshop, emphasizing ethical, effective, and critical use of ChatGPT.
- Remind students to be aware of ChatGPT's limitations.

<Student>

- Complete post-workshop questionnaires individually.
- Reflect on the workshop's key messages and the importance of considering ChatGPT's limitations in their future use.
- Share their thoughts, ask any final questions or seek clarification.

APPENDIX C: Workshop Slides

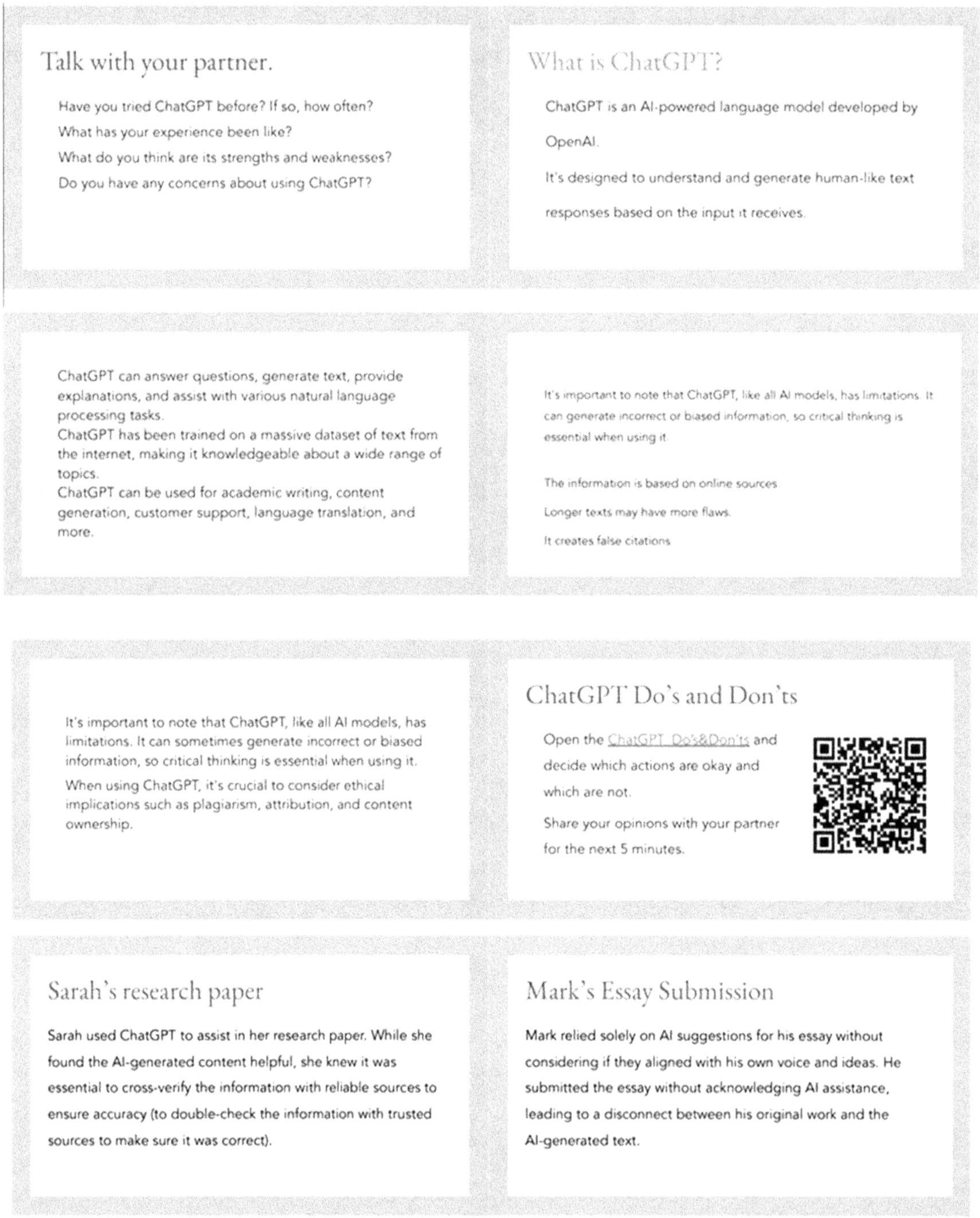
Talk with your partner.
Have you tried ChatGPT before? If so, how often?
What has your experience been like?
What do you think are its strengths and weaknesses?
Do you have any concerns about using ChatGPT?
What is ChatGPT?
ChatGPT is an AI-powered language model developed by OpenAI.
It's designed to understand and generate human-like text responses based on the input it receives.
ChatGPT can answer questions, generate text, provide explanations, and assist with various natural language processing tasks.
ChatGPT has been trained on a massive dataset of text from the internet, making it knowledgeable about a wide range of topics.
ChatGPT can be used for academic writing, content generation, customer support, language translation, and more.
It's important to note that ChatGPT, like all AI models, has limitations. It can generate incorrect or biased information, so critical thinking is essential when using it.
The information is based on online sources
Longer texts may have more flaws.
It creates false citations
It's important to note that ChatGPT, like all AI models, has limitations. It can sometimes generate incorrect or biased information, so critical thinking is essential when using it.
When using ChatGPT, it's crucial to consider ethical implications such as plagiarism, attribution, and content ownership.
ChatGPT Do's and Don'ts
Open the ChatGPT Do's&Don'ts and decide which actions are okay and which are not.
Share your opinions with your partner for the next 5 minutes.
Sarah's research paper
Sarah used ChatGPT to assist in her research paper. While she found the AI-generated content helpful, she knew it was essential to cross-verify the information with reliable sources to ensure accuracy (to double-check the information with trusted sources to make sure it was correct).
Mark's Essay Submission
Mark relied solely on AI suggestions for his essay without considering if they aligned with his own voice and ideas. He submitted the essay without acknowledging AI assistance, leading to a disconnect between his original work and the AI-generated text.

Tom's Schoolwork Ethics

Tom values academic integrity and uses ChatGPT for grammar and spelling checks. He proactively checked his school's guidelines on AI use, ensuring he would appropriately cite AI sources if he used them for content development.

Jessica's Fairness Check

Jessica was aware that AI models might produce biased content. She reviewed the AI-generated material for fairness and made necessary corrections. Before submitting her project, she reviewed and adjusted the AI-generated portions to ensure they reflected her voice and met her standards.

Chat GPT Walk-Through

openai.com

ChatGPT as a revision tool

What is a Chat GPT prompt?

A "ChatGPT prompt" refers to the input or query that a user provides to interact with the ChatGPT model. ChatGPT is a language model developed by OpenAI, and it is designed for natural language understanding and generation. To use ChatGPT, you provide it with a prompt or a question, and it generates a response based on its training data and knowledge.

Prompts can vary in complexity, from simple questions to more elaborate requests for information or assistance. ChatGPT is used in various applications, such as providing answers to questions, generating text content, assisting with language translation, and much more, all based on the input prompts it receives from users.

Scenario 1. "A student has written an email to their professor to explain his/her absence from class."

> Dear Prof.
>
> I am absent today. Smth came up.
>
> Sorry. Thanx

Scenario 2: "A student has written an email to his/her friend to explain his/her future absence"

> Hi, Tom
>
> can' meet u tomorow. Smth came up.
>
> Sorry, friend.

Keywords for ChatGPT Revision Prompt

1. Revise
2. Polite, Casual
3. Tone/ Style
4. Concise
5. Longer, more details

> 1. Who is the writer?
> 2. Who is the reader?
> 3. What are you writing about?
>
> (e.g., I am a university student. I wrote an email to my professor about my absence.)

Keywords for ChatGPT Revision Prompt

Please share your prompts and revised writings with your partner.

Please find similarities and differences.

e.g., ChatGPT chat share

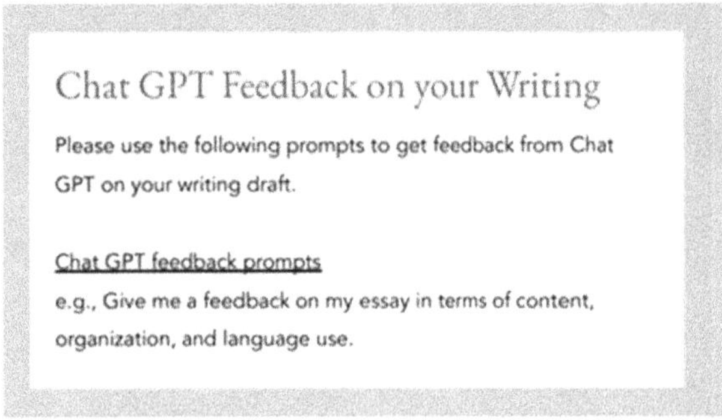
Chat GPT Feedback on your Writing
Please use the following prompts to get feedback from Chat GPT on your writing draft.
Chat GPT feedback prompts
e.g., Give me a feedback on my essay in terms of content, organization, and language use.

Keywords for ChatGPT Feedback Prompt
Please share your prompts and revised writings with your partner.
• Which keywords were effective?
• Do you think ChatGPT feedback is helpful? Why or why not?
e.g., ChatGPT chat share

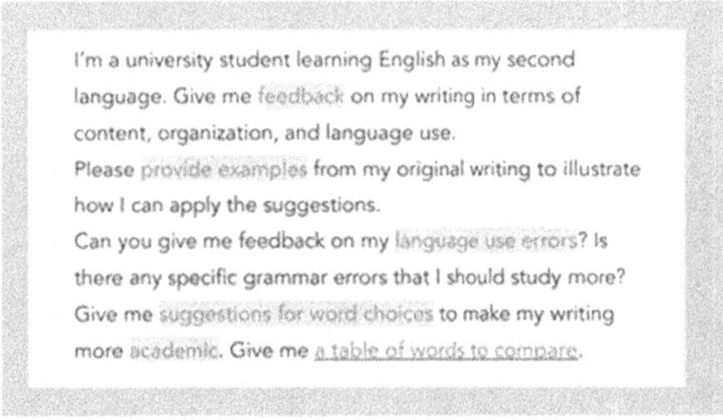
I'm a university student learning English as my second language. Give me feedback on my writing in terms of content, organization, and language use.
Please provide examples from my original writing to illustrate how I can apply the suggestions.
Can you give me feedback on my language use errors? Is there any specific grammar errors that I should study more?
Give me suggestions for word choices to make my writing more academic. Give me a table of words to compare.

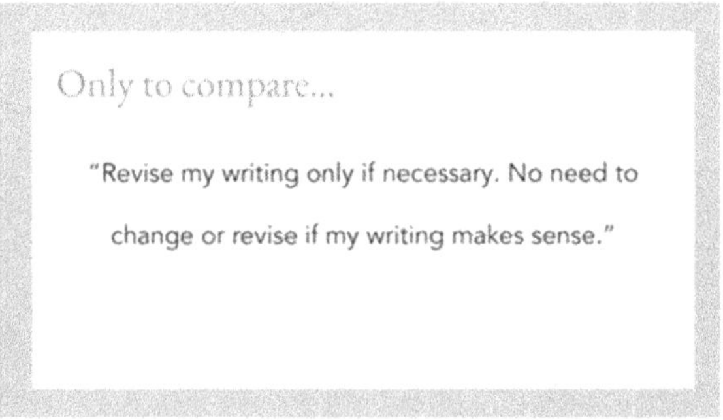
Only to compare...
"Revise my writing only if necessary. No need to change or revise if my writing makes sense."

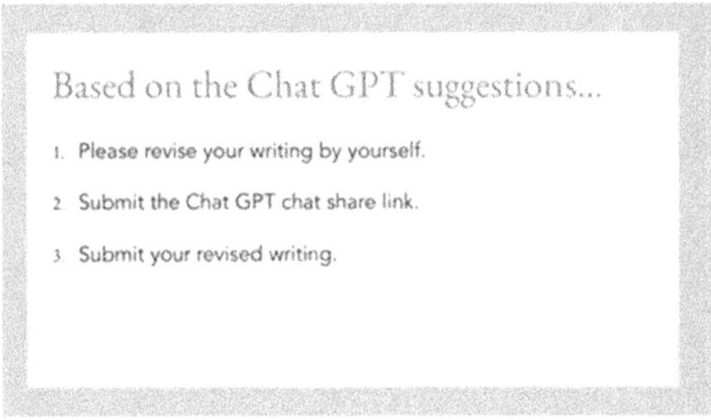
Based on the Chat GPT suggestions...
1. Please revise your writing by yourself.
2. Submit the Chat GPT chat share link.
3. Submit your revised writing.

Post-Workshop Questionnaires

Questions
sohyeon@hawaii.edu

APPENDIX D: Pre-Workshop Questionnaire

1. Name
2. Who is your ELI instructor?
3. What is your native language?

<Background information for writing competency>

1. Do you enjoy writing in English? (You might not be good at it, but you can still enjoy writing in English.) *rating: 1-5 (1=Not really, 5=Yes, I like writing in English.)*
2. Which English skill do you feel most comfortable with? *multiple choice*
    - Listening
    - Speaking
    - Reading
    - Writing
3. How would you rate your level of English writing? *Rating: 1-5 (1=beginner, 5 = advanced)*
4. How much time you typically spend revising a major written assignment? (for example, a final paper for a class) *multiple choice*
    - 30 minutes - 1 hour
    - 1 - 2 hours
    - 3 - 4 hours
    - More than 4 hours
    - Others
5. How confident do you feel about revising your own writing? *Rating: 1-5 (1=Not confident, 5 = Very confident)*
6. What kinds of feedback do you want to receive? What would be helpful for your writing revision process? (Check up to three) *Checkboxes*
    - spelling/grammar correction
    - word choices for natural language use (vocabulary/ expressions)
    - content (ideas)
    - structure (organization)
    - fluency (writing a lot)
    - research and citations
    - clarity and coherence
    - Other

<ChatGPT Usage>

1. Have you used ChatGPT before? *Multiple choice*
    - Yes, the free version.
    - Yes, the premium version (I'm paying monthly fees to use ChatGPT 4.0).
    - No
2. How often do you use ChatGPT for academic writing tasks? *multiple choice*

    - Daily/ Weekly/ Monthly/ Rarely/ Never/ Other
3. For which occasions do you utilize ChatGPT for academic writing tasks? (Check all that apply.) *Checkboxes*
    - Research papers and essays
    - Thesis or dissertation writing
    - Homework assignments
    - Proofreading and editing assistance
    - Generating ideas or brainstorming
    - Citing sources and references
    - Other
4. When using ChatGPT for writing assistance, what type of feedback are you looking for? (Select all that apply) *Checkboxes*
    - Grammar and punctuation corrections
    - Vocabulary suggestions
    - Sentence structure improvements
    - Guidance on organizing ideas
    - Recommendations for improving clarity and coherence
    - Assistance with academic style and tone
    - Help with research and citations
    - Other
5. How confident are you in your ability to use ChatGPT for academic writing? *Rating: 1-5 (1=Not confident, 5 = Very confident)*
6. Using ChatGPT can raise several ethical concerns including plagiarism (students submitting AI-generated content as their own work, etc.). Do you have any concerns about using ChatGPT? *Rating: 1-5 (1=I'm not concerned, 5 = I'm concerned)*
7. How satisfied are you with the feedback and suggestions provided by ChatGPT for your writing? *Rating: 1-5 (1=Not satisfied, 5 = Very satisfied)*
8. Could you please provide a detailed explanation of your satisfaction level with ChatGPT?

APPENDIX E: Post-Workshop Questionnaire

1. Name
2. Who is your ELI instructor?
3. Please copy and paste the chatGPT link of the workshop activities.

<ChatGPT Workshop Feedback>

1. Based on my experience, the level of workshop activities was: *Rating: 1-5 (1=too elementary, 5 = too advanced)*
2. Overall, the quality of the workshop was *multiple choice*
    - Poor/ Fair/ Good/ Outstanding

3. The workshop materials (e.g. visual aids, writing samples, etc.) were: *multiple choice*
   - Poor/ Fair/ Good/ Outstanding
4. Should the content and/or activities for future chatGPT workshops be changed? Please share your comments below.

<Learning to Effectively and Critically Use ChatGPT>

1. As a result of this workshop, my confidence about my English writing has: *Rating: 1-5 (1=not increased at all, 5 = significantly increased)*
2. As a result of this workshop, I can now revise my own writing more effectively based on ChatGPT suggestions and feedback. *Rating: 1-5 (1=strongly disagree, 5 = strongly agree)*
3. As a result of the workshop, I now have a better understanding of ChatGPT's strengths and weaknesses. *(1=strongly disagree, 5 = strongly agree)*
4. As a result of the workshop, I now have a better understanding of how to use ChatGPT critically avoiding ethical issues. *(1=strongly disagree, 5 = strongly agree)*
5. What kind of ChatGPT's feedback was helpful for your own draft revision process? *Checkboxes*
   - spelling/grammar correction
   - word choices for natural language use (vocabulary/ expressions)
   - content (ideas)
   - structure (organization)
   - fluency (writing a lot)
   - research and citations
   - clarity and coherence
   - Other
6. How frequently will you use ChatGPT after this workshop? *Multiple choice*
   - I am not going to use ChatGPT frequently.
   - I will use ChatGPT the same amount as before.
   - I am going to use ChatGPT frequently.
   - Other
7. Please leave any other comments or suggestions you have for future workshops. Mahalo!

Chapter 14
Leveraging AI and Pluralistic Approaches for Language Teaching:
A Focus on Inter-Comprehension Between Related Languages

Lourdes Barquín Sanmartín
https://orcid.org/0000-0001-7892-2177
University College Dublin, Ireland

ABSTRACT

This chapter introduces the pluralistic teaching approach of inter-comprehension utilizing the AI tool ChatGPT. Its objective is to heighten inter-comprehensive awareness among native English speakers studying Spanish and facilitate the comprehension of structurally asymmetrical grammatical phenomena between Romance languages and English. Specifically tailored to the British educational context, where the typical language sequence comprises L1 English, L2 French, and L3 Spanish, this chapter draws support from L3 acquisition literature. Focused on the aspectual contrast perfective/imperfective, less prominent in English compared to Romance languages, the author showcases how to generate parallel contrastive analyses of Spanish/French/English translations through ChatGPT.

INTRODUCTION

This chapter advocates the integration of the Pluralistic Approach of Inter-Comprehension Between Related Languages into language classrooms, leveraging ChatGPT as a facilitative tool. Our primary focus is on assisting teachers instructing Spanish as a third language (L3) in the UK, a linguistic trend increasingly observed among British learners of Foreign Languages (FL). Specifically, we delve into the implementation within Scotland's Pluralistic 1+2 Approach and the incorporation of Spanish as an L3 within the English curriculum. In these contexts, Spanish is introduced as

DOI: 10.4018/979-8-3693-0872-1.ch014

the L3 after English, which acts as a first language (L1), and French, which is taught as a second language (L2). Moreover, the applicability of this model extends beyond the UK, potentially benefiting countries like the US, where English is the L1, Spanish the L2, and French L3 in their FL curricula (Lusin et al., 2023).

The focus of this chapter is to recommend the integration of ChatGPT as a tool to create engaging classroom activities that enhance students' understanding of how languages work together. We focus particularly on tackling challenging grammar concepts that lack direct equivalence or clarity in a student's native language or their previously learned languages. By employing ChatGPT for translation and developing side-by-side comparisons, students can grasp how different languages handle specific grammar rules. This approach nurtures students' ability to recognize similarities and differences between languages, a skill crucial not only for mastering an L3 like Spanish but also for learning additional languages (L*n*).

By comparing complex grammar rules in Spanish and languages students already know, they can identify the most helpful prior language to aid their learning of the new language. In the UK, students commonly know English as their L1 and French as an L2. Since students learn these languages sequentially, our goal is to take advantage of the similarities between French L2 and Spanish L3 to assist English-speaking learners in understanding broader grammatical concepts common to Romance languages. Specifically, we focus on the 'imperfective aspect,' expressed as *imparfait* in French and *imperfecto* in Spanish, a past tense that lacks a morphological equivalent in English, thus requiring English to employ different grammatical structures to convey a similar concept.

This chapter accentuates the pedagogical utilization of ChatGPT, specifically within the British FL education setting, aiming to enhance the comprehension of language as a universal concept. Rather than focusing solely on teaching a single language in isolation, as traditional methods often do, this approach advocates a pluralistic methodology that embraces the incorporation of two or more languages within the classroom. This method embraces the integration of multiple languages in the teaching of the target language, acknowledging language as a universal concept that manifests in diverse forms across different languages. By leveraging ChatGPT for translation, this approach promotes plurilingualism by highlighting shared linguistic patterns across different languages and, thus, promoting a more holistic approach to language acquisition. Teachers can utilize ChatGPT as a translation tool to create reflective in-class tasks. These tasks, employing parallel contrastive analysis across two or three translations, are valuable for introducing or reinforcing new grammatical elements and assessing students' progress.

The application of ChatGPT explored in this chapter primarily focuses on its value from a teacher's standpoint, aiding in planning and resource development through ChatGPT's translation tool. However, beyond its role in teaching, we argue that ChatGPT can also be harnessed for independent and self-directed learning from a student's perspective. As pluralistic approaches, especially the concept of Inter-Comprehension Between Related Languages, remain less widely understood in educational settings, the initial sections of this chapter aim to clarify these approaches and discuss the reasoning behind our interest in adopting this innovative teaching methodology.

TEACHING FOREIGN LANGUAGES IN ENGLAND

Before we expand on how we can leverage ChatGPT to design reflective tasks when introducing new and complex grammatical phenomena in the Spanish classroom, it is essential to provide an overview of the British foreign language teaching and learning landscape and its inclination towards multilingualism. The prevailing FLs in both British secondary schools (Collen, 2020; 2021; 2022; 2023; Tinsley & Board, 2013) and British Higher Education Institutions (Critchley et al., 2021; Critchley et al., 2022) are French, Spanish, and German. However, it is noteworthy that in primary schools, French takes precedence as the primary FL (Figure 1). This tradition dates back to the historical significance of France as a European power in the late 17th century and its role as a *lingua franca*. During that era, FL learners in the UK predominantly studied French, many of whom are now primary school French teachers. Consequently, almost 73% of primary schools offer French, while Spanish accounts for only 28% (Collen, 2023, p.8).

Amidst the general decline of FLs in the British compulsory education setting compared to other subjects (e.g. Sciences, English Language and Literature), the Language Trends surveys from the last few years show a gradual increase in the number of enrollments for Spanish in British secondary education, which aligns with Instituto Cervantes' latest annual report (Instituto Cervantes, 2023), where it is shown that Brexit has led to an increase in the relative importance of Spanish within the EU and has stimulated the demand for its study.

The dominance of French extends into compulsory secondary education in England, making it the FL with the highest number of enrollments in the final exams or GCSE. However, the trend shifts in the two years preceding university education, known as A levels. In 2018, Spanish overtook French for the first time in A-level examinations (Tinsley, 2019, p. 4-5) and has maintained its position as the most popular FL at this educational stage for four consecutive years (Collen, 2023).

Figure 1. Most frequently taught languages in English primary schools (Collen, 2023, p. 8)

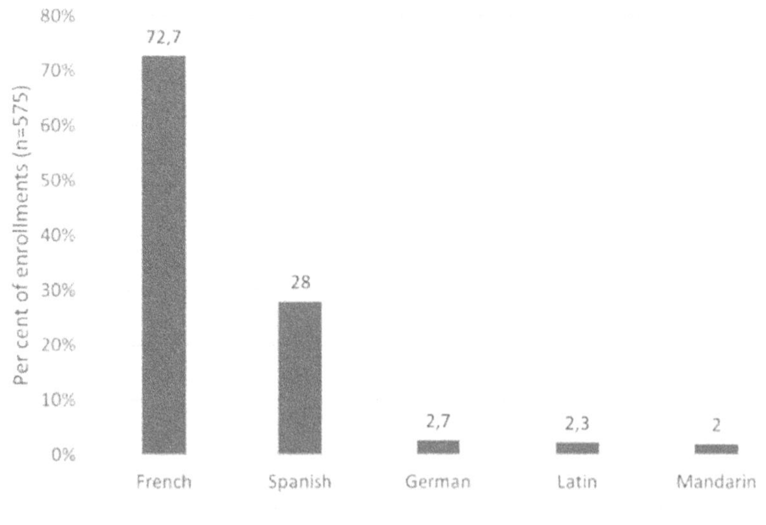

TEACHING FOREIGN LANGUAGES IN SCOTLAND

Scottish primary education mirrors England's sequential order of FLs, with French[1] being the most offered L2, taught in 98% of Scottish primary schools, and Spanish the most popular L3, being taught in 48% of schools that provided a third language (Scottish Government, 2022). This reflects a linguistic paradigm in Scottish primary education where French is introduced first as an L2 (Figure 2), and Spanish is later taught as an L3 (Figure 3).

Figure 2. Number of Scottish primary schools providing an L2 (Scottish Government, 2022)

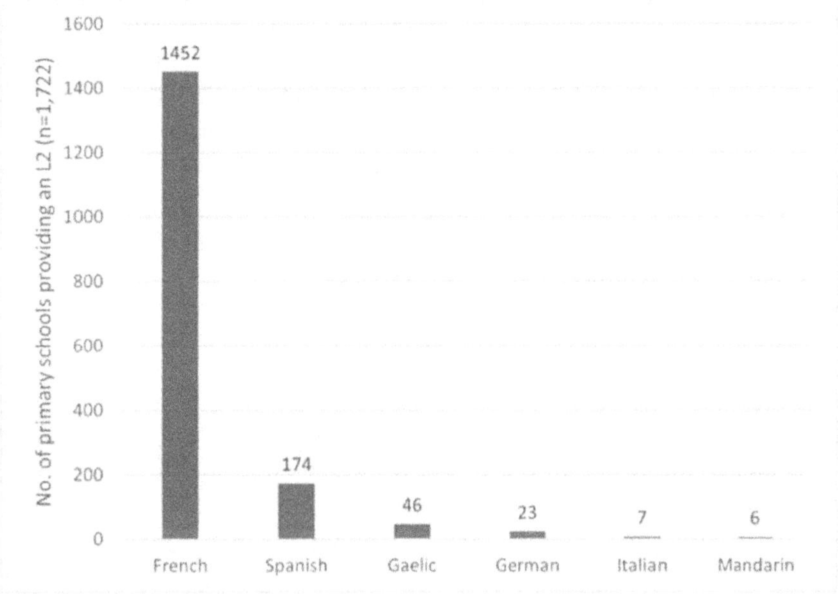

Figure 3. Number of Scottish primary schools providing an L3 (Scottish Government, 2022)

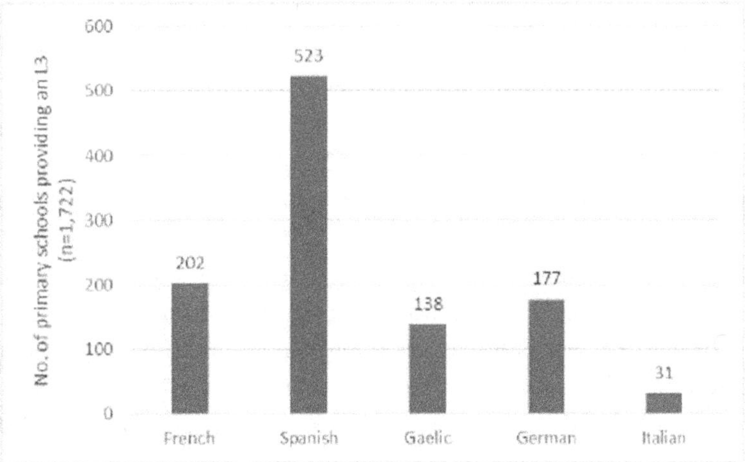

The language policy in Scottish primary education follows a plurilingual approach known as the *1+2 Approach* (Scottish Government, 2016, 2020). This is the only plurilingual language education program in the UK and aligns with the plurilingual initiatives of UNESCO (2003), the *Common European Framework of Reference for Languages* (*CEFR* thereafter) (Council of Europe, 2001, 2021), and the *Framework of Reference for Pluralistic Approaches to Languages and Cultures* (*FREPA* thereafter) (Candelier *et al.,* 2013). This approach reflects the positive and European-oriented attitude of the Scottish population towards language teaching. Notably, the 2016 Scottish Social Attitudes Survey revealed an overwhelming 89% of Scottish respondents advocating for FL acquisition commencing at the age of five, a statistic that serves as a robust indication that the prevailing attitudes toward early FL education remain consistent in 2023 (Scottish Government, 2016).

It is important to note that Scotland's approach is an exception in what has been a predominantly monolingual tradition in the UK. In 2016, the UK had the highest number of monolingual individuals in Europe, with 65.4% of adults not speaking any foreign languages, compared to the European average of 31.8%. Additionally, there was a 30% increase in monolingual individuals from 2007 to 2016, indicating a marginalization of foreign languages in the UK (EUROSTAT, 2016; Kelly, 2018). This chapter challenges the notion that the UK is predominantly monolingual and highlights a growing cohort of plurilingual British students learning French L2 and Spanish L3.

TEACHING FOREIGN LANGUAGES IN THE BRITISH HIGHER EDUCATION SETTING

The most recent Language Provision surveys in British universities reveal a similar language landscape to previous educational cycles. French, Spanish, and German remain the top three languages offered, with French and Spanish being the only ones available in 100% of surveyed institutions (Collen, 2023; Critchley et al., 2021; Critchley et al., 2022; Polisca et al., 2019). French continues to dominate British universities, boasting the highest number of enrollments in undergraduate studies and non-credit language courses. However, Spanish is closely following, and a paradigm shift is expected in the near future (Critchley et al., 2021; Critchley et al., 2022). It is essential to note that British universities annually receive a considerable influx of international students, a significant portion of whom are English as an Additional Language (EAL) speakers. While not all students possess the language profile of French L2 and Spanish L3, a substantial number are engaged in learning Spanish as an L3, with English as their L2. This diverse linguistic blend accentuates the critical need for distinguishing between the methods involved in teaching an L2 versus an L3 and, thus, catering to the distinct cognitive attributes of students engaged in learning more than one FL.

The sections above, which contextualize FL teaching curricula in the UK and advocate for the integration of ChatGPT into our teaching resources, intricately illustrate the evolving trends in plurilingual education within the UK. Notably, the increasing interest in achieving proficiency in multiple languages is not limited to the UK but extends to many European countries. In the current landscape, marked by the widespread normalization of technology and social media use, there arises a need to reassess our perception of FL learners. Rather than viewing them solely as monolingual individuals, it is crucial to recognize them as active participants woven into a vibrant tapestry of diverse cultures and languages. This societal and cultural shift underscores the necessity to move beyond terminology like 'complete beginner' or 'pure monolingual' as well as the conventional portrayal of FL/L2 learners, recognizing the increasing number of individuals embracing an L3 or L*n*.

In our dynamic and ever-evolving linguistic landscape, embracing plurilingualism has become a prominent trend. Translation, as a tool to foster inclusivity and pluralistic language teaching methodologies, assumes a crucial role within this context. By incorporating ChatGPT for translation purposes, students are exposed to multiple languages and empowered to tap into their existing linguistic knowledge bank, drawing from both their native language(s) and previously acquired foreign languages. This comprehensive approach not only widens students' lexical and grammatical understanding but also strengthens their meta- and inter-linguistic awareness, which can significantly enhance the acquisition of an L3 or subsequent L*n*.

INTRODUCTION TO PLURALISTIC APPROACHES

The so-called 'pluralistic approaches' are outlined in the *FREPA* (Candelier *et al.*, 2013), a framework rooted in the *CEFR* (Council of Europe, 2001, 2021), expanding upon it to meet the goal of updating our L2 teaching practices in a society where multiple languages coexist, and where every citizen, albeit at varying levels of competence, possesses knowledge of more than one language and, as a result of an increasingly hyperconnected society, is constantly exposed to other languages and cultures through different forms of media, such as social media or the television.

Every speaker, including our own learners, brings with them a linguistic background, which constitutes a key source of knowledge in L3 learning. Pluralistic approaches emerge in response to the rise of social multilingualism in the European continent and the consequent increase in plurilingual competence among citizens and language learners. This represents a paradigm shift that emphasizes the need to reinforce the 'multilingual competence' and 'multicultural competence' of L2 learners to equip them to effectively navigate the professional, academic, and sociocultural landscape of an increasingly hyperconnected and globalized society (Council of Europe, 2001, 2021). Despite the prevailing monolingual trends in the formal education system of the United Kingdom, the transition to pluralistic approaches is beginning to take shape through educational projects such as the *1+2 Approach* in Scottish primary education (Scottish Government, 2016, 2020). However, this initiative, as of now, stands as the sole indication of interest in pluralistic approaches within the British territory.

INTER-COMPREHENSION BETWEEN RELATED LANGUAGES

The concept of globalization, although present throughout human history, has notably surged in the early 21st century due to increased migration and heightened hyper-connectedness across social, communicative, and technological realms (Quan-Haase and Wellman, 2005). This era has seen English hold a dominant position as a global *lingua franca*; nevertheless, UNESCO (2003, 2021) emphasizes the importance of promoting FL education to support a plurilingual and pluricultural society.

Given our usage of the concept 'plurilingual', it is essential to distinguish between the notions of 'multilingualism' and 'plurilingualism'. The former refers to the coexistence of multiple languages within a specific nation or community, such as Europe being recognized as a multilingual continent. On the other hand, the latter operates at the individual level, extending beyond knowing multiple languages. It requires proactive utilization of one's complete linguistic and extralinguistic repertoire, enhancing communicative competence through the interaction and enrichment of languages, known as 'interlanguage.'

The prevalence of plurilingualism among FL learners has led to the emergence of 'pluralistic approaches' (Candelier et al., 2013; Council of Europe, 2021) to capitalize on these students' previous linguistic knowledge. The psycholinguistic premise that adult learners possess a wealth of life experiences before learning a new language challenges the concept of an absolute initial level or complete beginner, a perspective that encourages students to acknowledge that their language learning journey builds upon existing knowledge and experiences.

This paradigm shift in language acquisition moves away from considering languages as independent entities and instead embraces language as a fundamental principle inherent in all communication (Braunmüller, 2007). By adopting this mindset, learners realize that delving into a new language taps into a wealth of interconnected knowledge sources, as shown in Figure 4. This shift empowers students, reduces intimidation associated with language learning, and enhances their intrinsic motivation to master the language.

Figure 4. Sources of knowledge in foreign language learners

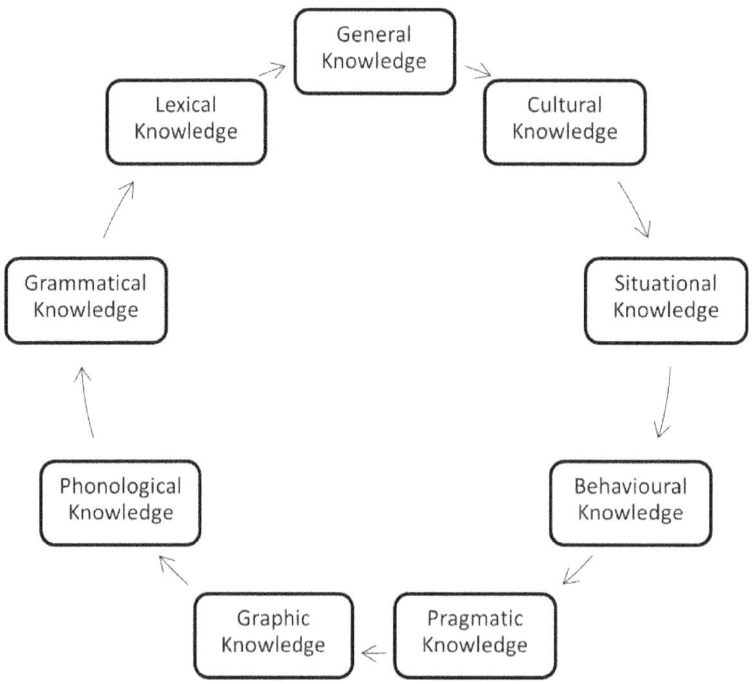

Therefore, it becomes evident that having prior knowledge of the target language, receiving formal instruction, or possessing an advanced level are not essential prerequisites for accessing and engaging with a new language. Rather, the focus is on tapping into the wealth of diverse knowledge and experiences that adult learners bring with them, capitalizing on the interconnected nature of language. This perspective aligns with the idea that learners are not starting from a blank slate but are building on their preexisting cognitive resources.

Collectively, the sources of knowledge shown in Figure 4 constitute our plurilingual competence, continuously available to students as a source of support in the acquisition process of the new foreign language. The Inter-Comprehension approach harnesses this prior knowledge, allowing teachers to guide students in recognizing these sources of knowledge and employing them effectively for comprehending new texts written in different languages. With this approach, students can draw upon their existing knowledge, actively applying it to enhance their proficiency in acquiring a new foreign language. Rather than starting completely anew, they rely on these well-established knowledge bases for support.

This chapter challenges the deficiencies of traditional teaching approaches and underscores the current acquisitive potential and relevance of pluralistic approaches. This chapter focuses on the Inter-Comprehension Between Related Languages, first, because it is an early approach in the UK, relatively unknown among teachers, with minimal presence in FL classrooms, and, thus, in need for wider outreach amongst teachers and researcher; second, because of its immense relevance in the context of FL education in the UK, where the two most offered and demanded FLs are French and Spanish, two Romance languages with high typological proximity and structural symmetry between them.

In order to showcase the potential of inter-comprehension combined with ChatGPT, we narrow its focus to one intricate morphosyntactic phenomenon that frequently presents challenges and pose a notable risk of fossilization for English-speaking learners of Spanish: the aspectual contrast perfective/imperfective. It is important to note that this grammatical feature is morphologically marked in inflectional languages like French and Spanish. In contrast, English, because of its limited use of inflections, relies on different morphosyntactic strategies such as word order or auxiliary verbs to express imperfective aspect.

British learners, typically equipped with French as their second language (L2) and Spanish as their third language (L3), can substantially enhance their approach to learning Spanish L3 by harnessing the positive transfer from their knowledge of French. From an educational perspective, artificial intelligence tools, exemplified by ChatGPT, offer exceptional utility in crafting teaching materials to bolster students' inter-comprehension abilities and exploit positive transfers as a learning tool. One practical approach is the generation of translations of Spanish texts into other Romance languages, whether they geographically coexist with Spanish or not, including languages like Galician, Catalan, Portuguese, French, or Italian, among others.

INTER-COMPREHENSION, NOTICING, LONG-TERM MEMORY, AND CHATGPT

The Noticing Hypothesis in Foreign Language Acquisition, introduced by Schmidt (1994, 2010), serves as a pivotal framework on how language structures assimilate into long-term memory. According to this well-established theory, learners acquire linguistic structures by consciously focusing on features embedded in the input – a cognitive process termed 'noticing.' The deliberate awareness and observation of these linguistic elements are instrumental in their absorption and eventual storage in long-term memory.

In the domain of language learning, ChatGPT's ability to translate into different languages plays a central role in facilitating the principles of the Noticing Hypothesis. Rather than directly engaging in the translation process themselves, learners benefit from ChatGPT's proficiency in generating translations across languages like English, French, and Spanish. Subsequently, students partake in reflective exercises, conducting contrastive and inter-comprehensive analyses among these translations, aimed at noticing, discerning, and comprehending underlying grammatical nuances. We argue that this is particularly beneficial when we are teaching grammar points that do not share structural symmetry with the student's mother tongue; for example, the imperfect tense is not morphologically marked in English, but it is in French and Spanish.

This approach instigates a critical examination of the divergences and convergences present within translations across the languages. By actively scrutinizing and comparing these translations, students immerse themselves in the process of 'noticing' grammatical patterns, syntactical variances, and linguistic intricacies across the linguistic spectrum. This analytical endeavor fosters a comprehensive understanding of grammar, fostering an awareness of the idiosyncrasies inherent in each language's structural makeup and, similarly, the underlying similarities across languages, despite their typological distance.

Guided by ChatGPT-generated translations, learners will actively engage in the process of 'noticing' grammatical subtleties, similarities, and discrepancies. Through observing how various linguistic elements manifest differently across languages, students develop a heightened ability to identify and understand grammatical disparities and resemblances. This not only fortifies students' retention of language structures, but it cultivates critical thinking around grammar and a more autonomous approach towards FL learning.

ASPECTUAL CONTRAST IN ENGLISH, FRENCH, AND SPANISH

To illustrate the practical application of ChatGPT in crafting inter-comprehension tasks, our focus centers on a specific grammatical aspect found in Romance languages like French and Spanish but notably absent in English: the perfective/imperfective aspectual contrast. This pertains to the choice between using the 'imperfect' and 'preterite' tenses in past narratives in Spanish.

This linguistic feature, prevalent in Romance languages, presents considerable challenges for English learners (Andersen, 1991; Hasbún, 1995; Ramsay, 1990; Salaberry, 1997). The complexity stems from French and Spanish expressing grammatical aspect at a morphological level, while English lacks a direct structural equivalent to the Romance imperfect tense. Consequently, English relies on alternative strategies like the Past Continuous (e.g., 'I was eating') and lexical constructions such as 'used to' and 'would' to convey habitual actions and continuity.

For instance, the phrase 'cocinaba un postre' (1) signifies an ongoing action without a specific temporal boundary. In English, this could be expressed using the Past Simple (1a) or the Past Continuous (1b). However, the Past Simple may lead to aspectual ambiguity by not conveying dynamism or duration. To compensate for this inflectional gap, English employs the progressive '-ing' form to impart the imperfective aspect (1b). Therefore, English effectively portrays aspectual differences through both the Past Simple and the Past Continuous, with the latter constructed using the 'be + -ing' periphrastic form (Declerck, 2006).

(1) Lucía cocinaba un postre
    a. *Lucía cooked a dessert*
    b. *Lucía was cooking a dessert*

As a general rule, the Spanish periphrastic 'estar + gerundio' cannot be considered equivalent to the imperfect tense since the latter encompasses a broader range of aspectual notions compared to the periphrastic form. The periphrasis specifically highlights actions (not states) in progress that align at a certain point (or interval) with the reference event (2b). Furthermore, the periphrasis emphasizes the internal dynamism of the event.

(2) a. *Raquel preparaba la comida cuando su hija llegó a casa.*
    b. *Raquel estaba preparando la comida cuando su hija llegó a casa.*

The distinction between the indefinite/imperfect contrast in Romance languages stands in contrast to English, which strictly relies on the progressive/non-progressive contrast (Montrul & Slabakova, 2003). This differentiation traces its origins back to the concept of 'co-preterite' (Bello, 1847), denoting an imperfect tense coexisting with another past event. For instance, in the context of example (3), the rain persisted for a delimited duration (i.e. hence the closed endpoints in the illustration) concurrent with the arrival, which acts as a temporal reference point. However, it remains unclear whether the rain was ongoing before the perfective event or if it continued after its culmination. This concurrent existence is articulated in English through the utilization of the Past Continuous (3), conveying simultaneity with the referenced event.

English lacks an equivalent past tense akin to the imperfect, prompting an approach through a temporal lens (Bello, 1847; Rojo, 1990) where the Past Simple, much like the *indefinido* tense, functions as the default perfective form. To differentiate Past Simple instances whose interpretation is not purely perfective, the perfective aspect can be regarded as a functional category [±perfective] (Giorgi & Pianesi, 1997).

In English, the value [-perfective] holds little relevance as the value [+perfective] is universally associated with all non-stative predicates. Conversely, in Romance languages, the perfective value may align with both [-perfective] and [+perfective] values due to the indefinite/imperfect contrast (Montrul & Slabakova, 2003). This [±perfective] system aims to enlighten native English speakers that certain past tense verbs do not consistently adhere to the [-perfective] value, a factor often leading to ambiguity in stative predicates.

The Past Simple in English is typically seen as conclusive. However, to convey the aspectual nuances akin to the imperfect tense, one must resort to using the Past Continuous. Unlike Spanish, stative predicates expressed in the Past Simple within English remain neutral in terms of aspect, disregarding the telicity of the predicate. Consequently, they can be understood either as prolonged states over time (imperfective value) or as specific, delimited events (perfective value).

This lack of alignment between Spanish and English creates confusion among learners of Spanish as a foreign language. For instance, in example (4), the state could be interpreted as 'John [was/was being] sick,' showcasing an aspectual difference not accounted for in English, as illustrated in Table 1.

Table 1. Examples of lexical aspect (Andersen & Shirai, 1994)

Examples	Interpretation	Lexical Aspect
(4) *Jonh was ill*	It is not known if John is still sick	State
(3) *John cleaned all evening*	John has finished cleaning already	Activity
(4) *John cooked dinner*	John has already finished making dinner	Accomplishments
(5) *John arrived home*	John has already arrived home	Achievements

Despite the differences between English and Spanish, there are some values of the preterite and imperfect tenses that can be considered equivalent to the Past Simple and Past Continuous, respectively. In perfective predicates, the Past Simple and the preterite express punctual events that have ended (6), and in imperfective predicates, the Past Continuous and the imperfect tense can also express past events that were in progress (7).

(6) *María llegó tarde al trabajo*
María arrived late to work

(7) *Cuando mama llegó a casa, veía la tele*
When mum arrived home, I was watching telly

Stative predicates are not compatible with the progressive form in English (8), thus constituting cases of interlinguistic inequivalence between English and Spanish. Although states in gerunds are not prototypical combinations in English, there are special uses where English speakers deliberately choose the -ing form to lend dynamism and temporality to the verb. In example (9), this strategy allows the speaker to distinguish between the fact that Mary's behavior was not appropriate in a past and transitory moment (9a) and another where the event becomes a property of Mary's personality (9b).

(8) *Había estudiantes en clase*
    *There were being students in class
(9) a. Mary was being rude and I grounded her
    b. Mary was rude and I grounded her

English relies on grammatical structures to compensate for its limitations in expressing aspectual nuances. In the context of the habitual imperfect, English utilizes various forms such as the Past Simple (10), the Past Continuous (11), the structure 'used to' (12), or its analogous form 'would' (13) (Cholij, 1994, p.87). The periphrastic constructions (12) and (13) serve to emphasize the habitual nature of the event and serve as equivalents to expressing actions or routines in the past, resembling 'used to' or 'would' followed by the infinitive (Kattan-Ibarra & Pountain, 2004)

(10) *Mi marido hacía la cena todos los días*
     My husband cooked dinner every day
(11) *María preparaba la cena cuando llegué*
     María was cooking dinner when I arrived.
(12) *El año pasado iba al gimnasio dos veces por semana*
     Last year I used to go to the gym twice a week.
(13) *Mamá se enfadaba si no hacíamos los deberes*
     Mum would get angry if we did not do our homework.

The absence of structural equivalence at a linguistic level among the three main languages in terms of aspectual contrast presents a significant opportunity for the incorporation of reflective tasks. These tasks primarily emphasize conscious attention to input, supported by parallel contrastive analyses among the three languages. By simultaneously presenting the same text in the past in these languages and highlighting their differences and similarities, it aims to train and enhance the learner's interlinguistic awareness and metalinguistic knowledge. This approach fosters the learner's metalinguistic consciousness about language as a universal concept and, more specifically, cultivates interlinguistic awareness regarding the internal dynamics of the Romance languages under study.

We believe it is both crucial and pressing to focus on the development of interlinguistic awareness, particularly among English-speaking learners. Oftentimes, due to a higher cultural interest in literature and the relatively straightforward linguistic and grammatical nature of the English language, these learners may not delve into deeper grammar or more terminological aspects while studying their native language in compulsory education. In the United Kingdom, the English Language and Literature curriculum in secondary schools mainly prioritizes oral and written comprehension and production skills. Consequently, students seldom have the chance to explore the morphosyntactic structure of their native language, resulting in a lack of a fundamental metalinguistic framework that would facilitate their engagement with subsequent languages.

To illustrate, we initially offer a concise overview of the English subject in the national curriculum for Key Stage 3 (11-12 years) and Key Stage 4 (13-15 years) in England. Subsequently, we present an excerpt from the National 3 curriculum (13-14 years) in Scotland, delineating the objectives of the English subject.

A high-quality education in English will teach pupils to speak and write fluently so that they can communicate their ideas and emotions to others and through their reading and listening, others can communicate with them. Through reading in particular, pupils have a chance to develop culturally, emotionally, intellectually, socially and spiritually. Literature, especially, plays a key role in such development. Reading also enables pupils both to acquire knowledge and to build on what they already know. (Department for Education, 2014, p.13)

The [English] Course offers learners opportunities to develop and extend a wide range of skills. In particular, the Course aims to enable learners to develop the ability to: (a) listen, talk, read and write, as appropriate to purpose, audience and context (b) understand, analyse and evaluate texts, as appropriate to purpose and audience in the contexts of literature, language and media (c) create and produce texts, as appropriate to purpose, audience and context (d) apply knowledge of language. (Scottish Qualifications Authority, 2014)

A well-developed awareness of linguistic and interlinguistic aspects, coupled with the strategic utilization of technological tools like ChatGPT, empowers students to become autonomous and independent learners. This proficiency enables them to autonomously identify both symmetrical and asymmetrical areas, particularly evident among British students, between French and Spanish. By leveraging ChatGPT's capabilities in providing translations and comparative analyses, learners can effectively enhance their learning process through conscious and deliberate utilization of positive transfer while simultaneously preventing or anticipating negative transfers.

This pluralistic philosophy transcends conventional didactic approaches. It perceives the learning of foreign languages as an ongoing and lifelong evolutionary continuum, further facilitated by innovative tools such as ChatGPT. Here, acquired skills are not confined solely to a single foreign language but are instead transferable across all known and future encountered foreign languages. This perspective emphasizes the continual growth and applicability of language skills throughout an individual's lifetime, with ChatGPT serving as a facilitator in fostering this multilingual and transferable proficiency.

DESIGNING INTER-COMPREHENSIVE RESOURCES WITH CHATGPT

This chapter proposes the use of ChatGPT as a translation tool to present new and complex grammatical phenomena, specifically those aspects that are not marked in the students' mother tongues. As an example of unmarked phenomenon in English but marked in Romance languages, we focus on the aspectual contrast perfective/imperfective as this is known to generate great difficulty when it comes to teaching it in class and, from a students' perspective, to understand it. Thus, this grammatical area lead often leads to fossilization of misconceptions and error due to lack of a proper comprehension of 'aspect'. The proposal is addressed at intermediate and upper-intermediate level Spanish classes ranging from A2-B2 (Council of Europe, 2001, 2021), where the past tenses are introduced.

This proposal does not present the results of an actual case study where ChatGPT has been used in a Spanish class. Rather, it proposes the potential benefits of using ChatGPT to promote plurilingualism and, thus, this proposal encourages further investigation. This idea endorses the inductive teaching approach, which initiates learning with specific examples or observations, guiding students to derive general conclusions or principles. Rather than relying solely on established theories or rules presented in textbooks that predominantly emphasize the target language and exclude references to other languages, this method encourages active learning from a pluralistic lens. The inductive nature of this proposal promotes observation, reflection, and pair discussions on how grammar works in the target language (i.e. Spanish) and recognizes similarities and differences with other languages students already know (i.e. English and French).

We utilize ChatGPT to generate translations in twos or threes for pedagogic purposes. These translations are then converted into well-designed and accessible reflective tasks to be explored conceptually in a classroom setting, with the support and guidance of the teacher. Given the high levels of difficulty encountered in teaching and learning the aspectual aspect in Romance languages, using contrastive analysis of translations and identifying differences and similarities across them can promote the 'noticing' of grammar in different languages.

From a learning perspective, translation can significantly enhance the 'noticing' process of the forms (i.e. grammar) and, adopting a pluralistic approach, can help increase students' interlinguistic awareness by highlighting differences and similarities between languages. ChatGPT serves as a key tool in designing in-class reflective tasks that encourage engagement and active learning and contributes to saving time in designing teaching resources. Nevertheless, the use of ChatGPT for translation purposes comes with its own challenges; notably having basic knowledge of all three languages involved before carefully proofreading all three translations.

Aside from its role in generating teaching materials, ChatGPT can serve as a valuable learning tool for students to independently review and practice Spanish at their own pace. Through incorporating reflective tasks prompted by ChatGPT within the classroom setting, we can showcase its capabilities and inspire students to autonomously explore using ChatGPT for their personal revision. This initiative has the potential to significantly enrich their language-learning journey by encouraging independent exploration and engagement with ChatGPT for Spanish revision.

To efficiently execute a reflective task using ChatGPT, we can use two stages. In Stage 1, it is crucial to formulate a prompt that encompasses all relevant contextual details. This includes the storyline, language requirements, desired level of difficulty, the linguistic profile of the students, and the specific grammar structures intended to be present in the text. Crafting a prompt of this nature ensures that the vocabulary and grammatical constructions used are comprehensible and suitable for the students' competency level.

Stage 1. *Please write an adapted version of the Beauty and the Beast in the past in Spanish. The level of difficulty must be addressed at a B1 Spanish class of native English speakers who are working towards a B2 by the Common European Framework of Reference. Make sure you include the three main preterites in Spanish: the pretérito indefinido, imperfecto and pluscuamperfecto.*

Following Stage 1, we proceed to Stage 2 where we utilize the Spanish version as a foundational reference for generating translations into English and French. It is imperative within the prompt to explicitly clarify that, despite their morphological differences, the '*passé composé*' in French and the '*pretérito indefinido*' in Spanish exhibit resemblances in their temporal and aspectual functions. While the archaic 'passé simple' in French has become obsolete, the '*passé composé*' stands as the predominant form for articulating past events in spoken French, primarily conveying perfectivity. Despite these disparities, we regard both tenses as equivalent given that they both serve the purpose of recounting past actions.

Stage 2. *Now, please translate this story into English and French. Use a table with three columns, one per language. Also, please highlight in bold all cases where you use verbs in the past, including indefinido, imperfecto and pluscuamperfecto. In English, you will have to look out for all Past Tenses. In French, you will have to highlight the imparfait (equivalent to Spanish imperfecto) and passé composé. Please treat the passé composé as the equivalent value to Spanish indefinido.*

Following Stage 2, upon receiving the three versions of the story (Spanish, French, and English) from ChatGPT, we can devise a reflective task that employs a square-coded system with (dis)continuous border lines (Table 2). This system aims to facilitate the identification and comparison of discrepancies and similarities across these languages. Utilizing a contrastive analysis between the Spanish *imperfecto* and the French *imparfait*, both depicted in continuous lines, we can uncover their structural symmetry (Westergaard, Mitrofanova, Mykhaylyk & Rodina, 2017), wherein the imperfective is used in precisely the same narrative positions in both Romance languages (Bardovi-Harlig, 1998, 2000).

Table 2. Parallel contrastive analysis of English/French/Spanish translations

Spanish Imperfecto Indefinido	**French** Imparfait Passé Composé	**English** **Past Simple**
Había una vez una joven llamada Bella a la que le gustaba mucho leer. Pasaba su tiempo libre devorando libro tras libro pues esta era su pasión. Era muy guapa y todas las chicas del pueblo querían ser como ella.	Il était une fois une jeune fille nommée Bella qui aimait beaucoup lire. Elle passait son temps libre à dévorer livre après livre car c'était sa passion. Elle était très belle, et toutes les filles du village voulaient lui ressembler.	Once upon a time, **there was** a young woman named Bella who **loved** reading very much. She **spent** her free time devouring book after book as this was her passion. She **was** very beautiful, and all the girls in the village **wanted** to be like her.
Un día, de repente, el padre de Bella se perdió en el bosque y se encontró con un castillo que no conocía. Como hacía mucho frío en la intemperie, decidió entrar. Llamó a la puerta varias veces, pero nadie contestaba. Como parecía que no había nadie, entró para buscar cobijo.	Un jour, soudainement, le père de Bella s'est perdu dans les bois et a découvert un château qu'il ne reconnaissait pas. Comme il faisait très froid dehors, il a décidé d'entrer. Il a frappé à la porte plusieurs fois, mais personne ne répondait. Comme il semblait qu'il n'y avait personne, il est entré pour chercher un abri.	One day, suddenly, Bella's father **got** lost in the woods and **stumbled** upon a castle he **didn't recognize**. Since it **was** very cold outside, he **decided** to enter. He **knocked** on the door several times, but nobody **answered**. As it **seemed** that **there was** nobody, he **entered** to seek shelter.

Furthermore, this comparative exercise allows students to observe that English (third column in Table 2) lacks morphological marking for the imperfect value, as the Past Simple tense encompasses both imperfective and perfective values (Giorgi & Pianesi, 1997). Through this parallel contrastive analysis, learners gain insights into the nuanced differences in how these three languages express past events, providing a deeper understanding of their structural and functional variations.

CHALLENGES AND PROPOSED SOLUTIONS

Challenge 1: Diverse Language Backgrounds

The most apparent challenge in this task proposal is assuming that all Spanish students possess prior knowledge of French. While our primary focus revolves around a growing cohort of British students proficient in French as a second language (L2) and Spanish as a third language (L3), it is crucial to recognize the diverse linguistic backgrounds within the class. Essentially, not all students may have a foundation in a Romance language.

This diversity extends to international students, many of whom are speakers of English as an Additional Language (EAL) and may not have a prior knowledge in a Romance language. Acknowledging the diversity of students enrolled in the British higher education is essential as the UK is the third country in the world to receive the most international students in the university context, following behind the United States and Australia (UNESCO, 2021).

Recognizing the widespread adoption of English as a global lingua franca among students worldwide, irrespective of their primary language (L1) or the foreign language (FL) they are studying, it remains within the teacher's discretion to opt out of including French in our comparative analysis. This stands as a choice best left to the teacher's discretion, given their familiarity with the diverse linguistic backgrounds of their students. Consequently, based on this nuanced understanding, the teacher maintains the authority to decide which language(s) can be incorporated into the contrastive analysis task during its design.

This discretion becomes particularly pertinent in scenarios where a teacher has a small group of Erasmus or international students in the class, possessing distinct linguistic backgrounds from the majority of the class. Such instances highlight the importance of tailoring teaching resources to suit the specific needs arising from varying language profiles within the classroom. By accommodating these differences, teachers can effectively cater to diverse student needs, ensuring an inclusive and adaptable learning environment.

While this approach represents a modified interpretation of the concept of 'inter-comprehension between related languages,' focusing solely on English and Spanish remains notably advantageous in both educational and language acquisition contexts, despite the considerable differences between these languages. In any classroom where a language is already in use as a primary means of instruction, there naturally emerges a level of mutual understanding between languages.

The key benefit of prioritizing a comparative study of English and Spanish lies in its inclusivity, catering to a diverse range of students without singling out specific language backgrounds. This inclusive approach cultivates an environment conducive to the comprehension of essential aspects of the target language, accommodating both native English speakers and those for whom English is an additional language (EAL).

This process unfolds through a reflective comparison between English and Spanish, fostering students' heightened awareness of linguistic disparities between the two languages. For instance, students can discern that English lacks a direct counterpart to the Spanish *imperfecto* verb tense, prompting them to delve into how English employs grammar rules to express similar concepts. This exploration can significantly deepen their comprehension of language structures across diverse linguistic systems, amplifying their capacity to understand and interpret languages. Moreover, this understanding builds upon their existing knowledge, empowering them to enhance their multilingual abilities, a proficiency that not only aids in their autonomous learning but also serves as a pivotal asset when acquiring future additional languages.

Challenge 2: Teacher Proofreading

In addressing the challenge of ensuring accurate translations produced by AI tools like ChatGPT, particularly with complex grammatical structures or idiomatic expressions, human oversight becomes essential. Teachers can encourage students to critically evaluate translations, pinpoint possible errors, or inconsistencies, and participate in discussions to understand why certain translations might deviate from expected outcomes. This collaborative method fosters a deeper grasp of linguistic subtleties and emphasizes the importance of human judgment alongside AI-generated outputs.

When integrating AI-driven language tools such as ChatGPT within educational contexts, it is imperative to acknowledge that teachers may not possess proficiency in all languages encompassed by these tools. Despite this limitation in comprehensive fluency, teachers frequently utilize these technologies to aid language learning. While teachers may lack extensive knowledge of the specific languages processed by AI tools, their role remains pivotal in guiding the learning process. They validate AI-generated content, initiate discussions on linguistic intricacies, and create an environment conducive to critical analysis among students regarding translation accuracy and linguistic frameworks.

Undetected errors in translations, despite thorough teacher review, offer valuable learning opportunities. Students actively engage with tasks and often discover these errors during reflection. Rather than being viewed negatively, these mistakes encourage deeper contemplation, observation, and discussion.

Contrary to tasks solely focused on correcting grammar, identifying errors in AI-generated translations prompts students to explore language intricacies. This process promotes critical thinking, analysis, and a richer understanding of grammar principles. Moreover, these errors stimulate discussions exploring language variations and contextual nuances, thereby enriching the learning experience beyond mere error correction. Ultimately, this approach fosters a more comprehensive grasp of linguistic complexities.

Within this framework, the primary responsibility of the teacher is twofold: to facilitate proficient use of AI-based language tools by students and to cultivate an environment encouraging comprehensive linguistic analysis. This approach goes beyond reliance solely on the teacher's language proficiency and grammar precision.

Challenge 3: Sociolinguistic Variations in Spanish

The vast array of language variations and dialects within Spanish poses a significant challenge. Spanish encompasses numerous regional and cultural variations, from idiomatic expressions to dialectal differences, which ChatGPT might not accurately capture, potentially causing confusion among students striving for a comprehensive understanding of the language's richness and diversity. These challenges underline the need for promoting awareness on the different dialects and variants of Spanish and, regardless of which one is being used in the translation, use supplementary human proofreading to ensure consistency using the same variant.

In our pursuit of a more inclusive approach to encompass diverse Spanish variants and contribute to curriculum decolonization, we can expand beyond ChatGPT's conventional use for translations and leverage ChatGPT's potential to 'translate' or adapt one Spanish variant into different ones (Table 3). This application of ChatGPT also serves as a powerful educational tool to highlight sociolinguistic phenomena and generate different Spanish variants of one same text. As shown in Stages 1-3 below, a contrastive analysis of Peninsular and Latin American Spanish can show students that the Spanish *pretérito indefinido* (Past Simple in English) and *pretérito perfecto compuesto* (Present Perfect in English) can be interchangeable in some cases.

Stage 1. *It's 5pm right now, but Julio is describing to me his morning routine earlier today. Julio is Spanish, so he prioritizes the pretérito perfecto compuesto (i.e. Present Perfect). Use vocabulary and grammar suitable for a B1 level (CEFR). Julio is the speaker, so write it in first-person singular and ensure it comprises at least 100 words. Write it in the past.*
Stage 2. *Now rewrite it in Mexican Spanish, prioritizing the pretérito indefinido (i.e Past Simple).*
Stage 3. *Now translate it into English*

Table 3. Parallel contrastive analysis of English/French/Spanish translations

Peninsular Spanish Pret. Perfecto Compuesto	**Mexican Spanish** Pret. Indefinido	**English** Past Simple
¡Hola! Esta mañana he tenido una rutina bastante ocupada. Me he levantado a las siete de la mañana. Primero, me he lavado la cara y me he cepillado los dientes. Luego, he desayunado con un café y unas tostadas. Después de eso, he ido al gimnasio y he hecho ejercicio durante una hora. Ha sido muy bueno para empezar el día con energía. Más tarde, he vuelto a casa y he tomado una ducha refrescante. Después, he repasado mis correos electrónicos y he hecho algunas llamadas importantes para el trabajo. A mediodía, he almorzado una ensalada con pollo.	¡Hola! Esta mañana tuve una rutina bastante ocupada. Me levanté a las siete de la mañana. Primero, me lavé la cara y me cepillé los dientes. Después, desayuné con un café y unas tostadas. Luego, fui al gimnasio e hice ejercicio durante una hora. Fue muy bueno para empezar el día con energía. Más tarde, volví a casa y me tomé una ducha refrescante. Después, repasé mis correos electrónicos e hice algunas llamadas importantes para el trabajo. Al mediodía, almorcé una ensalada con pollo.	Hello! This morning, I had a pretty busy routine. I woke up at seven in the morning. First, I washed my face and brushed my teeth. Then, I had breakfast with a coffee and some toast. After that, I went to the gym and worked out for an hour. It was really good to start the day with energy. Later, I came back home and took a refreshing shower. Afterwards, I checked my emails and made some important work calls. At noon, I had a salad with chicken.

The comparative approach in Table 3 highlights the similarities between English (i.e. Past Simple) and Mexican Spanish (i.e. Pretérito Indefinido) in the choice of the past tenses, where in both cases the aoristic value is prioritized. In this example, however, Peninsular Spanish employs the hodiernal past (i.e. Perfecto Compuesto) as the event took place earlier on the same day and the speaker wants to convey proximal relation to the moment of enunciation. In addition to a heightened inter-comprehensive awareness, this comparative analysis also nurtures an awareness of regional grammatical distinctions and the intricate linguistic diversity present within the Spanish language. By acknowledging and appreciating these diverse linguistic practices, students gain a more holistic view of the language's adaptability and evolution across different cultural settings, providing them with a more profound and multifaceted understanding of Spanish at a linguistic level.

These educational endeavors not only elevate students' linguistic competencies but also instill values of cultural empathy and awareness. They prompt students to acknowledge, honor, and value the multifaceted ways in which Spanish is utilized across various communities and regions, facilitating a profound comprehension of sociolinguistic dynamics inherent within the language.

CONCLUSION

As highlighted in this chapter, the integration of translation within a pedagogical framework, coupled with reflective practices such as self-reflection and classroom discussions, serves as a powerful avenue for enhancing students' meta- and inter-linguistic awareness. This heightened awareness plays a pivotal role in cultivating more autonomous learners, equipped to transfer these skills to grasp additional languages in the future. This emphasis on awareness proves particularly crucial for British learners, whose educational emphasis typically leans toward literature rather than comprehensive grammar exploration within the English Language and Literature curriculum.

In the realm of plurilingualism, utilizing ChatGPT for pedagogical translation stands out as a crucial strategy to cater to the diverse linguistic backgrounds prevalent in classrooms, particularly among overseas and Erasmus students, many of whom are proficient in English as an Additional Language. The efficiency of ChatGPT in saving time, alongside its effectiveness in customizing our resources and adapting contrastive analysis tasks to cater to various language combinations within the classroom, highlights its significance in cultivating a more inclusive learning environment.

Nonetheless, the role of ChatGPT transcends mere translation facilitation; its integration stands as a pivotal cornerstone in strengthening pluralistic approaches within conventional teaching methodologies. With heightened tourism, migration, and exposure to diverse languages via digital media, incorporating supplementary languages into the classroom alongside the primary target language cultivates a more enriched and holistic learning environment. This approach not only heightens linguistic awareness but also facilitates the acquisition of further languages in the future.

In essence, the utilization of pedagogical translation, augmented by ChatGPT's capabilities in translation, not only addresses the pressing need to enhance linguistic awareness but also champions inclusivity and pluralism within educational settings. Embracing this multifaceted approach acknowledges and leverages the richness of linguistic diversity, ultimately enhancing the learning experience and proficiency of students in a rapidly globalizing world.

REFERENCES

Andersen, R. (1991). Developmental sequences: The emergence of aspect marking in second language acquisition. In T. Huebner & C. A. Ferguson (Eds.), *Crosscurrents in second language acquisition and linguistic theories* (pp. 305–324). John Benjamins Publishing Company. doi:10.1075/lald.2.17and

Andersen, R., & Shirai, Y. (1994). Discourse motivations for some cognitive acquisition principles. *Studies in Second Language Acquisition*, *16*(2), 133–156. doi:10.1017/S0272263100012845

Bardovi-Harlig, K. (1998). Examining the role of text type in L2 tense-aspect research: Broadening our horizons. En P. Robinson y N. Jungheim (Eds.), Representation and process: Proceedings of the 3rd Pacific Second Language Research Forum (pp. 139–150). Tokyo: Pacific SLRF.

Bardovi-Harlig, K. (2000). *Tense and aspect in second language acquisition: Form, meaning, and use*. Blackwell., doi:10.1111/0023-8333.50.s1.7

Bello, A. (1847). *Gramática de la lengua castellana destinada al uso de los americanos*. Edición digital a partir de obras completas. Tomo Cuarto, 3ªed., Caracas, La Casa de Bello.

Braunmüller, K. (2007). Receptive multilingualism in northern Europe in the Middle Ages. In J. D. ten Thije & L. Zeevaert (Eds.), *Receptive multilingualism. Linguistic analyses, language policies and didactic concepts* (pp. 25–47). John Benjamins.

Candelier, M. (2013). *Janua linguarum – The gateway to languages – The introduction of language awareness into the curriculum: Awakening to languages*. Council of Europe.

Candelier, M., Daryai-Hansen, P., & Schröder-Sura, A. (2013). The framework of reference for pluralistic approaches to languages and cultures–a complement to the CEFR to develop plurilingual and intercultural competences. *Innovation in Language Learning and Teaching*, *6*(3), 243–257. doi:10.1080/17501229.2012.725252

Cholij, M. (1994). *Practice in Spanish Grammar*. Mary Glasgow Publications.

Collen, I. (2020). *Language Trends 2020. Language Teaching in primary and secondary schools in England*. British Council.

Collen, I. (2021). *Language Trends 2021. Language Teaching in primary and secondary schools in England*. British Council.

Collen, I. (2022). *Language Trends 2022. Language Teaching in primary and secondary schools in England*. British Council.

Collen, I. (2023). *Language Trends Northern Ireland 2023: Language teaching in Primary and Post-Primary Schools*. British Council.

Council of Europe. (2001). *Common European Framework of Reference for Languages: Learning, Teaching, Assessment*. Cambridge University Press.

Council of Europe. (2021). *Common European Framework of Reference for Languages: Learning, Teaching, Assessment—Companion Volume*. Council of Europe Publishing.

Critchley, M., Chaurin, T., & De Madeiros, A. (2022). *Survey of Language Provision in UK Universities in 2022*. Report no. 4, diciembre. University Council of Modern Languages (UCML), Association for University Language Communities in the UK and Ireland (AULC), United Kingdom.

Critchley, M., Illingworth, J., & Wright, V. (2021). *Survey of Language Provision in UK Universities in 2021*. Report no. 3, julio. University Council of Modern Languages (UCML), Association for University Language Communities in the UK and Ireland (AULC), United Kingdom.

Declerck, R. (2006). The grammar of the English verb phrase.: Vol. 1. *The grammar of the English tense system. A comprehensive analysis*. De Gruyter. doi:10.1515/9783110199888

Department for Education. (2014). *The national curriculum in England. Key stages 3 and 4 framework document* [DFE-00183-2013]. Retrieved from: https://assets.publishing.service.gov.uk/government/uploads/system/uploads/attachment_data/file/840002/Secondary_national_curriculum_corrected_PDF.pdf

EUROSTAT. (2016). *Number of foreign languages known (self-reported) by sex* [edat_aes_l21] Retrieved from: https://appsso.eurostat.ec.europa.eu/nui/submitViewTableAction.do

EUROSTAT. (2022). *Pupils by education level and number of modern foreign languages studied - absolute numbers and % of pupils by number of languages studied* [EDUC_UOE_LANG02] Retrieved from: https://ec.europa.eu/eurostat/databrowser/view/educ_uoe_lang02/default/table?lang=en

Giorgi, A., & Pianesi, F. (1997). *Tense and aspect: from semantics to morphosyntax*. Oxford University Press. doi:10.1093/oso/9780195091922.001.0001

Hasbún, L. (1995). *The role of lexical aspect in the acquisition of the tense/aspct system in L2 Spanish* [Doctoral dissertation]. Indiana University, Bloomington.

Instituto Cervantes. (2023). *El español en el mundo 2023*. Anuario del Instituto Cervantes.

Kattan-Ibarra, J., & Pountain, C. (2004). *Modern Spanish Grammar: A Practical Guide*. Taylor and Francis. doi:10.4324/9780203428313

Kelly, M. (Ed.). (2018). *Languages after Brexit: How the UK speaks to the world*. Springer International Publishing.

Lusin, N., Peterson, T., Sulewski, C., & Zafer, R. (2023). Enrollments in languages other than English in US institutions of higher education: Fall 2021. Modern Language Association of America. Retrieved from: https://www.mla.org/content/download/191324/file/Enrollments-in-Languages-Other-Than-English-in-US-Institutions-of-Higher-Education-Fall-2021.pdf

Montrul, S., and Slabakova, R. (2003). Competence similarities between Native and Near-Native speakers: An investigation of the Preterit/Imperfect contrast in Spanish. *Studies in Second Language Acquisition, 25*, 351–398. doi:10.1017/S0272263103000159

Polisca, E., Wright, V., Álvarez, I., & Montoro, C. (2019). *Language Provision in UK Modern Foreign Languages Departments 2019 Survey*. University Council of Modern Languages.

Quan-Haase, A., & Wellman, B. (2005). How computer-mediated hyperconnectivity and local virtuality foster social networks of information and coordination in a community of practice. *International Sunbelt Social Network Conference*. 10.1111/1468-2427.00309

Ramsay, V. (1990). *Developmental stages in the acquisition of the perfective and the imperfective aspects by classroom L2 learners of Spanish* [Tesis doctoral]. University of Oregon, Eugene.

Rojo, G. (1990). *Relaciones entre temporalidad y aspecto en el verbo español. Tiempo y aspecto en español*. Cátedra.

Salaberry, M. R. (1997). *The development of past tense verbal morphology in L2 Spanish classroom instruction*. Cornell University.

Schmidt, R. (1994). Implicit learning and the cognitive unconscious: Of artificial grammars and SLA. *Second Language Research, 10*(2), 93–119.

Schmidt, R. (2010). Attention, awareness, and individual differences in language learning. In Handbook of language teaching (pp. 27-63). Academic Press.

Scottish Government. (2016). *Children, Education and Skills. Attitudes Towards Language Learning in Schools in Scotland. Social Research*. Cabinet Secretary for Education and Skills. Learning Directorate, Education.

Scottish Government. (2020). *1+2 Languages Implementation Findings from the 2019 local authority survey*. Cabinet Secretary for Education and Skills. Learning Directorate, Education.

Scottish Government. (2022). *1+2 languages policy - local authority survey 2021: findings*. Cabinet Secretary for Education and Skills. Learning Directorate, Education.

Scottish Qualifications Authority. (2014). *National 3 English Course Specification* [C72473]. Retrieved from: https://www.sqa.org.uk/files/nq/CfE_CourseSpec_N3_Languages_English.pdf

Tinsley, T. (2019). *Language Trends 2019: Language Teaching in Primary and Secondary Schools in England. Survey report*. British Council.

Tinsley, T., & Board, K. (2013). *Languages for the future: What languages the UK needs most and why*. British Council and Alcantara Communications.

UNESCO. (2003). *Education in a multilingual world*. UNESCO Education Position Paper. Paris: UNESCO. Retrieved from: https://unesdoc.unesco.org/ark:/48223/pf0000129728

UNESCO. (2021). *Education: Outbound internationally mobile students by host region*. Institute of Statistics.

Westergaard, M., Mitrofanova, N., Mykhaylyk, R., & Rodina, Y. (2017). Crosslinguistic influence in the acquisition of a third language: The Linguistic Proximity Model. *The International Journal of Bilingualism, 21*(6), 666–682. doi:10.1177/1367006916648859

KEY TERMS AND DEFINITIONS

Aspect: Grammatical phenomenon found in many languages, including Romance languages like Spanish, French, Italian, and Portuguese. It refers to the temporal nature of an action, describing how an action unfolds over time rather than focusing solely on its completion. Aspect deals with the internal structure of the action, such as whether it is ongoing, completed, repeated, or continuous, rather than when the action occurred. In Romance languages, aspect is often marked by verb conjugation or auxiliary verbs and can indicate whether an action is ongoing, completed, habitual, or repeated. For instance, in Spanish, the distinction between the preterite (simple past) and imperfect tenses illustrates aspect. The preterite often represents completed actions in the past, while the imperfect indicates ongoing or habitual actions in the past. Aspectual distinctions can significantly impact the meaning and interpretation of sentences by providing information about the nature and duration of an action, adding depth to the temporal context of language.

Inter-Comprehension: This is the ability of speakers of closely related languages, such as Romance languages, to understand one another even if they do not speak the same language. This is facilitated by the linguistic similarities among these languages.

Pedagogic Translation: Deliberate use of translation as an educational tool to enhance language learning, cultural understanding, and linguistic proficiency. The approach combines the act of translating texts with structured reflection. This reflection prompts students to analyze their translation choices, linguistic challenges, cultural nuances, and strategies employed during the task. By integrating reflection, learners gain metalinguistic awareness, develop deeper language understanding, and improve translation skills while fostering critical thinking and self-awareness.

Pluralistic Approaches: These approaches in language teaching advocate for recognizing and embracing linguistic diversity, which is especially relevant when teaching or learning multiple languages or dialects.

Positive or Facilitating Transfer: Positive transfer occurs when similarities between one's native language and the target language make language acquisition easier. This often happens when linguistic features are shared between the two languages. For example, in the context of Romance languages, which are typologically-related, learners might find commonalities in vocabulary, grammar, and even sentence structure due to their shared Latin origins. This shared linguistic heritage can significantly ease the transition for learners, making it more intuitive to pick up the new language. Positive transfer serves as a bridge that helps learners harness their existing knowledge and skills to make sense of the target language, accelerating the learning process.

Romance Languages: These are a group of languages that have evolved from Latin and are predominantly spoken in Southern Europe. Among the prominent Romance languages are Spanish, French, Italian, and Portuguese. While all of these languages share a common Latin origin, they have also evolved distinctively in terms of vocabulary, grammar, and pronunciation due to a range of historical and geographical factors. For instance, Spanish and Italian have relatively high mutual intelligibility due to similarities in vocabulary and grammatical structure, while French exhibits more pronounced differences, especially in pronunciation and vocabulary, which can pose challenges for learners. These variations reflect the influence of historical events, such as the Roman Empire's expansion and later invasions, on the development of these languages, resulting in a rich linguistic landscape within the Romance language family.

Transfer: This concept refers to the influence of one's native language on the acquisition of a new language. It can either aid or impede the learning process, depending on how similarities and differences are managed.

ENDNOTE

1 This percentage includes primary schools that provide an L2 entitlement both fully (L2 is taught continuously from P1 to P7) and particularly (not taught continuously from P1 to P7).

Chapter 15
Designing Language Learning Experiences With Generative AI Tools

Betül C. Czerkawski
https://orcid.org/0000-0002-4189-4042
College of Applied Science and Technology, University of Arizona, USA

ABSTRACT

Artificial intelligence (AI), particularly generative AI, can present many opportunities for language learners to practice and improve their language skills, receive timely feedback on their performance, and customize their learning based on their needs and language proficiency. AI's benefits are not limited to second language (L2) learners. Instructors can also benefit from the novel generative AI technologies by using them in curriculum and lesson design, developing new teaching and assessment materials, or addressing diverse learner skills and needs. Despite AI's advantages, the main issue is how to design L2 environments effectively so learners can receive the best benefits from AI while reducing some associated drawbacks. This chapter argues that learning experience design (LXD) presents a road map for L2 instructors as they incorporate generative AI into their instruction. If the learning design is random and left to good intentions, achieving meaningful learning outcomes will also be left to chance. Following proven LXD guidelines may help alleviate the confusion around AI.

Artificial intelligence (AI) can be defined as a computer or a robot performing specific tasks that humans usually perform, such as finding solutions to problems, synthesizing information, analyzing data, or identifying patterns. The idea of AI that can analyze information is not new. Traditionally, AI uses discriminative modeling, making AI efficient and cost-effective. As a specific form of AI, generative AI, on the other hand, goes further than traditional AI. Relying on transformer-based machine-learning algorithms, generative AI can produce new and high-quality content using multiple modalities, such as text, images, audio, and videos. Compared to the traditional option, generative AI is less cost-effective but more efficient in producing new content that is coherent and conceptually appropriate (Hsu & Ching, 2023). The much-talked-about ChatGPT from Open AI, Bard from Google, Claude from Anthropic, and Bing from Microsoft are examples of generative AI.

DOI: 10.4018/979-8-3693-0872-1.ch015

Many fields, from medicine to security systems to businesses, have used AI in recent years. In the beginning, what started with simple text suggestions, grammar checks, and email prompts turned into a completely new direction with the automation of writing whole essays and even books. In education, the adoption of AI tools has been relatively slow. According to a national survey in the U.S. (Sebesta & David, 2023), 60% of higher education personnel reported scattered conversations around AI, while 75% stated a lack of incentives for using AI technologies. However, this situation is quickly changing as higher education institutions try to adapt to rapid developments.

In second language (L2) studies, AI has increasingly been used. For instance, voice-based AI tools such as Amazon Alexa and Apple Siri can increase communication skills (Underwood, 2017), while chatbots can provide unlimited and real-time practice options (Jeon, 2022), coach students as they study a language and improve their language skills (Wang et al., 2022), help with conducting critical research and evaluation (Hsu & Ching, 2023), and assist in translating, editing, paraphrasing, revising, researching and generating text (Warschauer et al., 2023). Researchers also reported some limitations with AI that learners and instructors need to be aware of. For example, the current AI tools may not offer "a broad enough view of language and culture, limiting students' exposure to diverse perspectives" or work well with students with accents (Wang et al., 2023, p. 2). In addition, generative AI tools can produce non-existent sources in writing prompts or hallucinate while presenting template rigidity (Barrot, 2023). As with any new emerging technology, the novelty effect of AI technologies may also subside over time (Fryer et al., 2017). Finally, Zhao (2023) argues that most-AI based digital writing tools for L2 focus on revisions and editing, while tools for completing higher-order tasks such as formulating ideas are still lacking. An effective and careful learning design may guide to mitigate the adverse impact of generative AI for L2.

This chapter aims to present a learning experience design (LXD) approach for the effective integration of generative AI so this new technology can lead to meaningful learning experiences in L2 instruction. According to a recent report, all uses of AI in education "must be grounded in established, modern learning principles" (U.S. Department of Education, 2023, p. 60), prioritizing learning design. Other scholars also argued that "it takes careful planning and learning to optimally leverage GenAI's capabilities" (Hsu & Ching, 2023, p. 606). The chapter, therefore, will start with presenting LXD models and practices applicable to L2 and discussing the contemporary design frameworks commonly used for emerging technologies. From there, design implications specific to generative AI in the context of L2 will be presented after synthesizing contemporary learning experience design (LXD) models.

LEARNING EXPERIENCE DESIGN (LXD) FOR L2

In a report published in 2007 by the Modern Languages Association, the authors call for new structures in teaching languages. While they never mention instructional design (ID) or LXD in this report, they call for a curriculum reform that includes "explicit, principled educational goals and expected outcomes" (MLA, 2007, para.14). The report focuses on the new type of content that needs to be included in the curriculum with little attention to the methodology of doing it. Unfortunately, most language teacher training curricula rarely include teaching subjects such as instructional design or learning experience design. Hence, a comprehensive and holistic approach to learning design can provide much-needed intentionality to deliver successful language instruction.

Instructional Design (ID) is a systematic approach to deliver effective and efficient instruction. With the advance of digital technologies via computers and mobile devices, concepts like *user interface interaction* or *online learning* are now at the forefront of education. Today, most instructors and designers adopt a more targeted approach to curriculum design rather than designing prescriptive and limiting curricular systems with carefully planned teaching and learning activities. This new targeted approach is labeled as Learning Experience Design or LXD, although it should be emphasized that not all scholars have reached a consensus on this new term. Clark (2021) even calls the LXD a field with an identity crisis. However, he also emphasizes the importance of learning from past ID experiences and moving into a new vantage point with LXD, where educators can resolve today's complex learning problems by creating context-specific learning opportunities.

LXD refers to designing learning activities, experiences, or materials using user experience design principles to achieve expected learning outcomes. Clark (2021) points out the primary goal of LXD: learning that puts the learner at the center of every educational endeavor. Learning outcomes are achieved by selecting the right experiences for learners and the design processes needed to create those experiences. In other words, LXD presents a multiple-step approach to achieving its goals: first, clear and realistic learning objectives aligned with the learner's needs and proficiency level are identified; then, teaching and learning activities that use human-computer interaction principles and the most recent findings of learning science are created; content and learning activities are sequenced so students would gradually connect the new knowledge with the prior knowledge; collaborative and social learning is supported, and finally, authentic and meaningful assessment procedures are arranged. In the context of L2, it is also essential to include culturally sensitive experiences for the learners to increase their intercultural competence. Moreover, considering the complexity of digital technologies and AI-supported platforms, LXD also provides an understanding of how students make choices and self-regulate their experiences.

DESIGN MODELS FOR EMERGING TECHNOLOGIES

Traditional ID practices utilize well-established models to guide the design process. Because the learning environment could be open-ended and fluid, ID models provide a framework for designers to conceptualize, plan, and execute instructional activities. Traditional models, such as the **A**nalysis, **D**esign, **D**evelopment, **I**mplementation, and **E**valuation or ADDIE (Branson et al., 1975) and Dick and Carey Model (1978) use behavioristic learning theory, while Gagne's Nine Events of Instruction (1965) and Merrill's Principles of Instruction (Merrill, 2002) use cognitivist learning theory. These older models also predominantly follow a linear design process. Compared to the behaviorist ID models, cognitivist models offer more flexibility; nevertheless, they are still structured models with little attention to technological developments and their impact on education.

Recently, a group of new design approaches flourished, inspired mainly by the computing fields. Unlike ID, LXD highly favors the latter computing-based approaches because of their connection to new technologies and emerging ideas in the learning sciences. One of the main differences between the traditional and contemporary models can be found in the linearity of the models and the learning theories on which they are based. For instance, a traditional model like Dick and Carey Model follows certain steps linearly, paying little attention to the contextual changes in the learning environments or differences in learner backgrounds. On the other hand, an iterative ID model like the Successive Approximation Model or SAM (Allen Interactions, 2021) considers the differences in each learning setting and makes adjustments for different learner needs via iterative learning design processes. The other difference between a traditional and contemporary ID model is the scope of the design activities. While ID is more appropriate for top-down comprehensive program-level designs, LXD focuses on course or unit-level designs that focus on learner experiences. Regarding learning theories, contemporary LXD models frequently use constructivist and connectivist learning theories, building on learners' prior knowledge, personal interpretations, and individual discoveries.

Moreover, LXD has been heavily influenced by the developments in the computing fields, such as human-computer interaction and software development. For instance, *agile design* provides a highly flexible activity or task-focused design technique; *rapid prototyping* helps designers in creating low-fidelity learning and teaching materials to move to high-fidelity materials; and *interface and interaction design* techniques consider the user experiences with the computing systems to generate meaningful learning experiences. Finally, modern LXD models are highly customizable based on the learner's needs and circumstances; therefore, LXD presents a flexible approach to the learning process that is much needed for an emerging technology such as AI.

INCORPORATING GENERATIVE AI IN L2

While applying LXD to the design of L2 environments, an instructor makes decisions in three main areas: How do the L2 learning objectives change due to using generative AI technologies? How can the affordances of the AI tools be used to create L2 learning and teaching activities? Finally, How does the use of generative AI impact assessment procedures? Addressing these questions would help instructors integrate generative AI in their L2 classrooms.

Learning Objectives and Generative AI

Learning objectives concern what learners should be able to achieve as a result of formal learning experiences. In addition, learning objectives do not only refer to cognitive level objectives (e.g., knowledge and intellectual skills) but also to affective (e.g., attitudes, emotions, interests, values, etc.) and psychomotor skills (e.g., physical coordination, motor skills). In schools, these objectives are also used to set up criteria for assessment and evaluation.

Generative AI may impact how students learn languages and what they learn. Judging by the rapid developments in AI technologies, learning objectives also need to change to reflect the circumstances of modern education settings. In other words, instruction time could focus on L2 learning objectives that are on the higher end of Bloom's Revised Taxonomy (Krathwohl, 2002), such as analyzing, evaluating, and creating, while AI could be employed to save time on lower-level learning objectives, such as remembering, understanding, and applying. For instance, rather than spending valuable instructional time with lower-level cognitive tasks that require memorization of language concepts, instructors can use AI applications with students to practice those tasks in a safe and non-judgmental AI environment. Similarly, drill-and-practice exercises, such as the practice of simple grammar structures or pronunciation of vocabulary, can be practiced using an AI program. This way, students can spend more class time on higher-level cognitive tasks, such as critically evaluating one's speaking performance, making cross-cultural references, and studying linguistic pluralities that can help understand the target language's culture.

While determining what L2 learners need to learn, instructors should consider learner perceptions of AI tools to tailor them to their needs. According to Chan and Hu (2023), user acceptance plays a significant role in the effective use of AI. As the learners trust their abilities in the learning environment, their positive perceptions lead to deeper learning experiences, while negative perceptions may lead to superficial learning. Therefore, including learners in setting learning objectives and outcomes could also be worth considering.

L2 Activities and Generative AI

Learning experience design has important implications when creating teaching and learning activities with AI. First, a well-grounded learning design framework assists educators in being aware of both the affordances and limitations of chatbots and generative AI so the learners get the best benefit. Regardless of the framework chosen, using LXD, L2 educators can start with the desired learning outcomes and find learning activities that AI can support. Second, AI can be a complementary tool to enhance instruction with close instructor guidance, monitoring, and modeling rather than replacing classroom instruction led by a teacher. Finally, in selecting and evaluating which AI tool to use, the educators weigh in on their usability and feasibility (U.S. Department of Education, 2023).

Regarding learning activities, generative AI can create engaging and interactive learning experiences, offering practice in language skills, grammar, and vocabulary. Chatbots, for instance, are the most commonly used AI tools as they can converse with the learners in the target language. What makes chatbots effective is their ability to respond to queries, continuously learn and improve the quality of their output, and act as tireless language-teaching assistants (Kohnke et al., 2023). In the new iteration of chatbots, in addition to voice recognition, integration with third-party applications is also possible, expanding chatbots' ubiquitous use. In addition to maintaining conversations, chatbots can respond to learner questions and assess their language skills in a written or spoken manner. Language instructors can also develop their chatbots using a visual chatbot development system. According to a systematic review of empirical studies, Huang, Hew, and Fryer (2021) found that chatbots have many pedagogical affordances, from being an interlocutor (e.g., language and skill practice, group discussions) to simulative practices (role-playing, learning scenarios in authentic learning environments), general assistance (helpline), and providing recommendations (providing need-based content).

The recent L2 literature has shown that chatbots can be effective technologies for language learning. They can decrease language anxiety (Hapsari & Wu, 2022), enable students to interact multimodally, develop vocabulary, provide feedback (Haristani, 2019), and improve their reading skills (Bailey et al., 2021). Chatbots can also engage learners in human-like conversations (Fryer et al., 2020) and increase their motivation (Jeon, 2022). Despite this generally positive outlook, there is also research that cautions about the limitations of chatbots. For instance, the researchers found that speaking with chatbots creates an environment lacking emotions. Additionally, chatbots may feed learners with inaccurate information (Annamalai et al., 2023; Kohnke et al., 2023). Similarly, AI technology can create an unnatural environment for students, making it difficult for authentic interactions. According to Wang et al. (2023), AI-based applications may be constraining in offering a broad range of cultural experiences and diverse opinions in the target language. Other scholars found that learners speak with shorter sentences while conversing with chatbots and use restricted vocabulary and even profanity (Hill et al., 2015). Finally, not every L2 student may take advantage of the generative AI, as different students may need different types of assistance when using chatbots (Wang et al., 2023).

Besides chatbots, language educators can use generative AI to foster traditional language tasks, such as mastering grammar rules, teaching new vocabulary (Jia et al., 2022), practicing pronunciation or listening exercises, and assisting students with reading, writing, and translation tasks. Generative AI can present more creative ways of teaching languages, including mime, poetry, lyrics, puzzles, and game creation in the target language, script-writing, or cultural immersion activities. Furthermore, AI can provide additional cultural context by explaining cultural nuances and offering practices that reflect regional differences in the target language. Finally, generative AI has great potential to individualize instruction for different student needs. Language instructors can curate language resources for a specific learning need and create tailored learning materials for their students (Pratama, Sampelelo, and Lura, 2023).

L2 Assessment and Generative AI

Some early research shows promising results concerning using generative AI in achieving learning outcomes in L2 classrooms. In a study by Wei (2023), generative AI improved student achievement and motivation and fostered self-regulated learning strategies among EFL learners. Despite such studies, generative AI has been central to many heated discussions, creating confusion about what students gain if they employ AI in their learning. For instance, the initial reactions from writing and translation instructors were highly cautious towards using AI in learning assessment. Lately, most L2 instructors are reflecting deeply on how learner assessments can be re-imagined (Amin, 2023; Richardson & Clesham, 2021). From the LXD perspective, it is essential to note that assessments should align with the learning outcomes. This criterion should be supported when a new technology like AI is brought into the classroom. Additionally, traditional assessments, such as take-home translation exercises and essays, should be re-considered for their relevancy in the age of generative AI. Authentic assessments, such as video-based portfolios, chats, or discussions, could be used whenever possible.

Generative AI can help language learning in three ways regarding the creation of assessments. First, using generative AI, language instructors easily create customized assessment materials, such as quizzes, worksheets, exams, and study materials. Some of these assessments could be used for student practice so that they can master language skills independently. Second, instructors can provide immediate and comprehensive feedback to their students using automated AI systems. While practicing themselves, learners also receive immediate feedback from the AI platform. Most language programs, such as Duolingo and Rosetta Stone, already use AI technology to customize language practices to the level of students. Finally, generative AI can be used as an adaptive learning tool where the difficulty level of questions can be adjusted based on student responses. The same adaptive systems also give information about students' learning difficulties by analyzing where their errors are. For instance, adaptive AI tools such as Cerego and 360Learning can provide feedback to students using different formats so they can correct their errors.

Table 1 summarizes the questions the instructors can ask themselves about learning design processes for generative AI.

Table 1. LXD questions for Generative AI

Learning Design Elements	Questions that Guide Learning Design
Learning Objectives and Outcomes	What do students need to learn? What objectives could be gained or practiced with generative AI? Which cognitive, affective, and psychomotor level learning objectives generative AI support? How can generative AI be tailored for different learner needs, language proficiency, and experience levels with technology? What digital competence skills do learners need to develop to use generative AI responsibly?
Learning Activities	What generative AI activities can support specific language skills (grammar, vocabulary, pronunciation, practice for mastery, speaking, writing, reading, listening, and intercultural skills)? How can generative AI support student motivation, participation, and engagement? What specific generative AI tools could be used?
Assessments	How can students use generative AI to get immediate feedback on their learning? How can learning proficiency be assessed using a generative AI tool? What self-regulation and metacognitive skills do learners develop when using generative AI?

GENERATIVE AI TOOLS FOR L2

With the growing number of generative AI tools emerging every day, it is impossible to capture all the tools that can be used in L2 here, but a few of them will be discussed to give an idea about the potential of AI. These tools can be categorized around L2 material development, formative assessment, and improvement of speaking skills.

Supermeme AI (https://www.supermeme.ai) and LingoTeach (https://lingoteach.ai)

AI can help instructors create L2 materials for instructional use. One such tool is called Supermeme AI. Memes are fun ways of looking at an idea using an unrelated image, animation, or video. The contradiction and interplay between the concept and the visual make memes entertaining for students. Supermeme AI can generate memes by typing simple prompts into the program. The program then generates a meme using an extensive multimedia database under fair-use policies. Memes can teach vocabulary, grammar concepts, trends, and culture (Huang, 2023), and Supermeme AI is available in over 110 languages. Using this app, L2 instructors can create memes for their classes or let their students find captions for a given meme. Huang also suggests various activities that use memes, such as writing a story for a meme, interpreting a meme, and voting for a favorite meme. The instructor can edit the meme caption to tailor the AI-generated materials for age-appropriateness. There are other meme-generating websites, but using the power of AI, this tool can generate random images that align with the spirit of memes better. While Supermeme is not a free tool, some free credits are available for new users.

The other AI tool that can be used for creating instructional materials is LingoTeach. LingoTeach allows instructors to start with selecting language structures they want their students to practice and a topic or scenario they want them to use with the chosen language structure. Then, the program generates text for reading or listening comprehension. For listening, instructors can record their own voice or utilize the system-generated recording. LingoTeach is available in five languages and is a fee-based tool.

Figure 1. Supermeme, an example of a creating writing prompt

Figure 2. Supermeme, an example of a creating writing prompt

Figure 3. LingoTeach, an example of a translation exercise from French to English

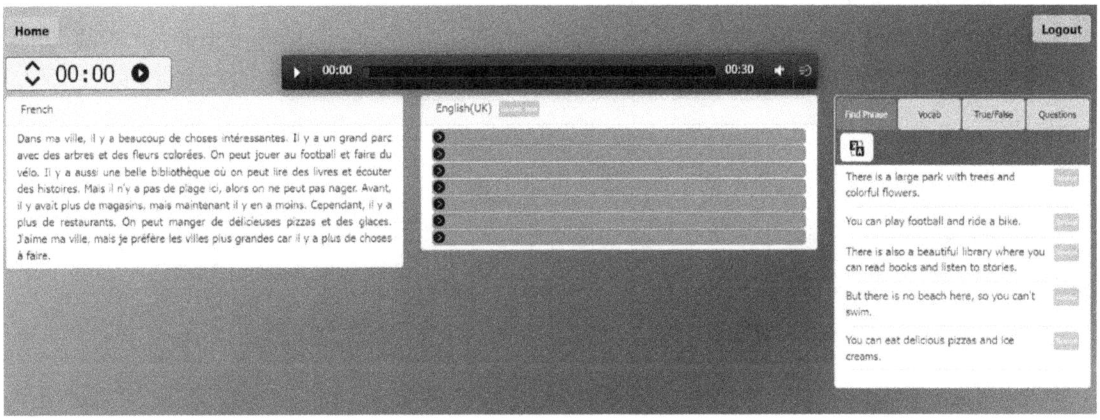

Formative (https://www.formative.com/ai-powered) and Quizlet Q-Chat (https://quizlet.com/)

The second set of AI tools that can be used with L2 relates to assessment. Using Formative, instructors can upload their text-based documents into the software, and then the AI tools generate auto-graded quizzes, assessment tools, or presentation slides, which students can study at their own pace. The presentation slides also include built-in questions to enforce student understanding as they view the content. As an assessment tool, Formative allows instructors to select various questions, embed their time-stamped videos into presentations to generate questions, check answers to detect plagiarism, and monitor student progress over multiple assignments. Formative is a fee-based tool, but a free version with limited functions is available. The tool can be integrated with learning management systems or Google Classroom. While it is not specific to languages, the support for a wide range of languages allows Formative to be an ideal tool for L2.

Figure 4. Formative AI, question bank for Spanish

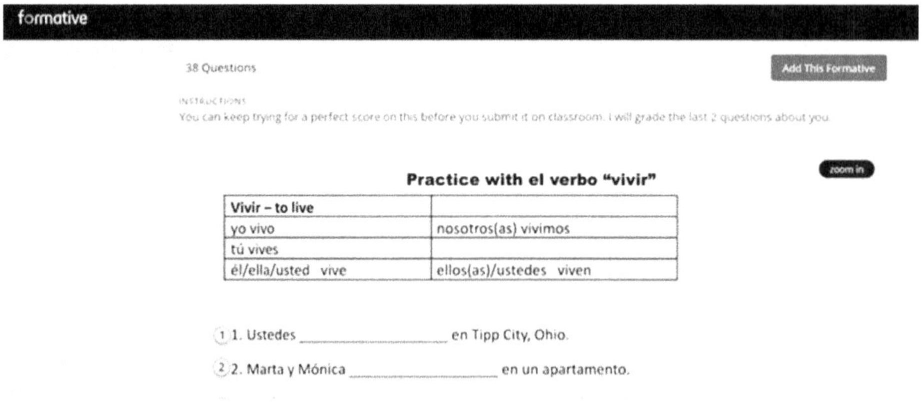

Quizlet is a well-known assessment tool for all content areas, but Quizlet Q-Chat is an AI-powered addition that helps learners assess their learning on a given topic by conversing with the Quizlet bot. Q-Chat guides and coaches students, similar to Formative AI. Instructors who want to use their own assessment options can use a fee-based option, Quizlet Plus, but the program is free for students. Currently, Q-Chat is available in five languages.

Figure 5. Quizlet-Q-Chat, practicing Ukrainian

Replika (https://replika.com) and TalkPal (https://talkpal.ai)

The third type of tool for L2 is AI intelligent agents for speaking. Although Replika is currently only available in English, the company plans to expand its language capacity soon. Replika can understand conversations in all languages but can respond in English. The basic version is free, and the program mainly involves conversing with a chatbot using an avatar, although learners can also type their conversations using the written mode. In ESL/EFL classrooms, Replika can encourage students to speak without fear, judgment, or social anxiety about how they sound in the target language. Replika does not conduct any translations or Internet searches, so its primary purpose is to chat on topics learners wish or mentor or coach them to improve their conversational skills. Each Replika offers a private chat platform, meaning only one user can speak to their Replika. In one study on higher education EFL students' views on Replika, the author found that students enjoyed using Replika and valued the immediate feedback they received about their conversations (Kılıçkaya, 2020). The same group of students also commented that when Replika had problems understanding their conversations, they edited or changed their prompts, which helped them correct their mistakes immediately. The author concluded that Replika can be used in the classroom but also outside of the school to develop confidence in speaking.

Figure 6. Replika, chat window with the personalized avatar

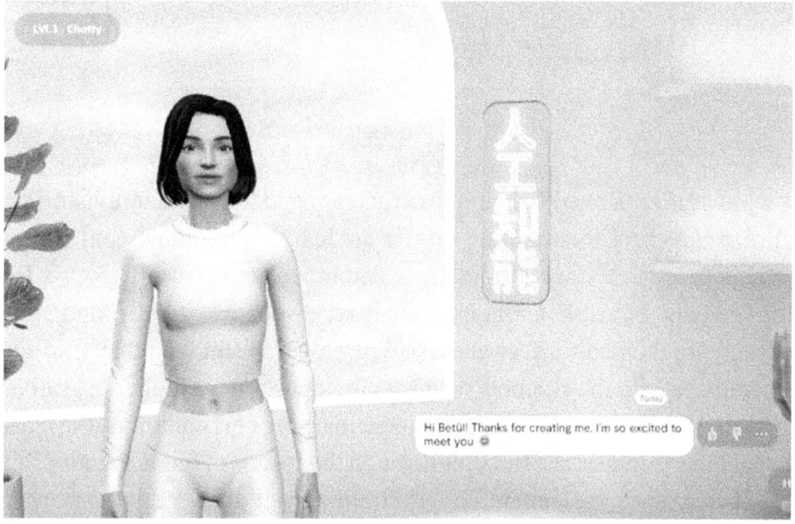

TalkPal is an AI tool very similar to Replika, but the main difference is that TalkPal was explicitly created for language learners. Therefore, it is available in a large number of languages. TalkPal aims to strengthen all four language skills with a wide range of options for continuous practice. While a fee-based program, TalkPal also has a free service for 10 minutes of daily practice. TalkPal can use different language registers, such as formal, informal, and fictional conversations so that students can practice their language skills in different modes. Like Replika, TalkPal can be used outside of the classroom to provide additional student practice options.

It should be noted that there are other AI-powered chatbots to practice languages. For instance, traditional language software programs like Rosetta Stone, Mondly, Babbel, Duolingo, and Memrise have AI chat options for learners. However, these programs are limited in functionality compared to Replika and TalkPal.

FURTHER IMPLICATIONS FOR LEARNING DESIGN

The following section presents some of the implications of LXD for generative AI. As the research into generative AI grows, further guidelines can be added to this list.

Figure 7. TalkPal, homepage for language skill selection

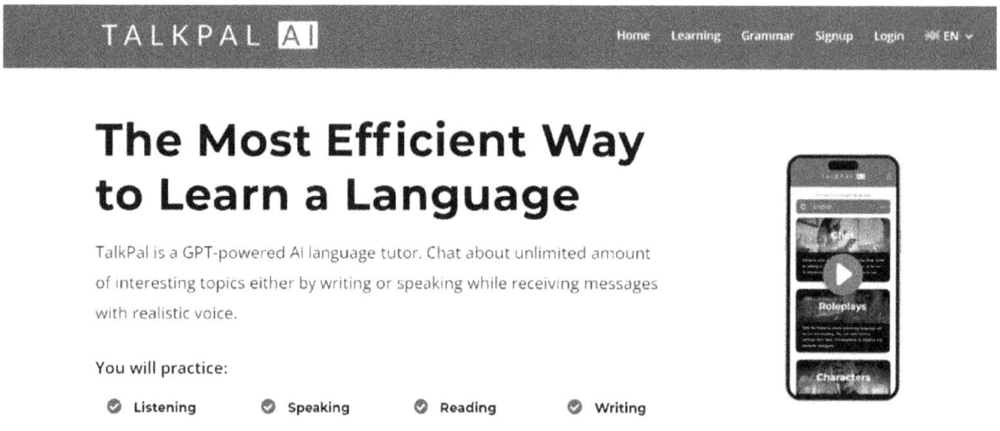

Reflecting on what students need to learn. Instructors need to consider revising course/unit/activity objectives to maximize class time for attaining significant learning outcomes and minimize the class time for repetitive language practices. Course objectives can be selected from Bloom's Revised Taxonomy higher level cognitive goals to enable learners to analyze, evaluate critically, and apply what they have learned while they increase their cultural awareness. The research conducted by Cao et al. (2023) showed that students engaged more with the chatbots when asking questions at higher cognitive levels than those at lower cognitive levels. Furthermore, "Most language learning curricula start the learning process with the acquisition of vocabulary and lexical bundles through the means of memorization" (Wilson & Marcin, 2022, p. 2). For advanced learners, Generative AI could help reduce redundant instructional practices by increasing the time spent on tasks such as examining and critically assessing cultural, political, and social elements from the target language. Some example learning objectives would be studying regional linguistic differences, the historical reasons for the differences, creating original works in the target language, or analyzing the development of the language in the historical context. For beginner learners, AI tools may offer much-needed practice options without any fear of judgment.

Expanding learning experiences with fun, engaging, and motivating activities. Considering that early research with AI chatbots shows a novelty effect that wears off quickly (Fryer et al., 2017), AI tools should be used occasionally and cleverly to expand classroom instruction rather than trying to replace essential teaching tasks, such as content presentation, explanations, probing student understanding and providing individualized feedback. Content creation for stimulating language tasks or finding connections between the native and target language requires intense work on the instructor's part. Generative AI can help develop engaging activities for the students with memes, debate ideas, and brainstorming options while customizing these activities for different student levels and needs.

Customizing learning experiences with diverse tasks created by AI. Tailoring AI-based programs for learner needs has different implications for learning. The first implication is the possibility of creating experiences for different learner needs and proficiency levels. Development of teaching materials that fit a specific learner's needs may be time-consuming and labor-intensive. L2 instructors could use generative AI to save time on creating visually rich content materials, fun games, or age-appropriate, exciting materials for their students. Second, as the mostly text and speech-based generative AI becomes more multimodal, instructors can also transform traditional language textbooks and web-based materials into a highly interactive environment. According to Pokrivcakova (2019), using AI to create personalized materials works against the "one-size-fits-all" approach to schooling and helps better meet individual learner needs. Finally, applications that "utilize AI can capture, aggregate, and analyze students' learning performance data in real time from different sources to develop a student learning profile and automatically provide customized content, feedback, and learning parameters" (Kim et al., 2022, p. 6070). Moreover, learning management systems (LMS) are expected to integrate AI into their system in the near future, providing more customizable learning experiences for students. Currently, the learner progress and grades are tracked with AI, but LMSs do not offer adaptive learning experiences where each learner customizes their experiences with the course content creating personalized pathways.

Expanding class time with cultural and authentic L2 learning experiences. Authentic learning helps make learning relevant to the students while bridging the content learned in the classroom to real-world situations. Research in teaching culture in L2 classrooms with the help of AI tools is scarce. However, some research exists on the authenticity and effectiveness of AI-generated content. According to Kim et al. (2022), using AI was beneficial to achieving learning outcomes when teachers implemented AI-generated authentic tasks. However, teachers here engaged students in AI by not leaving them alone with the activity but guiding them along the way. In their research, teachers took a proactive role when using AI and assisted students regularly and carefully.

Targeting all language skills holistically. According to a study conducted by Woo and Choi (2021) in L2, AI research is mainly focused on speaking and listening (14%), writing (11%), pronunciation (11%), grammar (7%), vocabulary (6%) and reading (5%). Intercultural competence, or teaching of culture in general, is the area that should be addressed the most. This study shows that the full potential of generative AI tools is only partially realized, and language skills are treated individually by most L2 instructors. The authenticity of the AI-generated tools to teach the cultural content of the target language is an area that needs to be investigated further, as not everyone agrees that AI can generate authentic content for instruction; hence, AI-created content falls short regarding authentic learning experiences.

Using AI-based assessments for practice and evaluation purposes. Grading student work can often be tedious and time-consuming. AI can provide faster and more detailed assessment feedback, sometimes even more detailed than the instructor's (Alharbi, 2023). The research on the consistency of AI-based evaluations is mixed. For instance, Ranalli (2021) suggests that automated writing evaluation tools such as Grammarly fall short of expectations because the feedback provided by the writing tools does not guarantee writing improvement. The success of the AI feedback depends on the learner and context. Therefore, student's proficiency level, content, instructional context, and comfort level using AI-based tools should be taken into account by the L2 instructors when using AI for learning assessment.

Creating a space for the discussion of ethical use. With all its advantages, the use of AI also poses serious ethical challenges, not to mention critical limitations, including the issues surrounding data privacy, bias, lack of diversity, reliability, authenticity, and academic dishonesty. Maintaining the integrity of educational practices in the increasingly AI-driven world is the topic of ardent discussions in every society today that should be taken seriously. While the examination of such ethical issues is beyond the scope of this paper, for L2 instructors, there are specific implications. L2 instructors have always been keen on incorporating new literacies in their teaching. Nash et al. (2023) argue that controversy around new literacies has always existed. Consequently, engaging with AI technologies should also be part of the literacy education the L2 instructors have spearheaded for decades. Modeling responsible use of AI by the L2 instructors, having classroom debates, or creating a safe environment for learners to discuss their own experiences could be part of language education.

Developing digital competency and AI literacy. Although generative AI can be highly useful, in order to limit the wide range of issues about its use, both learners and teachers "must develop the specific digital competencies needed to use such tools in ways that are pedagogically beneficial and ethical" (Kohnke et al., 2023, p. 546). In the last two decades, educational institutions have trained many students in using emerging technologies. However, the rapid growth of generative AI tools showed that this time, schools and universities fell short of training their faculty and students to gain digital competency skills, causing much confusion regarding AI. Moreover, most instructors are left alone without a clear instructional strategy and adequate infrastructure, causing further misunderstanding and chaos. A recent study showed that an "overwhelming majority of institutions do not offer incentives to encourage faculty to use AI, and a majority also reported no faculty development or training around AI" (Sebesta & Davis, 2022, p. 6). Digital competency with AI can be developed by continuously fact-checking the reliability of the information, being aware of the potential ethical issues and underlying biases, and understanding AI's technical underworking, social, pedagogical, and technological affordances.

RECOMMENDATIONS FOR FURTHER LXD RESEARCH

L2 instruction is complex and requires further empirical research due to the increased interest in generative AI and L2. In the last decade, most of the research attention was on AI technology; however, nowadays, more attention is paid to developing educational AI platforms that consider learning characteristics, educational context, and instructor capabilities. Customizable or adaptive AI-supported language instruction requires deeper pedagogical research using diverse language content and context. In L2, context is critical, as educators need to understand what system works for whom and why. Sound teacher training programs for integrating AI tools into language classrooms also need to be studied to understand how teachers can effectively employ AI. If some students cannot take advantage of AI technology because of their lack of vocabulary or accent, educators need to be aware of these limitations. Research into context-sensitive AI models must ensure that "they are effective, safe, and trustworthy for use with varied learners in diverse settings" (U.S. Department of Education, 2023, p. 59). Along the same lines, instructor guidance is vital when learning with AI, and more research is needed to establish effective teaching strategies that can help learners.

The student-AI interface interaction should be studied to respond to diverse user needs. Considering that there is a "dearth of knowledge regarding how students interact with AI agents for language learning and what differences may exist among distinct types of students in human-AI interactions" (Wang et al., 2023, p. 2), more research is needed to understand learner-AI interaction processes as well as the design considerations for AI interfaces. For instance, most AI tools used in L2 are not explicitly designed for L2 learners. L2 learner needs, their skill level with AI interfaces, and expectations may differ; therefore, research that includes diverse learner perspectives is needed to employ AI effectively in L2 classrooms.

Another consequence of AI use in L2 is related to reliance on technology. Considering that most AI tools are used in conjunction with online education, an added layer of complexity should be examined further. Likewise, research investigating the interactions between the learners and technology affordances is needed to craft a balanced use of AI applications. In addition, more longitudinal studies should be undertaken to understand the long-term effects of AI on L2 learning.

Finally, there is a need for more research on issues related to the accuracy of AI applications, user data, privacy, transparency of the platforms, and ethical issues surrounding AI. As with any emerging technology, instructors need to think carefully about generative AI and its use before employing it in their classrooms. While the ethical use of AI for L2 learners is beyond the scope of this paper, as a learning tool, the reliability of the information gathered via AI and its responsible use is part of the new literacies in which L2 instructors can lead the way for other disciplines. A research-informed AI literacy instruction and digital competency skills could help solve some issues and generate a solid ground to promote desired AI use for L2 learners.

CONCLUSION

The leading AI program, ChatGPT, launched on November 30, 2022, attracting millions of users worldwide. Although chatbots and AI applications are not new, with the introduction of ChatGPT, the education world witnessed a storm of new applications accompanied by a considerable interest similar to none. It can be argued that generative AI can arguably be used in L2 education in endless ways. While AI technology is still developing, educators lack data-driven teaching and learning strategies and proven pedagogical approaches.

The many research studies conducted only in the last year prove the interest in AI, mainly discussing the affordances and drawbacks of using AI in language settings. Many L2 scholars expressed their concerns about using AI for instruction (Dakakni and Safa, 2023). Considering how ubiquitous AI is, this idea is unrealistic because most web-based programs for writing and searching information have already integrated AI into their system. Then, the question is *how* to use AI for the best results in L2. Currently, there is little research on this issue, but the research is evolving.

This paper argued that learning experience design, as a contemporary, practical, and realistic strategy using instructional design guidelines, provides valuable insights for educators as it shows a pedagogically sound method of using AI in L2 instruction. More specifically, reflecting on new learning outcomes in the age of AI, creating AI-powered activities that will enhance student learning, and using an assessment approach that provides accurate and immediate feedback would structure some of the early excitement and discussions around AI and offer a sound foundation for L2. The suggestions provided in this paper can be used as a starting point while stimulating much-needed pedagogical research on AI integration.

REFERENCES

Alharbi, W. (2023). AI in the foreign language classroom: A Pedagogical overview of automated writing assistance tools. *Education Research International*, *2023*, 1–15. doi:10.1155/2023/4253331

Allen Interactions. (2021). *E-Learning development with SAM.* Allen Interactions. https://www.allen-interactions.com/services/custom-learning/sam/elearning-development

Annamalai, N., Elmagzoub, E. M., Zyoud, S. H., Soundrarajan, D., Zakarneh, B., & Al Salhi, N. R. (2023). Exploring English language learning via Chabot: A case study from a self-determination theory perspective. *Computers and Education: Artificial Intelligence*, *5*, 100148. Advance online publication. doi:10.1016/j.caeai.2023.100148

Bailey, D., Southam, A., & Costley, J. (2021). Digital storytelling with chatbots: Mapping L2 participation and perception patterns. *Interactive Technology and Smart Education, 18*(1), 85–103. doi:10.1108/ITSE-08-2020-0170

Barrot, J. S. (2023). Using ChatGPT for second language writing: Pitfalls and potentials. *Assessing Writing, 57*, 1–4. doi:10.1016/j.asw.2023.100745

Branson, R. K., Rayner, G. T., Cox, J. L., Furman, J. P., King, F. J., & Hannum, W. H. (1975). Interservice procedures for instructional systems development.: Vol. 1-5. *TRADOC Pam 350-30, NAVEDTRA 106A)*. U.S. Army Training and Doctrine Command.

Cao, C. C., Ding, Z., Lin, J., & Hopfgartner, F. (2023). *AI chatbots as multi-role pedagogical agents: Transforming engagement in CS education*. arXiv.org. https://doi.org//arxiv.2308.03992. doi:10.48550

Chan, C. K. Y., & Hu, W. (2023). Students' voices on generative AI: Perceptions, benefits, and challenges in higher education. *International Journal of Educational Technology in Higher Education, 20*(1), 43. doi:10.1186/s41239-023-00411-8

Clark, D. (2021). *Learning experience design: How to create effective learning that works*. Kogan Page Limited.

Dakakni, D., & Safa, N. (2023). Artificial intelligence in the L2 classroom: Implications and challenges on ethics and equity in higher education: A 21st century Pandora's box, Computers and Education. *Artificial Intelligence, 5*, 100179. Advance online publication. doi:10.1016/j.caeai.2023.100179

Dick, W., & Carey, L. (1978). *The systematic design of instruction*. Scott, Foresman.

Fryer, L., Coniam, D., Carpenter, R., & Lăpuşneanu, D. (2020). Bots for language learning now: Current and future directions. *Language Learning & Technology, 24*(2), 8–22.

Gagné, R. M. (1965). *The conditions of learning*. Holt, Rinehart, and Winston.

Hapsari, I. P., & Wu, T. T. (2022). AI chatbots learning model in English speaking skill: Alleviating speaking anxiety, boosting enjoyment, and fostering critical thinking. In *Innovative Technologies and Learning. ICITL 2022*. Springer. doi:10.1007/978-3-031-15273-3_49

Haristiani, N. (2019). Artificial Intelligence (AI) chatbot as language learning medium: An inquiry. *Journal of Physics: Conference Series, 1387*(1), 12020. doi:10.1088/1742-6596/1387/1/012020

Hill, J., Ford, W. F., & Farreras, I. G. (2015). Real conversations with artificial intelligence: A comparison between human-human online conversations and human–chatbot conversations. *Computers in Human Behavior, 49*, 245–250. doi:10.1016/j.chb.2015.02.026

Hsu, Y.-C., & Ching, Y.-H. (2023). Generative Artificial Intelligence in education, Part One: The dynamic frontier. *TechTrends: Linking Research & Practice to Improve Learning, 67*(4), 603–607. doi:10.1007/s11528-023-00863-9

Huang, W. (2023). Memes in Language Classrooms: From Traditional to AI-Generated. *FLTMagazine*. https://fltmag.com/memes-in-language-classrooms-from-traditional-to-ai-generated/

Huang, W., Hew, K. F., & Fryer, L. K. (2022). Chatbots for language learning—Are they really useful? A systematic review of chatbot-supported language learning. *Journal of Computer Assisted Learning*, *38*(1), 237–257. doi:10.1111/jcal.12610

Jeon, J. (2022). Exploring AI chatbot affordances in the EFL classroom: Young learners' experiences and perspectives. *Computer Assisted Language Learning*, •••, 1–26. doi:10.1080/09588221.2021.2021241

Jia, F., Sun, D., Ma, Q., & Looi, C.-K. (2022). Developing an AI-based learning system for L2 learners' authentic and ubiquitous learning in English language. *Sustainability (Basel)*, *14*(23), 15527. doi:10.3390/su142315527

Kılıçkaya, F. (2020). Using a chatbot, Replika, to practice writing through conversations in L2 English: A case study. In M. Kruk & M. Peterson (Eds.), *New Technological Applications for Foreign and Second Language Learning and Teaching* (pp. 221–238). IGI Global. doi:10.4018/978-1-7998-2591-3.ch011

Kim, J., Lee, H., & Cho, Y. H. (2022). Learning design to support student-AI collaboration: Perspectives of leading teachers for AI in education. *Education and Information Technologies*, *27*(5), 6069–6104. doi:10.1007/s10639-021-10831-6

Kohnke, L., Moorhouse, B. L., & Zou, D. (2023). ChatGPT for language teaching and learning. *RELC Journal*, *54*(2), 537–550. doi:10.1177/00336882231162868

Krathwohl, D. R. (2002). A revision of Bloom's taxonomy: An overview. *Theory into Practice*, *41*(4), 212–218. doi:10.1207/s15430421tip4104_2

Merrill, M. D. (2002). First principles of instruction. *Educational Technology Research and Development*, *50*(3), 43–59. doi:10.1007/BF02505024

Modern Language Association. (2007). *Foreign languages and higher education: New structures for a changed world*. https://www.mla.org/Resources/Guidelines-and-Data/Reports-and-Professional-Guidelines/Foreign-Languages-and-Higher-Education-New-Structures-for-a-Changed-World

Nash, B. L., Hicks, T., Garcia, M., Fassbender, W., Alvermann, D., Boutelier, S., McBride, C., McGrail, E., Moran, C., O'Byrne, I., Piotrowski, A., Rice, M., & Young, C. (2023). Artificial Intelligence in English education: Challenges and opportunities for teachers and teacher educators. *English Education*, *55*(3), 201–206.

Pokrivcakova, S. (2019). Preparing teachers for the application of AI-powered technologies in foreign language education. *Journal of Language and Cultural Education*, *7*(3), 135–153. doi:10.2478/jolace-2019-0025

Pratama, M. P., Sampelolo, R., & Lura, H. (2023). Revolutionizing education: Harnessing the power of artificial intelligence for personalized learning. *Klasikal: Journal of Education, Language Teaching and Science*, *5*(2), 350–357. doi:10.52208/klasikal.v5i2.877

Ranalli, J. (2021, June). L2 student engagement with automated feedback on writing: Potential for learning and issues of trust. *Journal of Second Language Writing*, *52*, 100816. Advance online publication. doi:10.1016/j.jslw.2021.100816

Richardson, M., & Clesham, R. (2021). Rise of the machines? The evolving role of Artificial Intelligence (AI) technologies in high stakes assessment. *London Review of Education*, *19*(1), 1–13. doi:10.14324/LRE.19.1.09

Sebesta, J., & Davis, V. L. (2023, June 30). Supporting instruction and learning through Artificial Intelligence: A survey of institutional practices & policies. *WICHE Cooperative for Educational Technologies*. https://wcet.wiche.edu/resources/wcetreport-supporting-instruction-learning-through-artificial-intelligence-a-survey-ofinstitutional-practices-policies

Underwood, J. (2017). Exploring AI language assistants with primary EFL students. In K. Borthwick, L. Bradley, & S. Thouësny (Eds.), *CALL in a climate of change: Adapting to turbulent global conditions – short papers from EUROCALL 2017* (pp. 317–321). doi:10.14705/rpnet.2017.eurocall2017.733

U.S. Department of Education, Office of Educational Technology. (2023). *Artificial Intelligence and Future of Teaching and Learning: Insights and Recommendations*. https://tech.ed.gov/ai-future-of-teaching-and-learning

Wang, T., Lund, B. D., Marengo, A., Pagano, N. R., Mannuru, N. R., Teel, Z. A., & Pange, J. (2023). Exploring the potential impact of Artificial Intelligence (AI) on international students in higher education: Generative AI, chatbots, analytics, and international student success. *Applied Sciences (Basel, Switzerland)*, *13*(11), 6716. doi:10.3390/app13116716

Wang, X., Liu, Q., Pang, H., Tan, S. C., Lei, J., Wallace, M. P., & Li, L. (2023). What matters in AI-supported learning: A study of human-AI interactions in language learning using cluster analysis and epistemic network analysis. *Computers & Education*, *194*, 104703. Advance online publication. doi:10.1016/j.compedu.2022.104703

Wang, X., Pang, H., Wallace, M. P., Wang, Q., & Chen, W. (2022). Learners' perceived AI presences in AI-supported language learning: A study of AI as a humanized agent from the community of inquiry. *Computer Assisted Language Learning*, 1–27. doi:10.1080/09588221.2022.2056203

Warschauer, M., Tseng, W., Yim, S., Webster, T., Jacob, S., Du, Q., & Tate, T. (2023, December). The Affordances and Contradictions of AI-Generated Text for Second Language Writers. *Journal of Second Language Writing*, *62*. Advance online publication. doi:10.1016/j.jslw.2023.101071

Wei, L. (2023). Artificial intelligence in language instruction: Impact on English learning achievement, L2 motivation, and self-regulated learning. *Frontiers in Psychology*, *14*, 1261955. Advance online publication. doi:10.3389/fpsyg.2023.1261955 PMID:38023040

Wilson, D. V., & Marcin, M. (2022). Building connections and critical language awareness between learning communities collaborating across two distant States. *Languages (Basel, Switzerland)*, *7*(4), 257. doi:10.3390/languages7040257

WooJ. H.ChoiH. (2021). *Systematic review for AI-based language learning tools*. Ithaca: Cornell University Library. https://arxiv.org/abs/2111.04455v1

Zhao, X. (2023). Leveraging Artificial Intelligence (AI) Technology for English Writing: Introducing Wordtune as a Digital Writing Assistant for EFL Writers. *RELC Journal*, *54*(3), 890–894. doi:10.1177/00336882221094089

ADDITIONAL READING

Almelhes, S. A. (2023). A review of Artificial Intelligence adoption in second-language learning. *Theory and Practice in Language Studies*, *13*(5), 1259–1269. doi:10.17507/tpls.1305.21

Amin, M. Y. M. (2023). AI and Chat GPT in language teaching: Enhancing EFL classroom support and transforming assessment techniques. *International Journal of Higher Education Pedagogies*, *4*(4), 1–15. doi:10.33422/ijhep.v4i4.554

Geçkin, V., Kızıltaş, E., & Çınar, Ç. (2023). Assessing second-language academic writing: AI vs. Human raters. *Journal of Educational Technology and Online Learning*, *6*(4), 1096–1108. doi:10.31681/jetol.1336599

Liang, J.-C., Hwang, G.-J., Chen, M.-R. A., & Darmawansah, D. (2023). Roles and research foci of artificial intelligence in language education: An integrated bibliographic analysis and systematic review approach. *Interactive Learning Environments*, *31*(7), 4270–4296. doi:10.1080/10494820.2021.1958348

Pokrivcakova, S. (2019). Preparing teachers for the application of AI-powered technologies in foreign language education. *Journal of Language and Cultural Education*, *7*(3), 135–153. doi:10.2478/jolace-2019-0025

Song, C., & Song, Y. (2023). Enhancing academic writing skills and motivation: Assessing the efficacy of ChatGPT in AI-assisted language learning for EFL students. *Frontiers in Psychology*, *14*, 1260843–1260843. doi:10.3389/fpsyg.2023.1260843 PMID:38162975

Yuan, Y. (2023). An empirical study of the efficacy of AI chatbots for English as a foreign language learning in primary education. *Interactive Learning Environments*, 1–16. doi:10.1080/10494820.2023.2282112

KEY TERMS AND DEFINITIONS

Artificial Intelligence (AI): Machines or software completing intellectual tasks usually completed by humans.

Emerging Technology: A newly created technology or improvements in an old technology that are being discovered or realized.

Generative AI: Multimodal artificial intelligence that can produce text, images, and other forms of data.

Instructional Design: An applied field for designing, developing, and delivering learning experiences using a systems approach.

Learning Experience Design (LXD): Method of creating learner-centered learning experiences to achieve learning outcomes.

Second Language (L2): A language spoken in addition to one's native language.

Second Language Acquisition (SLA): Sometimes called, second language learning, SLA refers to the process of a learning a new language.

Compilation of References

AbdAlgane, M., & Othman, K. A. J. (2023). Utilizing artificial intelligence technologies in Saudi EFL tertiary level classrooms. *Journal of Intercultural Communication*, *23*(1), 92–99. Advance online publication. doi:10.36923/jicc.v23i1.124

Abdul Rahman, N. A., Zulkornain, L. H., & Hamzah, N. H. (2022). Exploring artificial intelligence using automated writing evaluation for writing skills. *Environment-Behaviour Proceedings Journal*, *7*(SI9), 547–553. doi:10.21834/ebpj.v7iSI9.4304

Abu Melhim, A. (2014). The Status of Arabic in the United States of America post 9/11 and the Impact on Foreign Language Teaching Programs. *Advances in Language and Literary Studies*, *5*(3), 70–81. doi:10.7575/aiac.alls.v.5n.3p.70

Academic Integrity at UBC. (2023). *CHATGPT Q&A*. https://academicintegrity.ubc.ca/chatgpt-faq/

ACTFL. (2024). *ACTFL performance descriptors for language learners*. https://www.actfl.org/educator-resources/actfl-performance-descriptors

Adams, D., & Chuah, K.-M. (2022). Artificial Intelligence-Based Tools in Research Writing. In P. P. Churi, S. Joshi, M. Elhoseny, & A. Omrane (Eds.), *Artificial Intelligence in Higher Education: A Practical Approach* (pp. 169–184). CRC Press. doi:10.1201/9781003184157-9

Adipat, S., Laksana, K., Busayanon, K., Piatanom, P., Mahamarn, Y., Pakapol, P., & Ausawasowan, A. (2022). The world of technology: Artificial intelligence in education. *Special Education*, *2*(43), 2142–2146.

Ahmed, M. A. (2023). ChatGPT and the EFL classroom: Supplement or substitute in Saudi Arabia's eastern region. *Information Sciences Letters*, *12*(7), 2727–2734. doi:10.18576/isl/120704

Aikins, R., & Kuo, A. (2023). *What Students Said About the Spring of ChatGPT.* Inside Higher Ed. https://www.insidehighered.com/opinion/views/2023/09/07/what-students-said-about-spring-chatgpt-opinion?fbclid=IwAR0vUM4HY5ideFrvGVABp2sz8MZGuzEss4EH-YiXtaUZZ1_UsZA0xKar8kk_aem_AaflEkiAJcqt065wZj0M4DpuY4xmlkyGMn-z6JBFWzOh8ZjZMuKvLmriGOa6Cr1rHDho&mibextid=Zxz2cZ

Ajit, G., Lucas, T., & Kanyan, R. (2022). Design and Technology in Malaysian Secondary Schools: A Perspective on Challenges. *Malaysian Journal of Social Sciences and Humanities*, *7*(1), 335–351. doi:10.47405/mjssh.v7i1.1219

Ajzen, I. (1991). The theory of planned behavior. *Organizational Behavior and Human Decision Processes*, *50*(2), 179–211. doi:10.1016/0749-5978(91)90020-T

Akgün, S., & Greenhow, C. (2021). Artificial intelligence in education: Addressing ethical challenges in K-12 settings. *AI and Ethics*, *2*(3), 431–440. doi:10.1007/s43681-021-00096-7 PMID:34790956

Akter, S., McCarthy, G., Sajib, S., Michael, K., Dwivedi, Y. K., D'Ambra, J., & Shen, K. N. (2021). Algorithmic bias in data-driven innovation in the age of AI. *International Journal of Information Management, 60*, 102387. doi:10.1016/j.ijinfomgt.2021.102387

Al Darayseh, A. (2023). Acceptance of artificial intelligence in teaching science: Science teachers' perspective. *Computers and Education: Artificial Intelligence, 4*, 100–132. doi:10.1016/j.caeai.2023.100132

Alam, A. (2021, November). Possibilities and apprehensions in the landscape of artificial intelligence in education. In *2021 International Conference on Computational Intelligence and Computing Applications (ICCICA)* (pp. 1-8). IEEE. https://doi.org/10.1109/ICCICA52458.2021.9697272

Aldeman, N. L. S., Aita, K., Machado, V. P., da Mata Sousa, L. C. D., Coelho, A. G. B., da Silva, A. S., Mendes, A. P. D., Neres, F. J. D., & do Monte, S. J. H. (2021). Smartpath (k): A platform for teaching glomerulopathies using machine learning. *BMC Medical Education, 21*(1), 248. doi:10.1186/s12909-021-02680-1 PMID:33926437

Alexander, K., Savvidou, C., & Alexander, C. (2023). Who wrote this essay? Detecting AI-generated writing in second language education in higher education. *Teaching English with Technology, 23*(2), 25–43. doi:10.56297/BUKA4060/XHLD5365

Alhalangy, A., & AbdAlgane, M. (2023). Exploring the impact of AI on the EFL context: A case study of Saudi universities. *Journal of Intercultural Communication, 23*(2), 41–49. doi:10.36923/jicc.v23i2.125

Alharbi, W. (2023). AI in the foreign language classroom: A pedagogical overview of automated writing assistance tools. *Education Research International, 2023*, 1–15. doi:10.1155/2023/4253331

Allen Interactions. (2021). *E-Learning development with SAM.* Allen Interactions. https://www.alleninteractions.com/services/custom-learning/sam/elearning-development

Almelhes, S. A. (2023). A Review of Artificial Intelligence Adoption in Second-Language Learning. *Theory and Practice in Language Studies, 13*(5), 1259–1269. doi:10.17507/tpls.1305.21

Almutairi, A., Gegov, A., Adda, M., & Arabikhan, F. (2020). Conceptual artificial intelligence framework to improving English as second language. *WSEAS Transactions on Advances in Engineering Education, 17*, 87–91. doi:10.37394/232010.2020.17.11

Alshumaimeri, Y. A., & Alshememry, A. K. (2023). The extent of AI applications in EFL learning and teaching. *IEEE Transactions on Learning Technologies*. Advance online publication. doi:10.1109/TLT.2023.3322128

Alzahrani, F. K., & Alhalafawy, W. S. (2023). Gamification for Learning Sustainability in the Blackboard System: Motivators and Obstacles from Faculty Members' Perspectives. *Sustainability (Basel), 15*(5), 4613. doi:10.3390/su15054613

American Council on the Teaching of Foreign Languages (ACTFL). (2017). *NCSSFL-ACTFL Can-Do Statements.* Retrieved from https://www.actfl.org/resources/ncssfl-actfl-can-do-statements

Andersen, R. (1991). Developmental sequences: The emergence of aspect marking in second language acquisition. In T. Huebner & C. A. Ferguson (Eds.), *Crosscurrents in second language acquisition and linguistic theories* (pp. 305–324). John Benjamins Publishing Company. doi:10.1075/lald.2.17and

Andersen, R., & Shirai, Y. (1994). Discourse motivations for some cognitive acquisition principles. *Studies in Second Language Acquisition, 16*(2), 133–156. doi:10.1017/S0272263100012845

Annamalai, N., Elmagzoub, E. M., Zyoud, S. H., Soundrarajan, D., Zakarneh, B., & Al Salhi, N. R. (2023). Exploring English language learning via Chabot: A case study from a self-determination theory perspective. *Computers and Education: Artificial Intelligence, 5*, 100148. Advance online publication. doi:10.1016/j.caeai.2023.100148

An, X., Chai, C. S., Li, Y., Zhou, Y., Shen, X., Zheng, C., & Chen, M. (2023). Modeling English teachers' behavioral intention to use artificial intelligence in middle schools. *Education and Information Technologies*, *28*(5), 5187–5208. doi:10.1007/s10639-022-11286-z

App Store. (2015). *Tandem: Language exchange*. https://apps.apple.com/us/app/tandem-language-exchange/id959001619

Arnold, K., & Pistilli, M. (2012). Course signals at Purdue: Using learning analytics to increase student success. *Proceedings of the 2nd international conference on learning analytics and knowledge* (pp. 267–270). New York: ACM. 10.1145/2330601.2330666

Arnó-Macià, E., & Barés, G. M. (2015). The Role of Content and Language in Content and Language Integrated Learning (CLIL) at University: Challenges and Implications for ESP. *English for Specific Purposes*, *37*, 63–73. Advance online publication. doi:10.1016/j.esp.2014.06.007

Asiksoy, G. (2018). ELT students' attitudes and awareness towards the use of Web 2.0 technologies for language learning. *Journal of Language and Linguistic Studies*, *14*(2), 240–251.

Auer, M. E., Pester, A., & May, D. (Eds.). (2022). *Learning with Technologies and Technologies in Learning: Experience, Trends and Challenges in Higher Education* (Vol. 456). Springer International Publishing. https://link.springer.com/10.1007/978-3-031-04286-7

Awad, A. (2023). *Interview by author*. MESA.

Aziz, R. (2023). Creativity in higher education: The effect of personality on students' creative thinking skills. *Thinking Skills and Creativity Journal*, *6*(1), 44–51. doi:10.23887/tscj.v6i1.54916

Azzo, A. (2023). *Teaching Artificial Intelligence Literacy: 'AI Is for Everyone.'* Artificial Intelligence at Northwestern. https://ai.northwestern.edu/news-events/articles/2023/teaching-artificial-intelligence-literacy-ai-is-for-everyone.html

Bacon-Shone, J., Bolton, K., & Luke, K. K. (2015). *Language use, proficiency and attitudes in Hong Kong*. Social Sciences Research Centre, HKU.

Baha, T. A., Hajji, M. E., Es-Saady, Y., & Fadili, H. (2023). The impact of educational chatbot on student learning experience. *Education and Information Technologies*. Advance online publication. doi:10.1007/s10639-023-12166-w

Bai, B., Wang, J., & Zhou, H. (2020). An intervention study to improve primary school students' self-regulated strategy use in English writing through e-learning in Hong Kong. *Computer Assisted Language Learning*, *35*(9), 2265–2290. doi:10.1080/09588221.2020.1871030

Baïdoo-Anu, D., & Ansah, L. O. (2023). Education in the era of generative artificial intelligence (AI): Understanding the potential benefits of ChatGPT in promoting teaching and learning. *Journal of AI*, *7*(1), 52–62. doi:10.61969/jai.1337500

Bailey, D., Southam, A., & Costley, J. (2021). Digital storytelling with chatbots: Mapping L2 participation and perception patterns. *Interactive Technology and Smart Education*, *18*(1), 85–103. doi:10.1108/ITSE-08-2020-0170

Bardovi-Harlig, K. (1998). Examining the role of text type in L2 tense-aspect research: Broadening our horizons. En P. Robinson y N. Jungheim (Eds.), Representation and process: Proceedings of the 3rd Pacific Second Language Research Forum (pp. 139–150). Tokyo: Pacific SLRF.

Bardovi-Harlig, K. (2000). *Tense and aspect in second language acquisition: Form, meaning, and use*. Blackwell., doi:10.1111/0023-8333.50.s1.7

Barrot, J. S. (2023). Using ChatGPT for second language writing: Pitfalls and potentials. *Assessing Writing*, *57*, 100745-. doi:10.1016/j.asw.2023.100745

Baskara, R., & Mukarto. (2023). Exploring the implications of ChatGPT for language learning in higher education. *Indonesian Journal of English Language Teaching and Applied Linguistics, 7*(2), 343–358. https://eric.ed.gov/?id=EJ1391490

Baskara, R. (2023). Exploring the implications of ChatGPT for language learning in higher education. *Indonesian Journal of English Language Teaching and Applied Linguistics*, *7*(2), 343–358.

Basturkmen, H. (2023). Explicit versus implicit grammar instruction and knowledge. In J. I. Liontas (Ed.), *The TESOL encyclopedia of English language teaching* (pp. 1–7). doi:10.1002/9781118784235.eelt0060

Behrens, H. (2021). Constructivist approaches to first language acquisition. *Journal of Child Language*, *48*(5), 959–983. doi:10.1017/S0305000921000556 PMID:34382923

Belda-Medina, J., & Calvo-Ferrer, J. R. (2022). Using chatbots as AI conversational partners in language learning. *Applied Sciences (Basel, Switzerland)*, *12*(17), 8427. doi:10.3390/app12178427

Bello, A. (1847). *Gramática de la lengua castellana destinada al uso de los americanos.* Edición digital a partir de obras completas. Tomo Cuarto, 3ªed., Caracas, La Casa de Bello.

Bibauw, S., François, T., & Desmet, P. (2019). Discussing with a computer to practice a foreign language: Research synthesis and conceptual framework of dialogue-based call. *Computer Assisted Language Learning*, *32*(8), 827–877. doi:10.1080/09588221.2018.1535508

Bilquise, G., & Shaalan, K. (2022). AI-based Academic Advising Framework: A Knowledge Management Perspective. *International Journal of Advanced Computer Science and Applications, 13*(8), 193–203. doi:10.14569/IJACSA.2022.0130823

Bin-Hady, W. R. A., Al-Kadi, A., Hazaea, A., & Ali, J. K. M. (2023). Exploring the dimensions of ChatGPT in English language learning: A global perspective. *Library Hi Tech*. Advance online publication. doi:10.1108/LHT-05-2023-0200

Birck, J. (2017). *Zarah und Zottel: ein Pony auf vier Pfoten*. Fischer Sauerländer Verlag.

Birdsell, B. (2022). Student Writings with DeepL: Teacher Evaluations and Implications for Teaching. *JALT Postconference Publication*, *2021*(1), 117. doi:10.37546/JALTPCP2021-14

Birks, M., Chapman, Y., & Francis, K. (2008). Memoing in qualitative research: Probing data and processes. *Journal of Research in Nursing*, *13*(1), 68–75. doi:10.1177/1744987107081254

Bolton, K., Bacon-Shone, J., & Lee, S.-l. (2020). Societal multilingualism in Hong Kong. In P. Siemund & J. Leimgruber (Eds.), *Multilingual global cities: Dubai, Hong Kong and Singapore* (pp. 160–184). Routledge. doi:10.4324/9780429463860-12

Bolton, K., & Lee, S.-l. (2020). A socio-historical approach to multilingualism in Hong Kong. In P. Siemund & J. Leimgruber (Eds.), *Multilingual global cities: Hong Kong, Singapore, and Dubai* (pp. 38–62). Routledge. doi:10.4324/9780429463860-4

Bonner, E., Lege, R., & Frazier, E. (2023). Large Language Model-Based Artificial Intelligence in the Language Classroom: Practical Ideas for Teaching. *Teaching English with Technology*, *2023*(1). doi:10.56297/BKAM1691/WIEO1749

Bonner, E., Lege, R., & Frazier, E. (2023). Large language model-based artificial intelligence in the language classroom: Practical ideas for teaching. *Teaching English with Technology, 23*(1).

Borenstein, J., & Howard, A. (2021). Emerging challenges in AI and the need for AI ethics education. *AI and Ethics*, *1*(1), 61–65. doi:10.1007/s43681-020-00002-7

Bostrom, N., Yudkowsky, E., & Frankish, K. (2014). The Cambridge handbook of artificial intelligence. In K. Frankish & W. M. Ramsey (Eds.), *The ethics of artificial intelligence* (Vol. 316, p. 334). Cambridge University Press.

Bozkurt, A. (2023). Generative artificial intelligence (AI) powered conversational educational agents: The inevitable paradigm shift. *Asian Journal of Distance Education, 18*(1).

Branson, R. K., Rayner, G. T., Cox, J. L., Furman, J. P., King, F. J., & Hannum, W. H. (1975). Interservice procedures for instructional systems development.: Vol. 1-5. *TRADOC Pam 350-30, NAVEDTRA 106A).* U.S. Army Training and Doctrine Command.

Braunmüller, K. (2007). Receptive multilingualism in northern Europe in the Middle Ages. In J. D. ten Thije & L. Zeevaert (Eds.), *Receptive multilingualism. Linguistic analyses, language policies and didactic concepts* (pp. 25–47). John Benjamins.

Braun, V., & Clarke, V. (2006). Using thematic analysis in psychology. *Qualitative Research in Psychology, 3*(2), 77–101. doi:10.1191/1478088706qp063oa

Braun, V., Clarke, V., Boulton, E., Davey, L., & McEvoy, C. (2020). The online survey as a qualitative research tool. *International Journal of Social Research Methodology, 00*(00), 1–14. doi:10.1080/13645579.2020.1805550

Brena, R. F., Zuvirie, E., Preciado, A., Valdiviezo, A., Gonzalez-Mendoza, M., & Zozaya-Gorostiza, C. (2021). Automated evaluation of foreign language speaking performance with machine learning. [IJIDeM]. *International Journal on Interactive Design and Manufacturing, 15*(2–3), 317–331. doi:10.1007/s12008-021-00759-z

Briggs, N. (2018). Neural Machine Translation Tools in the Language Learning Classroom: Students' Use, Perceptions, and Analyses. *The JALT CALL Journal, 14*(1), 3–24. Advance online publication. doi:10.29140/jaltcall.v14n1.221

Brownell, J., & Swaner, L. (2010). *Five High-Impact Practices: Research on Learning Outcomes, Completion, and Quality*. Association of American Colleges and Universities.

Bruffee, K. A. (1984). Collaborative learning and the "Conversation of Mankind.". *College English, 46*(7), 635. doi:10.2307/376924

Buchanan-Shrader, H. (2023). Top 8 *Ways Chinese Teachers Can Use ChatGPT to Create Lesson Plans*. https://www.thechairmansbao.com/blog/chatgpt-teach-chinese/

Burgsteiner, H., Kandlhofer, M., & Steinbauer, G. (2016). Irobot: Teaching the basics of artificial intelligence in high schools. *Proceedings of the AAAI Conference on Artificial Intelligence, 30*(1). Advance online publication. doi:10.1609/aaai.v30i1.9864

Burkhard, M. (2022). Student Perceptions of Ai-Powered Writing Tools: Towards Individualized Teaching Strategies. *Proceedings of the 19th International Conference on Cognition and Exploratory Learning in the Digital Age, CELDA 2022, Celda*, 73–81. 10.33965/CELDA2022_202207L010

Busch, W. (2015). *Max und Moritz: eine Bubengeschichte in Sieben Streichen*. Esslinger Verlag.

Byram, M. (2020). *Teaching and assessing intercultural communicative competence: Revisited*. Multilingual Matters. doi:10.21832/BYRAM0244

Byrnes, H., & Manchón, R. M. (2014). Task-based language learning: Insights from and for L2 writing. An Introduction. In H. Byrnes & R. M. Manchón (Eds.), *Task-based language learning—Insights from and for L2 writing* (pp. 1–23). John Benjamins. doi:10.1075/tblt.7.01byr

Cai, W. (2023, February 24). ChatGPT can be powerful tool for language learning: The innovation offers multiple opportunities for language teaching and learning. *University Affairs*. https://www.universityaffairs.ca/career-advice/career-advice-article/chatgpt-can-be-powerful-tool-for-language-learning/

Camacho, A., Alves, R. A., & Boscolo, P. (2021). Writing motivation in school: A systematic review of empirical research in the early twenty-first century. *Educational Psychology Review*, *33*(1), 213–247. doi:10.1007/s10648-020-09530-4

Candelier, M. (2013). *Janua linguarum – The gateway to languages – The introduction of language awareness into the curriculum: Awakening to languages*. Council of Europe.

Candelier, M., Daryai-Hansen, P., & Schröder-Sura, A. (2013). The framework of reference for pluralistic approaches to languages and cultures–a complement to the CEFR to develop plurilingual and intercultural competences. *Innovation in Language Learning and Teaching*, *6*(3), 243–257. doi:10.1080/17501229.2012.725252

Cardona, M. A., Rodríguez, R. J., & Ishmael, K. (2023). *Artificial Intelligence and the Future of Teaching and Learning: Insights and Recommendations*. U.S. Department of Education, Office of Educational Technology. https://policycommons.net/artifacts/3854312/ai-report/4660267/

Carlson, M., Pack, A., & Escalante, J. (2023). Utilizing OpenAI's GPT-4 for written feedback. *TESOL Journal*, *759*, e759. Advance online publication. doi:10.1002/tesj.759

Carrington, V. (2005). Txting: The end of civilization (again)? *Cambridge Journal of Education*, *35*(2), 161–175. doi:10.1080/03057640500146799

Carvalho, L., Martinez-maldonado, R., Tsai, Y., & Markauskaite, L. (2022). Computers and Education : Artificial Intelligence How can we design for learning in an AI world ? *Computers and Education: Artificial Intelligence, 3*(July), 100053. doi:10.1016/j.caeai.2022.100053

Cavalcanti, A. P., Diego, A., Carvalho, R., Freitas, F., Tsai, Y. S., Gaˇsevi´c, D., & Mello, R. F. (2021). Automatic feedback in online learning environments: A systematic literature review. *Computers and Education: Artificial Intelligence*, 100027.

Cavanagh, S. R. (2020). How to make your teaching more engaging. *The Chronicle of Higher Education*.

Celik, I., Dindar, M., Muukkonen, H., & Järvelä, S. (2022). The promises and challenges of artificial intelligence for teachers: A systematic review of research. *TechTrends*, *66*(4), 616–630. doi:10.1007/s11528-022-00715-y

Chan, C. K. Y. (2023). A comprehensive AI policy education framework for university teaching and learning. *International Journal of Educational Technology in Higher Education*, *2023*(20), 38. doi:10.1186/s41239-023-00408-3

Chan, C. K. Y., & Hu, W. (2023). Students' voices on generative AI: Perceptions, benefits, and challenges in higher education. *International Journal of Educational Technology in Higher Education*, *20*(1), 43. doi:10.1186/s41239-023-00411-8

Chang, D. H., Lin, M. P.-C., Hajian, S., & Wang, Q. Q. (2023). Educational Design Principles of Using AI Chatbot That Supports Self-Regulated Learning in Education: Goal Setting, Feedback, and Personalization. *Sustainability*, *15*(17), 12921-. doi:10.3390/su151712921

Chassignol, M., Khoroshavin, A., Klimova, A., & Bilyatdinova, A. (2018). Artificial Intelligence trends in education: A narrative overview. *Procedia Computer Science*, *136*, 16–24. doi:10.1016/j.procs.2018.08.233

Chaudhry, M., & Kazim, E. (2021). Artificial intelligence in education (AIEd): A high-level academic and industry note 2021. *AI and Ethics*, *2*(1), 157–165. doi:10.1007/s43681-021-00074-z PMID:34790953

Chavez, M. (2016). Students' accounts of grammatical forms of German that are difficult, unattainable, and irrelevant for self-expression. *Language Awareness*, *25*(3), 197–221. doi:10.1080/09658416.2016.1165238

Chavez, M. (2017). Hard rules and bad memories: College learner's accounts of what makes learning German grammar difficult. *Die Unterrichtspraxis*, *50*(1), 1–21. doi:10.1111/tger.12018

Chen, L. (2023, June 23). Hong Kong rolls out first AI curriculum for junior secondary students, including lessons on ChatGPT, with 'lives definitely affected by artificial intelligence'. *South China Morning Post.*

Chen, L., Chen, P., & Lin, Z. (2020). Artificial intelligence in education: A review. *IEEE Access : Practical Innovations, Open Solutions*, *8*, 75264–75278. doi:10.1109/ACCESS.2020.2988510

Chen, X., Xie, H., & Hwang, G. J. (2020). A multi-perspective study on Artificial Intelligence in Education: Grants, conferences, journals, software tools, institutions, and researchers. *Computers and Education: Artificial Intelligence*, *1*(October), 100005. doi:10.1016/j.caeai.2020.100005

Chen, X., Zhou, D., Xie, H., Cheng, G., & Liu, C. (2022). Two decades of artificial intelligence in education: Contributors, collaborations, research topics, challenges, and future directions. *Journal of Educational Technology & Society*, *25*(1), 28–47.

Chen, X., Zou, D., Xie, H., & Cheng, G. (2021). Twenty years of personalized language learning. *Journal of Educational Technology & Society*, *24*(1), 205–222.

Chin, A. C. (2023). A corpus-based approach to learning and teaching Cantonese. In S. L. Lee (Ed.), The learning and teaching of Cantonese as a second language (pp. 184–195). Routledge.

Chin, K. Y., Wu, C. H., & Hong, Z. W. (2011). A humanoid robot as a teaching assistant for primary education. In *2011 Fifth International Conference on Genetic and Evolutionary Computing* (pp. 21-24). IEEE. 10.1109/ICGEC.2011.13

Chiu, T. K. F., Meng, H., Chai, C.-S., King, I., Wong, S., & Yam, Y. (2022). Creation and Evaluation of a Pretertiary Artificial Intelligence (AI) Curriculum. *IEEE Transactions on Education*, *65*(1), 30–39. doi:10.1109/TE.2021.3085878

Chmarkh, M. (2021). "Writing to learn" research: A synthesis of empirical studies (2004-2019). *European Journal of Educational Research*, *10*(1), 85–96. doi:10.12973/eu-jer.10.1.85

Choi, Y., & Suh, K. H. (2022). Verifying the usefulness of the theory of planned behavior model for predicting illegal use of online content: The role of outcome expectancies and social loafing. *BMC Psychology*, *10*(1), 1–12. doi:10.1186/s40359-022-00978-3 PMID:36371253

Cholij, M. (1994). *Practice in Spanish Grammar*. Mary Glasgow Publications.

Clark, D. (2020). *Artificial intelligence for learning: How to use AI to support employee development*. Kogan Page Publishers.

Clark, D. (2021). *Learning experience design: How to create effective learning that works*. Kogan Page Limited.

Cohen, I. L., Liu, X., Hudson, M., Gillis, J., Cavalari, R. N., Romanczyk, R. G., Karmel, B. Z., & Gardner, J. M. (2017). Level 2 Screening With the PDD Behavior Inventory: Subgroup Profiles and Implications for Differential Diagnosis. *Canadian Journal of School Psychology*, *32*(3-4), 299–315. doi:10.1177/0829573517721127

Cohen, M. D., & Téllez, K. (1994). Implementing cooperative learning for language minority students. *Bilingual Research Journal*, *18*(1–2), 1–19. doi:10.1080/15235882.1994.10162655

Collen, I. (2020). *Language Trends 2020. Language Teaching in primary and secondary schools in England*. British Council.

Collen, I. (2021). *Language Trends 2021. Language Teaching in primary and secondary schools in England*. British Council.

Collen, I. (2022). *Language Trends 2022. Language Teaching in primary and secondary schools in England*. British Council.

Collen, I. (2023). *Language Trends Northern Ireland 2023: Language teaching in Primary and Post-Primary Schools*. British Council.

Coniam, D. (2014). The linguistic accuracy of chatbots: Usability from an ESL perspective. *Text & Talk*, *34*(5), 545–567. doi:10.1515/text-2014-0018

Connor, U. (1998). Contrastive rhetoric: Developments and challenges. *Studia Anglica Posnaniensia*, *33*, 105–116.

Cope, B., Kalantzis, M., & Searsmith, D. (2021). Artificial intelligence for education: Knowledge and its assessment in AI-enabled learning ecologies. *Educational Philosophy and Theory*, *53*(12), 1229–1245. doi:10.1080/00131857.2020.1728732

Council of Europe. (2001). *Common European Framework of Reference for Languages: Learning, Teaching, Assessment*. Cambridge University Press.

Council of Europe. (2021). *Common European Framework of Reference for Languages: Learning, Teaching, Assessment—Companion Volume*. Council of Europe Publishing.

Council of Europe. (n.d.). *Common European Framework of Reference for Languages: Learning, teaching, assessment*. https://www.coe.int/en/web/common-european-framework-reference-languages

Creswell, J. W. (2012). *Educational research*. Pearson.

Critchley, M., Chaurin, T., & De Madeiros, A. (2022). *Survey of Language Provision in UK Universities in 2022*. Report no. 4, diciembre. University Council of Modern Languages (UCML), Association for University Language Communities in the UK and Ireland (AULC), United Kingdom.

Critchley, M., Illingworth, J., & Wright, V. (2021). *Survey of Language Provision in UK Universities in 2021*. Report no. 3, julio. University Council of Modern Languages (UCML), Association for University Language Communities in the UK and Ireland (AULC), United Kingdom.

Crompton, H., & Burke, D. (2023). Artificial intelligence in higher education: The state of the field. *International Journal of Educational Technology in Higher Education*, *20*(1), 22. doi:10.1186/s41239-023-00392-8

Dakakni, D., & Safa, N. (2023). Artificial intelligence in the L2 classroom: Implications and challenges on ethics and equity in higher education: A 21st century Pandora's box, Computers and Education. *Artificial Intelligence*, *5*, 100179. Advance online publication. doi:10.1016/j.caeai.2023.100179

Dale, R. (2021). GPT-3: What's it good for? *Natural Language Engineering*, *27*(1), 113–118. doi:10.1017/S1351324920000601

Dalton-Puffer, C. (2011). Content-and-Language Integrated Learning: From Practice to Principles? *Annual Review of Applied Linguistics*, *31*, 182–204. Advance online publication. doi:10.1017/S0267190511000092

Danan, M. (2004). Captioning and subtitling: Undervalued language learning strategies. *Meta*, *49*(1), 67–77. doi:10.7202/009021ar

Davenport, T. H., & Ronanki, R. (2018). Artificial intelligence for the real world. *Harvard Business Review*, *96*(1), 108–116.

De Oliveira, L. C., Jones, L., & Smith, S. L. (2019). Multimodal literacies in the english language arts classroom for english language learners. In English language education (pp. 21–31). doi:10.1007/978-3-030-02245-7_2

Declerck, R. (2006). The grammar of the English verb phrase.: Vol. 1. *The grammar of the English tense system. A comprehensive analysis*. De Gruyter. doi:10.1515/9783110199888

Department for Education. (2014). *The national curriculum in England. Key stages 3 and 4 framework document* [DFE-00183-2013]. Retrieved from: https://assets.publishing.service.gov.uk/government/uploads/system/uploads/attachment_data/file/840002/Secondary_national_curriculum_corrected_PDF.pdf

Dewey, J. (2023). *Experiential Education: Complete Collection: Problem-Based Learning, Pragmatic Philosophy of Scholarship, Democracy & Education*. Sharp Ink Publisher.

Dewi, H. K., Putri, R. E., Rahim, N. A., Wardani, T. I., & Pandin, M. G. R. (2021). *The use of AI (artificial intelligence) in English learning among university student: Case study in English Department, Universitas Airlangga*. https://doi.org/ doi:10.31235/osf.io/x3qr6

Dick, W., & Carey, L. (1978). *The systematic design of instruction*. Scott, Foresman.

Dincer, S. (2018). Are preservice teachers really literate enough to integrate technology in their classroom practice? Determining the technology literacy level of preservice teachers. *Education and Information Technologies*, *23*(6), 2699–2718. doi:10.1007/s10639-018-9737-z

Dizon, G., & Gayed, J. M. (2021). Examining the Impact of Grammarly on the Quality of Mobile L2 Writing. *The JALT CALL Journal*, *17*(2), 74–92. doi:10.29140/jaltcall.v17n2.336

Dodigovic, M. (2007). Artificial intelligence and second language learning: An efficient approach to error remediation. *Language Awareness*, *16*(2), 99–113. doi:10.2167/la416.0

Dooly, M. (2023). Moving Back into the Classroom while Moving beyond Current Paradigms: Lessons for Post-Covid Language Education. *Technology-Enhanced Language Teaching and Learning: Lessons from the Covid-19 Pandemic*, 213.

Dörnyei, Z., & Ushioda, E. (Eds.). (2009). *Motivation, language identity and the L2 self*. Multilingual Matters. doi:10.21832/9781847691293

Dreibelbis, E. (2023). *Google Translate vs. ChatGPT: Which One Is the Best Language Translator?* PCMag UK. https://uk.pcmag.com/ai/147242/google-translate-vs-chatgpt-which-one-is-the-best-language-translator#:~:text=AI Will Level Up Web Translation&text=But as we saw with,Translate's capabilities across the board.

Dwivedi, Y. K., Kshetri, N., Hughes, L., Slade, E. L., Jeyaraj, A., Kar, A. K., Baabdullah, A. M., Koohang, A., Raghavan, V., Ahuja, M., Albanna, H., Albashrawi, M. A., Al-Busaidi, A. S., Balakrishnan, J., Barlette, Y., Basu, S., Bose, I., Brooks, L., Buhalis, D., ... Wright, R. (2023). Opinion Paper: "So what if ChatGPT wrote it?" Multidisciplinary perspectives on opportunities, challenges and implications of generative conversational AI for research, practice and policy. *International Journal of Information Management*, *71*, 102642. doi:10.1016/j.ijinfomgt.2023.102642

East, M. (2015). Task-based teaching and learning: Pedagogical implications. In N. Van Deusen-Scholl & S. May (Eds.), *Second and foreign language education. Encyclopedia of language and education* (pp. 85–95). Springer. doi:10.1007/978-3-319-02323-6_8-1

Educause. (2018). *Horizon report: 2018 higher education edition*. Author.

Edwards, B. I., & Cheok, A. D. (2018). Why not robot teachers: Artificial intelligence for addressing teacher shortage. *Applied Artificial Intelligence*, *32*(4), 345–360. doi:10.1080/08839514.2018.1464286

Eguchi, A. (2021). AI-powered educational robotics as a learning tool to promote artificial intelligence and computer science education. In Advances in intelligent systems and computing (pp. 279–287). doi:10.1007/978-3-030-82544-7_26

Ehara, Y. (2023). *Innovative Software to Efficiently Learn English Through Extensive Reading and Personalized Vocabulary Acquisition*. Academic Press.

Ellis, R. (2009). Implicit and explicit learning, knowledge, and instruction. In R. Ellis, S. Loewen, C. Elder, H. Reinders, R. Erlam, & J. Philp, J. (Eds.), Implicit and explicit knowledge in second language learning, testing, and teaching (pp. 3–26). Multilingual Matters. doi:10.21832/9781847691767-003

Ellis, N. C. (2015). Implicit AND explicit learning of language. In P. Rebuschat (Ed.), *Implicit and explicit learning of language* (pp. 3–24). Benjamins. doi:10.1075/sibil.48.01ell

Ellis, R. (2006). Current issue in the teaching of grammar: An SLA perspective. *TESOL Quarterly*, *40*(1), 83–107. doi:10.2307/40264512

Ellis, R. (2016). Focus on form: A critical review. *Language Teaching Research*, *20*(3), 405–428. doi:10.1177/1362168816628627

El-Sabagh, H. A. (2021). Adaptive e-learning environment based on learning styles and its impact on development students' engagement. *International Journal of Educational Technology in Higher Education*, *18*(1), 53. Advance online publication. doi:10.1186/s41239-021-00289-4

Ennis, R. H. (2015). Critical thinking: A streamlined conception. In M. Davies & R. Barnett (Eds.), *The Palgrave Handbook of Critical Thinking in Higher Education*. doi:10.1057/9781137378057_2

Esplugas, M. (2023). The use of artificial intelligence (AI) to enhance academic communication, education and research: A balanced approach. *The Journal of Hand Surgery*, *48*(8), 819–822. doi:10.1177/17531934231185746 PMID:37417005

Eun, B. (2010). From learning to development: A sociocultural approach to instruction. *Cambridge Journal of Education*, *40*(4), 401–418. doi:10.1080/0305764X.2010.526593

EUROSTAT. (2016). *Number of foreign languages known (self-reported) by sex* [edat_aes_l21] Retrieved from: https://appsso.eurostat.ec.europa.eu/nui/submitViewTableAction.do

EUROSTAT. (2022). *Pupils by education level and number of modern foreign languages studied - absolute numbers and % of pupils by number of languages studied* [EDUC_UOE_LANG02] Retrieved from: https://ec.europa.eu/eurostat/databrowser/view/educ_uoe_lang02/default/table?lang=en

Fan, Y., Saint, J., Singh, S., Jovanovic, J., & Gasevic, D. (2021). A learning analytic approach to unveiling self-regulatory processes in learning tactics. *LAK21: 11th international learning analytics and knowledge conference*, 184–195.

Ferris, D., & Hedgcock, J. (2014). *Teaching L2 composition: Purpose, process, and practice* (3rd ed.). Routledge.

Fink, L. D. (2016). *Creating significant learning experiences: An integrated approach to designing college courses*. John Wiley& Sons.

Fink, L. D. (2016). *Five High-Impact Teaching practices* (Vol. 9). Collected Essays on Learning and Teaching.

Fitria, T. N. (2021). Grammarly" as AI-powered English Writing Assistant. *Journal of English Language Literature and Teaching, 5*(1), 65-78.

Flower, L., & Hayes, J. R. (1981). A cognitive process theory of writing. *College Composition and Communication*, *32*(4), 365–387. doi:10.2307/356600

Foltýnek, T., Bjelobaba, S., Glendinning, I., Khan, Z. R., Santos, R., Pavletic, P., & Kravjar, J. (2023). ENAI Recommendations on the Ethical Use of Artificial Intelligence in Education. *International Journal for Educational Integrity*, *19*(1), 12. Advance online publication. doi:10.1007/s40979-023-00133-4

Fryer, L. K., Nakao, K., & Thompson, A. (2019). Chatbot learning partners: Connecting learning experiences, interest and competence. *Computers in Human Behavior*, *93*, 279–289. doi:10.1016/j.chb.2018.12.023

Fryer, L., Coniam, D., Carpenter, R., & Lăpuşneanu, D. (2020). Bots for language learning now: Current and future directions. *Language Learning & Technology*, *24*(2), 8–22.

Fulford, M. (2023). *In the AI age, it's time to change how we teach and grade writing: If we continue to treat the use of AI as plagiarism, we're doomed to fail. Here's what we should be doing instead.* Chalkbeat Colorado. https://co.chalkbeat.org/2023/8/4/23820783/ai-chat-gpt-teaching-writing-grading?fbclid=IwAR2IuQa23f0M6dxmfay5nB_DlQgrJfMf-Pmm9hMbrWYVMW3WKAaruL3XrNKE

Fu, S., Gu, H., & Yang, B. (2020). The affordances of AI-enabled automatic scoring applications on learners' continuous learning intention: An empirical study in China. *British Journal of Educational Technology*, *51*(5), 1674–1692. doi:10.1111/bjet.12995

Gado, S., Kempen, R., Lingelbach, K., & Bipp, T. (2022). Artificial intelligence in Psychology: How can we enable psychology students to accept and use artificial intelligence? *Psychology Learning & Teaching*, *21*(1), 37–56. doi:10.1177/14757257211037149

Gagné, R. M. (1965). *The conditions of learning*. Holt, Rinehart, and Winston.

Gallacher, A., Thompson, A., Howarth, M., Taalas, P., Jalkanen, J., Bradley, L., & Thouësny, S. (2018). "My robot is an idiot!"–Students' perceptions of AI in the L2 classroom. *Future-proof CALL: language learning as exploration and encounters–short papers from EUROCALL*, 70-76.

Gandhi, T. K., Classen, D. C., Sinsky, C. A., Rhew, D. C., Garde, N. V., Roberts, A., & Federico, F. (2023). How can artificial intelligence decrease cognitive and work burden for front line practitioners? *JAMIA Open*, *6*(3), ooad079. Advance online publication. doi:10.1093/jamiaopen/ooad079 PMID:37655124

GaoC. A.HowardF. M.MarkovN. S.DyerE. C.RameshS.LuoY.PearsonA. T. (2022). Comparing scientific abstracts generated by ChatGPT to original abstracts using an artificial intelligence output detector, plagiarism detector, and blinded human reviewers. doi:10.1101/2022.12.23.521610

Gartner, S., & Krašna, M. (2023). Artificial intelligence in education - Ethical framework. In *12th Mediterranean Conference on Embedded Computing (MECO)* (pp. 1-7). 10.1109/MECO58584.2023.10155012

Gaudioso, E., Montero, M., & Hernandez-del-Olmo, F. (2012). Supporting teachers in adaptive educational systems through predictive models: A proof of concept. *Expert Systems with Applications*, *39*(1), 621–625. doi:10.1016/j.eswa.2011.07.052

Gayed, J. M., Carlon, M. K. J., Oriola, A. M., & Cross, J. S. (2022). Exploring an AI-based writing assistant's impact on English language learners. *Computers and Education: Artificial Intelligence*, *3*(100055), 100055. Advance online publication. doi:10.1016/j.caeai.2022.100055

Ghali, M. A., Ayyad, A. A., Abu-Naser, S. S., & Abu, M. (2018). An Intelligent Tutoring System for Teaching English Grammar. *International Journal of Academic Engineering Research*, *2*(2), 1–6.

Gilakjani, A. P. (2012). The significant role of multimedia in motivating EFL learners' interest in English language learning. *International Journal of Modern Education and Computer Science*, *4*(4), 57–66. doi:10.5815/ijmecs.2012.04.08

Gilmore, A. (2007). Authentic materials and authenticity in foreign language learning. *Language Teaching*, *40*(2), 97–118. doi:10.1017/S0261444807004144

Ginn, J., Salas, C. B., Barlowe, S., & Lehman, W. (2021). A novel framework for integrating mobile machine learning and L2 vocabulary acquisition. *Journal of Computing Sciences in Colleges*, *36*(5), 47–56.

Giorgi, A., & Pianesi, F. (1997). *Tense and aspect: from semantics to morphosyntax*. Oxford University Press. doi:10.1093/oso/9780195091922.001.0001

Godwin-Jones, R. (2022). Partnering with AI: Intelligent writing assistance and instructed language learning. *Language Learning & Technology*, *26*(2), 5–24.

Golonka, E. M., Bowles, A. R., Frank, V. M., Richardson, D. L., & Freynik, S. (2014). Technologies for foreign language learning: A review of technology types and their effectiveness. *Computer Assisted Language Learning*, *27*(1), 70–105. doi:10.1080/09588221.2012.700315

Gong, X., Tang, Y., Liu, X., Jing, S., Cui, W., Liang, J., & Wang, F. Y. (2020, October). K-9 artificial intelligence education in qingdao: Issues, challenges and suggestions. *IEEE international conference on networking, sensing, and control (ICNSC),* 1–6.

Graham, M., Milanowski, A., & Miller, J. (2012). *Measuring and Promoting Inter-Rater Agreement of Teacher and Principal Performance Ratings*. Online Submission.

Grassini, S. (2023). Shaping the Future of Education: Exploring the Potential and Consequences of AI and ChatGPT in Educational Settings. *Education Sciences*, *13*(7), 692-. doi:10.3390/educsci13070692

Griffin, P., & Care, E. (Eds.). (2014). *Assessment and teaching of 21st-century skills: Methods and approach*. Springer. doi:10.1007/978-94-017-9395-7

Grimes, D., & Warschauer, M. (2010). Utility in a fallible tool: A multi-site case study of automated writing evaluation. Journal of Technology. *Language, and Assessment*, *8*(6), 1–43.

Guo, K., & Wang, D. (2023). To resist it or to embrace it? Examining ChatGPT's potential to support teacher feedback in EFL writing. *Education and Information Technologies*. Advance online publication. doi:10.1007/s10639-023-12146-0

Haenlein, M., & Kaplan, A. (2019). A brief history of artificial intelligence: On the past, present, and future of artificial intelligence. *California Management Review*, *61*(4), 5–14. doi:10.1177/0008125619864925

Hagendorff, T. (2020). The ethics of AI ethics: An evaluation of guidelines. *Minds and Machines*, *30*(1), 99–120. doi:10.1007/s11023-020-09517-8

Haleem, A., Javaid, M., & Pratap, R. (2023). BenchCouncil Transactions on Benchmarks, Standards and Evaluations An era of ChatGPT as a significant futuristic support tool : A study on features, abilities, and challenges. *BenchCouncil Transactions on Benchmarks. Standards and Evaluations*, *2*(4), 100089. doi:10.1016/j.tbench.2023.100089

Hall, S. (1996). Introduction: Who needs "identity"? In S. Hall & P. Du Gay (Eds.), *Questions of Cultural Identity* (pp. 1–17). Sage.

Hammerly, H. (1986). *Synthesis in language teaching: An introduction to languistics*. Second Language Publications.

Hang, N. T. T. (2023). EFL Teachers' Perspectives toward the Use of ChatGPT in Writing Classes: A Case Study at Van Lang University. *International Journal of Language Instruction*, *2*(3), 1–47. doi:10.54855/ijli.23231

Hapsari, I. P., & Wu, T. T. (2022). AI chatbots learning model in English speaking skill: Alleviating speaking anxiety, boosting enjoyment, and fostering critical thinking. In *Innovative Technologies and Learning. ICITL 2022*. Springer. doi:10.1007/978-3-031-15273-3_49

Haristiani, N. (2019). Artificial Intelligence (AI) chatbot as language learning medium: An inquiry. In Journal of Physics: Conference Series (Vol. 1387, No. 1, p. 012020). IOP Publishing. doi:10.1088/1742-6596/1387/1/012020

Harklau, L., & Pinnow, R. (2009). Adolescent Second-Language Writing. In L. Christenbury, R. Bomer, & P. Smagorinsky (Eds.), *Handbook of Adolescent Literacy Research* (pp. 126–134). Guilford Publications.

Harvard Business School. (2023). *2.1 Academic Standards of Conduct.* Harvard Business School MBA. https://www.hbs.edu/mba/handbook/standards-of-conduct/academic/Pages/chatgpt-and-ai.aspx

Hasbún, L. (1995). *The role of lexical aspect in the acquisition of the tense/aspct system in L2 Spanish* [Doctoral dissertation]. Indiana University, Bloomington.

Hassan Taj, I., Ali, F., Sipra, M., & Ahmad, W. (2017). *Effect of technology enhanced language learning on EFL reading comprehension at tertiary level. Arab World English Journal*, 8.

Heffernan, N. T., & Heffernan, C. L. (2014). The ASSISTments ecosystem: Building a platform that brings scientists and teachers together for minimally invasive research on human learning and teaching. *International Journal of Artificial Intelligence in Education*, *24*(4), 470–497. doi:10.1007/s40593-014-0024-x

Heil, C. R., Wu, J. S., Lee, J. J., & Schmidt, T. (2016). A review of mobile language learning applications: Trends, challenges, and opportunities. *The EuroCALL Review*, *24*(2), 32–50. doi:10.4995/eurocall.2016.6402

Hejazi, S. Y., & Sadoughi, M. (2023). How does teacher support contribute to learners' grit? The role of learning enjoyment. *Innovation in Language Learning and Teaching*, *17*(3), 593–606. doi:10.1080/17501229.2022.2098961

Hill, J., Ford, W. F., & Farreras, I. G. (2015). Real conversations with artificial intelligence: A comparison between human-human online conversations and human–chatbot conversations. *Computers in Human Behavior*, *49*, 245–250. doi:10.1016/j.chb.2015.02.026

Hodges, C. B., Moore, S., Lockee, B. B., Trust, T., & Bond, M. A. (2020). *The difference between emergency remote teaching and online learning*. Academic Press.

Hoffmann, H. (2005). *Der Struwwelpeter*. Loewe Verlag GmbH.

Holmes, W., Porayska-Pomsta, K., Holstein, K., Sutherland, E., Baker, T. T., Shum, S. B., Santos, O. C., Rodrigo, M. M. T., Cukurova, M., Bittencourt, I. I., & Koedinger, K. R. (2021). Ethics of AI in education: Towards a community-wide framework. *International Journal of Artificial Intelligence in Education*, *32*(3), 504–526. doi:10.1007/s40593-021-00239-1

Hong, W. C. H. (2023). The impact of ChatGPT on foreign language teaching and learning: Opportunities in education and research. *Journal of Educ. Technol. Innov.*, *5*, 37–45.

Hong, W. C. H. (2023). The impact of ChatGPT on foreign language teaching and learning: Opportunities in education and research. *Journal of Educational Technology and Innovation*, *5*(1). https://jeti.thewsu.org/index.php/cieti/article/view/103

Hooda, M., Rana, C., Dahiya, O., Rizwan, A., & Hossain, M. S. (2022). Artificial intelligence for assessment and feedback to enhance student success in higher education. *Mathematical Problems in Engineering*, *2022*, 1–19. Advance online publication. doi:10.1155/2022/5215722

Hopkins, E. (2022). Machine learning tools, algorithms, and techniques. *Journal of Self-Governance and Management Economics*, *10*(1), 43–55.

Hou, Y. (2020). Foreign language education in the era of artificial intelligence. In Advances in Intelligent Systems and Computing (pp. 937–944). doi:10.1007/978-981-15-2568-1_128

Howard, K. B. (2023). Supporting learners with special educational needs and disabilities in the foreign languages classroom. *Support for Learning*, *38*(3), 154–161. doi:10.1111/1467-9604.12449

Hsu, Y.-C., & Ching, Y.-H. (2023). Generative Artificial Intelligence in education, Part One: The dynamic frontier. *TechTrends: Linking Research & Practice to Improve Learning, 67*(4), 603–607. doi:10.1007/s11528-023-00863-9

Huang, W. (2023). Memes in Language Classrooms: From Traditional to AI-Generated. *FLTMagazine*. https://fltmag.com/memes-in-language-classrooms-from-traditional-to-ai-generated/

Huang, W., Hew, K. F., & Fryer, L. K. (2022). Chatbots for language learning – are they really useful? A systematic review of chatbot-supported language learning. *Journal of Computer Assisted Learning*, *38*(1), 237–257. doi:10.1111/jcal.12610

Huang, X., Zou, D., Cheng, G., Chen, X., & Xie, H. (2023). Trends, Research Issues and Applications of Artificial Intelligence in Language Education. *Journal of Educational Technology & Society*, *26*(1), 112–131.

Huang, X., Zou, D., Cheng, G., Chen, X., & Xie, H. (2023). Trends, research issues and applications of artificial intelligence in language education. *Journal of Educational Technology & Society*, *26*(1), 112–131. https://www.jstor.org/stable/48707971

Huang, Y., & Wilson, J. (2021). Using automated feedback to develop writing proficiency. *Computers and Composition*, *62*, 102675. doi:10.1016/j.compcom.2021.102675

Hussherr, F.-X., & Hussherr, C. (2017). *Construire le modèle éducatif du 21e siècle-Les promesses de la digitalisation et les nouveaux modes d'apprentissage*. FYP éditions.

Huttenlocher, J., Haight, W., Bryk, A., Seltzer, M., & Lyons, T. (1991). Early vocabulary growth: Relation to language input and gender. *Developmental Psychology*, *27*(2), 236–248. doi:10.1037/0012-1649.27.2.236

Ifelebuegu, A. O., Kulume, P., & Cherukut, P. (2023). Chatbots and AI in Education (AIEd) tools: The good, the bad, and the ugly. *Journal of Applied Learning and Teaching*, *6*(2).

Immordino-Yang, M. T. (2015). *Emotions, Learning, and the Brain: Exploring the Educational Implications of Affective Neuroscience*. Norton Professional Books.

Incecay, V., & Dollar, Y. K. (2011). Foreign language learners' beliefs about grammar instruction and error correction. *Procedia: Social and Behavioral Sciences*, *15*, 3394–3398. doi:10.1016/j.sbspro.2011.04.307

Indiana University Knowledge Base. (2023). *Acceptable uses of generative AI services at IU*. https://kb.iu.edu/d/biit

Instituto Cervantes. (2023). *El español en el mundo 2023*. Anuario del Instituto Cervantes.

Ironsi, C. S. (2022). Navigating learners towards technology-enhanced learning during post COVID-19 semesters. *Trends in Neuroscience and Education*, *29*, 100189. doi:10.1016/j.tine.2022.100189 PMID:36470617

Jaiswal, A., & Arun, C. J. (2021). Potential of artificial intelligence for transformation of the education system in India. *International Journal of Education and Development Using Information and Communication Technology*, *17*(1), 142–158.

Janisch, H., & Zwerger, L. (2008). *Die Arche Noah*. Minedition.

Jatzlau, S., Michaeli, T., Seegerer, S., & Romeike, R. (2019). *It's not magic after all–machine learning in snap! Using reinforcement learning*. Academic Press.

Jean, G., & Simard, D. (2011). Grammar teaching and learning in L2: Necessary, but boring? *Foreign Language Annals*, *44*(3), 467–494. doi:10.1111/j.1944-9720.2011.01143.x

Jeon, J. (2021). Exploring AI chatbot affordances in the EFL classroom: Young learners' experiences and perspectives. *Computer Assisted Language Learning*, 1–26. doi:10.1080/09588221.2021.2021241

Jeon, J. H., & Lee, S. (2023). Large language models in education: A focus on the complementary relationship between human teachers and ChatGPT. *Education and Information Technologies*, *28*(12), 15873–15892. doi:10.1007/s10639-023-11834-1

Jia, F., Sun, D., Ma, Q., & Looi, C.-K. (2022). Developing an AI-based learning system for L2 learners' authentic and ubiquitous learning in English language. *Sustainability (Basel)*, *14*(23), 15527. doi:10.3390/su142315527

Jiang, R. (2022). How does artificial intelligence empower EFL teaching and learning nowadays? A review on artificial intelligence in the EFL context. *Frontiers in Psychology*, *13*, 1049401. Advance online publication. doi:10.3389/fpsyg.2022.1049401 PMID:36467167

Jiang, X., Rollinson, J., Plonsky, L., Gustafson, E., & Pajak, B. (2021). Evaluating the reading and listening outcomes of beginning-level Duolingo courses. *Foreign Language Annals*, *54*(4), 974–1002. doi:10.1111/flan.12600

Jian, X., Wang, J., Jia, J., & Feng, C. (2016). *Perform Suzhou: A course in intermediate to advanced spoken Mandarin*. Soochow University Press.

Ji, H., Han, I., & Ko, Y. (2023). A systematic review of conversational AI in language education: Focusing on the collaboration with human teachers. *Journal of Research on Technology in Education*, *55*(1), 48–63. doi:10.1080/15391523.2022.2142873

John, P., & Woll, N. (2020). Using grammar checkers in an ESL context: An investigation of automatic corrective feedback. *CALICO Journal*, *37*(2), 169–172. doi:10.1558/cj.36523

Kaddari, Z., Mellah, Y., Berrich, J., Belkasmi, M. G., & Bouchentouf, T. (2020). Natural language processing: Challenges and future directions. In Lecture Notes in Networks and Systems (pp. 236–246). doi:10.1007/978-3-030-53970-2_22

Kamarinou, D., Millard, C., Singh, J., & Leenes, R. (2017). Machine learning with personal data. In *Data protection and privacy: The age of intelligent machines*. Hart Publishing.

Kanellopoulou, C. (2019). Film subtitles as a successful vocabulary learning tool. *Open Journal of Modern Linguistics*, *9*(02), 145–152. doi:10.4236/ojml.2019.92014

Kang, B., & Kang, S. (2022). Construction of Chinese Language Teaching System Model Based on Deep Learning under the Background of Artificial Intelligence. *Scientific Programming*, *2022*, 1–10. doi:10.1155/2022/3960023

Kannan, J., & Munday, P. (2018). New trends in second language learning and teaching through the lens of ICT, networked learning, and artificial intelligence. *Círculo de Lingüística Aplicada a la Comunicación*, *76*, 13–30. doi:10.5209/CLAC.62495

Karoui, A., Alvarez, L., Geoffre, T., Guin, N., Lefèvre, M., Lachand, V., & Ramalho, M. (2022). Towards an automated adaptive learning web platform through personalization of language learning pathways. In Lecture Notes in Computer Science (pp. 448–454). doi:10.1007/978-3-031-16290-9_35

Kasepalu, R., Prieto, L. P., Ley, T., & Chejara, P. (2022). Teacher artificial intelligence-supported pedagogical actions in collaborative learning coregulation: A wizard-of-oz study. *Frontiers in Education*, *7*, 736194. Advance online publication. doi:10.3389/feduc.2022.736194

Kashdan, T. (2009). *Curious? Discover the Missing Ingredient to a Fulfilling Life*. Harper Collins.

Kasneci, E., Sessler, K., Küchemann, S., Bannert, M., Dementieva, D., Fischer, F., Gasser, U., Groh, G., Günnemann, S., Hüllermeier, E., Krusche, S., Kutyniok, G., Michaeli, T., Nerdel, C., Pfeffer, J., Poquet, O., Sailer, M., Schmidt, A., Seidel, T., ... Kasneci, G. (2023). ChatGPT for good? On opportunities and challenges of large language models for education. *Learning and Individual Differences*, *103*, 102274. doi:10.1016/j.lindif.2023.102274

KasneciE.SeßlerK.KüchemannS.BannertM.DementievaD.FischerF.NerdelC. (2023). Chatgpt for good? on opportunities and challenges of large language models for education. https://doi.org/ doi:10.35542/osf.io/5er8f

Kasper, G. (2006). Beyond Repair: Conversation Analysis as an Approach to SLA. *AILA Review*, *19*, 83–99. doi:10.1075/aila.19.07kas

Kataoka, S. (2023). Textbook Cantonese romanization. In S. L. Lee (Ed.), *The learning and teaching of Cantonese as a second language* (pp. 196–216). Routledge.

Kattan-Ibarra, J., & Pountain, C. (2004). *Modern Spanish Grammar: A Practical Guide*. Taylor and Francis. doi:10.4324/9780203428313

Kaufman, D. (2004). Constructivist issues in language learning and teaching. *Annual Review of Applied Linguistics*, *24*. Advance online publication. doi:10.1017/S0267190504000121

Keating, E., & Egbert, M. (2004). Conversation as a cultural activity. In A. Duranti (Ed.), *A companion to linguistic anthropology* (pp. 169–188). Blackwell Publishing Ltd.

Kehoe, F. (2023). Leveraging generative ai tools for enhanced lesson planning in initial teacher education at post primary. *Irish Journal of Technology Enhanced Learning*, *7*(2), 172–182. doi:10.22554/ijtel.v7i2.124

Kelly, M. (Ed.). (2018). *Languages after Brexit: How the UK speaks to the world.* Springer International Publishing.

Kessler, G. (2017). Technology and the future of language teaching. *Foreign Language Annals*, *2018*(51), 205–218.

Khan, I., Ahmad, A. R., Jabeur, N., & Mahdi, M. N. (2021). An artificial intelligence approach to monitor student performance and devise preventive measures. *Smart Learning Environments*, *8*(1), 17. Advance online publication. doi:10.1186/s40561-021-00161-y

Kharb, L., & Singh, P. (2021). Role of machine learning in modern education and teaching. In Impact of AI Technologies on Teaching, Learning, and Research in Higher Education (pp. 99–123). IGI Global. doi:10.4018/978-1-7998-4763-2.ch006

Kılıçkaya, F. (2020). Using a chatbot, Replika, to practice writing through conversations in L2 English: A case study. In M. Kruk & M. Peterson (Eds.), *New Technological Applications for Foreign and Second Language Learning and Teaching* (pp. 221–238). IGI Global. doi:10.4018/978-1-7998-2591-3.ch011

Kim, D.-E., Hong, C., & Kim, W. H. (2023). *Efficient Transformer-based Knowledge Tracing for a Personalized Language Education Application*. Academic Press.

Kim, J. (2023). Leading teachers' perspective on teacher-AI collaboration in education. *Education and Information Technologies*. Advance online publication. doi:10.1007/s10639-023-12109-5

Kim, J., Lee, H., & Cho, Y. H. (2022). Learning design to support student-AI collaboration: Perspectives of leading teachers for AI in education. *Education and Information Technologies*, *27*(5), 6069–6104. doi:10.1007/s10639-021-10831-6

Kim, N.-Y., Cha, Y., & Kim, H.-S. (2019). Future English learning: Chatbots and artificial intelligence. *Multimedia-Assisted Language Learning*, *22*(3), 32–53.

King, I. (2016, July 29). E-learning is the way forward for quality education. *South China Morning Post.*

Kitamura, F. C. (2023). ChatGPT Is Shaping the future of medical writing but still requires human judgment. *Radiology*, *230171*(2). Advance online publication. doi:10.1148/radiol.230171 PMID:36728749

Klimova, B. (2021). An insight into online foreign language learning and teaching in the era of COVID-19 pandemic. *Procedia Computer Science*, *192*, 1787–1794. doi:10.1016/j.procs.2021.08.183 PMID:34630743

Klímová, B., Pikhart, M., & Kacetl, J. (2023). Ethical issues of the use of AI-driven mobile apps for education. *Frontiers in Public Health*, *10*, 1118116. Advance online publication. doi:10.3389/fpubh.2022.1118116 PMID:36711343

Knox, J. (2020). Artificial intelligence and education in China. *Learning, Media and Technology*, *45*(3), 298–311. doi: 10.1080/17439884.2020.1754236

Koedinger, K. R., Corbett, A. T., & Perfetti, C. (2012). The Knowledge-Learning-Instruction framework: Bridging the science-practice chasm to enhance robust student learning. *Cognitive Science*, *36*(5), 757–798. doi:10.1111/j.1551-6709.2012.01245.x PMID:22486653

Kohnke, L. (2023). L2 Learners' perception of a chatbot as a potential independent language learning tool. *Int. J. Mobile Learning and Organization*, *17*(1/2), 214–226. doi:10.1504/IJMLO.2023.128339

Kohnke, L., Moorhouse, B. L., & Zou, D. (2023). ChatGPT for language teaching and learning. *RELC Journal*, *54*(2), 537–550. doi:10.1177/00336882231162868

Kolb, D. (1983). *Experiential Learning: Experience as the Source of Learning and Development*. Prentice Hall.

Kolovou, T. A. (2021). Recreating Cultural Immersion in an Online Environment. *Journal of Teaching and Learning with Technology*, *10*, 408–413.

Kong, S. C., Cheung, W. M. Y., & Zhang, G. (2021). Evaluation of an artificial intelligence literacy course for university students with diverse study backgrounds. *Computers and education. Artificial Intelligence*, 100026.

König, J., Bremerich-Vos, A., Buchholtz, C., Fladung, I., & Glutsch, N. (2019). Pre–service teachers' generic and subject-specific lesson-planning skills: On learning adaptive teaching during initial teacher education. *European Journal of Teacher Education*, *43*(2), 131–150. doi:10.1080/02619768.2019.1679115

Koraishi, O. (2023). Teaching English in the age of AI: Embracing ChatGPT to optimize EFL materials and assessment. *Language Education and Technology*, *3*(1).

Korkmaz, G., & Toraman, Ç. (2020). Are we ready for the post-COVID-19 educational practice? An investigation into what educators think as to online learning. *International Journal of Technology in Education and Science*, *4*(4), 293–309. doi:10.46328/ijtes.v4i4.110

Kormos, J. (2023). The role of cognitive factors in second language writing and writing to learn a second language. *Studies in Second Language Acquisition*, *45*(3), 622–646. doi:10.1017/S0272263122000481

Kostka, I., & Toncelli, R. (2023). Exploring applications of ChatGPT to English language teaching: Opportunities, challenges, and recommendations. *TESL-EJ*, *27*(3). Advance online publication. doi:10.55593/ej.27107int

Krathwohl, D. R. (2002). A revision of Bloom's taxonomy: An overview. *Theory into Practice*, *41*(4), 212–218. doi:10.1207/s15430421tip4104_2

Kuh, G. D. (2008). High-impact educational practices: What they are, who has access to them, and why they matter. Washington, DC: Association of American Colleges and Universities.

Kuh, G. D., & O'Donnell, K. (2013). Ensuring Quality & Taking High-Impact Practices to Scale. Washington, DC: Association of American Colleges and Universities.

Kuh, G., O'Donnell, K., & Schneider, C. (2017). HIPs at Ten. *Change*, *49*(5), 8–16. doi:10.1080/00091383.2017.1366805

Kukulska-Hulme, A., Bossu, C., Charitonos, K., Coughlan, T., Deacon, A., Deane, N., Ferguson, R., Herodotou, C., Huang, C.-W., Mayisela, T., Rets, I., Sargent, J., Scanlon, E., Small, J., Walji, S., Weller, M., & Whitelock, D. (2023). *Innovating Pedagogy 2023: Open University Innovation Report 11*. The Open University.

Kuleto, V., Ilić, M. P., Bucea-Manea-Țoniș, R., Ciocodeică, D. F., Mihălcescu, H., & Mindrescu, V. (2022). The Attitudes of K–12 Schools' Teachers in Serbia towards the Potential of Artificial Intelligence. *Sustainability (Basel)*, *14*(14), 8636. doi:10.3390/su14148636

Kurni, M., Mohammed, M. S., & Srinivasa, K. G. (2023). Natural language processing for education. In Springer eBooks (pp. 45–54). doi:10.1007/978-3-031-32653-0_3

Kwon, S. K., Shin, D., & Lee, Y. (2023). The application of chatbot as an L2 writing practice tool. *Language Learning & Technology*, *27*(1), 1–19.

Lai, V. D., Ngo, N. T., Veyseh, A. P. B., Man, H., Dernoncourt, F., Bui, T., & Nguyen, T. H. (2023). *ChatGPT Beyond English: Towards a Comprehensive Evaluation of Large Language Models in Multilingual Learning.* /arxiv.2304.05613 doi:10.18653/v1/2023.findings-emnlp.878

Lai, Y., Saab, N., & Admiraal, W. (2022). University students' use of mobile technology in self-directed language learning: Using the integrative model of behavior prediction. *Computers & Education*, *179*, 104413. doi:10.1016/j.compedu.2021.104413

Lakkala, M., Toom, A., Kangasharju, A., & Ilom, L. (2022). *Computers and Education : Artificial Intelligence Lower secondary students ' poetry writing with the AI-based Poetry Machine.* doi:10.1016/j.caeai.2022.100048

Lameras, P., & Arnab, S. (2021). Power to the teachers: An exploratory review on artificial intelligence in education. *Information (Basel)*, *13*(1), 14. doi:10.3390/info13010014

Langran, E., Searson, M., Knezek, G., & Christensen, R. (2020, April). AI in teacher education. In *Society for Information Technology & Teacher Education International Conference* (pp. 751-756). Association for the Advancement of Computing in Education (AACE).

Larsen-Freeman, D., & DeCarrico, J. (2019). Grammar. In *An introduction to applied linguistics* (pp. 19–34). Routledge. doi:10.4324/9780429424465-2

Last, R. W. (1989). *Artificial intelligence techniques in language learning*. Halsted Press.

Leavy, S., Meaney, G., Wade, K., & Greene, D. (2020). Mitigating gender bias in machine learning data sets. *Bias and Social Aspects in Search and Recommendation: First International Workshop, BIAS 2020, Lisbon, Portugal, April 14. Proceedings*, *1*, 12–26.

Lee, E., Lee, Y., Kye, B., & Ko, B. (2008). Elementary and middle school teachers', students', and parents' perception of robot-aided education in Korea. In EdMedia+ Innovate Learning (pp. 175-183). Association for the Advancement of Computing in Education (AACE).

Lee, D., Kim, H., & Sung, S. (2022). Development research on an AI English learning support system to facilitate learner-generated-context-based learning. *Educational Technology Research and Development*, *71*(2), 629–666. doi:10.1007/s11423-022-10172-2 PMID:36533222

Lee, H., Ahn, H., Nguyen, T. G., Choi, S. M., & Kim, D. J. (2017). Comparing the Self-Report and Measured Smartphone Usage of College Students: A Pilot Study. *Psychiatry Investigation*, *14*(2), 198–204. doi:10.4306/pi.2017.14.2.198 PMID:28326119

Lee, I., & Perret, B. (2022). Preparing high school teachers to integrate AI methods into STEM classrooms. *Proceedings of the AAAI Conference on Artificial Intelligence*, *36*(11), 12783–12791. doi:10.1609/aaai.v36i11.21557

Lee, N. T. (2018). Detecting racial bias in algorithms and machine learning. *Journal of Information. Communication and Ethics in Society*, *16*(3), 252–260. doi:10.1108/JICES-06-2018-0056

Lee, S. L. (2011). 高班閱讀課的網上課件 [Online components for advanced Chinese reading classes]. *Journal of Technology and Chinese Language Teaching*, *2*, 1–22.

Lee, S. L. (2016). E-Learning Readiness in Language Learning: Students' Readiness Survey and Normalization Process. *Journal of Technology and Chinese Language Teaching*, *7*(2), 23–37.

Lee, S. L. (2018). Modular approaches in eLearning design. *Journal of Technology and Chinese Language Teaching*, *9*, 48–61.

Lee, S. L. (2022). Synchronous online language teaching: a reflection from Hong Kong. In S. Liu (Ed.), *Teaching the Chinese language remotely: Global cases and perspectives* (pp. 235–251). Palgrave Macmillan. doi:10.1007/978-3-030-87055-3_10

Leow, R. P. (2019). ISLA: How implicit or how explicit should it be? Theoretical, empirical, and pedagogical/curricular issues. *Language Teaching Research*, *23*(4), 476–493. doi:10.1177/1362168818776674

Lew, R. (2004). *Which dictionary for whom? Receptive use of bilingual, monolingual and semi-bilingual dictionaries by Polish learners of English*. Robert Lew.

Liang, W., Yuksekgonul, M., Mao, Y., Wu, E., & Zou, J. (2023). GPT detectors are biased against non-native English writers. *A Cell Press Journal, 4*(7). doi:10.1016/j.patter.2023.100779

Li, B., Bonk, C. J., & Kou, X. (2023). Exploring the multilingual applications of ChatGPT: Uncovering language learning affordances in YouTuber videos. *International Journal of Computer-Assisted Language Learning and Teaching*, *13*(1), 1–22. Advance online publication. doi:10.4018/IJCALLT.326135

Lidén, A., & Nilros, K. (2020). *Perceived benefits and limitations of chatbots in higher education* (Dissertation). Retrieved from https://urn.kb.se/resolve?urn=urn:nbn:se:lnu:diva-96327

Limna, P., Kraiwanit, T., Jangjarat, K., Klayklung, P., & Chocksathaporn, P. (2023). The use of ChatGPT in the digital era: Perspectives on chatbot implementation. *Journal of Applied Learning and Teaching*, *6*(1).

Lim, W. M., Gunasekara, A., Pallant, J. L., Pallant, J. I., & Pechenkina, E. (2023). Generative AI and the future of education: Ragnarök or reformation? A paradoxical perspective from management educators. *International Journal of Management Education*, *21*(2), 100790. doi:10.1016/j.ijme.2023.100790

Lin, Z., Zhang, D., Tao, Q., Shi, D., Haffari, G., Wu, Q., He, M., & Ge, Z. (2023). Medical visual question answering: A survey. *Artificial Intelligence in Medicine*, *143*, 102611. Advance online publication. doi:10.1016/j.artmed.2023.102611 PMID:37673579

Li, P., & Yu, L. (2021). Digital Language Learning (DLL): Insights from behavior, cognition, and the brain. *Bilingualism: Language and Cognition*, *25*(3), 361–378. doi:10.1017/S1366728921000353 PMID:35669733

Li, R. (2020). Using artificial intelligence in learning English as a foreign language: An examination of IELTS Liulishuo as an online platform. *Journal of Higher Education Research*, *1*(2). Advance online publication. doi:10.32629/jher.v1i2.178

Li, S. (2010). The effectiveness of corrective feedback in SLA: A meta-analysis. *Language Learning*, *60*(2), 309–365. doi:10.1111/j.1467-9922.2010.00561.x

Liu, O., & Yau, C. (2023, March 22). Who needs a teacher? As ChatGPT takes off in Hong Kong, educationists worry about impact on teaching, learning. *South China Morning Post*.

Liu, G., & Ma, C. (2023). Measuring EFL learners' use of ChatGPT in informal digital learning of English based on the technology acceptance model. *Innovation in Language Learning and Teaching*, *0*(0), 1–14. doi:10.1080/17501229.2023.2240316

Liu, Y., & Quan, Q. (2022). AI recognition method of pronunciation errors in oral English speech with the help of big data for personalized learning. *Journal of Information & Knowledge Management*, *21*(Supp02), 2240028. doi:10.1142/S0219649222400287

Li, W., Zhang, H., Zhang, C., Luo, J., Wang, H., Wang, H., Zhu, Y., Cui, H., Wang, J., Li, H., Zhu, Z., Xu, Y., & Li, C. (2021). The Prevalence of Psychological Status During the COVID-19 Epidemic in China: A Systemic Review and Meta-Analysis. *Frontiers in Psychology*, *12*, 614964. Advance online publication. doi:10.3389/fpsyg.2021.614964 PMID:34017278

Li, X., Li, B., & Cho, S. J. (2023). Empowering Chinese language learners from low-income families to improve their Chinese writing with ChatGPT's assistance afterschool. *Languages (Basel, Switzerland)*, *8*(4), 238. doi:10.3390/languages8040238

Lobel, O. (2022). The equality machine: Harnessing digital technology for a brighter, more inclusive future. Hachette UK.

Lochtman, K. (2002). Oral corrective feedback in the foreign language classroom: How it affects interaction in analytic foreign language teaching. *International Journal of Educational Research*, *37*(3–4), 271–283. doi:10.1016/S0883-0355(03)00005-3

Loder, C., Minadeo, L., Jiménez, L. E. C., Luna, Z., Ross, L. J., Rosenbloom, N., Stalburg, C. M., & Harris, L. H. (2019). Bridging the expertise of advocates and academics to identify reproductive justice learning outcomes. *Teaching and Learning in Medicine*, *32*(1), 11–22. doi:10.1080/10401334.2019.1631168 PMID:31293184

Loewen, S. (2018). Focus on form versus focus on forms. In J. I. Liontas (Ed.), *The TESOL encyclopedia of English language teaching* (pp. 1–6). doi:10.1002/9781118784235.eelt0062

Loewen, S., Li, S., Fei, F., Thompson, A., Nakatsukasa, K., Ahn, S., & Chen, X. (2009). Second language learners' beliefs about grammar instruction and error correction. *Modern Language Journal*, *93*(1), 91–104. doi:10.1111/j.1540-4781.2009.00830.x

Lowe, R., & Leike, J. (2022). *Aligning language models to follow instructions.* OpenAI. https://openai.com/research/instruction-following

Lu, X. (2018). Natural Language processing and intelligent computer-assisted language learning (ICALL). *The TESOL encyclopedia of English language teaching*, 1-6. doi:10.1002/9781118784235.eelt0422

Luan, H., Geczy, P., Lai, H., Gobert, J., Yang, S. J., Ogata, H., Baltes, J., Guerra, R., Li, P., & Tsai, C. C. (2020). Challenges and future directions of big data and artificial intelligence in education. *Frontiers in Psychology*, *11*, 580820. doi:10.3389/fpsyg.2020.580820 PMID:33192896

Luckin, R., Holmes, W., Griffiths, M., & Forcier, L. B. (2016). *Intelligence unleashed: An argument for AI in education.* Pearson Education.

Lusin, N., Peterson, T., Sulewski, C., & Zafer, R. (2023). Enrollments in languages other than English in US institutions of higher education: Fall 2021. Modern Language Association of America. Retrieved from: https://www.mla.org/content/download/191324/file/Enrollments-in-Languages-Other-Than-English-in-US-Institutions-of-Higher-Education-Fall-2021.pdf

Lys, F. (2013a). Computer-mediated grammar teaching and its effect on different language tasks. In P. Hubbard, M. Schulze, & B. Smith (Eds.), Learner-computer interaction in language education: CALICO Journal: A Festschrift in Honor of Robert Fischer (Vol. 30, pp. 166–186). Academic Press.

Lys, F. (2013b). The development of advanced learner oral proficiency using iPads. *Language Learning & Technology*, *17*(3), 94–116.

Machwate, S., Bendaoud, R., Henze, J., Berrada, K., & Burgos, D. (2021). Virtual exchange to develop cultural, language, and digital competencies. *Sustainability (Basel)*, *13*(11), 5926. doi:10.3390/su13115926

Mackenzie, D. (2023). Surprising Advances in Generative Artificial Intelligence Prompt Amazement — And Worries. *Engineering (Beijing)*, *xxxx*, 4–6. doi:10.1016/j.eng.2023.04.004

Mageira, K., Pittou, D., Papasalouros, A., Kotis, K., Zangogianni, P., & Daradoumis, A. (2022). Educational AI chatbots for content and language integrated learning. *Applied Sciences (Basel, Switzerland)*, *12*(7), 3239. doi:10.3390/app12073239

Malik, G., Tayal, D. K., & Vij, S. (2019). An analysis of the role of artificial intelligence in education and teaching. In *Recent Findings in Intelligent Computing Techniques: Proceedings of the 5th ICACNI 2017,* Volume 1 (pp. 407-417). Springer Singapore. 10.1007/978-981-10-8639-7_42

Manyika, J., Lund, S., Chui, M., Bughin, J., Woetzel, J., Batra, P., Ko, R., & Sanghvi, S. (2017, December). Jobs lost, jobs gained: Workforce transitions in a time of automation. *McKinsey Global Institute.*

Maria, G., Sousa, B. De, Cardoso, L., & Toassi, P. (2018). *Duolingo As a Tool to Improve Vocabulary Writing in English as a No Inglês Como Língua Estrangeira.* Academic Press.

Marzuki, W., Widiati, U., Rusdin, D., Darwin, & Indrawati, I. (2023). The impact of AI writing tools on the content and organization of students' writing: EFL teachers' perspective. *Cogent Education*, *10*(2), 2236469. Advance online publication. doi:10.1080/2331186X.2023.2236469

McGee, R. W. (2023). Is Chat Gpt biased against conservatives? An empirical study. SSRN *Electron. J.* doi:10.2139/ssrn.4359405

McGill Library. (2023). *AI Literacy Guide*. https://libraryguides.mcgill.ca/ai/literacy

Meng, N., Dhimolea, T. K., & Ali, Z. (2022). AI-enhanced education: Teaching and learning reimagined. In *Educational Communications and Technology* (pp. 107–124). Issues and Innovations. doi:10.1007/978-3-030-84729-6_7

Mensah, C., Azila-Gbettor, E. M., & Asimah, V. (2018). Self-Reported Examination Cheating of Alumni and Enrolled Students: Evidence from Ghana. *Journal of Academic Ethics*, 89-102. doi:10.1007/s10805-017-9286-x

Merrill, M. D. (2002). First principles of instruction. *Educational Technology Research and Development*, *50*(3), 43–59. doi:10.1007/BF02505024

Meyer, J. G., Urbanowicz, R. J., Martin, P. C. N., O'Connor, K., Li, R., Peng, P.-C., Bright, T. J., Tatonetti, N., Won, K. J., Gonzalez-Hernandez, G., & Moore, J. H. (2023). ChatGPT and large language models in academia: Opportunities and challenges. *BioData Mining*, *16*(20), 20. Advance online publication. doi:10.1186/s13040-023-00339-9 PMID:37443040

Miller, T. (2019). Explanation in artificial intelligence: Insights from the social sciences. *Artificial Intelligence*, *267*, 1–38. doi:10.1016/j.artint.2018.07.007

Mills, A., Bali, M., & Eaton, L. (2023). How do we respond to generative AI in education? Open educational practices give us a framework for an ongoing process. *Journal of Applied Learning and Teaching*, *6*(1), 16–30. doi:10.37074/jalt.2023.6.1.34

Ministry of National Education. (2018). *Ortaöğretim İngilizce dersi (9, 10, 11 ve 12. sınıflar) öğretim programı* [Secondary school English course (grades 9, 10, 11 and 12) curriculum]. http://mufredat.meb.gov.tr/ProgramDetay.aspx?PID=342

Misiejuk, K., Ness, I. J., Gray, R. M., & Wasson, B. (2023). Changes in Online Course Designs: Before, During, and After the Pandemic. *Frontiers in Education, 7*, 996006. Advance online publication. doi:10.3389/feduc.2022.996006

Mittal, A. (2023, July 26). *The essential guide to prompt engineering in ChatGPT* [Blog post] Retrieved from https://www.unite.ai/prompt-engineering-in-chatgpt/

Modern Language Association. (2007). *Foreign languages and higher education: New structures for a changed world.* https://www.mla.org/Resources/Guidelines-and-Data/Reports-and-Professional-Guidelines/Foreign-Languages-and-Higher-Education-New-Structures-for-a-Changed-World

Moeller, A., & Catalano, T. (2015). Foreign language teaching and learning. In J. D. Wright (Ed.), *International Encyclopedia of the Social & Behavioral Sciences* (2nd ed., Vol. 9, pp. 327–332). Elsevier. doi:10.1016/B978-0-08-097086-8.92082-8

Mohamed, A. M. (2023). Exploring the potential of an AI-based Chatbot (ChatGPT) in enhancing English as a foreign language (EFL) teaching: Perceptions of EFL faculty members. *Education and Information Technologies*. Advance online publication. doi:10.1007/s10639-023-11917-z

Mohan, D. D., Jawade, B., Setlur, S., & Govindaraju, V. (2023) Chapter 4 - Deep metric learning for computer vision: A brief overview. Handbook of Statistics, 48, 59–79. doi:10.1016/bs.host.2023.01.003

Montrul, S., and Slabakova, R. (2003). Competence similarities between Native and Near-Native speakers: An investigation of the Preterit/Imperfect contrast in Spanish. *Studies in Second Language Acquisition, 25*, 351–398. doi:10.1017/S0272263103000159

Moorhouse, B. L., Wong, K. M., & Li, L. (2023). Teaching with Technology in the Post-Pandemic Digital Age: Technological Normalisation and AI-Induced Disruptions. *RELC Journal, 54*(2), 311–320. doi:10.1177/00336882231176929

Moser, K. M., Wei, T., & Brenner, D. (2021). Remote teaching during COVID-19: Implications from a national survey of language educators. *System, 97*, 102431. doi:10.1016/j.system.2020.102431

Nagata, N. (1996). Computer vs. workbook instruction in second language acquisition. *CALICO Journal*, 53–75.

Nash, B. L., Hicks, T., Garcia, M., Fassbender, W., Alvermann, D., Boutelier, S., McBride, C., McGrail, E., Moran, C., O'Byrne, I., Piotrowski, A., Rice, M., & Young, C. (2023). Artificial Intelligence in English education: Challenges and opportunities for teachers and teacher educators. *English Education, 55*(3), 201–206.

Nation, K., Dawson, N. J., & Hsiao, Y. (2022). Book language and its implications for children's language, literacy, and development. *Current Directions in Psychological Science, 31*(4), 375–380. doi:10.1177/09637214221103264

Nazaretsky, T., Ariely, M., Cukurova, M., & Alexandron, G. (2022). Teachers' trust in AI-powered educational technology and a professional development program to improve it. *British Journal of Educational Technology, 53*(4), 914–931. doi:10.1111/bjet.13232

Nazari, N., Shabbir, M. S., & Setiawan, R. (2021). Application of Artificial Intelligence powered digital writing assistant in higher education: Randomized controlled trial. *Heliyon, 7*(5), e07014. doi:10.1016/j.heliyon.2021.e07014 PMID:34027198

Ng, D.T.K., Luo, W., Chan, H.M.Y., & Chu, S.K.W. (2022). Using digital story writing as a pedagogy to develop AI literacy among primary students. *Computers and Education: Artificial Intelligence,* 100054.

Ng, D. T. K., Lee, M., Tan, R. J. Y., Downie, J. S., & Chu, S. K. W. (2023). A review of AI teaching and learning from 2000 to 2020. *Education and Information Technologies, 2023*(28), 8445–8501. doi:10.1007/s10639-022-11491-w

Ng, D. T. K., Leung, J. K. L., Chu, S. K. W., & Qiao, M. S. (2021). Conceptualizing AI literacy: An exploratory review. *Computers and Education: Artificial Intelligence*, *2*, 100041.

Nguyen, A., Ngo, H. N., Hong, Y., Dang, B., & Nguyen, B. T. (2022). Ethical principles for artificial intelligence in education. *Education and Information Technologies*, *28*(4), 4221–4241. doi:10.1007/s10639-022-11316-w PMID:36254344

Niepel, C., Burrus, J., Greiff, S., Lipnevich, A. A., Brenneman, M. W., & Roberts, R. D. (2018). Students' beliefs and attitudes toward mathematics across time: A longitudinal examination of the theory of planned behavior. *Learning and Individual Differences, 63*(June), 24–33. doi:10.1016/j.lindif.2018.02.010

Nikitina, L. (2011). Creating an authentic learning environment in the foreign language classroom. *International Journal of Instruction*, *4*(1).

Noda, M. (2007). Performed culture: Cataloguing culture gains during study abroad. *Japanese Language and Literature*, *41*(2), 297–314.

Nunes, A., Cordeiro, C., Limpo, T., & Castro, S. L. (2021). Effectiveness of automated writing evaluation systems in school settings: A systematic review of studies from 2000 to 2020. *Journal of Computer Assisted Learning*, *38*(2), 599–620. doi:10.1111/jcal.12635

O'Brien, P. (1993). eL: AI in CALL. In M. Yazdani (Ed.), Multilingual multimedia. Bridging the language barrier with intelligent systems (pp. 85–139). Intellect.

O'Malley, J. M., Chamot, A. U., & Küpper, L. (1989). Listening comprehension strategies in second language acquisition. *Applied Linguistics*, *10*(4), 418–437. doi:10.1093/applin/10.4.418

Okada, A., Whitelock, D., Holmes, W., & Edwards, C. (2019). e-Authentication for online assessment: A mixed-method study. *British Journal of Educational Technology*, *50*(2), 861–875. doi:10.1111/bjet.12608

Open, A. I. (2023b). *ChatGPT - Release Notes*. OpenAI. https://help.openai.com/en/articles/6825453-chatgpt-release-notes

OpenA. I. (2023a). *ChatGPT.* https://chat.openai.com/c/02af3cf9-1598-4fa1-882b-f543a27b21cc

Öztürk, G., & Aydin, B. (2019). English language teacher education in turkey: Why do we fail and what policy reforms are needed? *Anadolu Journal of Educational Sciences International*, *9*(1), 181–213. doi:10.18039/ajesi.520842

Paas, F., & Van Merriënboer, J. J. G. (2020). Cognitive-load theory: Methods to manage working memory load in the learning of complex tasks. *Current Directions in Psychological Science*, *29*(4), 394–398. doi:10.1177/0963721420922183

Pace-Sigge, M., & Sumakul, D. T. (2021). What teaching an algorithm teaches when teaching students how to write academic texts. *Linguistic, Educational and Intercultural Research 2021 (LEIC Research 2021)*, 78.

Pack, A., & Maloney, J. (2023). Using generative artificial intelligence for language education research: Insights from using OpenAI's ChatGPT. *TESOL Quarterly*, *57*(4), 1571–1582. doi:10.1002/tesq.3253

Palermo, C., & Wilson, J. (2020). Implementing automated writing evaluation in different instructional contexts: A mixed-methods study. *Journal of Writing Research*, *12*(1), 63–108. doi:10.17239/jowr-2020.12.01.04

Paltridge, B. (2018). Graduate student writing. In D. Belcher & A. Hirvela (Eds.), *The TESOL Encyclopedia of English Language Teaching* (pp. 1–6). Wiley Blackwell. doi:10.1002/9781118784235.eelt0516

Paribakht, T. S., & Wesche, M. (1997). Vocabulary enhancement activities and reading for meaning in second language vocabulary acquisition. *Second Language Vocabulary Acquisition: A Rationale for Pedagogy, 55*(4), 174–200.

Paschal, M. J., & Melly, I. K. (2023). Ethical Guidelines on the Use of AI in Education. In *Creative AI Tools and Ethical Implications in Teaching and Learning* (pp. 230–245). IGI Global. doi:10.4018/979-8-3693-0205-7.ch013

Pasden, J. (2023). *Using ChatGPT to learn Chinese* [Blog post]. Retrieved from https://www.sinosplice.com/life/archives/2023/02/03/using-chatgpt-to-learn-chinese

Pawlak, M. (2021). Implicit versus explicit grammar learning and teaching. In E. Macaro & R. Woore (Eds.), *Debates in second language education* (1st ed., pp. 165–182). Routledge., doi:10.4324/9781003008361-12

Pedró, F., Subosa, M., Rivas, A., & Valverde, P. (2019). *Artificial Intelligence and Language Learning: Opportunities and Challenges*. Working Paper on Language Policy. UNESCO. Retrieved from https://unesdoc.unesco.org/ark:/ 48223/pf0000366994

Pedró, F., Subosa, M., Rivas, A., & Valverde, P. (2019). *Artificial intelligence in education: Challenges and opportunities for sustainable development*. UNESCO.

Pérez-Núñez, A. (2023). Exploring the Potential of Generative AI (ChatGPT) for Foreign Language Instruction: Applications and Challenges. *Hispania*, *106*(3), 355–362. doi:10.1353/hpn.2023.a906568

Pike, K. L. (1967). Language in relation to a unified theory of the structure of human behavior (2nd, revised edition). Mouton & Co., Publishers.

Pikhart, M. (2020). Intelligent information processing for language education: The use of artificial intelligence in language learning apps. *Procedia Computer Science*, *176*, 1412–1419. doi:10.1016/j.procs.2020.09.151 PMID:33042299

Piotrowska, M., Czyżewski, A., Ciszewski, T., Korvel, G., Kurowski, A., & Kostek, B. (2021). Evaluation of aspiration problems in L2 English pronunciation employing machine learning. *The Journal of the Acoustical Society of America*, *150*(1), 120–132. doi:10.1121/10.0005480 PMID:34340465

Pokrivčáková, S. (2019). Preparing teachers for the application of ai-powered technologies in foreign language education. *Journal of Language and Cultural Education*, *7*(3), 135–153. doi:10.2478/jolace-2019-0025

Polisca, E., Wright, V., Álvarez, I., & Montoro, C. (2019). *Language Provision in UK Modern Foreign Languages Departments 2019 Survey*. University Council of Modern Languages.

Pouresmaeil, A., & Vali, M. (2023). The effects of incidental focus on form on learning vocabulary, grammar, and pronunciation. *Language Teaching Research*, *0*, 1–24. doi:10.1177/13621688231185419

Prasad, B. N., & Jaheer, B. (2023). The Use of AI (artificial Intelligence) in English Learning Among Engineering Students: A Case Study. *International Journal of English Learning & Teaching Skills*, *5*(4), 3500–3508. doi:10.15864/ijelts.5410

Pratama, M. P., Sampelolo, R., & Lura, H. (2023). Revolutionizing education: Harnessing the power of artificial intelligence for personalized learning. *Klasikal: Journal of Education, Language Teaching and Science*, *5*(2), 350–357. doi:10.52208/klasikal.v5i2.877

Preis, R., Bećirović, S., & Geyer, B. (2023). EFL Teaching in a Digital Environment. *Map Education and Humanities*. doi:10.53880/2744-2373.2023.3.1.56

Preussler, O., Preussler-Bitch, S., & Napp, D. (2017). *Die kleine Hexe: Ausflug mit Abraxas*. Thienemann Verlag.

Pujiani, T., Sukmawati, I. D., & Indrasari, N. (2022). Teachers' Readiness Toward the New Paradigm of English Language Teaching: A Narrative Inquiry. *Uc Journal Elt Linguistics and Literature Journal*. doi:10.24071/uc.v3i2.5363

Puspitasari, E., & Tsara, E. (2022). Learning Tools for EFL Writing: What and How based on Upper Secondary School Students' Perspectives. *VELES: Voices of English Language Education Society*, *6*(2), 488–499. doi:10.29408/veles.v6i2.5878

Qadir, J. (2022). *Engineering Education in the Era of ChatGPT: Promise and Pitfalls of Generative AI for Education.* TechRxiv xiv. 21789 434. v1 doi:10. 36227/ techr

Qin, F., Li, K., & Yan, J. (2020). Understanding user trust in artificial intelligence-based educational systems: Evidence from China. *British Journal of Educational Technology*, *51*(5), 1693–1710. doi:10.1111/bjet.12994

Quan-Haase, A., & Wellman, B. (2005). How computer-mediated hyperconnectivity and local virtuality foster social networks of information and coordination in a community of practice. *International Sunbelt Social Network Conference.* 10.1111/1468-2427.00309

Radić, N., Atabekova, A., Freddi, M., & Schmied, J. (2021). *The world universities' response to COVID-19: Remote online language teaching*. Research-publishing. net.

Ramirez-Anormaliza, R., Sabaté, F., & Guevara-Viejo, F. (2015). Evaluating Student Acceptance Level of E-Learning Systems. *8th Annual International Conference of Education, Research and Innovation*, 2393–2399. https://library.iated.org/view/RAMIREZANORMALIZA2015EVA

Ramsay, V. (1990). *Developmental stages in the acquisition of the perfective and the imperfective aspects by classroom L2 learners of Spanish* [Tesis doctoral]. University of Oregon, Eugene.

Ranalli, J. (2021). L2 student engagement with automated feedback on writing: Potential for learning and issues of trust. *Journal of Second Language Writing*, *52*, 100816. doi:10.1016/j.jslw.2021.100816

Ray, P. P. (2023). ChatGPT: A comprehensive review on background, applications, key challenges, bias, ethics, limitations and future scope. *Internet of Things and Cyber-Physical Systems*, *3*(March), 121–154. doi:10.1016/j.iotcps.2023.04.003

Rebolledo Font De La Vall, R., & González Araya, F. (2023). Exploring the benefits and challenges of AI-language learning tools. *International Journal of Social Sciences and Humanities Invention*, *10*(01), 7569–7576. doi:10.18535/ijsshi/v10i01.02

Reichelt, M., Lefkowitz, N., Rinnert, C., & Schultz, J. M. (2012). Key issues in foreign language writing. *Foreign Language Annals*, *45*(1), 22–41. doi:10.1111/j.1944-9720.2012.01166.x

Reid, J. (2006). "Eye" learners and "ear" learners: Identifying the language needs of international student and US resident writers. In P. K. Matsuda, M. Cox, J. Jordan, & C. Ortmeier-Hooper (Eds.), *Second-language writing in the composition classroom: A critical sourcebook* (pp. 76–88). St. Martin's.

Reigeluth, C. M., & An, Y. (2019). *Merging the instructional design process with learner-centered theory: The holistic 4d model.* Taylor & Francis Group.

Reiss, M. J. (2021). The use of AI in education: Practicalities and ethical considerations. *London Review of Education, 19*(1). doi:10.14324/LRE.19.1.05

Republic of Türkiye Ministry of National Education. (2018). *English Curriculum for Primary and Secondary Schools.* Retrieved from: https://mufredat.meb.gov.tr/Dosyalar/201812411191321-%C4%B0NG%C4%B0L%C4%B0ZCE%20%C3%96%C4%9ERET%C4%B0M%20PROGRAMI%20Klas%C3%B6r%C3%BC.pdf

Rettberg, J. W. (2022, December 6). *ChatGPT is multilingual but monocultural, and it's learning your values* [Blog post]. https://jilltxt.net/right-now-chatgpt-is-multilingual-but-monocultural-but-its-learning-your-values/

Richardson, M., & Clesham, R. (2021). Rise of the machines? The evolving role of Artificial Intelligence (AI) technologies in high stakes assessment. *London Review of Education*, *19*(1), 1–13. doi:10.14324/LRE.19.1.09

Roche, C., Wall, P. J., & Lewis, D. (2022). Ethics and diversity in artificial intelligence policies, strategies and initiatives. *AI and Ethics*, *3*(4), 1095–1115. doi:10.1007/s43681-022-00218-9 PMID:36246014

Roe, J., Renandya, W. A., & Jacobs, G. M. (2023). A review of AI-powered writing tools and their implications for academic integrity in the language classroom. *Journal of English and Applied Linguistics*, *2*(1), 22–30. doi:10.59588/2961-3094.1035

Rojo, G. (1990). *Relaciones entre temporalidad y aspecto en el verbo español. Tiempo y aspecto en español*. Cátedra.

Roll, I., & Wylie, R. (2016). Evolution and revolution in artificial intelligence in education. *International Journal of Artificial Intelligence in Education*, *26*(2), 582–599. doi:10.1007/s40593-016-0110-3

Roschelle, J., Lester, J., & Fusco, J. (Eds.). (2020). AI and the future of learning: Expert panel report [Report]. *Digital Promise*. https://circls.org/reports/ai-report

Roumeliotis, K. I., & Tselikas, N. D. (2023). ChatGPT and open-AI models: A preliminary review. *Future Internet*, *15*(6), 192. doi:10.3390/fi15060192

Rudolph, J., Tan, S., & Tan, S. (2023). ChatGPT: Bullshit spewer or the end of traditional assessments in higher education? *Journal of Applied Learning & Teaching*, *6*(1), 342–363.

Rudolph, J., Tan, S., & Tan, S. (2023). ChatGPT: Bullshit spewer or the end of traditional assessments in higher education? *Journal of Applied Learning and Teaching*, *6*(1).

Rundell, K. (2023, July 11). *Why adults should read children's books*. https://www.bbc.com/culture/article/20230711-why-adults-should-read-childrens-books?mibextid=Zxz2cZ

Rundell, K. (2019). *Why you should read children's books, even though you are so old and wise*. Bloomsbury Publishing.

Ryan, J., & Viete, R. (2009). Respectful interactions: Learning with international students in the English-speaking academy. *Teaching in Higher Education*, *14*(3), 303–314. doi:10.1080/13562510902898866

Sabuncuoglu, A. (2020). Designing one year curriculum to teach artificial intelligence for middle school. In *Proceedings of the 2020 ACM Conference on Innovation and Technology in Computer Science Education (ITiCSE '20)*. Association for Computing Machinery. 10.1145/3341525.3387364

Sahami, M. (1999). *Using machine learning to improve information access*. Stanford University.

Salaberry, M. R. (1996). A theoretical foundation for the development of pedagogical tasks in computer-mediated communication. *CALICO Journal*, *14*(1), 5–34. doi:10.1558/cj.v14i1.5-34

Salaberry, M. R. (1997). *The development of past tense verbal morphology in L2 Spanish classroom instruction*. Cornell University.

Salas-Pilco, S. Z., Xiao, K., & Hu, X. (2022). Artificial intelligence and learning analytics in teacher education: A systematic review. *Education Sciences*, *12*(8), 569. doi:10.3390/educsci12080569

Samea Qoura, A., & Moustafa Elmansi, H. (2023). *Artificial intelligence in language education: Implementations and policies required* [Conference presentation]. The first national conference for the educational studies sector. 10.21608/foej.2022.180319.1169

Samochowiec, J. (2020). *Future skills: Four scenarios for the world of tomorrow*. Jacobs Foundation. doi:10.59986/WGTT6117

Sari, S. N., & Aminatun, D. (2021). Students' perception on the use of English movies to improve vocabulary mastery. *Journal of English Language Teaching and Learning*, *2*(1), 16–22. doi:10.33365/jeltl.v2i1.757

Schieffelin, B. B., & Ochs, E. (Eds.) (1986). *Language socialization across cultures: Studies in the social and cultural foundations of language*. Cambridge University Press.

Schiff, D. (2021) Out of the laboratory and into the classroom: the future of artificial intelligence in education. *AI & Soc*, 331–348. doi:10.1007/s00146-020-01033-8

Schmidt, R. (2010). Attention, awareness, and individual differences in language learning. In Handbook of language teaching (pp. 27-63). Academic Press.

Schmidt, R. (1994). Implicit learning and the cognitive unconscious: Of artificial grammars and SLA. *Second Language Research*, *10*(2), 93–119.

Schmidt, T., & Strasser, T. (2022). Artificial Intelligence in Foreign Language Learning and Teaching: A CALL for Intelligent Practice. *Anglistik: International Journal of English Studies*, *33*(1), 165–184. doi:10.33675/ANGL/2022/1/14

Schreiber-Wicke, E., & Holland, C. (2017). *Zwei Papas für Tango*. Thienemann Verlag.

Schuengel, C., & van Heerden, A. (2023). Editorial: Generative artificial intelligence and the ecology of human development. *Journal of Child Psychology and Psychiatry, and Allied Disciplines*, *64*(9), 1261–1263. doi:10.1111/jcpp.13860 PMID:37528517

Schulhoff, S., Khan, A., & Yanni, F. (2023). *Your guide to communicating with artificial intelligence*. Retrieved from https://learnprompting.org/

Scottish Government. (2016). *Children, Education and Skills. Attitudes Towards Language Learning in Schools in Scotland. Social Research*. Cabinet Secretary for Education and Skills. Learning Directorate, Education.

Scottish Government. (2020). *1+2 Languages Implementation Findings from the 2019 local authority survey*. Cabinet Secretary for Education and Skills. Learning Directorate, Education.

Scottish Government. (2022). *1+2 languages policy - local authority survey 2021: findings*. Cabinet Secretary for Education and Skills. Learning Directorate, Education.

Scottish Qualifications Authority. (2014). *National 3 English Course Specification* [C72473]. Retrieved from: https://www.sqa.org.uk/files/nq/CfE_CourseSpec_N3_Languages_English.pdf

Sebesta, J., & Davis, V. L. (2023, June 30). Supporting instruction and learning through Artificial Intelligence: A survey of institutional practices & policies. *WICHE Cooperative for Educational Technologies*. https://wcet.wiche.edu/resources/wcetreport-supporting-instruction-learning-through-artificial-intelligence-a-survey-ofinstitutional-practices-policies

Seedhouse, P. (2004). The organization of turn taking and sequence in language classrooms. *Language Learning: A Journal of Research in Language Studies*.

Seemiller, C., & Grace, M. (2019). *Generation Z: A century in the making*. Routledge.

Self, J. (1998). The defining characteristics of intelligent tutoring systems research: ITSs care, precisely. *International Journal of Artificial Intelligence in Education*, *10*, 350–364.

Sellar, S., & Gulson, K. N. (2021). Becoming information centric: The emergence of new cognitive infrastructures in education policy. *Journal of Education Policy*, *36*(3), 309–326. doi:10.1080/02680939.2019.1678766

Selwyn, N. (2019). *Should robots replace teachers? AI and the future of education*. John Wiley & Sons.

Selwyn, N. (2019). *Should robots replace teachers?: AI and the future of education*. John Wiley & Sons.

Selwyn, N. (2019). What's the problem with learning analytics? *Journal of Learning Analytics, 6*(3), 11–19. doi:10.18608/jla.2019.63.3

Selwyn, N., & Gasevic, D. (2020). The datafication of higher education: Discussing the promises and problems. *Teaching in Higher Education, 25*(4), 527–540. doi:10.1080/13562517.2019.1689388

Seo, K., Tang, J., Roll, I., Fels, S., & Yoon, D. (2021). The impact of artificial intelligence on learner–instructor interaction in online learning. *International Journal of Educational Technology in Higher Education, 18*(1), 54. Advance online publication. doi:10.1186/s41239-021-00292-9 PMID:34778540

Shadiev, R., Liu, T., & Hwang, W. (2020). Review of research on mobile-assisted language learning in familiar, authentic environments. *British Journal of Educational Technology, 51*(3), 709–720. doi:10.1111/bjet.12839

Shadiev, R., & Yang, M. (2020). Review of studies on technology-enhanced language learning and teaching. *Sustainability (Basel), 12*(2), 524. doi:10.3390/su12020524

Shaikh, S., Yayilgan, S. Y., Klimova, B., & Pikhart, M. (2023). Assessing the usability of ChatGPT for formal English language learning. *European Journal of Investigation in Health, Psychology and Education, 13*(9), 1937–1960. doi:10.3390/ejihpe13090140 PMID:37754479

Shortt, M., Tilak, S., Kuznetcova, I., Martens, B., & Akinkuolie, B. (2023). Gamification in mobile-assisted language learning: A systematic review of Duolingo literature from public release of 2012 to early 2020. *Computer Assisted Language Learning, 36*(3), 517–554. doi:10.1080/09588221.2021.1933540

Shumin, K. (2002). Factors to consider: Developing adult EFL students' speaking abilities. *Methodology in Language Teaching: An Anthology of Current Practice, 12*(35), 204–211. doi:10.1017/CBO9780511667190.028

Singer, N. (2023). Ban or embrace? Colleges wrestle with A.I.-generated admissions essays. *The New York Times*. https://www.nytimes.com/2023/09/01/business/college-admissions-essay-ai-chatbots.html

Singha, R., & Singha, S. (2023a). Economic sustainability, mindfulness, and diversity in the age of artificial intelligence and machine learning. In P. Raj, P. B. Soundarabai, & P. Augustine (Eds.), *Machine Intelligence: Computer Vision and Natural Language Processing* (pp. 273–285). Taylor & Francis Group. doi:10.1201/9781003424550-15

Singha, S., & Singha, R. (2023). Protecting data and privacy: Cloud-based solutions for intelligent transportation applications. *Scalable Computing: Practice and Experience, 24*(3), 257–276. doi:10.12694/scpe.v24i3.2381

SlimiZ. (2021). The impact of AI implementation in higher education on educational process future: A systematic review, Research Square. doi:10.21203/rs.3.rs-1081043/v1

Sok, S., Kang, E. Y., & Han, Z. (2019). Thirty-five years of ISLA on form-focused instruction: A methodological synthesis. *Language Teaching Research, 23*(4), 403–427. doi:10.1177/1362168818776673

Soomro, S. A., Kazemian, B., & Mahar, I. H. (2015). The Importance of Culture in Second and Foreign Language Learning. SSRN *Electronic Journal, 15*(1), 1–10. doi:10.2139/ssrn.2656713

Southern, M. G. (2023, February 8). Google Launches Ai-Powered Contextual Translations. *Search Engine Journal*. https://www.searchenginejournal.com/google-launches-ai-powered-contextual-translations/478863/#close

Steenbergen-Hu, S., & Cooper, H. (2014). A meta-analysis of the effectiveness of intelligent tutoring systems on college students' academic learning. *Journal of Educational Psychology, 106*(2), 331–347. doi:10.1037/a0034752

Stephenson, B., & Harvey, A. (2022). Student equity in the age of AI-enabled assessment: Towards a politics of inclusion. In *Assessment for Inclusion in Higher Education* (pp. 120–130). Routledge. doi:10.4324/9781003293101-14

Sternberg, R. J. (2014). Most vocabulary is learned from context. In *The nature of vocabulary acquisition* (pp. 89–105). Psychology Press.

Street, B. V. (1993). Culture is a verb: Anthropological aspects of language and cultural process. In D. Graddol, L. Thompson, & M. Byran (Eds.), *Language and Culture* (pp. 23–44). BAAL and Multiple Matters.

Su, J., & Yang, W. (2023). Unlocking the power of ChatGPT: A framework for applying generative AI in education. *ECNU Review of Education.*

Su, J., Tsz, D., Ng, K., Kai, S., & Chu, W. (2023). Computers and Education : Artificial Intelligence Artificial Intelligence (AI) Literacy in Early Childhood Education : The Challenges and Opportunities. *Computers and Education: Artificial Intelligence*, *4*(January), 100124. doi:10.1016/j.caeai.2023.100124

Sumakul, D. T. (2019). When robots enter the classrooms: Implications for teachers. In *International Conference on Embedding Artificial Intelligence (AI) in Educational Policy and Practice for Southeast Asia, Jakarta, Indonesia.* SEAMEO SEAMOLEC.

Sun, Z., Anbarasan, M., & Kumar, D. (2020). Design of online intelligent English teaching platform based on artificial intelligence techniques. *Computational Intelligence*, *37*(3), 1166–1180. doi:10.1111/coin.12351

Sun, Z., Yu, Z. C., & Xu, F. Y. (2023). Analysis and improvement of classroom teaching based on artificial intelligence. In H. Niemi, R. D. Pea, & Y. Lu (Eds.), *AI in Learning: Designing the Future*. Springer. doi:10.1007/978-3-031-09687-7_7

Suresh, A., Jacobs, J., Lai, V., Tan, C., Ward, W., Martin, J. H., & Sumner, T. (2021). Using transformers to provide teachers with personalized feedback on their classroom discourse: The TalkMoves application. *arXiv Preprint arXiv:2105.07949.*

Sütçü, S. S., & Sütçü, E. (2023). English Teachers' Attitudes and Opinions Towards Artificial Intelligence. *International Journal of Research in Teacher Education*, *14*(3).

Sutton, R. S., & Barto, A. (1998). Reinforcement Learning: An Introduction. *IEEE Transactions on Neural Networks*, *9*(5), 1054. Advance online publication. doi:10.1109/TNN.1998.712192

Sweller, J. (2012). Cognitive load theory. In Springer eBooks (pp. 601–605). doi:10.1007/978-1-4419-1428-6_446

Swiecki, Z., Ruis, A. R., Gautam, D., Rus, V., & Williamson Shaffer, D. (2019). Understanding when students are active-in-thinking through modeling-in-context. *British Journal of Educational Technology*, *50*(5), 2346–2364. doi:10.1111/bjet.12869

Tafazoli, D., María, E. G., & Abril, C. H. (2019). Intelligent language tutoring system. *International Journal of Information and Communication Technology Education*, *15*(3), 60–74. doi:10.4018/IJICTE.2019070105

Tan, S. (2023). Harnessing artificial intelligence for innovation in education. In *Learning Intelligence* (pp. 335–363). Innovative and Digital Transformative Learning Strategies. doi:10.1007/978-981-19-9201-8_8

Teubner, T., Flath, C. M., Weinhardt, C., van der Aalst, W., & Hinz, O. (2023). Welcome to the Era of ChatGPT et al. *Business & Information Systems Engineering*, *65*(2), 95–101. doi:10.1007/s12599-023-00795-x

The Chinese University of Hong Kong. (2021, 24 August). A 30-minute EEG Test Forecasts Children's Language Development. *CUHK in Touch.* Retrieved from https://cuhkintouch.cpr.cuhk.edu.hk/2021/08/7463/

The Chinese University of Hong Kong. (2023). *Use of Artificial Intelligence Tools in Teaching, Learning and Assessments: A Guide for Students.* Hong Kong: The Chinese University of Hong Kong. Retrieved from https://www.aqs.cuhk.edu.hk/documents/A-guide-for-students_use-of-AI-tools.pdf

The Hong Kong Polytechnic University. (2023). *Guidelines for Students on the Use of Generative Artificial Intelligence*. Hong Kong: The Hong Kong Polytechnic University of Hong Kong. Retrieved from https://www.polyu.edu.hk/ar/ doc-drive/polyu-students/Student-guide-on-the-use-GenAI.pdf

Tinsley, T. (2019). *Language Trends 2019: Language Teaching in Primary and Secondary Schools in England. Survey report*. British Council.

Tinsley, T., & Board, K. (2013). *Languages for the future: What languages the UK needs most and why*. British Council and Alcantara Communications.

Toncic, J. (2020). Teachers, AI Grammar Checkers, and the Newest Literacies: Emending Writing Pedagogy. *Digital Culture & Education*, *12*(1), 26–51.

Toquero, C. M. D. (2020). *Challenges and Opportunities for Higher Education Amid the COVID-19 Pandemic: The Philippine Context*. Pedagogical Research. doi:10.29333/pr/7947

Towle, B., & Halm, M. J. (2006). Designing adaptive learning environments with learning design. In Springer eBooks (pp. 215–226). doi:10.1007/3-540-27360-3_12

Tseng, W., & Warschauer, M. (2023). AI-writing tools in education: If you can't beat them, join them. *Journal of China Computer-Assisted Language Learning*, *3*(2), 258–262. Advance online publication. doi:10.1515/jccall-2023-0008

Tumbal, S., Liando, N. V., & Olii, S. T. (2021). Students' perceptions toward the use of Google Translate in translating. *Kompetensi*, *1*(02), 313–320. doi:10.53682/kompetensi.v1i02.1853

Tuomi, I. (2018). The Impact of Artificial Intelligence on Learning, Teaching, and Education Policies. Science for Policy. doi:10.2760/12297

U.S. Department of Education, Office of Educational Technology. (2023). *Artificial Intelligence and Future of Teaching and Learning: Insights and Recommendations*. https://tech.ed.gov/ai-future-of-teaching-and-learning

UBC. (n.d.). *Generative AI Resources*. The University of British Columbia: Generative AI. https://genai.ubc.ca/resources/

Ünal, E., & Güngör, F. (2021). The continuance intention of users toward mobile assisted language learning: The case of DuoLingo. *Asian Journal of Distance Education*, *16*(2).

Underwood, J. (2017). Exploring AI language assistants with primary EFL students. In K. Borthwick, L. Bradley, & S. Thouësny (Eds.), *CALL in a climate of change: Adapting to turbulent global conditions – short papers from EUROCALL 2017* (pp. 317–321). doi:10.14705/rpnet.2017.eurocall2017.733

UNESCO. (2003). *Education in a multilingual world.* UNESCO Education Position Paper. Paris: UNESCO. Retrieved from: https://unesdoc.unesco.org/ark:/48223/pf0000129728

UNESCO. (2021). *Education: Outbound internationally mobile students by host region*. Institute of Statistics.

UNESCO. (2023). *UNESCO survey: Less than 10% of schools and universities have formal guidance on AI*. UNESCO. https://www.unesco.org/en/articles/unesco-survey-less-10-schools-and-universities-have-formal-guidance-ai

University of Toronto. (n.d.a). *ChatGPT and Generative AI in the Classroom.* Office of the Vice-Provost, Innovations in Undergraduate Education. https://www.viceprovostundergrad.utoronto.ca/strategic-priorities/digital-learning/special-initiative-artificial-intelligence/

University of Toronto. (n.d.b). *Using ChatGPT or Other Generative AI Tools on a Marked Assessment.* https://www.academicintegrity.utoronto.ca/perils-and-pitfalls/using-chatgpt-or-other-ai-tool-on-a-marked-assessment/

Urlaub, P., & Dessein, E. (2022). From Disrupted Classrooms to Human-Machine Collaboration? The Pocket Calculator, Google Translate, and the Future of Language Education. *Journal of Linguistics and Language Teaching*, *14*(1). Advance online publication. doi:10.5070/L214151790

UW–Madison Information Technology. (2023, August 24). *Generative AI @ uw–madison: Use & policies*. https://it.wisc.edu/generative-ai-uw-madison-use-policies/

van den Berg, G., & du Plessis, E. (2023). ChatGPT and Generative AI: Possibilities for Its Contribution to Lesson Planning, Critical Thinking and Openness in Teacher Education. *Education Sciences*, *13*(10), 998. doi:10.3390/educsci13100998

Van Dijk, T. A. (1977). Context and cognition: Knowledge frames and speech act comprehension. *Journal of Pragmatics*, *1*(3), 211–231. doi:10.1016/0378-2166(77)90035-2

van Dis, E. A., Bollen, J., Zuidema, W., van Rooij, R., & Bockting, C. L. (2023). ChatGPT: five priorities for research. *Nature, 614*, 224–226. doi: m10.1038/d41586-023-00288-7

Vaswani, A., Shazeer, N., Parmar, N., Uszkoreit, J., Jones, L., Gomez, A. N., Kaiser, L., & Polosukhin, I. (2017). *Attention Is All You Need*. https://doi.org//arxiv.1706.03762 doi:10.48550

Vazhayil, A., Shetty, R., Bhavani, R. R., & Akshay, N. (2019, December). Focusing on teacher education to introduce AI in schools: Perspectives and illustrative findings. In *2019 IEEE tenth international conference on technology for education* (pp. 71–77). IEEE.

Verdegem, P. (2021). Introduction: Why We Need Critical Perspectives on AI. In P. Verdegem (Ed.), *AI for Everyone?: Critical Perspectives* (pp. 1–18). University of Westminster Press. doi:10.16997/book55.a

Vij, S., Tayal, D., & Jain, A. (2020). A machine learning approach for automated evaluation of short answers using text similarity based on WordNet graphs. *Wireless Personal Communications*, *111*(2), 1271–1282. doi:10.1007/s11277-019-06913-x

Wahyuni, D. S. (2022). Integrated classroom-chatbot experience: An alternative solution for English as foreign language learners. *English Language Education and Current Trends*, *1*(1), 63–68. doi:10.37301/elect.v1i1.36

Walker, G. (2010). Performed culture: Learning to participate in another culture. In G. Walker (Ed.), *The pedagogy of performing a culture* (pp. 1–21). National East Asian Languages Resource Center.

Walker, G. (2021). Why we perform. In X. Zhang & X. Jian (Eds.), *The third space and Chinese language pedagogy: Negotiating intentions and expectations in another culture* (pp. 139–158). Routledge.

Walker, G., & Noda, M. (2010). Remembering the future: Compiling knowledge of another culture. In G. Walker (Ed.), *The pedagogy of performing a culture* (pp. 22–48). National East Asian Languages Resource Center.

Walsh, M. (2017). Multiliteracies, Multimodality, New Literacies and…. What Do These Mean for Literacy Education? *Inclusive Principles and Practices in Literacy Education*, *11*, 19–33. doi:10.1108/S1479-363620170000011002

Wang, J. (2016). *Ecology of literacy: A context-based inter-disciplinary curriculum for Chinese as a foreign language* (Doctoral dissertation). Retrieved from https://rave.ohiolink.edu/etdc/view?acc_num=osu1461251633

Wang, J. (2023a, March 25). *Xiang ChatGPT qingjiao "ba" zi ju – xisijikong de liangge quehan*向*ChatGPT*请教"把"字句——细思极恐的两个缺憾 [Consulting ChatGPT on the "ba" sentence – Two terrifying deficiencies upon careful reflection] [Blog post]. Retrieved from https://mp.weixin.qq.com/s/dXvedrVHrdtJKJ9Yda6qpQ

Wang, J. (2023b, March 18). *ChatGPT neng fou zhuli tiyan wenhua chuji xuecai zhizuo? ChatGPT能否助力体演文化初级学材制作?* [Can ChatGPT assist in creating beginner-level learning materials for performing the culture?] [Blog post]. Retrieved from https://mp.weixin.qq.com/s/rY4GkQYw7umEqRfEQVepmQ

Wang, T., & Cheng, E. C. K. (2021). An investigation of barriers to Hong Kong K-12 schools incorporating Artificial Intelligence in education. *Computers and Education: Artificial Intelligence, 2*.

Wang, J., & Jia, J. (Eds.). (2022). *Performed Culture in action to teach Chinese as a FL: Integrating PCA in curriculum, pedagogy, and assessment*. Routledge.

Wang, T., Lund, B. D., Marengo, A., Pagano, N. R., Mannuru, N. R., Teel, Z. A., & Pange, J. (2023). Exploring the potential impact of Artificial Intelligence (AI) on international students in higher education: Generative AI, chatbots, analytics, and international student success. *Applied Sciences (Basel, Switzerland)*, *13*(11), 6716. doi:10.3390/app13116716

Wang, X., Liu, Q., Pang, H., Tan, S. C., Lei, J., Wallace, M. P., & Li, L. (2023). What matters in AI-supported learning: A study of human-AI interactions in language learning using cluster analysis and epistemic network analysis. *Computers & Education*, *194*, 104703. Advance online publication. doi:10.1016/j.compedu.2022.104703

Wang, X., Pang, H., Wallace, M. P., Wang, Q., & Chen, W. (2022). Learners' perceived AI presences in AI-supported language learning: A study of AI as a humanized agent from the community of inquiry. *Computer Assisted Language Learning*, 1–27. doi:10.1080/09588221.2022.2056203

Warschauer, M., & Healey, D. (1998). Computers and language learning: An overview. *Language Teaching*, *31*(2), 57–71. doi:10.1017/S0261444800012970

Warschauer, M., Tseng, W., Yim, S., Webster, T., Jacob, S., Du, Q., & Tate, T. (2023, December). The Affordances and Contradictions of AI-Generated Text for Second Language Writers. *Journal of Second Language Writing*, *62*. Advance online publication. doi:10.1016/j.jslw.2023.101071

WarschauerM.TsengW.YimS.WebsterT.JacobS.DuQ.TateT. (2023, October 31). *The affordances and contradictions of AI-generated text for writers of English as a second or foreign language*. doi:10.2139/ssrn.4404380

Webb, S. (2007). The effects of repetition on vocabulary knowledge. *Applied Linguistics*, *28*(1), 46–65. doi:10.1093/applin/aml048

Wei, L. (2023). Artificial intelligence in language instruction: Impact on English learning achievement, L2 motivation, and self-regulated learning. *Frontiers in Psychology*, *14*, 1261955. Advance online publication. doi:10.3389/fpsyg.2023.1261955 PMID:38023040

Westergaard, M., Mitrofanova, N., Mykhaylyk, R., & Rodina, Y. (2017). Crosslinguistic influence in the acquisition of a third language: The Linguistic Proximity Model. *The International Journal of Bilingualism*, *21*(6), 666–682. doi:10.1177/1367006916648859

Willems, J. (2023). *ChatGPT at Universities – The Least of Our Concerns* (*SSRN* Scholarly Paper No. 4334162). doi:10.2139/ssrn.4334162

Williams, J. (2012). The potential role(s) of writing in second language development. *Journal of Second Language Writing*, *21*(4), 321–331. doi:10.1016/j.jslw.2012.09.007

Williamson, B., & Eynon, R. (2020). Historical threads, missing links, and future directions in AI in education. *Learning, Media and Technology*, *45*(3), 223–235. doi:10.1080/17439884.2020.1798995

Williamson, B., Eynon, R., Knox, J., & Davies, H. C. (2023). Critical perspectives on AI in education: Political economy, discrimination, commercialization, governance and ethics. In B. du Boulay, A. Mitrovic, & K. Yacef (Eds.), *The handbook of artificial intelligence in education* (pp. 555–573). Edward Elgar Publishing Ltd. doi:10.4337/9781800375413.00037

Wilson, D. V., & Marcin, M. (2022). Building connections and critical language awareness between learning communities collaborating across two distant States. *Languages (Basel, Switzerland)*, *7*(4), 257. doi:10.3390/languages7040257

Wilson, J., Ahrendt, C., Fudge, E. A., Raiche, A., Beard, G., & MacArthur, C. (2021). Elementary teachers' perceptions of automated feedback and automated scoring: Transforming the teaching and learning of writing using automated writing evaluation. *Computers & Education*, *168*, 104208. doi:10.1016/j.compedu.2021.104208

Wittgenstein, L. (1958). *Philosophical investigations* (3rd ed.; G. E. M. Anscombe, Trans.). Prentice Hall. (Original work published 1953)

Wong, J., & Waring, H. Z. (2020). *Conversation analysis and second language pedagogy: A guide for ESL/EFL teachers*. Routledge. https://books.google.com/books?hl=en&lr=&id=fybxDwAAQBAJ&oi=fnd&pg=PP11&dq=conversation+analysis+language+teaching+correction&ots=5gbus7JfWb&sig=-mgbXRuvOTp4vHDNcMaVDgQTAcs

WooJ. H.ChoiH. (2021). *Systematic review for AI-based language learning tools*. Ithaca: Cornell University Library. https://arxiv.org/abs/2111.04455v1

Woo, J. H., & Choi, H. (2021). Systematic Review for AI-based Language Learning Tools. *Journal of Digital Contents Society*, *22*(11), 1783–1792. doi:10.9728/dcs.2021.22.11.1783

Wu, L., Wu, Y., & Zhang, X. (2021). L2 Learner Cognitive Psychological Factors About Artificial Intelligence Writing Corrective Feedback. *English Language Teaching*, *14*(10), 10. Advance online publication. doi:10.5539/elt.v14n10p70

Xiao, Y., & Zhi, Y. (2023). An exploratory study of EFL learners' use of ChatGPT for language learning tasks: Experience and perceptions. *Languages (Basel, Switzerland)*, *8*(3), 212. Advance online publication. doi:10.3390/languages8030212

Xi, X. (2010). Automated scoring and feedback systems: Where are we and where are we heading? *Language Testing*, *27*(3), 291–300. doi:10.1177/0265532210364643

Xu, L. (2020, December). The dilemma and countermeasures of AI in educational application. In *2020 4th international conference on computer science and artificial intelligence* (pp. 289–294). ACM.

Yaacob, Z., & Saad, N. H. M. (2020). Acceptance of YouTube as a learning platform during the Covid-19 pandemic: The moderating effect of subscription status. *TEM Journal*, *4*, 1732–1739. doi:10.18421/TEM94-54

Yan, D. (2023). Impact of ChatGPT on learners in a L2 writing practicum: An exploratory investigation. *Education and Information Technologies*, *28*(11), 13943–13967. Advance online publication. doi:10.1007/s10639-023-11742-4

Yang, H., & Kyun, S. (2022). The current research trend of artificial intelligence in language learning: A systematic empirical literature review from an activity theory perspective. *Australasian Journal of Educational Technology*, *38*(5), 180–210. doi:10.14742/ajet.7492

Yau, K., Chai, C., Chiu, T., Meng, H., King, I., & Yam, Y. (2022). A phenomenographic approach on teacher conceptions of teaching artificial intelligence (AI) in K-12 schools. *Education and Information Technologies*, *28*(1), 1041–1064. doi:10.1007/s10639-022-11161-x

Yeadon, W., Inyang, O.-O., Mizouri, A., Peach, A., & Testrow, C. (2022). *The Death of the Short-Form Physics Essay in the Coming AI Revolution*. arXiv. . 2212. 11661 doi:10. 48550/arXiv

Yeşilyurt, Y. E. (2023). AI-enabled assessment and feedback mechanisms for language learning. In Advances in Educational Technologies and Instructional Design book series (pp. 25–43). doi:10.4018/978-1-6684-9893-4.ch002

Yildirim, Y., Arslan, E. A., Yildirim, K., & Bisen, I. E. (2021). Reimagining education with artificial intelligence. *Eurasian Journal of Higher Education*, *2*(4), 32–46. doi:10.31039/ejohe.2021.4.52

Yin, J., Goh, T. T., Yang, B., & Xiaobin, Y. (2021). Conversation technology with micro-learning: The impact of chatbot-based learning on students' learning motivation and performance. *Journal of Educational Computing Research*, *59*(1), 154–177. doi:10.1177/0735633120952067

Young, J. C., & Shishido, M. (2023). Investigating OpenAI's ChatGPT potentials in generating chatbot's dialogue for English as a foreign language learning. *International Journal of Advanced Computer Science and Applications*, *14*(6), 65–72. doi:10.14569/IJACSA.2023.0140607

You, Z. J., Shen, C. Y., Chang, C. W., Liu, B. J., & Chen, G. D. (2006). A robot as a teaching assistant in an English class. In *Sixth IEEE International Conference on advanced learning technologies (ICALT'06)* (pp. 87-91). 10.1109/ICALT.2006.1652373

Yu, L. (2021). The Performed Culture Approach. In Z. Ye (Ed.), New trends in teaching Chinese as a foreign language (pp.1–34). Singapore: Palgrave Macmillan. doi:10.1007/978-981-13-6844-8_7-1

Yuan, S., He, T., Huang, H., Hou, R., & Wang, M. (2020). Automated Chinese essay scoring based on deep learning. *CMC-Computers Materials & Continua, 65*(1), 817-833. https://doi.org/.2020.010471 doi:10.32604/cmc

Yueng, P. (2019, 31 January). AI will be a game changer for Hong Kong education. *China Daily Hong Kong*.

Yu, H. (2023). Reflection on whether Chat GPT should be banned by academia from the perspective of education and teaching. *Frontiers in Psychology*, *14*, 1181712. doi:10.3389/fpsyg.2023.1181712 PMID:37325766

Yurtseven Avci, Z., O'Dwyer, L. M., & Lawson, J. (2020). Designing effective professional development for technology integration in schools. *Journal of Computer Assisted Learning*, *36*(2), 160–177. doi:10.1111/jcal.12394

Zablotsky, B., Black, L. I., Maenner, M. J.; Schieve, L. A., Danielson M. L., Bitsko, R. H., Blumberg, S. J., Kogan, M. D. & Boyle C. A. (2019). Prevalence and trends of developmental disabilities among children in the United States: 2009–2017. *Pediatrics 144*(4). doi:10.1542/peds.2019-0811

Zai, X., Chu, X., Chai, C. S., Jong, M. S. Y., Istenic, A., & Spector, M. (2021). A review of artificial intelligence (AI) in education from 2010 to 2020. *Complexity*, *2021*, 1–18. Advance online publication. doi:10.1155/2021/8812542

Zawacki-Richter, O., Marín, V. I., Bondand, F., & Gouverneur, M. (2019). Systematic review of research on artificial intelligence applications in higher education–Where are the educators? *International Journal of Educational Technology in Higher Education*, *16*(39), 39. Advance online publication. doi:10.1186/s41239-019-0171-0

Zeng, Z. (2023, February 25). *Yu ChatGPT zuo pengyou!与ChatGPT做朋友!* [Befriending ChatGPT] [Blog post]. Retrieved from https://mp.weixin.qq.com/s/LLruwI7bWpSuCkAUx5BkiA

Zhai, X. (2022). *ChatGPT User Experience: Implications for Education* (*SSRN* Scholarly Paper No. 4312418). doi:10.2139/ssrn.4312418

Zhai, X. (2022). ChatGPT User Experience: Implications for Education. SSRN *Scholarly Paper*. . 43124 18 doi:10. 2139/ ssrn

Zhang, M., & Li, J. (2021). A commentary of GPT-3 in MIT Technology Review 2021. *Fundamental Research*, *1*(6), 831–833. doi:10.1016/j.fmre.2021.11.011

Zhao, J., Wu, M., Zhou, L., Wang, X., & Jia, J. (2022). Cognitive psychology-based artificial intelligence review. *Frontiers in Neuroscience*, *16*, 1024316. Advance online publication. doi:10.3389/fnins.2022.1024316 PMID:36278021

Zhao, X. (2023). Leveraging Artificial Intelligence (AI) Technology for English Writing: Introducing Wordtune as a Digital Writing Assistant for EFL Writers. *RELC Journal*, *54*(3), 890–894. doi:10.1177/00336882221094089

Zheng, L., Niu, J., Zhong, L., & Gyasi, J. F. (2021). The effectiveness of artificial intelligence on learning achievement and learning perception: A meta-analysis. *Interactive Learning Environments*, 1–15. doi:10.1080/10494820.2021.2015693

Zhu, Y. (2020). The application of artificial intelligence in foreign language teaching. *2020 International Conference on Artificial Intelligence and Education (ICAIE)*. 10.1109/ICAIE50891.2020.00024

Ziegler, N., & González-Lloret, M. (2022). *The Routledge Handbook of Second Language Acquisition and Technology* (1st ed.). Routledge. doi:10.4324/9781351117586

Zou, B., Guan, X., Shao, Y., & Chen, P. (2023). Supporting speaking practice by social network-based interaction in artificial intelligence (ai)-assisted language learning. *Sustainability (Basel)*, *15*(4), 2872. doi:10.3390/su15042872

Zou, D., Xie, H., & Wang, F. L. (2018). Future trends and research issues of technology-enhanced language learning: A technological perspective. *Knowledge Management & E-Learning*, *10*(4), 426–440.

About the Contributors

Fang Pan has a Master's Degree in Chinese Language Pedagogy. The editor is an experienced teacher of Mandarin in different settings. Before joining London School of Economics and Political Science (LSE), the editor taught all levels of Chinese at Harvard University and won Teaching Distinction Certificates in three consecutive years. The editor has experience in teaching a wide range of Mandarin courses in different settings, including pre-school classes, high school summer programs and university intensive programs. At the LSE, the editor is involved in teaching BSc International Relations and Chinese and BSc Language, Culture and Society undergraduate degree programmes. He was awarded LSE Teaching Excellence Awards several times. In addition to in-class teaching, the editor is one of the writers of the book Cases on Audio-Visual Media in Language Education. The editor attended and presented at several regional and international language conferences. The editor's past presentation topics include video project, grammar teaching, essay writing and curriculum design.

* * *

Samet Bal Samet Bal is an experienced educator and researcher who worked at Turkish Airforce Academy, Yildiz Technical University, and currently studies at Turkish Airlines Flight Academy as an air cadet. With a Master's degree in English Language Education and ongoing pursuit of a Ph.D. in the same field, he specializes in education technology and language teaching. His research and presentations have revolved around these areas, exploring innovative approaches to enhance language learning experiences.

Lourdes Barquín Sanmartín is a Teaching Fellow at University College Dublin and holds a PhD in Language Acquisition and Language Teaching from the University of Edinburgh. She is also a Fellow of the Higher Education Academy (FHEA). Her research centers on Spanish acquisition by native English speakers, particularly focusing on positive grammatical transfers between proximal languages. With a background in British education, Lourdes specializes in students with English as their first language (L1), French as their second language (L2), and Spanish as their third language (L3). Her work emphasizes the similarities between French and Spanish to aid in learning past aspectual and modal contrasts. To address this, Lourdes advocates for the pluralistic teaching approach of Inter-comprehension, which helps students utilize their previously-acquired languages as a tool to enhance both their linguistic awareness and comprehension, offering a holistic strategy for language learning.

Dimaris Barrios-Beltran received her PhD in Language Sciences (with minors in General Linguistics and Hispanic Linguistics) from Indiana University-Bloomington (IUB) in 2016. With over 16 years of teaching experience, she has held positions at various institutions, including IUB, Amherst College, and Mount Holyoke College. She has taught a range of courses, including Spanish language at various levels, Spanish culture, and Latin American and Caribbean cultures and histories. Her areas of expertise encompass Linguistics, Syntax-Semantics Interface, L1 and L2 Language Acquisition, Pedagogy, Spanish Heritage speakers, Communication Disorders, Specific Language Impairment, Autism, Disability-Inclusive classrooms, and Technology in the classroom. She has also served as AP Spanish reader, table leader and question leader for the College Board, and she has led several talks and workshops on linguistic research, teaching practices, Caribbean culture, and improving classroom dynamic through games, multimodal activities and technological tools.

Banu Çiçek Başaran Uysal works at the English Language Teaching Department within the Faculty of Education at Eskisehir Osmangazi University, Turkey. She received her Ph.D. in ELT from Middle East Technical University (2020). Currently, she is offering English teacher education courses at the undergraduate level. Her research interests are pre-service teacher education, in-service teacher training, technology integration, online education, artificial intelligence in education, and corpus linguistics

Géraldine Bengsch is a language tutor for German in the Department of Language and Linguistic Science at the University of York and a Visiting Lecturer in the Department of Sociology at City, University of London. She is passionate about technology in teaching and developing interactive educational resources to make learning enjoyable and accessible to all students.

Yongyin Chen is an experienced language teacher. Her research interests include applied linguistics, educational technology, and language education.

Betül Czerkawski is an instructional design and technology professor from the University of Arizona. She is also a Second Language Acquisition and Teaching Program faculty member. Her research interests include learning design, foreign language teaching and learning, and emerging learning technologies.

Nazmi Dinçer serves as an English Language Instructor at the Turkish National Defence University, primarily within the Department of Foreign Languages. Presently, he is responsible for conducting specialized courses designed to equip aspiring pilots with essential communication skills, specifically tailored to adhere to the International Civil Aviation Organization (ICAO) standards.In addition to his instructional duties, Mr. Dinçer is engaged in advanced academic pursuits as a Ph.D. candidate at the Department of Educational Technology, Bahçeşehir University. His research ambitiously explores the intersection of educational technology and foreign language education. His areas of focus include distance education, multimedia learning, the application of artificial intelligence in educational contexts, and the integration of game-based learning. His scholarly work contributes significantly to the evolving landscape of educational technology in language instruction.

Sylvia Gaspari is a Ph.D candidate in the Department of Italian Studies at the University of Toronto. She is finishing work on her thesis about the rhetoric of prayer within the invocations of Dante's Divine Comedy. She has also translated several Renaissance letters for a publication on Renaissance Grotesques, and has contributed to a translation of a book on Aristotle's peripatetic school.

Mohammad J. Jamali is a Ph.D. Candidate at the Department of Italian Studies of the University of Toronto. Since 2016, he has worked on Mario Pratesi's archives at the E.J. Pratt Library of Victoria University in Toronto. In 2019, when he started his doctoral studies in the Department, he began a sociolinguistic project focusing on the issue of gender disparity and gender identity in Italian, which he continues to carry forward, parallel to his main thesis on Pratesi.

Elizabeth Jasmine is a highly regarded Professor of Psychology at the Indian Institute of Psychology and Research (IIPR) in Bengaluru, Karnataka, India. Her distinguished academic career is marked by significant contributions to psychology, evidenced by her extensive publication history in national and international journals. As a dedicated educator and researcher, Dr. Jasmine imparts knowledge to the next generation and conducts ground-breaking research, exploring various aspects of human behavior and cognition. Her influence extends globally, with her work reaching international audiences through reputable journals, reflecting a profound understanding of psychology and offering insights that could shape the discipline's future.

Natalie Khazaal, PhD, is Associate Professor in the School of Modern Languages, Georgia Institute of Technology who studies the links between disenfranchisement, media, and language. She is an American Council of Learned Societies (ACLS) fellow for her work on Arab atheists. She has authored the book "Pretty Liar: Television, Language, and Gender in Wartime Lebanon" and coedited the book "'Like an Animal': Critical Animal Studies Perspectives on Borders, Displacement, and Othering."

Siu-lun Lee is Senior Lecturer at the Chinese University of Hong Kong. His research interests include applied linguistics, Cantonese studies, Chinese linguistics, sociolinguistics, language teaching pedagogy, technology and language learning. He is the author of the book series Modern Cantonese and the editor of The learning and teaching of Cantonese as a second language published by Routledge.

Sohyeon Lee is a graduate student in the Department of Second Language Studies at the University of Hawaii at Manoa. With a background spanning two decades in teaching L2 English to adolescents in various public schools in Seoul, Korea, she had the privilege of working extensively in curriculum design, instructional development, and textbook publications through her employment with the Seoul Metropolitan Office of Education. Her growing interest in Language Testing and Assessments has driven her to explore the intricacies of evaluating L2 English productive skills, particularly in the domains of writing. She is deeply committed to addressing validity and fairness issues in L2 English assessments within EFL contexts, aiming to promote fairness and justification in language assessment practices. She is also exploring how AI can be integrated into language teaching curricula and assessments.

Weiming Liu holds the position of Assistant Professor in the School of Applied Language and Intercultural Studies at Dublin City University, Ireland. His scholarly pursuits revolve around language teacher education and foreign language teaching and learning, with a particular focus on exploring the intricacies of language pedagogy.

Teresa Lobalsamo is Associate Professor, Teaching Stream, of Italian Studies at the University of Toronto Mississauga. Her current research includes curating a digital repository of archival materials related to Italian Canadiana, pedagogical considerations on the effective delivery of online courses, and work-integrated learning modules. In 2018, she received the University of Toronto Mississauga Teaching Excellence Award for Junior Faculty.

Franziska Lys is Professor of German and Director of Undergraduate Studies in the department of German as well as the Director of the MENA Languages program at Northwestern University. Dr. Lys is an internationally recognized expert in the integration of culture in the language classroom and widely published in that subject including a co-edited volume on the cultural integration of both Germanys 25 years after the "Wende." She has co-produced four foreign documentaries which are the main educational material for language learning software she designed.

Lee-Luan Ng obtained her PhD in Applied Linguistic from University of Otago, New Zealand. She teaches postgraduate courses at the Faculty of Languages and Linguistics. She is also a certified trainer for the software, NVivo. She has been invited to conduct workshops on using computer-assisted qualitative data analysis software in deciphering research data at various public and private universities locally and abroad. She was involved in international scholar exchange at Beijing Foreign Studies University as well as participated in research projects with an interdisciplinary focus with organizations such as the British Council. Her current research interest includes computer assisted language learning, online learning, learning in higher education, the use of AI, VR and gaming in language learning. Lee Luan has also been invited to review journal articles for overseas and local publications such as Frontiers in Psychology - Language Sciences, Pertanika Journal, Malaysian Journal of ELT Research, and The Malaysian Journal of Learning and Instruction.

Venosha Ravana, a distinguished academic at Tunku Abdul Rahman University of Management and Technology, holds degrees from Universiti Sains Malaysia and the University of Malaya. Specializing in instructional design and technology, language teaching, and teacher training, she actively contributes to these fields. During her Bachelor's degree, she volunteered at an INGO in Hanoi, Vietnam, teaching English to underprivileged students, showcasing her commitment to inclusive education. As prolific author, she penned two influential books in 2022 and 2023, providing practical insights for collaborative learning approaches. Engaged in collaborative research, Venosha collaborates with researchers from other institutions, fostering interdisciplinary contributions. As the coordinator of language courses at her institution, she plays a vital role in enhancing language education. From her early volunteer work to her current administrative and collaborative roles, Venosha's contributions exemplify a holistic dedication to education and community service. Her multifaceted approach makes her a respected and influential figure in academia.

Dellannia Segreti is a current graduate student at the University of Toronto. Her interests lie in equitable and accessible pedagogies, with a focus on experiential learning, research, and technologies.

Ranjit Singha, a doctoral research fellow at Christ University and distinguished member of the American Psychological Association (APA), excels in research and development across diverse domains: Mindfulness, Addiction Psychology, Women Empowerment, UN Sustainable Development Goals, and Data Science. Certified by IBM and The University of Oxford Mindfulness Centre, he also holds credentials as a Microsoft Innovative Educator, Licensed Yoga Professional, Certified Mindfulness Teacher, and CBCT Teachers Training from Emory University, USA. With educational qualifications spanning PGDBA (GM), MBA (IB), MSc in Counselling Psychology, and a Senior Diploma in Tabla, Mr. Ranjit has an extensive publication record, mentors research projects, teaches diverse subjects, and actively contributes to journals and publications, solidifying his impactful role in psychology.

Surjit Singha is an academician with a broad spectrum of interests, including UN Sustainable Development Goals, Organizational Climate, Workforce Diversity, Organizational Culture, HRM, Marketing, Finance, IB, Global Business, Business, AI, K12 and Higher Education, Gender and Cultural Studies. Currently a faculty member at Kristu Jayanti College, Dr Surjit also serves as an Editor, reviewer, and author for prominent global publications and journals, including being on the Editorial review board of Information Resources Management Journal and contributor to various publications. With over 13 years of experience in Administration, Teaching, and Research, Dr. Surjit is dedicated to imparting knowledge and guiding students in their research pursuits. As a research mentor, Dr. Surjit has nurtured young minds and fostered academic growth. Dr. Surjit has an impressive track record of over 75 publications, including articles, book chapters, and textbooks, holds two US Copyrights, and has completed and published two fully funded minor research projects from Kristu Jayanti College.

Jianfen Wang has a Ph.D. in Chinese Pedagogy and MA in TESOL from The Ohio State University. She is currently an Associate Professor of Chinese and Asian Studies at Berea College. She has 20 years of experience teaching and researching foreign language teaching and learning. She is a co-author of "Perform Suzhou: A Course in Intermediate to Advanced Spoken Mandarin" and the primary editor of "Performed Culture in Action to Teaching Chinese as a Foreign Language," a volume on innovative Chinese language pedagogy.

İlknur Yuksel works as an Associate Professor at the English Language Teaching Department within the Faculty of Education at Eskisehir Osmangazi University, Turkey. She received her Ph.D. in ELT from Anadolu University (2012). She offers several teacher training courses including Assessment and Testing in English Language Teaching. Her research interests include vocabulary teaching, teacher training, second language acquisition, instructional technologies in language teaching, and artificial intelligence for teacher education.

Index

S

T

W

www.ingramcontent.com/pod-product-compliance
Lightning Source LLC
LaVergne TN
LVHW080630011026
849160LV00014B/1170